THE REVIEW AND ABSTRACT

of the

COUNTY REPORTS

to the

BOARD OF AGRICULTURE

by

WILLIAM MARSHALL

DAVID & CHARLES REPRINTS

7153 4366 1

This edition first
published 1809

Printed in Great Britain by
Clarke, Doble & Brendon Ltd Plymouth
Published by David & Charles (Holdings) Limited
South Devon House Railway Station Newton Abbot

COUNTY REPORTS
To The
BOARD OF AGRICULTURE

COUNTY REPORTS
To The
BOARD OF AGRICULTURE

THE

REVIEW AND ABSTRACT

OF THE

COUNTY REPORTS

TO THE

BOARD OF AGRICULTURE;

FROM THE SEVERAL

AGRICULTURAL DEPARTMENTS OF ENGLAND.

By Mr. MARSHALL.

IN FIVE VOLUMES.

VOLUME THE SECOND,

(Which was first Published, in 1809, and is now combined with the other Volumes of the same Work;)

Comprizing those from the

WESTERN DEPARTMENT.

Which includes

CHESHIRE,
FLINTSHIRE,
SHROPSHIRE,
HEREFORDSHIRE,
WORCESTERSHIRE,
GLOCESTERSHIRE,
NORTH WILTSHIRE,
NORTH SOMERSETSHIRE.

York:

Printed by Thomas Wilson & Sons,

FOR LONGMAN, HURST, REES, ORME, AND BROWN, LONDON; CONSTABLE, AND CO. EDINBURGH; AND WILSON AND SONS, YORK.

1818.

THE

C O N T E N T S,

SYSTEMATICALLY ARRANGED.

Here-

POLITICAL ECONOMY.

Institu-

Drink-

Gloces-

Agriculture.

Glo-

Glo-

ADVER-

ADVERTISEMENT.

PREFIXED to the first volume of this Work, I offered a sketch engraving of the Northern Department, to show, with better effect than the verbal descriptions could convey, the several districts into which it naturally separates. And it was my wish to have accompanied the succeeding volumes with similar sketches. But finding the attention and time which it required, and the difficulty, in a recluse situation, of getting the engravings executed, satisfactorily; and, further, being aware (as is expressed in a note, p. 1. of the Nothern Department) that nothing short of an actual and deliberate survey can determine the outlines with due precision;—I have deemed it right to bestow the time and thought that, in the present instance, such a sketch would have required, in a way which, I conceive, will be more profitable to the public;—trusting that the verbal descriptions will be found to be fully sufficient, as a GROUNDWORK for the required SURVEY.

30 *November*, 1809.

SO FAR, the Advertisement prefixed to the REVIEW of the NORTHERN DEPARTMENT.

It will, here, be proper to notice an insinuation, intended to injure that work in the public mind, which appeared, soon after its publication, in a periodical work of considerable merit, and wide circulation, the property of the Board's publisher.

In the Monthly Magazine of August, 1808, in the annunciatory department of that publication, is the subjoined *entry**.

P. 53. "The public will observe with satisfaction, that Parliament has voted 3000*l.* to the Board of Agriculture, to enable it, with greater rapidity, to complete the Surveys of the kingdom. A full account of the labors and progress of this highly important Board will be found under the head *Proceedings* of *Public Societies.* As soon as the whole of the County Reports have been printed, it is intended to publish an analysis of the whole, to lay before his Majesty and both Houses of Parliament, a work which for useful and authentic information relative to the actual state of the empire, is likely to prove never to have had its equal in any country."

And, to this modest intimation is appended the following note.—"It may not be improper in this place

actual and deliberate Survey can determine the outlines with due precision,—I have deemed it right to bestow the time and thought, which in the present instance such a sketch would have required,—in a way that I conceive will be more profitable to the public;—trusting that the verbal descriptions will be found to be fully sufficient, as a GROUNDWORK of the required SURVEY.

* It did not, I believe, come out, on a late trial, that a certain publisher, not only vends *anonymous criticisms,* half yearly, on books recently published, but monthly annunciations of those in embryo: in which annunciations,—doubtlessly to excite the curiosity and whet the appetite of the public,—his own and his *friends'* bantlings (that are to be) are ostentatiously proclaimed to be babes of great promise; while the productions of others, which interfere with his or their schemes, are tauntingly spoken of, and attempted to be depreciated;—as in the instance before us.

place to notice a late extraordinary publication of a Mr. Marshall, which professes to divide the counties into *departments*, and give the substance of the County Reports of each department in a single volume. It is unfortunate for this work that its author should in his first volume have included some of the first *Proof Reports* of the Board, which it is well known were printed merely as skeletons, for completion and improvement, and these he gravely analyzes, and introduces as the basis of a regular abstract of the acknowledged Reports of the Board; of course such an analytical view of its own labors will be the business of the Board itself, as soon as those labors are finished."

"Oh! paragon of wisdom! fine suggestion! But how? and who's to *do* it, is the question." Surely not the compiler of the Code of Health.*

Respecting the "Proof Reports"—that is to say, the ORIGINAL REPORTS—the very "Reports of Counties"—which the first President of the Board (probably the writer of the note transcribed above) *swaggered* about, so *audaciously*, in 1795, *twice seven years since*, threatening, *forthwith*, to astonish with them, not only the three Estates of Parliament, but all the World,—even as he is now *puffing* and *promising*, about the "reprinted Reports,"—I have only to remark, that many of them are the works of PROFESSIONAL MEN,—of men writing from the dictates of THEIR OWN EXPERIENCE and (as this volume sufficiently shows) contain more *useful* and *practical* knowledge, than is to be found among the "Philosophy"! and "Literature"! of the now bepraised, "reprinted Reports." They are, of course, much better adapted to my purpose, and to the attention of the agricultural public, than those which, we are given to understand, are now costing the

* This is another plagiary, another adoption of my designs. See the INTRODUCTION to the NORTHERN DEPARTMENT.

public at large a handsome price. For what is it to *me* whether the Reports are original or secondary, gratuitous or purchased, provided they contain information that may be rendered useful to the permanent prosperity of the Country.

The view of the Editor of the Board has ever been that of making *great books*,—no matter as to their contents; he being, as has, I trust, been sufficiently shown (in the Introduction to the Northern Department) altogether unqualified to judge of the merit or demerit of the materials spread before him. He has, therefore, no other mean of endeavoring to procure for his productions a temporary celebrity and sale, than that of PUFFING.

Reader, take a sample!—In a provincial Newspaper of November last, appeared, in a long Advertisement, the following information extraordinary: *headed*, "ENGLISH LITERATURE." (ha! ha! ha!)

"It affords us the highest satisfaction to see another edition *announced* of Mr. Young's able survey of Lincolnshire; because this circumstance proves that the taste of the public is not vitiated so far as to encourage nothing but what is *crude* and *trifling* (!) and that *solid* and *useful literature* (!) has still remaining a sufficient number of effective patrons.

"On the subject of our own local and national history, we were once of opinion that nothing would succeed but transcripts of tomb stones, and views of country seats; but it appears from the great encouragement given to the sensible and rational Country Reports of the Board of Agriculture, that Political Economy, Statistics, Commerce, and Agriculture, in short, that common sense and the public good are now studied through the country, as much as were the reveries of parish clerks in a former age. The Board of Agriculture has happily given a new direction to the pursuits of the curious and inquisitive, and we now find its valuable Reports, in every

every library, by the side of Camden and the best local histories.

"We have long watched, with interest, the progress of this great national undertaking, which is calculated to bring us ultimately acquainted with the present state and the resources of our own country, and which in those respects as a *book* of *authority* (!) is unequalled in any other nation in the world." (Good heavens!) "Parliament has expended large sums upon it, and the intelligence of the ablest writers has for years been employed, in *actual surveys* (!) of the several counties.* It becomes, necessarily, therefore, a sort of Bible to every politician, philosopher, and lover of his country; and will be to future ages what the famous doomsday book has been to us; improved, however, by the enlarged views of modern inquiry."—Haa! ha! ha! ha! haa! †

In the annunciatory department of the Monthly Magazine of May 1808, stands the following passage.—P. 343. "This important Board proceeds with increased zeal and alacrity, in the preparation of the County Reports; twenty-eight of which have already appeared; and Oxfordshire, by Mr. Young, and Bedfordshire, by Mr. Batchelor, are ready to be put to press. New editions of Lancashire, Staffordshire, and Lincolnshire, are also in forwardness. It is impossible to speak in terms of praise equal to the intrinsic worth, and national importance of this series of books."

In the same publication of August 1808, p. 47, is printed

* Pray, reader, peruse *this* volume through.

† I hope to be pardoned for involuntarily exclaiming, here,—how can the right honorable, and honorable, the vice presidents, and other members of the Board, suffer such barefacedly charlatanic—such ranting, raving, besotted stuff—to go abroad, *as it were*, by their sanction.

printed the "Address to the Board of Agriculture, by Sir John Sinclair, Bart. the President" (dated the 7th June 1808): and in this we are told, unconditionally, that "all the counties of England will be completed in the course of this year" (1808).

But so far from that promise being fulfilled, not a single volume (if the Monthly Magazine is to be relied on) made its appearance, for more than twelve months after that assertion was made; and not more than three or four, even to this time, November 1809 *.

Further, in the same, of November, 1808, p. 363. —"The Board of Agriculture proceed in their grand design of completing the County Reports; a work which will bespeak the magnificent character of

* In the newspaper advertisement, is inserted a list of "the Counties of which Surveys are already completed and *published;*" in which list, several are included that were then, *not published,* and which did not come before the public for nearly twelve months afterward. Mention is also there made of "six others" as being "in the press and will be published before Christmas." But of those six which were promised to be published before Christmas, 1808, not one was heard of, until September 1809; when one of them was *announced,* as being then in the press!

What legitimate "authority" can belong to books thus *basely* born? Surely, some one must have an interest in those *lingering* births.

Of the twelve counties, which come within the Midland Department, only six "reprinted Reports," as they are falsely termed, (see pages 298 and 420 of this volume,) have yet made their appearance; or, judging from those dilatory and *mysterious* goings on, are likely soon to appear. I am, therefore, constrained to relinquish the natural line of procedure—the geographical order of succession—and to enter, next, on a Review of the Reports from the Eastern Department.

For, if no more dispatch be used than has hitherto been, another century may pass away, before the "labors" of the "Board" be "finished"! It is, therefore, surely right to proceed,—in the work of analysis and concentration,—with the materials we have, and in the best manner we are able; in order that the present generation may receive some benefit from those astonishing works.

of the present age. Thirty counties are now published, and less than as many more will perfect our knowledge of the whole island. Berkshire, Leicestershire, Oxfordshire, and Derbyshire are all in the press, and will appear before Christmas. We are happy to say that the encouragement of the public keeps pace with the importance of the work, and the entire series are now to be found, in every public and private library. But what is of more consequence to the agricultural interest of the empire, the intelligent landowners, and practical farmers, are every where emulous to possess one or more of these volumes; and country gentlemen in general are possessed of the entire series."

May it not, here, be fairly asked---*if* the sale is so extensive, why apply to Parliament for *extra supplies*, to keep the press in motion?

Other specimens of the puff audacious might possibly be found in the same publication; but scarcely any one equal in boldness to that which gives point to the newspaper advertisement, above quoted.

Having enumerated the volumes, asserted to have been then published, and some of the more respectable authors of them,—it is there said,—"Fourteen other volumes will complete the work; and as Parliament voted 5000*l* * on the last day of the last sessions, expressly to pay the expence of the various surveys, and to hasten the completion of this great *literary* undertaking (!) it may be supposed that it will be completed in the course of the ensuing year. *Every volume*, and *every survey*, is, however, *complete*, in

* In a recent Advertisement, of the same complexion, and in the same paper, we are told, that "This great national Work"—"is now publishing, at an aggregate expence of FIFTY THOUSAND POUNDS."

If this be *true*, it is an unwarrantable waste of money; if *not true*, it is an imposition on the public, and a libel on Government.

in itself, as far as relates to its own county" (assurance ineffable!) "and is to be purchased separately. Indeed, in favor of a work of such genuine worth, the booksellers throughout the kingdom, have, with laudable zeal, exerted themselves to promote the circulation, and they generally keep on hand copies of their own and of the neighbouring counties."—Yes, I am well informed I believe, until the groaning shelves are ready to break down under their *heavy* loads.

But success to puffing!—If the public can be brought to believe, that the Reports at large—that the ore, encumbered, as it is, with all its dirt and dross—may be considered as of high value,—its precious metal, in a concentrated form, must needs be estimated above all price.

30 *November*, 1809.

THE

WESTERN DEPARTMENT

OF

ENGLAND.

IN an INTRODUCTION to the NORTHERN DEPARTMENT of England (recently published) I noticed, at some length, the Origin and Progress of the Board of Agriculture;—

Described the Plan and Execution of the *original* Reports; also the Plan of the *reprinted* Reports;—

Defined the requisite *qualifications* of a *Reporter*;—

Explained my Plan of Reviewing them, by DEPARTMENTS;—and sketched the Outlines and Characteristics of the six *Agricultural* Departments, into which England aptly separates.

The WESTERN DEPARTMENT is thus distinguished:—

'This extends from the banks of the Mersey to the Somersetshire Avon and its banks. On the west, it is bounded by the Welch mountains; on the east, by the minor hills of Staffordshire, and the uplands of Warwickshire and Oxfordshire;—its southern bounds being given by the Chalk Hills of Wiltshire, and the Sedgemoors of Somersetshire.

'It comprises an almost uninterupted succession of VALE DISTRICTS, which accompany the Mersey, the Dee, the Severn and the Avon, to their respective confluxes with the sea. Thus, by natural character, it is discriminately marked.

'And it is not less so, by Agricultural produce. The entire Department, excepting the higher Lands of Shropshire and Herefordshire, the Cotswold Hills of Glocestershire, and the higher parts of the Mendip Hills of Somersetshire,—may be said to be almost wholely applied to the produce of the DAIRY: Cheeses of different qualities being its

its common (or prevailing) production. Fruit liquor, however, may be mentioned as another product that signalizes this natural division of the kingdom.'

This Department comprizes within its outlines,—part of *Lancashire* (the north side of the Vale of Warrington),—parts of *Flintshire* and *Denbighshire*,—nearly the whole of *Cheshire*, *Shropshire*, *Herefordshire*, *Worcestershire*, and *Glocestershire*,—with parts of *Wiltshire* and *Somersetshire*.

The REPORTS which will require to be examined, as relating to this Department, are the following; namely,

CHESHIRE, by Wedge, also by Holland.

FLINTSHIRE and DENBIGHSHIRE, by Kay.

SHROPSHIRE, by Bishton, also by Plymley.

HEREFORDSHIRE, by Clark, also by Duncumb.

WORCESTERSHIRE, by Pomeroy.

GLOCESTERSHIRE, by Turner, also by Rudge.

WILTSHIRE, by Davis.

SOMERSETSHIRE, by Billingsley.

CHESHIRE.

CHESHIRE.

THE NATURAL DISTRICTS, incident to this County and its environs, are the vale of Warrington,—the valley or district of the Wyches,—and the vale or district of Chester. The northeastern quarter of Cheshire forms part of the *Mountain*, or *Northern* Department; and has been noticed. See NORTH. DEPART. P. 522.

MY OWN knowledge of the three natural districts, now to be considered, has arisen in the following manner:—

In September, 1792, I first entered the county, by the Bridgewater Canal, from Manchester toward Chester; where I stopt some days, to examine its ample vale, and to gain some knowledge of its Cheese Dairy.

In August, 1798, I entered it, by Congleton; and spent some days, in the valley of the Wyches; where I saw somewhat more of its Dairy, in that most celebrated district of Cheshire Cheese making;—thence passing from Northwyche to Warrington.

In 1799, I entered the vale of Chester, by the way of Llangollen and Wrexham, to Chester;—passing, thence, by Frodsham, to Warrington.

In July, 1800, I entered it by Ruthen and Mold, to Chester; thence, by Eastham-Ferry, to Liverpool.

And, in August, 1800, I crossed the northwestern peninsula,—from Rock House to Parkgate; thence, to Chester; leaving the county, by the great road to Shrewsbury.

THE VALE of WARRINGTON.—This district was spoken of, in reviewing the Lancashire Report (see the NORTH. DEPART.:)—It extends from the head of the estuary of the Mersey, to near Manchester:—a distance of about twenty miles. Its width is irregular; as it spreads, on both sides, among the rising grounds which form its outlines. About Warrington, it is eight or ten miles in width; extending from near Newton, in Lancashire, to the gently rising grounds

grounds about Budworth, in Cheshire; which form its natural division from the valley of the Wyches.

Its *elevation* is inconsiderable, and its surface extraordinarily level. The Bridgewater Canal passes from end to end of the vale, without a Lock; but is of course somewhat elevated above the river at its lower extremity.

The *soil*, as far as my observations have gone, is principally of a rich sandy nature. Nevertheless, much cool strong Land is observable: notwithstanding the prevailing substratum would seem to be soft, red-sand rock.

The whole appears to be in a state of mixed cultivation. Much Arable, as well as much perennial Herbage, is seen on both sides of the vale.

The VALLEY of the WYCHES*.—This district accompanies the Wever and its principal branch, the Dane, from Congleton, to its junction with the Mersey; where it unites with the base of the vale of Warrington, (as has been noticed)—from which it is principally separated, by the rising grounds of Budworth, &c.,—situated between the Ring and the Wever; and from the vale of Chester, by Delamere Forest, and an irregular line of Hills, which stretch across the country, in a north-and-south direction. The towns of this district are NORTHWYCHE, MIDDLEWYCHE, NANTWYCHE and CONGLETON.

The *surface* of the upper parts of the district, between the Dane and the Wever, is extraordinarily flat, and of considerable width. The central parts are somewhat more diversified, in surface; and more contracted in extent. The lower part is still more confined,—almost closed,—by the near approach of the Delamere Hillocks. At its base, below Frodsham, a flat of rich Marsh Land is seen.—A proof of the extraordinary levelness of this quarter of the Island is given by a Canal, which reaches from Manchester to Middlewyche,—a distance of forty miles,—without the assistance of a single Lock.

The *Soil* varies. The banks of the Dane are mostly sandy;—with a few heathlets interspersed; much resembling the Lands of East Norfolk.—But those of the Wever, toward Nantwyche, are of a cold clayey nature;—a true cheese-dairy Soil. In the environs of the towns, the Soil is mostly rich; and, in the lower parts of the district,

* In the established pronunciation of the County and its neighbourhood, the *y*, in this appellation, is pronounced long.

district, much strong good Land is found;—mostly on a sandy base.

The *Climature* is remarkably forward. In 1798, Wheat was nearly ripe, and many Oats cutting, the latter end of July:—quite as forward, that year, as the southern counties.

The prevailing *produce* of this part of Cheshire may be said to be Cheese. Much Corn, however, is grown in the district. It is, strictly speaking, in a state of mixed Cultivation:—Arable crops, dairy produce and grazing, being joint objects of its occupiers. The last, however, is, I believe, confined to the practice of some comparatively few individuals.

But, viewed in a political light, the most valuable product of the district of the Wyches is the SALT which is therein produced;—partly in a fossil state, or *Rock-Salt*, and in part from *Salt-Wells*, out of which brine is raised; and, from this, immense quantities of salt is manufactured.

The VALE or DISTRICT of CHESTER. The widely spreading country round Chester is one of the few districts of the kingdom that have heretofore borne the title of *Vale*:—this having been, by way of pre-eminence, styled "Vale Royal."

The outlines of the tract of country which has had this honorable distinguishment conferred on it, have never, perhaps, been accurately defined or understood. It probably was meant to include the whole of the lower lands of Cheshire and Flintshire, and the eastern margin of Denbighshire; but, as has been shown, the lower lands of Cheshire have a natural line of separation, in the Delamere and other hills, which divide the flat lands that lie round Chester, from the valley of the Wyches,—a distinct tract of country.

The vale lands of Denbighshire and Flintshire, tho of different degrees of elevation, are wholely marked by the vale character. In approaching Chester, from North Wales, by the way of Llangollen, these lands are entered, at Wynstay, a few miles to the westward of WREXHAM. Eastward of that point of entrance, every thing is *English*,--every thing bears the *English vale* character. There, the natural characteristics and management of Cheshire may be said to commence in an extended flat of productive lands, appropriated to mixed cultivation and the cheese dairy.

On

On the north, the district of Chester is bounded by the Irish Channel, and the estuary of the Mersey. To the south, its limits are less accurately defined:—it follows the Dee, several miles above Chester;—to where its valley is contracted by hillocks, in the neighbourhood of MALPAS.

Measuring from the forest hills, on the east, to the broken grounds or uplands of Flintshire, on the west (about twenty miles); and from the northern extreme of the vale lands of the peninsula of Wirral, to the feet of the Malpas hillocks, on the south (about thirty miles,)—the extent of the vale lands of the district of Chester, may be estimated at five to six hundred square miles; and, of course, ranks among the larger vale districts of the island.

The *elevation* of this extensive tract varies. The neighbourhood of Chester, to some distance, is very little above the tide, and its surface extraordinarily flat,—much of it being level, as if water-formed:—a very low flat country. The upper or north end of the peninsula is broken in surface; is raised into hillocks,—some of them heathy;—its upper grounds being more elevated than those at its southern base; which resembles the environs of Chester and the body of the county.

The Wrexham quarter is still more elevated. But its surface is equally flat, as that of Cheshire; having every appearance, in crossing them, of low-lying vale Lands.

The *soils* of the district of Chester are less uniform than its surface. The east side, toward the Forest Hills, is mostly light and of a redish cast: but with some stronger red Land; the whole appearing to be incumbent on soft red-sand rock; of which the hills, on this side of the district, seem to be formed. Much of the northern peninsula is of a cool weak nature; the east side of it resting on a deep bed of clay; as appears by the banks or minor cliffs of the estuary of the Mersey. The west side of the district of Chester is of a cool, but mostly of a productive, quality;—interspersed with some weaker Lands:—the northwest quarter, toward Mold, affording coals.

In *Agricultural products* the three districts, here spoken of, are similar. The arable crops (which are frequently abundant) are Wheat and Oats*; with a little Barley; some

* The *Tartarian* or *Reed Oat* I observed to prevail, on the cooler weaker Lands of the Peninsula:—a further instance of their having found their most appropriate soil.—See NORTH. DEPART. p. 78.

some Clover; many Potatoes (especially on the Lancashire side of Cheshire); but, speaking with very little latitude, even in 1800,—*no Turnips!*—not even on the Turnip Lands, with which the county abounds.

But this may be in some measure owing to the species of LIVESTOCK prevalent in those districts;—namely, *Cattle;*—mostly *Cows.* In the lower Lands, not a *Sheep* is seen; excepting a few " Forresters." I have not *observed* any appearance of lowland Sheep, being bred, or even fatted, in the county.—*Cheese* is the principal product. Yet the management of *Grass Land* is reprehensible, throughout the County.

Hedge-row Timber is a prevailing product of the lower Lands of Cheshire; excepting its northern peninsula; where timber Trees are prevented from rising, by reason of the sea winds, to which it is peculiarly exposed. In Flintshire, plots of woodland of some extent are seen.

All in all, Cheshire and its environs, may well be classed among the most productive passages of the kingdom.

The prevalence of hedge trees, mostly full topped, added to the flatness of the surface, render the lower lands uninteresting, to the mere traveller. But no sooner is any of its eminences surmounted, than extensive views break upon the eye. Even from the ramparts of Chester (admirably and exemplarily kept) interesting views are seen. From the insular hillocks, in the southern part of the county, extraordinary circles of views are commanded:—nearly equal in extent to those seen from the Charnwood Hills of Leicestershire:—than which they are rendered more striking, by the estuaries, the sea, and the mountains, that give feature to the offscapes.

" GENERAL

"GENERAL VIEW
OF THE
AGRICULTURE
OF THE
COUNTY PALATINE OF CHESTER.
WITH
OBSERVATIONS ON THE MEANS OF ITS IMPROVEMENT.

BY MR. THOMAS WEDGE.

1794."

CONCERNING the REPORTER, or his MODE of SURVEY, I have no information; saving that which is to be gathered from his Report.

It was my intention, when I first undertook this Work, to have given a biographical sketch of each Reporter. But this I found a difficult, and it might have proved an *ungrateful*, task. And, unless so far as his *profession*, or habit of life, is concerned (and this the SURVEYORS, themselves, or the EDITOR of the BOARD, ought surely to have furnished) it is well, perhaps, for a Reviewer to depend wholely on the work before him, and to form his judgement from it alone; without regard to its author, personally considered.

In the Cheshire Report, there is ample testimony of the ability of Mr. WEDGE, as a *Reporter*. His manner is very much what I conceived it ought to be. His mind appears to be fixed on the best established practice of the County he is writing upon. Seldom do we find him endeavoring to impose on his Readers his own Opinions, or preconceived Sentiments. In this respect, Mr. Wedge surpasses all his Coadjutors, hitherto appreciated.

And even as a *Surveyor*, so far as his particular examinations have extended, he appears to have been duly assiduous. His Report, in most cases, agrees with my own Observations. It is, however, to the Manufacture of Cheese, which Mr. W. has evidently paid the most elaborate attention. The more ordinary articles of Information read as if they had arisen from a previous knowledge of the practice of the County, rather than from an actual Survey of its several Parts.

This being an *original* Report, there are not any Annotators. The number of Pages Eighty eight.

SUBJECT

SUBJECT THE FIRST.

NATURAL ECONOMY.

EXTENT.—Cheshire, Mr. Wedge observes, p. 7,—"contains, as appears by Burdett's map, exclusive of the estuary of the river Dee, about 1040 square miles, or 665,600 acres. Within the estuary of the river Dee, there are in Cheshire about 10,000 acres of naked sands, and 400 acres of marsh land."

ELEVATION and SURFACE.—P. 8. "The general appearance of Cheshire is that of an extended plain; but on the eastern side there is a range of hilly, or rather mountainous country, connected with the Derbyshire and Yorkshire hills, of about twenty-five miles in length and five in width, extending from near Congleton to the north eastern extremity of the county. From Macclesfield, in a north western direction, the surface is irregular and hilly; but continues of that description not further than to Alderly, about five or six miles from Macclesfield. On the Shropshire side, the surface is also broken and irregular. Approaching the western side of the county, (at the distance of about ten miles east from Chester) there is another range of irregular hills, which separates the waters of the Dee and Mersey" (Wever); "these hills are in a direction almost north and south, and extend about 25 miles from Malpas, on the south side of the county, to Frodsham, on the north side of it. The remaining part of the county amounting to nearly four fifths of the whole, is probably not more, on the medium, than from 100 to 200 feet above the level of the sea. Cheshire has formerly been celebrated as the vale royal of England; and if seen from the high lands about Macclesfield, the whole of the county to the westward has undoubtedly the appearance of one extended plain."

CLIMATURE.—P. 11. "With regard to the climate, it has been stated, that a large proportion of the surface of Cheshire is not more than from one to two hundred feet above the level of the sea: from this circumstance some idea of the climate of the county may be formed. It is, on the whole, more temperate and mild than the generality of other counties lying under the same latitude, owing

owing to the flatness of its surface (abounding as it does with much hedge row timber) and to its lying within the influence of the sea air." P. 24.—" Hay harvest commences in the beginning of July. Corn harvest commonly begins in the latter end of July, or the beginning of August, and ends, with some other exceptions, in the middle or latter end of September."

WATERS.—P. 9. " The principal rivers are the Mersey and the Dee; these receive, and carry off to the sea, all the smaller rivers and rivulets in Cheshire, viz. the Wever, the Dane, the Wheelock, the Goyte, the Bolling, &c. &c."

SOILS and SUBSTRATA.—P. 10. " There are a great variety of soils in Cheshire; clay, sand, black moor or peat; marl and gravel, in various intermixed proportions, abound in different parts of the county. The three first, however, form the most predominant parts in the generally prevailing soils, and of these the largest proportion is a strong retentive clay. The substratum is generally rammel or clay, marl, sand, gravel, or red rock; but most commonly one of the two former, viz. clay or marl. The numerous mosses, marshy meadows, and peat bogs, which abound in different parts of the county, seem sufficiently to prove, that either clay, marl, or some other unctuous earth, is very generally at no great depth below the surface."

MINERALS.—No direct mention is made of the *Salt Mines*, nor of the *Salt Springs*, of Cheshire; tho, even in an agricultural view, they form its greatest treasure. In " Covenants of Leases," however, not only " Rock Salt," but " Alum," is reserved to the Landlord, p. 14.—And refuse Salt is largely spoken of, as a " Manure." Salt is also incidentally enumerated among articles of " Manufacture." But of the mode of Manufacture, or of its History as a Fossil Production, we have no information.

SUBJECT THE SECOND.

POLITICAL ECONOMY.

STATE of APPROPRIATION.—P. 8. " The proportions of the cultivated parts of the county, and those which lie either waste, or in a state of little profit, are perhaps nearly as follows:

Arable,

Arable, meadow, pasture, &c. about - -	615,000
Waste lands, heaths, commons, greens, but few woods of any extent, - - - - -	30,000
Peat bogs and mosses, - - - - - - - - -	20,000
Common fields, probably, not so much as -	1,000
Sea sands within the estuary of the Dee, exclusive of what may be upon the shores of the river Mersey, - - - -	10,000
	676,000"

P. 63. "Several considerable tracts of waste lands have of late years been inclosed, and others are now in contemplation."

STATE of SOCIETY.—*Provisions.*—P. 25. "A family in Cheshire may be supplied with beef, mutton, and veal, taking the average of the whole year, at from four-pence to four-pence halfpenny per pound. Wheat, on the average of the last seven years, has been about 7s. 6d. per measure, weighing seventy-five pounds. Barley, during the like time, 3s. 6d. for thirty-eight quarts; oats 2s. 6d. for forty-six pounds; and cheese, about 46s. per hundred, of 120lb." (in 1793 or 4).

P. 25. "The sustenance of agricultural labourers in Cheshire, consists chiefly of potatoes, barley bread, and butter *(scarcely any cheese)* butter-milk, whey, and fleeting."—The last a peculiar product of the Cheshire Dairy; as will hereafter appear.

Manufactures of Cheshire.—P. 26.—"The Cotton Manufactories of Lancashire have extended very considerably into this county, and were making a rapid progress; but the late unfortunate failures, and the war, have at present stopped their further extension. There is some little cloth manufactured on the Yorkshire side of this district. In and near Stockport, there has been a considerable trade in hats, as well as in cotton and silk. There are silk-mills and copper-works at Macclesfield. A very considerable quantity of salt is manufactured in the neighbourhood of the Wyches."

Their *Effects* on *Agriculture.*—P. 26. "The effect of manufactories upon agriculture has been an increased demand for the produce of the land, and more especially for the luxuries of life: they have at the same time seriously increased the price of labour, and occasioned a scarcity of useful hands for husbandry. This was severely felt by the farmers, in the harvest of 1792, many of whom were obliged to pay for labourers at the rate of three shillings,

shillings, three shillings and six-pence, and upwards per day, besides victuals and drink. By lessening the number of hands, the price of labour is increased, and these effects must necessarily, in some measure, carry with them a depression of the spirit of agricultural improvement. The demand for corn, increased by the increase of trade, has diminished the size of dairies, and the more speedy returns, by the sale of oatmeal, (much used in Lancashire) has turned the attention of the farmers more to tillage than formerly, as many think, to the prejudice of the country.

"Manufactories have also had a tendency to increase the poor rates, in those parishes where they have been introduced, and have had a bad effect upon the morals of the people."

LOCAL TAXES.—*Poor Rates.*—In the Appendix is given, at some length, an "Extract from a Pamphlet, written in 1776, by a respectable Gentleman in Flintshire;"—containing some valuable Remarks, "on the Poor Laws;"—a work which appears, in those extracts, to be entitled to mature consideration, by those who may write, or legislate, on that very important subject of Jurisprudence. Though some of the positions may be erroneous, or doubtfully founded, it contains suggestions, I conceive, that might become practically useful to the Country:—a sufficient apology, I trust, for noticing it here.

Tithes.—P. 69. "In speaking of *obstacles* to general improvements, the present impolitic and, in many instances, oppressive mode of collecting *tithes in kind*, must present itself first to our notice. Their operation, as a bar to improvements, is so glaring, and, amongst disinterested men, so universally admitted, as to need no comment from us."

PUBLIC WORKS.—*Drainage.*—Mr. Wedge is friendly to COMMISSIONS of DRAINAGE:—Institutions that are requisite, in almost every quarter of the kingdom. Mr. W's Remarks, on this as on other subjects, are modest and sensible.

P. 62.—"With respect to the general improvement of this district, it is with much diffidence we presume to give any opinion; but from a hasty view of it, we are induced to think that the most material improvement which this county (speaking generally) is capable of, might be effected by means of a proper drainage, as the basis. Exclusive of the mosses, or peat bogs, which have been before stated to amount to about 20,000 acres, there are also

also numerous tracts of low and marshy meadow-lands; which either for want of a proper outfall, or owing to the water-courses not being sufficiently cleansed and kept open, are rendered, by land floods and stagnant waters, of little value. These marshy meadows, together with the whole of that description of land, might, if drained, &c. probably be improved to *more* than *double their present value.* There are, indeed, a great number of land-owners and occupiers interested in those flat situations, who are very desirous of improving them; but as the properties are generally intermixed, *particular* improvements cannot be effected, without the full execution of some *general* scheme of drainage. The greatest bars to such improvements chiefly arise either from the uncertainty, or short duration, of particular tenures, or the obstinacy and perverseness of individuals. We therefore think, that it would not only be much to the advantage of the land-owners and occupiers in general, but also greatly to the benefit of the county at large, if an act of Parliament, or other powers, applicable to the purposes of a general drainage, were obtained; not such as might *operate unjustly upon the tenantry*, but such as would compel every individual to contribute towards the general expence, *in proportion to their respective interests only.* A commission of sewers, which has lately been obtained, for four of the hundreds of this county, viz. Wirral, Broxton, Eddisbury, and Bucklow, will probably be the means of effecting, as far as the powers of it extend, in an equitable manner, this most essential and necessary improvement."

Inland Navigation.—P. 9. "The River Mersey divides Cheshire from Lancashire for near sixty miles; and is navigable about thirty-five miles from Liverpool, which is situated at a small distance from the mouth of the river, on the Lancashire side, as far up as to the mouth of the river Irwell, for vessels of sixty tons. The Dee forms a part of the western boundary of the county, and is navigable from the sea to the city of Chester, for vessels of considerable burthen.

"The river Wever falls into the Mersey about fifteen miles above Liverpool, and is navigable for vessels carrying sixty or seventy tons, near twenty miles from its junction with the Mersey, to Winsford Bridge, above Northwyche."

The Reporter's Remarks, in continuation, show the immense profit which, *in some cases,* may arise from improved River Navigations, and of course the great benefit that

that may accrue, from them, to the community; by lessening the quantity of land carriage; and thereby preventing the unnecessary consumption of the too scanty produce of our circumscribed territory.—P. 9. "The plan upon which the latter of these rivers was made navigable (by means of locks and wears) deserves to be noticed. The money raised for the purpose, amounting to about 49,000l. was subscribed by the gentlemen of the county, who were empowered by an act of parliament to divide on their respective subscriptions an interest of 6l. per cent. 5l. per cent. on the capital, and 1l. per cent. for the risk of the undertaking, until such time as the tonnage, arising from the trade on that river, should be sufficient, by instalments, to reimburse them. After such reimbursement, the whole amount of tonnage, first deducting the charges of necessary repairs and management of the river, "to be from time to time employed for and towards "amending and repairing the public bridges within the "said county of Chester, and such other public charges upon "the county, and in such manner as the magistrates shall "yearly direct." All vessels navigating in this river to pay one shilling per ton, whether they pass the whole length of the navigable part, or to any shorter distance; and the receipt amounted, as we are informed, last year, to near 8000l. The debt has been paid off several years, and near 4000 has been annually drawn from this resource, for the last four or five years, in aid of the expence of building a new county gaol at Chester."

Canals.—P. 10. "The Duke of Bridgewater's canal for fourteen feet boats from Runcorn (which is about thirteen miles above Liverpool) to Manchester, runs at no great distance from the Mersey, about twenty miles through the county, before it crosses to the Lancashire side of that river. The Staffordshire, or Grand Trunk Canal, joins the Duke's canal at Preston Brook, about five miles from Runcorn; and passes in a south eastern direction through nearly the middle of the county: The Chester canal extends from Chester to Nantwyche, in an eastern direction, about twenty miles."

In 1792, the Canal last mentioned was at a stand; with every symptom of abortion:—owing, as I was informed, to a want of due foresight in the projectors of it; as to the quantity of traffic it could command. The navigation of the Wever has the Saltworks to support it: whereas that between Chester and the valley of the Wyches had not more in prospect, than what "two waggons,

waggons, a week, might convey." Whether this was strictly the case is not essential to the intention of these Remarks;—which are purely meant to put projectors of this sort of improvement on their guard, and to intimate that, although inland Navigation is, in some instances, highly beneficial to adventurers and the community, it is capable of being greatly injurious to both,—when set about without due consideration. These remarks, however, are now become less necessary than they were, at the time they were first made; as the mania of Canal making no longer rages, in the manner it did at that time; when I was detained some days at Shrewsbury (where not a horse nor scarcely a bed was to be had) by a "Canal Meeting," and the myriads of eager candidates for shares, thereby drawn together*.

Roads.—The more public roads of Cheshire, are mostly *paved:* a practice that is more prevalent, here, even than in Lancashire. See NORTHERN DEPARTMENT, p. 265.

P. 26. "The great public roads, in general, are not very good; being most commonly either rough pavement, called causeways, or deep sand. Within the last twenty years considerable improvements have been made, and greater attention has been paid than formerly was to the private roads.

"*The Parochial Roads*—in the clay parts of Cheshire, are generally bad for carriages; but a small horse pavement on one side of the road, renders them conveniently passable at all times for horsemen: their want of improvement is in some measure owing to the scarcity of good materials, there being gravel but in few situations. The expence of pavement roads in Cheshire is about one shilling per superficial yard."

The subjoined remarks and suggestions, tho scarcely in any particular novel, are entitled to a place, here; as they contain truisms that cannot be too often empressed on the mind of the public. The present laws and regulations, relating to the public roads of this kingdom, are in some particulars shamefully irrational, and would be discreditable to a Nation, even in the dawn of civilization.

P. 63. "The present mode of committing the care of the roads to an officer *chosen annually, and by rotation, without any regard to abilities, &c.* in each parish, or township,

* By subsequent projects, as will be seen, some part of this canal has been rendered productive.

township, seems to be one chief cause of the neglect and insufficiency of their repairs. Sometimes, though seldom, an active intelligent man is in that office; but no proper system of repairs being laid down, and pursued, an ignorant, or indolent officer succeeding the former, suffers what has been properly done to go to decay. The idea of not doing any thing till it is necessary, viz. till the way is nearly impassable, is too prevalent; and there is little chance of roads left to the care of officers *so chosen*, ever being properly taken care of. The following hints are therefore submitted to the consideration and correction of the Board. The plan which has occurred to us, as most likely to remedy the evil complained of, is to empower and direct the justices, at their several quarter-sessions, to appoint proper officers (removable at their discretion) for districts of such a size, as they shall find most adequate to the purpose, with suitable salaries, to be paid out of the county rates. Those surveyors to have the sole management and direction of the roads which are put under their care; and to be accountable to the justices at their monthly meetings, in the several hundreds, where such surveyors are appointed. The usual annual surveyors to be chosen and appointed as heretofore, and their only business to be, on proper notice from the district surveyor, to summon the persons liable to do duty in the high-ways; and to collect the assessments within their several parishes, or townships. The justices to be impowered, on proper application, to make such rates as the nature and publicity of the road may require. Whether it would be proper that the counties at large, under particular modifications, should repair their several roads, by means of regular assessments in lieu of statute duty, may well deserve the consideration of the Board."

Rural Institutes.—Still more sensible and judicious are the following observations, on the promotion and diffusion of agricultural knowledge. They are highly creditable to the good sense and discernment of the writer.—I have great pleasure in transcribing them, at length.

P. 72. "The Agricultural Society of Manchester has produced, from time to time, some good effects in this district; but has not excited that general spirit of improvement in agriculture, which was so laudably intended by the society. Premiums, as an encouragement to particular modes of husbandry, or improvements, in any country, where the prevailing system of practice is different to that proposed, have little or no effect with common practical farmers.

"The

"The judicious cultivator, however, wants no pecuniary reward to stimulate his industry, and spur him on to rational improvements: nothing more is wanted, than to convince him that the thing proposed is attainable in *common practice;* and that it is more eligible and advantageous, than what he has been accustomed to. If that can be done, the improvement, whatever it may be, carries with it, in itself, a more substantial reward, than can be conveyed by any other common means. Without such a conviction, any attempts to encourage improvements, through the help of premiums, will probably be found expensive, and in the end fruitless.

"Much injury has, doubtless, been done to the cause of agriculture, by the sanguine, partial, and exaggerated accounts of fancied improvements of *book-farmers.* In almost every neighbourhood there are speculative men, of an enterprising turn of mind, who have a taste for agriculture; who read the various publications on that subject; and are forward to put in execution each newly supposed improvement. The real practical farmer observes closely these lettered experimentalists; and seeing, as he too often does, a tedious and expensive process end in disappointment, his prejudices are strengthened, and he sneers at what he contemptuously calls *book-farming.* It is an easy thing for a man to sit in his closet, and without any reference either to seasons, markets, or the objects of general practice, in particular districts, to frame such a course of crops as he may think applicable on all soils, in all situations; to suggest implements of husbandry equally well adapted to every required purpose; to recommend different sorts of stock suitable and proper for every kind of soil and climate; and to chalk out what he may conceive to be proper plans of management, applicable to every necessary occasion of husbandry. But when he has so done, even though his schemes of improvement may be sanctioned by the *appearance* of actual experience, yet it will avail but little; there must be something more than mere assertion, for the reasons before alluded to, to have due weight with the generality of farmers: the proofs, as to profit or loss, must lie open to their own observation. This train of reasoning naturally leads us to suggest the propriety of establishing, under the immediate direction and patronage of the Board, farms of *actual experiment,* in various parts of the kingdom. This is a plan which has long been thought of; but should it be carried into execution, upon an extensive scale,

scale, and the different farms be conducted by men of real experience and knowledge (upon a proper system of œconomy and prudence) it would, as we think, more effectually promote the laudable and patriotic intentions of the Board, than could be done by any other means whatsoever."

SUBJECT THE THIRD.

RURAL ECONOMY.

DIVISION THE FIRST.

TENANTED ESTATES,

Their IMPROVEMENT *and* MANAGEMENT.

ESTATES.—*Sizes and Proprietors.*—P. 11. "There are in Cheshire many very considerable estates possessed by gentlemen who have residences within the county. The number of proprietors of land, possessing from 500l. to 1000l. per annum rent, are also many. But the race of yeomanry is supposed to be much diminished; another species of freeholder, however, has increased in those parts bordering on Lancashire and Yorkshire, where a number of small farms have been purchased by the manufacturers of cotton, &c."

"The *tenure* is almost universally freehold. There are some few copyholds, or what may be called customary freeholds paying fines and rents certain, in Macclesfield, Halton, and one or two other manors."

The IMPROVEMENT of Estates,—On this important topic, *practically* considered, we find nothing to notice, in this Report, (excepting what has been transcribed on public drainage):—a circumstance which renders it probable that Mr. Wedge is not a practical man, in the higher departments of Rural Economy. The subjoined remarks, on the *tax* on *draining bricks*, are nevertheless admissible to a place here.—P. 25. "Proper attention, generally speaking, is not in Cheshire paid to the draining of land, particularly amongst the tenantry; and this may

may be chiefly attributed to the short terms of their leases. The tax upon bricks is a great discouragement both to the land-owners, and occupiers, in this most essential branch of improvement. The drains in common use are either made with bricks, loose stones, or brush wood; but chiefly the former."

The EXECUTIVE MANAGEMENT of Estates.—*Tenancy.*—P. 13. "*Leasing* for *lives* was formerly a very constant and general practice in Cheshire; and is still the custom in some parts of the county, although there are, comparatively speaking, few leases for lives remaining. Farms are now more generally set for a *term* of seven, eleven, fourteen, or twenty-one years; not many for a longer term than fourteen, and more probably for eleven years, than any other term. There are also many farms let from *year to year* only, particularly in the neighbourhood of gentlemen's residences.

"The usual *time of entry* is at Candlemas, the off-going tenant having the use of the buildings, and a pasture field near the house, as an outlet for his cattle, until the 1st of May; the off-going tenant is also intitled, by the custom of the country, to three-fourths of what fallow wheat there may be growing on the premises at the time of quitting."

"The *covenants* between landlord and tenant are various and uncertain. The following are some of the most general clauses:—The tenant agrees to pay his rent half-yearly; to pay all levies and taxes whatsoever; perform statute-duty in the high-ways; carry any materials that may be wanted for the repair of his buildings, &c. To keep the buildings, fences, &c. in good, sufficient, tenantable repair, being allowed timber and other necessary materials in the rough for that purpose. The tenant is confined to a certain quantity of tillage, usually about one-fourth of his farm, exclusive of meadow and summer fallow; he is restrained from ploughing any of the lands for more than three, or at most four years, in one course of tillage, and covenants to lay the land down in a husband like manner, with clover and grass seeds. He is also restrained in some instances from sowing brush wheat, and also from setting more potatoes than are necessary for the use of the family; and is not to set or assign any part of the premises without the consent of the landlord. All mines, minerals, salt springs, rocks of salt and alum, are reserved; and also all timber trees, with full liberty to fell, work, and carry away the same. The tenant is

not

not to crop or lop any timber trees, but to endeavour to preserve the same from injury, by cattle or otherwise: not to sell or carry off the premises any straw, dung, soil, ashes, or compost; but to use, spend, or leave the same upon the premises at the end of the term. The tenant is frequently restrained from paring and burning. In some instances, he agrees to lime or marl annually a certain number of acres, and to lay his dung on the pasture land. (?) This last clause has been lately introduced, and seems likely to become general. The injury done to land, by suffering weeds to run to seed, is guarded against in some leases, by the landlord's reserving to himself the power of cutting them down at the tenant's expence, if he shall neglect to do it after being called upon." An admirable clause.

In enumerating "Obstacles in the way of Improvement," Mr. Wedge resumes the subject of leases; and, having intimated the insufficiency of the present lease of Cheshire, as being equally insecure for proprietors and tenants, he hazards the following novel suggestion.—P. 70. "Suppose a lease was made so that (with some of the usual clauses) it might operate as a bond of arbitration between the parties. At the beginning of the term, let an exact report of the state of every part of the premises be made, and signed by both landlord and tenant: at the end of the term, let a survey be made by two persons indifferently chosen, and their award be final. If the estate, at the end of the term, was found to be improved, let the award direct what allowance should be made by the landlord for such improvements. If the estate, in the opinion of the referees, should appear to have been impoverished, let them be authorized to award the amount of damages to be payed by the tenant. But as such a contract would give a greater degree of security to the tenant than to the landlord, the landlord should be at liberty to order one or more views of the premises to be made during a term of twenty-one years. If any mal-practices appeared to be carrying on, then the lease to become void, if from those practices the injury should exceed a certain sum; and if the injury should not exceed that sum, then the tenant to be answerable for damages only. There are objections which may be made to such a lease; but are they greater than what might be urged against the present modes of letting land? and would not such leases, on the whole, be liable to fewer objections, and be more likely to encourage and secure

cure improvements, than what the present usual leases are?"

I have thought it right to insert the above proposal, which is very ingenious. But it is by no means equally practicable, I conceive, with the plan of the *triennial lease**; which is a continual check upon the tenant; yet secures to him, by arbitrative remunerations,—whenever he may quit possession,—the value of any extra improvements he may have executed, to the benefit of the farm in his occupation. There is, nevertheless, one part of Mr. W's plan, which, under certain circumstances, might be incorporated with that of the running lease:—as, when a farm, at the time of letting, is in a *superior state* of improvement or cultivation;—whether by the exertions of a spirited tenant, or the judicious management of its proprietor. In a case of this kind, it may be prudent to let its existing state, at the time of entry, be accurately taken, by men of judgement; and a bond or other security be given, by the tenant, to leave it, at the time of quitting, in a similar state; or pay what men of judgment may estimate the deterioration. But, in more ordinary cases, this regulation can seldom be requisite.

Rent.—On this important consideration, in the management of estates, Mr. W's remarks are superiorly entitled to attention, by men of large landed property. They show that Mr. Wedge (professionally or otherwise) has had considerable experience, or thought maturely, concerning this nice matter; and carry with them more force and conviction, than all the visionary, or interested, insinuations of theorists, necessitated proprietors, and land valuers by percentage.

P. 71. "The idea that high rents operate as a spur to improvements, seems to be too prevalent; as far as an advance of rent can so operate, it has been very freely applied in many parts of this district, and perhaps with greater freedom than success. We think, that gentlemen, by going too far on this plan, not only check, but in a great measure extinguish the spirit of improvement. The zeal of those who expect improvements, *by such means*, overlook the *necessity* of the persons who will comply with the terms proposed; and they also forget, the absolute necessity of a sufficient capital. A man of property

* See Treatise on Landed Property.

property is generally cautious of making an engagement where the rent is oppressive. He sees the success of those who invest their capital in trade, and thinks himself (with justice) intitled to something more than common interest for his money; and to an adequate return for his labour and attention. But those men who have the least to lose, are commonly the most forward to offer the highest rents. Let a farmer be ever so enterprizing and intelligent, yet if he is screwed up in his rent to the utmost, shackled by a short or precarious tenure, or in want of a sufficient capital, he will not have the courage to attempt, nor the *means* to accomplish any material schemes of improvement; but reverse those circumstances, and he will then give scope to his genius, and complete such improvements as must, in the end, conduce to the landlord's interest, to his own emolument, and to the benefit of the public."

DIVISION THE SECOND.

WOODLANDS.

NATURAL WOODS and HEDGE TIMBER.—P. 25.—"There are very few woods of any considerable extent in Cheshire, but there is an abundance of timber, principally oak, in the hedge rows, particularly on the Lancashire side of the county, to a degree which is frequently detrimental to the farms. The injury, however, arising therefrom seems annually to be diminishing."

PLANTING.—P. 25. "There are some few gentlemen of large property, who have paid great attention to planting, and have considerable plantations of young thriving timber upon their estates; but the sorts chiefly planted of late years, have been of the quick growing, or ornamental kinds, and the oak has been too much neglected, owing perhaps to the slowness of its growth."

DIVISION

DIVISION THE THIRD.

AGRICULTURE.

FARMS.—*Sizes.*—P. 12. "The land is occupied in farms of various extent; some may contain 500 acres, and upwards; there are few, however, of more than 300 acres; though the practice (but too frequently a pernicious one) of laying farms together, seems to be increasing; on the whole, it is probable that there is at least one farmer to every eighty statute acres. In a parish, which is nearly in the centre of the county, the following is an exact statement:

	£.		£.		*Tenants.*
From	300	to	150	per annum, there are -	6
	150	to	100	- - - - - - - - - -	11
	100	to	50	- - - - - - - - -	18
	30	to	15	- - - - - -	3
	15	to	8	- - - - - - - - - -	28"

Homesteads.—P. 12. "The farm buildings are in various states, and in various situations; but, for the most part, in good repair, although few can be said to be well situated. They are too often, without considering the advantages of situation, crowded together in villages, and the lands occupied with them confused and intermixed with each other; and the wash of the yards, a thing of material consequence, often lost to the occupiers. Many of the newly erected buildings are conveniently situated, and properly arranged; but as it does not very frequently happen, that the houses and offices are new at the same time, the ancient scite is usually retained for the sake of such buildings as may happen to remain in tolerably good repair."

Building Materials.—P. 12. "The new erections are either of stone or brick, and slated; the old ones are commonly built with timber, framed, and the spaces filled up with brick; some only with hazles twisted, and daubed with clay. The covering of the old buildings is mostly of thatch."

PLAN of MANAGEMENT of Farms.—P. 14. "It scarcely need to be observed, that dairying is the principal object of of Cheshire husbandry. It is, however, a fact well known here, that this county was formerly as celebrated for its wheat, as it is at present for its cheese; though it may, perhaps, be difficult to account for this change of management in its occupiers. In one instance, a dairy farm, of two hundred and forty acres, is nearly thus employed: from one hundred and fifty to one hundred and sixty acres of pasture; thirty-five acres of meadow; from twenty-five to thirty acres of oats; from eight to ten acres of barley; from seven to ten acres of wheat; and occasionally as many acres of summer fallow. Upon another dairy farm of one hundred acres, there is from ten to fourteen acres of oats; from six to eight acres of fallow wheat; and the like quantity of summer fallow: the remainder in pasture and mowing for hay; of the latter about twelve acres."

WORK PEOPLE.—P. 24. In 1793,—"A day labourer in winter has from seven to eight shillings per week; in the spring months from eight to nine shillings; and in harvest from nine to fifteen shillings per week. A waggoner has from nine to ten guineas per annum. Home servants, from six to nine pounds; and boys, from one and a half to three and a half guineas per year. A dairy maid, who has the whole care and management of the dairy, from eight to ten pounds per annum. An assistant to the mistress in the dairy, about 5l. 5s. Common maid servants, from 3l. 10s. to 4l. 10s. and girls, from thirty to fifty shillings a year. Mowing grass, from eighteen-pence to two shillings per acre; oats and barley, from sixteen-pence to two shillings; and reaping, from six shillings to eight shillings per acre. Threshing wheat, from three-pence to four-pence a measure of thirty-eight quarts; oats, from 2s. to 2s. 6d. and barley, 3s. to 3s. 6d. for twenty measures. Blacksmith's work is from four-pence halfpenny to five-pence, per pound."

WORKING ANIMALS.—P. 27. "Horses are universally used by the farmers, (drawn at plough three or four in length); some gentlemen are making experiments with oxen."—"There does not appear to be any thing in the breed of horses here employed in husbandry, that is much worthy of notice; they are of the strong black kind, generally about fifteen hands in height; those purchased in Derbyshire are thought to be the best, although the Leicestershire kind have, as is supposed, improved the general breed of the country."

MANURES.——*Marl.*—On this prevalent manure of Cheshire

Cheshire (judging from the number of "Marl Pitts" almost every where seen) the information here given is very brief; and, the specific qualities of the different Marls employed, not being noticed, it is unsatisfactory. The following particulars constitute the Report concerning this subject.—P. 22. "On the eastern part of the country, lime is chiefly used; and on the west and south, marl is the most general manure; of which there are various sorts, viz. the clay marl, the blue slate marl, the red slate marl, stone marls, &c. The clay marl is supposed to prevail most. The quantity of marl used, varies according to its quality, and the quality and nature of the soils on which it is laid. The quantity is from one to two roods, each rood being seventy-two solid yards and upwards, on an acre; the expence of it filled into the cart is about twopence a yard. Marl is generally laid upon the turf, and after the frost has had its effect upon it, it is sometimes harrowed before the field is broken up."

Lime, P. 22.—"When Lime is used, it is commonly mixed with gutter clods, scouring of ditches, or soil; and laid on the land for barley. Farm-yard dung is frequently mixed with the soil off the sides of lanes, with furrows drawn from between the butts of pasture land, with gutter clods, ditchings, &c. and to these marl or lime are sometimes added."

Sand, P. 22.—"Sand is also frequently used as manure on stiff lands, and with great success."—In compost, I have observed Sand employed.

But the Manure which principally engages Mr. Wedge's attention is foul or dirty *Salt;* which is repeatedly brought forward, in this Report and its Appendix. And although it may be considered in a great degree as a local Manure (being "the sweepings of storerooms, pan houses, &c."), it may be right to collect facts respecting it, at, this, its principal source in the Island.

Refuse Salt.—P. 22. "Foul or dirtied salt is a most excellent manure, either for pasture land, or fallows, when properly incorporated with soil, or other substances. And it is much to be regretted, that so large a quantity as 7 or 800 tons should annually, in Cheshire alone, be lost to the community. The heavy duty laid upon refuse, or dirtied salt, almost totally prevents its use for manure."

In setting forth Obstacles to Improvement; Mr. Wedge favors us with some interesting particulars, relating to the Rise and Operation of the *Imposts* levied on refuse Salt.

P. 67.

P. 67. "The Duty on foul or dirtied salt is an obstacle' also, in the way of improvement. We are informed, that prior to any duty being laid on *foul salt*, every person wishing to use it for manure, paid a salt-officer to attend and see it laid upon the land, or mixed with compost. In 1768 a duty of fourpence the bushel was laid upon it, with a penalty of sixty pounds (two thirds to the informer) if used for any other purpose than the improvement of land. This duty, it seems, was intended to support officers to accompany the salt into the country, and see it rendered useless for any other purpose but manure; yet no addition of officers took place. In 1782 the duty of fourpence a bushel was repealed. From that time refuse salt became, and has continued subject to the same duties as white salt. The reason alledged for this proceeding was, that salt was dirtied purposely, and sold in large quantities, to soap-boilers, skinners, and others, to the injury of the revenue. The fraud, however, was not practised by the farmer, or occupiers of land, in the neighbourhood of the manufactories; but by sending it free of duty to different parts of the kingdom, *coastways*. From twenty to thirty tons, and upwards, had frequently been shipped at once, for London, and other places; the importer paying a penalty of 60l. only, was but a trifling sum, upon a considerable quantity, compared to the duty, which white salt was subject to. The foul or dirtied salt (which is the sweepings of store-rooms, panhouses, &c.) has paid little, or nothing, to Government, since the time the duty was altered: the present duties operate, almost, as a total prohibition of it as manure."—Adding, p. 69.—"When it is considered that the refuse salt, thus unnecessarily destroyed, would be of *vast importance* in the agricultural improvements of this county, it is hoped, the Board will be induced to use their influence to obtain a relaxation of the present duties. And if they should see no impropriety in doing so, we may venture to say, that those very officers and watchmen, who now attend to see the foul salt destroyed, might and would be glad, for a small compensation from the farmer who came to purchase it, to attend him to his land (as was formerly the case) without any neglect of their other duty. It would, perhaps, effectually prevent any defraud in the revenue, if the use of it was confined to the farmers only, and the shipping of it coastways prohibited."

On the *Efficacy* of Salt as a Manure, we are furnished with the following particulars.—P. 67. "A difference of opinion

opinion having been entertained as to the utility of salt as a manure, we insert the following experiments, which we have been favoured with by a gentleman of Northwich: 'After draining a piece of sour rushy ground, about the middle of October, some refuse salt was spread upon a part of the land, after the rate of eight bushels to the acre, and on another part sixteen bushels. In a short time the vegetation disappeared totally, and during the month of April following, not a blade of green grass was to be seen. In the latter end of the month of May a most flourishing crop of rich grass made its appearance on that part where the eight bushels had been laid.

'In the month of July the other portion produced still a stronger crop; (the cattle were remarkably fond of it) and during the whole ensuing winter (which is ten or twelve years since) and to this day, the land retained, and yet exhibits, a superior verdure to the neighbouring closes. Another experiment was made in a meadow, where the after grass being of a coarse rank nature, which the cattle refused to eat, salt being laid upon a part of this meadow, they have ever since preferred the grass growing on that ground to every other part of the field, and eaten up every blade. He also states, that the good effects of salt are particularly seen, by mixing it even with the coarsest manure. A gentleman lately carried a small quantity of couch-grass roots, and other rubbish, harrowed off his land to the salt works, and laid it some time on the ground, where the foul salt, by the direction of the officer, is destroyed; he then carried it back and mixed it with other manure. His barley and his hay-grass were strong, from this composition, beyond his most sanguine expectations. A small quantity of foul salt was also laid upon a court pavement with a view to destroy the vegetation with which it abounded: the first summer after it was laid on, not a weed or a blade of grass appeared, but in the summer following its vegetation was *considerably* more abundant than it was before the salt was used. Its effects on fallow land are equally advantageous; by sowing it at the time of breaking up the land for a fallow, its strong saline quality destroys vegetation, and every noxious insect; but by being mixed sufficiently with the soil, before the wheat is sown, it adds a strong nutriment, and insures the best of crops.' Salt probably acts as a septic on vegetable substances; is an excellent manure, and may be used in all cases where either lime or marl are proper. The price of foul salt from

from the stoves, if free of duty, would now be about four-pence per bushel of fifty-six pounds; and of salt not stoved, about two-pence per bushel."

Surely, if refuse Salt is capable of being rendered thus beneficial to Agriculture, even *locally*, some measure might be hit upon that would prevent any serious Defalcation of the Revenue. To *waste* a valuable Article of the Produce of a Country, and especially one that is conducive to the prosperity of its Agriculture, and this merely for want of due regulations, or to secure some paltry pittance of Revenue, would be disgraceful to any Government.

In the Appendix, to this Report, is a Paper by John Hollingshead, Esquire, of Chorley, in Lancashire, "relative to common Salt as a Manure." But it is mostly of a speculative nature;—vainly indulging in the wildnesses of modern *Philosophers*. In the subjoined passage, however, there is much common sense.

P. 88. "A minister merits reproach who lays a duty, equal to a prohibition, on any article that would so essentially promote the interests of agriculture. High duties may be proper when there is a probability of the article being exhausted, which makes it necessary to limit the consumption; but that is not the case with salt, for on a thorough investigation of the salt rocks, and springs of Cheshire, they appear sufficient to supply the demands of all Europe for ever."—Mr. H. does not say on what authority he grounds his assertions, or by whom the "thorough investigation" was performed.

Arable Crops.—On the business of aration,—which including improvements, as well as the perennial routine of management, constitutes the most difficult and essential part of the business of Agriculture,—we have scarcely any thing that is peculiarly intitled to consideration, in this Report; excepting what relates to the Potatoe crop. I will, nevertheless, notice a few particulars that are found in it.

Species of Crops.—P. 16. "The grains mostly cultivated in Cheshire are, oats, wheat and barley. The milch cattle in winter being in a great measure fed with straw, peas and beans are, on that account principally, very rarely sown."

On the Succession of Crops, I see nothing that requires to be inserted, at length here. A long list of rotations is given (p. 16); from which it appears that three, or even four, Corn Crops are taken from Ley Grounds; the seeds of herbage being sown with the last crop;—in order to produce a foul ley, to lie three or four years; with the intent

intent that the Land may be able to throw out another succession of Corn Crops;—conformably with the practice of the MIDLAND COUNTIES; and similar to that of WESTMORELAND.

On *Tillage* we find the following loose particulars.—P. 15. "It may be necessary to explain as follows, viz. 1st. That when oats on stiff land are sown on one furrow, it is generally ploughed soon after Christmas. 2d. When oats on light land are sown on one furrow, it is generally turned at the time of sowing, or a little while before. 3d. When land is winter fallowed for oats, the number of ploughings are in general two: the first ploughing is in November, the second at the time of sowing. 4th. A winter fallow for barley; three ploughings generally: the first in November, stirred across and harrowed in March, and the third ploughing at the time of sowing. 5th. A pin fallow for wheat; two ploughings after a previous crop, which has been gathered in the same year the wheat is sown. 6th. Brush wheat, is wheat sown on one furrow after a previous crop. 7th. Summer fallowing of stubbles; the number of ploughings generally four: the first ploughing in February or March; and 8thly, Summer fallowing of turf, or what in Cheshire is called "a fork." Number of ploughings three or four: the first at Midsummer, or a little before."

On *Manuring*, the Reporter, for the first and almost only time, ventures to censure the established practice of Cheshire; and to urge, in a didactic way, an alteration of management. His animadversions, however, are much too general to be just; and only prove the Writer's want of extensive practice.

P. 65. "There is evidently a mistaken practice in Cheshire, with respect to the application of manure: it is not, however, an error peculiar to this county, for there are, perhaps, few parts of the kingdom where it is not to be met with. The practice alluded to, is that of laying manure upon land of inferior quality, while that of a better kind remains in a state which wants improvement. This is the general custom of the country, not only with respect to manure which is purchased, but with that also which arises from the consumption of produce on the premises. The better part of almost every farm in the kingdom is robbed, and in some degree impoverished, by attempting to improve, at an evident loss, the poorer parts of it. Where a farm has justice done it, every part in rotation should receive the manure arising from its own produce. There

There are, indeed, some instances of lands being of so rich a quality, either for tillage or pasture, that by laying any manure upon them, an injury would be sustained; but on the whole, it is an evident fact, that any manure whatever, (if not in its nature unsuitable to the soil) *will always* be attended with a *much more* profitable return, when laid on *good land*, than it will when laid upon land of inferior quality."

This general principle of management (which the Reporter continues to recommend) if operated upon, would only tend to bring husbandry back to the obsolete system of *infield* and *outfield*,—of occasionally plowing and cropping the inferior lands situated at a distance from the homestead, and bringing home the produce, to enrich the better lands:—a practice which, within memory, I believe, prevailed in most parts of Scotland; and which has probably heretofore prevailed in England. See NORTHERN DEPART. p. 515. But the inferior lands, thus treated, and of course impoverished by such treatment, have, by a change of practice,—by a right application of manure, and the turnip culture,—been raised to a state of productiveness.

So much depends on soils, subsoils, and situations (both in regard to soil and manure) that all *general rules*, respecting this matter, must be in a degree futile. Even the obsolete plan of infield and outfield, may, in some cases, be proper. Every judicious husbandman will, in this part of his conduct, as in others, be guided by a variety of given circumstances.

Semination.—P. 24. "Wheat is generally sown about Michaelmas, but when it follows a crop of potatoes, it is rarely sown before the end of October; oats from the middle of March, to the end of April; and barley usually in the beginning of May."

Of the management of *growing crops*, of *harvesting*, or of the *homestead* management, we have no notice;—either generally, or as being applicable to any particular crop; excepting what relates to

POTATOES.—Cheshire (as well as Lancashire) having long been celebrated for its potatoes, it will be right to pay close regard to its modes of culture. Judging from the produce of a single parish, we may conceive the entire produce of the county to be immense. P. 19. "Potatoes are cultivated in the parish of Frodsham, (which is near to the Mersey, and near to Runcorn) with as much success, and probably to as great an extent as in any other parish in in the kingdom. It is estimated, that not less than 100,000 bushels, of 90 lb. weight, have annually, for some years past, been grown in this parish; and a ready sale has generally been found for them, owing to the great demand for this root in Lancashire, and to an easy and cheap communication with Liverpool, by means of the river Mersey, and with Manchester, by the Duke of Bridgewater's canal."

Mr. Wedge has furnished us with many particulars concerning the culture of this valuable root. These I will endeavour to arrange, in the progressive order of practice.

Soil.—P. 19. "To plant potatoes in (what is here thought to be) the most approved manner, a considerable depth of dry, light, or loamy soil, is necessary."

Tillage.—P. 19. "The mode of culture is generally this: The land is ploughed before Christmas to receive the meliorating influence of the frosts; in April it is ploughed across, torn and pulverized with the harrow; after which it is ploughed deeply into butts of about five feet broad."

Manure.—P. 20. "The quantity of manure used for potatoes, is generally from 20 to 40 tons on a statute acre, worth from three to four shillings per ton; and is spread upon the land previous to the last ploughing."

Planting.—P. 19. "In the latter end of April, or the beginning of May, the sets are put into holes made with a setting stick, at the distance of eight or ten inches from each other."

Cleaning.—P. 19. "About three weeks after, or as soon as the buds begin to appear, they are covered with about two inches of soil, spread equally from a trench which is dug between the beds; and this not only adds fresh mould for the benefit of the potatoe plants; but also checks the growth of couch grass, which it will nearly destroy. When the plants appear in full row the ground is hoed, and afterwards kept clear from weeds by hand, till such time as the plants have covered the ground."

Harvesting.—P. 20. "In digging up the potatoes, which is usually done with a three pronged fork, care should be taken to pick out all the couch grass, and to carry it off the field. If this is properly done, the land in general is left in a state of most excellent preparation for a crop either of wheat or barley; unless, however, in situations, where foreign manure can be purchased, or the crop is consumed by stock upon the premises."

 Expence.

Expence.—P. 20. "Three ploughings and harrowing may be estimated at from twenty to twenty-five shillings per acre. In planting, a peck of sets to a rood of 64 yards is used: making the holes, putting in the sets, and covering them, costs about three halfpence per rood; and soiling the like expence: the expences of weeding are uncertain; getting up the crop at about sixpence per rood."

Produce.—P. 20. "The produce in a general way, on good land, may be stated at about four bushels, of 90lbs. each, to a rood, or 300 bushels on an acre."

Markets.—The present places of *sale*, have been mentioned, aforegoing.

The *Home Consumption* is as follows:—P. 19. "In years of plenty, when the market is overstocked with potatoes, and the price so low as one shilling per bushel, considerable quantities have been given to different kinds of stock, viz. to feeding cattle, milch cows, horses, and hogs, and we are informed with great success: this is an interesting subject of inquiry."

Effects of Potatoes on Land.—P. 20. "The culture of potatoes must certainly have a tendency to impoverish every estate on which it is practised. The yard dung, in many parts of Cheshire, is too much lavished on the potatoe ground; but this practice is, as has been stated, in some instances guarded against by the covenants between landlord and tenant."

Letting Potatoe Grounds.—P. 21. "Land for potatoes is very frequently hired of the farmers, by gardeners, or labouring people, at from five to six pounds per acre; and when it is considered, that the interest of the *hirer* extends no farther than for *one* year, it is not to be wondered at, if (as frequently happens on light and weak soils) the land is left, after a crop of potatoes, in a much worse state than it was in before: on the contrary, if the crop is a good one, and the ground is properly worked and cleaned at the time of getting it up, the land may be made as clean from couch grass and weeds, as any other kind of culture can possibly make it. But the object of the poor man is to free the land of the potatoes, not of the couch grass which it may contain; and it will generally be found to require a very constant attendance from the farmer, to see that the latter is properly effected."

The mode of practice, above described, is spoken of by the Reporter as "the most approved manner." He mentions, however, a *variety* of practice, for shallow soils. P. 20.

P. 20. "On shallow soiled land, potatoes are generally planted and soiled with the plough; a method which consumes less manure than that before described. In this method of planting, (the land being prepared as before) a furrow about four inches deep is turned; the manure is spread lightly in the hollowed space of it, the potatoe sets having been previously dropt at the distance of about eight or ten inches asunder; the same furrow is then turned back upon the sets; the next row of sets are dropt, and covered with manure in the hollowed space of a furrow, which is turned towards the first row at the distance of about 18 inches from the first line of sets, viz. leaving something more than two furrows width of soil untouched with the plough: the sets and manure are then covered as before; and the same method pursued, till the whole of the ground intended to be planted, is finished. Soiling with the plough is thus performed: As soon as the plants begin to appear, the ground which had been balked is split, or turned both ways upon the young plants, with a long wrested plough, so as effectually to cover them. After this has been done, the crop is to be kept clear of weeds by the hand and hoe."

Of the method of cultivating *early Potatoes*, we have the following account.—P. 18. "The improved method, or what is yet called the secret of raising early potatoes, was first practised in this county by one Richard Evans, late of Wellazey, in Wirrall, deceased. The secret consists in nothing more than to keep the sets, (which should be of the earliest kind), during winter, carefully guarded from the frost, in a warm place, where they may sprout at least three inches, by the beginning of March. As soon after that time as the season happens to be favourable, they are, with the sprout on, to be carefully planted in a dry soil, in drills, with a small rib of earth between each drill, and the end of the sprout just under the surface of the ground. The plants should be kept covered with straw or rushes, &c. every night, as long as the frosts continue, and uncovered every favourable day. By this method, early potatoes have been as plentiful in Liverpool market, for some years past, in the middle of May, as they used to be, before this method was known, in the middle of June. A second crop of potatoes is sometimes grown on the same field, in the same year."

Concerning the *varieties* of Potatoes, the *choice* and *method of cutting* the *sets*, the *diseases* of potatoes, the method of *preserving* the crop in winter, or the *crops* that usually

usually *precede* and *follow* potatoes, we find no mention made, in this Report.

GRASS LANDS.—On this principal division of his subject (duly considered);—namely the Grass Lands of Cheshire, their Nature and Management;—the Reporter is almost silent: and this notwithstanding Cheshire is a Dairy, and of course a grass land County. Its management, it is true, is far from being proper to be held up as a pattern to the rest of the kingdom. On the contrary, it appears, in a general view, to be behind almost every other part of it. Nevertheless, on closer examination, minutiæ of excellence might probably be found: and its present state ought certainly to have been reported.

In the following unintelligent paragraph about "watered meadows," is comprised the whole of the information, directly given on this subject.—P. 21. "The meadows which lie near to the rivers are frequently overflowed, and produce great abundance of rich hay and aftermath. The country in general being flat, and the brooks and rivulets running in small confined dingles, there is not any great extent of land capable of this improvement; but in those situations where the land might be floated, there seems very often to want an attention to it."

In the section "Implements," we find the following method of destroying Rushes.—P. 23. "*The hodding scythe*—is an implement, we believe, but little known. It is much used in some parts of this country, for the purpose of freeing land from the common rush, and with good effect.

"Since this method of eradicating rushes has been known, many scores of acres of low and marshy meadow lands have been cleared; and with the aid of gutters more than doubled in their value. This implement is nothing more, than a short strong scythe: the blade is about twenty inches in length, but curves in a different manner to the common scythe; the edge is nearly one way of it, in a straight direction from heel to point, but the flat part of the blade forms a curveture which varies about four inches from a straight line. The sneath, or sneyd, to which the blade is fixed, is about three feet six inches long, and has one scythe like handle, placed about eighteen inches from the top: when the work is performed, one hand is placed upon the top of the sneath, and with the handle in the other, the crown of the rush roots, by a smart stroke of the implement, is scooped out by the convex part of the blade.

blade. The most proper season for this business is early in the spring. The rush roots should be carried off to form a compost, and the hod holes, or cavities, filled level to the surface of the land with soil, and hay seeds be sown therein."

ORCHARDS.—P. 13. "Considering how well adapted to fruit trees, both the soil and climate are in many parts of the country, there has been a very great neglect in respect to the planting of orchards."

This remark, so far as relates to the paucity of orchard grounds in Cheshire, is strikingly just. But whether this privation is owing altogether to neglect, or whether the natural economy (the climature, soil, or subsoil) of Cheshire, as of Lancashire (which in many respects have a close resemblance of each other) is unfriendly to orchard fruits, is not for me to determinine, here.

HORSES.—See the section *Working Animals*, p. 24, for information on this subject.

SHEEP.—On this subject, likewise, Mr. W's information is narrowly circumscribed.—P. 28. "There is not any generally fixed breed of sheep in Cheshire; each common or waste maintains a few; but on the forest of Delamere great numbers are kept. The wool of the forest sheep is fine; it sold in 1792 as high as thirty shillings the tod of twenty pounds; but last year did not reach twenty-six shillings; and some was sold as low as a guinea."

P. 29. "The Dairy—being the main object, there are very few sheep kept on the farms in Cheshire; what are kept, the farmers are supplied with chiefly from the Welch and Scotch markets, and from the neighbouring counties of Salop, Derby, &c. In general, no more sheep are kept on the farms, than can be supported by '*running in the stubbles, and picking the fallows.*'"

Cheshire, as has been said, resembles Lancashire, in this and many other particulars. A traveller might pass through them without observing a sheep. The forest and common sheep of Cheshire are similar to those of Shropshire; namely, a fine wooled variety of the ancient stock of the kingdom.

CATTLE.—*Breed.*—To this subject Mr. Wedge has paid more attention; and speaks of it, with a degree of intelligence.

P. 29. "There is no species of cattle which is peculiar to this county, and that being the case, the nature of the breed is scarcely to be described. The long-horned Lancashire, the Yorkshire short-horned or Holderness, the

the Derbyshire, the Shropshire, the Staffordshire, the Welch, Irish, Scotch, and the new Leicestershire cattle, have at different times been introduced in different parts of the county, and the present stock of dairy cows is a mixture of all these breeds. It is impossible to say which of the intermixed breeds are the most approved of as milkers, milk being the general object. To describe the variety of opinions on this head, would be almost an endless task."

P. 30. "The milking cows of Cheshire will not, it is thought, weigh more than seven scores per quarter, on the average, when fattened; their prevailing colours are red, brindled, and pied; with almost universally "finched," or white backs."

These two passages may seem to be at variance:—the first asserts that there is no established breed in the county; while the latter tends to do away that idea. And, in speaking of "Improvements," toward the end of the volume, the Reporter expresses a doubt of whether the existing breed is capable of any improvement; and, contrary to his usual practice, enters at some length into the general subject, in a manner that will not be well relished by *refined* breeders.

P. 64. "In the present breed of milch-cattle (profitable as they undoubtedly are) the general opinion seems to be, that there is very little room for improvement: considerable attention having already been paid to them. That there is *some* room for improvement, must be admitted; it has probably, however, no great degree of reference either to *bone* or *offal*. We have noticed before, that the milch cattle of Cheshire are frequently continued as milkers to too great an age, before they are slaughtered; but we are at the same time inclined to think, when the cattle of this county are properly fattened, and killed at a proper age, that our *roasting pieces* are not inferior in flavour, &c. &c. to those of any other breed of cattle in the kingdom. Much has been said about a waste of the produce of the land, in the production of bones and offal,—perhaps it is so. It cannot be denied, that improvement may be made in the general breed of, almost, every county in the kingdom; but still *refinements* may be carried too far; nor is it judiciously promoting the ends of such improvements, to induce the country to expect a greater degree of success than what, in general practice, is commonly attainable. The professed objects of fashionable breeders are, to lessen the quantity of bone and internal fat, reduce the weight of inferior pieces, and add to the

the bulk and quality of the prime joints; such as rumps, sirloins, &c. &c. We admit (for the sake of argument, *what is doubtful)* that these objects have been attained; but has it been shewn, or can it be proved, that, at the same time, when the quantity of bone and offal have been reduced, that there has been, upon the whole, a greater acquisition of prime flesh and fat produced at *less expence*, than what is attained *in the common practice of the kingdom at large?* If such proofs can be adduced, they will certainly promote the ends in view much more effectually, than the *assertions of interested individuals*."

Had Mr. W. argued that "fashionable breeders" have been doing more for *graziers* than for *dairymen*, and that fashionable graziers have been wasting more sustenance on superfluous fat, than unfashionable breeders and graziers ever did on superfluous bone and offal,—his arguments might have been considered as more revalent, in a Report of a Dairy County.

Choice of Cows.—P. 30. "The size, form, and production of the udder, is more attended to than the figure and bulk of the beast: and it seems to be universally allowed, that there is very little, if any, connection between utility for the dairy, and the much extolled points of fashionable breeders, as to shape, beauty, &c. Where larger, and what are called finer shaped breeds, have been tried, they do not in general appear to have answered so well as those smaller hardy ones before described. The general practice in breeding here, is to cross; and it seems to be admitted, that such cows as are bred "upon the land," are found to answer best; for when a purchased cow happens to have been bred upon poorer land than what she is brought to, it is generally not till the second year, at the earliest, that she comes to her full milk." Again—"The points which are generally thought to indicate a good milker, we believe, are as follows, viz. a large thin-skinned udder, large milk-veins, shallow and light fore quarters, wide loins, a thin thigh, a white horn, a long thin head, a brisk and lively eye, fine and clean about the chap and throat; and, notwithstanding some of these points will be allowed, in feeding cattle, to be good ones, yet, upon the whole, a good milker is generally ill-shaped. These indications, as a general rule to judge by, like all other general rules, have many exceptions. It is found, however, by experience, that those cows which possess an aptitude to fatten, very seldom, if ever, are profitable milkers."

The

The *Rearing* of *Cows*.—P. 31. "When calves to keep up the dairies are home bred, they are generally reared from the best milkers; and this is the case with respect to bull calves, as well as heifers. Those which are reared are generally calved in February or March, and are kept on the cows most commonly for about three weeks; afterwards they are fed with warm green whey, scalded whey, and butter-milk mixed, or hard fleetings: of the latter food, about five quarts are given at a meal to each calf. With the green whey, water is frequently mixed, and either oatmeal, wheat, or bean flour, is added; about a quart of meal or flour is generally thought to be enough to mix with forty or fifty quarts of liquid, which is sufficient for a meal for ten calves: if flax seed is given, a quart of boiled seed is added to the whey, &c. for a like number of calves; oatmeal gruel, and butter-milk, with a little skimmed milk mixed in it, are also frequently used for the same purpose: some one of these foods is given night and morning; but at the latter part of the time only once a day, with few exceptions, till, and for some time after, the calves are turned out to grass, and continued in the whole for ten or twelve weeks. The first winter a good pasture is reserved for the calves, and a little hay is given to them night and morning, as soon as hard weather sets in. The second winter their dry food is straw, having an open shed occasionally to shelter under, near their pastnre; they are, however, frequently foddered with straw in the open fields.

"The summer following, the heifers, at two years old off, are put to the bull. During the third winter, in some parts of the county, they lie out in the fields till near calving time; in other parts of the county, the heifers are tied up at the same time as the milking cows are: in both cases, they are fed with straw night and morning, till about a month before calving: hay is afterwards given during the whole of the time they continue to be housed, and sometimes crushed oats when they calve early."

The *Management* of *Cows*.—P. 32. "They are taken up into the cow houses about the middle of November, or as soon as the weather begins to be bad. It is commonly intended that the cows should be permitted to go dry, about ten weeks before the time of their calving; as it is thought to render them less profitable the ensuing season if kept to their milk too long.

"The usual dry foods are, wheat, barley, and oat straw, hay, and crushed oats; the two former kinds of straw are found

found to make cows go dry much sooner than the latter; and another generally allowed effect, attributed to such straw, is, that more than the usual time will be required to churn the cream of cows when so fed; but wheat straw is esteemed much more wholesome than barley straw, and as having less of those effects attending it. Those cows, which, at the time of housing, are not expected to calve till rather late in the spring, are fed with oat straw, and sometimes hay, during the time they are milked; afterwards either wheat or barley straw is given to them. The forward in calf cows, on the contrary, when taken up, are put either to wheat or barley straw, as circumstances may suit; and oat straw is not given to them till the whole of the other straw is consumed. This, however, depends upon the price of markets for grain. The straw fodder is continued in either case, till about three or four weeks before the time the cows are expected to calve: when hay is given to them, the quantity is from two to two and a half (?) per week, per cow. From the time the cows have calved till they are turned out to grass, some ground or crushed oats are given them twice a day, generally, from twenty to twenty-five quarts per week to each cow. In years when hay has been scarce, many farmers have given chopped straw, and a little corn mixed in it, with two small fodderings only of hay per day, and occasionally a foddering of straw at night.

"The cows are turned into an 'outlet' (a bare pasture field near the buildings) about ten o'clock in the morning, and housed again about four in the afternoon, the winter through; but have no fodder in the outlet. It is the practice of many, after the cows have been turned into the outlet, as soon as they shew a desire of being taken up again, they are let into the yard, and housed; and this in very cold, or in wet weather, must be a much better practice, than suffering them, as is usually done, to stand shivering with cold in a field without shelter.

"Turning the cows out to grass in good condition, is a matter much attended to, in order that they may, as the term is, 'start well;' for if a cow is not in good condition when turned out to grass, or has been too much dried with barley straw, it is a long time before she gets into full milk."

P. 33. "The *quantity* of *land* sufficient to keep one cow the whole year, must of course vary with the quality and produce of different soils; and the size and nature of the beast, probably on the average, having reference to the

the quantity of hay and corn consumed, as well as to the grass and straw, a cow, in the course of the year, will consume the produce of three statute acres of land."

P. 59. " The frequent *change* of *pasture* is thought to be very material to the milk product of cows. In the height of summer they have frequently a day pasture and a night pasture; and this is governed by the circumstances of water and shade; but there are those who prefer a range of pasture, and a frequent change also, as most desirable for milking cattle."

P. 33. " The *season* of *calving* is March and April; some few cows drop their calves about Christmas and in February; and the heifers in the beginning or middle of May."

Attendance in the *House.*—P. 34. " *In the Management and Care of a large Dairy of Cows*—(or a pack of cows, as is the term in Cheshire) a constant and almost an unremitting attention is required. At calving time the cowman, or the master, are frequently up two or three times in the course of a night, to see whether 'any thing is amiss.' The racks and mangers are every day well cleaned out; due attention is paid to the appetites of the different beasts, and the quantity of food is governed accordingly. After this is done, the master himself, generally, goes round from stall to stall just before bed time, and adds to or diminishes the quantity of fodder as occasion may require."

On the *Diseases* of *Cows*, the Reporter is not silent. He enumerates " the most usual maladies to which dairy cattle in Cheshire are subject, and the remedies most commonly administered for them,"—p. 34.

Few of these, however, appear to be sufficiently *authentic*, or *probable*, to be here inserted. Nevertheless, the following facts, which Mr. Wedge says he had " from good authority," and the observations thereon, are interesting.

Cows casting their Calves.—P. 35. " A whole dairy of near twenty cows cast their calves in one year. The farmer sold the bull, which he had used, to a neighbour, and the whole number of cows to which he was put the following year cast their calves also. The original owner bought the bull again, and three of his cows only, that were put to him, had the like misfortune. These few instances, although very strongly indicative of some defect in the male, cannot be considered as being absolutely conclusive as to the cause of the complaint; and more particularly

particularly so, as it seems (in Cheshire at least) to be almost generally admitted, that this misfortune most frequently happens, either in wet seasons, or when the cattle are in very high condition; and generally continues for two or three years together. As a confirmation in some degree of this opinion, it is said, that in those parts of North Wales, where the cattle through necessity are kept in lower condition, instances of the kind very rarely happen."

The *proper Age* for *Milking*.—P. 30. "It is admitted also, that milking stock is frequently kept too long without changing. If a cow happens to prove a good milker, she is commonly kept for that purpose, until she is of little value for any other. An old cow may give more milk than a young one, but it is not of so rich a quality; and this is not all, for an old beast will require more, and better food, to keep her in condition and in full milk, than one of a proper age; which age is thought to be between four and ten years; but there are many who think a milker is not in her prime till five years old."

On the *Sizes* of *Dairies*, in Cheshire, or the *Disposal* of *Dairy Cows*, there, we do not find any direct information, in this Report.

MANAGEMENT of the CHESHIRE DAIRY.

THE objects of the Dairy of Cheshire are (as that of other districts, at a distance from the metropolis, or other populous town)—Calves, Butter, Cheese, Hog Liquor.

CALVES.—All that we find, in this Report, respecting calves, as a product of the dairy, is comprized in the subjoined extract.- P. 33. "In a stock of twenty cows, the ten first dropped calves, at a month old, fetched to be slaughtered, from twenty to twenty-five shillings each; the remainder, upon an average, not more than eight shillings; for when the cheese-making season comes on, the calves, whether young or old, fat or lean, are all hurried away to the butcher. Allowing, however, for those cows which are barren, those which cast their calves, and other casualties, the average price of the calves does not amount to more than about twelve shillings, the dairy through."

The following remedies, for the *scour* in calves, are sufficiently *probable* to be registered, here. P.36. "Skimmed

med milk, or, new milk and water thickened with bean or wheat flour, is usually given, and contined for their food till the scouring is removed; sometimes the steep liquid, or rennet, is given for the same purpose; one or two half pint drenches, it is said, will be sufficient."

MILK BUTTER.—In the butter manufacture of Cheshire, we perceive a striking difference from the practice of the rest of the kingdom: the West of England practice of raising the cream by heat, and churning it with the hand and arm, is scarcely a more singular variety, in the English butter dairy, than that of Cheshire, in which the milk and cream are churned together, without any previous separation. The public are, therefore, greatly indebted to Mr. Wedge, for a valuable detail of this extraordinary practice. It is at least ingenious.

P. 37. "There does not appear to be any thing particularly worthy of notice, in the process of making butter; unless it be the common practice of churning the 'whole milk,' instead of setting up the milk for the cream to rise, and churning it alone, as is the custom in most other parts of the kingdom. In Cheshire, the whole milk (viz. cream, and all without being skimmed) is churned together; and preparatory to that, the meal is immediately, after milking in summer, cooled in quantities proportioned to the heat of the weather, previous to its being put together, which from time to time is done in earthen 'cream mugs,' or jars. In these jars (containing four or six gallons each) it is intended to stand till it is 'carved' (as the term is) or clotted in a proper degree for churning, and this is judged to be the case sufficient for the intended purpose, as soon as the whole is coagulated, and has acquired a small degree of acidity, which will generally take place in warm weather, in the course of a day or two. In winter, the cream mugs are placed near a fire, to forward the 'carving' or clotting of the milk. If the milk in warm weather has not been sufficiently cooled before it is put to the former meal, or if in winter the mugs have been set too near the fire, it curdles the whole mass, making it (as the phrase is) 'go all to whig, and whey;' and afterwards heave in the mug. Again, if in summer, or, when kept in a warm situation, the milk is not churned within a day, or a little more, after it is sufficiently 'carved,' a kind of fermentation and heaving also ensues; in both cases, the butter will be rank, and ill tasted; nor will the milk produce so much butter, as when it has been properly managed, and churned in proper time. We do not find, that any

any comparative experiments have in this part of the country been made, so as to ascertain, with any degree of certainty, which of the two common modes of obtaining butter is best, in regard to quantity, flavour, &c. This matter, however, well worth attending to, might easily be ascertained by experiments both simple and unexpensive.

"In most parts of Cheshire, butter is made up for sale in lumps, that have the term 'dishes' applied to them; the weight of a 'dish' is one pound and a half, or twenty-four ounces."

CHESHIRE CHEESE.

BEFORE the method of manufacturing, this valuable article, was described, it would have been desireable to have looked into the DAIRY ROOM, most prevalent in Cheshire; as well as into the milking yard of that county. But for a description of the former, we look in vain, in Mr. Wedge's Report. We must therefore be content with Mr. W's own ideas, respecting a milk house. They are by no means inappropriate, and may have been the result of some experience.

P. 42. "*Milk-House.*—A northern aspect is the best for a milk-house, and it should be so sheltered by buildings, or trees, as to keep it from the rays of the sun during the whole day. The perfection of a milk-house is to have an uniform temperature in its contained air, the whole year round. If this is not attainable, recourse must be had in hot seasons to cold spring water, which should be daily and plentifully poured on the floor: nor is cleanliness, at any time, in any of the departments of the business to be neglected."

MILKING.—The Cheshire practice, in this particular, is well described.—P. 60. "There is in general on dairy farms, one woman servant to every ten cows, who are employed in winter in carding, spinning, and other housewifery business; but in milking, the women, both night and morning, during summer, where large dairies are kept, are assisted by all the other servants, men and boys, except the man who drives the team."

P. 42. "The hour of milking, during the summer season, is six, both night and morning. It is a general, and very

very prudent practice for the farmer himself to attend the milking, to assist in carrying the milk into the milk-house, and to see that the cows are properly dripped; for as each succeeding drop which a cow gives at a meal exceeds the preceding one in richness, it is an important point to have the cow's bags completely emptied, and the more particularly so, because if that is not done, it has a tendency gradually to make them go dry. The milking pails commonly used, will hold about two gallons each, which, when full, are emptied into a bowl, or large wooden vessel, that will contain three such pails full, and in that the milk is carried to the milk-house, where it is poured through a sieve into a leaden milk cooler. The sieve is supported over the cooler by a cheese ladder. This cooler is framed on legs like a table, on the top of which legs is a leaden cistern about nine inches deep, five feet long, and two feet and a half wide. In the bottom of the cistern is a vent hole, to which is fitted a wooden spiggot, or plug. In some dairies, there are coolers sufficient to hold a full meal's milk. In this case the milk stands in them all night, and after its cream is skimmed off in the morning, it is drawn out through the vent hole, into brass pans, and so carried into the cheese tub. Where there is only one cooler, and that insufficient to hold a meal's milk, the milk is drawn off into pans as soon as the cooler is full, which is again filled as it is brought to the house, observing to leave the milk last brought in, to stand in the cooler all night. The expeditious cooling of the milk has considerable influence in preventing its tendency to acidity in the heat of summer. When the weather is cold, the use of the leaden cooler is generally set aside.

"If milk was repeatedly drawn off into pans, and again returned into the cooler until quite cold, perhaps the quality of the cheese might thereby be improved, and the difficulty in making it be lessened."

MANUFACTURE of CHESHIRE CHEESE.

MR. WEDGE's account of this process forms, by far, the most valuable part of his Report; and is entitled to much attention.

The heads and the mode of registering are similar to those which I adopted in GLOCESTERSHIRE (have mostly been copied from them). But the natural order of arrangement

ment is not always adhered to; being, in some instances, inverted, and of course rendered ridiculous: a defect, however, which I will here endeavor to rectify.

I have the greater satisfaction in giving Mr. Wedge's account a place, here; as he has judiciously entered into the *detail* of the several processes; without which, as has been said, no *practical* knowledge of them can be conveyed. Yet there are many surface-skimming theorists who will, no doubt, censure it, on that account. I transcribe it with greater confidence, as it corresponds with my own observations, on the Cheshire practice.

Mr. Wedge commences his account with the subjoined preliminary remarks.—P. 40. "CHESHIRE CHEESE MAKING*. It is not supposed, that any improvement of consequence has taken place in cheese-making during a great length of time, except only the improved method of preparing steep. In all dairies, the same points are admitted to be the essential; but although the means of attaining those points are, upon farms similar circumstanced, so far alike, as to differ materially in the minutiæ only, yet upon those minutiæ much of the art of cheese-making depends.

"That an exact uniformity does not prevail, in every part of the process, is no wonder; for there is not any of the business which is conducted in a dairy, that tends in the least to chymical exactness. And where there is no precision, there can be no just comparison; and where no comparison can be made, there exists no foundation for an attempt at uniformity. The degree of heat at setting the milk together, is never measured; the quantity of steep is guessed at, and its quality not exactly known, the quantity of salt necessary is undefined; and the 'sweating' or fermenting of the cheese when made is accidental. Under these circumstances, we cannot help expressing, by the way, a wish that a cheese farm of experiment might be established in this county, under the patronage of the Board of Agriculture, and under the management of a person well skilled in chymistry, that something like scientific principles might be discovered on which to conduct the process."

The different operations, &c. as described by Mr. W. I arrange in the order in which they succeed each other, in practice.

1. The

" * The whole of this account refers to cheese of 60 lbs. weight.—Cheese of this weight is susceptible of every excellence to be found in Cheshire cheese."

1. The QUALITY of the MILK, subjected to this particular species of cheese.—P. 43. "Cheshire cheese is generally made with two meals milk, and that in dairies where two cheeses are made in a day. In the beginning, and end of the season, three, four, and even five or six meals milk are kept for the same cheese. It is difficult to say what proportion of the cream is withheld from the milk, before it is put together; the quantity may be varied, either through supposed judgment and skill in the art, or from other motives. The general custom, however, in the best dairies, is to take about a pint of cream, when two meal cheeses are made from the night's milk of twenty cows."—P. 59. "The Milk of Cows—which have newly calved, if the quantity of it be considerable, has a tendency to cause the cheese to heave: the first meal's milk that goes into the cheese-tub, is generally the sixth or seventh from calving. Others never having observed this tendency, always put the third meal from calving into the cheese-tub."

2. The PREPARATION of the MILK, for Coagulation.—*Degree* of *Warmth*.—P. 46. "It is, we believe, generally admitted, that not only the quantity, but the quality of the curd, as to texture, (viz. toughness, or otherwise) depends in a great measure upon the length of time the cheese is in coming, and that the time again depends on the quantity, and strength of the coagulum used, the state of the atmosphere, and the heat of the milk when put together. In this stage of the art, where a degree of accurate certainty seems to be required, there is no other guide but the hand, and the external feelings: the thermometer of a Cheshire dairy-woman is constantly at her fingers ends. Accordingly, the heat of the milk, when set, is endeavoured to be regulated by the *supposed* warmth of the room, and the heat of the external air (having reference also to the quantity, and strength of the steep) so as that the milk may be the proper length of time in sufficiently coagulating, which is generally thought to be about an hour and half. The evening's milk (of suppose twenty cows) having stood all the night in the cooler and brass pans, the cheese-maker, (in summer) about six o'clock in the morning, carefully skims off the cream from the whole of it, observing first to take off all the froth and bubbles, which may amount to about a pint; this not being thought proper to put into the cheese, goes to the cream mug to be churned for butter, and the rest of the cream is put into a brass pan. While the dairy-woman is thus employed,

ployed, the servants are milking the cows, having previously lighted a fire under the furnace, which is half full of water. As soon as the night's milk is skimmed, it is all carried into the cheese tub, except about three-fourths of a brass pan full (three or four gallons), which is immediately placed in the furnace of hot water in the pan, and is made scalding hot; then half of the milk thus heated in the pan is poured also into the cheese tub, and the other half is poured to the cream, which, as before observed, was skimmed into another brass pan. By this means all the cream is liquified and dissolved, so as apparently to form one homogeneous, or uniform fluid, and in that state it is poured into the cheese tub. But before this is done, several bowls, or vessels, full of new milk, will, generally, have been poured into the cheese tub, or, perhaps, the whole morning's milk. Care is taken to skim off all the the air bubbles, which may have formed in pouring the new milk into the cheese tub."

P. 45. "The *Colouring* for cheese is, or at least should be, Spanish arnotta; but as soon as colouring became general in this county, a colour of an adulterated kind was exposed to sale in almost every shop. The weight of a guinea and a half, of real Spanish arnotta, is sufficient for a cheese of 60 lbs. weight. If a considerable part of the cream of the night's milk be taken for butter, more colouring will be requisite. The leaner the cheese is, the more colouring it requires. The manner of using arnotta is to tie up in a linen rag the quantity deemed sufficient, and put it into half a pint of warm water over night; the infusion is put into the tub of milk, in the morning (with the steep infusion) dipping the rag into the milk, and rubbing it against the palm of the hand as long as any colour comes out."

Some *varieties* of practice are enumerated. But I find nothing that arrests attention; excepting that—"in many celebrated dairies, during the whole summer, they do not heat a drop of the night's milk, only dissolve the cream in a brass pan floated, or suspended in a furnace of hot water; and this (we are credibly informed) was the practice of a person, who made more than five hundred weight of cheese of the very best quality per cow (of 120 pounds each hundred) in one season:"—and that—"the lowest degree of heat on setting together, viz: putting the milk into the cheese tub, is one half cooler, than milk from a cow, the highest about twice the warmth of that animal's milk;

milk; and this is meant as the practice in *summer*, speaking *generally*." p. 47.

An idea, however, is thrown out, p. 47,—that—"it is generally on poor clay lands, that the milk most requires warming; on good rich soils the milk will not bear much heating; at least, by so doing the process of cheese-making is rendered more difficult."

Quere, does this account for the best cheese being, every where, made from lands of a cool nature? And, quere, is it not coagulating the milk for Cheshire cheese, very hot, that gives it the harshness which it often possesses? But, quere, is it not necessary to set the milk, hot, for large cheeses? These, by way of agitating the theory of a difficult art.

3. COAGULUM, or *Rennet*.—In Cheshire, not only the "mawskin," or stomach of the calf, is used for the purpose of coagulation; but also the curd, or "chyley matter," which therein happens to be contained, at the time of slaughter; agreeably with the practice of Norfolk. This circumstance, perhaps, may seem to account for the rank disagreeable flavor, which some Cheshire cheeses emit.

The *Choice* and *Curing* of "*Mawskins*," or Bags.—In most dairy districts, the skins are usually *purchased*, by dairy women, in a *cured state*:—Butchers, or persons who make a business of it, performing this part of the process. However, as I have not before met with the operation; and as Mr. Wedge's account of it, as well as of the choice of the skins, appears to be, in the principal parts, rational, if not authentic, I will here insert it.

P. 41. "*Rennet or Steep*—is an infusion of the prepared stomach of a sucking calf, usually called the bag or mawskin: in order to have this in perfection, the calf should have lived on new milk only, and be quite in health at the time of being killed. Under these circumstances, the maw-skin is always found to contain, when taken out of the calf, more or less of a firm, white, curd-like matter. This chyly matter is frequently salted for present use, and is generally esteemed a proof of its being a good skin; but this proof of excellence is not always to be depended on. When calves are sold, it is the custom of Cheshire to have the maw-skins returned; and it is also customary for such farmers who live near to a butcher's shop, to attend the killing of calves, in order to choose the best. If the skins of their own calves prove bad ones, they

they pick those that have curd in them, and taking it out, put it into such of their own skins as happen to have none of it, and leave the empty ones for somebody else. Amongst imported skins, the farmers often meet with those of lambs and kids; which answer the intended purpose but indifferently.

"When it comes from the butcher, the chyly matter is taken out, and the skin cleared from slime, and every apparent impurity, by wiping, or a gentle washing; the skin is then filled nearly full of salt, and placing a layer of salt upon the bottom of a mug, the skin is laid flat upon it; this mug is large enough to hold three skins in a course; each course of skins should be covered with salt, and when a sufficient number of skins are thus placed in the mug, that mug should be filled up with salt, and with a dish, or slate over it, be put into a cool place, till the approach of the cheese-making season, in the following year."

Preparing Rennet for *Use*.—In this, the Cheshire practice differs from that of Glocestershire. In Cheshire, the cured skins, at the approach of the cheese-making season, are "all taken out, laid for the brine to drain from them, and being spread upon a table, they are powdered on each side with fine salt, and are rolled smooth with a paste roller, which presses in the salt; after that, a thin splint of wood is stuck across each of them, to keep them extended while they are hung to dry" (p. 42); agreeably to the practice of the North of England.

In *using* the skins, the under-mentioned is the practice of Cheshire.—P. 44. "In the evening, part of a dried maw-skin is cut with a pair of scissars, and put into half a pint of luke-warm water, to which is added as much salt as will lie on a shilling. In the morning, this infusion (the skin being first taken out) is put, as hereafter mentioned, into the cheese tub of milk; but so great is the difference in quality, of these skins, that it is difficult to ascertain what quantity will be necessary for the intended purpose. A piece, the size of a half crown, cut from the bottom end of a good skin (the bottom end being strongest) will commonly be enough to give sufficient strength to the coagulum for a cheese of 60 lb. weight; although ten square inches of skin are often found too little.

"It is customary to cut two pieces for each cheese; one from the lower, the other from the upper part of the skin. The cup in which this skin is infused, ought to be well scalded every day."

Mr.

Mr. W. mentions an "improved method of preparing steep." This is nearly the same as that of GLOCESTERSHIRE, which I have described. There are, however, shades of difference between them. I therefore insert Mr. W's description.

P. 44. "Take all the maw-skins provided for the whole season, pickled and dried as before; put them into an open vessel or vessels, and for each skin pour in three pints of pure spring water; let them stand twenty-four hours, then take out the skins, put them into other vessels; add for each one pint of spring water, and let them stand twenty-four hours as before: on taking the skins out the second time, gently stroke them down with the hand into the infusion. The skins are then done with. Mix those two infusions together, pass the liquor through a fine linen sieve, and add to the whole a quantity of salt, rather more than is sufficient to saturate the water, viz. until a portion of salt remains undissolved at the bottom of the vessel. The next day, and also the summer through, the scum, as it rises, is to be clearly taken off, and as the liquor should not be suffered to remain, without a portion of undissolved salt at the bottom, it will be necessary frequently to add fresh salt, as that which was dissolved will gradually form itself into crystals, and be taken off with the rising scum. Somewhat less than a wine half pint of this preparation will generally be sufficient for 60 lbs. of cheese. Whenever any of this liquid is taken out for use, the whole should be well stirred up."

4. The PROCESS of COAGULATION.—P. 48. "The rennet and colouring being put into the tub, the whole is well stirred together; a wooden cover is put over the tub, and over that is thrown a linen cloth. The usual time of coming is one hour and a half, during which time it is frequently to be examined: if the cream rises to the surface, before the coming takes place, as it often does, the whole must be stirred together so as to mix again the milk and cream, and this as often as it rises, until the coagulation commences. A few smart strokes on different sides of the tub, with the cheese ladder, &c. will forward the coagulation if it is found to be too long in forming. If the dairy woman supposes the milk, &c. to have been, accidentally, put together cooler than she intended, or that its coolness is the cause of its not coming, hot water, or hot milk, may be poured into it, or hot water in a brass pan partially immerged therein. But this must be done

done before it is at all coagulated; for after that takes place. though but imperfectly, it must not be tampered with so as to break the forming curd: a considerable part of the cream would thereby be diverted into the whey, and the quantity of curd much lessened. Before the coagulation takes place, an additional quantity of rennet may also be put in, if thought necessary; but this will, after coagulation, be added with little effect, as no means can be used to mix it with the whole mass, without disturbing the forming curd. If the cheese has been set together hotter than it was meant to be, the opposite means, under the same precautions, may be recurred to. But the more general practice is, to suffer the process to proceed, hot as it is, until the first quantity of whey is taken off; a part of which being set to cool, is returned into the tub to cool the curd. When the cheese happens to come much sooner than a proper time, owing to too great a degree of heat in the milk on setting, or putting together, or too great a strength of steep, there is less curd; and it is considerably tougher, than when the milk has been set cooler together than usual, or when, rather, too little steep has been used. In the latter case, the curd is exceedingly tender, and when that so happens, a part of the whey is taken out of the cheese tub, and heated as much as may be thought sufficient, to give to the curd, on being mixed with it, a proper degree of toughness. In an hour and a half (as mentioned before) if all goes on well, the coagulation will be formed. This point is determined by gently pressing the surface of the milk with the back of the hand. Experience alone is the only guide in this test, for the firmness of curd will, (as before stated) from the milk set hot together, be much greater than that from milk which has been set cold together. Another criterion to judge whether the milk be sufficiently coagulated, is, to lift up the skimming dish, which is always left inverted on the surface of the milk. If the cheese be properly come, the whey and curd will distinctly appear where the skimming dish lay."

5. The Management of the Curd.—In this stage of the process, the Cheshire practice nearly corresponds with that of Glocestershire, &c. Nevertheless, it will serve to show the utility, if not the necessity, of the minutial operations of this tedious part of the process; more especially as the two practices seem to have grown out of distinct courses of experience; as will pretty plainly appear, in the next division of the subject.

Dis-

Discharging the *Whey.*—P. 49. "If the milk has been set together very warm, the curd (as before observed) will be firm; in this case the usual practice is to take a common case knife, and make incisions across it, to the full depth of the knife blade, at the distance of about one inch, and again crosswise in the same manner; the incisions intersecting each other at right angles. The whey rising through these incisions is of a fine pale green colour. The cheese-maker and two assistants then proceed to break the curd: this is performed by repeatedly putting their hands down into the tub (the cheese-maker with the skimming dish in one hand) and breaking every part thereof as they catch it. Raising the curd from the bottom, and still breaking it—This part of the business is continued till the whole is broken uniformly small: it generally takes up about forty minutes, and the curd is then left covered over with a cloth for about half an hour, to subside.

"If the milk has been set cool together, the curd will (as mentioned before) be much more tender, the whey will not be so green, but rather of a milky appearance. The cheese-maker in this case, instead of the knife, has recourse to the skimming dish, the edge of which she holds perpendicular to the surface of the whey in the tub, and dips it gently an inch or two into the curd, and turns it over until the whole surface is thus turned. The breaking then proceeds as before, but a cautious and gentle mode of doing it, is more necessary than in the former case. Rather more time of course is requisite for breaking down a cold, than a hot cheese; but when sufficiently broken, it is covered over, and left to subside as before. After standing about half an hour, as much whey is taken out of the tub into the brass pans, as conveniently may be, without taking any of the curd with it. In some dairies this whey is occasionally heated, in others cooled (or at least a part of it) and returned into the cheese-tub again, as the weather, or other circumstances, may require. In general, however, it is not returned to the curd, but the whey being laded out of the tub, the breaking recommences as before for about one quarter of an hour; it is then left to settle for a few minutes, when the whey is again laded out with the former precaution.

"The bottom of the tub is now set rather a tilt, the curd is collected to the upper side of it, a board is introduced of a semicircular form, to fit loosely one half of the tub's bottom. This board is placed on the curd and a sixty

sixty pound weight upon it, to press out the whey, which draining to the lower side of the tilted tub is laded out into brass pans. Such parts of the curd as are pressed from under the board, are cut off with a knife, placed under the weighted board, and again pressed. This is repeated again and again, the whey being constantly laded out as it drains from the curd. The whole mass of curd is then turned upside down, put on the other side of the tub, again pressed, pared, and pressed as before. The board and weight being removed, the curd is cut into several pieces of about eight or nine inches square, piled upon each other, and pressed with the board and weight (repeating the cutting and piling) as long as any whey drains from it. A stranger to the business would conclude that much stress was laid upon breaking the curd, just on the surface of the whey, for he observes that the whole of the curd is broken there, and the palms of the women's hands being turned upwards, keep continually raising, and buoying up a portion of curd to the surface, with a seeming intention to delay the crushing of it, until it floats upon the top; but this circumstance is owing to the lightness of the curd in that state, and which on that account escapes the grasp, until it comes in contact with a lighter medium, the air. It scarcely need be added, that the more gentle the whole of the business in the tub is performed, the more perfect will be the separation of curd and whey."

Salting the *Curd.*—P. 51. " The next thing is to break the curd in a brass pan. After being pressed in the tub as long as any considerable quantity of whey drains from it, the curd is cut into three (nearly) equal portions, one of which is taken into a brass pan, and is there by two women broken exceedingly fine. As soon as it is coarsely broken, a large handful of salt is added, which in the subsequent breaking is well mixed with the curd; that portion of curd being sufficiently broken, is put into a cheese vat which is placed to receive it, on a cheese ladder over the cheese-tub. The vat is furnished generally with a coarse cheese-cloth. The second and third portions of the curd are treated in the same manner, and emptied into the vat; except, that into the middle portion, eight, nine, or ten times" (?) " the quantity of salt is usually put. By some dairy-women, however, each portion is salted alike, and with no more than three large handfuls to each. The breaking takes up more, or less time, as the cheese was set together hotter or colder; half an hour is, perhaps, the longest time."

Scalding

Scalding the *Curd.*——This does not enter into the Cheshire, (as into the Glocestershire, &c.) practice; excepting so far as is rather unintelligibly intimated, aforegoing.

Vatting the *Curd.*—P. 52. " The curd, when put into the cheese-vat, in its broken state, is heaped above the vat in a conical form; to prevent it from crumbling down, the four corners of the cheese-cloth are turned up over it, and three women placing their hands against the conical part, gently, but forcibly, press it in near a horizontal direction, constantly shifting their hands when any portion of the curd is starting from the mass, and turning down, and folding up the cloth as occasion requires. As soon as the curd adheres together so as to admit it, a small square board with a corner of the cloth under it, is put on the top of the conical part of the curd, with a sixty pound weight upon the board. Several iron skewers are, at this time, stuck in the cone, and also through holes in the side of the vat. In many dairies, a lever is used to thrust or press the cheese; this is a long substantial pole, one end of which is fastened in the wall, in a direction nearly parallel to the top of the cheese, on which (the cheese) a small board is placed to receive the lever. The power gained by it is used at discretion. In other dairies, they use thrusting screws, which are fixed to the floor above, the power whereof may be regulated at pleasure. The employment of the women is now drawing out, and putting in the skewers*, thrusting and keeping together the portions of curd that the power of the weight, or lever, &c. displaces. This operation is continued till the whey, which at first ran from it freely, begins to be discharged by drops; the weight, &c. and skewers are then removed, and one woman takes up the corners of the cloth, while the others break the curd half way to the bottom of the vat as small as they can. Some people use a wooden, or tin hoop, about nine inches broad, instead of holding up the corners of the cloth, during this breaking. After the upper half of the cheese is thus broken, it has again a weight, or other power, applied to it, and is skewered and thrusted as before; at first the whey, again, runs freely, and the operation is continued as long as those means will press out a drop of whey. Two of the women then

* This operation, I believe, is peculiar to Cheshire and its environs.

then take the four corners of the cloth, (the skewers, &c. being removed) and the other woman lays hold of the vat, which is drawn from the cheese, and after rinsing it in warm whey, and putting another clean cloth over the upper part of the cheese, it is returned inverted into the vat again; and being placed on the ladder over the tub, is broken half way through as before: the thrusting, weighting, and skewering, &c. is repeated, and continued from two to four hours, or as long as a drop of whey can be extracted from the cheese."

Spare Curd.—P. 53. "In the practice of some dairy-women, some spare curd is kept to mix with the following day's cheese, from an opinion that it will prevent the cheese swelling under the press, &c. But on the whole this method is but seldom practised."

6. MANAGEMENT of the WHEY.—In this particular, the Cheshire practice differs widely from that of the rest of the kingdom. I have not, at least, met with any thing, out of this quarter of the island, which bears the smallest resemblance to it. It is probably of Celtic origin; arising from the same root, as the practice of the West of England, in raising the buttery matter of milk; tho produced in a somewhat different manner:—both of them, however, are effected by heat of the same degree. In Devonshire, &c., milk butter is the ordinary product, in Cheshire, &c., whey butter; and the two expedients are equally ingenious, to promote, in the most efficient manner, the respective ends proposed.

Separating the Butyraceous Particles of Whey.—P. 39. "*Scalding Whey.*—The whey, when taken out of the cheese-tub into brass pans, or other convenient vessels, is suffered to stand about a quarter of an hour; when it is put out into other vessels, in which vessels it again stands as long, and is then poured into the furnace-pan. In each of these intervals, it deposits a sediment of curd, which is collected in the bottoms of the vessels, and returned to the mass of curd in the cheese-tub.

"That whey which drips into the tub while the cheese is being pressed over it, is always kept by itself, and set by till it is at least a day old; as soon therefore as the green whey, in the furnace-pan, becomes so hot as to throw up a little white froth, or foam, *(it must not boil)* the 'thrustings' of the preceding day are put into it (unless as before stated they are otherwise disposed of): these cause the whey to break, and throw up a substance, something in appearance between cream and curd, which is is constantly skimmed off, as long as it rises, and put into the cream mugs to be churned for butter.

"This whey cream, as it is called, is churned up thrice a week, and the average produce of butter which it yields, from one dairy cow, is from eight to ten ounces weekly. The difference of price between this and milk butter is generally from one penny to two-pence per pound."

P. 38. "*Whey Butter.*—It may not be improper to explain, that what is here called 'green whey,' is the clear whey which is taken from the curd out of the cheese tub; the 'white whey' is what is pressed out of the curd by hand, &c. after being put into the cheese-vat: the general term of whey is given only to such part of the liquid as remains after the fleetings (made by scalding the whey) have been skimmed therefrom. In the process of making whey butter, in some instances, the 'thrustings,' or white whey, is set in 'cream mugs,' to 'carve,' and acidulate for churning, either by the warmth of the season, or of a room, in the same manner as in the mode described for making milk butter. In other instances, the green and white whey are both *boiled* together for fleetings (the accounts of which *follow*): in this case, or when the green whey is *boiled* alone, (the boiler, if an iron one, being previously rubbed with butter, to prevent the whey from catching, or acquiring a burnt like taste) such a fire is kept, as will make the whey as hot as possible, *without boiling*, and as soon as they have acquired that degree of heat, the buttery matter, which the whey contains, will break, or separate from it, and rise to the surface. This generally takes place in the course of about an hour; but when the whey is perfectly sweet, a little souring is sometimes added, to produce the breaking effect. In other respects, the process of making whey butter is the same as that of milk butter."

In the Report, these matters are rather whimsically arranged. The method of separating the buttery matter from the whey is spoken of, before the whey has been separated from the curd, and the method of making whey butter, before the cream has been disengaged from the whey. Even when the arrangement is reversed, the information is deficient in perspicuity, and the language, in correctness. Indeed, the contents of the last extract are so very different from the rest of the account of the Cheshire dairy, one is led to the idea that they are the "carved thrustings" of some other hand.

Fleetings.—P. 39. "As soon as the whey is exhausted of its

its cream," (in the manner above described) "about two quarts of butter-milk is poured into it, which again breaks into what are called 'fleetings,' or 'flit milk,' and these are skimmed off, for the use of the servants, &c. &c. As it is matter of surprize to many, that so few pigs (about one pig and not more, weighing about 18 scores when fat, is usually fed from the remaining offal of every eight or ten cows) are kept on Cheshire dairy farms, it may not be improper to observe, that except in corn harvest, the produce of the dairy, such as whey, butter-milk, and fleetings, is the constant beverage of the servants and labourers; and to this consumption may be added the constant aid of 'supping,' as it is called, which each dairy furnishes daily to the numerous cottagers around, who fetch it from the houses."

7. The MANAGEMENT of the CHEESES.—*Pressing.*—P. 53. "When no more whey can be extracted by the aforesaid means," (see p. 55.) "the cheese is again turned in the vat, and rinsed as before in warm whey. The cloth now made use of is finer and larger than the former, and is so laid, that on one side it shall be level with the edge of the vat, and on the other wrap over the whole surface of the cheese, and the edges put within the vat: thus perfectly inclosing the whole cheese in the cloth. In this stage of the business the cheese is still higher than the edge of the vat; and to preserve it in due form, recourse is had to a tin binder or hoop, about three inches broad, which is put round the cheese, on the outside of the cloth, and the lower edge of the binder pressed down within the vat, so low as that the upper edge of it may be level with the surface of the cheese. The cheese is then carried to the press, and a smooth strong board being placed over it, the press is gently let down upon it; the usual power of which press is about fourteen or fifteen hundred weight. In most dairies there are two presses, and in many three or four, of different weights. The cheese is, by some, put under the heaviest press first, and by others under the lightest. Some dairy-women, instead of the tin binders, use cheese fillets, which are a strong, broad, coarse sort of tape; one end of which they thrust down with a thin wooden knife between the cheese-cloth and vat, and then draw it tightly several times round the cheese, and fasten it with a strong pin. As soon as the cheese is put into the press it is immediately well skewered. The skewers are of strong iron wire, eighteen or twenty inches long, sharp at the points, and

and turned with a bow at the other end. The vat and tin binder have holes to receive those skewers, especially the binder, which holes are seldom more than an inch from each other. As the press always stands close to a wall, only one side of the cheese can be skewered at a time; on that side, therefore, as many skewers are stuck in different directions, as conveniently may, leaving as many holes unskewered as are skewered, to give an opportunity of changing the holes. The business of skewering continues till the next morning, at six o'clock, and in that time the oftener they are shifted the better; every second time of shifting them, the cheese is turned halfway round in the press, to come at the other side of it. In half an hour from the time the cheese is first put into the press, it is taken out again, and turned in the vat, into another clean cloth. At this time the edges of the cheese are pared off, if they have become sharp under the press (but as the vats are now made usually with the angles rounded, the paring is rendered unnecessary) the vat being wiped dry before the cheese is returned to it."

Scalding the *Cheeses*.—P. 54. "When the cheese is thus first time taking out of the press, it is the custom in some places to put it naked into warm, and in other places into hot whey, where it stands an hour or more; it is then taken out, wiped dry, and after it has stood till cool, is returned to the press. This is done with a view of hardening its coat, that it may stand the better. By rarefying the air near the surface of the cheese, it perhaps may cause its discharge, and prevent blisters."

Further on *Pressing*.—P. 55. "At six o'clock in the evening, the cheese is again turned in the vat into another clean cloth. At this and the former turning, some dairy-women prick the upper surface of the cheese all over, an inch or two deep, before it is replaced under the press, with a view also of preventing blisters. At six o'clock in the morning it is again turned in the vat, with a clean cloth as before: The skewers are now laid aside. When the next day's cheese is ready for the press, the former one is again turned in the vat, with a clean cloth, and put under another press. At six o'clock in the evening, and at six in the morning following, it is again turned in the vat, using at these two last turnings two cloths finer than those which were before used, in order that as little impression as possible from the cloth may remain on the coat of the cheese."

Salting the *Cheeses.*—P. 55. "*Salting-House.*—At noon the cheese is taken from the press (after having been there about forty-eight hours) a fresh fine cloth being put under it, which serves only as a lining to the vat; and is not turned over the upper surface of the cheese, as has been hitherto the case.

"It is then taken and placed nearly midside deep in brine, in a salting tunnel, or tub; the upper surface of the cheese being covered all over with salt. It stands generally about three days in the salting tunnel, is turned daily, and each turning well salted; the cloth being twice changed in the time. The cheese is then taken out of the vat, and in lieu of which a wooden girth, or hoop, is made use of, equal in breadth to the thickness nearly of the cheese: in this it is placed on the salting benches, where it stands about eight days, being well salted all over, and turned each day. The cheese is then washed in luke-warm water, and after being dried with a cloth, it is placed on the drying benches, where it remains about seven days; it is then washed in warm water as before, with a brush, and wiped dry with a cloth. After it has stood about two hours from this washing, it is smeared all over with about two ounces of sweet whey butter, and then placed in the warmest part of the cheese room.

"*Variation of Management.*—On the cheese coming into the salting-house, it is in some dairies taken out of the vat, and after its sides are well rubbed with salt, is returned into the vat, with a clean fresh cloth under it; the top being covered with salt, it is placed on the salting benches, turned and salted twice a day, and the cloth changed every second day. On the salting benches it is continued seven or eight days, when it is taken out of the vat, and with a wooden hoop round it, or cheese fillet, is put into the salting tunnel, and managed therein as before described. When cheese is salted on the benches, before it goes into the tunnel, it is only washed once, viz. before it is smeared with butter."

P. 60. "Twenty-eight pounds, or half a bushel per week, on the average, is sufficient through the summer for dairies where sixty pound cheeses are made, including the other domestic uses of a moderate sized family. The greatest quantity of salt expended on one sixty pound cheese, that we have heard of, is about three pounds; but how much of that actually remains in the cheese, no one is able to say: of the salt put in it when breaking, much is discharged by the thrusting, &c. Whether it acquires much

much saltness in the salting-house, dairy-men themselves are doubtful, although much salt is there expended."

The *Cheeses* on the *Floor.—Cheese Rooms.*—P. 56. "The cheese rooms are commonly placed over the cow-houses, and this is done with a view to obtain that moderate and necessary degree of temperature so essential to the ripening of cheese, to which the heat arising from the cattle underneath, is supposed very much to contribute.

"The most desirable covering for a cheese room, as contributing to that even temperature so much desired, is thatch, for reasons that must be obvious."

Preparing the *Floor.*—P. 56. "Before the cheese is brought into the rooms, the floors are mostly well littered with what the farmers here call 'sniddle;'" (sedge—*carex)* "though wheat straw is frequently made use of for this purpose; but the knots of it are apt to leave an impression in the cheese. The afterneath of grass, well dried, seems to be a good substitute for sniddle. The labour of turning and cleaning cheese is performed almost universally by women; and that in large dairies where the cheeses are upwards of 140 lb. each, upon an average: this they do without much appearance of exertion, and with a degree of ease, which is matter of surprize even in this country."

Management on the *Floor.*—P. 56. "During the first seven days, it is every day well rubbed all over, and generally smeared with sweet whey butter; afterwards a circular space is left, unrubbed, of four or five inches diameter; in the centre of each side the cheese, which, as long as it is afterwards kept, is, or should be turned daily, and rubbed three times a week, in summer, and twice in winter. Scraping the rind should be rendered unnecessary by frequent cleanings. In a warm room, the coat will easily be prevented from rising."

Diseases of *Cheeses.*—At the close of his valuable account of the Cheshire Dairy Management, Mr. Wedge offers some "miscellaneous observations and opinions." These mostly relate to the diseases of cheeses. They are, however, in most part, unavailing. They appear not to have resulted, either from mature practice, or sound science; but rather to have arisen from slight inquiries, and popular notions. One or two of them may be noticed.

On *Cracks.*—P. 57. "Cracks in cheese are supposed to be owing to the use of lime as a manure; to their being exposed,

exposed, at any time after taking out of the press, to a current of air; but especially if so exposed, before it has sweated in the cheese-room."

On "*hove cheese*," the Reporter expatiates, at length. I insert his remarks, here; not as being in themselves of direct value; but as they may lead to the discussion of an important matter, in the manufacture under notice:—namely, what dairy-women term the "sweating of cheese."

P. 57. "*Hove Cheese*.—This is an imperfection derived from *flatulence*, as the general cause. The sweating of cheese is, undoubtedly, a *fermentation*, and if this process of nature has been regular and complete, the *flatulence is thereby expelled*, and cheese is never subject to heave afterwards.

"But if the *fermentation, or sweating*, has been imperfect, which may happen from a variety of causes, indeed from all the causes that check other fermentations, the cheese will be liable to become hove at any time, by the approach of a thunder cloud, by sudden changes of the weather from dry to rain; which effecting an alteration in the state of the air contained in cheese, will cause those to be most hove, in which the most impure air abounds; and that is in cheese made from *rich*, and at the same time, *various* herbage; but more especially *clover*, though the cows should pasture *uniformly* upon *it*. Hence it appears adviseable, to get the cheese to sweat as soon as may be, after it comes into the cheese-room, as that is the only method to prevent the possibility of its heaving, if it be flatulent.

"It is strange, however, that so far from any means being used to give a cheese-room the temperature most favourable to fermentation, nothing has been done to ascertain the degree of heat which usually prevails in it. Every dairy should be furnished with a regular sweating-room. When a cheese is made, there is certainly a specific time when its contained air and juices incline to fermentation; and that natural tendency should at that time be assisted. At present the whole is left to chance; and at the very period, probably, when a cheese is beginning to ferment, the weather becomes suddenly cool; if the process is then checked, the inclosed air becomes putrid, especially if the cheese has been ill made; and the next fermentation is really putrefactive.

"It must be admitted, that the more perfectly the whey is got out of the cheese, by skewering, thrusting, and pressing,

pressing, the less air will be left in it, and less will be the probability of air generating in the cheese. Perhaps cheese would be less subject to heave, if it were made of all cold, or all warm milk; viz. of one equal temperature, as the mixing of warm and cold fluids together generates air. The usual remedy for this evil (heaving) is to weigh it down."

After long observation, and the experiments which I have made, on the defects of cheeses (and published in the *first* edition of my GLOCESTERSHIRE) I perceive nothing in the foregoing unscientific remarks that merits observation, in this place; excepting Mr. W's proposals for "sweating rooms;" which to me convey a new idea. It may well be remarked, however, that as every cheese, or class of cheeses, would require different degrees of heat, to bring them to the desired state of "sweating,"—not one room but a series of rooms would be required, to bring on a due degree of exudation. I have seen rich well manufactured cheeses, in warm weather, throw off, by exudation, (not fermentation) no inconsiderable quantity of oleaginous liquid (resembling that from toasted cheese) so as to reduce, at once, their richness and weight: while others of a dry harsh quality, would receive, manyfoldly, the same degree of heat, before the exudation, or what Mr. W. terms the "fermentation," could be induced. That some cheese, as some hay, is susceptible of fermentation (proper) is evident; but it arises not from "flatulency," or "inclosed air," but from the PRINCIPLE of FERMENTATION being previously lodged in its bulk,—and still remaining in an active state.

8. PRODUCE of CHESHIRE CHEESE.—P. 34. "The quantity of cheese made per cow (varying from 50 lb. to 500 lb. and upwards) must also be governed by circumstances.—The nature of the land, the oldness of the pastures, and the seasons, together with the wintering of the stock, have each a separate influence: on the whole, perhaps the quantity may be stated at 300 lb. from each cow, 'slinkers' (such as cast their calves) and bad milkers included, the dairy through. The quantity of milk, agreeably to this estimation, if a gallon is supposed to produce a pound (sixteen ounces) of cheese, will be eight quarts a day each cow, for twenty-two weeks (nearly) through the dairy. It must, however, be understood, that a number of the cows (which has been intimated before) continue in profit till about ten weeks before the time of calving. There are cows that will give twelve quarts of milk twice aday,

a day, for three or four months together; but it is remarked that those cows, who give much more than eight quarts at a meal, either go off their milk much sooner, or else their milk has less richness in it, than that of others who do not give so large a quantity."

9. DISPOSAL of CHEESE.—The Reporter, quitting his usual manner, speaks with somewhat unguarded warmth, on this subject. In Glocestershire, &c. a practice, similar to that of Cheshire, prevails. The same sort of *confidence* exists. Mischievous consequences may possibly result from it; but none fell under my notice, in that principal district of the cheese dairy of England. I do not see how the business of the dairyman could be conveniently conducted, without some kind of "contract;" few men having room for their whole year's making. Nor does the Reporter propose any other method of dealing, between the "factor," or purchaser, and the producer. His remarks are these:

P. 61. "*Cheese Factors.*—The absurd custom of making contracts between the cheese-factor and the dairy-man, we cannot pass unnoticed. The bargain most frequently is only verbal, and seldom any one present, except the purchaser and the seller, (sometimes, indeed, his wife). This vague contract has been frequently broken by dishonest persons, and although the price is fixed, yet the delivery and payments are often put off from time to time, to the manifest injury of the dairy-man, whose cheese is continually diminishing in weight, till it suits the *convenience* of the *factor* to come and weigh it. We are but little versed in commercial transactions, yet we presume, however, to think, that neither in the East Indies, nor on the desolate wastes of Africa, does British commerce assume a much more despotic shape, than in the cheese-room of a Cheshire dairy-man. The business of the dairy is, in general, admirably well attended to, by a laborious and careful set of women, who are the support, and ought to be the pride of the country: their husbands degrade themselves, are ungrateful, in undervaluing the produce of *their* toil and care, and but too often injure themselves and families, in compliance with the foolish custom before alluded to. What regret, therefore, must one feel in contemplating the insignificance of a man who rents three or four hundred pounds a year, and yet dares not free himself from such a tyrannical custom!"

SWINE.—P. 27. "The species of hogs generally kept in Cheshire, is a mixture between the long and short-eared

eared breeds, weighing, when fattened, from ten to twenty score each, (twenty pounds to the score).

"An easy method of preventing pigs from rooting is here practised by some gentlemen, and although a trifling circumstance, it may not be thought unworthy of notice. The gristley or horney part of the snout, through which the ring is usually put, is cut away with a sharp knife; by this means alone, without the least injury arising from it to the animal, the mischief of rooting is effectually prevented."

For the *Hog Liquor* of the Cheshire Dairy Farms, and the small number of swine kept upon them, see the article WHEY, p. 57.

"GENERAL VIEW

OF THE

AGRICULTURE OF CHESHIRE;

WITH

OBSERVATIONS DRAWN UP FOR THE CONSIDERATION

OF

THE BOARD OF AGRICULTURE

AND INTERNAL IMPROVEMENT.

By HENRY HOLLAND,

MEMBER OF THE ROYAL MEDICAL SOCIETY OF EDINBURGH.

1808."

THIS REPORTER of the County of Chester appears, by the title page, to be a medical man. And, in a modest and appropriate "preface," there is evidence of his being a native of Cheshire; as, in enumerating the instances of assistance he has received, from his friends, he mentions his father, and another relative.

Of his MODE of SURVEY, not a word is said. Indeed, his book, in many parts, shows him to be, strictly speaking, a *Reporter;* not a *Surveyor.* He appears to write, "on Agriculture and internal Improvement," at least, from the authority of others, rather than from his own observation.

As a REPORTER, however, Mr. HOLLAND has very considerable merit. His language, tho sometimes too copious, is generally clear: it is the appropriate language of science; in whose best school Mr. H. would seem to have been educated. On *general topics,* too, and more especially on NATURAL HISTORY, Mr. Holland appears, from different parts of his performance, to be well informed. But he is too ingenuous to assume any pretension to a *practical knowledge* of the subjects of RURAL ECONOMY, or to claim the merit of being even an *amateur,* in any one of its branches. He seems, however, to have spared no pains in collecting information from his friends.

The

The principal CONTRIBUTORS to this Report are *John Thomas Stanley, Esquire*, of Alderley Park; *Mr. Holland*, of Sandlebridge; and *Mr. Fenna*, of Blackburn.

In the close of his acknowledgements, Mr. H. mentions Mr. WEDGE's REPORT, in the following mannner. "From the original Report of the County, by Mr. Wedge, I have likewise derived great assistance; and more especially in that part of the work which relates to the system of dairy management pursued in Cheshire." p. viii. And on that and a comparatively few other occasions, only, is it noticed:—notwithstanding it contains more *practical* knowledge, and useful information, applicable to the *rural* concerns of Cheshire, in almost any one of its sheets, than is to be found in the entire volume now before me. Was it, then, intended, by the Editor of the Board that Mr. Wedge's Report should, in the greater part, be lost to the public? And this merely because the "original Reports" have been ridiculed, in the mass, as too trifling for public attention? Is the Board's Editor incapable of distinguishing between those which have merit, and those that have none? Alas! into what hands have the gratuitous labors of the primary Surveyors fallen! And this merely, perhaps, because they were gratuitous. While those which now, I understand, cost two or three hundred, a piece, are valued, it would seem, and published, merely on that account. The Board's Moderator is not the only one who estimates things according to their costs.

It remains to be noticed of Mr. Holland, as an Author, that his work is well digested: that is to say, we *seldom* find several distinct topics thrust together into the same section; as they are by most others of the Board's Authors. Moreover, Mr. H. has favoured his Readers, not only with a "*Running Title*," but an INDEX.

The number of pages three hundred and seventy-eight.

SUBJECT THE FIRST.

NATURAL ECONOMY.

EXTENT.—P. 2. "It contains, as appears by a reference to Burdett's map, about 1040 square miles, or 665,600 acres, exclusive of the sands in the estuary of the river Dee, which may be reckoned at nearly 10,600 acres; a cena considerable part of these is now however secured by embankments from the sea, and still more may be, in process of time."

SURFACE.—Much of what we find under this head, as well as under that of extent, agrees with *Mr. Wedge's* Report.

The following description of a striking feature in the face of Cheshire is Mr. H's own.—P. 7. "The most singular feature in it, is the insulated rock of Beeston, situated about two miles to the south of Tarporley; which forms a most striking object from the whole of the surrounding country, and even from the neighbourhood of Liverpool. This rock, which on one side rises almost perpendicularly to the height of 366 feet, is composed of sandstone. Its summit is crowned with the ruins of Beeston castle, a fortress erected A. D. 1220, and formerly esteemed impregnable."

WATERS.—Under this head, likewise, we perceive some original writing. Mr. Wedge has only *enumerated* the rivers,—Mr. Holland has *described* them. But nothing of use, or even of interest, arises from the description,—other than what occurs in looking over a map of the county.

For an account of one species of waters in Cheshire, however, we are obliged to Mr. H.; Mr. W. having entirely omitted them;—namely, the *lakelets,* or "meres," with which Cheshire abounds.

P. 77. "Besides these streams, we have in Cheshire a number of small lakes, both natural and artificial, many of them of considerable extent and depth. The natural lakes are called Meres or Meers, an appellation probably derived from the French *Mer*. The principal of these are Rosthern Mere, Budworth Mere, Mere Mere, Tatton Mere, Pickmere Mere, all in Bucklow hundred; Comber Mere, in Namptwich hundred; Oak Mere on Delamere forest; and Reed's Mere in Macclesfield hundred. Comber Mere, Rosthern Mere, and Budworth Mere, are the most considerable in point of extent. The first of these is nearly two miles in length, and half a mile in breadth; the latter are smaller. All these Meres abound with fish, chiefly pike, bream, perch, dace, and eels. If to these natural lakes be added the artificial pieces of water, of which there are several extensive ones in the county; and the numerous marl pits which are to be met with in every farm; it may perhaps be stated as a fact, that a greater surface of land is covered with water in Cheshire, than in any

any other county in England, Cumberland and Westmoreland only excepted."

CLIMATURE.—*Quantity* of *Rain*.—P. 5. "It is generally supposed that more rain falls in Cheshire than on the same surface of land in any other part of the kingdom, Westmoreland and the neighbouring county of Lancashire perhaps only excepted."

Mr. H. proceeds to account for this fact (which I conceive to be controvertible) by ascribing it to the Irish sea, and westerly winds. Now the westerly and south-west winds, which most of all bring rain from the Atlantic, have a wide tract of mountain to cross, in their way to Cheshire. In Devonshire, it is well ascertained, that the vale of Exeter which lies to the east of Dartmore (an inferior mountain, whether in extent, or elevation, to those of Wales) is much less liable to rains, than the banks of the Tamer and Tavey, which lie to the west of it. An inconsiderable part of Cheshire lies open to the Irish sea;—merely the point of one of its "horns;"—and that opens to the *north*, rather than to the *west*, or *south-west*.

What Mr. Holland says of the *temperature* of the *atmosphere* of Cheshire, is, I conceive, much more judicious.—P. 6. "Owing to the relative situation of the county, and the general flatness of its surface, Cheshire enjoys, on the whole, a more mild and temperate climate than many counties situated under the same, or even a more southern latitude. In winter the frosts are not often severe, or of long duration; and the snow seldom continues on the ground more than a few days. The range of hills dividing the county from Derbyshire, which, from its situation and extent, may with propriety be denominated the English Apennines, breaks the force of those easterly winds, which are so peculiarly prejudicial to vegetation on the opposite coasts of the island; while the prevalence of the westerly breezes, during a large proportion of the year, produces an equality of temperature favourable both to the agriculture of the county, and to the general salubrity of the climate."

SOILS.—On this subject, Mr. H. greatly surpasses his predecessor. His intention and endeavours were highly laudable; as they were directed toward forming an accurate map of the soils of Cheshire.—P. 7. "It was my original intention to have procured for this Report, an accurate map of the soils in Cheshire; and, with this view, I sent several sketches to different parts of the county, to be filled up by delineations of the soil in each particular

particular district. I was under the necessity, however, of relinquishing this design, in consequence of the very great intermixture of soils in the county, which rendered it difficult, if not impossible, to obtain information sufficiently correct for their delineation in a map. For this reason, it will not be in my power to give so clear and precise a view of the subject, as I could have wished; but I may remark at the same time, that the circumstance which makes it a matter of so much difficulty to procure an accurate representation of the soils, would have the effect of rendering such a representation, if procured, less valuable and interesting than it would be, were they more distinctly marked out by nature."

This passage, alone, might have served to establish Mr. Holland's fitness for scientific observation, on matters falling immediately under his own experience, had not his chapter on climature preceded it. What is here said of the soils of Cheshire might be repeated of many other parts of the kingdom; especially those situated at, or near, the feet of mountains, or broken hilly districts. Mr. H. however, in compliance with the expressed desire of the Board, attempted a sketch of the soils of the county, under his inspection, and has prefixed it to his literary performance. At the close of his "preface," he thus appropriately speaks of it —"The desire, (p. viii.) expressed by the Board of Agriculture, to procure some delineation of the soils in the several districts surveyed, has induced me, subsequently to the completion of the Report, to attempt such a delineation on the general map of Cheshire. For the reasons, however, stated in the section on soil and surface, this sketch is necessarily extremely imperfect, and must be regarded as communicating only a very general view of the subject."

This map, as it is, may, I believe, be considered as the very best and most accurate of the soil maps of the Board's Reports that have yet fallen under my particular examination; those of Northumberland, Cumberland, and Westmoreland excepted. Had the soils of Cheshire been permanently distinguished by the graving tool, as those of the three counties abovenamed, it would have had a better claim to praise. In *probable accuracy*, it certainly exceeds all the other blotch maps of the Board's Reporters, which I have hitherto inspected. No stripes, nor long straight lines, declare it to be an imposition on the public.

In his letterpress, Mr. H. takes a glance at the several hundreds of the county, and speaks of their respective soils.

soils. But I perceive nothing in the detail that could add to the value of this register.

SUBSOILS.—P. 8. "The substrata are of various kinds, clay, marl, sand, rammel, foxbench, gravel, or red rock; but most commonly one of the two former, viz. clay or marl. The term *rammel*, or *rammelly soil*, is usually applied in this county to a composition of various kinds of clay, white sand, and gravel, intimately mixed with a small proportion of oxide of iron. It is generally met with under a weak brown, or grey soil, which seldom exceeds four or five inches in depth. It lies in strata, from eighteen to thirty inches in thickness, upon white or red sand, or clay marl: the latter frequently partaking of its nature for the depth of a few feet. Rammel is penetrable by the roots of trees, but is notwithstanding very unfavourable to the vegetation of the places where it is met with. Still more injurious in its effects on vegetation is the substance called *foxbench*. This is very frequently met with in Cheshire, lying in beds from six inches to three or four feet in thickness; and, like rammel, is usually covered with a thin weak soil."

FOSSILS and MINERALS.—It is on the subject of GEOLOGY we see Mr. Holland to the best advantage, as a writer. It is in *subterranean* Cheshire he would seem to be most at *home*. When I expressed my surprize, and regret, at Mr. Wedge's remissness, relating to these topics, I was not aware that Mr. Holland was employing himself so profitably upon them. To render his remarks the more intelligible, Mr. H. has given an engraved sketch (a very sketch, by the way) of "the minerals in Cheshire;" showing the relative situations of the mines and quarries.

Freestones, of a superior quality, are raised, in various parts of the county; for the purpose, not only of masonry; but, formerly, of covering. The latter use, however, is now giving way to that of Welch slate. Alderley Edge (a prominent feature of the eastern part of Cheshire), Runcorn (on the north), Manley (toward the west), and Styperson (on the eastern margin), are spoken of as the principal quarries of this useful fossil.

Limestone is found in one part of the county, only; namely, near Congleton, on the eastern border.

Copper and *Lead* ores have been extracted, at different periods, with varied success, out of Alderley Edge, abovementioned. Copper ore is found, likewise, in the Peckferton Hills, in the south-western quarter of the county, and is at present working, there, with a fair prospect of success.

success. On the whole, however, Cheshire can scarcely be ranked as a *metallic* county.

But it contains treasure of far greater value to society. Its *Salt Mines* confer on it a pre-eminence of distinction, which no other county of the kingdom can claim. We must not, however, pass, unnoticed,

The *Coal Mines* of Cheshire. For altho they are much inferior to those of other districts, Mr. Holland's account of them is too interesting to be neglected. I lay up, with pleasure, the whole of it.

P. 12. "This valuable mineral is worked to a very considerable extent in Cheshire, in the district of country between Macclesfield and Stockport, and in the township of Little Neston in the hundred of Wirrall. At the latter place, the seam of coal is, I understand, five or six feet in thickness; and the workings are carried to a considerable distance under the channel of the Dee. No coal has been met with in the range of hills which runs through the middle of Cheshire, nor in any of the flat part of the county. It was remarked, however, by the late ingenious Mr. Whitehurst, that 'the sand-beds in Cheshire are frequently accompanied with a very curious phenomenon. At Mere, near the seat of Peter Brooke, Esq., I saw a sand-pit containing the fragments of pit-coal, and cinders deposited in a stratified manner through a considerable extent of the bank*. I have also observed the same appearances at Mobberley, near Knutsford. The above fragments of coal and cinders lay six or seven feet below the surface of the earth; and I have lately been informed, by a gentleman of that neighbourhood, that such appearances are not peculiar to the sand-beds of Mere and Mobberley, but that they are almost universal, wherever sandpits are dug in Cheshire †.'

"This

" * The small fragments, and thin layers of coal, which are often found in beds of sand and other strata in Cheshire, have evidently been brought from a distance, and deposited by the same floods or torrents which have deposited the sand. The quantity is too insignificant to be worthy of any attention, otherwise than as the smallest quantity of any substance must prove that a portion of the same substance has had an existence in the place from which it had been originally conveyed. So many changes have taken place on the surface of the country over which the water depositing the strata of Cheshire has flowed, that it would be now impossible to ascertain where the substances forming these strata were detached from their primary positions. J. T. S."

" † Whitehurst's inquiry into the original state and formation of the earth. p. 16."

"This stratified appearance of a carbonaceous substance, in many places of the thickness of six or eight inches, may frequently be observed, especially in beds of sand, as described by Whitehurst. In boring, however, a few years ago, to the depth of sixty yards, in the lands of Lawrence Wright, Esq. in Mobberley, no coal was discovered. A considerable quantity of gypsum was found at different depths, mixed with the strata of earth which were passed through; and it seems probable, that either rock salt, or brine, rather than coal, would have been met with, had the boring been continued to a greater depth.

"The range of high ground running between Macclesfield and Stockport, and connecting itself with the Derbyshire hills, is the principal source of the coal worked in this county. Collieries are established in the townships of Hurdsfield, Rainow, Bollington, Adlington, Pott-Shrigley, Lyme, Worth, Poynton, and Norbury; including a district, from south to north, of about ten miles. In all these townships, the principal seam of coal is found nearly at the same level, from 70 to 100 yards below the surface. Various strata are passed through in getting down to it, among which are several other beds of coal, but not of sufficient thickness, or quality to bear the expences of working. The seam of coal that is worked is usually met with under a stratum of sand-stone. It varies very considerably in thickness; but generally speaking, a gradual increase in this respect is found to take place, as it is traced towards the north. In the immediate neighbourhood of Macclesfield, it is so thin as scarcely to repay the expences of working. Through Hurdsfield, Rainow, Bollington, Adlington, and Pott-Shrigley, the thickness of the bed increases from one to two feet. From Lyme, through Worth, Poynton, and Norbury, it swells into ten feet. The quality of the coal is very various in different parts of the district, but is, generally speaking, exceedingly good.

"There is no peculiarity worthy of notice in the mode of working these mines. The water is in most instances raised from the pits by the aid of the steam engine; in Pott-Shrigley, however, there is a considerable colliery, where it is drained from the bottom of the works, which are at the depth of one hundred yards from the surface, by a tunnel cut under the hill for that purpose. Through this tunnel the water is conveyed into a brook, running in a deep valley, at a distance of nearly a mile from the works.

"The

"The town of Macclesfield, and the middle and southern parts of the hundred, are principally supplied with coals from the collieries in the first five of the townships, which have been named. The largest colliery in any of these townships is that now working at Pott-Shrigley; the coals from which are esteemed of a very superior quality. Stockport, and its populous neighbourhood, derive their supply of fuel from the collieries in the townships more nearly adjacent. Those at Worth and Poynton, are much the most considerable, affording an inexhaustible supply of excellent coal, which is worked with much spirit, and to great profit. The prices at the different collieries vary, of course, according to the quality of the article; and as no coals in this neighbourhood are sold by weight, it becomes difficult to ascertain the relative proportion which the prices at the several pits bear to each other, and to those in other coal districts *."

SALT.—But it is to the salt rocks and subterranean brines of Cheshire that the Reporter has properly paid the most assiduous attention. And his endeavours have not been fruitless. Had his Report of Cheshire no other merit, than what is found in his account of its salt-works, this, alone, would render it valuable. For, as Mr. Holland truly says (p. 19.)—"there are few objects more interesting in the natural history of this island, than the rich brine springs, and extensive beds of fossil salt found in the county of Chester; and there are none more important in its political economy, whether we consider the manufactures and commerce to which they give rise, or the fertile source of revenue which they afford to the country."

In the digestion and arrangement of the materials adduced, Mr. H. has not been unsuccessful. Nevertheless, by some transpositions, with respect to the latter, the facts, and the observations thereon, will rise more aptly to the mind of the reader.

On the HISTORY of the salt-works of Cheshire, we have, in this Report, some interesting particulars.—P. 23. "Of the *Discovery of the Brine Springs*, and the time when they were first worked, we have no certain accounts. There can be little doubt, but that at a very early period, salt must have been procured from the brine springs which found their way to the surface. This, as has been mentioned,

"* For the information with respect to the collieries in Macclesfield hundred, I am indebted to Edward Downes, Esq. of Shrigley Hall."

tioned, is particularly the case with the springs in the neighbourhood of Nantwich and Middlewich; and we learn from Doomsday book that, at the time of Edward the Confessor, brine-pits were wrought at all the wiches in Cheshire. It seems however that, even several centuries afterwards, the art of making salt was very imperfectly understood in any part of England; and that the quantity manufactured was very inconsiderable. Henry VI., being informed that a new method of making salt had been invented in the Low Countries, by which it might be made more abundantly in England than it had hitherto been, invited John de Sheidame, a gentleman of Zealand, with sixty persons in his company, to come into England, to instruct his subjects in the new method of making salt, promising them protection and encouragement*. Whether they came, or what their improvements were, does not appear; but it is probable that these were not of much importance, or that they were lost; for we find the Royal Society, soon after its institution, very intent upon improving the art of manufacturing white salt, and publishing, towards the close of the 17th century, the histories of several modes of making it; particularly Dr. William Jackson's account of the brine springs, and the mode of making white salt at Nantwich, in Cheshire; and Dr. Thomas Rastel's account of the manufacture of it at Droitwich, in Worcestershire. These are rather reports of the methods of manufacture then used, than suggestions of improvements. The salt made in England was still considered inferior to that made abroad; and what was manufactured in Cheshire was confined to the supply of its own consumption, and that of a few neighbouring counties.

"The want of knowledge in the manufacture, and the supposed superiority of foreign over English salt, attracted in the beginning of the last century, the attention of the House of Commons; and Mr. Lowndes, a Cheshire gentleman, received a reward from parliament, in consideration of his making known some improvements he was imagined to have made in the manufacture of salt. Soon afterwards the late Dr. Brownrigg published his ingenious and philosophical work on 'the art of making common salt;' in which, in addition to a full and detailed account of the processes in the manufacture of it, at that time used,

"* Rymeri Fœdera, Vol. x. p. 761."

used, he suggested a variety of alterations and improvements. Some of these were adopted, though not to the extent which was admitted of by the state of the manufacture. In consequence however of these and various subsequent improvements; joined to the increased commercial spirit of the country; and the facility of communication with Liverpool, which was added to by rendering the Weaver navigable for vessels of considerable burthen from Northwich and Winsford; the manufacture of white salt in Cheshire, as well for home consumption, as for exportation, has exceedingly increased in the course of the last century, more particularly towards the close of it; and the support of it is now become an object of the first consequence, not only to the county itself, but to the nation at large.

"Though the brine springs appear to have been known and worked in the earliest periods of the history of this country, the *discovery of the beds of Fossil or Rock Salt* is of much more recent date. The first of these was found in the year 1670, about 34 yards from the surface, in searching for coal in Marbury, about a mile north of Northwich. The bed of it which was met with was 30 yards in thickness; and underneath it was a stratum of indurated clay. The discovery of this bed of rock salt in Marbury, led to other attempts to find it; and on sinking a shaft any where within half a mile of the place where it was first found, it was met with, about the same distance from the surface, if the access to it was not prevented by brine or fresh water.

"This continued to be the only part of the county in which rock salt was found, till the year 1779; when in searching for brine, near Lawton, it was there met with, about 42 yards from the surface. The stratum of it was only four feet in thickness. Beneath this was a bed of indurated clay, 10 yards thick; on penetrating which, a second stratum of rock salt, 12 feet in thickness, was found. On continuing the sinking, another stratum of indurated clay, 15 yards thick, was passed through; and underneath this appeared a third stratum of rock salt; which was sunk into 24 yards. The lowest 14 yards being the purest, these only were worked.

"Hitherto no attempts had been made to find a lower stratum of rock salt in the neighbourhood of Northwich; for as the one first met with was so thick, and furnished such abundant supply for every demand, there could be no other inducement to this than the hopes of meeting

meeting with a stratum, at greater depth, containing a smaller admixture of earth. It appears too that the fear of meeting with springs below, which might impede the working of the pits, or even render this entirely impracticable, prevented the owners of them from sinking deeper*. As however no inconvenience of this kind had occurred, on sinking through several alternate strata of rock salt and clay at Lawton; and it had been found that there was a lower stratum of rock salt there, more pure than those nearer the surface; the proprietors of one of the mines near Northwich were led, in 1781, to sink deeper than had yet been done, and to pass through the bed of indurated clay, lying underneath the rock salt which had been so long known and worked. This indurated substance was found to be from 10 to 11 yards in thickness; and immediately beneath it a second stratum of rock salt was met with, the upper portion of which differed little in purity from the higher stratum; but on penetrating into it from 20 to 25 yards, it was there found much more pure and free from earthy admixture. It continued to have this increased degree of purity for four or five yards only; and for 14 yards still lower, to which depth the shaft was sunk, the proportion of earth was again as large as in the upper part of the stratum. It was therefore thought useless to sink further.

"Several other proprietors of mines in the neighbourhood followed the example which had been set them; and penetrated through the bed of indurated clay lying beneath the upper stratum of rock salt. A second stratum of rock salt was always met with below this; and on passing down into it, the same order of disposition as to purity was met with, as in the mine in which it had been first examined; and the same has been found to prevail in all the mines since sunk in this neighbourhood."

The Locality of the various Brine Springs and Salt Rocks, that have yet been discovered, will be seen, in the following extracts.—P. 19. "The principal *Brine Springs* in Cheshire are found in the valleys through which the Weaver, and the little rivulet the Wheelock have their course; and generally near the banks of these streams. If we except a spring of weak brine at Dunham, near the Bollin;

" * Dans la crainte de rencontrer des sources d'eau; qui genesoient, ou peut-etre detruiroient l'exploitation, on n'a pas approfondi dans la masse de sel au dessous de 10 toises.

" Jar's Voyages Metallurgiques. Tome 3, p. 95 "

Bollin; and the springs at Dirtwich, in the most southern part of the county, no others have ever been worked. By their means an importance is given to the Weaver, which it would not otherwise possess; and there is probably a greater bulk of carriage on this stream, than on any other river in the island, of itself so little considerable.

"Tracing the Weaver from its source, at the Peckferton hills, we do not find any springs strongly impregnated with salt near it, till it approaches Namptwich. That brine does exist as high up as Bickley, though it has not been ascertained at what depth, or of what strength, appears probable from a sinking of ground, and consequent filling of the cavity with brine, which took place in this neighbourhood in 1657; a relation of which is given by Dr. Jackson in the Philosophical Transactions*, and a still more particular account by Childrey†. Leland gives the history of a very similar occurrence at an earlier period, a few miles south of this. He relates that, 'about a mile from Combermere abbey, part of a hill with trees upon it, suddenly sunk down, and was covered with salt water, of which the abbot being informed caused it to be wrought; but the proprietors of the wiches compounding with him, he left off working.' He adds, 'that this salt pool still continued in his time, but that no care was taken of it‡.'

"A few miles lower down the Weaver than Bickley, in Baddiley, and one or two adjoining townships, springs are met with impregnated with salt in various degrees. Brinefield, is the name given to several of the inclosures in Baddiley. When the river takes a northerly direction at Audlem, brine is met with on each side of it, and may be found, on sinking near its banks, all the way from thence to Namptwich. About midway between Audlem and Nantwich, there is a farm, which retains the name of Brinepits farm, where salt was formerly manufactured. A little further down, brine was found, and salt made, on each side of the river, at Austaston, and Baddington‖. At the present time, however, none is manufactured till we get to Nantwich, where numerous brine springs are met with. Continuing our course down the river, we find brine

"* Lowthorp's Abridgement of the Philosophical Transactions, Vol. II. page 352."

"† Childrey's Britannia Baconica, page 132."

"‡ Leland's Itinerary, Vol. I. p. 82."

"‖ King's Vale Royal, p. 66."

brine at Winsford. Betwixt Winsford and Northwich, attempts have been made to get down to it; but these have hitherto been rendered unsuccessful by the quantity of fresh water which has been met with. It is again found at Leftwich, in the angle betwixt the Dane and the Weaver; at Northwich; at Witton, half a mile north of Northwich, on a small brook of the same name, which falls into the Weaver at Anderton; and at Anderton, a township about a mile below Northwich. At Barnton, a mile still lower down the river, a weaker brine has been found; and again at Saltersford, about a mile below Barnton. Two miles still lower, in Weverham, brine has been found, and was worked as early as the time of William the Conqueror. It does not appear that any has been discovered below this place.

"Following the course of the little stream, the Wheelock, we first meet with brine at Lawton, on the very confines of the county; then three or four miles lower at Roughwood, in the township of Bechton; again at Wheelock; and, lastly, at Middlewich, where the Wheelock falls into the Dane.

"No brine has been found in the valley through which the Dane flows from Middlewich to Northwich. Higher up this stream, in the neighbourhood of Congleton, some of the enclosures have the name of Brine-field, Brine-hill, &c.; whence we may conclude, that brine has some time or other been discovered there.

"Though the places which have been mentioned are the only ones where brine has been found, and works for its evaporation erected, there is little doubt but it might be met with in almost every part of the valleys through which the Weaver and Wheelock take their course, did not the fresh water springs prevent the access to it."

Again, p. 36. "Rock salt has occasionally been met with in a few other parts of the county; betwixt Middlewich and Winsford; again, a little lower down the river than Winsford, in sinking for brine; and about four years ago, in boring for coal at Whitley, six or seven miles below Northwich, and about two miles north of the Weaver, a bed of rock salt was discovered, about forty yards from the surface. At none of these places, however, was it thought worth while to get it, chiefly on account of their distance from water-carriage; and as the working of the pits at Lawton was soon discontinued, it is only from the pits in the neighbourhood of Northwich that the rock salt is now procured. These are at present ten or twelve in number;

at

at all of which the rock is worked in the lower stratum only."

The DEPTH, at which the rocks and brines are severally deposited, beneath the surface of the ground, Mr. H. thus briefly relates.—P. 22. "The *Depth from the Surface* at which the brine springs are found; the level they take when the stratum which immediately confines them is penetrated; and the abundance of the springs, are very various. At Nantwich, the brine is met with about ten or twelve yards from the surface; and in sinking for fresh water it is necessary to do this with caution, that the brine may be avoided. In sinking for the foundation of a bridge, a few years ago, just above this town, a very copious brine spring was found about eight yards from the surface; and the workmen were much incommoded by it. The brine springs rise nearly to the surface. When we get to Winsford, to which place the Weaver is made navigable, we find the brine at a much greater distance from the surface; and it is generally necessary to sink from 55 to 60 yards before it is met with, when it is found in great abundance. It has its level 12 yards from the surface. At Northwich, it is found at a depth from 30 to 40 yards, the springs being very fluent; its level is about 20 yards from the surface. At Witton, it is met with about the same depth, and rises to the same level, the springs being equally copious. Through the whole of Anderton, the quantity of brine is most abundant; at the higher end of this township, it is found about 40 yards from the surface, and the level is nearly the same as that at Witton. Somewhat lower down, it is necessary to sink from 50 to 55 yards before it is met with. Still keeping the course of the river, at Barnton, about a mile below Anderton, on sinking 65 yards, and boring 50 yards below this, a very weak brine was discovered, and that in small quantity.

"If we trace the different brine springs along the little stream, the Wheelock, we find that at Lawton they are met with about 85 yards from the surface, and have their level at 70 yards. The springs are much less copious than many of those on the Weaver. At Roughwood, the brine is 50 yards from the surface, and rises 15 yards; the spring is by no means abundant, and is often pumped dry. At Wheelock it is found at the depth of 70 yards, and rises within 30 yards of the surface; the springs being very copious. At Middlewich, the brine is at different depths, from 35 to 84 yards; in one pit, in which it is found at 70 yards deep, it rises to the surface. The springs

springs here are by no means fluent, and are occasionally pumped dry."

The SHAFTS.—P. 37. "The shafts are usually square, and constructed of timber; we find one, however, about a mile from Northwich, circular, and of brick."

The STRATA, passed through, in sinking the shafts, are as follow.—P. 27. "There is great uniformity in the *Strata* which are passed through in sinking for brine or rock salt. They very generally consist of clay and sulphate of lime, mixed in various proportions; that of the latter somewhat increasing as the shaft approaches the brine or rock. The workmen distinguish the clay by the appellation of *metal*, giving it the name of red, brown, or blue metal, acoording to its colour; and the sulphate of lime" (gypsum) "by that of *plaister*. The strata formed by these are, in general, close and compact; allowing very little fresh water to pass through them. In some places, however, they are broken and porous: and they admit so much fresh water into the shaft, that whenever this shaggy metal, as the workmen call it, has been met with, it has been usual to discontinue any attempts to pass through it. It was thought not only impracticable to overcome a water, which vulgar prejudice had magnified into a great stream running under ground; but it was believed, even if the sinking could be continued below this, that the water could not be kept out of the shaft; and that it would either weaken the brine so as to destroy its value, or would find its way into the cavity of any rock pit which might be found below it. Later experience has proved that these ideas were not altogether well founded. A few years ago an attempt was made in Witton to pass through this porous stratum, in order to get to the brine. It was met with about 28 yards from the surface; the thickness of it, was about 13 feet; and the quantity of water, which was forced through it into the shaft, was 360 gallons a minute. By means of a steam engine, the sinkers were enabled to pass through this water; to fix a guage, or curb, a few yards below it, in a stratum of indurated clay" (clay stone); "and thence to bring up a wooden frame, supporting a wall of puddle, 12 inches thick; by which the access of the fresh water into the shaft was, in a great degree, prevented, and an opportunity given to pass down to the brine below. A shaft was afterwards sunk through this porous stratum, for the purpose of obtaining rock; which object was after a short time defeated, by the influx of brine into the shaft, at the surface

surface of the upper stratum of rock: an accident originating in a cause completely distinct from the fresh water in the porous stratum."

The strata found, in sinking the shaft, at Witton, are shown in an engraved section; which, however, is not at all necessary to the right understanding of the thickness, the succession, and the nature of each stratum. They are equally well comprehended, by the following list; which forms one column of the plate.

		Yds.	Ft.	In.
Plate I.	" 1. Calcareous Marl - -	5	0	0
	2. Indurated Red Clay - -	1	1	6
	3. Indurated Blue Clay with Sand	2	1	0
	4. Argillaceous Marl - -	1	2	0
	5. Indurated Blue Clay - -	0	1	0
	6. Red Clay with Sulphate of Lime irregularly intersecting it - - -	1	1	0
	7. Indurated Blue and Brown Clay with grains of Sulph. of Lime interspersed - -	1	1	0
	8. Indurated Brown Clay with Sulph. of Lime, crystallized in irregular masses, and in large proportion - -	4	0	0
	9. Indurated Blue Clay, laminated with Sulph. of Lime	1	1	6
	10. Argillaceous Marl - -	1	1	0
	11. Indurated Red Clay, laminated with Sulph of Lime -	1	0	0
	12. Indurated Blue Clay, with laminæ of Sulph. of Lime -	1	0	0
	13. Indurated Red and Blue Clay	4	0	0
	14. Indurated Brown Clay with Sand and Sulph. of Lime interspersed through it. The fresh water (360 gallons per minute) finds its way through holes in this stratum, and has its level at 16 yards from the surface - - -	4	1	0
	15. Argillaceous Marl - -	1	2	0
	16. Indurated Blue Clay, with Sand and grains of Sulph. of Lime	1	0	9
	Carried forward	33	1	9

17. Indurated

	Yds.	Ft.	In.
Brought over	33	1	9
17. Indurated Brown Clay, with a little Sulph. of Lime - -	5	0	0
18. Indurated Blue Clay, with grains of Sulph. of Lime -	0	1	6
19. Indurated Brown Clay, with Sulph. of Lime - -	2	1	0
20. The first bed of Rock Salt -	25	0	0
21. Indurated Clay or Stone, with veins of Rock Salt running in it - - -	10	1	6
(76 2 9)	76	1	3

"The second bed of Rock Salt has been sunk into, 35 or 36 yards."

P. 29. "The *inclination* in this shaft, was from N. W. to S. E.; and the *dip* about one yard in nine. No. 14 is the stratum through which the fresh water flowed; and the level it found was 16 yards from the surface, which nearly corresponds with that of the brook below. The line of separation between the lowest stratum of earth, and the first of rock salt, is very exactly defined; they are perfectly distinct, and do not at all run into each other. On carrying a horizontal tunnel for 100 yards along the upper stratum of rock salt; this was found to be irregular and unequal on its surface; the irregularities, in great degree, corresponding with those on the surface of the ground above." (!)

P. 30. "The *thickness* of the upper bed of rock salt, in those pits lying most to the N. E., is thirty yards; and it appears gradually to decline in thickness towards the S. W.: losing, in the course of a mile, five yards. In the pit last sunk in the neighbourhood of Northwich, which is the one most to the S. W., it is only twenty five yards thick."

On the ORIGIN of Salt Rocks, much is adduced by Mr. H. Seventeen or eighteen pages (in the body of the work, p. 30, &c., or the Appendix No. 2) are filled with strictures on this topic. But few of them, there are, which do not, to my conception, *dip* toward the improbable, if not the ridiculous. There is abundant evidence, in the foregoing extracts, to convince any man, that the salt rocks of Cheshire were not formed, where they are now found.

Of the CONSTRUCTION of these rocks we have a much more interesting and satisfactory account.—P. 34. "On making

making a *horizontal section of the bed of Rock Salt*, a singular appearance presents itself; on the whole of the surface made by this section, various figures may be observed differing in form and size; some of them being nearly circular, others approaching more to an oval form, whilst in others an irregular pentagon may be traced. Some of them are not more than two or three feet in diameter; others are ten or twelve feet. The lines which form the boundaries of these figures are white; and from two to five or six inches wide: on examination, these appearances are found to be owing to the rock salt, in the white lines forming the divisions of the figures, being perfectly pure, and free from earthy admixture. Combined with the salt, having earth in various proportions mixed with it, a general effect is produced, not very distantly resembling mosaic work. (Pl. II. is a representation of a portion of the roofing of a rock-pit.) This disposition is uniformly observed through the whole thickness of the stratum of rock salt; and in whatever part of it an horizontal section is made, similar appearances are found. To what causes it has been owing that the rock salt has been deposited in this singular manner, it is difficult to conceive. The whole stratum of rock salt may be compared to a mass of basaltic columns; the lines of separation in each pillar being marked by the pure and transparent white salt.*

"The division betwixt the lower portion of the upper bed of rock salt, and the indurated clay or stone beneath it, is as exactly defined as that betwixt the upper portion of it, and the earth above. In passing through this stone, small veins of rock salt are found, here and there running in it, in various directions; and wherever there has been any little crevice in it, this is found filled up with rock salt, to which the clay and oxide of iron have given a deep red tinge. (Plate III. is a representation of a portion of this, taken from the part where it joins the upper bed of rock salt.)

"The thickness of this stratum of stone is uniformly found to be from 10 to 11 yards; and the lower part of it is as distinct from the second bed of rock salt, as its upper part

* In p. 38, Mr. H. says, "From some experiments made on different specimens of rock-salt, it appears that the transparent rock salt is an almost pure muriate of soda, and contains no admixture of either earth or earthy salts. The colour of the less transparent and brown specimens is derived from the earth which enters, in greater or less proportions, into their composition."

part is from the first; and its termination is equally abrupt.

"The perpendicular section of the second bed of rock salt varies little from that of the upper bed, till it has been penetrated about 20 yards from the surface, when it assumes a more stratified appearance; and is here found, as before mentioned, to have a much smaller proportion of earth combined with the muriate of soda.

"The horizontal section of this stratum exhibits the same figured appearance in the roof, as the upper stratum."

Respecting the *firmness* of *texture*, belonging to the salt rocks of Cheshire, we can only judge, from what appears in this Report, by the circumstance of their being blasted with gunpowder, in working them.

On this subject, the WORKING of the Rocks, we find a few particulars noticeable.—P. 37. "With respect to the mode of working, no peculiarity of moment is observable in these mines. By the operation of blasting, and the mechanical instruments usually employed in mining, the rock salt is obtained in masses of considerable size, differing in form and purity. Previously, however, to the extension of the workings in any particular direction, care is taken to secure a good roofing for the cavity which is to be formed. In doing this, the men employ picks of the common description; working horizontally, so as to form a roofing of the rock, and making this as plane as possible. From its situation, a few feet above the purer part of the stratum, the rock obtained during this process is usually of inferior quality, and is for the most part employed in the refineries. The depth of the workings from the roofings depends in a great measure on the nature of the stratum, and the proportion of it occupied by the rock of the purer quality, or, as it is termed, *Prussian Rock*. Fifteen or sixteen feet may perhaps, however, be taken as the average depth of the workings. The cavity thus formed presents a striking appearance; and, when illuminated by candles fixed in the rock, the effect is highly brilliant. In some of the pits the roof is supported by pillars, eight or ten yards square, which are in general regularly disposed; others are worked out in aisles; the choice here however seems to be wholly arbitrary.

"Till within the few last years, horses were in every instance employed in raising rock salt, from the pits at Northwich. This method has, however, in some measure been superseded by the improved steam-engine; and the substitution of this invaluable machine has now taken place at several of the pits, out of which rock salt is obtained. At the others, horses are still used. The men employed in working the rock are paid by the ton, usually receiving two shillings for this quantity, they finding both the tools and the powder."

Brine.—The *origin* or cause of subterranean brine, and consequent brine springs,—now that salt rocks have been found, in their neighbourhood,—might seem to be too obvious, even to notice.—Nevertheless, before the discovery of the rocks, much theoretic ingenuity (similar to that now exercised, concerning the origin of the rock itself) would doubtlessly be expended.* Mr. Holland's notice of this is of course brief.—P. 39. "Previously to the discovery of the beds of fossil salt in Cheshire, various erroneous and absurd opinions were formed, as to the origin of the brine; to enter into any detail of which, would, at the present time, be perfectly useless. Since this discovery was made, no doubt has been entertained, that the saline contents of this fluid are derived from the water of springs, or rain water, penetrating down to the surface of the rock salt, or the head of the rock, as it is usually called, and effecting the solution of a certain portion of the salt, with which it then comes into contact."

Here, the *natural expenditure*, or bent, of the fluent brine, aptly suggests itself.—There does not appear to be, at present, any copious surface springs, by which it is drawn off. It is plain that there are subterraneous channels of communication (doubtlessly formed by the wasting away of the surface of the rock, which has been taken up by the water in contact with it) between the wells. (See p. 87.). And, by the falling in of the ground (see p. 77.), it would seem that the solution had (previously to the establishment of manufacturies) been, there at least, considerable. And it is not at all improbable that other cavities had been formed, and are forming, in various parts of the salt-rock district. Even the artificial expenditure of brine, in the numerous manufactures now carried on, must necessarily reduce the parts wherever the saline matter, which the brines contain, is taken up.

On following the Wever from Nantwyche toward the estuary of the Mersey, the depth at which the brine is found

* See North. Depart. p. 140.

found is greater as it approaches the sea *. But it is evident that there is no *deep*-lying communication with the sea; as the water constantly rises considerably above the level (probably the top or "head" of a salt rock) at which it is found lodged (see p. 79.). Even admitting that the height to which it rises, at Anderton (where I had the best opportunity of examining the saltworks of Cheshire) to be on a level with the sea; yet this would not prevent the flow of the brine; which is much heavier than sea water. If there really is a channel of communication, between the subterranean brines of Cheshire, and the estuary of the Mersey, its issue, it is probable, may be detected by the superior weight and saltness of the water, in that part.

These reflections arising in the course of my examination of Mr. H's valuable paper, I have thought it right to give them a place, here.

Of the *qualities* of the different brines of Cheshire, Mr. Holland has bestowed ample attention: more, perhaps, than the subject requires.—P. 39. "Several circumstances will, of course, influence the quantum of this solution, or the strength of the brine, some of which it may not be uninteresting to mention. One of the most obvious is, the extent of surface of the rock salt exposed to the action of the water: the greater this is, and the more completely the water and rock salt are brought into contact, the greater will be the consequent solution, and the stronger the brine. Independently, however, of such an immediate operation, the strength of the brine will be varied by the manner in which any pit is worked, and the circumstances attending the raising the brine; for if it is pumped up seldom, it is found to be weaker than it would be, was it drawn up more frequently. The explanation of this seems to be that the water which finds its way to the stratum of fossil salt, probably remains, in great degree, at rest, till put into motion by raising the brine; while in this state, the portion of it which is immediately in contact with the rock becomes saturated; but acquiring at the same time a greater degree of specific gravity than it had as pure water, it thereby prevents the water above from sinking down so as to act upon the rock; and the sum of solution is consequently less than when the pit is frequently worked, and the rock salt exposed to a more

* Above Nantwyche, the brine still breaks out, naturally, at the surface. See MANURES, ensuing.

more constant action of the water. This is particularly the case in a brine pit, not immediately connected with any other; and the same observations will be applicable to those pits which have a communication; with this difference only, that the mode of working in one pit is to be taken into consideration in the effect produced on the strength of brine in another, independently of its own particular operations. Most of the pits in the neighbourhood of Northwich and Winsford have such a communication at the rock-head, as is made apparent by the brine in one pit having its level lowered, when another pit is at work, at some distance. At Northwich, this has been further evinced when the brine has found its way into the cavity of a rock salt pit, an accident which has frequently occurred. When this has happened, six or eight brine pits, at the distance of nearly a mile from each other, have often been laid dry, and have continued so till the rock pit has been filled, and the brine has again found its level. On some occasions, where the cavity of the rock pit has been large, four or five weeks have elapsed before this has been completed.

"The strength of the brine will also be materially affected by the quantity of fresh water which finds access to it, either directly through the sides of the shaft out of which the brine is drawn, or by any fissures in the earth with which these are nearly connected. The proportion of salt held in solution, will bear a ratio to the fresh water thus introduced, and to the subsequent opportunity this has of acting upon the rock.

"With regard to the quantity of salt, which a given portion of water will, when fully saturated, hold in solution, very different estimates have been formed. These differences appear to have arisen, on some occasions, from confounding a given quantity of brine with the same measure of water, and not discriminating betwixt the quantity of salt contained in the one, and that which the other was capable of dissolving. Other causes of variations in the reports which have been given, appear to have arisen from the different state of the salt used in making the experiments, the specimens of which may have possessed various degrees of dryness, and have contained a larger or smaller proportion of the water of crystallization. The learned bishop of Llandaff, who made several experiments with a view of ascertaining which report came nearest to the truth, made use in these of the pure fossil salt; the proportion of water of crystallization in which is probably little

varied

varied. He found that, "he could never dissolve quite six ounces of rock salt, in sixteen avoirdupoise ounces of water."* This result nearly corresponds with that afforded by the experiments of Hoffman,† and Brownrigg,‡ and there is little doubt of its accuracy."

P. 43. "The workmen, or the *wallers* as they are called, usually form their estimate of the strength of brine from its specific gravity; and a new laid egg is their common hydrometer. This sinks in pure water; is suspended in water which has a small quantity of salt dissolved in it; and has a greater or less portion of its surface exposed, as the brine holds more or less salt in solution. They also use an hydrometer graduated upwards, like the common spirit hydrometer, the zero point of which is a fully saturated or leach brine; by these means, however, they know only the comparative strength of the different brines, and are not able to ascertain the exact proportion of salt, contained in a given quantity of the liquor."

Mr. H., therefore, enters upon a course of experiments, with Beaume's hydrometer, to ascertain the quantity of pure salt (otherwise muriate of soda) contained in the waters of the most celebrated brine wells, in Cheshire.

Having found, by one of Beaume's instruments, "the scale of which," says Mr. H. "was, with his usual accuracy, fixed by my friend Mr. C. R. Aikin,"—that "a cold saturated solution of the muriate of soda, in pure water, contains, according to this scale, 27.812, per cent. of this salt," (p. 44.) Mr. H. proceeded to prove, by the same instrument, the strength of nine or ten different brines, now in work:—the result of which appears to be (though not summed up) that the subterranean brines of Cheshire afford about 25, per cent. in weight, of pure salt; which is only 2.812, per cent. less than brine that is raised to the point of saturation.

It may be said to be generally known that water can dissolve, and suspend, only a certain portion of salt. If more than this proportion be added, it will fall down, and remain undissolved, at the bottom of the water; which is thus shown to be completely saturated.

In a note, Mr. H. compares the brines of Cheshire, with those

* See Watson's Essays, Vol. II. p. 46.

† Hoffman de Salinis Halensibus.

‡ Brownrigg, p. 64.

those of France.—N. P. 46. "It may here not be uninteresting to compare the strength of the Cheshire brine springs with that of similar springs in France. We have a memoir on the national salt works in the departments of la Meurthe, Jura, Doubs, and Mont Blanc, by citizen Nicholas, an associate of the national institute; who was required, by a decree of the committee of public safety, August 14th, 1795, to visit the national salt-works; to collect all the necessary observations concerning their actual situation; and procure means for their improvement.

"It appears from this memoir, that there are three establishments in the department of la Meurthe, namely, at *Chateau Salins*, at *Mozenvie*, and at *Dieuze;* two in the department of Jura, at *Salins* and *Mont-Morot;* one in the department of Doubs, at *Arc;* and two in the department of Mont-Blanc, at *Montiers*, or *Mont-Salin;* and at *Conflans*.

"At *Chateau Salins*, *Mozenvie*, and *Dieuze*, the brine pretty regularly contains from 13 to 14 per cent. of muriate of soda, though, after long pumping, it comes up stronger.

"At *Salins* (department of Jura) the average degree of saltness is 11.86 of the hydrometer. At *Mont-Morin*, from $1\frac{1}{3}$ to $8\frac{1}{2}$ of the hydrometer.

"At *Arc*, the brine contains from 3 2-7ths to $7\frac{1}{8}$ per cent. of muriate of soda.

"The result of a particular analysis of the brine at *Chateau Salins* was, that one pound of the water gave 1 oz. 7 grains of pure salt; 23 grains of selenite; 75 grains of Glauber's salt; and $81\frac{1}{2}$ grains of muriated lime and magnesia."

The MANUFACTURE of "White Salt."—On the proper *site* of manufactures, we have the following judicious observations.—P. 42. "In the establishment of any manufacture for the crystallization of salt, the first objects of consideration, undoubtedly, are the strength and purity of the brine, which is to be used in the manufacture. Independently, however, of these circumstances, the advantages derived from several other adventitious ones, may render it better worth while to manufacture salt from a weaker brine, in one situation, than from a stronger in another. One of the most important points influencing the choice of a situation for the establishment of a manufactory of salt, exclusive of the strength and purity of the brine, is the opportunity it may afford, of erecting this so as to enjoy the advantages of water carriage, as well for the convenience of the exportation of the manufactured salt, as as for the ready conveyance of coals to the works. Much too will depend on the price and supply of coals, where the consumption is necessarily so large as it is in this manufacture. The fluency of the spring is another consideration, which, as Dr. Jackson observed, 'may be rich or poor in a double sense; for a spring may be rich in salt, but poor in the quantity of brine it affords.' The opportunity of strengthening a weaker brine with rock salt, may also render it more advantageous to work this, than a stronger brine differently circumstanced.

"With respect to the strength and purity of the Cheshire brines, it appears by analysis, that the greater proportion of them possess these requisites in a very superior degree; many of those which are less impregnated with salt, have rock salt in their neighbourhood, affording a ready means of strengthening them; while the springs are in general copious, and coals readily procured, though of late years at a considerably increased price; at the same time, the extension of the navigation of the Weaver, and the contiguity of the Grand Trunk canal furnish every convenience of water carriage."

Raising the *Brine*.—P. 48. "From the pits in which the brine is found, it is pumped up into cisterns, or reservoirs formed near the works. In a few situations which admit of the assistance of a stream of water, the brine is raised by this means. This is the case at Lawton, at Roughwood, at the old works at Weelock, and at one of the pits both in Northwich and Middlewich. Where this assistance could not be procured, it was formerly the custom to draw it up by horses*. As the demand for salt increased, in addition to these, small windmills were employed in raising the brine; with the increasing consumption, various inconveniences were found to arise from trusting to a machine depending on the uncertain operation of the weather, which led to the use of steam engines; and at almost all the newly erected works, the brine is raised by means of these."

Saturating the natural Brine.—P 49. "The *reservoirs*, into which the brine is pumped up, are either large ponds, formed

"* In Camden's time even the assistance of horses was not called in for raising the brine. He says, "At Northwich there is a deep and plentiful brine-pit, with stairs about it, by which, when they have drawn the water in their leathern buckets, they ascend, half naked, to their troughs, and fill them, from whence it is conveyed to the wich-houses." *Camden's Britannia*, p. 561.

formed in clay, and generally lined with brick, capable of containing the consumption of several weeks; or they are wooden cisterns, pitched within, which will hold a supply of brine for the consumption of a few days only.

"From the account which has been given of the Cheshire brines, it will have been seen that the greater number of them contain a very large proportion of salt, and that many of them very nearly approach to saturation. Though however approaching to this, there are none of them which are completely saturated, or which will not dissolve an increased portion of salt; and as it is of so much importance in the economy of the fuel, to have as little superfluous water as possible to evaporate, it is always an object with the manufacturer to obtain a fully saturated brine. Where then either the brine is weak, or a convenient opportunity is found of saturating a brine already strongly impregnated with salt, this is done by placing a quantity of rock salt in the cistern into which the brine is pumped, and allowing the liquor to act upon it, till it is entirely saturated. A strong wooden frame is fixed in the cistern, at about half its depth, upon which the rock salt is thrown; and the earthy residuum is occasionally removed from thence, after all the salt has been dissolved *."

Evaporating the water of the saturated brine;—and thereby *chrystalizing* the salt it contains.—P. 50. "From the reservoirs the brine is drawn, as it is wanted, through wooden pipes, or by troughs into the *evaporating pan.*

"The pans used in Cheshire, for the evaporating of the brine, are now made of wrought iron. The dimensions of these vary very much; but, in general, those of modern erection are considerably larger than what were in use a few years ago; and they usually contain from 600 to 800 superficial feet. One or two pans of still larger dimensions have been erected, containing each nearly 1000 feet. Their usual form is that of an oblong square, and their depth

"* It is probable that this mode of strengthening a weak brine was put in practice soon after the first discovery of the rock salt. Dr. Leigh claims the merit of having first introduced it. *See Leigh's Natural History of Lancashire and Cheshire*, p. 43.

"In like manner the sea or river water slightly impregnated with salt, is brought to a perfect state of saturation, by the addition of rock salt; and works for the preparation of white salt from such a solution, are erected at Frodsham, near the junction of the Weaver with the Mersey, and on the Lancashire banks of the Mersey. The rock salt is conveyed down the Weaver to these works, and is there refined."

depth from 12 to 16 inches*. To a pan containing from 6 to 800 superficial feet, there are usually three furnaces, from six and a half to seven feet long; and 20 to 24 inches wide. The grates are from two and a half to three feet from the bottom of the pan. The furnace-doors are single, and there are no doors to the ash-pits.

"The different pans are usually partitioned out from each other, and there is a separate *pan-house* to each pan. Within this pan-house, at one end is the coal-hole; the chimney occupies the other end; there is a walk along the two remaining sides of the pan, five or six feet wide; and between these walks and the sides of the pan-house, which are generally of wood, long benches, four or five feet wide, are fixed, on which the salt is placed in conical baskets to drain, after it has been taken out of the pan: a wooden or slated roof is placed over the pan-house, with l'œuvres to allow the steam to pass freely out.

"After the brine has been drawn from the cistern into the evaporating pan, the process of the manufacture is varied, according to the state in which it is wished to have the salt procured, and the uses to which it is intended to be applied. The effects of these variations will be best understood, by first examining what is the process of nature in forming the crystals of muriate of soda; and then by stating the different ways in which the manufacture is conducted.

"The natural form of the crystals of muriate of soda, is that of a perfect cube; and they regularly assume this figure, when the due arrangement of their particles has not been interrupted by agitation, or the application of strong heat. 'These cubes exhibit diagonal striæ, and frequently on each side produce squares parallel to the external surface, gradually decreasing inwards; circumstances which shew the vestiges of their internal structure: for every cube is composed of six quadrangular hollow pyramids, joined by their apices and external surface; each of these pyramids filled up by others similar, but gradually decreasing, completes the form. By a due degree of evaporation, it is no difficult matter to obtain these pyramids separate and distinct; or six of such, either hollow or more or less solid, joined together round a centre. If we examine the hollow pyramid† of salt farther,

* A *profile sketch* is given of the pan and flues. It is not, however, required.

"† The bases and altitudes of these little pyramids are in general equal; thus shewing the disposition of the salt to form a cube."

farther, we shall find it composed of four triangles, and each of these formed of threads parallel to the base; which threads, upon accurate examination, are found to be nothing more than series of small cubes*.' The perfect crystallization of the salt can, however, take place only under the circumstances above mentioned, a freedom from agitation, and from too rapid an evaporation of the water which holds the salt in solution: and it is principally on the presence or absence of these causes, that the variation in the appearance of the manufactured salt depends.

"The manufacture is conducted in several different ways, or rather heat is applied in various degrees, to effect the evaporation of the water of solution; and according to these different degrees of heat, the product is the stoved or lump salt; common salt; the large grained flaky; and large grained or fishery salt.

"In making the *stoved*, or *lump salt* as it is called, the brine is brought to a boiling heat; which in brine fully saturated, is 226 degrees of Fahrenheit. Crystals of muriate of soda are soon formed on the surface; and almost immediately, by the agitation of the brine, subside to the bottom of the pan. If taken out, each of them appears, at first sight, to be granular or a little flaky; but if more accurately examined, it is found to approach to the form of a little quadrangular, though somewhat irregular, pyramid. The boiling heat is continued through the whole process; and, as the evaporation proceeds, similar little crystals continue to form themselves, and to fall to the bottom of the pan. At the end of twelve hours, the greatest part of the water of solution is found to be evaporated; so much only being left as is sufficient to cover the salt and the bottom of the pan. The fires are then slackened, and the salt is drawn to the sides of the pan with iron rakes. The waller then places a conical wicker basket, or barrow as it is called, within the pan; and having filled this with salt, by means of a little wooden spade, he suffers the brine to drain from it for a short time into the pan; and then carries it to one of the benches, at the side of the pan-house, where the draining is completed. It is afterwards dried in stoves, heated by a continuation of the same flues which have passed under the evaporating pan, and is reckoned to lose in this about $\frac{1}{7}$th of its weight. In making this salt the pan is twice filled in the course of twenty-four hours.

"On

" * See Bergman's Essays, Vol. II. p. 12 and 13."

"On the first application of heat, if the brine contains any carbonate of lime, the acid may be observed to quit the lime, and this being no longer held in solution, is either thrown up to the surface, as the ebullition takes place, along with the earthy or feculent contents of the brine, whence it is removed by *skimmers;* or it subsides to the bottom of the pan, along with the salt first formed, and with some portion of the sulphate of lime; and is raked out in the early part of the process. These two operations are called *clearing* the pan; some of the brines scarcely require them at all, and others only occasionally.

"An analysis of these *clearings* was made by my friend, Mr. William Henry. He found 480 parts, containing 384 of muriate of soda, 20 of carbonate of lime, and 76 of sulphate of lime. Circumstances however are continually occurring to vary these proportions, even in the same brine; and the proportion is generally less than he found it.

"In making the *common salt,* the brine is first brought to a boiling heat, as in making the stoved salt; with the double view of bringing it as soon as possible to a state of perfect saturation, and of more readily clearing from it any earthy contents. When these purposes have been effected, the fires are slackened, and the crystallization is carried on with the brine heated to 160 or 170 degrees of Fahrenheit. The salt formed in this process is in quadrangular pyramids or hoppers, close and compact in their texture, frequently clustered together, and larger or smaller according to the degree of heat which has been applied. Little cubical crystals will often be intermixed with, and attached to these. The remainder of the process is similar to that of the stoved salt, except that after draining in the baskets, it is immediately carried into the store-house and not afterwards exposed to heat. The pan is filled only once in 24 hours in making this salt.

"The *large grained flaky* salt is made with an evaporation conducted at the heat of 130 or 140 degrees. The salt formed in this process is somewhat harder than the common salt, and approaches nearer to the natural form of the crystals of muriate of soda. The pan is filled once in 48 hours. As salt of this grain is often made by slackening the fires betwixt Saturday and Monday, and allowing the crystallization to proceed more slowly on the intermediate day, it has got the name of *Sunday salt.*

"To

"To make the *large grained* or *fishery salt* the brine is brought to a heat from 100 to 110° of Fahrenheit; and at this heat, the evaporation of the water, and the crystallization of the salt, proceed. No agitation is produced by it on the brine; and the slowness of the evaporation allows the muriate of soda to form in large, nearly cubical crystals, seldom however quite perfect: with this heat it takes five or six days to evaporate the water of solution."

Clarifying, &c. the evaporating liquor.—P. 56. "In the course of these several processes various additions are often made to the brine, with the view of promoting the separation of any earthy mixture, or the more ready crystallization of the salt. These additions have been different at different works; and many of them seem to have been made from particular, and often ill-founded prejudices; and without any exact idea as to their probable effects. The principal additions which have at various times been made are, acids; animal jelly and gluten; vegetable mucilage; new or stale ale; wheat-flour; resin; butter; and alum."

These several additions are spoken of, in detail; but little of a practical nature arises from it. It gives Mr. Holland, however, an opportunity of showing how much he has attended to the subject, and his acquaintance with the writers that have treated upon it. Many, if not most, of the additions that are, or have been, in use, would seem to be little more than the nostrums of quackery, whereby to give an air of mystery to the art of salt making; as the additions to the coagulum of milk are, in like manner, used by dairywomen.

The subjoined passages contain what I conceive to be proper to extract, for the guidance of inexperienced salt-boilers.

P. 57. "Blood is still occasionally used at some of the salt works in Cheshire,* and, when fresh, is found highly useful; but the difficulty of procuring it in the quantity wanted, and of keeping it without putrefaction, are objections to its general use. *Whites of eggs* have been frequently added to the brine for the same purpose as blood."

P. 58. "The white of eggs are not much used in Cheshire for clearing the brine. It is not supposed that they would not answer the purpose, but the same object is effected by means

"* It is the only substance used at Birtley in Durham for clarifying the brine."

means less expensive. *Glue* is frequently used for clearing the brine, and is found to answer the purpose perfectly well; and this is the only substance used at many works. The addition most frequently made to the brine for assisting in clearing it, is the jelly procured by boiling *cows'* or *calves' feet.* The consumption of these at some of the works is very considerable. They are salted, dried, and laid up ready for using. When wanted, they are either boiled in a separate pan, and the broth carried to the evaporating pan; or a stew-pot is placed in one of the corners of the evaporating pan, and the feet being put into this, the jelly is extracted from them by the heat of the brine in the pan, and is added as the waller sees occasion."

P. 59. "*Butter* or some other oily substance is very generally added to brine during the evaporating process, and after the clearing has been made, to assist the granulation of the salt, and to make the brine 'work more kindly.' Dr. Brownrigg seems to think it produces no good effect, and that 'the salt-boilers have little to plead in its favour, besides the immemorial custom.' This opinion of his appears not to have been well-founded; and the experience of the wallers leaves little room for doubting that the addition of the butter enables the salt to crystallize more readily. While the evaporating process is going on, it frequently happens that an adhesion takes place betwixt the sides of the little crystals of salt, which form on its surface; and that, instead of falling to the bottom of the pan, these adhere together, producing a kind of incrustation to a considerable extent on the surface of the brine, which prevents the evaporation from going on regularly, and by confining the steam occasions the brine underneath to acquire too much heat. When a crust of this kind forms, the salt boilers say that 'the pan is set over:' It is somewhat raised above the surface of the brine, is usually of an opaque whiteness, and has lost a large part of its water of crystallization. The great use of butter seems to be to prevent the pan from 'setting over.' If a very small portion of this or any other oily substance is added to the brine in one of the largest pans, it may be seen in a very few minutes to diffuse itself over the whole surface, and in its progress to occasion any crust, which may have been formed on the brine, to subside to the bottom of the pan. At the same time a great steam is observed to rise; the superabundant heat is carried off; and

and the crystallization afterwards proceeds with regularity."

Salt-boilers, it appears, have long been, and still are, in the "habit of adding *alum* to their brine, when they wish to procure a hard firm salt of large grains," and, Mr. H. seems to be of opinion, with the desired effect. His words are:—P. 61. "Notwithstanding the opinion which Dr. Brownrigg entertained on this subject, the addition of alum does appear to assist in promoting the crystallization of the salt in large grains; but in what manner its effects are produced, I am unable to ascertain."

The *Residue* of Crystallization.—P. 61. "By the application of heat and the assistance of the different additions which have been mentioned, a large proportion of the carbonates of lime, and of iron, if any are contained in the brines, is separated and cleared out. Some part of these is still left in the pan, and as the evaporation proceeds, subsiding to the bottom, together with the sulphate of lime, they form an incrustation there, called by the workmen *pan-scratch* or *scale;* which gradually accumulating along with such portion of the muriate of soda, as is mixed with them, it becomes necessary to remove from the pan every three or four weeks, by *picking;* an operation consisting in the separation of this scale from the pan, by heavy blows with sharp iron picks. These pickings were analysed by the excellent chymist before-mentioned, Mr. William Henry. He found 480 parts of them to contain 40 of muriate of soda, 60 of carbonate, and 380 of sulphate of lime. Circumstances of course are occurring to vary these proportions. Where the brine is weak, the proportion of muriate of soda is still smaller than in Mr. Henry's analysis; since on any fresh addition of brine to the pan, the muriate of soda which had been deposited, would be re-dissolved; on the contrary, if the brine approached to saturation, it would remain united with the scale upon the pan.

"The pan-scratch accumulates most towards the close of the evaporation; for when there is much salt deposited in the pan, it forms such a heavy mass at the bottom, that the water cannot penetrate into it; and hence the portion which is lowest undergoes a sort of calcination and fusion, which gives it extreme hardness, and a very strong adhesion to the pan *."

The

"* At Salins, and at several of the salt works in France, the scales picked from the pans are lixiviated, in order to extract from them the muriate

The *Fuel* used in making Salt.—P. 71. "The progress of improvement in any art, especially in the early and unlettered ages, has usually been made by slow and gradual advances. Simple as the process of making salt from brine, by the application of heat to an evaporating vessel, now appears; it was long before the manufacture attained this degree of perfection. The rude mode of preparing it consisted only in pouring the brine upon burning wood, for which the oak and the hazel were preferred, and then collecting the salt deposited upon the ashes of the wood *. When evaporating vessels were at length brought into use, wood was the only fuel employed to effect the evaporation. Camden, speaking of the salt works at Droitwich, says, 'what a prodigious quantity of wood these salt works consume, though men be silent, yet Feckenham Forest, once very thick with trees, and the neighbouring woods will by their thinness declare daily more and more †." King published his Vale Royal in 1656; and it appears from his account, that wood continued to be the fuel at that time most used at the Cheshire salt works; and that a general preference was given to it. Coal however began to be employed at, or about that period; and King mentions, as a new and singular circumstance, that it had been substituted for wood at some recently erected salt works above Namptwich ‡.

"The considerable extension which has taken place during the last century in the manufacture of salt in Cheshire, has been necessarily accompanied with a proportionate demand for fuel; and the use of wood, of which it would have been impossible to have found a supply at all adequate to the consumption of the different salt works, is now entirely discontinued, and coal substituted for it."

P. 72. "The importance of having a supply of this article, convenient of access, and moderate in price, may be conceived from a statement of the quantity annually brought up the Weaver, for the supply of the works in its immediate neighbourhood. Taking the average of the last ten years, ending April 5th, 1806, I find that 57,780 tons have been brought up to Northwich, Anderton, and Witton;

muriate of soda they contain. When the water has acquired a strength of 14 per cent. it is added to the brine in the pans. See Memoir on the National salt works of France by Citizen Nicholas."

"* See Plinii Hist. Nat. XXXI. c. 7, & Varro de re rustica, L. I. c. 6."

"† Camden's Britannia, p. 518."

"‡ King's Vale Royal, p. 66."

Witton; and 30,860 to Winsford; making a total annual average of 88,640 tons. The last of these ten years, the quantity brought up exceeded that of any former year. To Northwich, Anderton, and Witton, it amounted to 70,580 tons; and to Winsford, to 36,460 tons; making a total of 107,040 tons.

"The entire quantity of coal thus conveyed up the Weaver, it is true, is not consumed in the manufacture of salt; a small proportion of it being applied to domestic purposes at Northwich, Winsford, and their neighbourhood; but this cannot amount to a tenth part of the whole consumption, probably much less. The remainder is used in the manufacture of salt."

The RENTAL VALUE of *Brine Wells.*—P. 48. "It appears from Doomsday book that the king had formerly a claim on all the brine springs in Cheshire. In the time of Edward the Confessor, 'there was a brine spring at Namptwich, and eight salterns betwixt the king and earl Edwin; of which the king bore two thirds of the expences, and received two thirds of the returns; the earl the other third.' The earl had also a saltern for the particular use of his own family: if, however, he sold any salt from this, the king had two thirds of the receipts, the earl one third. Several private individuals had also salterns for the use of their own families; but if they sold any salt, a certain sum was paid to the king.

"No right over these springs is now claimed by the crown; and they are the sole property of the owners of the land in which they are found. Few of them, however, are occupied by the land-owners; and they are in general let out to tenants, either at a fixed annual rent, without any restriction as to the working them, or at a rent proportioned to the extent of the manufacture, and the quantity of salt made."

The PRODUCE of the Salt Mines, and Salt Works of Cheshire.—This is not well stated, by Mr. Holland. In the section "Commerce," it is true, he has taken commendable pains to make out distinct parts of the expenditure; but has not clearly stated the whole amount of annual produce. I will, here, insert his statements at large; and refer to them from the head *Commerce.*

P. 317. "It has been mentioned under the section above referred to, that though rock salt has been found in several parts of the county, no pits are now worked, except in the neighbourhood of Northwich. Part of the inferior rock salt which is procured there, is used at some of the

the refineries in the neighbourhood: a further quantity is sent down the Weaver for the supply of the refineries at Frodsham, and of those in Lancashire, on the banks of the Mersey. The purer rock salt, or what is usually called Prussia rock, is carried by the same conveyance to Liverpool; whence it is exported chiefly to Ireland, and the ports in the Baltic. I find that the quantity of rock salt sent down the Weaver,

from April 5th, 1796,	to April 5th, 1797,	was	55,633 tons.
—— 1797,	—— 1798,	—	34,028 ——
—— 1798,	—— 1799,	—	33,983 ——
—— 1799,	—— 1800,	—	46,206 ——
—— 1800,	—— 1801,	—	54,103 ——
—— 1801,	—— 1802,	—	56,403 ——
—— 1802,	—— 1803,	—	53,861 ——
—— 1803,	—— 1804,	—	60,946 ——
—— 1804,	—— 1805,	—	59,826 ——
—— 1805,	—— 1806,	—	56,104 ——

giving an annual average for the last ten years of 51,109 tons. In this, is included what is used at the Frodsham and Lancashire refineries, which may probably amount to about a third of the whole. By the report from the committee of the house of commons, appointed to inquire into the laws relating to the salt duties, ordered to be printed 30th of June 1801, it appears that

in 1798 were exported	20,168	tons of rock salt.
in 1799 ——	33,913	——
in 1800 ——	34,939	——

Of the above quantity,

in 1798 ——	16,095 tons.
in 1799 ——	22,374 ——
in 1800 ——	19,663 ——

were sent to different ports in Ireland: the remainder was exported principally to Denmark, Russia, Sweden, Prussia, and Germany; and a small quantity to Guernsey, Jersey, and the West Indies.

"The white salt manufactured in Cheshire forms a still more important commercial object than the rock salt. While endeavouring to trace the rise and gradual progress of this manufacture in a former section, I stated that, a little more than a century ago, the quantity of salt made in Cheshire appeared scarcely more than adequate to its own supply, and that of a few adjoining counties. The rapid increase which, since that time, has taken place in this manufacture, exclusive of the active spirit of commerce and enterprize which has existed in the country, may be attributed to the formation of internal canals,

which

which have furnished a more ready means of intercourse with the inland counties; and to the facility of communication with Liverpool, which the extension of the navigation on the Weaver, as high up as Winsford, where large salt works are erected, has been the means of effecting.

"As a consequence of the opportunity, which is afforded by the Staffordshire canal, of conveying this necessary article into the interior of the country, the greater part of the salt manufactured at those works situated near this canal, is disposed of for home consumption. Some portion of what is made at Winsford and the neighbourhood of Northwich, is also thus applied; but by much the largest proportion of the salt manufactured at these latter places is exported.

"It appears, from the accounts I have received, that from May 24, 1805, to May 24, 1806, there were disposed of for home consumption,

	Bushels.		Tons.	Bushels.
At Lawton - - -	156,071	or	3,901	31
At Wheelock - -	181,297	—	4,532	17
At Roughwood - -	56,529	—	1,413	9
At Middlewich - -	97,292	—	2,432	12
At Winsford - -	32,004	—	800	4
At Northwich and its neighbourhood -	140,444	—	3,511	4
Giving a total of -	663,637 bu.	or	16,590 tons,	77 bu.

and paying a duty to government of 475,728*l.* 15*s.* This is exclusive of the salt manufactured at Namptwich and Frodsham; and of that made at the works on the Lancashire side of the Mersey, from the solution of the rock salt procured in the neighbourhood of Northwich; the greatest part of which is used for home consumption.

"Though so large a quantity of salt is manufactured in Cheshire for home consumption, by far the largest proportion of what is made is sent down the Weaver to Liverpool, for exportation. Winsford, and the neighbourhood of Northwich, peculiarly enjoying the advantages of the navigation on this river, and having an abundance of brine, the salt exported has been in great degree furnished from the works established at these places. Whatever surplus there has been at the manufacturies in other parts of the county, above the demand for home consumption, has also been similarly disposed of. I have received an account of the quantity of white salt, which has been conveyed down the Weaver, during the last ten years,

years, nearly the whole of which has been exported. What is stated as from Northwich, includes not only the salt manufactured in the immediate neighbourhood of that place, but whatever has been sent down from the different works, situated near the banks of the Staffordshire canal; a communication by means of an inclined plane, betwixt this canal and the Weaver at Anderton, affording a greater facility of conveyance down to Liverpool, than was possessed before such a communication was established.

"Account of white salt sent down the Weaver from Winsford and Northwich.

"From April 5th, 1796, to April 5th, 1797.
Winsford, 24,335 tons. Northwich, 75,820 tons.

From April 5th, 1797, to April 5th, 1798.
Winsford, 30,222 tons. Northwich, 70,322 tons.

From April 5th, 1798, to April 5th, 1799.
Winsford, 38,611 tons. Northwich, 70,181 tons.

From April 5th, 1799, to April 5th, 1800.
Winsford, 38,423 tons. Northwich, 67,690 tons

From April 5th, 1800, to April 5th, 1801.
Winsford, 52,881 tons. Northwich, 89,594 tons.

From April 5th, 1801, to April 5th, 1802.
Winsford, 61,586 tons. Northwich, 92,290 tons.

From April 5th, 1802, to April 5th, 1803.
Winsford, 47,825 tons. Northwich, 90,921 tons.

From April 5th, 1803, to April 5th, 1804.
Winsford, 3,820 tons. Northwich, 78,060 tons.

From April 5th, 1804, to April 5th, 1805.
Winsford, 48,207 tons. Northwich, 99,230 tons.

From April 5th, 1805, to April 5th, 1806.
Winsford, 63,552 tons. Northwich, 115,226 tons.

The annual average of the last ten years, according to this account of salt sent down the Weaver, is, from Winsford, 44,384 tons; and from Northwich, 84,933 tons; giving a total average of 139,317 tons.

"The greater proportion of the salt sent down the Weaver, exclusive of that part of it which supplies the fisheries in Scotland and the home consumption, is exported to Ireland; to the ports in the Baltic; to the States of America; to Newfoundland; and the British continental colonies. A small quantity is sent to the West Indies; to Asia; and to Africa.

"Though the manufacture of white salt, and the commerce

merce to which it has given rise, have experienced so large an increase during the last twenty years, there seems reason to believe that they still admit of considerable extension. One of the obstacles to this is the state of the navigation of the Weaver, which does not furnish depth of water sufficient for the flats to convey the salt down during the neap tides; as a consequence of which, the merchant at Liverpool, rather than suffer the evils and expense arising from the detention of his vessel, either suffers it to sail with half a cargo, or seeks out some other article of loading. Should a more ready communication be formed betwixt the Weaver and the Mersey, by means of the projected canal from the former to Weston point, which would admit of the flats passing down at even the lowest tides, (see the article *Canals)* this inconvenience would be, in a great degree, removed.

"Another circumstance which has operated as a check to the extension of the salt trade, has been the inequality of the duty betwixt foreign and British salt imported into Ireland. Whilst the former pays only 1s. 5d. per bushel, all British salt imported pays 2s; the difference in the import duty being more than the original invoice cost of the British salt. (!) What possible reason there can exist for such a preference being given to a foreign manufacture, it is difficult to conceive! We cannot, however, be surprized that the effect of it has been to lead the Irish to believe, that bay salt possesses a superior efficacy, in the curing of provisions, to salt of British manufacture; or that the quantity of the former imported into Ireland should be so considerable. By the report from the committee of the House of Commons appointed to inquire into the laws relating to the salt duties, we find that there were imported into Ireland

in 1799, 262,351 bushels of foreign salt.
1800, 225,040 ditto.
1801, 136,109 ditto.

"Were the import duties upon foreign and British salt made equal, there can be little doubt but that the large sums, which are at present annually paid for bay salt, would be saved to the country; since, from the analysis which has been given of the British salt, made from natural brine springs, in the account of its manufacture (see the section *Minerals*), it appears to be at least equally free from the admixture of earthy salts, with the bay salt; and the size of the crystal can be readily varied by the manufacturer,

facturer, so as to adapt it to whatever is its intended application."

The IMPORTANCE of the salt works of Cheshire, considered in a political point of view, is highly honourable to that county. P. 316. "Under the section of *Minerals*, I have given a detailed account of the natural history of the rock salt, and of the manufacture of white salt in this county. The commerce which these give rise to, and the number of hands for which they directly or indirectly find employ, render them objects of the first importance, in a commercial and political point of view. By a memorial of the manufacturers of white salt, proprietors of rock salt pits, and exporters of salt, presented, in 1805, to the late Mr. Pitt, against an export duty he had it in contemplation to lay upon rock and white salt exported to any part of Europe; it appears that the number of hands, employed in the various branches of the salt trade, amounted, at that time, to 2,950, exclusively of their families; and that the sum invested in salt works, rock pits, and lighters, amounted at a moderate valuation to 436,000*l.* over and above the capital employed to carry on the trade. The evils which would have resulted to the trade from the export duty which was intended to have been imposed, were so strongly pointed out in this memorial, that the minister was induced to abandon the tax he had proposed."

By the *tax* on *salt*, for home consumption, manufactured in Cheshire only, beside what is drawn from the rock salt sent out of it, for the purpose of saturating sea water,—Government appears, from the foregoing extract, p. 101, to receive an annual revenue of little less than half a million, sterling.

On the QUALITIES of the different varieties of salt, (produced in the manner described aforegoing p. 93,) and their EFFECTS in CURING ANIMAL FOOD,—Mr. Holland has favored us with some luminous and satisfactory observations; which he thus introduces.—P. 62. "We have remarked that the salt formed from the same brine, by the application of different degrees of heat, varies very much in external appearance; and it has been very generally imagined that the salts produced by these variations in the process of the manufacture, were equally different from each other in their component parts, and in their qualities, as in outward form. It has also been the prevailing opinion, that any salt formed from natural brine was inferior in its power of preserving animal flesh from putrefaction to bay salt, or the salt procured from sea water. It is of much

much importance to ascertain, how far the ideas which have been formed on these different points, are well founded; that if they owe their origin to groundless prejudices, these may be removed; that if, on the contrary, there is any foundation for them, the causes of the difference in the quality of the salt made from the same brine, and those of the inferiority of the salt made from natural brine, to that from sea water, may be ascertained.

"It is allowed by all that pure muriate of soda is the salt, of all others known, which is best fitted for the preservation of animal flesh, and provisions of every kind; and that the goodness of any salt depends on its containing a perfectly neutralized muriate of soda, free from the admixture of other alkaline or earthy salts.

"The difference in the quality of the salt made by a boiling heat, and that by a low degree of heat, has been supposed to be owing,

"1. To a portion of the muriatic acid being expelled from the muriate of soda, by the high degree of heat, while a superabundance of alkali has been left.

"2. To the greater combination of the earthy salts contained in the brine with the muriate of soda, by the agitation in the boiling process."

These received opinions, Mr. H. refutes, by experiments and arguments, in a masterly manner, and in the face of the most celebrated chemists of the age, who had adopted them.

This done, Mr. Holland proceeds to show, in a more familiar way, that, not only the different varieties of manufactured salts, from fossil rock, and subterranean brine, but those produced from sea water, in a more natural manner, are equal in their specific virtues, for the preservation of animal matter, from corruption. But, owing to their different forms and textures, they are severally adapted to different purposes, in that process.

P. 68. "As a still further proof that the stoved salt, or the salt prepared by a boiling heat, and the large grained salt, or that prepared by a low degree of heat, though differing in form, have scarcely any difference in their component parts, we have only to re-dissolve a portion of each in pure water. By applying to the solution of the large grained salt a boiling heat, we obtain a granular flaky salt, resembling stoved salt; while on the other hand, by carrying on the evaporation of the water of solution of the stoved salt at a heat of 100 degrees, we obtain large cubical crystals of muriate of soda; and these operations

operations may be repeated, *ad infinitum*, with correspondent results. The component parts of these two salts are in fact the same: their only difference is in outward form, and in the hardness and compactness of their crystals.

"Though however differing little in purity; and though from the experiments which have been given, it has appeared that they were each nearly a pure muriate of soda; yet it will readily be conceived that their difference in form and in compactness, may fit them for very various application in the preservation of animal flesh and provisions.

"For table use, for the salting of butter, and for various domestic purposes, a preference is given to the salt prepared by a boiling heat; the smallness of its grain better fitting it for these purposes.

"For the same reason, and from its consequent readiness of solution, this salt is well adapted for making the pickle for *striking* the meat, which is the first part of the process in curing fish, and preserving animal flesh.

"For the *packing* of fish and provisions, it is by no means so proper as the common or large grained fishery salt; and, as might be expected, it is found, when applied to this purpose, not to preserve them equally well from putrefaction. This however arises, not from any want of purity in the salt, nor from any admixture of earthy salts with it; but from its small grain, and its want of hardness and compactness, derived from its containing more of the water of crystallization than the larger grained salt. Being so ready of solution, the whole of it is formed into brine; which being forced out from betwixt the layers of flesh or fish, by the pressure of these on each other, the different portions of animal matter come into close contact, without having any salt interposed. Whereas when the salt of larger grain is used, a considerable part of it long remains undissolved; separating the different portions of meat; admitting, in some degree, the brine to flow betwixt the layers; and furnishing a constant supply of saturated brine, from the solution of the salt in the fluids exuding from the animal matter, to every part of the packed provision.

"The action of bay salt is exactly similar to that of the large grained salt; and neither the one nor the other appears to have any advantage over the salt prepared by a boiling heat, except in the size and compactness of its crystals; and in its containing a somewhat smaller proportion

tion of the water of crystallization: and as the large grained fishery salt, prepared by a low degree of heat from natural brine, is more than equal to the bay salt in these important points; there can be no doubt, whatever prejudices to the contrary may have existed, that it at least equals the latter in its power of preserving animal flesh, or provisions.

"Experience, however, has much more weight than any theory on the subject. This experience we have, on an extensive scale, at the navy office at Deptford, where the large grained salt, manufactured in Britain from natural brine springs, has for several years been the only salt used for *packing* provisions; after they have been first salted with common salt, or that prepared by a heat of 180 degrees. Though these provisions have been afterwards carried to the hottest climates, the strength and purity of the salt used in preserving them have never been called in question. The provisions have kept perfectly well; and it has never been doubted that the salt here used, was in every respect equal to the St. Ubes salt; or to any other salt prepared from sea water, by the natural heat of the sun*."

To corroborate the evidence of experience, in England, Mr. Holland laudably extended his enquiries to Ireland, where most of the salt provisions, sent to distant markets, are cured; and from thence received the satisfactory information which follows.—P. 323. "I received the following answer to some enquiries I made of a very intelligent gentleman at Cork, as to the comparative advantages of the bay, and large grained fishery salt of British manufacture, in the curing of provisions. 'The large grained fishery salt is not used here; and I am doubtful whether any fair trial has been made of it. The St. Ubes salt comes cheaper, and perhaps is more solid in the crystal or grain; and unless the import duty on British salt was lowered, I expect it would be very difficult to lead the provision merchants to use it in preference to the Portugal salt. They know that the latter answers their purpose; and nothing but a material difference in cost, would be likely to alter their opinion, or prejudice. I have myself no doubt of the large grained fishery salt curing provisions quite as well as the St. Ubes salt." (!)

It would be injustice to the merit of Mr. Holland not to

"* What is sold in London as bay salt, is almost entirely the large grained salt of home manufacture from natural brine springs."

to pay due tribute of praise to him, for his ingenuity, industry, and perseverance, in adducing fit subject matter for his valuable account of the salt works of Cheshire;—much too valuable to be buried in a "County Report." I have, therefore, bestowed more attention upon it, and taken up with it a greater portion of this volume, than may, perhaps, be thought requisite to the more especial intention of my present pursuit. Every thing that is *practically* useful, I believe, will be here found arranged in the most natural, and of course the most intelligible form.

SUBJECT THE SECOND.

POLITICAL ECONOMY.

STATE of APPROPRIATION.—For the quantity of *unappropriated lands*, in Cheshire, see Mr. *Wedge's* statement, p. 11.

In his chapter "Enclosing," (p. 118.) Mr. *Holland* enters, in a speculative way, on the *general subject* of appropriation. But, after the ample discussion it has had, it were in vain to look for any thing in his strictures, that can entitle them to a place, here.

In the chapter "Waste Lands," we find this Reporter more at his post, while giving us the *progress* of *appropriation* in *Cheshire*.—P. 208. "Though enclosing has taken place to a greater extent of late years, there still remains a very considerable proportion of uncultivated land in this county. The forest of Delamere, in Eddisbury hundred, though somewhat diminished in size by late enclosures, still contains about 10,000 acres, in a state of little or no profit. In Macclesfield hundred, besides the very extensive district of hilly uncultivated land on the Derbyshire border, there are several large tracts of peat moss, as Lindow Common, Featherbed Moss, &c. In Northwich hundred, we meet with another considerable district of waste land, called Rudheath; part of which has, however, been planted within the last few years, chiefly with Scotch fir; the plants appearing vigorous and healthy: while another considerable tract of land upon it has been enclosed, and, at considerable expense, brought into a state of cultivation by the spirited exertions of Strethill Wright, Esq. Besides these, there is in very many of the townships

townships in the county, some heath, common, or moss land; the whole or part of which might be brought into a state of profitable cultivation.

"The scarcity, which prevailed throughout the kingdom a few years ago, acted as a powerful stimulus to the enclosure of waste land in this county; and the spirit which was then excited, has still by no means subsided. Many extensive mosses and commons, by the aid of draining, marling, &c. have, within the last two or three years, been brought into a state of cultivation; and additional improvements of a similar kind are at present either projected, or actually carrying into execution. What proportion of the remaining waste land in the county may be enclosed and cultivated, with benefit to the occupiers, is somewhat doubtful. Though considerable success has attended some of the late attempts of this nature on Delamere forest, it seems highly probable that a large part of this tract might be more advantageously occupied in planting, than in any other mode. The same remark may be made with respect to Rudheath, and several other districts of waste land in Cheshire."

PROVISIONS.—The following account of the provisions of Cheshire may be said to be written in the appropriate language of Report. It is the more valuable, as coming from one, who, in the pursuits of his profession, has peculiar opportunities of witnessing the truth.—P. 298. "The price of provisions is so continually varied by the operation of seasons more or less favourable, and by different external causes, that it is difficult to give any average statement on this subject. Generally speaking there has been a gradual increase of price, proportioned to the decreasing value of the circulating medium; and all kinds of animal food sell for, at least, one third more than they did ten years ago.

"Beef and mutton average from 7*d.* to 8*d.* per lb.
Veal and pork from 6*d.* to 7*d.*
Rabbits, poultry, and eggs in proportion.
Butter from 1*s.* 2*d.* to 1*s.* 6*d.* per lb. avoirdupois.
Cheese from 2*l.* 15*s.* to 3*l.* 10*s.* per cwt. of 120 lb *.

Wheat

"* The constant average price of some dairies is much greater than the highest here stated, a circumstance which depends principally on the length of time the cheese is kept. By long keeping, cheese is considerably diminished in weight; so that the actual difference in price between that sold early, and that kept for one or two years, is not so much as at first view it might appear."

Wheat from 9*s.* to 12*s.* the bushel of 75 lb.
Barley from 5*s.* 6*d.* to 7*s.* 6*d.* the bushel of 60 lb.
Oats from 3*s.* 6*d.* to 4*s.* 6*d.* the bushel of 45 lb.

"The middle and lower class of farmers seldom, however, indulge themselves with much fresh animal food. At the close of the market they frequently purchase a little, at a cheaper rate, for the supply of a few days; the remainder of the week they content themselves with bacon or beef of their own curing; a little of which serves to give a relish to their large dish of potatoes or cabbages. Whey or buttermilk from the dairy contribute to complete their meal.

"The cottagers and labourers have, in like manner, their dishes of potatoes with bacon or butter; and where they can buy or beg a little whey or buttermilk from the farm, this supplies their drink. The farmer, however, is usually so fearful of robbing his calves or his pigs, that he seldom grants this indulgence, excepting to the cottagers in his immediate employ.

"Bread made of wheat, or of barley and wheat mixed, is almost the only kind used in the houses of the more opulent farmers; and even the smaller farmers are much less in the habit of using bread made of barley alone, than they were a few years ago. Oat bread is seldom seen in Cheshire: oat meal made into cakes, or boiled with water or milk into hasty pudding, is a frequent article of diet.

"Tea is in common use amongst the cottagers and labourers: and, with the usual additions, generally constitutes at least one of their daily meals."

Mr. H. advocates the use of *Tea,* among the lower classes. And altho we perceive not much, that is strikingly observable, advanced on the subject; yet the sentiments of a medical man, on a topic of high consideration, in the science of dietetics, and the welfare of the most useful class of society, cannot be undeserving of attention. The use of tea appears to be little else than an innocent indulgence. But, quere, has not longevity rather encreased, than diminished, since its introduction*?

P. 299.

* On the 25th January 1796, I united strong infusions of teas (green and bohea) with tartarized steel; and thereby formed *inks* of a quality similar to that of the common ink of the shops. I wrote with them, severally, on the same slip of paper,—"common ink;"—"bohea tea and tartarized steel;"—"green tea and tartarized steel;" and,

P. 299. "It is, I confess, by no means clear to me that this ought to be made the subject of that indiscriminate censure which I have so often heard pronounced upon it. It is objected to from its supposed tendency to debilitate and relax, and from its leading to great waste of time. With respect to the first point, it may admit of much doubt, whether it does produce the evils imputed to it. Who, after excess of fatigue, has not experienced the enlivening and invigorating effects of this pleasant astringent beverage; and without feeling any subsequent debility?—It may not agree with every constitution, or it may be taken to an injurious excess; but if we are to bring arguments against it from the abuse of it, will not these be at least equally applicable to any substitute for it? Besides I would ask what substitute, so little expensive, can be found for the labourer? The produce of the dairy he is very generally debarred from; whilst the high tax upon malt renders even small beer scarcely accessible to him; and I will not suppose that those who regard tea as unwholesome and pernicious, would recommend the substitution of spirits for it. It is to be considered too that tea is made the vehicle of bread, butter, sugar, and cream; all of which will be allowed to contribute importantly to nutriment. With regard to the time consumed by the cottager in tea drinking, it is not necessarily more than in taking any other meal; and if, by the little rest it affords him, he is better enabled to resume his labour, that time can hardly be considered as lost. The means of enjoyment in the possession of the poor are too scanty to admit of diminution."

FUEL.—P. 300. "A few years ago, the fuel used by the farmers and cottagers consisted almost entirely of wood, and peat, or turf as it is here called, from the peat mosses. Each farm, where there was a peat moss in the township, had its moss room allotted to it, from which peat was procured. Though this is still used amongst the cottagers and small farmers, pit coal is now the general article of fuel in Cheshire. Macclesfield hundred is supplied in great measure from its own collieries; which also furnish a supply to the eastern part of Bucklow hundred*. The other-

and, to this day (23d June 1809) there is barely a shade of difference in their permanency.—Is not this good evidence of that the teas are *astringent*;—consequently, *corroborant*, and what is termed *stomachic*? Their *aroma* is acceptable to most stomachs.

"* See the Section *Minerals*."

other districts of the county procure it either by the canals, which convey it into the interior from Staffordshire and Lancashire; or by land carriage immediately from the collieries in the hundred of Wirrall, Flintshire, and the two counties above mentioned. Cannel or *candle* coal, a fuel incomparably pleasanter than any other, is also in frequent use in the northern parts of the county; the best is brought from Haigh in the neighbourhood of Wigan; an inferior kind from Worsley in Lancashire, and from Staffordshire. The price of coal has been gradually increasing for many years, but apparently not more than in proportion to the increased price of labour: and the large demand for the use of the manufactories: on the banks of the canals it is 12*s*. 6*d*. or 13*s*. per ton."

MANUFACTURIES.—P. 325. "Little remains to be said on this subject after the detailed description of the salt manufacture which has been given under the section on *Minerals*. This indeed is the only manufacture, for which Cheshire is peculiarly distinguished, unless the making of cheese can with propriety be so termed. From its immediate neighbourhood to Manchester, it has of course participated in the great extension of the cotton manufacture which has taken place in that town, and the surrounding country; and there are few situations in the county, favourable to the erection of cotton mills, where such edifices are not now to be met with. This is particularly the case in the part more immediately adjoining to Lancashire: and it has invariably been accompanied by a proportionate increase in the population and wealth of the country. From its vicinity to Manchester, and its large participation in the trade of that place, Stockport has now become one of the most flourishing towns in the kingdom; having acquired a degree of consequence and population, which render it an object of great importance in the political economy of the county. A serious check has indeed been lately given to the prosperity of the cotton manufacture, by the unfortunate aspect of our foreign connections, and the consequent uncertainty of all commercial speculation; but this, it may be hoped, is an evil of a temporary nature, which will yield to the influence of better times, and a more happy system of continental policy.

"At Macclesfield and Congleton there are large silk mills, and handkerchief weaving is carried on to a considerable extent." A few other manufactories of minor note, are enumerated.

Mr.

Mr. Holland mentions some experiments that have been made, by the *tanners* of Cheshiré (who are spoken of as being very numerous) to find out a *substitute* for *oak bark*; and particularly on grinding "the twigs and ends of the boughs of oak." But tho adopted, by different tanners, the plan is given up. The barks of several trees are enumerated, by Mr. H. as a substitute for that of the oak. But none of them, I fear, will answer the end desired. That of the elm mixed with oak bark, is now under trial, in the West of England. The bark of the birch (not here enumerated) has long been in use, in the Highlands of Scotland, for tanning shoe leather; and is yet, I believe, clandestinely used, by the small occupiers, there, for the same purpose,—without admixture. A substitute for oak bark, in the operation of tanning, is most anxiously to be desired.

On the question, whether manufactures are favorable to Agriculture, Mr. Holland "feels himself inclined to answer in the affirmative."—P. 328. "The increase of wealth" (Mr. H. says) "and population, which is the never failing result of a *flourishing* manufacture, by the additional demand which it creates for the products of the earth, communicates a powerful stimulus to agricultural industry."—Yes, certainly,—"while the wind blows—then the mill goes."

For lengthened remarks, on this subject, see the NORTHERN, or *Manufacturing*, DEPARTMENT.

See also the ensuing head, *workpeople*.

COMMERCE.—From the foregoing account of the manufactures of Cheshire, little of a *commercial* nature can strictly belong to it. Indeed, it has no *port*, from whence to carry on any *foreign* trade. Chester is a *coasting* port; and Frodsham may be termed a carrying place to the port of Liverpool. The cotton mills of Cheshire are but branches, or twigs, of the Manchester manufacture. And the cheeses of this county are mostly sent, by trading vessels, to the London market. What relates to the export of salt appears aforegoing. p. 99.

POOR LAWS and REGULATIONS. The following remarks of J. T. Stanley, esq. in the section "Cottages," are entitled to attention.—P. 87. "The country is absolutely losing population by the operation of the law which gives a settlement to the occupier of ten pounds a year. Nothing can be more absurd than the assertion, that the occupation of lands worth 10*l.* per annum, supposes a man to have had credit and estimation above the class of people

people likely to become paupers. As the law is explained, a man may occupy the land in two different counties, and a settlement be gained where he has slept, and where no one would have trusted him with the occupation even of a garden. It enables paupers to be continually throwing themselves upon the townships where they find charitable institutions, or other advantages; in consequence of which, land-owners either pull down their cottages, or let them, without land, to such persons as belong to their townships, to diminish the chance of new rent charges falling on their properties. A good cottage, with land sufficient to keep a cow, is worth eight or nine pounds a year; a person holding such a tenement can therefore at any time gain a settlement where he resides, by renting an acre of aftergrass, and a little potatoe land. The law by this means actually operates against the poor; and many more might have opportunities of renting land sufficient for the keep of a cow, were it not so easy for them to obtain a new settlement by these means. A holding of at least 20*l.* per annum, should be made requisite to confer a settlement, were it for no other purpose than to prevent cottages being let without land; and the land occupied ought to be in the same township where the man resides, and under the same landlord. The alterations in the law need not be applied to towns, if it be thought unwise to encrease the difficulty of obtaining settlements on a general principle; as it now stands, it evidently does mischief in the country, and defeats one great object which the Board of Agriculture has in view, the increase of the number of cottagers holding land."

For this very reason, I conceive, should the present laws be continued. Scarcely any thing that can defeat so baneful a measure,—so destructive to the agricultural interest of the country,—can be injurious to its welfare.

More is said (by the Reporter, p. 88.) on the subject of *cottage cow grounds;* and Mr. Boys's Report of Kent is combated, without success.—Until the principles laid down, and, I trust, firmly established, in my Treatise on Landed Property, be overthrown, I must consider all cursory remarks on the subject, as unworthy of notice. Let men of fortune indulge their benevolence toward the few who happen to be situated round their residences; and whom they keep in their own desultory employments. But let not the more urgent and necessary business of their tenants, and of occupiers in general, be impeded by the necessity of employing laborers, who will work, only, when their

their own conveniency, or humor, may suit. Farmers, like manufacturers, mechanics, and tradesmen in general, require *constant laborers*,—men who have no other means of support than their daily labor,—men whom they can *depend upon*. Mr. Boys is an extensive and well experienced practical husbandman,—he speaks from *his own experience*, on *a large scale*;—not from *enquiries* made among *small occupiers*,—*working farmers*,—who want occasional assistance, only,—or *gentlemen* who employ laborers for their own amusement; or who have various operations going on,—as farming, gardening, building, planting, and other improvements, and, of course, can shift them from one employment to another, as occasion may require. Had Mr. Boys sat down to write of medicine, he might have been as much at a loss, as Mr. Holland may be when he ventures to expatiate on rural subjects. This is assuredly not wantonly intended to hurt Mr. H's feelings; but to endeavor to give him due rank as a Reporter of *rural* practices. I can rather commiserate Mr. H's situation; as he appears, by his preface, to have been *pressed* into the service.

In the section "Poor Rate," Mr. Stanley is respectfully introduced—"as a most active and intelligent magistrate, whose situation has afforded him every opportunity of making observations on the subject," of the Poor Laws. After describing, in forcible language, the depravity of the lower classes, under the existing law, Mr. S. says—P. 107. "Whatever the law is, it should be imperious; and the overseers should be allowed no choice in the distribution of their charities. They should be compelled to find work for the idle, and not suffered to give them money. For the maimed and the sick there should be public hospitals. There should be punishment for the depraved: and magistrates and constables should be armed with a power that could reach petty offences. No woman ought to have a right to call on the public for the maintenance of an illegitimate child, without suffering some punishment for her misconduct. More should be left to private charity than is at present. Indeed, who now will give money to relieve distress, which, if charity does not, the law must relieve? Charity now only goes in aid of the poor rate; and whoever maintains a poor labourer or sick widow, exempts his neighbours from a portion of their tax."

This I insert as the opinion of Mr. Stanley, a most respectable country gentleman. I cannot, however, agree with

with Mr. S. when he says—"that "Charity now only goes in the aid of the poor rate."—This, indeed, is a false axiom that is capable of doing serious injury to many of the most deserving; who, tho able to *exist*, without parochial relief, might only drag on a wretched existence without the charitable aid of their humane and benevolent neighbours. It must be allowed, however, that there is much good sense, tinctured with severity, contained in Mr. Stanley's proposed regulations.

In the section "Poor,"—Mr. Holland touches on the now trite topics—of promoting, among the laboring classes, a "spirit of independence," and of encoraging provident societies—"box clubs"—for that purpose.

In the same section, Mr. H. censures the absurd custom, or law, of appointing, annually, overseers who are ignorant of the office they are to fill; and offers a practical plan for alleviating the evil.

P. 330. "It is by no means an uncommon case for a man when he first enters on this office, to be completely ignorant of the actual state of the poor in his township; he distributes money, without knowing the rights of the claimants, or the proportion of assistance to which they are entitled; and by the time he has acquired this information, he quits his office. Attempts have been made, in some instances, to remedy this evil. In one of the townships in Macclesfield hundred, a plan has been adopted to ascertain the real state of all those who claim relief from the overseers, by annually drawing up a register of various circumstances connected with their situation; on a reference to which, the overseers may be enabled, in every instance, to ascertain what are the real necessities of the claimants, and to proportion their distributions accordingly. Some idea of the nature of this register may be procured from the annexed paper. The pursuance of the plan has had the effect of diminishing greatly the amount of the poor-rates, in the particular townships alluded to.

" Former Residence.	Present Residence.	Father.	How employed.	Wages he earned per week.	Mother.	How employed.	Wages she earns per week.	How many children.	Their different ages.	How many actually employed.	How many capable of being employed.	Earnings of the whole family per week.	What relief they receive per week.	What occasional relief within the last year.	Character of the family.	Rents paid.	Remarks.
				s.			s. d.					l. s. d.	s. d.	l. s. d.		l. s. d.	
Radcliff -	Sunderland	B. C.	Dye house.	14	B. C.	Chair woman.	3 0	3	5, 8, 10.	1	1	0 19 0	2 0	2 0 6	Good.	1 11 6	House rent withdrawn.
Styall - -	Stockport.	Dead.	—	—	A. B.	Sundries.	3 0	4	All girls. 7,10,12,16.	1	2	0 7 6	3 0	—	Ditto.	2 2 0	
Ditto - -	Ditto - -	C. D.	Weaving.	14	C. D.	Nurse.	4 6	3	3, 6, 9. Girl.	—	—	0 18 6	2 0	1 18 7½	Ditto.	2 0 0	
Wilmslow	Bollington.	Dead.	—	—	D. E.	Reeler.	6 0	5	9, 12, 14, 16, 21. Girls	5	5	1 9 6	2 0	0 14 6	Indifferent.	2 15 0	This family earns 1*l*. 9*s*. 6*d*. per week... Have notice they are to receive no more aid from the township.
Ditto - -	Chorlton.	F. G.	Blind and incapable of working.	—	E. G.	—	—	—	— —	—	—	—	2 6	3 0 2	Good.	0 14 0	Had sickness."

TITHES.—P. 103. "The quantity of land exempt from the collection of tithes is very inconsiderable in Cheshire. On the College lands, which are extensive in this county, they are all held by lay proprietors; chiefly on leases of twenty-one years, renewable at the end of every seven years. These proprietors usually collect a portion of their tithes in kind, and let out the remainder; or, as is the case in many instances, make an annual composition with the farmer, sending a person to value the produce of the corn land, and allowing the farmer the option of taking or refusing the titheable portion, at the valuation that is made. A similar plan is almost invariably pursued when the tithes are in the immediate possession of the clergy. In many places the hay is valued in the same manner; but, in general, a trifling modus is paid in lieu of tithes on this article of produce. In some parishes it is tithed in kind."

INLAND NAVIGATION.—*Navigable Rivers.*—The *Mersey.*—P. 74. "The tides flow up the Mersey as high as Warrington, where their course is interrupted by a weir thrown across the river. To obviate this impediment to the navigation, and the difficulties arising from the naturally winding course of the stream; an artificial cut of considerable length has been made, which passes to the south of Warrington, and being connected with the Mersey again, at some distance above the town, enables vessels, of sixty or seventy tons burden, to navigate as high up as the place where the Irwell empties itself into this river. The navigation is continued up the Irwell; by which means a water communication is established between Manchester and Liverpool; inferior however in point of commercial convenience to that afforded by the Duke of Bridgewater's canal, for an account of which see the article on *Canals.*"

Speaking of the estuary of the *Dee,* Mr. Holland says, p. 75, "This estuary, from the small proportion which the body of water brought down bears to the breadth of the channel, is left almost entirely dry when the tide is out; presenting to the eye of the spectator, a bed of sand, covering several thousand acres. These sands were, however, at a former period much more extensive than they are at present. By means of embankments a large tract of land has been gained from the sea; while an artificial channel formed for the river affords sufficient depth of water to bring vessels, of between three and four hundred tons, up to the quays at Chester. The navigation is partially

partially interrupted at Chester bridge by a stone causeway, which makes a fall in the river of thirteen feet. The spring tides however flow over the causeway, and allow a navigation for small barges as high up as the village of Bangor, in the detached part of Flintshire, nearly 20 miles above Chester."

The *Wever*.—P. 306. "The river Weaver was in its natural state navigable by the high tides only about six miles above Frodsham Bridge. The demand for salt being considerably increased, and there being scarcely any conveyance for it but by land, one act of parliament was obtained in 1720, and another in 1759, to make this river navigable from Frodsham Bridge to Winsford Bridge. By the latter act, the management of the navigation was committed to the principal gentlemen of the county, as trustees; under whose superintendance most of the locks have been rebuilt; and (with the exception of one, which will soon be removed) these are now in excellent condition. In consequence, however, of the prodigious extension of the salt trade, the present accommodations on the Weaver navigation have been for some time found insufficient; and it is in contemplation to make an additional cut, of about four miles in length, from the weir near Frodsham Bridge, to a place called Weston Point. The execution of this plan will enable the flats to proceed to Liverpool in neap, as well as spring tides; and thereby to avoid the delay which they now experience at Frodsham Lock; below which, the river is so shallow and full of sand banks, that vessels are detained there, from four to six days, every neap tide, to the great detriment of the salt proprietors on the river, as well as of the merchants in Liverpool.

"The river was made completely navigable from Winsford to Frodsham, and a considerable debt, thereby incurred, was discharged many years ago; since which time, the surplus arising from the tonnage has been regularly paid to the county treasurer; and disposed of by the magistrates, at each Michaelmas quarter sessions, according to the provisions of the two acts.

"The length of the navigation from Winsford to Frodsham is about twenty miles, with a fall of forty-five feet ten inches divided between ten locks. The flats employed upon it carry from sixty to eighty tons, and some few one hundred. The total number is at this time two hundred and fifty. Rock salt, white salt, and coals, are the principal articles of carriage upon the navigation; all others being of an amount very inconsiderable.

"Except

"Except in a few instances where the trustees have thought proper to reduce the tonnage, it is now, and can never exceed, one shilling per ton; a lower rate perhaps than is charged on any other navigation in the kingdom."

Canals.—P. 306. "Few counties in the kingdom derive so many advantages from internal intercourse of this kind as Cheshire; and in few are the effects of it more generally important. The immediate proximity of the county to the towns of Manchester and Liverpool, has been highly favourable in this respect. The facility of communication with the latter town, afforded by the Weaver, has given to the salt manufactories in the interior of Cheshire, an extent and importance which renders the navigation on this river an object of interest not only to this particular district, but to the nation at large; while the numerous canals, intersecting the county, afford a cheap and easy conveyance of goods of every description to the most distant parts of the kingdom."

P. 312. "The benefits resulting to the agriculture of Cheshire, from its large participation in the system of internal navigation, are very considerable at present, and will, in all provability, become much more so. The cheap introduction of lime into the county, and the opportunity which is afforded of conveying marl at a slight expense to places where that valuable article is not met with, are both in themselves objects of great moment to the farmer. Another very important advantage is the cheap supply of fuel, afforded by these means, and the greater facility with which it is procured in every part of the county."

The Duke of Bridgewater's Canal,—(P. 308.) "enters Cheshire near Stretford; and passing about half a mile to the north of Altringham, pursues a westerly course to Runcorn, where it is lowered precipitously into the Mersey, by a series of locks, fourteen in number, admirably constructed, and furnished with spacious reservoirs, to supply the waste of water occasioned by the continual passage of vessels. These are in fact the only locks on the canal, in a course of about thirty miles; so strictly has the principle of keeping the level been adhered to. Between Altringham, and the romantic village of Lymm, a stupendous mound has been constructed to carry the canal over the vale of the Bollin, a few miles above the place where this river empties itself into the Mersey. By means of this canal, Manchester is supplied from Liverpool with raw articles of foreign growth, cotton, dyewoods, &c. while in return large quantities of manufac-

tured

tured goods are sent to the latter place for exportation. Coals too are carried from the pits at Worsley in Lancashire, to various parts of the county, through which the canal passes; and large supplies of provisions are, by this means, conveyed to the Manchester markets, with little expense to the farmer, and with all the speed and regularity of land carriage. The vessels employed on this canal are of various sizes. Those which convey bulky goods, between Manchester and Liverpool, are usually from fifty to one hundred tons burthen; the coal is conveyed in long, narrow boats, several of them drawn by one horse. Boats resembling the Dutch treckschuyts, are used for the convenience of passengers, and pass daily between Manchester and Runcorn, producing a considerable revenue to the proprietor."

P. 309. "At Preston Brook, about five miles from Runcorn, the Duke of Bridgewater's canal is joined by the GRAND TRUNK, one of the greatest undertakings of this nature in the kingdom. By its means an internal communication is established between the Mersey, the Trent, the Thames, and the Severn, so that goods may be sent by water carriage from the interior of Lancashire and Cheshire, to Birmingham, Bristol, London, and Hull; while collateral canals or navigable rivers extend the intercourse to almost every place of importance in the kingdom. The Grand Trunk crosses Cheshire, in a direction from north west to south east, pursuing a course of about thirty miles in this county. At the distance of a mile from Preston Brook, it is carried under a hill, by a tunnel one thousand two hundred and forty-one yards in length, seventeen feet four inches in height, and thirteen feet six inches wide. At Saltersford, a few miles further, is another tunnel, three hundred and fifty yards in length, and of the same internal dimensions as the former. A third tunnel at Barnton, close to Saltersford, is five hundred and sixty yards in length. Few articles, the immediate produce of Cheshire, are at present conveyed along this canal. Though its course lies for many miles in the immediate neighbourhood of the salt manufactories and rock salt pits, it has hitherto been employed to a very trifling extent in the conveyance of these articles. A large quantity of coal is, however, brought along it from the Staffordshire collieries. The boats upon this canal are about twenty-five tons burthen. The tonnage paid to the proprietors is three halfpence per mile."

P. 310. "The ELLESMERE canal, forming a direct junction between the Mersey, the Dee, and the Severn, is another undertaking of much importance to the internal prosperity of the country. The act for it passed A. D. 1793. It leaves the Mersey, about eight miles above Liverpool, and crossing the peninsula of Wirrall to Chester, communicates with the navigable channel of the Dee. It then pursues its course by Wrexham, Ruabon, Chirk, and Ellesmere, to Shrewsbury. At Frankton common, in the neighbourhood of Ellesmere, a branch is set off to Whitchurch, whence it has lately been extended to Namptwich; joining the Chester canal, near that town. The Ellesmere canal communicates with many extensive collieries, and with valuable quarries of slate and limestone: it has likewise a connexion with several iron works and lead mines in Shropshire and Denbighshire; and the facility of conveyance which it affords, will, in all probability, be the means of extending these sources of public wealth, and of disclosing others, hitherto unexplored."

The CHESTER canal.—P. 311. "Till its junction with the Whitchurch branch of the Ellesmere canal was completed, the canal between Chester and Namptwich proved a most burdensome concern to the proprietors, and was productive of no advantage to the internal intercourse of the country. The carriage on it was insufficient to pay for the necessary repairs; and shares were, in many instances, sold at one per cent. of their original cost." See p. 14.

ROADS.—On this subject, the present Reporter appears pretty evidently to be deficient in practical knowledge. He might, therefore, have prudently passed it, in silence. Cheshire is unfortunate in a supply of road materials; and, judging from Mr. H's Report, it is not more fortunate in road makers.

MARKETS.—*Fairs.*—P. 313. "At Chester there are three very considerable fairs in the year. The first, held on the last Thursday in February, is principally for cattle and horses; and is called *Horn and Hoof* fair. The others are held on July 5th and October 10th; and by the city charter are kept open fourteen days. The principal object of these two fairs is the sale of Irish linen, which is brought over in great quantities, and exposed to sale in a large and convenient building, erected and solely appropriated to this purpose. Besides private purchasers, numbers of shopkeepers from different parts of the kingdom lay in their

their stock of linen at these fairs Very considerable quantities of Manchester and Yorkshire goods are likewise brought here, and sold in buildings conveniently fitted up for the purpose. At the October fair, there is a large sale of hops."

P. 314. "Namptwich in particular has a market for cattle, the first Saturday in February, called the *New Market*, equal to any of its fairs; and the sale of cattle continues here every Saturday till the latter end of May. Little corn or grain of any kind is now brought into the markets, being generally sold by samples to the dealers. Bacon, oatmeal, flour, bread, and other articles of this kind, are usually purchased out of the retail shops; which scarcely a village, consisting of a dozen houses, is without.

"Tolls are collected in many of the markets of this county, and are, of course, regarded with much dislike. Some few have, however, of late years been given up."

Surplus Produce.—P. 343. "From the relative situation of this county, it cannot be expected to contribute, in any great degree, to the supply of the metropolis. Indeed, cheese is almost the only article of agricultural produce, with which Cheshire furnishes the London markets. This is purchased by the cheese factors, and sent generally either to Chester and (or) Liverpool, where it is shipped for London, in vessels regularly employed in the trade.

"Considerable numbers of young cattle, which have been drifted from the dairy stocks in this county, are slaughtered in London, after having been previously fattened in some of the feeding" (fatting) "counties."

SOCIETIES of AGRICULTURE. The present Reporter's observations, on this topic, are unimportant. Had he inserted the *whole* of Mr. *Wedge's* remarks his book would have been the better.

EXPERIMENTAL FARMS.—P. 343. "Some years ago, an experimental farm was established at Waverham, near Northwich, by a few intelligent gentlemen and farmers in that neighbourhood, in which a good deal of draining was done, several of the improvements in modern husbandry practised, and new breeds of cattle and sheep introduced; but it being found upon the whole an expensive and losing concern, from the nature of the land and other circumstances, the attempt was abandoned, and has not since been resumed."

SUBJECT

SUBJECT THE THIRD.

RURAL ECONOMY.

DIVISION THE FIRST.

TENANTED ESTATES,

Their IMPROVEMENT and MANAGEMENT.

ESTATES.—*Sizes* and *Proprietors.*—P. 79. "There are few counties of equal extent with Cheshire, in which the number of wealthy land-owners seems so considerable. Whether the revenue derived from the soil is in itself greater, or that men of fortune reside more on their estates in this county than in others, may be a question; but from various accounts which I have received, it appears that not less than fifty noblemen and gentlemen are now resident in Cheshire, in possession of property within it of from 3 to 10,000 *l.* a year; and that there are at least as many others with properties of from 1 to 3,000 *l.* a year. At the same time the number of smaller land-owners is not apparently less than in other counties. The description of this latter class has however been very much altered of late years. From the advantages which have been derived from trade; and from the effects of the increase of taxes, which have prevented a man living with the same degree of comfort on the same portion of land he could formerly; many of the old owners have been induced to sell their estates; and new proprietors have spread themselves over the county, very different in their habits and prejudices. It may be doubtful whether the change on the whole has been disadvantageous. Land, when transferred, is generally improved by its new possessor. With a new, and often a more enlightened view of its advantages and resources, he brings with him the means and the disposition to try experiments, and give to his new acquisition its greatest value. He feels the want of comforts and conveniences, which custom had rendered familiar to a former occupier; he builds, drains, and plants; and by his spirit and example stimulates all around him to increased exertions."

Yeomanry.—

Yeomanry.—To the above passage, a Note signed "J. T. S." is appended. It is worthy of a place, as text, in any work of a kindred nature. It does the head and heart of its writer (doubtlessly Mr. STANLEY) infinite honor. It is sensible, judicious, and charmingly written. It is true, from the beginning to the ending. I have singular pleasure in having an opportunity of inserting it, here.

N. P. 80. "The loss of the old English yeoman will nevertheless be regretted: his attachment to his home, and to the laws and religion of the country; his submission to government; his respect for all who were above him, and affection for all who were below him, rendered him a most useful and valuable member of the community. He was a man contented with his situation, and anxious for the solid and permanent prosperity of the land in which he had been born and educated. He honoured antiquity of possession from principle, because he connected the permanence of families with the real welfare of the state; he encouraged the sentiment from prejudice, because it conferred honour on himself. He had his own pride of birth; and the property he had derived from ancestors he wished to leave unimpaired to posterity. But his pride never was, nor could be, offensive to the poor. He was too little raised above them for their envy: and they had always seen and known him what he was. He had been brought up amongst them, and on all occasions took part in their concerns. He was the link which connected the gentleman and the farmer; and as both were willing and desirous of associating with him on friendly terms, his existence gave a concord and harmony to society; created a common knowledge and interest in all that was passing; and blended into one whole the welfare of each respective neighbourhood."

IMPROVEMENT of Landed Property.—*Prosecuting Improvements.*—A very "intelligent friend" of the Reporter throws out, incidentally, some valuable suggestions, on this subject, in a note—P. 161. "A long course of experiment, by those who can afford to suffer loss, should follow every new suggestion. So many various circumstances affect success; so many objects are to be kept in view at the same time; such a balance must be made of the sacrifices necessary on the one hand, against the insurance of an advantageous result on the other; that on very few points indeed can any given system be pronounced either good or bad. The very best recommendation

dation of any new method, or any new discovery, is the constant steady prosecution of it, by the person recommending it. Few farmers are so prejudiced, or so blindly attached to old customs, as not to be convinced of the utility of what they see to be uniformly, and unequivocally productive of advantage."

Reclaiming Wild Lands.—On *Sod-burning*, we find several pages; but not a line that is entitled to public attention. It is not an established practice of Cheshire; and of course ought not to have been *dwelt upon*, in a Report of that county. For various remarks, on this topic, see NORTH. DEPART.

Draining.—Nearly the same may be said concerning this operation. Mr. Fenna's detail is well enough; but it contains nothing new or excellent.

Irrigation.—This operation, we are informed, is "still in its infancy," in Cheshire; p. 247.

EXECUTIVE MANAGEMENT of Estates.—P. 80. "There does not appear to be any peculiarity in the management of the estates in Cheshire."

Tenancy.—P. 108. "The practice of leasing for lives, which was formerly very generally in Cheshire, is now by no means so frequent. Most of the old leases of this description have now run out, and only a few of the land proprietors in the county retain the custom on their estates. Neither are leases of twenty-one, or fourteen years, by any means so frequent as formerly; few terms now given exceeding eleven years, and the generality not rising above seven; a circumstance which may be attributed to the operation of several causes, but principally, perhaps, to the rapid decrease in the value of the circulating medium. When leases of twenty-one years are given, it is generally under a condition that the tenant should incur some extraordinary expenses at the commencement of his term; or where the land is so rough, that it cannot soon be brought into a state of profitable cultivation. An exception must be made for the Church and College lands, which are all held either for the term of twenty-one years, renewable at the end of every seven years; or on leases for lives."

P. 111. "Several land proprietors have *of late years* adopted the practice of forming a new agreement with a tenant two or three years before the expiration of the old term; the rent continuing the same until the actual commencement of the new lease."

Mr.

Mr. H. I am happy to find, highly approves of this point of management.

Covenants.—See Mr. Wedge's account, p. 19; which Mr. H. has copied, with due acknowledgment.

In the section "weeding," we find the following passage —P. 246. "We have often occasion to regret that the clause, introduced into many leases, empowering the landlord to cut down weeds at the expense of the tenant, if the latter neglects to do it himself, is either not made general, or more frequently enforced."

See *Plan* of *Management*,—ensuing.

Time of *Entry*.—P. 110. "The usual time of entry upon a farm is at Candlemas, the off-going tenant being allowed the use of the buildings, and of a pasture field near the house as an outlet for his cattle, until the 1st. of May, old style; he is also entitled, by the custom of the county, to two-thirds, or, in a few instances, to three-fourths of the fallow wheat, and generally by agreement to half the eddish or brush wheat which may be growing on the premises at the time of his quitting *."

Rents.—Owing to a combination of circumstances, Mr. H. lays the average rent, of the cultivated lands of Cheshire, at thirty shillings, an acre. These circumstances are, chiefly, *manufactures* and *canals;* the higher rents being of course *local.*—P. 102. "Some land particularly favourable for the purposes of the dairy is let as high as 50 or 55s. per acre; which I find to be the case on a few farms in the middle, and southern parts of the county; but it is a circumstance of very rare occurrence. Taking then the average rent at 30s. per acre, and making a proper allowance for waste lands, the total annual rental of the county may, perhaps without any material error, be estimated at £900,000; a sum which bears a much higher proportion to the extent of surface, than is generally the case throughout the kingdom.

"The ancient custom of paying rents in kind is now almost entirely abolished. On some dairy farms the landlord, by a covenant in his lease, has the liberty of choosing a cheese at Christmas; in other instances he receives a goose or a couple of fowls. Personal services on the part of

"* In the original Report of Cheshire, I find it stated, that the off-going tenant is entitled by the custom of the county to three-fourths of the fallow wheat. Here however Mr. Wedge is not strictly accurate; two-thirds, and not three-fourths, being the quantity generally allowed throughout the county."

of the tenant are now seldom required; it being found in general more convenient for both parties that the rent should be paid entirely in money: in some cases, however, the landlord requires from his tenant a few days team work every year; or, where no team is kept, two days harvest work as a labourer."

Land Measure.—P. 342. "Land was formerly very generally measured in this county by what is called the Cheshire acre, containing 10,240 square yards; and this measure still continues to be employed to a certain extent, particularly in the northern part of the county. The statute acre, of 4,840 square yards, is now, however, in much more general use; and this accordingly is the measure to which I have invariably referred in the course of the Report."

DIVISION THE SECOND.

WOODLANDS.

TIMBER.—P. 197. "Though there are few woods or plantations of any large extent in Cheshire, yet the quantity of timber, growing in this county, very greatly exceeds what would be a fair average estimate for the kingdom at large. In the northern and middle parts, particularly, the number of trees in the hedgerows and coppices is so considerable, that, from some points of view, the whole country has the appearance of an extensive forest. The greatest part of this timber is oak, and the facility with which the bark of this invaluable tree was formerly obtained, has in all probability been the cause of the establishment of so many tanyards in the county. But the quantity of timber of all kinds in Cheshire, has, within the last few years, been so much diminished, and particularly the oak, that the tanners have now great difficulty in supplying themselves with a sufficiency of bark."—"The ancient woods in the park of the Earl of Stamford and Warrington, at Dunham Massey, are the most considerable in the county. The oaks here have attained a very unusual size. Individual trees of greater magnitude may be found in various parts of the kingdom; but few spots in the island, certainly none in this county, can boast such an assemblage of stately oaks, as ornament

ment one part of the park, raising their venerable heads above the rest of the forest trees. Those of an inferior size, in the same park, are numerous, and many of them promise to become very fine timber. The magnitude of the elms and beeches, is likewise a striking feature in the woods at Dunham. Of the early history of the large oaks, I have not been able to obtain any accurate account. From some deeds, in the possession of the noble owner, it appears, that, above two hundred years ago, they are mentioned as the trees in the *old* wood. During a violent storm of wind, on the 21st of January 1802, one of these immense oaks (the fourth or fifth only in point of size) shared the fate of several hundred small trees, and was torn up by the roots. The measurement of it, over the bark, was 481 feet: after the bark had been stripped off, it was found to contain 403 feet of timber. It appeared that it had lost its tap-root, having been supported entirely by the roots which had shot out in a lateral direction: the trunk, however, was so perfectly sound, and the timber was considered so valuable for the purposes of a mill-shaft, that 373½ feet of it were sold, to be applied to this use, at 6*s.* 6*d.* per foot, or for 121*l.* 7*s.* 9*d.* An elm, which was blown down at the same time, measured 146 feet, and was sold for 36*l.* 10*s.* at the rate of 5*s.* per foot *."

P. 199. "In the woods at Alderley Park, the seat of J. T. Stanley, Esq., the size, and beauty of the beeches, forms a striking and predominant feature. These venerable trees were planted about a hundred and fifty years ago. The trunks of many of them rise to the height of twenty feet, before they divide into branches; and measure four yards in circumference, from the surface of the ground to this height."

On the grounds and estates of Lords Grosvenor and Cholmondeley, and other large proprietors, we are told, great quantities of fine timber still remain.

PLANTATIONS.—The late EARL of WARRINGTON appears to have been the great planter of Cheshire. Some successful attempts, in more modern times, have been made on Delamere Forest, and, more particularly, at Taxall, on the borders of Derbyshire, on a large scale.

Great

* "A colony of herons had, for ages, fixed their residence on the summits of the lofty oaks in Dunham park. After the violent hurricane in January 1802, which tore up one of their favourite trees, and occasioned great devastation among the branches of several others, they retreated to a neighbouring grove of beeches, where they have ever since enjoyed a secure abode."

Great apprehensions are entertained, by the Reporter, as well as by his friend, Mr. Stanley (in a note on the subject) in regard to the extirpation of ship timber, in Cheshire, and the kingdom at large. The former says much on the subject; but without infusing any thing of plan, or of interest, into his pages. The latter, however, suggests, or rather intimates, something new, for its preservation.—N. P. 203. "If for one or more acres covered with a given number of thriving oak plants, the owner was to be exempted from the operation of certain taxes; if, for instance, his house was to be exempted from the window tax; or he was to be allowed the free use of bricks, to be employed upon his own land; or some gratification and exemption, equal to the good he did his country, new forests would soon spread themselves over the kingdom, and become a security for its future safety and prosperity. The value of the land given up to planting should be considered in the apportionment of the indulgence."—Again —"We pay heavy taxes now, that the national debt may be extinguished fifty years hence; why should not taxes be paid now, that the navy may exist a hundred years hence?"

See the NORTHERN DEPARTMENT, p. 224, for remarks on this subject.

The following regulations, probably instituted by the late Lord Warrington, will serve, at least, as an item of history, on the management of estates, and the propagation of timber, in former times.

N. P. 207. "Though too little regard is undoubtedly paid to planting in this county, yet there are individual instances, in which it is made an object of considerable attention. I have been informed that in Lord Stamford's leases for lives, the tenants are bound to plant every year a certain number of trees, oak, ash, elm, or poplar, proportioned to the extent of their farms. The plants are found by the owner of the land; and the tenants condition to preserve them. Similar clauses are inserted in the leases granted by other landed proprietors, but I doubt whether sufficient attention is paid to enforcing the execution of them."

DIVISION THE THIRD.

AGRICULTURE.

FARMS.—*Sizes.*—On this subject Mr. Fenna furnishes a "statement of the size of farms in four townships, situated in in different parts of the county." The inferences from which are thus drawn.—P. 92. "From this statement it appears that, in the townships in question, the greatest number of holdings, in any of the foregoing classes, are under one acre each; and that the greatest quantity of land is occupied by tenants renting from 50 to 100 acres. An extension of these results to the county at large might probably be made without any great inaccuracy of statement. By calculations, formed with an express view to the ascertainment of this fact, it would appear that the average size of holdings cannot be estimated at more than 70 acres; and, in this statement, all those under 10 acres are excluded. Some few dairy farms in this county run as high as 350 or 400 acres."

Having stated these facts, in a Reporterly manner, and of course done all that his duty required, Mr. H. ventures on the wide field of argument, relating to the sizes of farms, considered in a *political* light:—a field that has, of late years, been trodden, until it is almost bare. The combatants, however, have mostly ranged themselves on opposite sides of it; leaving an untrodden space between them.

Mr. Holland takes his stand on the large-farm side; and acquits himself with becoming ingenuity; and with fluency of language; but without advancing any thing new, or making out any one point, with peculiar clearness. Having spoken to the extent of five or six pages, in favor of large farms, he alters his position; and (as if he had had a rap on the knuckles,—perhaps by his friend Mr. T.) proceeds to cut down, and pare away, much of what he had been striving to establish; very judiciously bringing down his scale of tenements to a cottage with a cow-ground:—a very proper thing in its place: namely as a *first step*, in mounting the ladder of predial holdings.

Homesteads.—And *Plans* of *Farms.*—P. 82. "The state of the farm-houses and buildings attached to them, is very various in Cheshire. On some of the large dairy farms in the middle of the county, the buildings, in point of extent, and convenience of arrangement, are equal to those in most parts of the kingdom. In the hundred of Wirrall, the reverse is undoubtedly the case. Here, the farm-houses and buildings are all crowded together into villages, without any regard to the advantages of situation, or to regularity of construction. By this means the farmer is frequently thrown to the distance of two or three miles from his land, a circumstance productive of so many serious

serious inconveniences, as to render the removal of its cause a measure highly desirable."

Building Materials.—P. 83. "The covering of the old buildings is generally of thatch; and here it may be noticed that the dairy-maids usually give the preference to the thatched cow-houses, from their preserving a more uniform temperature than those covered with slate, or tiles."

In this Report are engravings of farmsteads. One of them is well enough, in itself; but not peculiarly eligible as a Pattern. Plates, however, are allowed, by the many, to "set off a book."

Cottages.—There does not appear to be any thing remarkable, in the plan or *construction* of the cottages of Cheshire. In a Note, signed "J. T. S." are some sensible remarks, on the *coverings* of *cottages.*—N. P. 86. "It may be doubted, whether the substitution of slate for thatch, in cottages and small farm-houses, is an advantage. Thatch renders a house warmer in winter, and cooler in summer, than slate. In winter, it prevents the warmth produced by the fires from escaping; and in summer it absorbs few of the sun's rays; at least it allows but little heat to penetrate through it. A room below thatch may be kept warm with half the fuel which it would be when below slate."

The rents of cottages are remarkably high in Cheshire. "When a garden, only, is annexed, they usually let for four or five pounds, per annum," p. 86.

I found occasion to speak on cottage *cowgrounds*, under the head *Poor Laws*, &c. p. 113; as the subject grew aptly out of an extract there made, relating to the settlements of paupers. This subject, indeed, is of so doubtful a nature that it is difficult to say, precisely, where it ought to be classed:—whether under *cottages*, *laborers*, *poor rates*, or *farms;* the last has the best claim to it; as appears, above, p. 131.

On *fences* and *gates*, we find lengthened remarks; but without any practical information arising from them, that can be useful or interesting, in other districts; excepting what is noticed of *iron* gates,—for farm uses, I take for granted.

P. 122. "In some few instances, gates made of bar iron have been substituted for oaken ones. The bars in these gates are circular; and are usually four or five in number, with a cross piece, as in the common gate. The original cost varies, of course, according to the number of bars, and the weight of iron employed; but it may be estimated, in general, at from two to three pounds for a gate of the ordinary size."

Mr.

Mr. Stanley's suggestion of a gate *law* is, however, entitled to a place, here; as coming from an "experienced magistrate."—P. 120. "Gates are becoming a very expensive article; and the stumps being no longer made of the heart of the tree, but of refuse timber, all outside, soon rot at the bottom. Some law is wanted to prevent people from injuring gates. Nothing is more common than for them to be broken wantonly; thrown off their hinges; and to have the irons, on which they are hung, drawn out. Indeed many laws are wanted for the preservation of property out of doors. The only remedy now, against mischief of various kinds, is an action of trespass; which cannot be resorted to against a pauper or stranger, with any good effect, or without gteat expence."

OCCUPIERS.—On this subject, Mr. H's remarks are sensible; but too *general* for a *provincial* Report. Suffice it to say, here, that the lower classes of Cheshire farmers are represented as adhering to *the customs* of their forefathers; but "that there are among the larger farmers in this county, a set of men, who for their general intelligence and respectability of character, and from the judicious and rational spirit of improvement by which they are animated, may deservedly rank among the first agriculturists in the country." p. 100. This is a fortunate circumstance, seeing how much they have on their hands, before they can raise the practice of Cheshire to a par with the best practice of the kingdom.

PLAN of MANAGEMENT of Farms in Cheshire.—P. 125. "The proportion of land occupied in tillage in Cheshire is by no means so considerable as in many other counties; though upon the whole, I believe, I should be justified in stating, that it is more so at present than it was some years ago. On the greater number of farms, the tenant is restricted, by the terms of his lease, from holding more than a fourth part of his land in tillage; the landlord being unwilling to allow a larger proportion to be employed in a way which is generally esteemed prejudicial to the fertility of the soil. In consequence of this restriction, the corn, raised on many of the smaller Cheshire farms, does not greatly exceed what is necessary for the consumption of the family, and the stock of the farmer. No considerable quantity of barley is sown, though there appear to be several districts of sandy loam favourable to its cultivation. Wheat and oats, but particularly the latter, constitute the principal objects of tillage in Cheshire."

Succession of Crops.—Mr. Holland copies Mr. Wedge's

round

round of rotations; and adds another by Mr. Fenna; and others from information. I do not, however, consider any of them to be particularly entitled to public attention.

WORKPEOPLE.—P. 296. "The wages of servants and labourers have been very considerably advanced within the last twenty years, in a proportion perhaps more than equal to the decreasing value of money. This is particularly the case in the neighbourhood of Macclesfield, Stockport, and the manufacturing parts of the county. Such high wages are occasionally obtained by children in these districts, that few are now brought up to husbandry and it is there as difficult to get a boy to drive the plough, as a man to hold it."

WORKING ANIMALS.—P. 289. "The number of oxen employed in husbandry in the county is exceedingly small: a few gentlemen have tried them in their teams, but the example does not seem likely to be followed."

The Reporter, then (somewhat adventurously) proceeds to argue on the *comparative merits* of oxen and horses, in the employment of husbandry; and this, it would seem, from the general tenor of his Report, without the smallest share of experience, with either of them, in that capacity. With just as much propriety, and benefit to society, might Mr. Boys, or any other of the Board's *agricultural* Reporters, have risqued his opinion, on the typhus fever, compound fractures, or any other difficult matter, in physic, or surgery. See NORTH. DEPART. p. 378.

IMPLEMENTS.—There does not appear, from this Report, to be any thing peculiar in the instruments of husbandry in use, in Cheshire; excepting the "*hodding scythe;*" an account of which is copied from Mr. Wedge's Report, (see p. 34.) What is said of the *mole plow*, belongs to

The *Draining* of Farm Lands.—P. 114. "The mole-plough for draining clay lands has been introduced on several farms; and, from the high and deserved estimation in which it is held by the farmers who have already adopted it, its use will, in all probability, become more general in the county."

TILLAGE.—The *summer fallow* appears, from Mr. Holland's uninteresting account of it (p. 127) to be still common, for wheat. "Green crops,"—*fallow crops,*—however are, it seems, annually increasing; but are not yet prevalent.

MANURES.—Experiencing in Mr. Holland's account of the salt mines and manufacture of Cheshire, that he is not merely acquainted with the new nomenclature of chemistry; but likewise with the best writings, of modern chemists;

chemists; together with some practical knowledge of chemical experiments; I was led to expect much useful information, concerning the manures of that county. I am not altogether disappointed.

Various species are enumerated, as "being employed to a greater or less degree, in Cheshire:"—namely, marl, lime, dung, sand, peat moss, ashes and soot, bone dust, rape dust, &c.: also refuse salt and marsh mold; which are separately treated of.

Marl.—In reviewing the Report of Lancashire (see NORTH. DEPART.) I paid particular attention to the nature and management of its marls; and intimated a hope that, in the Report of Cheshire, I might find a more intelligible and explicit account of the specific qualities, and component parts, of the marls of this quarter of the kingdom. But, in the original Report, I found no notice, whatever, concerning these particulars; and I was not, at the time I reviewed it, aware of any other account of the Natural Economy and practice of Cheshire being intended to be published. My hopes were of course renewed, and much heightened, when I understood that a scientific and chemical Reporter had been engaged to draw up a second Report of the county.

The popular descriptions, or rather provincial names, of "marls," in LANCASHIRE, are "shell marl;" "blue or reddish slate marl;"—"strong clay marl."—Of those found, and employed as manure, in CHESHIRE, Mr. *Wedge* enumerates,—"clay marl;" "blue slate marl;" "red slate marl;" "stone marl."

The following is Mr. *Holland's* description of the marls of Cheshire.—P. 221. "This is unquestionably one of the most important of the Cheshire manures, whether we consider the extent to which it is applied, or the great utility connected with its application. It is found in almost every part of the county, but in greatest abundance, where the prevailing soil is a clay, or clayey loam. Under sandy, or mixed soils, it is very frequently met with; but usually at a more considerable depth. In a few instances, it has been discovered between two strata of sand stone: this is the case in some parts of the hills, on the western boundary of Delamere forest; where the marl obtained is of a very superior quality. In the hundred of Wirrall, where there is a very considerable predominance of clay, it is met with in abundance; and is used to a greater extent there, than in any other part of the county.

"The term *marl* is employed in Cheshire in a most com-

comprehensive sense, including a variety of substances, very different in external appearance, and varying greatly if not in the nature of their constituent parts, at least in the proportions in which these are arranged in the mass. The most common varieties in the county are distinguished by the appellations of clay marl, slate marl, and stone marl; the first of these kinds is met with in the greatest abundance, and is perhaps the most generally beneficial. In some instances however the farmer mistakes a brown, shining clay for this description of marl; by putting which on his clay land, he throws away his labour, and rather injures than benefits the soil."—It thus appears that the Lancashire, and the Cheshire marls are very similar.

Mr. H. next points out the criteria whereby the *qualities* of the marls of Cheshire are to be ascertained.—P. 221. "The criteria of the excellence of marl must, of course, have a reference to the different kinds employed. Generally speaking that may be esteemed good, which is of a dark brown colour, intersected with veins of either a blue, or light yellow shade; it should be greasy to the touch, when moist; and friable, when dry. Marl of this description, when put into water, will fall to pieces, allowing a considerable portion of sand to sink to the bottom of the vessels; from the application of which simple test the farmer might, in many instances, derive much advantage. There is an excellent kind of marl sometimes met with, which is vulgarly called dove dung, from its resembling in appearance the dung of pigeons."

Thus, instead of a chemical analysis of the various sorts, we merely find the popular notions of the good people of Cheshire; and, indeed, of every other part of the kingdom, where "marls" are in use. This, I freely confess, was a serious disappointment. For Mr. H. immediately proceeds to speak of the *quantity to be used*, and the *method* of *using* it, in Cheshire:—Particulars which I could have more readily excused, in the work of an unpractised Reporter.

Mr. Holland, however, afterward treats of the *operation* of marls; and, in doing this, touches on their *properties*:—moreover, in a note, we are told that several specimens were sent to Mr. Davy, an "ingenious and accurate chemist," for examination. Those strictures not being of very great length, and it being on topics like that which is now under notice, (as has been before intimated) that we we can expect to reap useful information, from the Report under consideration, I will here insert them, entire.

P. 223. "That marl is actually productive of the greatest benefit to the lands on which it is used, is a fact which can admit of no doubt. Much variety of opinion however exists, as to the mode of operation by which this benefit is effected. Several intelligent persons, with whom I have spoken on the subject, consider the calcareous matter which it contains, as the principal, if not the sole agent, in the improvement of the land. Others have stated it as their opinion, that the principal advantage derived from marl, is the addition of bulk or quantity which it makes to the soil; while others again regard its action as of a mechanical nature; considering the improvement of the land, on which it is applied, as the consequence of an alteration which it makes in the texture or disposition of the soil*. Upon an attentive consideration of the subject, it appears to me in the highest degree probable, that marl may derive a certain portion of its utility as a manure, from each of the three causes which have been assigned. From analysis of the substance, it is found to be an intimate mixture of the aluminous and siliceous earths, usually combined with a certain portion of carbonate of lime, and not unfrequently deriving a tinge from the presence of an oxide of iron. The latter substance, however, from the smallness of its quantity, cannot be supposed to produce effects, either beneficial or the reverse. With respect to the calcareous earth contained in the marl, it must undoubtedly have, to a certain extent, the same action that would be produced by the direct application of lime as a manure; but as it is rendered clear, by actual experiment, that some descriptions of marl which are used with advantage, do not contain any portion whatever of carbonate of lime, we cannot certainly attribute the efficiency of marl to this cause alone†. It must have some

" * The best marl, is that which contains the largest proportion of lime. Its application is undoubtedly the most beneficial on light soils. —*A Correspondent.*

" The great advantage of marl seems to arise from its adding bulk to the soil. On light sandy land, it stiffens the soil, and prevents the rain water from passing through too rapidly.—*A Cheshire Farmer.*

" Marl appears to be principally of advantage from the increase which it gives to the quantity of soil.—*A Correspondent.*"

" † Out of twelve specimens of marl, which Mr. Wilbraham, of Delamere Lodge, sent to Mr. Davy for examination, eleven were found

some additional operation upon the land, from which a certain portion of its value, as a manure, is derived. This operation may consist either in the increase of soil obtained by its application, or in the change which it produces in the texture and quality of the land on which it is laid. Marl may itself be considered as a soil, capable of affording nutriment to every description of vegetable substance: when therefore it is ploughed into the ground, a positive addition of bulk is obtained, and, of consequence, a more abundant source of nutriment for succeeding crops procured. In the hundred of Wirrall, where the stratum of soil is, generally speaking, thin and poor, much advantage is derived from the application of marl, simply as an increase of quantity to the soil. On light sandy land, an additional advantage is connected with its use; the marl, from the large proportion of clay which it usually contains, having a tendency to stiffen the soil, and to bring it to that medium, or neutralized state, (if I may so express myself) which appears the most decidedly favourable to the purposes of vegetation. If this statement be accurate, (and I have every reason from enquiry and observation, to believe it to be so) the utility of marl is derived from three several sources; viz. from the calcareous earth, which it contains; from the increase of soil obtained by its application; and from the change which it effects in the disposition of the parts composing the soil. The last of these modes of operation, it is obvious, will be greatly varied by the nature of the soil to which the marl is applied. On stiff clay land its effect in altering the texture of the soil is less considerable than on any other."

Altho we find nothing new in those remarks,—every idea contained in them being either before the public, or are clearly understood by professional men, in marling districts,—yet the manner in which the different modes of operation are made out, does Mr. Holland much credit, as a writer.

In the Appendix to the volume, now before me, is a paper

found, by that ingenious and accurate chemist, to contain calcareous earth in various proportions. As the result of trials made upon a number of specimens procured from different parts of the county, I have found that, though the greater number contained a certain proportion of carbonate of lime, there are several kinds which do not effervesce in the slightest degree upon the addition of the dilute sulphuric acid, and consequently do not contain any portion of calcareous matter. Still, however, they are called marls by the farmer, and are found to produce an ameliorating effect upon the land."

paper "on the nature and origin of marls,"—by J. T. Stanley, Esquire, F. R. and A. S. &c.

This paper, in as much as it throws a few fresh rays of light on the *nature* of the marls found in Cheshire, is valuable. But what is said in it, regarding the *operation* of marls, appears to be ill founded. And the conjectures hazarded, respecting their *origin*, relate to fossils in general, rather than to marls in particular. I transcribe what concerns the marls of Cheshire.

P. 348. "Marl is a substance found in many parts of England, but in peculiar abundance in Cheshire, where it has been long used with great advantage for the improvement of the soil. It consists of clay, sand, and lime very intimately, but unequally mixed; and has the appearance of a clay of a dark brown colour, intersected with light blue veins; though, when freshly broken, it has rather a granular surface: on pressing it between the fingers, however, it has a softer feel than clay. It is seldom found as a stratum, or layer of any length; but generally a few feet below the surface, in detached masses of twenty or thirty roods in extent, and eight or ten yards in depth; covered with clay, and resting on a bed of sand or gravel. It has been spread over land in Cheshire for many centuries; and leases granted in the reigns of Edward I. and II. contain clauses obliging the tenants to make use of it.

"That marl is most esteemed which contains the most lime; but good effects are produced by such as contains scarcely a sufficient proportion to be perceptible. The farmers say, it strengthens the soil, enables the growing crops to maintain their vegetation during a dry season, and that it fills the kernels of corn. It does most good on light land; but even stiff lands derive a benefit from it. A field is said to be well marled when 128 solid yards are spread over a statute acre*. Marl falls into pieces, after having been exposed for a few months to the weather, and is then ploughed in. Its greatest effect is apparent when the field is brought into a second course of tillage; and after six or eight crops have been procured from it, it ceases to operate."

The *quantity*, used.—P. 222. "The quantity of marl used in this county, varies according to its quality, and the nature of the soils on which it is used. On a light or sandy soil, two cubic roods of marl, each rood containing

64 solid

* But see below.

64 solid yards, is reckoned a good covering for a statute acre. On strong retentive clay land, one rood is generally found sufficient for the same extent of surface."

The *application*.—P. 222. "The usual time of marling is in the summer months; beginning in May, when the ploughing is over, and continuing till the commencement of harvest. It is sometimes laid on the green sward in winter; and, after being acted upon by the frost, is ploughed in the following spring, generally for oats. Marling on fallows is also practised to a very considerable extent."

The *expence* of marling, in Cheshire, Mr. Holland makes out (p. 223) to be "five pounds per statute acre."

An ample detail of the marls; marl pits; method of working them; state of the land to receive them; the season of marling; the quantity set on; spreading them; and the expence attending those operations; in LANCASHIRE; may be seen in the REVIEW of the NORTHERN DEPARTMENT,—p. 286.

Those who are desirous of being more fully acquainted with the marls of this kingdom, may find in my registers of the nature and practice of its several departments, different species and varieties described and analyzed.

For general remarks on marls; the methods of searching for them; and that of employing them;—see the TREATISE on LANDED PROPERTY, p. 222; or the ABSTRACT of it,—p. 242.

Lime.—P. 226. "Lime is used to very considerable extent as a manure in most parts of Cheshire, but more particularly on the eastern side of the county, where it is procured in great abundance, and at a tolerably cheap rate, from Derbyshire. The lime kilns at Newbold-Astbury, near Congleton, likewise supply a large district, to the south-east of the county, with this valuable article. The larger proportion of the lime stone used in the middle and western parts of Cheshire, is procured from the Welch coast, and burnt at the different kilns in the county: some of it also is procured from Staffordshire. In the hundred of Wirrall, a comparatively small quantity is used as a manure; a circumstance which may be attributed principally to the nature of the soil in this district."

Of the qualities, or descriptions, of those several limes, —or of the limestones, whether of Cheshire or Wales, that are burnt in the county, we are not informed; either in a scientific, or a popular, way.

P. 227.

P. 227. "The *quantity* of lime laid on an acre varies, in this county, from 70 to 140 bushels. There is likewise a considerable variation in the *price* at which it is procured. The average price may perhaps be stated at seven-pence or eight-pence per bushel. Good lime, brought by the Staffordshire canal, in *iron boats*, from the neighbourhood of Leek, may be purchased, at the wharf at Acton bridge, at sixpence the bushel."

Dung.—I am happy to hear that the Cheshire farmers are beginning to *bed their dung yards*, with mold, &c.; as a foundation for their farm yard manure.—p. 227.

The average *price* of dung, in Cheshire—"may, perhaps, be stated at seven shillings per ton."—p. 229.

Sand.—Here, the reader must prepare himself for something new.—P. 229. "One of the principal agricultural improvements which has taken place of late years in Cheshire, is the introduction of sand as a manure for stiff clay lands. This practice is, indeed, still in its infancy in the county, but the success which has invariably attended its adoption, will, in all probability, render it much more general. The value of sand as an improvement to the soil was formerly little known; a few loads were sometimes carried into the farm yard, but even these instances were rare till about thirty years ago, when T. Corbett, Esq., of Darnhall, began to use very considerable quantities; sometimes mixing it with dung, sometimes laying it raw on his grass lands. The success which attended these experiments induced several farmers in the neighbourhood to follow the example of Mr. Corbett; and the practice has since been introduced on a number of the principal dairy farms in the middle of the county, where opportunities for its adoption occur. Such opportunities are by no means uncommon; deep beds of sand being frequently met with under the clay, which predominates as a superficial stratum.

"The kind of sand esteemed most favourable for laying on clay lands, is usually of a red colour, derived from an oxide of iron contained in its substance, and is *soft and unctuous to the feel.* No very accurate analysis has hitherto been made of it; but it certainly contains a considerable proportion of aluminous earth, combined with the siliceous particles of the sand. In none of the specimens, which I procured for the purpose of experiment, have I been able to detect the presence of any calcareous matter."

Let not, however, the occupiers of other districts *run*

at

at *sand*, "as a manure,"—from what is above stated. The "sand," used in Cheshire, appears, in the Reporter's unsatisfactory description of it, to be a rich silt;—perhaps of marine origin,—formed at the mouth of some muddy estuary of former times;—of a kindred nature (but disfigured by time) with the "sea mud" that will presently be mentioned.

Mr. Manley of Merton corroborates Mr. Holland's statement. He says, p. 231.—"It is excellent management in the farmer, before he ties up his cattle for the winter, to lay a coat of sand, at least a foot in thickness, where he intends to throw his dung out of the cow houses. The dung should be repeatedly levelled on the sand, and a second coat of the latter laid on toward the end of February; upon which should be put the remainder of the dung procured before the cattle go to grass. As soon after this time as possible, the compost should either be turned, and mixt well where it lies, or cut down *in breasts*, filled into the dung carts, and taken away to some situation near the land on which it is intended to use it. Here it should be laid in a heap of at least two yards in thickness. After remaining two or three months in this state, it is in excellent condition for putting upon the land; and will be found upon the whole, one of the most advantageous manures the farmer can employ, particularly on soils where there is a considerable predominance of clay."

This, it is highly probable, may be strictly true, with respect to the *Cheshire* "sand;" but let not *any* sand be thus applied, on a large scale, on the strength of what is above reported. Let it, nevertheless, be the business of every occupier of strong tenacious lands, who can procure sand of any sort, in his neighbourhood, to try its effects, on a moderate or smaller scale; and in Mr. Manley's manner. But let him not "poison" his whole dung hill with the meagre sandy grout, which is frequently found in cold clayey districts.

I recollect an instance, in Surrey, of an ingenious and well experienced practitioner (Mr. Arbuthnot) mixing ordinary infertile sand with his strong clayey land, by way of forming it into sandy loams. But he desisted; because he found, or fancied he found, that his soil, instead of being encreased in friability, became more binding than it was in its natural state; even as the purer clays, by adding sand to them, are rendered more eligible, as brick earths.

This circumstance, and the foregoing precautions are not

not brought forward to damp the spirit of experimenting; but as hints that may tend towards rendering it the more successful; and, of course, the more alert and durable. Grass land would seem to be the most eligible site of experiment.

Peat earth.—P. 232. "This substance, made into a compost with lime or dung, has been employed in several instances with great success."

The Reverend Croxton Johnson forms his compost on the spot,—*upon* the moss—(it does not appear that he cuts *through* it).—P. 232. "In the beginning of January the moss is trenched, and thrown up into ridges, that it may be dried and pulverized by the frost. Towards the latter end of February, it is turned over and laid flat, when it is usually found considerably lighter than when it was first dug up. It is then covered with dung, in the proportion of a fourth or fifth part of the weight, and left in this state for a fortnight or three weeks; after which it is turned over, mixed thoroughly with the dung, and thrown into heaps. A fermentation generally commences in a few days, which varies in continuance according to the degree of moisture in the moss. After it has subsided, the compost is turned over, as before, and the moss at the same time broken very small, that it may mix the more intimately with the dung. In consequence of this process a second fermentation usually takes place, and often to a more considerable degree than in the first instance. The compost is ready to put on the land about the middle of April. Where lime is used instead of dung, the proportion added to the peat moss is considerably smaller. The remainder of the process is conducted in a similar way." In what manner the dung or lime is got upon the moss, or how the compost is removed from it, is not reported; and, of course, no *practical* information is conveyed

Ashes.—P. 234. "An intelligent farmer informs me that he has been in the habit, for some years, of burning gorse" (furze—whins) "upon his summer fallows, and spreading the ashes over the land."

Salt, as a manure.—Notwithstanding what Mr. Wedge has advanced, on this subject, (see p. 25.) Mr. Holland doubts, at least, its efficacy, as such. Experiments are detailed; but their results contradict each other. He attempts to account for this disagreement, and to reconcile them; but without success. He, therefore, prudently leaves the matter nearly where he found it. The following natural facts, however, are worth registering.

P. 239.

P. 239. "On the banks of the Weaver, above Namptwich, several brine springs break out upon the surface, which have the effect of destroying all vegetation, for several yards round. On the marshes in the neighbourhood of Frodsham, the natural application of the muriate of soda seems to produce effects of a somewhat contrary nature. A considerable extent of these marshes, is overflowed by the salt water, every spring tide: and in the intervening period, is used as a pasture for horses, cattle, &c. The vegetation here is by no means deficient in vigour; the cattle are extremely partial to the grass, and very speedily fatten upon it."

All the world know the value of the herbage of salt marshes, for the feedage of livestock. And the value of the EARTH of SALT MARSHES, as a manure, for other lands, appears to be well attested; tho not generally known. In Lancashire, "sea slutch" is successfully used as manure."—(See NORTH. DEPART.) And, in the Appendix to the Report of Cheshire, now under consideration, is a circumstantial and satisfactory account of its efficacy, as such, in that county.

It has long been understood, or believed, that salt on its application, in quantity, is inimical to vegetation; but that time changes its effect. And this popular idea, it is possible, may be founded in fact. Mixing it with wet soil, or pouring it upon dry mold, in a liquid state, and letting such saline earth remain for a length of time, before it be used (repeatedly moving it, and thereby exposing fresh surfaces to the air) may perhaps be the most eligible mode of applying it. Has it been tried as a *liquid manure*,—as urine and yard liquor have not unfrequently been applied?

After all, while salt is forbidden to be used as a manure, it may seem to be a waste of words to treat of it, as such. Let us hope, however, that a time may come when more political regulations, than at present would seem to exist, may be instituted, respecting it.—And, until such a measure take place, let us turn our attention to what is here termed "sea mud," or the earth of salt marshes.

Marsh mold.—This, it is probable, may be found at the mouths of many or most of the estuaries of the kingdom,—of a sufficiently rich quality to be profitably used as manure. The evidence of its extraordinary effect, as such, in Cheshire, is given by Mr. Orred of High Runcorn, in the following words.—P. 368. "After experiencing, for fifty years, the advantage of the use of sea-sludge as a manure,

manure, I can positively assert, that no other is equal to it, either for corn or grass. We have what we call the *green sod sludge*, and the *slob:* the former is the strongest, and is consequently always preferred when it is to be had. We generally get four rood to the (Cheshire) acre*. I have frequently carried it near a mile, when I had good marl on the spot; as it is got with so much less expense, and answers so much better. We take one graft off the lower part of the marsh, never going deeper. One man gets it with the shovel, whilst another puts it into the cart with a pitch fork. We always lay it upon grass, and plough it in the spring following. If the ensuing March is dry, and there has been much frost in the winter, a heavy pair of harrows will prepare it for the plough; otherwise it must be chopped with spades; but this is seldom necessary. We always sow the land with oats the first year, and have generally 140 bushels to the acre, I mean the Cheshire acre, eight yards to the perch. After oats, we either sow barley, or plant potatoes. If barley, we have, on an average, 100 bushels per acre: I have had 160. If planted with potatoes, we have seldom less than 400 bushels per acre, 90 lb. to the bushel †. The third year, we have always as much wheat as can grow upon the land. The fourth year, the land is laid down, either with oats and clover, or barley and clover. We always mow the clover once, and have as much as can possibly be cut out: it is then kept in pasturage four or five years, and though I have been in most counties in England, I never saw richer or better. If a field is over marled, it is spoiled for grass; but this is never the case when the sea mud is used, and the latter remains much longer in the land. I make no doubt but there are many situations in England, where the sea mud might be made as profitable as it is here, were the proprietors of land apprized of its advantages."

The above evidence may seem to corroborate the idea, that

* Which is about 120 cubic yards to the statute acre.

† In the section "potatoes," we are told that, at Weston near Frodsham, "sea mud is used as a manure for crops of potatoes; twenty loads being the quantity usually laid on an acre. The ground thus manured not only gives a large produce of potatoes, but is in a state of excellent preparation for a succeeding crop of either wheat or barley. The adoption of this practice has increased very greatly the value of land about Weston." P. 143.

that salt not only requires to be a length of time incorporated with the soil, before it act profitably, as manure; but that the compost should have free communication with the atmosphere. The older banks that have grown green with herbage, are preferable to the more recent mud banks; and of the former, only one spit, or spadegraft, in depth, is taken.

It may be, however, that the fertilizing quality of marsh mold chiefly resides in the nature of the mud itself, together with the vegetable matter which the first spit necessarily contains; without much aid from the salt, which it contained in its recent state. But this by the way.

The practitioner, who is fortunately situated where the earth of a salt marsh may be conveniently procured, and where the practice of applying it, as manure, is not yet established,—will,—free from any preconceived theory,—try its effects, on his own lands; by applying it, in various proportions, on a moderate scale; until he has fully ascertained, whether under his own particular circumstances, it can (taking into his account the deterioration of his marsh land) be applied with sufficient profit; and having found that it may, to fix upon the proper quantity to be used:—leaving it to theorists to settle the controversy about the "muriate of soda," as a manure.

FOOD of PLANTS.—Mr. Holland closes his section, "manuring," with—"general remarks on the nature and application of manures:"—quoting foreign chemists, respecting the former, and Mr. Wedge's Report, concerning the latter.

His remarks on the *nature* of *manures* are all that require to be noticed, here. These being of moderate length, and it being (as has been repeatedly intimated) on *chemical*, rather than *agricultural*, topics, we are to look for useful information, from Mr. H. I insert them, entire. They have at least, a becoming modesty to recommend them

P. 241. "From the analysis of different vegetable substances, and from experiments made upon the growth of plants, it would appear that the siliceous and aluminous earths, carbonic acid, water, oxygen, and the remains of animal and vegetable matters, are the materials most essential to the growth and nutrition of vegetables. Analysis would likewise seem to indicate that some of the salts constitute a necessary part of the food for plants; though the variety in the nature and proportion of these salts

salts is greater than that prevailing among the other materials of vegetable nutriment. That a certain proportion of the mould, produced by the putrefaction of animal or vegetable matters, is essential to the fertility of every soil, has been proved by the experiments of Giobert, who found that the siliceous, aluminous, calcareous and magnesian earths, though mixed together in the proportions used to fertile soils, and moistened with pure water, never produced a vigorous vegetation, till he employed the water exuding from a dunghill to give moisture to the soil. We are at present too little acquainted with the mode of vegetable nutrition and growth to assign, with precision, the immediate causes of this fact. It would appear, however, from the experiments of Hassenfratz, Saussure, and other enquirers into this subject, that the value of putrid animal and vegetable matters, as ingredients in soil, depends principally, if not entirely, upon the peculiar state of combination in which the constituents of such substances exist; a state apparently the most favourable to their re-organization by the vegetative process. The experiments made by Saussure, on the mould procured from the decay of different vegetable matters, have shewn that the most usual constituents of this substance are carbureted hydrogen gas, carbonic acid, water, frequently containing a small portion of ammonia combined with a vegetable acid, charcoal, and an empyreumatic oil. It is probable that the decomposition of animal substances by putrefaction furnishes materials very similar for the process of vegetation, and that the fertility of any soil is derived principally from the due admixture of such substances with the simple earths; and perhaps also from the proportion of them capable of being held in solution by water. A general knowledge of these circumstances, and of the superior value of putrid animal and vegetable substances as additions to his soils, must induce every judicious agriculturist to bestow much of his attention upon the collection and preservation of all such manures, as well as upon their proper application and distribution to his lands."

For Mr. Wedge's strictures, on the *application* of manures, see p. 29, aforegoing.

Semination.—P. 126.—"*Drill husbandry for Corn.* The system of drill husbandry for corn has hitherto been introduced to a very trifling extent in Cheshire; and the generally prevailing opinion among the farmers in this district seems to be, that the adoption of the practice would

would be attended with consequences rather injurious than beneficial. Among those, however, who have made experiments on this mode of husbandry, there are some who regard the subject in a different point of view. Mr. Holland, of Sandlebridge, informs me, that he has made several trials, in which the application of drill husbandry to corn has been very successful."

P. 127. "Another intelligent farmer states it as his opinion, that drill husbandry for corn is not preferable to the old broad-cast system. He allows that a large produce has in many instances been the result of trials made on the former mode; but attributes this circumstance to the particular care which has been taken to have the land in a good state for the experiment, rather than to any peculiar advantages connected with this mode of husbandry.

"Dibbling for crops of corn is very little known or applied in this county."

GROWING CROPS.—In the Section, "weeding," much is said; but nothing that merits particular notice; excepting what relates to the weeding of highways and hedges; and this I had elsewhere said, before I saw Mr. Holland's Report; namely, the making it part of the business of road Surveyors to clear public lanes, and the sides of Roads in general, from weeds that bear winged seeds. In the foregoing head *Covenants*, p. 127, an extract from the Section under notice will be found.

WHEAT.—This crop is twice brought forward:—once in the Section "fallowing," and, again, under its legitimate head. But I have found nothing, in either, that is particularly entitled to public notice; excepting the following extraordinary instance of the mischievousness of the *berbery*, to the wheat crop. Tho of some length, I cannot refrain from copying it. Not that I think it necessary to the establishment of the fact; having already, I conceive, established it, by my own experiments and observations*.

P. 134.

* See NORFOLK. *Minutes*, 13 & 133. Also MIDLAND COUNTIES, *Min.* 7 I have observed similar effects in other instances.

I must be allowed to indulge myself, here, in saying, that what was rather exultingly brought forward, by botanists (previously to the publishing of those experiments and observations) as one of the palpable vulgar errors of farmers, which showed their want of botanical knowledge,—might now, with more truth, be retorted on themselves.

P. 134. "An opinion has long been entertained that the barberry *(berberis vulgaris)* produced some noxious effect upon corn, and particularly upon wheat and oats. Withering, speaking of it, says, "This shrub should never be permitted to grow in corn land, for the ears of wheat that grow near it never fill; and its influence in this respect has been known to extend as far as three or four hundred yards across a field*." Since no reason could be assigned for so extraordinary an effect, nor any analogous fact produced, this has generally been regarded as a popular error, and little credit attached to it. Such a strong confirmation of it has however lately come to my knowledge, that I think it proper to state it. About twenty years ago a young plantation on the lands of Sir J. F. Leicester, Bart. was fenced out with a barberry hedge, about a hundred yards in length. On the opposite side, to the north west of the plantation, was a small enclosure about ninety yards across, held by one of his tenants. Three years ago this was sown with wheat; the crop produced, although the land appeared in good condition, scarcely paid the expense of thrashing; the grain being extremely small, and the quantity of it very inconsiderable. On the following year the field was sown with oats, and the return of the crop was little more than equal to the seed. Last year the field was well limed, and was partly in fallow, and the remainder set with potatoes. In the autumn the whole was sown with wheat, which came up well, looked healthy, and shot into ear at the usual time; promising a crop at least equal to any in the neighbourhood. Soon after, the plant became brown and completely decayed, and when cut, it was thought not worth while even to carry it from the field. I had an opportunity of examining it as it lay there, a few days after it had been cut, and found all the straw was completely rotten, and that every ear of the plant within twenty yards of the hedge had been entirely unproductive, not yielding a single grain of corn. At the distance of twenty, or twenty-five yards, a few very small grains of wheat might be discovered in some of the ears. Still further from the hedge the grains were larger and more numerous; but in no part of the field was the produce sufficiently abundant to induce the farmer to carry it off the ground. The enclosure beyond the wheat field was sown with oats; and this

"* Botanical Arrangement, Vol. 1. p. 367."

this crop also seemed materially to have suffered from the influence of the same cause. All the crops of corn in the same neighbourhood were at least as productive as usual."

BARLEY,—is classed, by this Reporter of the Cheshire practice, among "crops not commonly cultivated." Any thing of excellence in its culture cannot, of course, be reasonably expected, in that county; where, nevertheless, there appears iu the map of its soils, as well as from a view of the soils themselves, an abundance of *barley lands.*

OATS.—Nor do I find any thing worthy of special attention belonging to the culture of oats, in Cheshire.

PULSE.—Nor is there aught that is related, either on the *pea*, or the *bean* crop, to instruct or interest the agricultural public.

BUCKWHEAT.—P. 167. "In the time of Gerrard, who published his herbal in 1597, it appears that buck-wheat was "very common about Namptwich in Cheshire, where they sow it as well for food for their cattle, pullen (poultry) and such like, as to serve instead of a dunging." Very little is now sown in this county, and the produce is either ploughed in, as a manure; or mowed, for fatting swine, and poultry with the grain."

CABBAGES.—P. 159. "This crop, like the former," (turnips) "is much more generally cultivated in Cheshire than formerly, and is held in equal, if not in greater estimation, as green food for cattle*."

Cabbages with *early potatoes.*—P. 160. "There is a sort of garden husbandry lately introduced into the neighbourhood of Warrington, which seems highly deserving of attention. It consists in the growth of early potatoes, with alternate rows of ox-cabbage. The potatoes are set as early as they can be, so as to be safe from the frosts; they are taken up in June, or the beginning of July; and the cabbages, which have been planted in alternate rows, left, to remain as winter food for the cattle."

TURNEPS,—are pretty evidently a *fresh* crop, in Cheshire.—P. 156. "The more general introduction of *green* crops,

"* The cabbage is, in my opinion, the best green crop for the dairy. The cattle fed upon it give more milk than when fed upon turnips; and it does not communicate that disagreeable flavour to milk, butter, and cheese, which is sometimes done by the latter food. —*Mr. Manley.*"

crops, and their extended application as food for cattle, is undoubtedly one of the greatest improvements which has taken place, *of late years*, in the agriculture of Cheshire. In the middle, and southern parts of the county particularly, every dairy farmer has *now* his field of turnips and cabbages; which he uses for his milch cows, during the winter and spring months. In the hundred of Wirrall, these crops are by no means so frequent; though an extension of their growth would in all probability be a source of considerable advantage to the dairies in that district."

The practice of *drilling* them,—of sowing them on ridgets,—has already found its way into the county:—where the "Swedish turnip" is not unknown.

POTATOES.—After the ample detail of useful information laid up, from the LANCASHIRE Report, and from Mr. *Wedge's* Report of Cheshire,—I shall, I find, be able to make very little addition, from that of Mr. *Holland*,—respecting the culture of this inestimable root; excepting what relates to the management of *early potatoe*, in *Wyrral;* and this it may be said, would better appear in a work concerning horticulture, than in one of agriculture.

Nevertheless, as WALLASEY (situated at the extremity of the Peninsula of Cheshire, nearly opposite to Liverpool) appears to have been the birth place of the early potatoe, and still takes the lead in its culture;—and as, in a year of scarcity of grain, a supply of potatoes during the summer months, might, as Mr. H. justly observes, be a seasonable relief—(provided, it should be added, some practical method can be hit upon to cultivate them, on a sufficiently large scale, *in the Field);* I will extract the account published by Mr. Holland; as it is, apparently, more accurate and practical, than that by Mr. Wedge.

P. 146. "*Potatoe culture in Wirrall**. From the situation of the hundred of Wirrall, between the estuaries of the Mersey and Dee, the climate of this district is mild and temperate, and peculiarly favourable to the cultivation of potatoes. The immediate vicinity of Liverpool, creating a large demand for this vegetable, has given rise to an improved mode of raising the early kinds, which deserves the attention of the practical agriculturist. The following is the method pursued. The potatoes designed for the sets are

"* With this account of the culture of early potatoes in Wirrall, I was favoured by the Rev. R. Jacson of Bebbington."

are got up in September or October, or even before; the sooner after they are mature, the better; and in November are laid up in a warm dry room, where they are spread rather thinly, not more than two or at most three potatoes in thickness, and covered with wheat chaff, or dry sand. They are further protected from frost, whenever it is necessary, by a blanket or rug spread over them. By this mode of management, they are generally well sprit by the month of February or the beginning of March; if this should not be the case, the sprouting is accelerated by sprinkling them from time to time with a little water. A potatoe is said to be well sprit, when it has a shoot from two to four inches long, as thick as a small quill, and terminated by two little leaves. In this state they are planted whole; all the shoots being cut off, excepting one, as early in February as the season will allow; they are set not more than five or six inches asunder, the tops just within the ground. As long as there is any danger from an exposure to the frosts, they are carefully protected by a covering of straw or pease-haum; which is taken off in the day, unless the weather be extremely severe, and put on again at night. By this management, potatoes are now as plentiful in the Liverpool market, in the middle of May, or even sooner, as they were, before it was practised, in the middle of June. At the same time, the culture of this vegetable is productive of very considerable profit to the farmer; a second crop being, in almost every instance, raised from the same land in the same year.

"The land is always manured for potatoes in Wirrall, except where a naturally rich spot, or one that has some time before been well manured, is allotted to the early crop. Under these favourable circumstances, both this crop, and that which is allowed to come to maturity, are generally much better in kind than is otherwise the case."

In a note, p. 150, Mr. H. reasoning, *professionally*, from the analogy between animals and vegetables, hazards the following assertions,—" On the same principle, when potatoes have been exposed to a sharp frost, the best method of counteracting its effects is to cover them with mats, or straw, before the morning sun can have any influence upon them: they will thus be secured against a too sudden transition from cold to heat. Water poured on them would have nearly the same effect; for, however cold, its temperature would have been always considerably above that of the frozen dew which hangs on their leaves; and it would gradually restore a healthy action of their vessels. The

The mortification of a frozen limb would be the inevitable consequence of a too sudden exposure of it to warmth; whilst the circulation is restored, and the life of the part preserved, by immersing it in snow, or bathing it with the coldest water which can be procured."—Admitting this to be strictly true, and practicable, it is still but *gardening*. The thought, however, is ingenious; and may be found valuable to the growers of early potatoes, in the environs of great towns.

The PRODUCE of Potatoes, *in the field*, Mr. H. estimates, as follows:—By the *Frodsham* practice (the lazybed method) at two hundred and fifty bushels,—of ninety pounds, each:—By the *Wirral* practice (not described) from one hundred and fifty to two hundred and fifty bushels. And by the *Altringham* practice ("in drills, either with the plow or spade") at three hundred bushels, each statute acre. The produce, by the *ordinary* practice of Cheshire (the lazybed method) is not mentioned.—On the whole, the products, in Lancashire, and in Cheshire, are much the same;—namely, about two hundred and fifty bushels of ninety pounds each.—Mr. Wedge's statement of three hundred is probably too high. (For a manure of Potatoes, see n. p. 145.)

CARROTS.—P. 164. "Though the cultivation of this vegetable is carried to a very considerable extent in the neighbourhood of Altringham, it cannot with propriety be reckoned among the crops commonly cultivated in this county. The mode of culture usually pursued, in this particular district, is exceedingly simple. A dry loamy soil is chosen, and is fallowed with a light furrow before Christmas; it is soon after dug, that the frost may act upon the soil, and prepare it for being *raked* fine, when the seed is sown, which is generally done towards the middle, or latter end of March. The only kinds of seed sown in the neighbourhood of Altringham, are, what are called the London, and home-seed. The latter is raised by the gardeners in the neighbourhood, and is very generally preferred to the London seed, being frequently sold for four times the price. The produce varies greatly, according to the nature of the soil, and of the season. Ten or twelve tons, or about 350 bushels per statute acre, are, I understand, reckoned a very fair produce; now and then the farmer obtains fifteen or sixteen tons; in other seasons not more than four or five.

"Manchester is the principal market for the carrots grown in the neighbourhood of Altringham; the conveyance

veyance to that town by the duke of Bridgewater's canal being at once cheap and expeditious."

Onions,—we are informed, are a profitable crop, in the neighbourhood of Altringham; where they are grown for the Manchester market. This, however, is still only gardening; and every gardiner is acquainted with the culture of onions.

P. 166. "The soil esteemed most suitable to the growth of onions is a black loam upon a cold bottom: land newly improved by draining, &c. is preferred to that which has been for some length of time in tillage:"—a hint, *this*, to small farmers, in the neighbourhoods of great towns.

CULTIVATED HERBAGE.—Of this we find a few gleanings, only; collected from different fields of information.

PERENNIAL GRASS LAND.—P. 169. "The natural meadows in Cheshire are numerous, and for the most part situated by the sides of the small streams, which intersect the county in every direction. They possess a remarkable degree of richness and fertility; a circumstance which may probably in part originate in other causes than the greater degree of moisture derived from their situation."

After noticing the soils of *cow grounds*, in Cheshire, (which will be mentioned under the head, *Dairy*) Mr. H. enters upon a long *catalogue raisonné* of the meadow plants of Cheshire; and enumerates some corn weeds and hedge plants. But I perceive nothing of useful information, that is not already known to the agricultural public, arise from any part of it.

Haymaking.—The Reporter, in a section bearing this appellation, joins the harvesting of the cultivated, and the natural, herbages; tho their methods of treatment ought to be very different.

The *Time* of *Cutting*.—P. 184. "Clover and rye grass, which are the artificial grasses most cultivated for hay in Cheshire, are frequently cut as early as the middle of June; whilst the natural meadow grasses are seldom cut in this county before the middle or latter end of July; and it is not uncommon to see many farmers in their hay harvest as late as the third or fourth week in August."

This, Mr. H. very properly censures; and, calling in the celebrated *poet* and *botanist*, DARWIN, to his assistance, endeavours to convince the occupiers, of Cheshire, of their error, in that particular of their management. Had he, instead of having recourse to the *saccharine theory*, told them that the grasses and other herbs, usually mown for hay, contain, in their *stems*, and *foliage*, during their state

state of growth, what will, in the state of maturity,—(if suffered to stand)—be lodged in their *seeds;* and that if they be injudiciously suffered to stand until they be matured, and *shed* their seeds on the ground, what remains of them will be mere *straw* or *pulse-halm;* and, moreover, that should any part of that nourishment which was intended, for their perfect maturation, be *left in the soil*, it will presently rise out of it, in the shape of *after-grass;*—he would probably have conveyed conviction more forcibly and clearly to their minds.

Mr. Holland's account of the Cheshire practice of making hay does the farmers of that county (who follow the methods Mr. H. describes) much credit. It is in the better manner of English haymaking. I find nothing in it, however, which is not understood, and practised, in different parts of the kingdom, and has been described, again and again. It is in MIDDLESEX, we must look for excellence in this art;—among the hay farmers round the metropolis.

In the Reporter's dissertation, concerning haymaking, hay stacks, and hay barns, (filling half a sheet of paper) I see nothing that could repay my readers for the trouble of perusal. He would seem to have had just sufficient experience, in those matters, to generate in his mind a fund of theoretic ideas.

HORSES.—P. 289. "No particular attention seems to have been paid to the breed of horses in Cheshire, though from the very great increase which has taken place, of late years, in the price of this highly useful animal, the improvement of the breed is considered as an object of more importance than formerly."

CATTLE.—Respecting this most important topic, in an *agricultural* Report of Cheshire, Mr. Holland, very judiciously, copies Mr. WEDGE's account:—giving the following substantial reasons for so doing.—P. 249. "The dairy constitutes so principal an object of attention to the Cheshire farmer, as to render the subject of this section highly interesting and important with a reference to the agricultural economy of the county. It will, therefore, be necessary to enter into a more particular detail of the system of dairy management, pursued in this district, than might otherwise appear consistent with the general plan of the Report. The papers on this subject, contained in the Original Report, are copious and by no means deficient in point of arrangement. To ascertain how

how far a reliance might be placed on their accuracy of statement, I took an opportunity of circulating them among several respectable and intelligent dairy farmers; requesting at the same time any additional remarks, which might appear necessary or important to the subject. Finding, as a result to this inquiry, that the entire accuracy of these papers might be depended on, I have judged it most adviseable to insert them here, as they stand in the Original Report; omitting, however, the account of the diseases of cattle, which appears superficial and trifling. The few remarks and comments, with which I have been favoured, are inserted as notes."

Those notes, together with what else I can collect from other parts of Mr. H's Report,—concerning cows, and the DAIRY,—I will insert, here, in their natural order; the better to enable my reader to combine them with Mr. Wedge's detail.

COWS.—The favorite *Soil* of *Cow Grounds*, in Cheshire. —P. 170. "From the great extent to which the making of cheese is carried on in Cheshire, the proportion of pasture land is very considerable; particularly in the middle and southern parts of the county. Its quality is of course varied by the nature of the soil, and other local circumstances. From the enquiries I have made of several intelligent farmers, with a view to ascertain what description of land is peculiarly suitable for a dairy pasture, I have found it to be the general prevailing opinion, that a tolerably stiff clay soil, especially with a substratum of marl, is, upon the whole, the most favourable for this purpose: more milk may be had from cows pastured on a rich loamy soil, but it is esteemed inferior in point of quality. This opinion is in a great measure confirmed by an actual reference to facts. The dairy farms in Namptwich, and the western part of Northwich hundred, which are, generally speaking, the finest in the county, are situated for the most part on a stiff clay land, with a strong marl below it. Throughout the greater part of Broxton hundred, which is completely a dairying district, the soil is either a strong clay, or a clayey loam; and the same observation may be extended to the hundred of Wirrall."

Management of *Cows*.—P. 256. "The more general introduction of green crops, and of the practice of stall feeding for dairy cows, may certainly be reckoned among the most considerable improvements which have taken place of of late years in the agriculture of Cheshire. With the dairy farmer, it is a principal object to increase the quantity of his milk, and to continue it as long as possible This can in no way be more effectually done, than by giving green food to his cattle; and I am informed by several intelligent farmers, that by this management the milk may be continued a month longer in the autumn than could be effected by trusting to the pastures only for a supply of food. The importance of this circumstance, in a dairy district, must be sufficiently obvious."—How far cabbages and turneps are consonant with the cheese dairy of Cheshire, we are not informed.

Disposal of *Cows*.—P. 192. "The dairy constituting the principal object of attention to the Cheshire farmer, the feeding of cattle is very little practised in this county; and consequently nothing peculiarly worthy of notice occurs on this subject. Some few farms in different parts of the county are held for the purpose of feeding: and it is a general practice with the occupiers of the larger farms, of from one to three or four hundred acres, to reserve a few acres of their aftergrass for feeding one or more of the refuse of their stock, or such as do not promise to be profitable for the next year's dairy. One of these is generally killed at Christmas for the family, part of it being salted, dried, and kept for the use of the succeeding year. Much the greater part of the refuse stock, however, is driven to the markets in the south of Lancashire; or sold at the Michaelmas and spring fairs, and carried off to some of the feeding counties nearer the metropolis."

The DAIRY.—*Dairy Women*.—Under the head "Character of Farmers," we find the subjoined flattering account of the DAIRY WOMEN of Cheshire.—P. 100. "I must not dismiss this subject without devoting a few words to the fair dairy women in this county, of whom indeed it is impossible to speak but in terms of approbation. The farmer has only to provide a proper stock of cattle, and to superintend the management of his white and green crops; he is secure of having his rent made up for his landlord, by the industry and excellent management of the female presiding in the dairy, who is usually his wife, daughter, or some other person connected with the family. To the same source too may be attributed the general appearance of neatness and comfort which is observable in the domestic economy of the dairy farmer; a circumstance of no trivial moment, when considered in its reference to the cha-

character, as well as to the happiness of an important and useful class of society."

Milking.—N. P. 259. "In the choice of a person for milking the cows, great caution should be employed; for if that operation be not carefully, and properly performed, the quantity of the produce of the dairy will be greatly diminished. It should be a rule never to allow this important department to be entrusted, without controul, to the management of any, but very trusty servants, as the cows should always be treated with great gentleness."

Churning.—N. P. 261. "I have met with one farmer who employs a small water wheel to work his churn; by means of which he can make the churn-staff work at pleasure from 1 to 108 strokes in a minute. He has experienced the greatest advantage from this mode of churning, and recommends its adoption whenever the situation of the dairy will admit of it."

Coloring Cheese.—N. P. 269. "It has been calculated, that not less than 5 or 6000l. is annually paid in Cheshire, for arnotta, for the colouring of cheese. If the gentry would prefer, and be particular in ordering for their own table, cheese that is not coloured, that ridiculous, and completely unnecessary expense would probably, in a great measure, be done away. *Mr. Fenna.*"

There appears, at the first glance, to be some egregious error in this estimate. The price of annatto, in Glocestershire, some years ago, was tenpence an ounce; which is enough to color two hundred-weight of cheese. A ton, on this calculation, costs eight shillings and four pence. But let us call it ten shillings. The produce of Cheshire is estimated, by Mr. Fenna (as will presently appear) at 11,500 tons; which, at ten shillings, a ton, gives a product of 5,750*l.* for the coloring used in Cheshire; provided the number of cows kept for sale cheese, alone, be 92,000.

Markets for *Cheese.*—P. 315. "The greatest proportion of the cheese, especially of that made in the large dairy farms in the southern and middle parts of the county, is disposed of to the cheesemongers in London; who usually employ factors or agents, resident in these districts, to purchase the dairies for them; the farmers agreeing to deliver the cheese either at Chester, where it is shipped directly for London; or at Frodsham, from which place it is conveyed by way of Liverpool to the same market. Some is sent up the Staffordshire canal, to the inland counties; while no inconsiderable part of the smaller sized dairies,

dairies, and a large proportion of the cheese made in the northern, and north east parts of the county, is purchased by the factors for the supply of the Stockport and Manchester markets; whence it is distributed through the populous districts in the south of Lancashire, and the west of Yorkshire."

Price of *Cheese.*—In the Section "Provisions," while enumerating their prices, we find the subjoined note attached to this item:—"Cheese from 2*l.* 15*s.* to 3*l.* 10*s.* per cwt. of 120 lb."—N. P. 298. "The constant average price of some dairies is much greater than the highest here stated, a circumstance which depends principally on the length of time the cheese is kept. By long keeping, cheese is considerably diminished in weight; so that the actual difference in price between that sold early, and that kept for one or two years, is not so much as at first view it might appear."

Produce of *Cheese* by the *Cow.*—N. P. 258. "In the hundred of Wirrall, where there is a dairy on most of the farms, the average annual produce of cheese from each cow cannot be stated at more than 2 cwt. This deficiency originates in several obvious causes; few of the pastures in this district are old grass land; they are in general very fully stocked with cattle; to the breed and condition of which, too little attention is usually paid by the farmer. The neglect of giving turnips, or some other description of green food to the cows in the months of October and November; and their bad wintering, which is, for the most part, of straw only, are additional circumstances, which account in a great measure for the comparative smallness of produce from the cattle on the Wirrall dairies. *Rev. R. Jacson.*"—Mr. WEDGE lays the produce of each cow at $2\frac{1}{2}$ cwt.

Produce of the *county*—N. P. 252. "The number of cows kept for the dairy in Cheshire may be about 92,000; from which are probably made annually about 11,500 tons of cheese.—*Mr. Fenna.*

"This calculation appears to be tolerably accurate. Estimating the number of cultivated acres of land in the county at 600,000, taking nearly a third of this number for dairy *pasture*, and allowing two acres to each cow, we shall approach very nearly to the statement made by Mr. Fenna of the number of dairy cows in Cheshire. Averaging the quantity of cheese made annually from each cow at $2\frac{1}{2}$ cwt., the result will correspond with his calculation of the quantity made every year in the county."

In

In the Vale of Berkeley, in Glocestershire, where the lands, I apprehend are of a richer quality than those of Cheshire,—four acres, or upward, are allowed to each cow*. But, there, cows eat hay, during the winter months:—whereas, in Cheshire, they consume, in winter, much produce of the arable lands; so that, here, three acres of *grass land* may be the outmost quantity occupied, by each cow; namely, two for *pasture* (as above stated) and one for *hay* and *aftergrass*.

I was led to these considerations, by finding the estimated produce of Cheshire to exceed greatly that of Glocestershire; and, by observing, in the markets (the *home* markets†) the proportion of "Cheshire cheese" to fall short of that of "Glocestershire cheese."—It is true, that under the name of "Gloster cheese" much of that made in North Wiltshire, and Somersetshire, and part of that made in the midland counties, may appear. But, on the other hand, quantities of cheese produced in the environs of Cheshire,—in North Wales and in Shropshire,—go to market, I believe, under the appellation of "Cheshire cheese." It will, therefore, be found perhaps on revision, that the estimate, by Mr. Fenna, has been laid too high, in the Cheshire Report.

Mr. Wedge estimates the arable, meadow and pasture lands, including parks and pleasure grounds, at 620,000 acres:—And Mr. Holland copies his estimate.—Supposing that one third of this aggregate quantity to be appropriated, *entirely*, to the production of *cheese*—for *sale*;—and allowing three acres to one cow, the number of cows, kept for the *sole* purpose of *sale cheese*, will be 68,888. Hence, on these premises, and allowing each cow to produce 2½ cwt. of cheese, the aggregate produce of the county will be 8,600 tons. This by way of exciting further calculation.

SHEEP.—P. 286. "The dairy being the object of greatest moment to the Cheshire farmer, less attention is paid to sheep in this than in most other counties. They are, however, to be found in large flocks on the hills bordering on Yorkshire and Derbyshire, and are of a good healthy kind, the wethers, at four years old, weighing from

* See RURAL ECON. of GLOCESTERSHIRE.—Subject *Dairy Management, Vale of Berkeley.*

† Is a greater quantity of Cheshire, than of Glocestershire, &c. cheese sent to *foreign* markets?

from 15lbs. to 18lbs. the quarter; but the wool is coarse. Besides this, there does not appear to be any peculiar breed in the county, except that on the forest of Delamere; which is small, the wethers, weighing from 8lbs. to 12lbs. the quarter, at four years old. The mutton of this breed is much esteemed, and the wool is valuable, selling this year at 2*l.* 12*s.* 6*d.* per stone of 20lbs.; the fleeces, however, are small, often not weighing more than 2lbs. The wool is purchased by the Yorkshire manufacturers of cloth. In point of shape, these sheep are not much unlike a diminutive Norfolk, with faces and legs black, grey, brown, and white, generally with small horns."—A variety of the true native, or naturalized, mountain breed of England. See NORTHERN DEPART. p. 200.

RABBITS.—P. 293. "There are but few rabbit warrens in this county: the principal are on Delamere forest: Sir J. F. Leicester has one in his park at Tabley. On several of the heaths and sand lands, rabbits are frequent, but not in number to constitute a warren."

There can be little doubt of that on the Delamere, and other insulated, hillocks of Cheshire,—seeing the markets of Manchester, Liverpool, and Chester are within view,—rabbit warrens might be stocked with profit.

PIGEONS.—P. 294. "The number of pigeons bred for sale in this county is very inconsiderable; it being the general opinion that they consume a greater quantity of produce than is compensated for by the profits they afford. They are generally kept at gentlemen's houses; few farmers having more than three or four couple; and many none. Where however an old hall or mansion house is occupied by the farmer, the number is frequently very considerable. Their dung is, I understand, particularly useful in the tan yards, in reducing the hides after they have been thickened by the action of the lime; and large quantities of it are purchased by the tanners, and applied to this purpose.

"The value of pigeons in this county is about a shilling or sixteenpence a couple."

BEES.—P. 294. "Hives of bees are to be met with at many of the farm houses in this county, as well as at some of the cottages, and in the small gardens in the immediate neighbourhood of towns."

To the silly injunction laid upon the Board's Reporters, respecting the "*expence* and *profit*" of farming,—Mr. H. has

has paid more serious attention than the matter required. By way of exhibiting in strong colors the uncapableness of him who imposed the task,—I will here insert Mr. H's sensible account of his endeavor,—notwithstanding the difficulties and embarrassments he had to encounter,—toward the accomplishment of his task, in this respect.

P. 111. "Nothing is more difficult than to ascertain with any degree of accuracy the actual expenses and profits attendant upon farming. So many circumstances are occurring to vary these on different farms; so few farmers are in the habit of keeping accounts, sufficiently regular for the formation of such calculations; and of those who keep accounts, so few are willing to communicate any information relative to their individual expenses and profits; that it becomes almost a matter of impossibility to procure statements which can convey any accurate ideas on the subject. These difficulties I have experienced, to their full extent, in endeavouring to obtain the information necessary to the drawing up this article. Readily conceiving that nothing could be procured by applications for the account of expenses and profits on particular farms; I stated my queries in a more general way, requesting information as to the probable expenses and profits on a dairy farm of 200 acres, without reference to any individual instance. Finding however that this mode of application was equally unsuccessful, I was induced at length to relinquish the design; and must plead as my apology for the omission of this part of the plan prescribed by the Board, the causes before mentioned. It cannot be reasonably expected that the farmer who rents his land should consent to have a statement of his profits brought forward, in a way which would naturally attract the attention of his landlord, and might have an effect in raising the rent of his farm; while among those farming their own land, there are few who note down, with sufficient accuracy for the purposes of such a statement, all the incidental expenses which they incur; and which, though small when taken individually, rise in conjunction to a very considerable amount. Even were one or two calculations of this kind obtained, the information communicated by this means would, I apprehend, be very trifling, and perhaps only accurate with respect to the farms from which they were respectively obtained; so great is the variety resulting from circumstances of a local and individual nature."

PART

PART OF

NORTH WALES,

SITUATED WITHIN THE

AGRICULTURAL DISTRICT of CHESTER.

IT has been said, aforegoing p. 5, that the NATURAL DISTRICT of CHESTER extends within the counties of *Flint* and *Denbigh*:—the lands and their management being the same, on either side of the fortuitous line of demarcation. The "Cheshire-cheese" dairy extends even into the VALE of CLWYD (one of the richest, most beautiful, and habitable, passages of country in the island); which, however is naturally separated (unless at its lowest extremity) from that of Chester, by a lofty ridge of hills; rising, southward, to mountain heights*.

To the southward, or rather south westward of those hills, are situated the VALE LANDS in the neighbourhood of WREXHAM; which are naturally, and agriculturally, a portion of the wide-spread DISTRICT of CHESTER. See as above.

NORTH WALES was surveyed, and reported to the Board of Agriculture, by GEO. KAY; who dates his letter of advertisement, at LEITH, in June 1794; when his Report was published.

Mr. KAY (tho the whole of his Reports are stitched up in one thick 4to pamphlet; they being *original* Reports) treats,

* The VALE of LLWYD;—(usually written *Clwyd;* and pronounced *Cloö-id*)—In July 1800, I spent a few days in this charming Vale. I forbear, however, to speak of it, in detail, here; as it would be attempting to rob NORTH WALES of its brightest and most valuable gem. The lower part of it is included in *Flintshire*, the upper part in *Denbighshire;*—and this notwithstanding its entireness, and peculiar uniformity, as a VALE DISTRICT,—whether it be viewed in a *natural*, or an *agricultural*, light. Hence, this Vale, alone, might serve to show the impropriety, if not the absurdity, of surveying and reporting, *by counties*.

treats, separately, of each county of North Wales:—first, of Flintshire; and, lastly, of Denbighshire.

The account of FLINTSHIRE is fuller of information, respecting the existing state of the country, than that of any other county of North Wales. That of DENBIGHSHIRE, on the contrary, is the least so; being rather a detail of the experiments of "Mr. Lovatt," and the recommendations of the Reporter, than of the nature and established practice of Denbighshire. I find in it not one period to place here.

I mean not, however, in saying this, to convey an idea that Mr. K's QUALIFICATIONS, as a REPORTER, are beneath those of the generality of the Board's Authors; the comparison in this respect being in his favor. Mr. Kay is evidently a man of observation, and not unacquainted with agricultural concerns. But his Report of North Wales would seem to have been done under difficulties, and on the spur of an occasion; as appears by the subjoined extract from a letter to the President of the Board, prefixed to his work.

P. i. "In obtaining an account of the present state of husbandry in North Wales, several difficulties occurred. Among others, no distinct map of it could be procured, although I enquired at all the shops in the principal towns, from Edinburgh to Chester. The only one I could obtain, was very obligingly furnished me by a gentleman in the last mentioned city; but it was old and indistinct; also the season of the year in which I commenced the survey, was by no means favourable*. In some instances, no opportunity was allowed me, either of showing or of explaining the plan of the board; and when it was, I sometimes found gentlemen averse from the scheme. These circumstances will account for what, to many readers, may appear material omissions in this performance; and will, I hope, be some apology for the many mistakes or inaccuracies into which I may have fallen."

"* Mr. Kay was appointed late in the season, in consequence of an accident having happened to the person who was originally nominated for that purpose, which prevented his fulfilling his engagement."

FLINT-

FLINTSHIRE.

NATURAL ECONOMY.

CLIMATURE.—P. 2. "The climate is by no means reckoned unfriendly to vegetation. From the situation and narrow form of the county, extending along the shore of the Dee, the sea breezes prevent the snow from lying any length of time. Frost or snow seldom interrupts the operations of husbandry three weeks in a year. Rainy weather is the greatest obstruction, especially where the soil is clay; and yet, the seed time and the harvest are not later than in the best counties in Scotland, and more early than in many northern counties in England. Harvest generally begins about the middle of August, and frequently earlier along the sea coast, and is commonly finished in September."

SURFACE.—P. 1. "The wild, rugged, and mountainous appearance of North Wales, is no where very conspicuously displayed in this county. Excepting the waste lands, it is all well wooded, and enclosed with hedges and other fences. Its surface throughout is varied by hill and dale. From the shore of the Dee, the land ascends gradually, by gentle rising arable hills, which fall by degrees into rich fertile plains. A ridge of higher hills on the south separates it from Denbighshire, which, in many places along their sides, produce corn, and in some parts are cultivated to the summit."

SOIL.—P. 1. "The soil most prevalent along the coast, and in the vales of Clwyd and Mould, is a strong clay, interspersed with gravel, loam and sand."

The prevailing soil of the VALE of CLWYD is of an extraordinary nature:—a pale-colored silt, or mud, rather than clay:—very similar to that of the Vale of Ilchester, in Somersetshire; and, like that, it is superiorly fertile. The Vale of Clwyd is, in this and other respects, dissimilar from that of Chester.

FOSSILS.—On the contrary, the eastern side of Flintshire agrees in soil and substrata with the western side of Cheshire; the two being, in reality, one and the same natural district. See the head *Manure*, ensuing.

POLI-

POLITICAL ECONOMY.

APPROPRIATION.—P. 2. "Although some small portions of the waste lands have lately been divided and inclosed, yet there are many thousand acres still left in their original state, which are very capable of being converted into arable and pasture lands. And, although all the waste lands or commons in North Wales, are denominated mountains, yet many of them are as level as a bowling green; and, in this county, they are, in general, not more hilly than the arable lands, nor is the soil inferior in quality, were it as well cultivated. In Flintshire, the commons are depastured by sheep, black cattle, horses, and asses, belonging to the neighbouring tenants, from which no possible advantage can be derived, as the poor animals, kept in this almost starved state, can never improve; on the contrary, the loss sustained by death throughout North Wales, is incredible. There are many farmers, who, rather than risk their stock on the commons, sell their privilege at the paltry sum of 4d. a head for sheep, during the season, and for other cattle in proportion. The expence of improvement cannot be great, inclosing and draining being the chief things required. Coal and limestone are got in abundance, and at an easy rate."

P. 4. "There are no common fields, or fields in *run rig*, in this county, as I am informed, except between Flint and St. Asaph, and it is in agitation to divide and inclose them. The difference of rent between open and inclosed fields, is estimated at one third."

TITHES.—P. 20. "The church rate in this county is one eleventh of the produce, in place of one tenth. This singularity has existed time immemorial."

TENANTED ESTATES.

EMBANKMENTS.—P. 3. "Two thousand acres were gained from the Dee, by embankment, about 12 years ago, the soil of which is for the most part clay, and is now rented at 20s. *per* acre. Two thousand four hundred more have been recently embanked in the vicinity of Chester, the soil whereof is a pure sand, on which a very great variety of artificial grasses have been sown, but the white clover

clover prevails, and already produces good pasture, appearing as if it would soon equal the best in the county."

TENANCY.—P. 7. "I cannot account satisfactorily for the backward state of agriculture throughout *North Wales*, unless from the want of leases. The lands being generally possessed by tenants at *will*, must, on their part, consequently act as a complete bar to improvement. From this cause, the present indolence and inactivity imputed to farmers, evidently proceed."

RENT.—P. 19. "The average rent of the best land lying along the coast, and in the fertile vales of Clwyd and Mould, is estimated at about 20s. *per* English acre, exclusive of land tax, poor and church rates, &c. which the farmers in many places throughout North Wales pay."

P. 20. "As a proof of the heavy taxes paid in this county, I shall only here mention a small spot of ground, consisting of 13 English acres, and let at 40s. *per* acre.

	£	s.	d.
The nominal rent amounts only to - -	£26	0	0
Poor rates 5s. *per* pound, - -	6	10	0
Church tax, - - -	3	4	0
Land tax, - - -	3	4	0
Assessment for roads, &c. - -	0	13	0
	£39	11	0

Which makes the actual rent above 3*l*. *per* acre."

AGRICULTURE.

FARMS.—P. 8. "The farms in this county are in general small, extending from 20 to 100 acres of arable land. A few amount to 300, and even more. They may average about 50 acres."

HOMESTEADS.—P. 9. "Where the farms are large, the tenants are very well supplied with housing; but the smaller ones, that rent from 20*l*. to 50*l*. a year, of which there are a greater proportion, are very ill accommodated."

PLAN OF MANAGEMENT.—In speaking of *farms*, Mr. K. says—p. 8.—They are "employed in pasture and husbandry in equal proportions, as nearly as could be ascertained; though I am inclined to think, that more than one *half* is kept for pasture."

P. 7. "In so fertile a county as Flintshire, it is to be regretted that no attempts have hitherto been made to introduce green crops, without which no proper system of of husbandry can be pursued; even clover and rye-grass are but seldom cultivated, and then, too, in a very slovenly manner by common farmers. Few pease and beans are sown, nor are potatoes so generally planted as they ought to be. A field of turnips is rarely to be met with."

MANURE.—*Marl.*—P. 10. "Clay marl is found in the eastern parts of Flintshire in great abundance, about three or four feet under the surface, and is laid on grass lands, for pasture and hay, in the month of November, or before winter. It is not of a very rich quality, therefore a great deal is applied, which requires the winter frost to pulverize it; and in the spring, when the lands are dry, they are harrowed with harrows interwoven with brushwood, and generally produce good crops of hay. There is also rock marl in the neighbourhood of Flint, which is most commonly applied to the barley lands, sometimes to pasture and hay, the soil gravel, yielding abundant crops."

CATTLE.—P. 20. "The breeding of *black** cattle in this county, is made a very principal object, and much more attended to than agriculture. Of the breeds there are none distinct or pure, because, as from their near connexion with England, constant supplies are brought of the most noted kinds. From 10*l.* to 12*l.* is the most common price of a good milch cow, yielding from 25 to 30 quarts of milk *per* day, for three or four months after calving, and fed on good pasture. Besides calves of their own breeding, great numbers are bought in, from the neighbouring counties, where the object is chiefly cheese. It is computed, that each cow shall produce 3 cwt. of cheese in a year."

* This epithet, as here applied, is doubly absurd :—it is not only an *expletive;* but is, in this place, *false.*

SHROPSHIRE.

SHROPSHIRE.

THIS county separates most reluctantly into NATURAL DISTRICTS. Notwithstanding the Severn runs through the centre of it, dividing it into nearly equal parts, it is not obviously accompanied by a *rivered vale;* unless at the southern margin, below Bridgenorth, where the vale of Worcester naturally terminates.

In the neighbourhood of its capital,—SHREWSBURY,—a wide extent of vale lands are observable. But they are not determined by boldly rising grounds, on either side.—Round WHITCHURCH, a more confined, but richer, passage is seen; which, however, may be considered as an extension, or appendage of the *district* of *Chester.*—Also, in the environs of LUDLOW, a rich and beautiful plot of country is found. But this, as the sites of STRETTON and BISHOP'S CASTLE,—and the entire southwestern quarter of the county,—is, by locality and natural economy,—*Welch.* While much of the southeastern quarter (the vale lands noticed above excepted) is occupied by *Mines* and *Manufactures.* It is, therefore, the more central parts that are best entitled to consideration, here—particularly,

The VALE OR DISTRICT of SHREWSBURY.—My own knowledge of this district, and the county at large, has arisen thus:—In September 1792, I viewed with attention, the line of country, between Whitchurch and Shrewsbury; where I stopped some days, and looked round its neighbourhood: thence by Coalbrokedale, and Bridgenorth, to Worcester, &c.—In March 1797, I entered it at Tenbury; thence, by Ludlow and Bishop's Castle, to North Wales. And, in April, I re-entered it, by the Welch Pool Road; in my way to Shrewsbury, &c.—In August 1800, I passed directly through the centre of the county; from Whitchurch, by Shrewsbury, and Stretton, to Ludlow, &c.*

The *surface* of the central parts of the county is remarkably flat:—an extended plain, beset with a few hillocks;

* RETROSPECTIVE VIEW of the WESTERN DEPARTMENT.—Since this volume was prepared for the press; namely, in the spring of the present year (1809); I passed through the entire department; —from

locks;—the *Wrekin* being the most conspicuous. Yet even this far seen, and therefore far famed, "mountain," —is, when approached, a very hillock! A proof, this, of the extraordinary levelness of this part of the island.

However, the low lands of Shropshire, tho forming a flat, cultivated country, must necessarily have a considerable degree of *elevation above the tide*; inasmuch as they occupy the highest ground,—the turn of the water,—between the Severn and the Dee; and are situated at one hundred miles' distance from the mouth of the former; that is to say, from the sea at low water.—By the devious course of the Severn, the distance must be much greater.*

In *soils*, as well as in *management*, the low lands of Shropshire resemble, in a striking manner, those of the midland counties;—of whose western margin this tract may be considered as an extension or continuation;—whereby the Lowlands of the central, or midland part of England are united with those of Wales. For the district of Shrewsbury extends, westward, to that of WELCH POOL;—(situated within the political bounds of Wales); which forms part of the rich and well cultivated VALE of MONTGOMERY, (extending from Pool to Newtown) which is altogether *English*.

Like those of other vale districts, the soils of Shropshire are various; as will appear by the Reports. To the westward, and in the environs, of Shrewsbury lies much rich powerful land; even where it is incumbent on coals:—an unusual circumstance.

I am the less solicitous, regarding the rural practices of Shropshire, as it may be considered rather as a *mining* and *manufacturing*, than as an *agricultural* county. Its dairy practice partakes of that of Cheshire; and its arable management (as has been said) of that of the midland counties. Nevertheless, it will be proper to pay due attention to such facts and suggestions concerning it, as may be deemed worthy of preservation; and which appear in the two Reports that have been printed by the Board of Agriculture.

"GENERAL

—from Manchester to Chester;—thence, by Wrexham and Ellesmere, to Shrewsbury (a line of country I had not before traced); and thence through Worcestershire, Glocestershire, and North Somersetshire, into the more Western Department;—in order to correct my judgement, and clear up a few doubtful points.

* See Plymley's Shropshire; art. Inland Navigation, ensuing.

"GENERAL VIEW

OF THE

AGRICULTURE

OF THE

COUNTY OF SALOP.

WITH

OBSERVATIONS ON THE MEANS OF ITS IMPROVEMENT.

BY J. BISHTON,

OF KILSAL, SHROPSHIRE.

1794."

THIS is the ORIGINAL "REPORT" of Shropshire;—if Report it may be deemed. Of the twentyseven pages, of which the *body* of the work consists, not seven relate, immediately, to the "Agriculture of the County of Salop."—The rest are filled with effusions relating to the writer's own practice and opinions;—some of which are entitled to a hearing.

The President of the Board being dissatisfied with the primary performance, sent a list of queries to the author; and his answers, to some of them, are given in a "postscript;"—by which means, the work is extended to thirty-eight pages.

The QUALIFICATIONS of this Reporter (for such let us designate him) may be gathered from his production. He is evidently a *professional* man of considerable experience; and has, formerly, cultivated a farm of full extent. He is, probably, more the man of business, than the—bookmaker. Yet on subjects that particularly engage his attention, we find no want of words.

His MODE of SURVEY cannot be an object of enquiry. His knowledge of the practice of Shropshire, no doubt, has been acquired in the prosecution of his profession.

No map.

SUBJECT

SUBJECT THE FIRST.

NATURAL ECONOMY.

SOILS.—Regarding this subject of Report, Mr. Bishton may be supposed to be professionally conversant.—P. 7. "From Over-Arely, in the south-east, to Melverley, in the north-west, the navigable river Severn divides this county nearly into two equal parts; the north-east side of which is chiefly of a turnip soil, intermixed with a tolerable proportion of meadow and pasture. The banks of the Severn, which are often overflowed, produce hay in great plenty. On the south west side of the river Severn, from Allerbury, about eight miles wide down to Cressage, the lands are chiefly pretty good, and contain pasture, wheat, and turnip land, but very variable; each sort lying in small quantities, and many farms containing each sort. That from Cressage, about six miles wide to Bridgenorth, and from thence to Cleobury and Ludlow, is chiefly mixt soil upon clay, and part thin.

"The remainder of the county, and lying more to the south-west side, is very variable, mostly thin soil, some upon clay, other upon rock, extensive tracts of hills, and waste; upon the whole, there is in this county, all sorts of land, except chalk and flint."

Concerning the *elevation*, the *turn* of *surface*, or the *climature*, which those lands enjoy, we have no account.

MINERALS, &c.—P. 7. "It abounds with coal pits, and has also valuable mines of iron, &c. a description of which, however, does not come within the scope of this Report."

And, in answer to the queries put to him, Mr. B. in his postscript adds,—P. 37. "There are very considerable mines of lead, iron, and coal, and also lime, rock and building stone, some of which are worked to considerable profit, by the liberality of the owners granting long leases, which encourage opulent companies, to search for, and work the same."

SUBJECT

SUBJECT THE SECOND.

POLITICAL ECONOMY.

STATE of APPROPRIATION.—P. 8. "This county does not contain much common field lands, most of those having been formerly enclosed, and before acts of parliament for that purpose were in use; but the inconvenience of the property being detached and intermixed in small parcels, is severely felt, as is also the inconvenience of having the farm buildings in villages."—And in his postscript, the Reporter replies to the queries sent him,—P. 30. "In comparison of many other counties this may be called an enclosed one, particularly in respect of field land; yet there certainly remain many commons, though few of large extent, which would still pay well the expense of enclosure. One of the most considerable is the Morf, near the town of Bridgenorth.

"As to the extent of the commons, I would beg leave to advise, that a surveyor may be sent into each county, with instructions to take as many lines over each common, as would pretty nearly ascertain the quantities; this method would not cost the Agricultural Board more than thirty guineas, on an average, for each county; and at the same time and expence, the worth of the wastes may be ascertained, by supposing them in a state for enclosing, for in their open state the value of the best is but trifling*."

On the "*Improvement* of *Commons*," Mr. Bishton speaks like a man of sense and feeling, whose mind has reached a maturity of judgement, by a length of observation and experience,—*on the spot*. His sentiments widely differ from those engendered *in closets*,—with which well meaning people have been long amused, and some, it is to be feared, misled.

P. 24. "On this head surely it is not necessary, at this time of day, for myself or any other person, to say any thing more than, inclose them all as soon as convenient. The idea of leaving them in their unimproved state to bear chiefly gorse bushes, and fern, is now completely scouted, except by a very few, who have falsely conceived that

* Have the Board profited by this hint?

that the inclosing of them is an injury to the poor; but if those persons had seen as much of the contrary effects in that respect, as I have, I am fully persuaded their opposition would at once cease. Let those who doubt, go round the commons now open, and view the miserable huts, and poor, ill cultivated, impoverished spots erected, or rather *thrown together*, and inclosed by themselves, for which they pay 6d. or 1s. per year, which, by loss of time both to the man and his family, affords them a very trifle towards their maintenance, yet operates upon their minds as a sort of independence; this idea leads the man to lose many days work, by which he gets a habit of indolence; a daughter kept at home to milk a poor half starved cow, who being open to temptations, soon turns harlot, and becomes a distressed ignorant mother, instead of making a good useful servant. The surrounding farmers, by this means, have neither industrious labourers, or servants, therefore, the commons with the cottagers around, become a great burden instead of a convenience; for most certain it is, that in all the countries where this is the case, the labourers are generally indolent,—and the contrary is the case where they live under the farmer, in comfortable cottages, with only a quarter of an acre of land, work every day in the year, and have their children taught to read, and put out to labour *early*. This I have been a witness too, not only in my own parish, where we enclosed a common and fields 25 years ago, but in many other places since, where I have been concerned. To do any thing for a poor man and his family (who are to be maintained by their own labour) which gives them the habit of indolence, is the same as taking the rich man's income, for both alike become helpless."

These arguments militate, with nearly equal force, against the scheme of cottagers keeping cows,—on inclosed lands.

PROVISIONS.—P. 38. "Butter, from one shilling to fourteen-pence per pound; the price of that article, is the best tacit proclamation of the luxury and prosperity of this kingdom; for I remember within the compass of forty-five years, families in my neighbourhood, supplied with butter, the year through, at four-pence per pound."

TITHES.—P. 31. "But little tithe is taken in kind—mostly by fair and equitable compositions, which are in in some places renewed every year, in others, are let for a longer term. I have, within the distance of twenty miles round my own neighbourhood, for these last twenty years,

years, valued yearly a great deal of tithe, which has been let to the occupiers of the respective farms from which it was issuable, and within that period, the same practice has become pretty general."

ROADS.—To this subject, Mr. Bishton appears to have paid extraordinary attention; and has spoken his sentiments upon it, at some length. Much of what he has said is well entitled to a place, here. The folly of appointing, annually, ignorant, dilatory, parochial Surveyors has, it is true, been repeatedly brought forward; but it cannot be too generally condemned.

P. 18. "The roads in this county, both turnpike and private, are generally bad; the private ones, particularly in the clay part of the county, are almost impassable to any but the inhabitants, notwithstanding there have been many acts of parliament, with a view to make them perfectly good, which end, if it could be obtained, would be a most important step to improvement in agriculture There are already sufficient resources given by divers acts of parliament, for enforcing statute duty, and raising the supplies by assessments upon the inhabitants; but in several of the arrangements, I humbly conceive, the acts are very deficient, and which occasions the general failure in the desirable end for which they were passed.

"In lieu of surveyors in each parish, (who are generally chosen in turn, and consequently have neither time nor experience sufficient to act properly, and are generally not inclined to exert themselves by enforcing the duty, &c.) I would propose for the magistrates to have power to appoint a proper surveyor with a salary, who should act under their direction, and be amenable to them for their conduct; such surveyor, to undertake the arrangement of a certain district, (say 10 miles square) whose duty it should be, to employ deputies, to call in and see the statute duty done under his direction: by this means the forming of the roads, which is the first principle, would be done in the most approved method, and the statute duty regularly called out. There may be an inspector, an inhabitant in each parish, appointed, and chosen yearly, whose interest it would be, as well as his duty, to act as a check upon the general surveyor and his deputy; this office being easy, might be filled by one of the most liberal persons in the parish. I apprehend that an arrangement of this sort would very soon insure good private roads. And something like the following would procure us good turnpike roads also."

This

This desirable effect is proposed to be obtained by erecting a weighing machine, at every turnpike gate, and regulating the load, to be carried, on each width of felly; not by the *number* of *horses* employed; but by the actual *weight* of the *load* to be sustained:—an accurate mean of regulation, which science and common sense require. A ton is a definite term which is mathematically understood; but the power of a horse is altogether indeterminated; one horse being possessed of twice the power of another.

Mr. B. enters into particulars respecting his plan. But his remarks are too *wordy* for insertion, here. And the following items of his proposed regulations, simply set down, will be more intelligible to the reader, than his pages of *broken* law language.

Waggons.

16 inch fellies to carry 8 tons, in summer, or 7 tons, in winter.

9 inch fellies,—rolling 16 inches,—$6\frac{1}{2}$ tons, in summer,—6 in winter.

9 inch fellies,—6 tons, in summer,—$5\frac{1}{2}$ in winter.

6 inch fellies,—rolling 11 inches,—$5\frac{1}{2}$ tons in summer,—5 in winter.

6 inch fellies,—$4\frac{1}{4}$ in summer,—$3\frac{3}{4}$ in winter.

Less than 6 inches,—$3\frac{3}{4}$ in summer,—$3\frac{12}{20}$ in winter.

Carts.

9 inch fellies to carry 3 tons, in summer, or $2\frac{3}{4}$, in winter.

6 inch fellies,—$2\frac{12}{20}$, in summer,—$2\frac{7}{20}$, in winter.

Less than 6 inches,—$1\frac{3}{4}$ in summer,—$1\frac{12}{20}$ in winter:—*including the weights of the carriages.* And every hundred weight, above those standards, to pay ten shillings.

I insert the above scale without comment; excepting that the weights appear to me to be too high. This, however, may easily be rectified. The thought, and the attention bestowed upon it, do Mr. Bishton very great credit.

To enforce these regulations, Mr. B. proposes that, after a certain day to be named, in a law for the above purposes, every turnpike road, without a weighing machine, shall be *free*.

The *good effects* of such regulations, Mr. B. enumerates, in the following sensible manner.—P. 22. "The weighing engines will sufficiently prevent carriages of all sorts being over loaded, which will be a preservation of the road, whereas, the restraint upon the number of horses does not answer the purpose; for a short and overpowered team, does

does more damage to the roads, than a great number of horses, which draw easy, and consequently pass along much quicker. That disagreeable restraint will be thereby made unnecessary, which empowers and encourages some poor indolent wretches to wander about the country, with their ready printed notices, to catch a prey, which when got, is lavished away in drunkenness, debauchery, and disorder; and if they fail in their lawful attempt, which is often the case, and perhaps distressed to the greatest degree, being despised by persons of all denominations, pursue poaching and fowl stealing, which lead to greater acts of thievery, of which there are many instances; for all the convictions are grounded upon the poor wretches, as above described, being by the law allowed to be the credible witnesses, who obtain the reward to the amount of 5*l.* or more, when the team owner's servant or servants are all deemed perjured: so that as the act now stands, no one is safe from these convictions.

"The occupiers of farms in general, particularly those upon the middling sized ones, find themselves very much oppressed and injured by the law now subsisting for regulating the turnpike roads, by their being restrained from drawing more than four horses in waggons, the fellies of the wheels thereof being under six inches broad. Were farmers permitted to draw any number of horses, it would be of great public utility in lowering the price of those animals, which is now enormously high; the farmer would find it his interest, as formerly, to keep breeding mares, which, with the colts they breed, may be made useful great part of the year, provided they may be worked easy. The law as it now stands, acts nearly as a prohibition to farmers breeding horses; for a breeding mare, or a colt under 5 years old, is not fit to draw one of four in a waggon, with no more than 60 bushels of barley or wheat, which is the common load of the Shropshire or Staffordshire farmers, neither of which being more than two tons, which is considerably under the weight the present act allows to be drawn on the turnpike roads in winter. Before the said turnpike laws were in force, the farmer's team, to draw his 60 bushels of wheat or barley, consisted of six in number, two of which, at least, were mares either in foal or sucklers, two colts, one of them two, the other three years old, which were never oppressed or hurt by their work; consequently a succession came on, and the owner had one or two good sound colts to sell off every year to the harness or draught, as they best suited."

P. 23.

P. 23. "Another evil occasioned by this law is, that such farmers are obliged to keep horses of the largest size, which consume the produce of much land, by eating a large quantity of corn, when the smaller horses, working easy, seldom eat any."

Mr. Bishton's laudable anxiety, to put his plan in execution, is evident in his concluding proposal.—P. 23. "It is humbly conceived, that upon this principle, a law for regulating the roads may be enacted, so as to answer every good design of the present, and at the same time relieve those individuals who are exceedingly injured, and also be of general utility. I hope I shall not be thought to digress too much from the subject of agriculture, when it is considered, that good roads are the first improvement to be made upon an estate, where the roads are bad; and I verily believe, that a petition to parliament, to obtain the above alterations, would be signed by every person interested in the counties of Salop and Stafford. I have taken the liberty to send one enclosed, for the society's inspection, and if some such method shall be recommended by the society, I beg to be considered at their service, to send a clerk round the counties, for the signatures of those who may approve of the measure."

SUBJECT THE THIRD.

RURAL ECONOMY.

DIVISION THE FIRST.

TENANTED ESTATES,

Their IMPROVEMENT and MANAGEMENT.

ESTATES.—P. 31. "The *sizes* of both the estates and farms in this county are very various;—here are estates of noblemen and of several commoners, which cover from ten thousand to twenty-five thousand acres each; while there are an infinite number of freeholders and yeomen's estates of all inferior sizes."

Tenures.—P. 31. "There is much copyhold tenure, but of easier customs than in the neighbouring counties."

IMPROVE-

IMPROVEMENT of ESTATES.—On *Proprietors* improving tenanted Lands.—There is much good sense, arising no doubt out of practical knowledge, comprized in the subjoined remarks.—P. 27. "Where gentlemen have agents who are experienced in husbandry, they cannot do better than to suffer such to assist the tenants, by paying for part of their draining, marling, watering, embanking, &c. for which they may, in proper and fair time, obtain from 10 to 20 per cent. for their money: but, extraordinary it is, that very few gentlemen, will come into this measure, of assisting their tenants with money for improvements; not even those who are satisfied with 3 per cent. for their capital, when they purchase additions to their estates."

Embanking.—In the following observations, on this cardinal improvement of landed property, in many situations, there is nothing new. But they show that the most valuable improvements may be rendered abortive, under the guidance of ignorance; and that, by a more enlarged knowledge of the subject, they may be rendered superiorly beneficial.

P. 16. "There is another improvement, which is carried on to great perfection, upon the lands subject to the floods of the rivers Severn and Vernieu, in Montgomeryshire, bordering upon this county, by embankment; but the banks should be fixed at a discretional distance from the side of the river, so as when embanked on both sides, the course of the flood may not be too much narrowed. In many instances it should be from 40 to 50 yards; yet there has been a great inconvenience attending this improvement, for though the produce of hay, &c. has by this means been all saved, yet this land has been found to be much less fertile by the water being kept off, and in some places it has occasioned the banks to be disregarded; but there is an easy remedy for this, by fixing at proper distances, troughs with swing gates or valves, by which the water may be suffered to overflow as usual, from November to March inclusive, and be shut out in the summer months; thus the fertility would sustain no injury, and the produce be preserved.—This is an improvement of great utility, and more neglected than that of floating.

"Consider for a moment the immense quantity of hay, as well as pasturage, that may by this practice be saved particularly in wet seasons, and in most situations at a small expence. I may venture to say, that many thousand acres may be preserved at from 3d. to 6d. per yard in length, but 10s. per yard is trifling, compared with the improve-

improvement which may be made in many situations. There is a bar to this improvement, however, in many places, by property being intermixed, for which reason there should be commissioners appointed by parliament, with power to make such improvements, when called upon so to do, by the persons forming a majority of landed property in any certain district, which commissioners, should have such power as the commissioners of the Deytheur and Street-marshal in the Montgomeryshire Inclosure Act, where near 3000*l.* has been laid out for that purpose, and by which many thousand acres are preserved from floods."

On the banks of the Severn, in the neighbourhood of Glocester, the practice above recommended is in use. See the RURAL ECONOMY of GLOCESTERSHIRE.

Draining.—P. 8. "There is much draining done by the best farmers, both with stone and wood."—P. 17. "But in many situations, particularly in clay countries, the materials, as stone, &c. are very expensive, occasioned by getting, and the distance it is to be carried; and thin soil upon clay requires the drains in many places to be not more than from 6 to 8 yards asunder, which consumes large quantities of materials. I have made what I call, a brick arch, for that purpose, full an inch thick and a foot long, nearly of the shape of a ridge tile, but being not more than 5 inches wide at bottom, and 6 inches semi-diameter, it cannot possibly be used in building; but such having been made at a brick kiln, the excise-officer thought them taxable, and charged them 2s. 6d. per thousand, as common bricks."—P. 18. "These arches may be made, when common bricks are at 15s. per thousand, without tax, at about 30s. per thousand, which will lay a cavity of six by five inches, and near 340 yards long."

Mr. B's directions for using these draining tiles are by no means accurate. Nevertheless, in the hands of an intelligent practical drainer, they may in some cases, be very eligible.

Irrigation.—P. 9. "There are some meadows floated, by preserving levels from streams of water, but little of this improvement is done in a masterly manner; though floating has been long in practice by a few of the best farmers, and the use of the spirit level is known by many." What is to be understood by "preserving levels?" Is the practice of floating "upward," or "downward," here meant?

For *Sodburning*, see TILLAGE.

EXECU-

EXECUTIVE MANAGEMENT.—*Tenancy*.—P. 27. "Leases have of late years been much exploded by gentlemen of landed property, many of whom having formerly granted excessive long terms, have been induced, by the injury sustained thereby, and some other reasons, to object to any lease! This is a contrary extreme, and to obviate that difficulty, I have formed a lease (a copy of which is sent to the honourable Board) which has been so fortunate as to meet with the approbation of both landlord and tenants in general; the former being left in some degree at liberty, and the latter made confident of having an allowance for their improvements, from which they may not have had a proper return of profit, before they were compelled to quit."

Surely, a lease, which promised so much good to the landed interest, ought not to have been thrown by, as waste paper. An abstract of it, at least, should have been published.

AGRICULTURE.

FARMS.—P. 31. "The farms are as various," (as Estates) "from that of from one to five hundred acres on the eastern side of the county, to the little farm of twenty acres on the borders of Wales."

PLAN of MANAGEMENT.—P. 8. "The culture is as various," (as the soils are) "some exceeding good and other as bad; and I am sorry to say, more of the latter than the former; and the defect arises from a variety of causes—the want of judgment in cultivation—of sufficient property—of confidence in landlords—of sobriety and industry."—How much information (accurate or otherwise) is contained in those few lines!

Mr. B. then proceeds to give an account of his own practice,—"upon 400 acres, being part of a farm which was in my own occupation, for many years" (p. 11). But tho it takes up no inconsiderable portion of his Report "of the Agriculture of the County of Salop," it contains nothing new or excellent;—not even as a *paper* relating to the practice of an individual;—and is altogether out of place, in a Report to a public Board, concerning the established practice of a county.

WORKPEOPLE.—"The folly of Shropshire exceeds that of the MIDLAND COUNTIES, in regard to the *excessive quantity*

tity of *beverage* allowed to farm laborers.—P. 36. "The allowance of beer, in this county, both winter and summer, is generally given to those who take their work, in the winter 3 quarts each, in summer 4, and in harvest from 5 to 8 quarts of strong and small beer.—This customary allowance is excessive; but there are few parts of England, where the harvest is got in with such spirit and expedition: but the custom of such excessive drinking ought to be checked, and has been done in the best governed families."

WORKING ANIMALS.—P. 35. "In the strong lands, four or five *horses* are used to a plough, or six or eight *oxen;* the oxen are preferred for ploughing in the strong lands, but horses for the road business; that being the case, horses are best adapted for small farms, as oxen are for ploughing upon large ones."

Horses.—P. 11. "There is no particular breed, indeed very few foals are bred in this county; the supply is chiefly from Derbyshire and Leicestershire, by which means there are many valuable teams; and those farmers who can afford to purchase, find it their interest to have such, occasioned by the restraint laid by the turnpike laws from not drawing more than four horses."

See also the section *Cattle*, ensuing.

MANURES.—P. 8. "There is scarcely an instance of folding sheep, the commons being poor, and the farms chiefly small; the flocks are also small. The manure is chiefly farm-yard dung, lime, and marl."

TILLAGE.—P. 8. "The tillage part of what is called the wheat land, or mixt soil upon clay, is generally very ill cultivated by a fallow, prepared only by the first ploughing being performed in May or June, the next in August, and in September it is ploughed and harrowed, therefore sowed in the latter end of October; by this mode the land is not reduced, and consequently the seeds and weeds not killed. But it is fair to observe, that the mistaken people who cultivate thus, produce a reason for their conduct, by saying, that if they made their land too fine, it would produce less wheat, by the Autumnal rains beating the fine land into a crust, and thereby stopping vegetation."

This established "reason" corroborates, in my mind, the idea of our ancestors having raised commonfield lands (which were obliged to be fallowed every third year) into high sharp ridges, to prevent the malady here spoken of. See MIDLAND COUNTIES,—*Minute* 21.

Sodburning.—The subjoined account (unsatisfactorily as it is given) conveys ideas that are highly interesting to arable farmers, and is new to the kingdom at large. The Shropshire practice (if such is really the established practice of that county) may well be considered as a new or distinct method of reducing tough sward, by the mean of fire; and of meliorating rough grounds, in general. It does not reasonably follow, that, because the sward is separated from the soil, and exposed in grassy clods to a degree of heat, it should be reduced to *ashes.* This idea, it is true, I have had occasion to bring forward repeatedly (see NORTHERN DEPART.) but never in the striking manner in which it here appears.

P. 9. "There is some paring and burning done here in the thin soil, or sour swards upon clay; but the paring is performed near two inches thick, the sward is laid round a small faggot of wood, large enough, when burnt, to blacken and scorch the sward reared round it, these burners not holding it good to reduce it to red ash. Thus, in its coarse, but scorched state, it is spread upon the land when ploughed, being first got into rows to make way for the plough; and most certainly these blackened lumps, &c. do often produce an extraordinary crop of wheat, though upon land not worth more than seven shillings per acre, and the succeeding crops generally answer as well."

HOPS.—P. 36. "Hops are cultivated on a small part of the Herefordshire side of this county."

GRASS LANDS.—P. 9. "That for hay is seldom manured, except one field next the house, and that with such shovellings as are got near it by scraping near the house."

This sort of defective information may lead to error, but can scarcely be of any real utility. If it had been shown that hay grounds, in Shropshire, are universally or generally (except as above excepted) *mown every year,*—and of course without any intervention of summer *pasturage,*—yet throw out abundant crops, *without manure,*—the fact would have been highly interesting; tho discredited, perhaps, by the hay farmers round the metropolis.

There are, nevertheless, well ascertained instances, that have come within my own knowledge, in which hay grounds have borne *fair* crops, every year, during a length of years; without any *manure,* or any advantage from *pasturage,* except what the aftergrass has afforded. And what is still more interesting,—those who occupy such grounds (deep loams of a naturally fertile quality) *refrain* to manure them, under a conviction that, altho manuring might

might encrease the crop, for a few years, it would afterwards be injurious to them. That is to say—lands, once manured, will not afterward bear mowing, every year, without a repetition of manure. These facts and this opinion, however, I throw out, here, merely to agitate a most important topic in Rural Economy *.

CATTLE.—P. 10. "*Neat* † cattle, on the north east side the river Severn, are an inferior sort of the Lancashire long horn, in general for the dairies; the south eastern part of the district being chiefly light turnip land, the clover and pasture are mostly appropriated to the dairies, which are small; the cheese is rather ordinary, as much butter is gathered, which is taken off at a good price in the manufacturing towns. On the north west side of this district, and bordering upon Cheshire, the dairies are much larger and chiefly for cheese. Most farmers rear a few calves yearly for the regular supplies of their dairies, and the breed is by some made better, by the purchase of bulls from Leicestershire and Lancashire.

"On the south west side the river Severn, small dairies are kept both for butter and cheese; many calves are reared,—the bull calves are cut, and many heifers splayed; from three years old to six, they are worked easily by drawing double, eight in a team to a single furrow plough. The capital farmers do not work them more than six hours at a time, and in seed time, when more expedition is wanted, they change them by working one team in the morning and another in the afternoon; by this method, as they say, they get their team labour done at a small expense, for their oxen being sold lean, at from 25*l.* to 35*l.* per pair, they reckon their improvement to pay them near 2*l.* a year each. This is the sort of oxen that the Northamptonshire and Leicestershire graziers buy in the autumn at Shrewsbury, Bridgenorth, Bishop's-Castle, and Much-Wenlock fairs."—This might be termed lumping information.

DAIRY.—See the foregoing extract; to which may be added the following:

P. 38. "This county is not famous for dairying; but the best dairy-wives make about eight pounds of a cow, but those make much more, who are near enough to a town

* I have conceived a theory to account for this believed effect;—at least, on deep, sound, well bottomed lands. But it is not sufficiently matured to be ventured abroad, in this place.

† Another aukward expletive. See p. 168.

town to sell their milk, and those who keep new milched cows in winter, and sell their skim'd milk by the quart."

SHEEP.—P. 10. "The breeding flocks are few and small, where there are no commons, but are various in their sorts, as the fancy of the farmer leads him, for in this county there are sheep kept of most of the sorts in England; but those *farmers who have commons*, (?*) generally keep of a size from 11 lb. to 14 lb. per quarter, shear about 2 lb. of wool each, worth about 1s. 6d. per pound. Upon some commons, the aged wethers do not require much assistance in the winter, but the ewes and lambs, with the yearling sheep, are either wintered from home or kept in their own farms. This sort, which is kept to stock commons, is generally sold off or fed upon their own turnips, at from four to five years old."

GENERAL REMARK.

The original Report from Shropshire shows that a man of matured experience can scarcely sit down to write, on practical subjects, on which his experience has arisen, let the paucity of his matter, and the manner of expressing himself, be what they may, without furnishing some portion of valuable information.

* This wants explaining.
There are, I understand, on the verge of Delamere Forest, men who depasture some thousands of sheep upon it; without occupying any cultivated lands:—a practice which remains to be examined.

"GENERAL VIEW

OF THE

AGRICULTURE

OF

SHROPSHIRE:

WITH OBSERVATIONS.

DRAWN UP FOR THE CONSIDERATION OF

THE BOARD OF AGRICULTURE AND INTERNAL IMPROVEMENT.

BY JOSEPH PLYMLEY, M. A.

ARCHDEACON OF SALOP, IN THE DIOCESE OF HEREFORD, AND HONORARY MEMBER OF THE BOARD.

1803."

THE REPORTER, in a Preface, makes an apology of some length (and somewhat supererogatorily it would seem) for his—a Clergyman's—undertaking a work of a temporal nature. Rather, surely, ought some excuse to have been made for a deficiency of practical knowledge, respecting the leading subjects of the undertaking. But a spirit of philanthropy which is conspicuous throughout the work, was, doubtlessly, the amiable motive that induced the Archdeacon of Salop to comply with the request of the Board. The "Preface" closes with the following explicit statement.—P. xviii. "Having said thus much in explanation of the propriety with which a Clergyman may appear in a work of this kind, I have to add, that I am very little of a practical farmer, but, living chiefly in the country,

try, I have, from an early age, thought more or less of the improvement of its artificial state. In the parochial visitations of my Archdeaconry, a district for observation has occurred to me; and in inquiring into the state of the several parishes, facts, connected with the cultivation of the country, have come before me.

"The communications I have been directly favoured with, and those copied from such of the Original Reports for this county as were returned to the Board with marginal remarks, as well as the parts of the Original Report itself, will be given as quotations, as often as they occur, with the names of the gentlemen to whom the public are under obligations on this account. *Longnor, May* 25, 1801."

And the same candor is shown in the "conclusion" of the work:—together evincing a degree of ingenuousness that has not been excelled, by any other Reporter whose work has yet passed under review.—P. 354.—"Whatever has occurred to myself as matter of improvement, has been incidentally mentioned in the different sections, so that I have little to add in the conclusion of this Report, except an apology for not having confined myself so strictly to the subject of each section as the plan may seem to require; but, besides that the ideas were naturally suggested by the section then under consideration, in a work that is more likely to be looked into occasionally, than read through*, it may be better, perhaps, to repeat some ideas, as matter of explanation, or to guard against mistakes, than take it for granted that every division will be consulted, or brought to bear together upon the reader's mind. So far as I have been favoured with assistance, I have expressed my sense of its value as I went along. I have given every respectable opinion that was handed to me, either through the Board, or as matter of private favour, without encumbering the same with any observations of my own. If I appear to differ with any of those opinions, I say of those instances, and of every part of the Report for which I am responsible, that I sincerely and earnestly desire it may be regarded as a work of no pretensions on my part, beyond that of having attempted to give such information as may lead to inquiry. This county has not many legitimate objects of an Agricultural Report, strictly so called."—The fact is—Shropshire

* Rather the reverse, I conceive.

shire is rather a *mining* and *manufacturing*, than an *agricultural* county*.

The principal *economical* CONTRIBUTORS to this Report are—

EDWARD HARRIES, Esquire, "an active and attentive landlord of very considerable property"—"whose attention to and experience in the management of his valuable estates give weight to his observations."

The late Reverend Mr. LLOYD of Aston;—"who was a member of the Board, and whose opinions derived weight from his judicious management of his extensive property."

Mr. WILLIAM REYNOLDS of Colebrokedale; who, from what can be *gathered* from sundry parts of the Report, appears to be an Iron-master of eminence; also a canalist; miner; and *practical mineralogist.*

The Reverend Mr. ROWLEY.

The Reverend Mr. WILDING of All Stretton.

Mr. TELFORD, Engineer.

Mr. BOWMAN—"a respectable land agent."

Mr. FLAVEL of Alderbury.

Mr. TENCH of Broomfield—"a practical farmer of eminence."

Mr. PRICE, Mr. POWYS, Mr. COTES, &c.

In the *editorship* of this Report, there is cause of censure. The marginal notes of the original Reports, together with extracts from the original itself, and the private communications of the friends of the Reporter, are inserted, miscellaneously (in their respective sections)—as *text;* but without any other identification, than the name of the writer appended, in a note, *at the end* of each quotation:—for which name the reader has to *search* over two or three pages, perhaps, before he can learn even the *name* of him whose writing he is about to read; and, when he has found the name, it may be as totally unknown to him, as the *pretension* of its owner is to write on the subject under discussion:—beside this method being most liable to typographical errors; as will appear. It is true, that, after having repeatedly perused the book, he may have caught, incidentally, a few traits of the several writers,

* A passage in Mr. Plymley's Preface accords with this conclusion. —P. xvi.—"The scope of Shropshire farming being so general, and so much intermixed with improvements of all kinds from other parts of the kingdom, seemed to afford little room for appropriate information."

writers, and have made out an imperfect catalogue of their *qualifications*, like that which I have formed, above

Surely, the Board should have *required*, of its several Reporters, some explicit information regarding the *authenticity* of what is published—"by authority of the Board."

Were it requisite to speak of the *manner* of the Reporter, whose acquirements as a writer on Rural affairs are now under consideration, it might be said that, on practical subjects, his style is too diffusive, and frequently incorrect. But on subjects that are connected with the moral duties and well being of society, Mr. Plymley is more happy:—his philanthropy toward the lower classes, and his humanity to even the *animals of society*, (in one solitary instance excepted!) will be found, in the ensuing extracts, to infuse a well moderated warmth, and a facility of expression, into his language. The performance, altogether, (except as above excepted) abundantly evince the benevolent disposition of the Archdeacon of Salop.

The number of pages, three hundred and sixty six.

A small sketch map of the *hundreds* of Shropshire is prefixed!

SUBJECT THE FIRST.

NATURAL ECONOMY.

ELEVATION and SURFACE.—To these topics (blended with soils and fossils) the Reporter has appropriated some pages. The following short extract contains all that appears to be of sufficient importance to be transcribed.—P. 44. "Though no part of this county can be called flat, generally speaking, yet the N. E. parts are comparatively so, and as contrasted with the hills on its southern and western borders, leading on to the Welsh mountains, and with the hills of Derbyshire and Staffordshire to the E. unite with the still more level county of Chester, in forming a great plain, or valley. The Wrekin hill has been celebrated, from the circumstance of its detached situation, I should suppose, rather than its height. It rises in a flat part of the county. North of it, are excrescences of rock, and partial swells; to the S. W. the hills are more frequent;

quent; and on the W. and S. W. borders, there is a succession of hill and dale."

CLIMATURE.—On this subject, the Reporter has adduced some *interesting* particulars. But, in this as in other instances, his strictures possess more of the semblance, than the reality, of *importance*.

P. 37. "The climate, throughout this county, is so far altered by the irregularity of its soil and surface, that there is a considerable difference. The harvest on the eastern side, where the land is warm and flat, is frequently ripe about a fortnight sooner than in the middle of the county, where the vales are extensive, but where the surface is less light, and the bottom often clayey; and hay and grain are both gathered earlier there than on the western side, where the vales" (valleys) "are narrow, and the high lands frequent and extensive, although the ground is not in general so stiff, and lies for the most part on a semi-rock full of fissures. The easterly winds prevail in spring, and those from the west in autumn; but I believe the easterly winds are the most regular, those from the west generally blowing for a series of years (five or six perhaps) strong and frequent, and then for somewhat near a similar space less often and less violent. The same may be said of wet and dry seasons; but the periods of both appear to be much shorter."

The above is a literal transcript. To it is subjoined "a list of days upon which there was no rain, and upon which there was *some* rain within the day and night, for six years;"—(by whom is not mentioned). This table is, of course, no guide to the quantity of rain which fell. It, nevertheless serves to show that Shropshire is involved in a humid atmosphere. The writer adds—"I do not know of any rain guages that have been kept, in this county."

P. 39. "Mr. AIKIN, in his tour, 1797, observes, that common pluviameters afford no sufficient proof of the quantity of rain that falls in a country, because the most partial showers are often the heaviest; so that an inch or two of rain may be gained in one spot, whilst none has been received at the distance of a mile, or less; but he conceives, that proper observations made at the Iron Bridge, near Coalbrook-dale, would ascertain the superfluous water from about 1260 square miles. I have now before me an account of the height of the Severn upon each day, Sundays excepted, from October 17, 1789, to October 17, 1795, registered by the direction of Mr. WILLIAM REYNOLDS at Coal-port, and which will be inserted in in the Chapter upon Canals."—Some remarks on this suggestion will appear under the ensuing head, *Canals*.

The Reporter adds, p. 40—"an account of two thermometers;"—the one noted in Devonshire,—the other in Staffordshire. But so much depends on instruments,—the aspects in which they are placed,—and the several *accompaniments* which attend them, that I refrain from inserting it, here. The disparity of heat, in those two situations, I *find*, by the account given, is, on a par of several months' observation, about 7½ *degrees* in favor of Devonshire; but on what *scale* is not said.

WATERS.—After being informed that—"the river Severn passes thro the county, from N.W. to S.E.;"—(p. 82) "the contributory rivers within the county"—(p. 85) are enumerated;—amounting to—"a hundred or more rivers and brooks, or parts of rivers and brooks." (p. 88.) How much unnecessary labor must have been bestowed, on this unprofitable detail; which fills several pages. The graver, not the pen, is the appropriate instrument wherewith to delineate brooks and rivulets;—in cases, let it here be said, where delineations of them are requisite.

Whatever is *useful*, belonging to the rivers of Shropshire, will be found under the head, *Inland Navigation*, ensuing; excepting what relates to

Salmon.—In the section, Waters (of the Report) several species of fishes, that inhabit them, are mentioned,—to the number of twenty two ordinary species of English fresh-water fishes. The salmon, only, is noticeable, here, p. 84.—They "come up the river" (Severn) "with the first flush of water after Michaelmas, and are in high season till May. This fish often sells now from 1s. 6d. to 2s. 6d. per pound. Some years ago it was cheaper; but in the beginning of the last century, it was full as dear as as it is now, and was almost entirely bought up for the London market at that price; which is extraordinary, considering the value of money at that time, and the length of time necessary to convey it. At a former period, salmon is reported to have been so plentiful at Shrewsbury, that stipulations were made in the indentures of apprenticeship, fixing the number of days in a week on which the master may serve it as food to his apprentice."

Admitting the authenticity of this statement, it may be remarked, that, notwithstanding the present scarcity of this valuable fish, in the rivers of England, we may at least hope that it will only be temporary. It is much to be feared, however, that the quietude and security which those

those migrators, naturally, and formerly, enjoyed, have been broken in upon, of later years, by human arts,—by mining, manufactures, and river navigations; and still more, perhaps, by the unwarrantable traps and snares that are set for them, by millers, (of various descriptions) and *others*.

The *lakelets*, meres, or pools, with which Shropshire, as Cheshire, abounds, are enumerated p. 89. The largest (which has given name to Ellesmere) measures 116 acres. The rest are beneath 50 acres, each. The least 8 acres. The whole are nearly twenty in number.

SOILS.—P. 41. "Shropshire contains a great variety of soils and surface; and the former, in particular, have that variety so much intermingled, that any general account, especially such as has been incidentally given, in speaking of the climate, must be received with every allowance for exceptions, greater or less. And as the subject of this Section has been thus somewhat anticipated, so it will be difficult to treat of the soil and surface, without alluding to the minerals of the county. For a stone being only a hard mass of earth, and earth in powder being only an aggregate of minute stones, the compact and pulverized are best considered under the denomination of earths; but, in a popular work, it may be necessary to draw a broader line between them, and describe them, as much as may be, in words of common acceptation."

The learned Reporter then proceeds to define the several component parts of the geological system. But his labors are altogether inscientific and unavailing.

In the course of this Section, entitled "Soil and Surface," the several hundreds, or sub-divisions of the county are gone over, and *some account*, not only of the soils and surface, but of the fossils they include, is offered. I perceive nothing, however, that can claim a place, here; except what follows:—

P. 48. "In Cundover hundred, there is "a good deal of gravelly loam*," sand and clay, and oftentimes intermingled in very small beds; clayey soils lying over red sandstone, and others, with gravel or sand, under them. In the liberties of Shrewsbury, and hundred of Ford, there is also much pebbly loam: some reddish rock and clay, north of Shrewsbury, and some lighter coloured clays, lying over limestone, on the north borders of Ford hundred;

* EDW. HARRIES, Esq.

dred: its southern district is very much a deep clayey soil, with coal under, and becomes at last gravelly, rocky, and uneven. The hundred of Chirbury is still more uneven, but has plains of a deep light-coloured loam, or clay. Purslow and Clun are very uneven; but several of the hills are smooth, and fine sheep-walks, with a slaty rock under; in some places containing so much silex, as to form good roof-slate, and in others good building-stone; but most commonly the rock is argillaceous. There are some pale-coloured clays in these districts, and a considerable quantity of lighter soils, not so much gravelly perhaps, as mingled with argillaceous rock, and which becomes friable upon exposure to the air. In the vales, the meadow and pasture ground is very good.

"It has been observed, that there is a continuation of red soil from Northamptonshire to Devonshire, which is uniformly very good. The red soils of this county are, in general, productive."

Fossils.—See the last extract.—In the Section "Minerals," the following notices, concerning the fossil productions of Salop are found—

Limestone.—P. 65. "This county is also well supplied with lime, and in general the limestone is at no great distance from coal. It differs in colour, and in the quantity of flour, or powder, that it yields when slacked. The lime-works at Lilleshal are very considerable. There is plenty of limestone near the Wrekin and Coalbrook-dale, and it extends from Benthall-edge (on the opposite side of the Severn, to Coalbrook-dale), near to Wenlock, called there Wenlock-edge; and so, S. W. pointing towards Ludlow, it forms a ridge of rock, somewhat perpendicular on the N. W. side. It is worked in various parts, and yields a large quantity of white powder, though these properties degenerate as it extends south, till it becomes too argillaceous to be very valuable. Lime is found also in the Clee-hills; in a small degree in the S. W. district; in many places south of Shrewsbury, but of a brown colour, and less pulverising quality. West of Shrewsbury, it is gotten in considerable quantities, in the parishes of Cardiston and Alberbury; and at Porth y wain and Llanymynach, on the west confines, is a hill of limestone of an excellent quality. At the east end of the Wrekin, and at some other lime-works, is a red lime, that will set very hard in water. Mr. Smeaton discovered that lime, with a certain proportion of clay and iron, did best under water. And the

the colour of the lime here spoken of, indicates its having these component parts."

Ironstone.—P. 66. "Ironstone is found in the neighbourhood of Wellington, Coalbrook-dale, and Broseley In and near the Clee-hills, it is also met with; and Dr. TOWNSON has taken notice of a species of ironstone in the Llwynymain colliery, near Oswestry, which he ascertained to be a mixture of spatous iron-ore and the common argillaceous ironstone. He observes, that the best iron and steel, viz. those of Styria, are made of spatous iron-ore; and therefore he judges that this may be found very valuable. Mr. WILLIAM REYNOLDS informs me, that there is a very good stratum of spatous iron-ore found at Billingsley, but that it is not worked."

Building Stones.—P. 67. "This county is also well supplied with building-stone; and its north district, which could be but little noticed for the subterraneous treasures we have been speaking of, stands pre-eminent for its quarry at Grinsell, seven miles north of Shrewsbury, where is a white *sandstone*, superior, perhaps, to any in the kingdom: the top rock lies in thin strata; the bed is 20 yards thick. There is plenty also of good red sandstone in the neighbourhood. The same may be said of the east side of the county; and near Bridgenorth, beds of red sandstone are found under white sandstone; and again, beds of white sandstone under the red. This appears a singular division and alteration of the cements. Iron particles give their colour to the red stone; and it is on this account, probably, that the weather has more influence on it than on the white-stone, the iron absorbing so much air as to lose its tenacious quality.

"Farther south, sandstone prevails; and Dr. TOWNSON found at Orton-bank, a stratum of the *Bath* and *Portland-stone*, between strata of common *limestone*."—"Very good *stone slates*, for covering roofs, are met with in the parish of Bettus, on the S. W. confines of the county. And there is very good *flag-stone* in Corndon-hill, west of Bishop's-castle."

For an instance of *slate stone*, see the art. *Soil*, aforegoing; p. 193.

In a chaos, similar to that of old, we find the subjoined interesting account of

Fossil Pitch.—P. 70. "At Pitchford, about seven miles S. E. of Shrewsbury, is a red sandstone, approaching the surface in many places, and from which exudes a mineral pitch. The same substance is gathered from a well in in the neighbourhood, and in some quantity in warm weather; but in winter, very little is seen floating on the water. From the rock is extracted an oil, called BETTON'S British oil. The experiment was first tried at Broseley (at a place still called the Pitch-yard), about fourscore years ago, or more, and an account of which was published in No. 228 of the Philosophical Transactions: from near that period, the Pitchford rock has been gotten for that purpose, and sometimes 20 ton, or more, used in a year, for which the manufacturer paid 5s. per ton. It was carried from thence to Shrewsbury, where the oil was procured by distillation; but the process is kept secret; a patent was obtained for the discovery by the late Mr. BETTON; but his right to a patent was disallowed, by the decision of a court of law, some time after. The oil was used only medicinally, and has probably many of the properties of what is called FRIAR'S balsam, and in quality and appearance has a near resemblance to oil of amber, and is often sold as such. When the manufacture was carried on in its greatest extent, I have understood that a considerable quantity of the oil was exported, and principally to Germany. It is still to be bought in Shrewsbury, from the preparer. It is also from a rock of red sandstone that the fossil tar-spring near Coalbrook-dale, issues. Mr. AIKIN relates in his book, before quoted, p. 194. that this "spring was cut into, by driving a level in search of coal; that the quantity that issued at first, was to the amount of three or four barrels per day; but that, at present (1797), there seldom flowed more than half a barrel in the same period." And in 1799, Dr. TOWNSON states the produce at only 30 gallons per week (now, 1802, it is about half that quantity), though, he imagines, other fissures filled with the same substance, may be found, if there was a greater demand for it. The oil distilled from this tar, exactly resembles BETTON'S British oil, and is used as a solvent for Caoutchouc (commonly known by the name of elastic-gum, or Indian-rubber), which is now used as a varnish for cloth, and is particularly applicable to balloons."

MINERALS.—Shropshire abounds with mineral productions. The following account of them, tho without form, will not be found altogether void. The three Sections denominated "Climate"—"Soil and Surface" and "Minerals"—are but one continuous mass of mixed information; some particulars of which, as the extracts will evince, are valuable.

P. 50.

P. 50. "There are mines of *lead-ore*, of a good quality, on the western side of this county, which have been very productive. The Bog-mine, in the parish of Wentnor, and the white-grit mine, in the parishes of Shelve and Worthen, adjoin the Stiperstones: they are high hills, with bare and ragged summits, resembling the ruins of walls and castles: they are a "granulated quartz, much harder than common sandstone, but apparently not stratified*." The Bog-mine has been worked to the depth of 150 yards; a solid lump of pure ore of 800 lb. has been gotten up there: the vein is in some parts three feet thick, and generally bedded in white spar. One ton of this ore will run 15 cwt. of lead, besides slag. Dr. TOWNSON says, "these mines are in argillaceous schistus, and produce galena lead-ore †, sometimes spatous ‡ lead-ore, and blende §." The ores at the white-grit mine, are the common galena, and the steel-grained ores; sometimes the white spatous-ore, and considerable quantity of black-jack §. The ores from this mine are not smelted separately; they differ much in their product, and little experiment has been made to ascertain it. I have been informed, that they produce from 10 to 13 cwt. of lead, besides slags, from a ton of ore, and rarely more ‖. At Snailbach, in the neighbourhood of the same hills, but nearer Shrewsbury, lead has been gotten for a long time. "The vein was in some parts four yards wide. The vein-stones are heavy spar, mixt with calcareous spar and quartz. The ore here is the common galena and the steel-grained, and sometimes the white spatous-ore ¶." It has been "worked to the depth of 180 yards. The matrix of the ore is crystallized quartz and carbonate of lime. The ore is, 1. Sulphuret of lead, both galena and steel-ore, which latter con-

"* Dr. TOWNSON."

"† This is lead mineralized by sulphur, and is the most common lead-ore. It is sometimes called potters' lead-ore."

"‡ This term is not in NICHOLSON'S Dictionary, or in the 8vo. edit. of KIRWAN: it means lead-ore crystallized in the form of spar."

"§ Tracts and Observations in Nat. Hist. &c. p. 184."

"‖ Mr. PENNANT, in his Welsh Tour, vol. i. p. 447, says, 'the lamellated, or common kind of lead-ore, usually named potters'-ore, yields from 14 to 16¼ cwt. of lead from 20 cwt. of the ore, but the last produce is rare.'"

"¶ Dr. TOWNSON'S Tracts, &c. p. 183."

contains silver; 2. Carbonate of lead, crystallized; 3. Red-lead ore*; 4. Blende, or black-jack†." Lead-ore has been met with in many other places in this part of the county. As far west as Llanymynach, lead is found in small quantities, and *copper*, which the Romans are supposed to have worked to a great extent. Tools, judged to be Roman, have been found in these mines, and some of them are preserved in the library of Shrewsbury free-school. In this hill, the lead is met with in bellies of ore, that is, a small string leads often to a body of ore about four or five yards in diameter, but from which there is no vein issues, that may lead the miner to the other bodies of ore remaining in the hill. *Calamine* also is here met with. The rock at Pimhill is strongly tinctured with copper. Symptoms, both of copper and lead, appear also in the Cardington hills, many miles S. E. of the spot we are speaking of, and not very far south of the centre of the county. "Lead is also found at Shipton, in the road from Wenlock to Ludlow, but never yet in sufficient quantities to reward the adventurers‡." Full as far north of the centre, it is reported, in a MS. history of Bradford North (A. D. 1740), that "HENRY TENISON, Esq. got *copper-ore* in his estate about Red Castle; but it lay so deep, that it turned to little account;" and I believe we may apply the following paragraph from the same MS. to many adventures in mining in this and other counties; for the author proceeds to say, that "the Rev. Mr. SNELSON expected to find this hidden treasure at Weston, but had his labour for his pains, and his expence for his trouble."

Coals.—On this important subject, which is nearly connected with the lasting prosperity of the country, Mr. Plymley has been successful. The particulars of information which he has adduced, concerning it, are entitled to special attention.

P. 52. "Coal of an excellent quality is gotten on the eastern

"* Mr. AIKIN says this ore was discovered in these mines by RASPE, a German. Mr. NICHOLSON, in his Chemical Dictionary, 1795, remarks, that this ore had not then been found, except at Catharineburgh, in Siberia. I do not know that these two red-lead ores have been ascertained to be precisely the same, or that any difference between them has been discovered."

"† Vide AIKIN's Tour, p. 203."

"‡ Mr. WILLIAM REYNOLDS."

eastern side of the county, particularly in the parishes of Wellington, Lilleshall, Wrockwardine, Wombridge *, Stirchley, Dawley, Little Wenlock, Madeley, Barrow, Benthall, and Broseley, and which "promise a lasting and plentiful supply † for the great iron manufactures in that neighbourhood, for domestic use, and as an export to other counties by the river Severn, on or near the sides of which they lie."—South of these works, and on the other side of Bridgenorth from them, coal appears again. It may be found in most parts of the hundred of Stottesden; but the roads in general are an obstruction to its being removed. South again of these, and of the Clee hills, are very valuable coal-works, in some of which the canal, or kennel coal, is found. Mr. PENNANT, in his Voyage to the Hebrides, remarks, that the name is probably *candle*-coal, from giving a light that supersedes, in poorer houses, the use of candles; and the Bishop of LLANDAFF, in his Chemical Essays, has the same idea, supported by the circumstance, that in the northern counties candles are called cannels. The S. W. parts of this county have not yet been proved to contain coal; and the inhabitants purchase, at a great expence of land-carriage, coal from the Clee hills, or from collieries in the west parts of Shropshire: such there are W. and S. W. of Shrewsbury. Again, on the W. and N. W. borders of the county, coal of a good quality is gotten. Out of fifteen hundreds, the following large proportion of ten are known to produce coal, viz. Oswestry, Ford, Shrewsbury, Bradford South, Brimstry, Wenlock, Cundover, Munslow, Overs, and Stottesden. Mr. WILLIAM REYNOLDS has favoured me with the following lists of strata in five different collieries in the eastern district. His name will add an interest and value to the communication, in the opinion of all those who have the pleasure of knowing him."

I readily

"* In this parish, Mr. W. REYNOLDS, about ten years ago, put in practice an idea he had conceived some years before, of uncovering the strata of ironstone and coal which lay near the surface, so as to get the whole of the strata of ironstone and coal, clay, &c. to a certain depth; when in the old method, large quantities, both of ironstone and coal, were unavoidably lost, and which never afterwards would be of any use to the proprietor or occupier of the mines. This method is now followed in other works, where the strata lie sufficiently near the surface."

"† EDW. HARRIES, Esq."

I readily copy one of these stratifications; not for the use of coal miners; but as an additional fact in the science of geology, with which agriculture and the other branches of Rural Economy, are inseparably connected. See NORTHERN DEPARTMENT, p. 21.

P. 53. "STRATA IN LIGHTMOOR WIMSEY PIT.

	Yds.	Ft.	In.
A good loam, and mixed soil, - -	6	0	0
Pale blue clunch, - - - - - -	16	0	0
Dark-grey rock, not very strong, - -	5	0	0
Sky-blue clunch, - - - - - -	2	1	6
Three stinking coals, divided by pale-blue earth, two inches between each,	1	1	6
Strong clod mingled, pale-blue and red, -	16	0	0
Brown rock, called the stinking-coal rock, -	7	1	0
Three stinking coals, divided by pale-blue earth, four or five inches between each,	3	0	0
Blue clunch, - - - - - - -	4	2	0
Red clunch, pale, - - - - -	4	0	0
Rough rock, so called from being full of dark-brown hard pebbles and ironstone,	7	0	0
Bind, a pale-blue clod, - - - -	14	0	0
Stone-clod, ditto, in which lies a bed of ironstone, called ballstone,	5	0	0
Black slate, - - - - - - - -	0	1	0
Coal, called top-coal, exceeding good fuel, -	1	1	0
Top coal, tough, a dark-blue earth, and a very heaving measure,	0	1	0
Coal, called the foot-coal, - - - - -	0	1	0
Slumbs, black-slaty earth, and a heaving measure,	2	0	0
Coal, called the three-quarter coal, - -	0	2	0
Rotch, dark-grey hard rock, - - -	0	2	0
Coal, called the double-coal, - - -	1	0	0
Dark-grey clod; will fire from its own nature,	2	0	0
Coal, called yard-coal, - - - -	1	0	0
Black, (a black slate-coal, and rock, mixed)	2	1	6
Clod, a pale white, in which lies a bed of ironstone, called	2	0	0
Flan, a dark slate, - - - - -	0	0	6
Coal, called upper flint-coal, - - -	1	1	6
Upper flint, a dark-grey rock, - - -	7	1	0
Pinny-measure; a pale-blue clod, in which lies a large quantity of small balls of ironstone, called pennystone,	5	1	6

Stinking-

	Yds.	Ft.	In.
Stinking-coals; three beds, divided by three or four inches of dark-brown earth,	0	1	9
Pale-blue clod, - - - - - -	2	0	0
Coal, called the silk-coal, - - -	0	1	2
Clunch, of a dark blue, - - - - -	5	1	6
Coal, called the silk-coal, divided by a few inches of grey earth,	0	1	6
Clunch of a dark blue, with coal in the middle. seventeen inches thick; the coal is called silk-coal,	3	1	10
Coal, called the two-foot coal (feet), - -	0	2	0
Lintseed-earth (dark brown—a very shuttle measure),	0	1	2
A black slate, - - - - - - -	0	0	6
Coal, called the best coal, - - - - -	0	1	6
Black-bass, or slate, - - - -	0	0	6
Coal, called the middle coal, - - -	0	2	9
Dark-brown stony clod, - - - -	1	0	6
Coal, called clod-coal, - - - -	0	1	10
Clod, of a pale blue, - - - - - -	1	1	8
Coal, called little flint-coal, - - -	0	2	2
Little flint; a rock of a dark grey, mixed with pebbles and ironstone,	16	0	0
(156 0 4)	154	1	4
Die-earth; a pale-blue hard clunch: this measure continues the same, to the depth of more than	100	0	0

So far I have proved on the rise of the work. How much deeper it is, we know not."

The retrospective remarks, on four Sections previously detailed, are these.—P. 60. " We see then, that in the first-mentioned coal-pit, no coal was found within much less than 30 yards of the surface, and that then three small layers of bad coal only were gotten; that after sinking near 24 yards deeper, three other layers of the same coal were procured, but that the first vein of good coal lay 92 yards beneath the surface; that this vein was 4 feet thick; that none of the veins appear to have been more than 5 feet thick; and that in 154 yards, and more, regularly worked, or above 254, taking in the whole experiment, 13 yards 2 feet of coal were found. In the second pit specified," (at Wombridge) " the coal appears to have been met with in little more than 21 yards from the surface.

face. One of the veins proved 6 feet thick; and in sinking somewhat less than 44 yards, above 7 yards thickness of coal was discovered. In the third pit specified," (in Madeley field) "the sulphureous, or bad coal, was met with in 16 yards from the surface, and good coal in less than 28 yards; no vein exceeded 3 feet; and the aggregate in almost 68 yards, was not quite 9 yards of coal. In the fourth pit specified," (in Slaney's Dawley) "the first unmixed coal was fifty yards from the surface; and in sinking above 116 yards, it does not appear that here was any vein thicker than 2 feet; and the aggregate of unmixed coal measured only 5 feet 2 inches in thickness."

Further remarks,—P. 60. "Dr. TOWNSON, in his tracts, p. 166, has given the strata of two other pits in this district, and has added to the colliers' names for the different measures, his own definition of each. He observes, that "annually about 260,000 tons of coal are raised in this district," a very large proportion of which are consumed in the adjacent iron-works, I presume; for I have understood, that in the Ketley iron-works they use at least 6 ton of coal out of every 7 they raise. What I have called the collieries of the eastern district, comprehend pits on both sides the river Severn. The veins of coal in this district, are equal in thickness, I believe, to most in this county, but very inferior to those of the Staffordshire works, from 15 to 20 miles east of these, where, I have been told, there is a bed of coal measuring 13 yards or more."

P. 61. "The next coal-works to be mentioned, are those of the Clee-hill, from 20 to 30 miles south of those we have been describing*. Collieries indeed are now working at Billingsley, connecting them, in some measure, by their situation; and again, west of the eastern coal district, pits have been lately sunk with success. I am indebted to Dr. TOWNSON's tracts, before quoted, for the following lists of the strata in two of the Clee-hill collieries."

These I refrain to copy, but insert the remarks thereon. —P. 63. "In the first of these Clee-hill pits then, we find the first strata of coal 98 yards below the surface; that the thickest vein is 6 feet; and that the aggregate of coal in 107 yards 1 foot, is 12 feet 6 inches. In the second pit, they must sink 116 yards before coal is found, the vein

"* A coal-pit is now (1802) worked on the summit of the Brown Clee hill, within the encampment."

vein of which is also 6 feet thick; and the other veins, which are not pure coal, measure in the aggregate 10 feet; so that, in 137 yards, there are only 16 feet of coals, and of these, only six that are unmixed."

The collieries, in the west and northwest, extremity of the county are then mentioned. But nothing noticeable arises; except what appears to be a vague (or not well reported) opinion of the colliers.—P. 63. "The veins between the Dee and Ceiriog, are a lighter coal, burning more quickly, and the ashes are white. This difference is supposed, by the colliers, to arise from the less weight of water that is over these veins."

P. 64. "Mr. Arthur Davies, of Oswestry, has favoured me with the following list of the strata in the engine-pit at Chirk-bank coal-work, and which is the deepest pit he has sunk."

The depth of this pit is 102 yards 3 inches. The remarks thereon are these:—"We find then in this pit, a vein of 7 feet thick, 1 foot thicker than any mentioned in the other Shropshire coal works; and that in little more than 102 yards, 7 yards and 3 inches of coal are met with."

P. 65. "Having given these specimens of the strata in the collieries on the E. S. and N. W. borders of the county, I shall conclude with those in one of the deepest pits at Welbatch, the works there being the most considerable of what may be called the central collieries of this county."—The depth 52 : 2 : 3.—"We see then, that in near 53 yards there is only 1 yard 9 inches of coal, and no vein thicker than 2 feet; but, probably, there are veins of more substance, whenever it shall be thought expedient to sink these pits deeper."

It may have its use to remark, here, that of the eight sections, given in the Report, under Review, the first appearance of coal, in the first section, was ninety feet beneath the surface. In the second sixty feet. In the third, fifty feet. In the fourth, near one hundred and fifty. In the fifth, almost three hundred. In the sixth, three hundred and fifty feet. In the seventh, upward of one hundred feet. And in the eighth, nearly one hundred feet. Yet I have heard it significantly suggested, by a coal engineer of high consideration, that it is quite needless to look, in this island, for fresh coal districts. For wherever coals are deposited, the seams must necessarily "crop out:"—that is, must make their appearance, at or very near the surface; as in hollow ways, or deep-sunk ditches:—For the seams generally lying in a shelving posture,

posture, they must, somewhere or other, reach the surface.

But supposing the upper edge, even of a steeply shelving seam, to have been covered, in the convulsions of nature that gave the present form to the earth's surface, with a few feet of earthy matter, only,—the argument becomes vague. The proprietors of existing collieries, it is true, have an interest in propagating such a doctrine. But, in a country destitute of coals, let not the proprietors of estates listen to it, implicitly.

On the *internal supply* of coals, in Shropshire, we find, in the section "Manufactures," the following slight notice, by Mr. Harries.—P. 340. "The number of blast-furnaces for iron between Ketley and Willey, about seven miles distant, exceed any within the same space in the kingdom. We have no reason to apprehend that the coal will fail us. Some of our veins of coal and iron-stone are said to make iron of the first quality. The consumption occasioned by the number of hands employed in these works has been a great spur to our agriculture."

Some idea of the *consumption* of coals, in Shropshire, is given in p. 201, aforegoing. Also in the section *Manufactures*, ensuing.

Coal Tar.—P. 71. "Near Jackfield, on the south side the river Severn, is carried on the manufacture of coal tar, for which Lord DUNDONALD formerly obtained a patent. In coaking the coal, which is here done in close vessels, they obtain the volatile products which are raised in vapour by the heat of the operation of coaking, and condensed in a chamber covered with lead plates, over which water is constantly running. These products are a water and an oil; the former of which contains a portion of volatile alkali, and the latter is boiled down to the consistence of tar or pitch. The oil which is caught during the boiling down, is used as a solvent for resin, and forms an excellent varnish for ships, or any wood-work exposed to weather."

SALT SPRINGS.—P. 71. (from Dr. TOWNSON's Tracts) —"The MS. account of Bradford North, mentions a salt-spring at Smeithmore, in the Lordship of Longford; and Dr. TOWNSON states several springs of salt-water to have been found in the neighbourhood of the tar-spring; and that in the parish of Brosely, on the opposite side of the Severn, salt is said to have been made formerly, from water taken out of pits, still called the Salthouse Pits. At the Lyth, in the parish of Cundover, is a field, the soil of which

which is impregnated with salt; and there is no doubt but this commodity could be gotten in this county, though its proximity to the extensive and established salt-works of Cheshire, may prevent any profit from an adventure of this kind. At Kingley Wick, about two miles west of Lilleshall-hill, is a 'spring of salt-water, that yields 4 or 5000 gallons in the 24 hours. It is an impure brine, but was formerly used; the salt-pans and buildings are still remaining. It flows out of a reddish sandstone-rock, which rests upon a reddish chert, like that of the Wrekin *. And at Admaston, near Wellington, only two miles from Kingley Wick, there is a salt medical spring, chalybeate and hepatic. There are two springs; the one containing carbonated iron and lime, selenite, and sea-salt; the other hepatic air, aerated lime, selenite, and sea-salt.'"

Mineral Waters.—Several Wells are noticed; and "Sutton Spa" (near Shrewsbury) is copiously described.

SUBJECT THE SECOND.

POLITICAL ECONOMY.

Political Divisions.—On this topic, which is but distantly related to Rural Economy, Mr. Plymley has thought fit to employ thirty five pages of his volume.

After the *hundreds*, or other subdivisions of the county, have been enumerated,—we are favored with the following important information.—P. 3. "All these divisions are disproportionate in size, and irregular in shape. The same may be said of parishes. They have too, in common with our counties, insulated and detached parts: they vary, in point of extreme length, from one mile and under, to fourteen miles and more; and in extreme breadth, from half a mile to ten miles. A small proportion have the same extreme diameter, that is, are about as broad as long; but then the boundary is often irregular, and the length and breadth are, in general, disproportionate."

What succeeds, however, is of more serious import. —"Several parishes are intersected by other parishes, or have one or more of their districts detached, and, in some instances, at a considerable distance. Some are detached

"* This brine is now used for the making of soda, at a work established at Wormbridge, on the banks of the canal there."

detached parts of counties; others comprehend part of two counties; still more are composed of parts of different hundreds. They contain from one to sixteen townships. There are instances of a township being a detached part of an hundred. Townships, again, are not always bounded within their parishes, several being in part in one parish, and in part in another parish. They are composed of one or more hamlets, and do not always coincide with the townships, so called, by which the land-tax is gathered."

What a complication of absurdities! Surely there must have been intervals of peace, in which so much inconvenience, to magistrates, as well as to the owners and occupiers of land, might have been done away, or much ameliorated, without alarm to the constitution!

Even (p. 4) "the civil division of *manors*, though frequently confined to the whole or part of a parish, comprehends, in some instances, part of two parishes, and has within it parts of different townships; and the jurisdiction of court leets are not always confined to the hundred they are situated in. Thus difficult is it to speak of the divisions of a county, from the want of coincidence in boundaries and jurisdictions; many of them appearing independent of each other, rather than separate, but component parts, of one and the same scheme."

Many or most of those anomalies, no doubt, have grown out of *reasonable* circumstances, which existed at the times of their taking place; but which are, now, no more. How irrational, then, under a change of circumstances to suffer their *memory* to be the cause of grievance to the most useful part of the community. As well might the crutches of a cripple be handed down from father to son, aye and worn too, in compliment to the memory of a distant ancestor, to whom they happened to be useful.

The following conjectures on the *Origin* of *Parishes*, are ingenious, and probable. In the central Highlands of Scotland, where the building of churches is of comparatively late date, similar ideas, respecting the boundaries of parishes, prevail.

P. 4. "The history of that experience from whence our constitution has so happily arisen, points out circumstances from which these varied limitations of district have grown. With respect to parishes, for instance, they seem to have originated, however disputable the exact date of their origin may be, from lords of manors, and persons of extensive landed property, building churches, as Christianity advanced in these kingdoms, for the use of themselves and tenants,

tenants, and to which churches they procured the tithes arising from their estates to be paid, which, if not specially appropriated, would have been paid to the bishop of the diocese, for the use of the clergy in general, and of such pious purposes as he deemed necessary. Now the founders of any church would wish that all their lands should pay tithe thereto, rather than to any other, and in preference to their tithes being applied at the discretion of the bishop; so that where the estate of any founder of a church was scattered, the district appropriated to pay tithe to it, would be scattered also; and it was from the junction of these circumstances, a church being built, and a district appointed to pay tithe to its minister, that parishes had their beginning *. It is not, however, easy now to say what are parishes."

The archdeacon, after having attempted the definition of a *parish*, furnishes a long, and loosely printed list of *churches* and *chappels*—within the county. It were needless to observe that such a list would have been a more appropriate offering to the diocesans (three in number) whose dioceses reach within the county of Salop, from the archdeacon thereof, than to the Board of Agriculture.

STATE of APPROPRIATION.—In the chapter "Enclosing," the Reporter says, p. 144.—"A great deal of land has been inclosed, and is still enclosing, in this county, generally by Act of Parliament, but sometimes by private agreement. Very large wastes and commons still remain. Among these, Clun Forest deserves to be particularly noted. It contains above 12,000 acres."

In the chapter "Waste Lands," Mr. Harries tells us, p. 221.—"A large quantity of wastes have been enclosed and improved, but too many still remain. The Morf, near Bridgenorth, is five miles in length, and may be two or three miles in width, and there are smaller commons, amounting to some hundred acres, not far from it; all of which are highly capable of improvement from enclosure: these would soon be made of the value from 12*s*. to 1*l*. per acre. There are several large commons in the road from Shrewsbury to Drayton; these are of much inferior value, but still capable of being made profitable: on the very worst parts of them the Scotch fir would thrive. A general inclosure bill for commons not exceeding 500 or 600 acres, would very soon cause a many thousand acres, that

* Vide BLACKSTONE's Com. vol. i. p. 111. 8vo. 8th edit.

that are now in a very neglected and unprofitable state, to be brought into cultivation: the expense of a private act precludes the proprietors of such from applying to Parliament; and we know that one obstinate man will prevent its being done by private agreement. Such commons, therefore, are likely to remain as they are. The extensive commons between Church-Stretton and Bishop's Castle, and beyond Clun, to the borders of Radnorshire, are so elevated and so well calculated for sheep-pastures, that perhaps they cannot be better applied."

The Reporter adds, p. 222.—"Having made some observations under the heads of Enclosing, and of Cottages, that may with equal propriety have appeared in this chapter, I have little to add in this place, except that the extensive forest of Clun, the Longmynd, and other wastes alluded to by Mr. HARRIES, may certainly be enclosed to advantage."

The idea thrown out, above, by Mr. Harries, is entitled to the highest consideration. If a combination of ignorance, prejudice, and folly, bordering on idiocy, will not permit a *general* inclosure bill to pass, let a *partial* one, as suggested by Mr. Harries, be carried into effect. The smaller commons are frequently the best lands that are now unappropriated (those of some of the forests excepted); and it is against the enclosing of these, more particularly, that separate bills are *insuperable* bars.

POPULATION.—The following statement of the Reporter will tend to show the lax manner in which the *internal* regulations of Government, are planned and executed; and to put those on their guard who may have occasion to make use of the lately formed register of the population of the kingdom;—useful as it *might* have been!

P. 346. "Since writing the above, the return has been made under the Act of the 41st GEO. III.—That return states this county to contain 31,182 inhabited and 929 void houses, 34,501 families, 82,563 males, 85,076 females, 45,046 persons employed in agriculture, 35,535 mechanics, and 70,504 persons not comprised in either of those two classes. The total number of persons 167,639. It is possible that a very few districts may be omitted in this return, and that some may have been counted twice over, from the circumstance of townships and parishes not being always co-extensive. The inaccuracy of the return, with respect to the number of persons employed in agriculture, is very obvious. The Act does not say whether it was the intention

intention of the Legislature to confine this list to males, and there are three ways in which it has been made. In some returns, the males only employed in agriculture are given; in others, the list contains also women keeping farms, and dairy-maids: and again in others, all the men, women, and children of a farmer's family, or of a labourer's in farming business, are added to that class. The same is the case in the return of the mechanics, and this return is further doubtful, as miners are in some instances added to it, and in others stated as belonging to those not comprised in either of the specified employments; whilst the persons making the return in some parishes, have seemed to consider it necessary to class all the inhabitants under the head of agriculture or of trade; as I observe them so stated where I know there are resident clergymen, at least, of respectability, and who have families."

PROVISIONS.—P. 271. (by Mr. Tench)—"The present price of provisions (such as are used in the farmer's family) is as follows:—Flour 6s. per bushel, weighing 56 lb.; cheese 3½d.; beef 3 d.; mutton 3½d.; veal 3½d.; bacon 6 d. per lb.; and potatoes 1 s. 6 d. per bushel: this I consider the average price of the last five years."

The Reporter adds—"This account, though given in 1794, appears like a Report from ancient times; under a feeling of prices, double in the lowest instances, and quadruple in the highest."

From the above and other passages, it appears that laborers, in Shropshire, purchase flour;—do not send corn to the mill:—a practice which will be found to be censured, under the head, *Workpeople*, ensuing.

FUEL.—In the original Report, it is said "the whole county is plentifully supplied with coals, from four to six shillings per ton, at the pits."

On this Mr. Plymley observes, p. 272.—"The price of coal, as above mentioned, has risen considerably, and even then, that price was applicable only to the collieries of the East district. At the Clee-hill collieries, and all the smaller ones, the prices were 8s. and to 10s. 6d. the ton or stack. In the S. W. district are houses (I speak not of cottages) where no coal, perhaps, was ever burnt. Peat is a common fuel there, and wood. Coppice-wood of twenty years growth can be bought for 6 l. and 7 l. the acre, and cord-wood at 8s. and 9s. the cord. The only coals that can be brought to the S. W. district (except they should be imported by the Montgomeryshire canal) are

are those that are dearest at the pits, and the distance for land-carriage is very great: in some instances above 20 miles."

MANUFACTURES.—Shropshire, as will be seen, by the following extracts, is a manufacturing county of no small consideration.

P. 340. (by Mr. Reynolds)—"In the coal district are the following *iron-works*. In the south is Willey, Broseley, Calcot, Benthal, and Barnets Leasow: these are on the south side of the Severn. On the north side of this river is Madeley Wood, Coalbrook-dale, Lightmoor, Horsehay, Old Park, Snedshill, Ketley, Donnington, Queen's-Wood, and Wrockwardine Wood *."

P. 340. (from Dr. Townson's tract)—"These works employ about 6000 hands; and annually about 260,000 tons of coal are raised in this district. It is worth remarking, that Coalbrook-dale can justly claim the merit of having, in the beginning of this century, introduced upon a large scale the use of coaked coal, as a substitute for charcoal in making of iron."

P. 341. (by the Reporter)—"*Garden pots*, and other vessels of a coarse fabric, are made at Broseley. At Caughley, in that neighbourhood, is a *china manufacture* of great excellence. The blue and white, and the blue, white and gold china there, is, in many instances, more like that from the East than any other I have seen. These works have been purchased by the proprietors of a later establishment, the Coal-port China-works, and are confined to the ware specified above. At Coal-port coloured china of all sorts, and of exquisite taste and beauty, is made. More immediately at Coal-port, for the china-works are near it, is a manufacture of *earthen-ware*, in imitation of that made at Etruria, and called the Queen's, or Wedgewood's ware †. In the lordship of Cardington, in this county, a quartz and clay may be gotten for compounding this ware, the former superior, as I am well informed, to that imported out of Carnarvonshire to the Staffordshire potteries.

" * There are now (1802) on the south side of the river Severn, at the different iron and coal works, 25 fire-engines, and on the north side of the river 155, making together 180 fire-engines. Thirty years ago, I believe there were not 20 in the same district. The second lever-engine that was erected was upon a colliery in Madeley parish."

" † At Coal-port is also a manufacture of ropes and one of chains, now much used for the same purposes."—Mr. W. REYNOLDS.

potteries. There is a *glass manufacture* at Donnington. At Shrewsbury is a company of *shearmen*, who have been for a long time the shearers or finishers of the Welsh flannels.

" Various branches of the *flannel manufacture* are carried on near Shrewsbury, and a large mill for the purposes of spinning, fulling, &c. was erected at the isle, between four and five miles N. W of Shrewsbury, near where the Severn, by its windings, forms a peninsula. There are also mills for dying woollen cloth in this county; one of the more considerable is near Lebotwood, about nine miles north of Shrewsbury.

" Lately a large manufacture of *coarse linens*, and more particularly of *linen thread*, has been established near the north suburbs of Shrewsbury. A considerable wholesale trade in *gloves* is carried on at Ludlow, for the London market."

TRAFFIC.—Shrewsbury is figuratively called " the capital of North Wales " It is, literally, a place of intercourse, between England and that division of the principality:—furnishing it with English and foreign articles of consumption; and receiving, in return, its rough manufactures. The subjoined account of the Reporter, respecting this species of traffic, is satisfactory.

P. 338. " The staple trade of Shrewsbury is in fine flannels and Welsh webs. The flannels are bought at Welsh-Pool, in a market holden for that purpose, every other Monday. Most of these flannels are made in Montgomeryshire, and some are made and more spun in the neighbouring parts of Shropshire. The flannel in Pool market sells from 9d. to 4s. per yard, in pieces of 100 yards long on an average. They are chiefly re-sold to the London merchants, who are the exporters. The webs are fabricated in Merionethshire and Denbighshire, and brought to Shrewsbury, where they are sold in a close market, that is, in a hall, where none but the members of the drapers' company can enter; but of late years much of this market has been anticipated by buyers in the country, which often forces the Shrewsbury drapers to send there themselves. Webs are about 200 yards long, and may be worth from 1s. to 20d. per yard. The webs that are made in Merionethshire are about seven-eighths of a yard wide, and are called the *strong*, or *high country cloth*. Those made in Denbighshire, are called small, or low country cloth. The former, after they are bought by the drapers, have the wool raised and sheared by men, called

at

at Shrewsbury shearmen, or they are sent to the fulling-mill to be thickened, and are then exported in bales of different sizes, some containing even 2000 yards. The ultimate markets are Holland, Germany, and America. The *small cloth* is about the one-eighth of a yard narrower than the other. The web is the same length. Many of these are sold at Oswestry market, and are generally dyed before they are exported. They supply clothing for the slaves in the West Indies and South America. The manufacture in Wales, by means of jennies introduced into farm-houses and other private houses, is four times as great, I am told, as it was twenty years ago. Formerly the Shrewsbury drapers bought the whole that came to Pool; now drapers or shop-keepers from Wrexham and other places attend the Pool market. The wool of the country is insufficient for the manufacture."

POOR RATES.—The following observations of the Reporter, tho inconcise, are sufficiently interesting to be inserted, here.

P. 129.—" It is difficult to give a distinct view of the comparative pressure of poor-rates to the value of property, because in many parishes the rate is made according to an old valuation; and where there is a new valuation, it is frequently equalized upon a scale below the amount of the full value. For instance, the person or persons valuing, estimate, in the first instance, the real income that each estate should bring in, and then return two-thirds, three-fifths, or seven-tenths of such real amount, as the rent at which an assessment shall be made. I do not see the use of this secret ground-work of a rate; it may possibly help to abate the cavils of troublesome men, or puzzle them in their endeavours to find fault with an assessment; yet the open way of making it, according to the full computed value, would, upon the whole, give more satisfaction, as well as being strictly proper. It is very obvious, as the Original Report expresses it, that " the poor-rates are very various, and have been enormously increased of late years." Mr. BISHTON further states, that " in his parish, which has no tradesmen in it, the poor-rates have been raised from 25l. to 100l. per annum, within 30 years:" and I should think this may be taken as no improbable average, at the date of his Report. I say this with more confidence, from looking at notes I made in the parochial visitations of my archdeaconry (in the years 1793 and 1794 principally). The late seasons, and even that of 1795 and 1796, must have made a great alter-

alteration, from the extra price of all articles of food. Near the time Mr. BISHTON wrote his Report, I met with extreme instances of the rate having risen from 3½d. in the pound upon an old valuation, to 3s. upon the same valuation within memory; and from 8d. in the pound to 2s. within 13 years: but I met with a few instances where the rate had rather declined, and several where the advance in the last 20 years had not been very considerable."

What succeeds requires to be duly attended to, by those who treat of the subject of Poor Rates.—P. 130. "It should be recollected, however, that in this county, the county-rate, which is paid out of the poor's-rate, has been very high, from the circumstances of an extensive gaol and county-hall having been built, with several handsome bridges, within the said period of 30 years; thus, in one parish, the poor's-rate raised in the year 1723 was 5l. 3s. 8d.; in the year 1773, 15l. 17s. 3d.; and in 1792, 31l. 13s. 2d.; but in the last year, what they call the vagrant-money, *i. e.* the quota to the county-rates was 12l., which in some former years may not have been more than 1 l."

Mr. Plymley has evidently paid great attention to this important topic; as a few more extracts, from his Report, will sufficiently show.

On *Houses* of *Industry*, Mr. P. has inserted the following information, by Mr. Harries.—P. 131. "Till the late high price of grain the parish-rates may have been from 1s. to 2s. 6d. per pound full value. It is almost invariable, that the smaller the parish the easier the rate. In addition to the house of industry at Shrewsbury, there has been one lately erected at Ellesmere, including several adjoining parishes; another at Oswestry, and again at four miles from Shrewsbury, including several parishes. Great part of the hundred of Chirbury has united itself to a house of industry between Pool and Montgomery. As the houses of industry (except Shrewsbury) are new institutions, we cannot form any accurate judgment of the advantage or disadvantages of them. Many public expenses are now defrayed out of the poor's-rates, to the amount of perhaps one-third of the rate."

The succeeding remarks are from the philanthropic pen of the Reporter.—P. 131. "The desire that every person, who thinks fairly on the subject, must have, of seeing all his fellow-creatures who are grown up and settled in life, happy in a habitation suitable to their condition.

dition, makes houses of industry, at first view, objects of some suspicion. But when it is considered how many poor persons cannot procure comfortable houses; how many will not keep those clean or decent that they have; how many will not make the best of their lot by industry; and now many will not take care of the education of their children: when all these circumstances are considered, we become reconciled to institutions that force cleanliness upon those who are dirty; and wholesome food upon those of depraved appetites. In these houses, when properly conducted, some labour is procured from the indolent who are within, and an additional incitement given to the industry of those who are without: and the education of the children is uniformly better than they would probably have had, even from better parents, out of the house. These considerations should not slacken our endeavours to prevent the necessity of such receptacles. Every argument that can be brought in their favour, is an additional motive for attending to the comforts of the labouring class, and for encouraging them in right behaviour: but whilst the present want of education, and of proper disposition in so many of this class continues, we cannot regret that such fabrics have, in many instances, been built or furnished."

On *Overseers*, Mr. Plymley's observations are sensible and just.—P. 133. "The office of overseer is generally an annual office; though magistrates have a discretion in sanctioning the appointment, they can rarely do more than object to notorious characters, if there is no appeal against the parish return; and the parish return is generally that of indiscriminate rotation, among all those whose occupations render them liable to the office. These laws then are intrusted, in the first instance, to every diversity of temper and ability: to every degree of inexperience and self-interest. In large parishes, the office does not return to the same person above once or twice in his life. In a large parish, an annual overseer cannot become acquainted with the real situation of all the poor persons belonging to it, many of whom are dwelling out of the parish. An annual overseer has always his own business to attend to, and therefore may feel irritated, or injured, so often as he is called off from it; and hence the concerns of the poor are liable to be less kindly and patiently investigated."

On the *sizes* of *Parishes*, or *Townships*, the Archdeacon's remarks are equally judicious.—P. 133. "What Mr. HARRIES has observed, of the rate being uniformly lowest in in small parishes, is not only very true, but I doubt not, that all the real poor of small parishes are best provided for. The knowledge that each individual in a small parish generally has of every other, not only reveals the merit of the deserving, and prevents imposition from undeserving objects, but the publicity arising from it tends to encourage industry, and check vice."—P. 134. "There are two ways in which the benefits resulting from small parishes may be in part obtained, and instances of either mode may be met with. The one is appointing separate overseers to separate townships of a large parish; and if this plan is sufficiently extended, and a separate and independent rate made and collected for each township, great good will be done. The other is devolving the whole management upon one overseer, who shall be annually appointed, and who shall receive a sufficient salary to make him regard the office his business, as well as his duty."

There can be little doubt, I apprehend, of the position that *the smaller the parish or township, the easier the rate.* The larger parishes in Yorkshire are divided into townships; each having its own overseers. The parish in which I at present reside, comprizes seven or eight townships. That in which I live includes a middle sized village. Yet there is, at present, only one person, by whom relief is required.

Where parishes are small, or divided into small townships, the existing practice of appointing overseers appears to be fully adequate to the purpose desired. But in towns and populous, extensive country parishes, that are not yet divided into townships, more permanent managers of the poor are in a degree necessary. In these cases, let magistrates appoint PERENNIAL MANAGERS; as well as confirm the choice of *annual overseers*, chosen out of the inhabitants, as at present;—not to *direct*, but as *checks* on, the managers; as well as to ease the magistrates of much trouble; by their (the overseers) receiving the ordinary complaints of paupers;—and examining on all occasions, into the conduct of the manager. Thus, the inhabitants who pay, and those who receive, will have a fair chance of justice being done them,—by guardians of their own choice; or by an appeal to magistracy, in cases that may require it. In country parishes of moderate size, active school masters might undertake the management of the poor; with but little interruption to their school duties.

I can-

I cannot agree, entirely, with Mr. Plymley regarding the *existing poor laws:* altho I allow there is much truth in what he says on the subject. The present law, with respect to *settlements*, at least, is truly irrational, and altogether incompatible with wise government. I will, nevertheless, copy what Mr. P. advances. It is full of thought.

P. 132. "The more I consider the existing poor laws, the less I am convinced of the propriety of the outcry that has been against them. In this, as in many other instances, the complaint may be brought home rather to the want of a due administration of the law, than of the law itself. The provisions of the legislature in the time of Queen ELIZABETH are certainly so far wise, that relief may be given to the poor under them, in every possible case of distress. This then is one grand principle of an act to prevent absolute want. That worthy objects should not obtain their due proportion, or that unworthy ones should be able to procure too large a share, is not to be wondered at. Laws can rarely be framed so as to execute themselves. They must be put in force by men, subject, more or less, to the infirmities of our nature; and, independent of this general obstruction to the effect of the wisest regulations, their are peculiar sources of perplexity belonging to the management of the poor."

TITHES.—In the Chapter, "State of Property," is the subjoined passage on Tithes.—P. 92. "The landed income of this county may be about 600,000l. per ann. and of this, one-twentieth part may be paid in tithe by composition (for scarcely any is gathered) to the parochial clergy."

And in the Section "Tithes," we find the remainder of the Reporter's information respecting this subject.

P. 128. "Very little tithe is gathered. In the archdeaconry of Salop, in Hereford diocese, somewhat above one half of the land pays tithe to the parochial clergy; but as the rectories therein are above double the number of vicarages, and almost double the other churches, and as the rectories throughout England exceed the vicarages by somewhat more than one-fifth only, and the other churches by somewhat more than two-fifths only, it may be *presumed*" (what ought to have been *made out.*) "that scarcely half the land of the kingdom pays tithe to the church. The average of the compositions for tithes in this county, does not, *perhaps*, exceed the tithe of the rent, or 2s. in the pound. A few extreme cases may be pointed out, and such instances will be talked

talked of; but, again, there are other instances below the average mentioned."

GENERAL DRAINAGE.—In the "Conclusion" of this volume, Mr. Harries recommends—p. 353.—"A general act of parliament for the effectual draining of low lands; which should compel the carrying on of proper drains through different estates, so that the obstinacy of an individual should not hinder a general improvement; should provide for defraying the expense by a rate where necessary, and for settling disputes relative to the right of water for irrigation."

MILLS.—Mr. Plymley is an enemy to *wind mills;* and with good reason, when exposed near a road. They certainly are, in such situations, nuisances of a dangerous kind. A law to oblige proprietors, of those already erected, to enclose them with sufficiently high fences, to prevent their terrific and dangerous effects;—and also to prevent others from being erected in such situations;—would doubtlessly be salutary. But let not the mischievous effects of *water mills* be encreased, to prevent—"a nuisance to the eye in most prospects that exhibit wind mills." (p. 88). There are who view them in a different light.

INLAND NAVIGATION.—*Navigable rivers.*—P. 82. "The river Severn runs through this county, from N. W. to S. E. and is navigable the whole way; but its navigation is very much impeded by the lowness of the water in summer, and by floods in winter. It is the only navigable river. The vessels chiefly used on it, are barges, trows, wherries, and boats. The barges and trows have masts, which can be lowered, to go under bridges: the stream carries them down, with or without a sail, and they are towed up by men, assisted, or not, in the same manner, according to the wind. The barges are from 20 to 80 tons burthen, and trade very much between Shrewsbury and Gloucester. The trows are larger, and belong to the ports lower down the Severn. They fetch timber from Pool-quay, in Montgomeryshire, and are used to convey goods between Gloucester and Bristol, that are carried in smaller vessels to or from the first of those ports; but much the greatest number of barges is employed in carrying the produce of the mines near Coalbrook-dale into the counties of Worcester, Gloucester, &c. A horse towing-path is now established from Bewdley to Coalbrook-dale, which is more and more used, and, it is hoped, will soon be extended, the office of towing

towing barges by men, being looked upon as very injurious to their manners."

P. 85. "There is neither lock nor weir upon the Severn, from Pool-quay, in Montgomeryshire, to the mouth of the Avon, near Bristol; a distance of 155 miles. From its source in Plinlimmon-hill to the sea, it runs about 200 miles, but is navigable only from Pool-quay. Its course through Shropshire is between 60 and 70 miles. Some years ago, attempts were made to procure the improvement of its navigation, by deepening the shallows and erecting locks, but the scheme was opposed, and defeated."

In the chapter, "Political Economy," Mr. Telford, "so well known in many parts of England and Scotland, as an engineer and an architect,"—has given a circumstantial "Account of the Inland Navigation of the County of Salop."

This is a well written, scientific, valuable paper; and ill associates with the undigested materials of which the Reports to the Board of Agriculture are principally made up. As a "Communication" to the Board; or as a separate publication; it would have appeared with more propriety.

The first part (comparatively small) relates to the *Severn*, as a navigable river; and, having noticed its defects, as such, points out the causes from which they arise; namely,

P. 286. "*First*, From the fords and shoals which are frequent in a river, the bed of which has a considerable declivity, and consists of matter of such different qualities.

"*Secondly*, From the deficiency of water in drought, and from the superabundance of it during rainy seasons; and,

"*Thirdly*, From the mode of hauling the barges by men instead of horses."

"These circumstances," (Mr. Telford continues) "taken together, render the navigation very imperfect; and the year 1796 afforded a striking instance of the degree of this imperfection, since during the whole of that year, there were not two months in which barges could be navigated, even down the river, with a freight which was equal to defray the expenses of working them. This interruption was severely felt by the coal-masters, the manufactures of irou, the barge-owners. and the county in general.

"The daily account of the state of the water in the river,

river, which has been kept for many years past at Coal Port, and which forms a part of this Report, will show the very irregular and imperfect state of the navigation.

"The inconveniences arising from the irregularities of the water have always existed in some degree, but they have been greatly increased by the embankments which have lately been raised to protect the low lands in Montgomeryshire, and in the upper parts of the county of Salop. Formerly, when the river had arrived at a moderate height, it overflowed these low lands to a great extent, which thereby operated as a side reservoir, and took off the top waters of the high floods; and these waters returning to the bed of the river by slow degrees, proved a supply for the navigation for a long time after the flood began to subside, but being now confined to a narrow channel, they rise suddenly to a greater height, and flow off with more rapidity than formerly; whereby the navigation is at one period impeded by uncontrolable floods, and, at another, left destitute of a sufficient supply for its ordinary purposes.

"To remedy the inconveniences attending the shallows, and the irregularities of the water, two plans have been recommended, the adopting of either of which would greatly improve the navigation.

"By the first of these plans, a constant and regular navigation is proposed to be established, by means of curing the shallows which are in the river between Gloucester and Worcester, and of forming locks and weirs from Worcester upwards."

P. 288. "The second plan is to collect the flood-waters into reservoirs, the principal ones to be formed among the hills in Montgomeryshire, and the inferior ones in such convenient places as might be found in the dingles, &c. along the banks of the river. By this means the impetuosity of the floods might be greatly lessened, and a sufficient quantity of water preserved to regulate the navigation of the river in dry seasons, and likewise to answer many other useful purposes, such as the forming ponds for inland fisheries, the supplying artificial canals, and the watering of land. This, it is thought, might even prove the simplest and least expensive mode of regulating navigable rivers, especially such as are immediately on the borders of hilly countries."

This is a magnificent idea, which is highly honorable to the mind that conceived it.

P. 289. "With regard to adopting the mode of hauling barges

barges by means of horses, instead of the present barbarous and expensive custom of performing this slave-like office by men, it is only necessary that a good towing-path for horses should be formed along the banks of the river, and which will no doubt take place, if any scheme of general improvements should ever be adopted. In the mean time, a laudable example has been shown by Mr. WM. REYNOLDS, of Ketley, who has formed a towing-path for horses near to the new manufactories at Coal-port, and has carried it on through his father's property to the iron bridge, a distance of about two miles: this being along some rugged banks, and over some of the worst fords which are on the river, proves beyond contradiction, that this sort of towing-path is practicable at no extravagant expense, and besides, completely destroys the common objection of horse towing-paths where many rapids or fords intervene."

Canals.—Mr. Telford next proceeds to his main subject —"the artificial canals" of Shropshire.—P. 290. "The county of Salop has been among the first to adopt this valuable improvement, and it is probable that this backwardness ought to be accounted for, from its enjoying the benefit of so fine a river. But the general consumption of the kingdom at large, continuing to create a still greater demand for the products of the county, in mines and manufactures, as well as agriculture, these likewise extending, in the natural progress of improvement, to a greater distance from the river, and the expence of conveyance being thus proportionally increased, it has of late become an object of importance to improve, by some means, the mode of conveyance from the more distant works to the banks of the river."

But Mr. T. observes in his "Conclusion," p. 307.—"Although Shropshire was behind most of the other counties in adopting the plan of forming artificial canals, it has of late made a rapid progress in the execution of this valuable improvement; and I may venture to say, that there has been more ingenuity displayed in the means taken for overcoming the various obstacles which lay in the way of the canals of this county, than has hitherto been shown in those of any other county in England.

"The inclined planes, the small boats, the ascending and descending by means of pits, with the various machinery connected therewith upon the Ketley and Shropshire canals, and the iron aqueduct upon the Shrewsbury canal,

canal, were each of them new with regard to British canal-making."

To these important inventions, Mr. WILLIAM REYNOLDS of Ketley (in or near Colebrokedale) appears to have the principal claim; as will be shown by the subjoined extract; which, tho of some length, I give a place, here; as a material of the HISTORY of CANALS, in ENGLAND. For, notwithstanding, *railways* are, at present, in high esteem, there are numberless situations in which canals will continue to be superiorly advantageous; and many, no doubt, in which the present number may be extended, with profit to the country;—in preventing a large portion of its produce from being consumed unprofitably, by animals of draft. In this point of view, CANALS and RAILWAYS are closely connected with RURAL ECONOMICKS.

P. 290. "The superior utility of navigable canals, had by this time been pretty generally ascertained, and they were found to be more especially advantageous in the removal of heavy articles; it therefore became evident, that a navigable canal was the means by which coal and iron could be sent from such distances as the *Oaken Gates* and *Ketley*, so as to reach the market on terms of competition with the same sort of articles which are procured nearer to the river.

"But how necessary soever a navigable canal might be for those purposes, it was for a long time deemed an impracticable project. The general summit over which it must pass, lying on that range which is considered as nearly the highest ground in the kingdom; this ground being also very rugged, and consisting of ridges which are insulated from the adjoining country, there was no prospect of procuring a sufficient quantity of water for the purposes of lockage, the only mode of conveying boats from a higher to a lower canal, which had at that time been practised in Britain.

"These seemed insuperable difficulties, and most probably might have proved so for ages to come, had not Mr. WILLIAM REYNOLDS, of Ketley (whose character is too well known to need any eulogium), discovered the means of effecting this desirable object: for he, about this time, having occasion to improve the mode of conveying ironstone and coals, from the neighbourhood of the Oaken Gates to the iron works at Ketley, these materials lying generally at the distance of about a mile and a half from the iron-works, and at 73 feet above their level; he made a navia navigable canal, and instead of descending in the usual way, by locks, continued to bring the canal forward to an abrupt part of the bank, the skirts of which terminated on a level with the iron-works. At the top of this bank he built a small lock, and from the bottom of the lock, and down the face of the bank, he constructed an *inclined plane* with a double iron railway. He then erected an upright frame of timber, in which, across the lock, was fixed a large wooden barrel; round this barrel a rope was passed, and was fixed to a moveable frame; this last frame was formed of a size sufficient to receive a canal boat, and the bottom upon which the boat rested, was preserved in nearly an horizontal position, by having two large wheels before and two small ones behind, varying as much in the diameters as the inclined plane varied from an horizontal plane. This frame was placed in the lock, the loaded boat was also brought from the upper canal into the lock, the lock-gates were shut, and on the water being drawn from the lock into a side pond, the boat settled upon the horizontal wooden frame, and as the bottom of the lock was formed with nearly the same declivity as the inclined plane, upon the lower gates being opened, the frame with the boat passed down the iron railway, on the inclined plane, into the lower canal, which had been formed on a level with the Ketley iron-works, being a fall of 73 feet. Very little water was required to perform this operation, because the lock was formed of no greater depth than the upper canal, except the addition of such a declivity as was sufficient for the loaded boat to move out of the lock; and in dry seasons, by the assistance of a small steam engine, the whole of the water drawn off from the lock, was returned into the upper canal by means of a short pump.

"A double railway having been laid upon the inclined plane, the loaded boat in passing down, brought up another boat containing a load nearly equal to one-third part of that which passed down. The velocities of the boats were regulated by a brake acting upon a large wheel placed upon the axis on which the ropes connected with the carriage, were coiled.

"It is proper to observe, that Mr. REYNOLDS reduced the size of his canal boats, for instead of making use of boats of 70 feet in length, each carrying from 25 to 30 tons, he made them only 20 feet in length, 6 feet 4 inches in width, and 3 feet ten inches deep; each capable of carrying eight tons. This inclined plane was completed in the year 1788.

"As

"As soon as the plan of ascending and descending by means of an inclined plane was fairly understood, every person was convinced that its principle was very applicable to the situation of the ground which lay between the Oaken Gates and the river Severn, and that this invention alone would obviate the difficulties which before had been considered as insurmountable. Under this impression, a subscription was entered into, and an act of parliament was obtained for the Shropshire canal."

Mr. Telford then proceeds to describe and explain, with the help of well executed engravings, "plans and elevations of the inclined planes upon the Shropshire and Shrewsbury canal."—Together with the direction, construction, general economy, and advantages, of the said united canal.

He then describes, in like manner, the "iron aqueduct which conveys the Shrewsbury canal over the river Tern, at Longdon in the county of Salop."—P. 300. "The idea of having this aqueduct made of cast-iron, was first suggested and recommended by THOMAS EYTON, Esq. then Chairman of the Committee; after due consideration it was approved of by the Committee, and the principles of construction, and the manner in which it should be executed, were referred to Mr. WILLIAM REYNOLDS and the Writer of this article, who, after several consultations, and forming and considering various plans, at last determined upon that which is represented by the annexed engravings, No. 3. The castings for the aqueduct were done at Ketley, and were removed to Long, a distance of five miles, partly by land and partly by water-carriage.

"This aqueduct was proposed in consequence of the great floods which happened in the beginning of the year 1795, and it was fixed up complete in March, 1796."

P. 301. "Besides the Shropshire and Shrewsbury canals, there is likewise another canal, which, although not wholly within the county of Salop, is yet so materially connected with it, as to require particular notice in this Report: it is called the *Ellesmere Canal*, and rather than one, is in fact a system of canals, distributed over that extensive and fertile district of country which lies between the banks of the Severn on the South, and those of the river Mersey on the North, and between the skirts of North Wales on the West, and the borders of Staffordshire on the East, a space of 50 miles in length, and more than 20 in breadth, exclusive of the valleys which open into North Wales.

"This

"This canal will unite the rivers Severn, Dee, and Mersey, and will, by this means, open a communication by water, from the above-mentioned districts to the ports of Liverpool and Bristol.

"Although it is certain that this part of the country, will reap many advantages (as to articles of commerce) from the communication which this canal will open to these two rival ports, yet it is true, that by far the most beneficial effects will follow from the influence which it will have upon the agriculture of the adjoining districts; and it is probably the first instance, in Great-Britain, in which the extension and improvements of agriculture have been the principal motives that led to the forming a navigable canal of so great an extent, and where manufactures, commerce, and the trade of large towns, have been only secondary considerations."

The section "Canals," closes with the register of the heights of the water in the Severn, at the iron bridge, near Colebrokedale (mentioned, aforegoing, under the head *Climature)* from the year 1789 to that of 1800, both inclusive.—Every day, in each year (Sundays excepted) during twelve years!

With a view to the improvement of the navigation of the Severn, this register does the scientific perseverance of Mr. Reynolds great credit. But its use, as an improvement of the "common pluviameter," is altogether imaginary; and ought not to have made any impression on the cultivated mind of the Reporter. The quantity of rain water which reaches a river is no guide, whatever, to that which falls in its neighbourhood. Fifty inches of rain might fall in a year, on many or most of the southern chalk hills, for instance, without even one inch of it reaching a river. What falls over open limestone rocks, as well as over deep sandy or gravelly substrata, is likewise almost wholley absorbed; except when it may happen to fall in very heavy showers.

Roads.—The following observations (by Mr. Lloyd) though nothing new, furnishes additional evidence concerning the irrationality of the present road laws.—P. 280. "The private roads are by no means properly attended to; and which may be attributed to the general highway act being so easy of evasion, that every farmer is able to avoid doing statute duty, or, at least, next to none. Nothing is more valuable than *time*, especially to a man of business, and a farmer who executes the office of surveyor of the highway, *impartially and effectually*, will find he must neglect

neglect no small part of his own business, and after all he might, perhaps, have been as little out of pocket, had he done the whole work with his own team and labourers. There is no trick, evasion, or idleness, that shall be deemed too mean to avoid working on the road: sometimes the worst horses are sent; at others a broken cart, or a boy, or an old man past labour, to fill: they are sometimes sent an hour or two too late in the morning, or they leave off much sooner than the proper time, unless the surveyor watch the whole day. It is true, that redress may be had by application to a magistrate; but then how often causes for complaint occur? and how many days must be lost to bring each home to the offender? who, *from custom*, thinks he is doing no harm; besides the constant breach of good neighbourhood that must be occasioned by these petty litigations. A remedy might easily be had in the following manner:—Abolish all personal service upon the highways. Let surveyors be appointed, as at present, who should have power, under the authority of two magistrates, to raise, by rate, certain sums that may be deemed necessary for the repair of the roads within the respective parishes and townships, and to account for the same at going out of office at the year's end."

P. 281. (by the Reporter) "In many of the midland and southern parishes of Shropshire, there is no tolerable horse-road whatever; and in some that have coal and lime, those articles are nearly useless, from the difficulty of bringing any carriage to them. This, like most other evils, in the political economy of this country, becomes ameliorated, in proportion as the proprietors of the larger estates reside upon them."

Materials.—P. 281. (by the same) "Our best roads are made by buying the stones that may be picked off clover leys, &c. and breaking them small before they are used; and by skreened gravel, of which there is a tolerable supply near several roads, though the country they go through may be in general clay, the soils being so various and intermixed."

Hedgerows of Roads.—A hint to the managers of estates. (by the same)—P. 282. "High hedges, and trees in hedges by the sides of roads, are inconvenient, not only as they keep off the sun and wind, and deny the traveller the solace of observing the country he is passing through, but the leaves that fall off in Autumn obstruct the water courses at a critical season. When landlords want to fell timber, they should make a point of cutting that down first

first which grows near roads, and they should not raise trees in such situations."

Width of Roads.—The Reporter *perfectly agrees* with me, respecting this particular.—P. 282. "The breadth of every road should be determined by the circumstances of the country it goes through. A road of 60 feet, is, in general, a baneful breadth, not only as it is an unnecessary waste of land, but as it invites trespass and obstruction from stray cattle, &c."

Road *Carriages*.—The following well conceived suggestion (by the Reporter) is worth preserving.—P. 283. "By the 13 Geo. III. it is enacted, that the name, &c. of the owner of every waggon, &c. shall be painted in *large letters upon some conspicuous part of such waggon, &c.*; perhaps it would be better if the words, *front, or right hand side*, were inserted, instead of *conspicuous part*, because that the name, &c. would be more certainly seen, carriages in passing taking the left hand side of the road. If the size of the letters also was fixed (as in the case of those on dairy doors, &c.) it may be an improvement. The value of all regulations depends so much upon their being enforced, and so few persons will take the trouble to enforce, even the best regulations, that whatever tends to facilitate the detection of offenders is worth regarding."

Markets.—*Weights* and *Measures*.—The subjoined *mass* of information will serve (with other instances already adduced) to show the uncivilized state of the markets of this supereminently *commercial* country!

P. 351. (by the Reporter) "Wheat, barley, and pease, are sold by the strike, or bushel, which in Shrewsbury market is 38 quarts, but in some other markets it is 40 quarts. The 38 quarts of wheat should weigh 75 lb., the 40 quarts 80 lb. In other markets in the county, the bushel of wheat does not weigh more than 70 lb.: this is chiefly applicable to the eastern district. The bushel of flour is every where 56 lb. Thirty-eight quarts of barley weigh about 65 lb. A bushel of oats means three half bushels of the customary measure at Shrewsbury, and should weigh better than 93 lb. In other markets it means $2\frac{1}{2}$ bushels, sometimes heaped, sometimes stricken, and sometimes a medium between both. A bag of wheat means three bushels customary measure. The quarter bushel is called a hoop, or peck; and the fourth of that is called *a quarter*. Butter, when fresh, weighs 17 oz. to the lb; when salted, 16 oz. The last is reckoned by gawns, which signifies 12 lb. of 16 oz. in Shrewsbury, and 16 lb,

16 lb. of 16 oz. at Bridgnorth. Cheese is sold by the cwt., which at Shrewsbury means 121 lb. and 113 lb. at Bridgnorth. Coals are sold by the ton, which is 20 cwt. of 112 lb. at some pits, and 120 lb. at others: the stack is now rarely used; it was a measure of four feet square, and would sometimes weigh 25 cwt. Hay is sold by the ton, of 20 cwt. of 112 lb. Home-made linen cloth is sold by the ell, which measures a yard and half.

"The acre is the statute acre.

"The workman's rood in digging is eight yards square; in hedging eight yards in length.

"An attempt was made by order of Sessions some years ago, to introduce an uniformity of weights and measures, and it was accomplished in Bishop's Castle market, by the perseverance and activity of a neighbouring magistrate; but as the same attention was not continued in other markets, the old measures were in time introduced again."

In p. 174, speaking of wheat, the Reporter says,—"the customary measure varies from 38 to 40 quarts in different markets, but the test of wheat is what it will weigh. The bushel is expected to weigh 75 lb. in the neighbourhood of Shrewsbury, and 80 lb. in that of Bishop's-Castle."

RURAL INSTITUTES.—P. 351. (by the Reporter)—"There are no agricultural societies of any standing in this county: one has been lately established at Drayton, upon the N. E. borders, and another at Shifnal, upon the east borders; both these districts adjoin, and are connected with Staffordshire."

SUBJECT THE THIRD.

RURAL ECONOMY.

DIVISION THE FIRST.

TENANTED ESTATES,

Their IMPROVEMENT and MANAGEMENT.

ESTATES.—*Proprietors.*—The following desultory remarks, tho they prove nothing, are at least ingenious.—P. 90. (by the Reporter) "Landed property is considerably

ably divided in Shropshire, more so, perhaps, than is generally imagined. In the parochial visitations of my archdeaconry, I have enquired the number of proprietors in a parish, and generally found them more numerous than I had expected. If I asked who were the proprietors of the next parish, a few of the most opulent were named; but when I arrived there, I again found the number far exceeding the general estimation. Manufactures and commerce, the professions of arms and of the law, raise men of small fortunes to affluence; and their riches enable them to concentre the estates of others. But again, men of hereditary fortune become forced to alienate their domains, and these, perhaps, are parcelled out among purchasers of inferior wealth. The thrifty farmer, or mechanic, supplies the place of those proprietors who have sold their lands for the sake of increasing their stock, or of trying their fortune in manufactures; and some of these may, in the first or second generation, again become purchasers of real estates. The number of gentlemen of small fortune living on their estates, has decreased: their descendants have been clergymen or attornies, either inthe country, or shopkeepers in the town of their own county; or more probably in this county, emigrated to Birmingham, to Liverpool, to Manchester, or to London: but then the opulent farmer, who has purchased the farm he lives upon, or some smaller estate, which he sets or holds, with the large one he before rented, is a character that has increased. Whether the proprietors of land in this county are more or fewer than heretofore, I have no practicable means of knowing."—Adding—"I am led to think, that the freeholders and copyholders cannot now be less than 3000."

I have great satisfaction in transcribing Archdeacon Plymley's strictures on magistracy, and the duties which men of large landed property owe to society;—in return, let it be added, for the many privileges and superior advantages, which therein they enjoy.—The Archdeacon's remarks are evidently the result of much thought, guided by good sense, and moderated feeling; and afford those for whom they were made, valuable means of reflection. Agriculture requires a greater number of existing laws to be strictly observed, than perhaps any other profession.

P. 348. "It may be said of legislation and police, as connected with agriculture, as well as with most other subjects, *that there is more want of a due execution of existing*

isting laws, than of new laws. The office of a justice of the peace is somewhat expensive and very laborious, more especially as the same persons are, in general, the acting commissioners for taxes. Still many country gentlemen do great service to the public, by submitting to what I may call this disagreeable necessity; for I know not whether it is not essential to the proper strength and harmony of our constitution, that persons of independent fortune should continue freely to execute the laws committed to their trust; that they should as magistrates, oversee and direct the police of the country; and as commissioners of taxes, judge between the executive power and the people, and that without fee or reward: because the notoriety of their having no other interest in the trouble they take, than what is common to all the subjects of the realm, ensures a more ready acquiescence in their decisions, and must add to the weight of beneficial influence. Still in the execution of most laws there must be some extent of co-operation. Few persons like to be informers—few like to be complainants, unless their passions are warmed, or their interests distinctly injured. From the former circumstance, many trivial accusations are brought forward: from the latter, thieves are apprehended and prosecuted. But that cattle are straying in the roads; that nuisances are left on the highway; that work is not provided for the poor; that servants are enticed to the ale-house—upon these and other occasions, individuals are rarely sufficiently injured to give their time and trouble in praying justice, though there are laws, which, if inquired after, would redress most of the evils complained of. A watchful magistrate may do much, but he cannot do every thing. Persons of large fortune (as has been observed before) should consider the burthen of this office as a kind of tax arising out of the interest they have in the welfare of the country; and though it is far from being the case, that there is no feeling of this kind, yet it were to be wished that this feeling stood higher, and that persons of property, instead of wishing to educate all their sons for situations, by which they may advance the honours or opulence of their families, would consider how the heirs to large estates could be best formed to that highly important, but oftentimes mistaken character, a *country gentleman.* Nothing low, or idle, or flippant, or profligate, belongs to this character. Like every other post in human life, it is a post of duty. Independent of the assistance required from him in administering the justice of the country, he should

be

be the adviser and peace-maker of his district; he should co-operate in the improvement of rural arts; he should be the pattern of improved husbandry; he should set an example of scrupulous obedience to the laws in his own person, and endeavour to sustain the tone of Christian morality throughout his neighbourhood. And in what situation of a country will the possessors of large fortunes, so acting, be deemed useless or inconvenient? Or can any country be endangered, that is cemented by a middle order, whose powers and services are so happily mingled?"

On the *sizes* of estates, in Shropshire, the conjectural account, which follows, may serve to convey some general ideas.—P. 91. (by the Reporter) "Estates vary in value, from 1*l.* per ann. to several thousand pounds per ann.; that the proportion of the estates of 10*l.* a year, and under, may be nearly one-third in number of the whole; and that those of more than 10*l.* a year, and not exceeding 100*l.* a year, are above one-half of the whole number; that the largest estates are, in general, parts of estates, *i. e.* the proprietors have estates in other counties; that of those who have no property out of this county, above one-half reside upon their estates; that the proportion of those who have estates in other counties, may be about one-twelfth in number, but that, in property, they possess full two-fifths of the whole; and that of these partial proprietors, one-fifth may reside a part of the year on their estates."—P. 92. "The landed income of this county may be about 600,000*l.* per annum"

Tenures.—P. 93. "There is much copyhold-tenure, but of easier customs than in the neighbouring counties.*" The lords of some customary manors" (says this Reporter) "have enfranchised the copyholders, upon receiving an equivalent in money. The customs of the greater number are preserved and acted upon. In the manors of Ford, Cundover, Wem, and Loppington, the lands descend to the youngest son, and in default of sons, to the youngest daughter. In the manors of Cardington and of Stretton, estates descend to the eldest son, and in default of sons, the daughters are coheireses. The fines and heriots also in these two manors, though somewhat different, are so fixed and easy, that it may be doubted whether the tenure is not preferable to freehold."

IMPROVEMENT of ESTATES.—There is some reason and truth, in the Reporter's observations, in p. 347.—"It seems best that the landlord should be the improver. He has an interest in making full and effectual improvements: for

"* Original Report."

for then he can set his lands for a fair price: whereas if tenants make, or rather attempt to make improvements, the effort will be limited, as their interest is limited, and an improvident saving will oftentimes counteract the good that was intended."

Somebody's remarks, in p. 237 *, are new and judicious. —"When a farmer has a crop of turnips, which he does not intend to clean by hoeing, let his landlord send a man to hoe a quarter, or even half an acre for him, as well as possible, but neither in the *best* nor *worst* place. The farmer should be present to see the process; the value of which will be demonstrated to him, when his crop is full grown, and he compares the hoed part of the field with the rest. The next year he should be allowed a man for two days, to instruct two of his own men, and to hoe between them; after which they will be able to do the business themselves."

For another instance of this sort, see the head *Turnips* ensuing.

Reclaiming watery and *wild Lands.*—P. 223 (by Mr. Lloyd) "About 20 years ago there were large tracts of lands (Baggymoor, and other moors from near Boreatton to St. Martin's) in the Winter usually covered with water, but which are now, in consequence of enclosures and drainage, at no great expense, rendered of considerable value. Hither wild-fowl of all sorts usually resorted, and astonishing quantities were annually taken at the decoy near Whittington, the property of Mr. Lloyd, of Aston, but which, from the above improvement, has been deserted by the ducks, &c. and has been suffered to go out of repair, never again, probably, to be appropriated to its former use. The lands have been laid dry by large open ditches, which have served as fences. The grass is of a coarse nature, but where *paring and burning* have been adopted, these meadows have amply paid for the improvement, so that all the farmers who have such land are treating it in the same manner."

Irrigation.—The watering of grass lands would seem to be partially practised, in Shropshire;—as well in the *Wiltshire*, as in the *Devonshire*, manner. But there is nothing noticeable on the subject, in this Report; excepting a novel suggestion (in the section "Draining") by Mr.

* These remarks are included between "turned commas," or marks of quotation; but no writer's name is appended. *One* instance, this, of the impropriety of the method censured, in p. 188.

Mr. Harries. P. 229.—"I would have an act of parliament, giving the use of water to the land-owners on the seventh day, when the millers might rest from their work; liberty to use it when there is a surplus, and no damage can be proved."

The insertion of this hint is highly creditable to the liberality and moderation of Mr. Plymley. Much good, doubtlessly, would accrue from such a regulation.

EXECUTIVE MANAGEMENT of Estates.—Again we find the Archdeacon of Salop, with becoming deference, stimulating landed gentlemen to a just sense of their duties, as such.

P. 96. "Without intending to interfere with the right of private judgment, which must always direct the operation of general rules, and without attempting to decide upon the influence, from circumstances, that must so frequently control the conduct of individuals, and whose conduct may be perfectly right, though contrary to the best general rules, still the suggestion of leading principles is sometimes useful, and I would offer to landed proprietors in this place, a consideration of how much their own good, and that of the community, may be oftentimes promoted, by a residence upon their estates; and by the concentration of their property, so that as much of it as possible may be within the sphere of their personal influence. I do not want persons of large fortune to become their own stewards; perhaps those who reside in the country, and are intent upon the general improvement of their neighbourhood, want professional assistance of this kind, even more than absent proprietors: they have not only the most use of this assistance, but they can see that it is beneficially exerted. It is a medium between their own ideas and the views of those who are uneducated; it is a medium of enquiry and of mutual information; it begets necessary explanations; it conveys necessary admonitions. Independent of what is more particularly business, it tends to preserve unbroken the connexion between the rich and the poor.

"When a resident proprietor acts from proper principles, excessive poverty is, of course, banished from his district: should he not be the benevolent or well-informed man that may be wished, still the income derived from the neighbourhood is circulated in the neighbourhood, and poverty is relieved. The difference between a village where the proprietor resides, and one where he does not, may perhaps exemplify the difference between England

and

and Ireland, where absent landlords are much more numerous."

Managers.—P. 92. (by the Reporter) "There are several respectable land-agents in this county, who are very generally employed in valuing and setting farms, and who receive the rents also from some estates. On other estates, the landlord, or a common steward, or sometimes an attorney, receives the rents. Several large estates have been materially improved by the judicious management of land-agents by profession; so much so, that the face of the country has become quite altered."

Tenancy.—P. 135. (by the same) "Leases for lives, or for a single life, were more common than they are now; though some very considerable proprietors have, at no great distance of time, leased farms for the term of the tenant's life. Sometimes a farmer has made a fortune by a beneficial lease; but it has more frequently happened that he has hurt the land and himself, by the indolence it has given rise to. One very considerable estate, set on leases for three lives, did not produce, a few years ago, more than one-tenth of the annual value to the landlord; and many of the farms so conditioned, and of the roads near them, appear worse managed than those in the neighbourhood that have not been in lease."

P. 136. (by the same) "The propriety of leases, like many other things, depends upon circumstances; therefore no general rule can well be given advising their use or disuse. Where neither a landlord nor his agent take any interest in the cultivation of an estate, or where the landlord is not willing to lay out money in improvements or repairs, the tenant cannot be expected to cultivate a farm to any advantage without the security of a lease; and where there is no confidence between landlord and tenant, the insertion of restrictions, or the prescription of a mode of culture, may also be necessary."—Again—"Where a landlord, by himself or agent, studies his own estate; and where the size and various branches of it are not too great to be understood thoroughly, a tenancy from year to year, unfettered by any restrictions, further than that of good husbandry, required by the law of the land, is perhaps best for both parties."—No:—six months, and even twelve months' notice is too short a warning for a good tenant. See NORTHERN DEPART. p. 359.

The following information, by the Reporter, will astonish the managers of estates, in these "improving," otherwise *rent-raising* times (owing *in part* to the rapid depreciation

ciation of money); when landlords are ready to take possession of a long-leased farm, in almost any state or condition.

P. 136. "One gentleman of this county set leases for 21 years certain, and for seven years more, at the option of the lessor. This was meant as a check against the tenant's impoverishing the land in the last years of his absolute term; at the end of which the lessor meant to part with him, or come to a new agreement for 21 years, with the threat of seven years beyond it, for which he might be obliged to hold it, had he treated it improperly. Thus, he could not hurt his landlord without hurting himself more."

Covenants.—P. 127. "In old leases, reserves were made of a day's ploughing, or of some days work in the harvest; some poultry at Christmas; the keep of fighting cocks, or of dogs; but I do not know that any such stipulations are now inserted or made. The rack-tenants of a sporting landlord are frequently subject to the inconvenience of keeping dogs; and rack-tenants are in many places expected to draw a load or a certain number of loads of coal annually."

Rent.—P. 127. (by the Reporter) "Land is measured by the statute acre, and it varies from 8s. or less per acre, to 12s. in districts where the roads are bad, and where the landlord has not interested himself in the improvement of his estate, or where the agent has gone on in the beaten track of superintendance: and from 15s. to 20s. per acre and more, the farm together, in more favourable situations. Near towns land lets from 2l. to 6l. an acre; and in the manufacturing parts of the county small parcels of land also let high."

Choice of Tenants.—P. 126. "Mr. William Flavel, of Alberbury, observes, in the margin of a Report returned to the Board, 'I am of opinion that landlords are chiefly in fault respecting ill husbandry, by not paying that attention to the management of their estates as they ought to do, and making a proper distinction between good and bad farmers.'"

DIVISION

DIVISION THE SECOND.

WOODLAND.

WOODS and HEDGEROWS.—P. 212. (by the Reporter) —"Notwithstanding large yearly falls of timber, there are still some very fine woods of oak growing in this county. There is a good deal of hedge-row timber also, consisting of oak and ash principally, a few wych and other elms, still fewer beech, lime, and sycamore. Poplars are not uncommon by the sides of brooks and small rivers. There are a few yew trees, and hollies have been plentiful, but that beautiful tree and useful fence appears to have been neglected or destroyed. *Birches*, both as *a tree* and *fence*, are common in the S. W. district."—The last period is a specimen of the want of neatness, in the language of the volume under Review.

P. 214. (by the same)—"There are many thousand acres of coppice-wood in this county. Their value depends much upon situations; but perhaps they do not pay more than 7s. an acre yearly, upon the average. As fire-wood, the demand is diminished, from the increased consumption of coal, and which is still increasing, by means of turnpike-roads and canals; and for forges, wood is in less request than heretofore. Many sorts of iron are now manufactured with preparations of coal, which could only be worked with fires of wood 20 years ago. It is no improbable supposition, that the demand for coppice-wood will continue to decrease, in proportion as the art of making iron is better understood."

P. 218. (by Mr. Harries) "This county was remarkably well furnished with oak timber, and still retains more than any other that I am acquainted with. Great supplies have been sent to Bristol for ship-building, and the stock has been greatly diminished within the last 30 years. There is still sufficient remaining for our domestic consumption, and other markets."—Again—"Underwoods are very extensive; they consist chiefly of oak, and the greater part are in such soils and situations, as make the best return that could be expected. Large quantities of oak poles are used for different purposes in the coal-pits; as they are required to have some strength, they are sel-

dom

dom fallen before 24 years growth, and the bark (used in tanning leather) is an object of great importance, and now sells at an high price. Birch will answer for coal-pit wood, but is not so valuable. Ash is used for hoops, and the tops are converted to chairs by the turners. On the side of Shropshire, near Bewdley, in Worcestershire, is a large tract of underwood fallen at 18 to 21 years growth, for converting into charcoal for making bar-iron."

P. 219. (by the same)—"Our hedge-rows have furnished a great quantity of oak and ash, and some elms, though generally much injured by cropping."

For a hint to the managers of hedge-rows,—see *Roads*, p. 224, aforegoing.

Planting.—P. 212. (by the Reporter) "There are many modern plantations of various sorts of firs and pine, generally mixed with different deciduous trees. At Linley near Bishop's Castle, are plantations of larch, Scotch and spruce firs, as old, I believe, as most plantations of the sort in South Britain. Mr. More planted each species in considerable masses, instead of mingling them. He raised also indigenous trees in considerable quantity, and had a large collection of the rarer sorts."

The sentiment which succeeds those facts, tho not *new*, is not the less just.—"Though there may be a call to plant in this country, still the duty is not so imperious a one, that it should be universally entertained. Like many general duties, it should yield to circumstances; and trees should not be reared in any quantity upon land that may be made subservient to agriculture or profitable pasture. When we are independent of foreign corn, we may calculate more minutely, probable importations of timber."—And Mr. Harries entertains the same opinion.—P. 214. "Timber in this county, like all others, has of late been infinitely more destroyed than preserved; nor does it seem to have been considered as an article of future value; crops of grain, &c. producing a more expeditious return of profit to the cultivator, the advantages to be derived from planting have seldom occupied his thoughts. Planting indiscriminately, is as absurd as a total neglect of it. Attention should be paid to the soil, situation, and other circumstances."

This rule has long been laid down. But the transgressions against it have been manyfold and great. Mr. H. (in the course of his lengthened remarks on this subject) brings a proof of its justness.—P. 218. "I know several woods,

woods, from 80 to 120 years growth, by no means at maturity, which, under a course of agriculture, would have produced ten times its value."

Either this writer's direction, for *lopping* trees, or the explanatory diagram, inserted in his account, is defective.

DIVISION THE THIRD.

AGRICULTURE.

FARMS.—*Size.*—Mr. Plymley, after quoting what Mr. Bishton has said, on this subject (p. 181); adds, p. 120,—" and even there, viz. on the west side of the county, are several farms as large as most in the east district; and the size has increased in all parts of the county, two, three, or four farms being put into one, though there are a few instances of large farms being again subdivided. There is a use, perhaps, in farms of all common sizes, so far as they are extended, at least in this county. The small farmer, for instance, brings his grain early to market, and the large farmer's hoard may prevent scarcity."

These are truisms that have been uttered, again and again, and cannot have too many tongues and pens to promulgate them.

Mr. Harries's observations, on the sizes of farms, are rather applicable to the stronger lands of Shropshire, than to lands in general, and of the kingdom at large. His conclusion, however, is just, and shows that he is practically acquainted with the management of an estate. —P. 122. "Large farms, where the occupier has abilities and capital, are the most profitable, or where entire new erections are to be made, are the most so to the owner; but where they are already built upon, I believe the owner will obtain a larger rent, and have his lands cultivated with more neatness, from the size I have recommended" (100 to 200 acres); "he will attend to several minutiæ that the large farmer neglects: it renders an independent situation for a greater number of families, and of that description of people so desirable to a state."

It appears, however, by Mr. H's statement, that it is the present practice of Shropshire to enlarge them.—P. 122. " The generality of farms rise from 50 to 200 acres; we have

have a few from 200 to 500 or 600 acres: it is a pretty general practice to enlarge them. In the last thirty years the number of our farms may have diminished one third."

On *laying out farms*,—see *Homesteads* below.

On *Farm Gates*,—An admirable idea is thrown out, by Mr. Lloyd,—p. 150.—"Farmers should contract with their wheel-wright to keep their gates in repair by the year, and to go over them regularly (exclusive of accidental repair) every quarter."—Rather say—whenever it may suit their own convenience. Gates, that swing clear, are not only more secure, and convenient, but last much longer, than those which drag on the ground. It would of course be the interest of the contracter, to keep them in the state most profitable to the farmer; as well as to the proprietor who allows gate timber.

Homesteads.—P. 102. (by Mr. Tench) "The farm-houses and buildings, in general, are very inconveniently situated and ill-constructed, many of them being at one extremity of the farm; but the greatest part are situated in villages; those that are not so, are mostly built in some very low situation, by which means the farmer entirely looses the drainings of his fold-yard, which, had he an opportunity of turning over his land, would render him infinite service."

P. 102. (by Mr. Lloyd)—"I have found it advisable, where a set of farm-buildings have required a thorough repair, to remove them to a more desirable situation, in chusing which, the following particulars should be attended to: 1st, A centrical part of the farm; 2dly, A proper distance from the road; 3dly, A high, but not an exposed, aspect; that the farm-yard may be warm for young cattle, that the manure may be carried *down-hill*, and that the liquid manure may run over as much land as possible."

Mr. Bishton, the original Reporter, too, complains of the inconveniences of farm houses being situated in villages (see p. 173). Nevertheless, in the Report under Review, we find a complete plan of a farm house village! —with cottages intermixed, and a church in the center: altogether, very much resembling those that other times and circumstances have thickly planted, in every quarter of the kingdom.

But the Reporter, it appears, formed his plan, some years ago; and, in 1794, made a communication to the Board of Agriculture; recommending, it would seem (see his Report, p. 103) not only villages of farm houses and cottages, but also cottage cow grounds;—in confor-

mity,

mity, it is probable, with the *fashion*, which *then* reigned, concerning the latter establishments. See p. 114, aforegoing.

Mr. Lloyd's suggestion, respecting farm house *windows*, deserves notice.—P. 105. "The windows of farm-houses should be large, and made to admit plenty of air; but never more than one in a room, or the farmer will inevitably stop them up to save the tax. They should open by sliding, not upon hinges, that the wind may not have power to break them: the same observation will hold good as to those of the out-buildings."—The Reporter adds, p. 106,—"It is melancholy to see the dark rooms, in which farmers' servants are often put to sleep, since the increase of the window-tax. It would be well, if landlords would see that a proper number of windows were kept open in farm-houses. An intelligent and active magistrate of this county, once favoured me with the following suggestion, for an alteration in the window-tax, with reference to this subject. 'No house used as a farm-house only, to pay for more than 12 windows, = 2l. 16s.; every farm-house with which lands of the value of 150l. per ann. are occupied, shall be rated for not less than 10 windows, = 1l. 14s.; the glass duty will be much increased, as well as the window-tax.'"—This well conceived suggestion seems to be entitled to the consideration of the Legislature.

The following remarks of the Reporter, regarding the *building materials* of *barns*, have much truth in them:—and, in situations where materials can be *chosen*, may have their use.—Wood (Studwork and weather boarding) is an ordinary material of barns, throughout the southern counties.

P. 107.—"Barns framed with timber and walled with boards, appear preferable to those built of stone or brick The grain will generally thrash out cleaner, and of a brighter colour, from a boarded barn: the air penetrates through all parts of a bay surrounded with boards; they are soon dried by the wind, and warmed by the sun, after rain, and are too close to admit birds; whereas the air-holes left in stone or brick-work, will not exclude them: the air so let in, acts partially: snow and rain also get in at times; the walls are always cold, and frequently damp."

For a well planned *fatting shed*, see the head *Turnips*, ensuing.

Cottages. In what might be termed a valuable moral essay,

essay, concerning country laborers, Mr. Plymley has thrown out some admirable ideas, respecting the *construction* of cottages:—a topic that has, of late, employed the pens and pencils of plannists, artists, and amateurs. There is scarcely any form, which fancy can devise, in which they have not been represented. But Mr. P. properly, and happily, ridicules all *fine* and *fancy* forms.—P. 109. "I would only suggest the impropriety of making them, or indeed, any other object, bear an outward appearance, intended to contradict their inward use—all castellated or gothicised cottages, all church-like barns, or fort-like pigstyes, I should conceive to be objectionable. They are intended to deceive, and they tell you that they are intended to deceive. It is not pleasant to encourage any thing like deceit; but in these instances, imposition effected is rarely gained; it amounts only to imposition attempted; or, could the deceit succeed, it would only present a prospect with fewer proprieties about it than there really are. Almost every species of country building has a good effect, if properly placed and neatly executed; and what are the least ornamental, or indeed the most disgusting, of their appendages, cease to shock, when supported by the relative situation they stand in, shewing their necessity and their use. A dunghill in a farm-fold creates no disagreeable idea, but connected with a Gothic gateway, or embattled tower, it is bad. Cattle protected by the side of a barn, form a picturesque group; but sheltering under a Grecian portico—the impropriety is glaring. Linen hanging to dry on the hedge of a cottage garden, may be passed without displeasure; but the clothes of men, women, and children, surrounding the cell of an anchorite, or the oratory of a monk, have their natural unseemliness increased by the contrast."

The following passage will, at least, show the humane disposition of its writer.—P. 112. "Where a ground-floor is made perfectly dry, there is a convenience in having the bed-room to open out of the kitchen, because the kitchen-fire is sufficient for the purposes of illness. Food or medicine, can be warmed at it, and an attendant can be kept warm, and near the patient."

P. 113. "Another observation, with regard to cottages, should not be forgotten. The persons living in them, should be tenants to the real landlord, paying a fair annual rent."

This, as an ordinary rule, has much propriety on its side. But, like most other rules, it is liable to exceptions.

On

On large farms, at least, it is convenient, if not necessary, to have some cottages *within* them,—with inmates over whom the occupiers have a degree of *command*. The Archdeacon's plan, and the practice of Scotland, are in direct opposition.—See NORTHERN DEPARTMENT, p. 370.

I must not pass over the Reporter's dissertation on cottages and cottagers, without noticing a hint relating to cottage pigsties.—P. 115. "Where it is not convenient or advisable to let him have land enough for a cow, he may have a large garden, and the necessary and pig-stye should be so placed, that the soak from them may be directed to manure the soil. The pig-stye should have a small court, to open into the garden only. When a pig is bought, it is small, and can be carried to the stye, where it may remain. I have found this the only way of preventing the labourer's pigs from wandering about a village. If the stye opens to a road, it will never be so well guarded as when the first act of trespass must be in the owner's garden."

A hint on cottage gardening is also well given.—P. 210. (by the Reporter) "The dwarf-pease should be given among the labourers by those who can procure the seeds, as they bear well, and want no rods."

OCCUPIERS.—N. P. 123. (by Mr. Price) "The Shropshire farmers, in general, are very industrious. There are few of them but what work hard along with their servants. Their grain is generally extremely well cleaned for market. In the women's department, in the farm-houses, there seems to be a greater exertion of industry than I have remarked in most other counties. Besides brewing, baking, providing for the family, where workmen are maintained in the house, and managing the dairy, the farmer's wife, with the assistance of her maid-servants, in the evenings, and at spare hours, carries on a little manufacture, and gets up a piece of linen cloth for sale, every year."

PLAN OF MANAGEMENT.—P. 123. (by the Reporter)—"The scope of Shropshire farming is perhaps less confined than that of many other counties. The farms, generally speaking, are arable, grazing, for hay, for the dairy, rearing, and feeding. There are some pigs, some sheep, some colts; though the proportion of these several objects varies from situation. As to further marks of character, they are probably as various as man. The slothful and the industrious; the indolent and the enterprising; the hard-hearted and the benevolent—may be in the same proportion as in other counties, under the same degree of improve-

improvement; for the dread of innovation, or the aversion to experiment, subside, as the profit of new systems is felt, or the advantages of practiced skill are perceived; and how far the spirit of improvement is introduced, it is the purport of the different Sections to explain. In all parts of this county, examples of superior husbandry may be met with. There are few breeds of cattle, or few mechanical improvements, but what may be found within the county. Several gentlemen, as well as farmers, have gone to great expense in importing them from other counties. And perhaps where, from natural causes, the husbandry is the worst, there is the greatest local collection of both. I mean the succession of improved breeds, and of improved farming instruments, that have been, and are, at Kinlet-hall, situated between Bridgnorth and Cleobury Mortimer. The immediate neighbourhood appears to have improved by the example set, and the information communicated to them. And if the eastern district of the county is in general better cultivated than any other spots of equal size, it must be recollected, that it is nearer to an improved part of the kingdom: the soil is more easily managed, from its lightness, because less strength is necessary to plough with, more seasons are suitable to work in, and there is less occasion for draining." How unlike is the language of this extract to that of pure science.

Mr. Lloyd, in p. 125, censures the farmers of Shropshire, for being—" too much tempted, and detached from agriculture, to carry for hire upon the road." This, however, can scarcely happen, to a serious extent, unless in *mining* districts.

Succession. P. 170. (by the Reporter) " To estimate the value of the improved husbandry, we should look at that which was not unusual formerly, and even specimens of which may now, or could lately have been met with in this county, viz. fallow, wheat, oats for two years, the second year's crop being sown with clover, and which clover was suffered to remain two or three years, whilst fresh land, or a clover-ley of three years growth was broken up for oats or a fallow. If barley was introduced, it was after the wheat and before the oats. Some unfavourable situation, formerly under this course, have lately, by a proper application of manure, been successfully varied with turnips and barley."

WORKPEOPLE.—P. 139. (by Mr. Flavel)—" At present (about 1795) I give my labourers 14d. a day all the year; when

when the hay-harvest commences, I allow them meat and drink until the end of corn-harvest. I allow each man two quarts of small beer till harvest, and then six quarts each of harvest beer, exclusive of small beer at meals. I agree with my workmen to thrash most of the wheat and barley by task, at 6s. the score wheat, and 3s the score barley.

" *N. B.*—The harvest beer is one bushel of malt to eleven gallons, which is always brewed in October."

Again (by Mr. Tench, in 1795)—P. 139. "The rate of wages is from 6l. to 9l. per annum; price of labour, from the close of corn-harvest till hay-harvest following, 1s. 2d. per day, and two quarts of beer; though much wheat is set to thrash at 6s. per score, thirty-eight quarts to the bushel, with two quarts of beer per day, and barley at 3s. per score; during the hay-harvest the price of labour is 1s. 6d. per day, with six quarts of beer; but a considerable quantity of hay is set to mow at 1s. 10d. per acre, with six quarts of beer: for the corn-harvest the price of labour is from 9s. to 12s. per week, with meat and beer, though great part of the wheat is set to reap at 5s. per acre, with meat and beer. From the close of corn-harvest, till hay-harvest following, labour begins at six in the morning, and ends at six at night; and when hay-harvest commences, from five in the morning till seven or eight at night; and during the corn-harvest from daylight till night."

In the section "Hogs."—P. 267. (by the Reporter) "A greater proportion of labourers fed a pig formerly than at present; though those who are industrious and rear plenty of potatoes, contrive still to kill a bacon pig in Winter. One reason why labourers have not a pig so frequently as heretofore, may arise from their buying flour or bread, instead of wheat. Farmers who refuse to sell wheat in small quantities, act very improperly, for the labourer who can buy wheat, gets better bread than he can otherwise procure, and he has the bran towards feeding a pig."

Working Animals.—On this subject, we find numerous remarks, by different hands, in the volume under Review. But scarcely one of them is entitled to special attention. Both oxen and horses are in use; but chiefly the latter.—pp. 263 & 4. The Reporter is evidently in favor of oxen (from different parts of his work) in preference to horses. No evidence, however, appears of his having had sufficient experience of both, to decide on their comparative value.

Mr

Mr. P. speaks, with feeling, on the barbarous practice, which still prevails in Shropshire, of docking cart horses, and "the cruel custom of setting the horns of oxen."

The only extractable passage, on this topic, is from Mr. Powys's paper, in the Appendix. Mr. P. occupies on a scale sufficiently large to acquire adequate experience. But his paper is written in the manner of a tyro in agriculture, rather than in that of an experienced farmer. The passage alluded to is this:—P. 363.—"I think cows are much more useful and beneficial than oxen, and that it would be an advantage to the kingdom if few or no oxen were reared. The uses of cattle are to work, milk, and feed. I have seen barren cows work as well as oxen; they require less keep, and walk faster. Oxen are of no use to the dairy, and they will not feed so fast as cows."

How far this plan may be eligible, in large undertakings, I will not attempt to decide. Small working farmers, who keep a few cows, and who are unable to support horses, sufficient to work their lands, properly,—might, doubtlessly, receive, on many occasions, essential benefit, from working their cows. It has long appeared, to me, a matter of astonishment that they should neglect so obvious a mean of immediate profit.

Manures.—P. 233. (by Mr. Tench)—"Dung and lime, or a compost of dung, lime, and soil, are used. Sometimes soot and malt-dust is sown on meadow or pasture land: two years ago, soap-ashes were much used, but now the price of them is advanced as high as 8s. per ton, at which price they will not answer for manure, but are sold to go to the glass-houses."

P. 233. (by Mr. Lloyd) "The manure most in use, is lime, with which every part of this county is tolerably well supplied. It is principally spread upon arable land, and by that means the farmer can reserve the dung for the grass. Lime, whem mixed with peat, will consume it to ashes; and was this practice to become common, an admirable manure for grass-lands, or young clover, would be procured."

P. 232. (by Mr. Harries)—"Lime is purchased at the different works in this county, for about 10s. or 12s. per waggon-load of from 40 to 50 bushels, and large quantities of it are used throughout the county."

P. 235. (by the Reporter)—"Turf is sometimes cut upon Clun forest, in May or June, and burned. The ashes are used as a manure for turnips, ten cart-loads to an acre."

Mr. Reynolds, in a note on "Soils and Surface"—p. 47, says—"this pale-coloured clay has the local and technical name of dye-earth; and though, where it lies deep, it is of a blue colour, yet, when near the surface, becomes a pale yellow, from the oxydation of the iron it contains: it consists of 26 parts of calcareous earth, 58 ditto argil, 16 silex and iron. Might it not be used on the sandy lands on the banks of the river between Bridgnorth and Worcester, as a manure? This dye-earth is stratified, and contains marine impressions."

This earth being met with, in immense quantities, in sinking coal pits, (see p. 200,) and containing, by the above analysis, more calcarious earth, than many of the marls in use,—sufficient experiments ought, surely, to be tried with it, as such.

TILLAGE.—P. 162. (by Mr. Harries)—"Though summer fallows are by no means so frequent as formerly, yet they are used on our strong lands, preparatory for wheat, if after a stubble it is generally ploughed over before Christmas, and has at least three more ploughings in the course of a summer; if, upon a clover ley that is foul, it is grazed in the spring with sheep, and the first ploughing not given before the month of June, and there is afterwards sufficient time to work and clean it. Sometimes the clover is mowed, and a tolerable good fallow is made previous to October. Though summer-fallows are not so frequent, turnip fallows have increased in a much greater proportion upon our dry soils that are not too strong."

Mr. Cotes, in two letters to Lord Carrington (at that time President of the Board) relates an extraordinary *discovery* which, he conceives, "may be an effectual means of contributing to the ample supply of the country."—The substance of his plan is this.—P. 164. "Plough a wheat-fallow in two, three, or even four, *bout-ridges*, dependent on the foul condition of the land. In the *furrow* put some dung, on that dung place the potatoe-sets, and then plough a *bout* upon them; a *ridge* thus formed, gives a double portion of earth for the plant to grow in, and it has the benefit of the dung to root in. This applies to that part of the land which bears the *crop*, and which will form so many rows. The remaining part of the land will form so many alleys, in which, during the summer, the common operation of the plough will make the *fallow*: and thus crop and fallow be had, without injury to the land."

Now, this is precisely the COMPOST FALLOW which I formerly

merly made, in Surry, and described in the MINUTES of AGRICULTURE;—*Minutes* 11 and 255.

On "Paring and Burning," the Reporter has favored us with some appropriate remarks. I copy them, not only as such; but as being the most *practical* suggestion, with which the Reporter, himself, has furnished us.—P. 231. "Where there is a surface of rushes, or of very coarse grass, and where the ground is laid down to grass after a single crop, paring and burning may answer well. But I have seen it practised on land in this county, where there was no weed of peculiar tenacity to be destroyed, and where the custom has been to take two or three crops of grain before the land is again converted to grass. Under this management, I should think paring and burning must be very prejudicial. The ashes so produced are undoubtedly a good present manure; but when old swards are ploughed in, the land becomes very luxuriant by the third year, in consequence of the grass and roots having rotted, and being mixed with the soil. If they are then laid down with grass-seeds, they answer well; and if they are continued in tillage, they are calculated to receive peculiar benefit from lime."

For a successful practice, by *sod burning*, see *Improvement* of *Estates*, p. 229, aforegoing.

MANURING.—What Mr. Rowley says of the "variation of manures,"—tho chiefly speculative,—I give a place, here.—P. 234. "For thus, not only new vigour is applied to the land, but also fresh compounds are formed, by combining the matter of the soil with a strange substance; and thus, in some degree, a different soil is formed, and a different aliment of vegetables."

SEMINATION.—P. 159. (by Mr. Tench)—"The usual seed-time for wheat, is October, and for lent grain, from the beginning of March till the latter end of April; and corn-harvest, from the beginning of August till the middle of September. The grain, in general, is sown broad-cast, though some of the neatest farmers make use of the drill-plough to great advantage, and turnips are found to answer admirably well."

The Reporter adds,—"The drill-husbandry may answer best in light and gravelly soils, such as require an extra quantity of seed; where the plant gathers, as the farmers express it, that is, where many plants or stalks put out from one root, dibbling appears preferrable. This" (dibbling) "is a very partial improvement, but it is worthy of being extended, when it is considered how much seed may be saved, and how many children may be taught to earn wages thereby."

WEEDING.—236. (by the Reporter) "The advantages from weeding ground seem not sufficiently attended to. Thistles are usually cut out of grain: the person doing it walks between the ridges, with two small iron hooks at the end of a stick of some length, and by that means cuts off the thistles, or other large weeds; and this is repeated, as the necessity of the case requires: but then the farmer who has been at this expense and trouble, will not go a step farther to cut down the weeds in the hedges of the same field even; therefore a succession of seed is at hand to blow over it."

P. 237. (by Somebody) —" Farmers are particularly inattentive to plants which produce winged seeds, and will suffer them to grow in the lanes, or wastes adjacent to their lands (which of course must receive a large proportion of the seed), rather than cut them; though attended only with slight trouble, and merely because, as they say, *it is not their business* "—And they say truly. It should be the business of the overseers of the highways; who ought to be compelled, not only to keep the roads in repair; but to free the lanes from winged weed seeds.

HARVESTING.—P. 142. (by the Reporter)—" Wheat, in general, is reaped with broad hooks, or saw sickles. Barley and oats are mowed. Pease are cut up or *bagged* with a bill or *bagging* hook. In some places wheat is mowed."

ARABLE CROPS.—Almost all that is valuable, in this Report, on the cultivation of *grain* crops, is comprized in the following extract —P. 171. (by Mr. Harries)— " Our crops commonly cultivated are wheat, barley, oats, pease, and turnips.

" *Wheat*, sown upon a clean clover ley of the first or second year (and no wheat yields better.) The red straw wheat, seed steeped in urine or salt and water, afterwards sprinkled over with lime, and well mixed together. From two to three bushels (of 38 quarts) per acre, is sown in October. If the land is in condition, and manured a little over, two bushels per acre is sufficient. October is the best month; but on sound lands wheat is sown till the middle of November. Dung is spread upon the leys and ploughed under; sometimes we cart and spread the dung after the seed is harrowed in. If turnips are to succeed wheat, we never manure for the wheat. If lime is the manure to be used, we sometimes spread it upon the clover in July; at other times harrow it in with the soil, during

during the Summer, in the proportion of three waggon-loads to two acres. Summer-fallows for wheat are either dunged or limed, and sowed the end of September or beginning of October, with a little over two bushels of seed per acre. Wheat frequently succeeds pease upon one, and sometimes two ploughings. When vetches or buck-wheat are sown, they are followed by wheat. Wheat is sometimes ate a little with sheep in the Spring, wed with the hand once or twice in the month of May or beginning of June, it produces from 10 to 25 bushels per acre, seldom more; 15 to 20 bushels may be looked upon as the more general produce. It will be recollected that by a bushel is meant 38 quarts, if no explanation of the measure is given.

" *Barley.*—When barley succeeds wheat upon strong soils, the stubble is generally ploughed under the end of December, or in January. The frost prepares such soils for working well with the harrows at seed-time. When barley follows wheat on sandy, gravelly, or pebbly loams, it has frequently three ploughings; if after turnips, one, and sometimes two; we sow $3\frac{1}{2}$ bushels per acre, from the 20th of March to the beginning of May; the produce is from 18 to 35 bushels; upon powerful land I have known 40 bushels of the sprat or broad barley.

" *Oats.*—Oats are sometimes sowed upon the turf after one ploughing, which is given in the month of January, frequently after wheat, upon stiff or shallow soils with one ploughing also. I am at a loss to state the produce, from the variety of our measures for oats, not any two markets agreeing together.

" *Pease.*—Pease are frequently sowed upon old pastures, or clover-leys, after one ploughing, in the month of March. They are uncertain in their produce; from 10 to 24 bushels per acre are raised. I believe they are more grown upon our sound soils than any other county. They are used in fatting our large stock of hogs, and for food for horses.

" *Rye.*—There is but little rye grown now, though formerly on the sandy loams it prevailed much, where now good wheat is grown, owing, as it is thought, to the change of the nature of the soil, from the great quantity of lime that has been bestowed upon it.

" *Vetches.*—A few vetches are sown for cutting to soil horses in the stable (an excellent practice) If left for seed, the following crop is wheat.

" *Buck-wheat.*—A little buck-wheat is sown on light soils,

soils, from the 20th to the end of May; by that time such lands may be well cleaned. It covers and shades the soil, and keeps the weeds under, and leaves it mellow, and in fine order for wheat after one ploughing: on this account I consider it as an improving crop, though not ploughed in, which is a practice with some farmers.

"*Beans.*— Scarcely any are grown in the county."

On the *produce* of grain crops, we find these particulars, —in addition to those above mentioned.—P. 174. (by Mr. Tench)—"The average of wheat per acre in this county, is 22 bushels of 38 quarts; of barley, 28 bushels; of oats, 18 bushels, each bushel containing three half-bushels, of 19 quarts each, or 57 quarts the bushel; pease, 18 bushels; beans, 18 bushels; vetches, 15 bushels, all customary measure of 38 quarts."—The Reporter adds,—"the soil Mr. TENCH cultivated, when he favoured the Board with this account, was, I believe, a gravelly loam. The average he states is, I fear, higher than that of the county at large."

TURNIPS.—The subjoined account of this valuable crop, (by Mr. Harries) shows that it was, at the time he wrote, not yet *fully naturalized*, in Shropshire;—at least on the Welsh side of the county.—P. 173. "On the east side of the county, turnips come in as a regular crop in a course, and are sown from the middle of June till the first week in July; the land is made clean and fine by frequent ploughings, the first before Christmas: they manure with 15 tumbril load of dung per acre: the produce is from 10 to 20 ton per acre. An acre of turnips will keep stock equal to 2 tons of hay. Two acres of good turnips will feed three middle-sized beasts, with barley-straw. In the parts of the county inclined to sand, the land is sound enough to eat the turnips upon the field they grow in, with sheep or young cattle: they are sometimes given on an adjoining ley or stubble, and often drawn home for stall-feeding: upon the gravelly loams scarce any are fed upon the lands: the increase of this crop has been very great in the last 20 years. Few good farmers that have sound land are without a field of them, and they are generally introduced in every other course."

P. 125. (by the Reporter)—"The management of the Walcot property has been very beneficial, and the cultivation of turnips upon Lord CLIVE's different estates has been encouraged by the annual distribution of six silver cups, varying in value from 16 guineas to 4 guineas."

For another, and more immediately practical, method

of encoraging the hoing of turnips, see Herefordshire, ensuing.

Expenditure of Turnips.—P. 175. (by the Reporter) "Turnips are sometimes stacked for winter use, by which means the young cattle have the benefit of the tops in their most luxuriant state, and the larger turnips are preserved from frost, and are easy of access in all weather. At Purslow-hall, in this district (the *seat* of the *bull* which won the prize at Shifnal last year), a shed for feeding oxen is built in a field of considerable declivity, and there is a passage to feed them, between the head of the stall and a wall that supports the earth. Under the bank, or declivity of the field, there is a vault, with a trap-door, level with the surface of the field, through which the turnips intended to be preserved through the winter, are easily unloaded, and another door from this vault opens into the passage at the head of the stalls before-mentioned. The vault being under ground, the turnips are preserved from damage by weather."

POTATOES.—This valuable and now long naturalized root, in most parts of England, would seem to have been, in 1803, a stranger to *agriculture*, in the county of Salop. Mr. P. therefore, properly classes it among "crops not commonly cultivated."

P. 176. (by the Reporter)—"The culture of potatoes increases annually, and some farmers plant them in fields."

Some novel and curious applications of—"the residuum or fibrous parts of the potatoes,"—after the farinacious parts had been extracted as starch,—are related to have been made by the Rev. Mr. Wilding. But they only serve to establish the idea, that potatoes had then been lately imported into the Salopian territory. Specimens of Mr. W's salop or sago, sea biscuits, sweet cakes, and muffins,—received, the "approbation" of the Board of Agriculture. —p. 176.

HEMP.—P. 177. (by Mr. Price) "There is a small plot of ground called the *Hemp-yard*, appendant to almost every farm-house, and to many of the best sort of cottages. Wherever a cottager has 10 or 15 perches of land to his cottage, for this purpose, worth, as let in farms, from 18d. to 2s. 6d. a-year, it will, with his wife's industry, enable him to pay his rent. A peck of hemp-seed, Winchester measure, which costs about 2s. will, on an average, sow ten perches of land. This will produce from two to three dozen pounds of tow, when dressed and fit for spinning. Each

Each dozen pounds of tow will make about ten ells of cloth, generally sold at about 3s. an ell. Thus a very good crop on 10 perches of land, or a very middling crop on 15 perches, will produce about 4*l.* 10*s.* about half of which, or 2*l.* 5*s.* may be reckoned for the woman's labour and profit, after the rent of the land, seed, dressing, whitening, and weaving expenses, are deducted. The process is easy. The hemp is pulled a little before harvest, and immediately spread on grass land; where it lies for about a month or six weeks; the more rain there is, the sooner it is ready to take off the grass. When the skin, or rind, will peel easily from the woody part, it is, in a dry day, taken into the house; and when the business of the harvest is over, they take the advantage of the finest sunshine weather to dry it well, and dress, or, as it is called, tutor it; that is, break, or divide the woody part from the skin, or rind; which is easily performed by a simple machine, called a break or tutor, which consists of three or four ribs of wood, or iron, which fall into each other. It is then fit for the tow-dresser, who brings it into a proper state for spinning. After it is spun, it is whitened, and then sent to the weaver, of which there are many who weave for the farmers, cottagers, &c. After the crop of hemp is pulled up, the land is sown with turnips, which prove a valuable resource for the family throughout the winter."

Less than a century ago, a similar practice prevailed, in the northeast quarter of Yorkshire. And, heretofore perhaps, in many other parts of England.

GRASS LANDS*.—*Mowing Grounds.*—P. 180. (by Mr. Harries)

* In this, as in the Cheshire Report, we find a *catalogue with remarks* of the grasses and other indigenous plants. That which is now under view fills a sheet and a half of paper. It is chiefly compilation, or trifling detail; and is fitter to *fill up* a *botanical* than an *agricultural* work. The following is an extract from the first item of the list. P. 184. " *Anthoxanthum odoratum*, sweet-scented vernal-grass. This is one of the earliest grasses. It will grow in almost any soil and situation. It is generally very abundant in uncultivated places, as commons, heaths, forests, as if it were an order of Providence, that where the food for cattle is least in quantity, it shall be of the *sweetest* kind!" What a confusion of ideas and *sensations!* It is true, that, in our language, *odoriferous* and *saccharine* are equally expressed by the epithet *sweet*. But in the mouths and stomachs of cattle, I believe, no two qualities of herbage have less affinity. *Lolium perenne*, not *anthoxanthum odoratum*, is *there* the "sweetest kind;" tho of all the grasses, perhaps the least odoriferous. Yet we find that first of English grasses slightly spoken of!—in a work on modern English Agriculture!!

This

Harries) "On the borders of the Severn, and other flat lands contiguous to lesser streams, that occasionally overflow their bounds, and enrich the adjoining lands by the particles of soil that *the subsiding of the waters* leave behind them, we have natural meadows, that are constantly mown without any other manure being bestowed upon them. These are subject to the crop being spoiled, from the waters overflowing during its growth, and before it is got in. An Act of Parliament to enable the occupiers to raise a rate for embanking, opening the channel, and making back-drains, would be a means of greatly improving such valuable tracts *. Upon upland meadows, the manure from the chaff at the barn-doors mixed with soil, ashes and shovellings, is very properly applied."

Pasture Grounds.—The same writer continues,—"the farmer's pastures I think are more neglected than any other part of his land, as very little manure is ever put upon them; they consider it as more wanting elsewhere." Quere, for "pastures" read *mowing grounds*, or *grass lands;* in contradistinction to *arable grounds?*

ORCHARDS.—P. 211. (by the Reporter) "Many farmers have small orchards, from whence they make a little cyder for home consumption, and on the confines of Herefordshire and Worcestershire the orchards are larger, and cyder is made for sale."

HORSES.—P. 262. (by Mr. Harries) "In my neighbourhood a considerable number of foals are bred. I think sufficient to keep up the stock of the district."

P. 262. (by Mr. Rowley)—"Many farmers in the neighbourhood have stallions of the cart breed, and almost every one wishes to keep up his stock in this manner, and for this purpose breeding mares constitute a part of every team. Many useful horses of this kind are brought to market. Likewise some saddle-horses are reared here."

P. 263. (by Mr. Price) "There are many small, hardy, compact and very useful working horses, bred in Shropshire."

P. 263. (by the Reporter) "The observation from the original Report, is most applicable I presume, to the

This encumbrance of "Plymley's Report of Shropshire," I have pleasure in saying, is not from the pen of the Reporter. The sin of insertion, only, is his.

"* An Act of Parliament was lately obtained, for compelling the owners of land near the river Rea to this management."

the eastern borders of the county, for the farmers in general breed a foal or two every year, some for the cart, but more for the road: several inferior hunters are also reared, and some of a better sort."—Again—" Upon Clun-forest many small horses are bred and reared, and some upon the Longmynd; but the breeds are not so valuable as they were formerly."

P. 264. (by Mr. Lloyd) "The breed of horses is not sufficiently attended to, farmers being apt to send their mares to the cheapest stallions, without any other consideration whatever, and consequently very few good stallions are brought into the country: were it considered that a bad horse eats as much as a good one, the advantage of being more particular would be very obvious. As the canals will reduce the carriage of heavy weights upon the roads, lighter horses, with more blood, will be found of greater use than the heavy Leicestershire sort."

CATTLE.—*Breeds*—P. 241. (by the Reporter)—" The *neat* cattle of this county cannot be referred to any of the distinct breeds that writers upon live stock have enumerated, though, probably, they are much the same breed as that spread over Warwickshire and Staffordshire. The old Shropshire ox was remarkable for a *large dewlap.* There have been many cattle reared within the last 20 years, from the improved breeds of Lancashire, Cheshire, Leicestershire and Staffordshire, and that of Mr. FOWLER, of Oxfordshire. Upon the south confines of the county, the Herefordshire breed is now gaining ground; and some Devonshire cattle have been brought to Kinlet-hall. About Bishop's Castle is a good breed of cattle, the colour a dark red; they are more uniform in shape and colour than in any other district in the county."

The following general reflections (by the same), like many others of this writer's observations,—tho they may not be uniformly just,—border, in some parts, very closely on accuracy In the close of the passage, we find a *truism* forcibly put.

P. 243. " What are called the Leicestershire breeds, are undoubtedly very quick feeders: they are always beef; but they appear less adapted to work than the Herefordshire and Devonshire breeds. The meat will be often too fat, and there will not be a proportion of tallow on the inside. This applies equally to the sheep and hogs of the same breeders. When the object is to lessen bone and muscular strength, a quiet, indolent, quick-feeding animal is produced; but an active strong animal is is wanted, if the oxen are to work. These different qualities appear to me to reconcile the seemingly different principles of breeding *in and in* (that is, from the same stock) and of crossing stock. The former may diminish bone and muscular strength, and the latter increase it, and thus each principal may be equally good, if applied according to the object aimed at. It seems desirable, how ever, to produce in the Leicestershire breeds, an aptness to increase in flesh as well as in fatness. Waste of any kind is wrong; but when provender is used in making an animal too fat to be eaten, the fault is double. It is consuming food of one species to spoil food of another species."

On the *Slaughtering* of Cattle, Mr. Plymley has adduced some interesting and valuable information. The substance of it is all that is requisite, here.

The people of SPAIN, it has been understood, have long slaughtered their cattle by severing what might be termed the stem of the nervous system from its root; and thereby cutting off all communication, between its several branches and their common parent, the brain;—whereby every sensation of the animal instantly ceases.

This generally received opinion, however, has recently been staggered, by the following circumstances. Mr. Du Gard, surgeon of the Shrewsbury infirmary, finding that a patient, who had injured his spinal nerve, not only lived, but preserved his intellects, some days, tho his body was insensible,—ingeniously, and humanely, considered this case with that of an animal after having been "pithed;" and, to convince himself of the truth, had several operations performed, in the *English* manner; all of which seemed to confirm his hypothesis. Hence he drew the following conclusion.

P. 250. "From all these circumstances I conclude that the new method of slaughtering cattle is more painful than the old. The puncture of the medulla spinalis does not destroy feeling, though it renders the body quiescent, and in this state the animal both endures pain at the punctured part, and suffers, as it were, a second death, from the pain and faintness from loss of blood in cutting the throat, which is practised in both methods."

Mr. Du Gard, in consequence, communicated his *discovery* to a surgeon in London,—a pupil of the celebrated JOHN HUNTER,—and he, to the Board of Ariculture;—to whom he afterwards presented a Paper, on the subject.

In

In relating several ingenious experiments, formerly made, by Mr. Hunter, and Mr. Cruikshanks—another of Mr. H's pupils,—and describing the operation as performed by a "pithing butcher," of some experience,—the writer (Mr. Everard Home) thus explains its want of due effect, when performed in the ordinary manner.

The cause of life remaining in the head and chest of the animal, after the ordinary operation, and this while the limbs are quiescent, and to appearance dead,—is owing to the spinal nerve being divided at too great a distance from the brain; namely, *below* the origin of the branch of nerves which supply the diaphragm;—by which mean respiration is continued, for a time, after the operation. But if the principal nerve, or "spinal marrow," be divided, or "punctured,"! *above* that branch of the system, instant death ensues.

This fact was known to, and perhaps discovered by, that extraordinary self-taught anatomist, the late JOHN HUNTER; as appears by the following operations performed by him.—P. 255. "Having explained" (says Mr. Home) "the causes of failure in the present mode of pithing animals, it becomes necessary to state, that *when the operation is properly performed, its success is complete.* Of this I will mention the following instance:

"A small horse was killed in this manner, that a cast might be made of its muscles in their natural state of action. The animal was allowed to stand upon a pedestal, and the operation was performed by Mr. HUNTER, with a large awl: the breathing ceased instantaneously, and the animal was so completely dead as to be supported by the assistants, without making the slightest struggle, and was fixed in the position in which he stood, without ever coming to the ground *.

"A dog was killed so instantaneously in the same way, by Mr. HUNTER, that Mr. CLIFT, the conservator of the Hunterian Museum, who held the legs, and did not see the awl introduced, was waiting till the animal should struggle, and had no knowledge of any thing having been done, till he was told to let go, and was surprized to find that the animal was completely dead.

"In these operations, the instrument was small, and directed by the skill of an anatomist upwards into the cavity of the skull, so as to divide the medullary substance

"* The cast of this horse has a place in the Hunterian Museum."

stance above the origin of the nerves which supply the diaphragm.

"*By adopting this method of performing the operation of pithing cattle, it will be attended with the same success.*"

In this, as in a thousand other instances, we see the necessity of attending to the MINUTIÆ of operations; not in anatomical and surgical matters, only; but in those of agriculture. It is not merely "performing" an operation; but performing it *properly*, that insures success. Yet how often do we see it happen that, because a bungler or two have executed a work, *improperly*, it is given up as "good for nothing," and cried down,—by chattering blockheads, who have no power of invention, in themselves, nor industry to improve on that of others,—as an "innovation."

The instance under notice is an extraordinary one; and shows to inventors and improvers, in general, how much depends on ACCURACY, in all practical matters; and warns them, that, when a great good is in view, no limits should be set to study and perseverance. Had not the genius and perseverance of a HUNTER developed the truth, in the case before us, the less profound experiments of Mr. Du Gard might have thrown into total disuse an operation which does honor to human nature:—and not to perform it, invariably, will, in my mind, be the greatest disgrace of humanity:—even as knocking down a bullock is the lowest degree of savage brutality *.

Calves.—P. 257. (By Mr. Rowley) "When the farmers in this district intend to rear calves, they wish the cows to bring them in February or before. When they propose to fatten them for the butchers, they do not desire them

* Could death be inflicted with *certainty*, by a *single blow*, this charge could not be brought against the present practice. In the slaughter-houses, in the metropolis, where, through constant habit, the knocking down art is best understood and executed, some degree of certainty may be approached. But not so in the country;—where I have *seen* many savage blows given, before the animal fell; and where I have *known* the head of the victim so much bruised and swollen, by the repeated strokes of the executioner, that his instrument had no longer any effect; the mangled wretch being obliged to be shot, in that horrible state of torture!

The above recited operations we are told were "directed by the skill of an anatomist." But, surely the hand of a butcher might be *taught* to perform it, with equal dexterity. If not, let us have anatomical "pithers," as well as veterinary surgeons.

Let pithing schools (or academies by some more appropriate name) be

them before the latter end of March."—P. 258. (by the same) "The manner of feeding them is various. Some mix oat-meal, some wheat-flour, some oil-cake, with milk. Some give them at an early period hay and oats. Some turn them out to grass, two to a cow. The calves which are not intended to be reared, are suckled till they are sold to the butchers. They are sold to advantage if they are kept till they are six weeks old."

Winter Management of Cattle.—P. 259. (by Mr. Price) "*Cows* in Shropshire are every where housed and tied up during the winter"

SHEEP.—P. 260. by Mr. Price) "The old Shropshire sheep are" (mostly) "horned, and have black or mottled faces and legs. They are about as large as the South-down sheep; but the neck rather longer, and the carcass, perhaps, not quite so compact. They are extremely hardy, and have never any dry food given them in the Winter, except in great snows which last for a considerable time. They are not attended by a shepherd, nor folded; nor do they generally *drink*. If any sheep is seen to drink, the farmer looks upon it as a sign that such sheep is rotten or tainted."

Again (by the Reporter)— "There is a breed of sheep on the Longmynd with horns and black faces, that seems an indigenous sort: they are nimble, hardy, and weigh near 10 lbs. a quarter when fatted. Their fleeces, upon an average may weigh $2\frac{1}{2}$ lbs. of which half a pound will be the breechen or coarse wool, and is sold distinct from the rest. Upon the hills nearer Wales, the flocks are without horns and with white faces, rather shorter legs, heavier but coarser fleeces than the Longmynd sheep, and of about the same weight per quarter. The farmers in different districts, have tried at one time or another almost all the improved breeds."

P. 261. (by the same) "Farmers complain of a want of sale for the Leicestershire sorts, as the meat is too large and fat for private families. They are generally bought for the Liverpool and Manchester markets. In manufacturing

be immediately established. And let it be deemed *murder* (and a suitable punishment be assigned for it) to slaughter domestic animals in the present barbarous manner.

The operation is, in its nature, so simple that, with a crooked lancet, even a child might, doubtlessly, be taught to perform it. Whereas, not one butcher in five, probably, has strength and slight enough, to deprive the animal of all sensation, *with certainty*, at the *first blow*.

turing towns this sort may answer well, because where dinners are cooked by baking, a joint of this mutton may be cut into small pieces, and one of them put into a dish of potatoes through the week, and sent to the oven, when the quantity of fat will be an advantage, as it will make a large dish of potatoes palatable without other sauce."

SWINE.—P. 266. (by Mr. Harries)—"Perhaps no county of its extent grows so many" (?) "or rears or fats so many hogs."

Again (by the Reporter)—"The original hog of this county was a high-backed, large-eared animal. This has been crossed by various breeds, and is rarely to be met with unmixed. Several Berkshire and Leicestershire boars have been introduced, and the Chinese breed has declined."

P. 267. (by Mr. Lloyd) "Pork and bacon are much used among the poorer people, when they can procure them; therefore the sort which is to be fed with the least trouble is to be preferred. A mixture of the Shropshire and Chinese has in this respect been found to answer for bacon, and a cross of the wild breed for pork."

RABBITS.—P. 268. (by the Reporter) "There are some considerable warrens upon the Longmynd, the brown Clee-hill, and on the Morf. Those in Longnor Park, and in Frodesley Park, have been destroyed, and I do not know of any in private grounds that are regularly preserved."

Again (by Mr. Lloyd) "Rabbits have of late been much destroyed, by reason of the commons upon which they were bred having been enclosed; and in some parts of the county they are seldom to be met with, except in a tame state."

POULTRY.—P. 268. (by the Reporter)—"There is not any particular breed of poultry in this county. Geese are reared on the commons, and sold to the farmers, who fatten them in their stubbles, and with grain afterwards. Some farmers rear large quantities of turkeys, particularly within the Honour of Clun, though I know of no local circumstances that influence their doing so. These turkeys are bought up by persons who drive them to Birmingham and other large towns. The markets of the county are well supplied with turkeys, geese, fowls, and ducks. It is to be lamented that they are generally carried alive to market. Death is no misfortune to an animal that has no previous apprehension of it. But poultry,

carried

carried in bags or baskets to market, have several hours of previous suffering, and the burthen and trouble of carrying them thither seems much increased thereby. It is a point of duty, not to put any animal to needless pain."

Yet it is not more strange, than it is true, that the same Archdeacon Plymley, in remarking on the humane practice of "pithing cattle"—(see p. 253,) the most humane act that man can administer to domestic animals, does not follow up, and recommend, the operation which causes *no pain* to the animal; but gives into, and in effect recommends, that which is capable of subjecting it to the most excrutiating torture!—merely, it would seem, to gain an opportunity of giving a false turn to the subject:—thro some *motive* which does not *appear*.—P. 246. "We may the less regret the difficulty in getting new modes established, when we thus see the superiority of an old custom under very improbable circumstances; and if well-meant reformers wanted any additional motives to care and circumspection, a very forcible one is furnished in the instance of the time and trouble taken to introduce this operation, and which, as it has been hitherto practised, is the very reverse of what was intended."

Now, the very reverse of this is the TRUTH, (as clearly appears aforegoing p. 254.) Unfounded insinuations, like this, cannot be too severely censured. They are calculated to sap the root, not of *political*, but of SCIENTIFIC REFORM, and thereby to arrest the advancement of the human understanding; and, in the instance under view, to stifle the virtuous flame of humanity!

PIGEONS.—P. 269. (by the Reporter) "There are few pigeons bred for sale in this county. Though pigeons pick up grain that would otherwise be lost, yet they do much damage in fields newly sown with grain, as well as where the grain is almost ripe. They are also very detrimental to thatched roofs, and more so to those with tile and slate, as they pick out the mortar and so loosen the cover, and especially the crests, where they can get at the cement easily. If there is any profit in pigeons, it probably is from the manure gotten out of the dove-houses."

P. 270. (by Mr. Lloyd) "Pigeons, probably, are more expensive than profitable, for though you do not see what they eat, yet it is to be remarked, that when there is no plunder for them in the fields, they are in a poor hungry state."

A law to prevent their being let loose, or to allow them to

to be destroyed in the act of pillage, in SEED TIME and HARVEST, might be, at once, salutary and equitable. See NORTHERN DEPARTMENT, p. 409.

DECOYS.—For an instance of draining being an enemy to decoys; see p. 230.

BEES.—P. 270. (by the Reporter) "Several of the farmers and cottagers keep a few stalls of bees, and sell the honey."

HEREFORDSHIRE.

THIS county, like Shropshire, is without striking features to distinguish and separate it, into well determined NATURAL DISTRICTS. The Wye worms its course through the heart of Herefordshire, as does the Severn through Shropshire. But not in either of them do we find any thing of the nature of a rivered vale. Indeed, the whole of Herefordshire, its marginal heights excepted, is one wide district of vale lands,—studded with hills, hillocks, and minor swells, of various heights and dimensions. The most natural division, and at the same time, the best agricultural distinction, is into *strong* and *light* lands.

The lower lands, which form, principally, the base of the county, are of a clayey nature—mostly CLAYEY LOAMS of a superior quality:—much of them rich *red land,* interspersed among soils of a browner color; but frequeutly of equal or superior fertility. And, interwoven among those, are lines of water-formed lands (on the banks of its brooks and rivers); and some of them of superior quality.

The lighter lands, the SANDY LOAMS, are principally confined to the southeast quarter of the county;—to what are termed the "Rye lands of Herefordshire;"—a name that has, doubtlessly, arisen from their prevailing produce, in former times.

HEREFORDSHIRE is almost, exclusively, *agricultural.* There are neither mines, nor manufactures, of any considerable extent, in the county:—in this, particularly, varying from the county of Salop.

My own knowledge of Herefordshire was chiefly acquired, in 1788, previously to my writing on the orchards and fruit liquors of that part of the kingdom;—when I took a general view of the county. I have, since that time, crossed it, incidentally, but with attention, in different directions; and at different seasons.

BEFORE I enter upon a Review of the two Reports to the Board of Agriculture, from HEREFORDSHIRE, it may be proper

per to notice the eastern side of MONMOUTHSHIRE;—which, tho its inhabitants are, in language and manners, *Welch*:—yet, in natural economy, and agricultural management, it may be deemed *English*:—and may, without disparagement to either county, be considered as a continuation of Herefordshire;—and, as such, I intended to have comprized the Report of it, within the limits of my present work.

But, on examining the only account of it, that has yet been printed by the Board, I find nothing to induce me to bring it forward, here:—not a line of it is fit to be extracted!

I will, therefore, only notice, in this place, that the DISTRICT of RAGLAND, and the entire VALE of USK,—from Abergavenny to Newport,—rank, in richness and beauty, among the first passages of British territory.—The vale of Usk is, to South Wales, what that of Clwyd is to North Wales, and that of Montgomery to the midland parts of the principality.

"GENERAL VIEW

OF THE

AGRICULTURE

OF THE

COUNTY OF HEREFORD.

WITH

OBSERVATIONS ON THE MEANS OF ITS IMPROVEMENT.

BY JOHN CLARK,

OF BUILTH, BRECONSHIRE.

1794."

CONCERNING the REPORTER, in this instance, or his QUALIFICATION for the post assigned him, not a trace of information appears; excepting what may be detected, relative

lative to the latter, in his performance. In the section, Roads, he speaks of his "pretty long experience," and, in other parts of his production, some evidence of his acquaintance with men and things, in the county of Hereford may be seen; together with some general knowledge of its rural concerns. But we have no proof, whatever, of his possessing a mature knowledge of PRACTICAL AGRICULTURE. Nor does he *speak* at all, on the MANAGEMENT of LANDED PROPERTY.

In regard to his MODE of SURVEY, we are left entirely in the dark. Builth is situated at some distance from the county of Hereford. But Mr. Clark, perhaps, had some general knowledge of the county, as a professional man, previously to his sitting down to make his Report of it. This, however, is mere conjecture.

Mr. Clark's being an *original Report*, we find no *annotators.*—The only contributor to it is Mr. Joseph Harries; who, in the Appendix, furnishes a valuable Paper, on a disease peculiar to oxen.

As to the *authorship* of this performance, little requires to be said. It is a mere sketch;—the writer having, in a *good* measure, set the Board's rules of arrangement at naught. It will be seen, in several of the extracts, that the Reporter, in this case, *can* write. But his passion for *fine* writing too frequently involves his good sense in a degree of obscurity; or, by exciting a smile, it is passed over unheeded.

The number of pages, in the body of the work, sixty six: —in the Appendix, twelve.

No map.

SUBJECT THE FIRST.

NATURAL ECONOMY.

ELEVATION and SURFACE.—On these particulars we find little: excepting what can be gathered from the Reporter's elevated descriptions of the general appearance of the county:—of which presently.

The following passage, however, is admissible, in this place.—P. 11. "On viewing this county from the summit of any of its hills, the idea presented to the spectator, on either

either side, is that of an extended flat; but when he descends to the plains below, he finds the face of the country to be very different from what it seemed to be from the former station. On examination he finds what seemed a flat to be gentle swells, resembling small *segments* seemingly cut off a large globe."

CLIMATURE.—P. 8. "The climate of this district is remarkably mild."

P. 9. "The *situation* of *most* of this county is so placed as to add, in some degree, to the mildness of the climate and the fertility of the soil. It is sheltered in a great measure, on the north-west and south-west, by a *border* of mountainous district.

"Most of the long continued rains, in this quarter of the kingdom, are from a *south-west* point. The Welsh mountains, which are situate in that point, by their great elevation, partly intercept, and partly attract the clouds in wet weather, and by stripping them of a portion of that superabundant moisture with which they are charged, may contribute to the mildness of this district."

P. 25. "Harvest begins the first week in August, and ends the first in September, in general."

WATERS.—P. 12. "The Wye is the only river of which this county can boast, although the Lugg is sometimes honoured with that appellation by the natives.

"The Wye rises from Plinlimon-hills, in Montgomeryshire, and entering Radnorshire at Cefinycoed, passeth through that county, until it receives the Elan, two miles below Rhaydergowy. From thence it separates the counties of Brecon and Radnor to Hay, a distance of thirty-three miles. Leaving Breconshire at Hay, and Radnorshire at Rhydspence, two miles lower, it enters this county with a slow but majestic pace. The Wye having now travelled sixty miles from its source, is strengthened and augmented to no small size by the wealth which it has collected from a large district of hills and vallies on either side, whose numerous rivers and streams have united to add to its importance, by consigning to it, at once, their respective contents, and their respective names.

"The Wye moves slowly through this county, by the city of Hereford and market town of Ross, until it reaches Gloucestershire; then by Monmouth to Cheapstow, where it joins the Severn *sea*, disdaining to resign its contents to any other stream."

SOILS, &c.—P. 13. "*The soil* of this country is very different, and the difference often becomes striking in the space

space of a few yards only; from a strong clayey to the kindly sandy mould: yet all are rich, productive, and wonderfully adapted by nature for the nourishment of the different species of vegetables which she had destined to become the tenants of these different species of soils.

"Excepting the skirts of this county, on the south, all the land that has a sufficient quantity of sand in its composition is, in a very high degree, friendly to vegetation: the only defect to which the soil inclines, is, when it contains too large a proportion of clay. But although the soil be often stiff here, it does not come under the description of what is called in some places, "poor stiff clay." This is easily accounted for, because

"*The sub-soil* uniformly partakes of the nature of the *superficial.* No stratum of poisonous *tell,* hostile to vegetation, lurks beneath the plough, to intimidate the farmer from a deep furrow; nor to send up its offensive moisture to contaminate the roots of the plants, and chill their growth."

The APPEARANCE of the face of the country.—As Herefordshire is certainly one of the most beautiful counties in the kingdom, let us indulge its Reporter in listening to his splendid description of it.

P. 8. "The county of Hereford is equalled by few spots in the island of Great Britain for the production of every article that can contribute to the comfort, the happiness, and, in some degree, the luxury of society. Here a verdure almost perpetually reigns. The wide flats, extended for many miles, are clothed in Nature's fairest robes, and enriched by a profuse distribution of her most chosen gifts. When the hills rear their mild heads, they do it, seemingly, with a view to captivate the eye by their sylvan charms, and invite the traveller to partake of an air less luxuriant and satiating than that of the plains below. On the flats the atmosphere is so loaded with the riches which it collects from the sweet-scented herbs around, that the inhaled air gives a glow of health and vigour to the surrounding vegetables on which it breathes; hence the ancients, with much propriety, complimented this favourable district with the appellation of the GARDEN OF ENGLAND."

P. 9. "The *features of the country* exhibit a striking variety of beauties, but it all partakes of that variety from which every idea of inferiority is excluded: no barren spot, that by the humility of its deportment would form a contrast to the general claim to pre-eminence. The idea of *richness* is *rather prevalent,* and apt to over-awe the mind by by that self-sufficiency, and those assumed airs of superiority, of which it is, perhaps, not easy for Wealth to divest herself. Cornfields, meadows, orchards, extended lawns, and hop-grounds, satiate the eye by one continued scene of luxury.

"From the top of any part of that range of hills called *Dinmore*, between Leominster and Hereford, this county may be viewed to much advantage, so far as its *agricultural wealth* can be examined; indeed any other eminence within the county will serve the same purpose. It is, in fact, of very little importance from what station it is viewed, so that it can be seen; for when there is no natural nakedness to cover, nothing can be seen from any position, which the traveller would not wish to view."

P. 10. "On whatever side the spectator turns his eyes, the prospect before him is equally inviting; whether to gratify the fanciful sallies of a wandering taste, by their external charms, or the daily demands, and more peremptory cravings of human wants, by their store of internal wealth. The GENTLEMEN'S seats, where Art occasionally steals, imperceptibly, to assist Nature in her endeavours to please, gives the spectator an idea of *taste*. The farmhouse, surrounded by large fields of yellow corn, green meadows, blooming orchards, and wide lawns covered with herds of cattle, that of *wealth*: the towering spire and neat village, that of *devotion* and *decorum*: and, what is peculiarly gratifying to the humane mind, the cottage gives the idea of *comfort*."

SUBJECT THE SECOND.

POLITICAL ECONOMY.

STATE of APPROPRIATION.—*Common Pastures.*—P. 27. "*The waste lands*, in this county, may be estimated at *twenty thousand acres*. One-half of the waste land is situate in those quarters that join the counties of Brecon or Radnor, and the other half dispersed in several small parcels over the remainder of the county. Excepting some part of the former division, every acre might be converted into meadow, arable, pasture, or *woodlands*: the last probably the most beneficial of all, on account of the great increase

increase in the demand for "*hop-poles*." At a moderate computation, the land, when so employed, would be worth from twelve to fifteen shillings annually per acre."

P. 28. "The most extensive districts of *waste lands*, in this county, are situate at the foot of the Black Mountains, above the Golden Valley. I do appeal to such gentlemen as have often served on *grand juries* in this county, whether they have not had more FELONS brought before them from *that* than any *other* quarter of the county. Yet the people there are not *naturally* more vicious than their neighbours. IDLENESS, that *fell* ROOT on which VICE always finds it easy to graft her most favourite plants, and which is found to contribute so much to their future health and prosperity, alone form the characteristic difference.

"A *cottage*, with a few acres of inclosed land, gives the occupier a right to turn stock to these common hills. The profit of that stock is expected to supercede the necessity of labour, in cultivating the few acres which he possesses: should these *hopes*, however, not be *realized*, any method of providing for the *demands of the day* is preferred to the drudgery of labour."

Mr. Clark brings forward other arguments to show that the appropriation of common pastures ought not to be obstructed by the claims of cottagers. But they are too valuable, as strictures on the poor laws, to be detached from the general subject. I therefore reserve them for the section *Poor Rates*.

Common Fields.—In the Appendix, Mr. Clark enters largely into the propriety of completing the appropriation of these under-productive lands; and combats the objections, said to be made against so obviously wise a measure, —even by some of the occupiers of them, in Herefordshire; —in which this species of imperfect property prevailed, in 1794, over "a great part of the best lands of the county."

P. 69. "The invariable rotation of crops in all the common fields is, first year, a fallow; second year, wheat; third year, pease or oats; then begin again with a fallow.

"It is not requisite to point out to an agriculturist, the wretched state of *aration* in a country in which the above destructive system prevails. The misfortune is still increased by the humiliating reflection, that some of the best land in England is thus condemned to lie idle every *third* year; and that by a species of rebellion against nature, her children are robbed of a considerable portion of that ample provision which *she had made for them*." Again —"there

—"there are, however, few subjects on which men differ so much as the advantage to be derived from inclosure of *common fields*; and since a great part of the best land in this county still remains in that state, I have taken the liberty of submitting to the Honourable Board, the arguments for and against such a measure, so far as I have been able to judge from the information which I have received concerning it in this district."

Mr. Clark then proceeds to obviate the alleged objections to the measure. They are chiefly two:—namely lessening the production of corn, and lowering the population of the country.

Mr. C. elicits an admirable general argument, in favour of Inclosing,—p. 70.—"If it be an advantage to the public to keep the common fields in their present state, it would be a very great additional advantage to turn the fields that are now inclosed into common fields, for what is good for a part, is good for the whole."

Mr. Clark estimates the value of inclosed lands, and the amount of their produce of food, for society, at double what they let for, and produce, in their open common field state (pp. 70 and 71.) If an increase of fifty per cent. be gained, by inclosure, surely, proprietors and the community have a sufficient motive toward completing their appropriation.

The fact is—common fields (unless in some particular situations) *cannot* be converted, immediately, into perennial grass lands, with full profit to occupiers and the community. Speaking of them, in a general way, they will not continue in a state of profitable herbage, more than a few years (more or less according to the nature of the land:)—after which, they require, in propriety of management, to be broken up for a succession of corn crops. It may be said, with little risk, that common-field lands, even under ordinary management, furnishes the markets with as much, or more, *corn*, after their inclosure, as they did in their open state:—beside a large addition of *animal food*, from the herbage they produce;—on lands, it may be put, that previously lay fallow, *unnecessarily*.

To show the effect which inclosing common fields has on population, Mr. Clark has had recourse to Mr. HOWLET'S enquiries on the subject; and has inserted a table of eighty-nine parishes, situated in various counties, that had recently (within twenty years) been inclosed, and of four hundred and ninety, in the same counties, that had not been recently enclosed:—by which it appears that the increase

crease of baptisms, in the recently inclosed parishes, was in the ratio of one hundred to one hundred and twentyone,—or twentyone per cent; while, in the parishes not recently inclosed, the increase was only nine, per cent.

That table appearing to have been formed with much deliberation, and in a manner that reflects infinite credit on the patriotic views and perseverance of Mr. Howlett;—(who first made out a list of inclosure bills, from the Journals of the House of Commons, and then circulated letters among the Clergy of the several parishes),—the result (as above stated) I presume, may be received with confidence; and be deemed conclusive*.

Poor Rates.—Mr. Clark,—to obviate the appropriation of common pastures, by removing the objections arising against it, on account of the claims of cottagers,—takes a more enlarged view of the claims of the indigent on landed property, than I have before met with.—Some of the remarks, it is true, may appear "harsh;" but others, we may venture to allow, are practically just.

P. 27. "To deprive the *poor* of that benefit, which, in their present state, they derive from the *waste land*, must, no doubt, at first view sound *harsh*. But it ought to be remembered, that in this wealthy county, where there is so much work to be done, and so few hands, comparatively, to perform it, there are few *poor* that do not deserve to be so. Those persons who are disqualified to provide for the calls of human nature, by the feebleness of *infancy*, the crushing hand of *disease*, or the infirmities of *old age*, cannot be said to be poor, because ALL the *landed property*, situate *within* their respective parishes, is always liable to be charged with their maintenance, whatever changes may take place in respect to its owners, or occupiers.—Extravagance, folly, or profligacy, may induce the owners of these lands to dispossess themselves of their right in them, but the right of the poor remains *unalienable*, while our present

* One cause of the increase of inhabitants, by inclosure, is evident; not only to reason, but to experience, in every quarter of the island. The operations of fencing, draining, roadmaking, building, and other improvements, draw together a number of hands, from the surrounding country; some of whom settle and rear children, in the parish inclosed; where they become permanent inhabitants. For an inclosed parish or township requires, in *most* instances (not all) *much more* manual labor, than it did while it lay open. Hence, necessarily arises a permanent increase of *useful* inhabitants in a country, by the appropriation of its territory.

present just, humane, and wise laws have an existence. Ample provision for the want of every person that falls under *either* of these descriptions, is chearfully submitted to by the inhabitants of districts less distinguished for benevolence than those of that under review.—Whatever be the *means*, however, that put it in the power of any *other* class of the people to live in idleness, except these, must even prove hurtful to the public and to *themselves*. The *industrious* are not only oppressed by supporting the idle and the profligate, but the public in general are injured, by leaving in the *uncultivated soil* that portion of the food of society, which their being compelled to labour, would add to the general mass."

In speaking of the late Lord Viscount BATEMAN, as a farmer of eminence, in the county, Mr. C. mentions the laudable attention which his Lordship paid to the poor of the parish in which he resided; and recommends his plan as an example to other men of fortune.

P. 17. "It is worthy of remark, that the *noble farmer* is also *poor house-keeper* of the parish. The consequence is, that in place of six or seven shillings in the pound of poor's rate, it is only ninepence!!!—and not threepence in the *real rent*.

"It is scarcely necessary to add, that the poor are more comfortably maintained than probably any equal number of the same station in the kingdom. Every one that is able to work is employed on the farm. The children are taught the different branches of agriculture; and such as are of a *delicate* constitution are bound to trades, and at a proper age sent out to masters, to make room for others. Was the example of the HEAD of *the parish of* SHOBDON followed by men of landed property throughout the kingdom, we should seldom hear of the *poor's* envying the *rich*, as they would then be *employed* not *oppressed*."

By extending this sort of attention, over the several parishes of an estate, and thereby training up children in the way they should go, something considerable might be done, toward meliorating the condition of the laboring classes, and preventing their becoming an unnecessary burden on those who are bound, by the law of the land, to support them, if reduced to a state of indigence.

INLAND NAVIGATION.—P. 12. "The Wye is neither beneficial nor hurtful to the agriculture of this county, in any considerable degree. To the city of Hereford, and its vicinity, it is of service, as coal and other heavy articles are brought there from the forest of Dean and Bristol.

It

It also enables the inhabitants to send cider, bark, timber, &c. back by the same conveyance to the Severn: even the counties of Brecon and Radnor derive some little benefit from the Wye, as it is in floods navigable six miles above Hay."

ROADS.—Mr. Clark's strictures on roads are entitled to particular attention*. They appear to be the result of much thought on the subject; and to have arisen in "the course of pretty long experience." They are of some length; but not uniformly valuable. Some of them are (to me at least) new. How far they may be practical is not necessary here, to decide. They will serve, at least, to agitate the subject:—And others may be useful in corroborating what I have long been urging. I have long been of opinion, that nearly one moiety, more than one third, of the labor and materials that are expended on the roads of this country is thrown away; through ignorance, prejudice, (otherwise obstinacy) and the present road laws.

P. 51. "The situation of the high-ways reflect no inconsiderable portion of disgrace upon the notice of this district. To say that the roads are bad is, in fact, saying nothing. They are bad over most of the kingdom, and must ever continue so while the present laws respecting them are suffered to continue in force; but here they are so in a very uncommon degree; and what is peculiarly mortifying, they are, in their present local situation, incapable of being made good, although they may be mended."

This radical defect, it would seem, from Mr. C's Report, is owing to the unlevelness of the present lines;—not only of the parochial, but of the turnpike roads; all (the latter) of which have been made,—"during the present century; and the direction in which many of them are laid out exhibits marks of folly and stupidity uncommonly striking; or, more properly speaking, there seems to have been a malignant degree of ingenuity displayed by the persons (whoever they were) that laid out the roads, in entailing upon posterity so provoking an evil as that of unnecessary hilly roads." p. 52.

P. 53. "There is an error of a most fatal tendency in the present laws of this kingdom respecting turnpike roads;

* In the RURAL ECONOMY of GLOCESTERSHIRE, &c. I found ample occasion to censure the *roads* of *Herefordshire;* which were, at the time I wrote, in a most shameful state.

roads; the laying out of which is entrusted to the owners of the lands through which they pass, who are generally the Commissioners: hence they are made judges in their own cause. When, therefore, their own interest, real or imaginary, and the ridiculous prejudices of their tenants, whispered in their ears, are opposed to the interest of the public, it would betray an ignorance of the frailty of human nature, to conclude that the balance of the scale would not bear to the usual quarter.

"It frequently happens, that the horrible demon of discord, that destroys the peace of almost every neighbourhood at contested elections, sallies forth upon these occasions. If the great man, who generally takes the lead in laying out the turnpike road, has no immediate interest himself, he has often a friend to oblige, or an enemy to mortify, by sending the road up hill, to save the land of the one, or through the middle of a meadow, to hurt the other. A tippling-house on the top of a hill, or a favourite piece of land at the bottom, compels the husbandman, at this day, in many parts of this kingdom, to keep one-third more cattle in his team, than there would otherwise have been occasion for.

"In the course of pretty long experience, I have, very rarely, seen a great man take it into his head to ruin a turnpike road, who did not succeed, in the face not only of reason, but of facts reducible to mathematical demonstration. Pride, more than interest, often influences the conduct on such occasions. A majority of votes, at a turnpike meeting, keeps up the spirit of the party, and serves to intimidate the enemy. The same party spirit is sometimes visible, in passing the road, by the Commissioners after it has been made. If the contractor be of the strong party, three or four inches of gravel will do in place of twelve, to which his contract bound him; but if he gave his vote with the weak party, "woe be to him!"

To remedy this evil, Mr. C. proposes, in a note, p. 54,— "An act of legislation, empowering government to appoint surveyors, with salaries moderately competent to make it worth the attention of men of character. Twenty might be sufficient over the whole island. That no bill, for a new turnpike, should be received by the House of Commons until the surveyor of the district transmitted an affidavit to the House, that he had marked the intended road on the ground; and that it was, in his opinion, the shortest and the levellest that could be laid out between the two ends of the district through which the road passed.

Should

Should it be made to appear by measurement, and taking the elevations, that a shorter or a leveller road might have been made, the surveyor should be dismissed from his office, as incapable; and if it should be found that partiality had influenced his conduct, the usual punishment in cases of perjury should be inflicted."

P. 55. "I cannot see any probability of making the parochial roads in this county even tolerably safe, until the statute labour be entirely abolished; as well as the ridiculous farce of appointing one of the parishioners annually (at no salary) to inforce them from his relations, friends, and neighbours, a strict performance of a duty which probably he never discharged himself; and from which, by shewing lenity to his neighbours, he will expect to be excused in his turn, when they shall respectively succeed him in the office of surveyor. But admitting the surveyor to be influenced by the most earnest desire of discharging his duty, by the time that he knows a little of his business, and the best method of minding the road, his year is out, and he is dismissed from his office, which, by the present laws, is destined to be eternally in the occupation of one novist after another. The days set aside for the performance of the statute labour are, by long established custom, considered as allotted to play and merriment; and the man who can continue to do the least work with his master's cattle, thinks he does him a kindness."

P. 56. "Excepting some parts of the turnpike, almost every road in this county is liable to be indicted. The money annually paid by the land-holders, in consequence of indictments, I am informed would go a great way towards paying the interest of a sum sufficient to put all the roads in the county in good repair.

"Under all these disagreeable circumstances, nothing seems so likely to relieve the inhabitants of this county from the insufferable evil of the present uncommon bad roads, as an act of the legislature to empower the landholders in the different parishes (under certain restrictions) to borrow a sum sufficient to put their roads in repair, and make the lands, in proportion to their real annual value, chargeable with the payment of the interest, in lieu of the statute labour.

"I have communicated this idea to some of the most intelligent farmers in this county, and it has met with the approbation of all with whom I have conversed on the subject: and it can scarcely be suspected, that the land-owners would lose sight of their own interest, so far as to give

give it any opposition; good roads being a requisite prelude to the admission of many great and important improvements, of which this county is still capable."

P. 57. "It is often mentioned as a reason for not making amendments in turnpike acts when they are renewed, that if any alteration be made, the Clerks of the House of Commons will charge additional fees: hence the old act is renewed, with all its load of original deformities.

"However pure the intention of the framers of the present laws respecting turnpikes might have been, they operate in a peculiar degree as an inducement to continue bad roads in their present state; since the inhabitants of a district, oppressed by bad roads, must pay 300l. or 400l. before they can be at liberty to borrow money to mend them."

To obviate this hardship, Mr. C. in a note, p. 57, intimates that—"a power vested in the judges to regulate all matters respecting the high-ways, within their respective districts, on the circuits, without the necessity of expensive applications to parliament, especially when there was no opposition to the proposed measure, would be attended with consequences highly beneficial to the public, and would remove several barriers, which, at present, obstruct the improvement of the kingdom."

Those several suggestions I insert, without comment, for the use of those whom they may concern.

SOCIETIES for the Encoragement of Agriculture.—P. 59. "There are none in this county. This is the more to be wondered at, as this comes under the denomination of a residing county; and abounds with men of extensive landed property, enterprise, and liberality of mind. Such an institution seems to be much wished for by every man of a rational turn of thinking, with whom I have conversed on the subject; and in order to carry it into effect, nothing more seems to be wanting than just to begin; merely to hand about a subscription paper at one of the county meetings, which I have reason to conclude would be filled up, almost instantaneously, to a respectable amount. For, on such an occasion, where is that man occupying any respectable rank in society, who would not throw aside all party considerations."

SUBJECT

SUBJECT THE THIRD.

RURAL ECONOMY.

DIVISION THE FIRST.

TENANTED ESTATES,

Their IMPROVEMENT and MANAGEMENT.

ESTATES.—*Proprietors.*—P. 10. "The numerous seats of the nobility and gentry, environed by their respective plantations, dispersed in various directions over the extended prospect, decorate the scene with considerable elegance; whilst the proprietors of these splendid mansions, by their *personal* residence, confer a dignity upon the district, and by their countenance and example strengthen and invigorate the spirit of its agriculture. The contemplative mind is here in a peculiar degree gratified, by the pleasant reflection, that the husbandman in this county, seldom toils for an absent landlord; equally a stranger to the vices and the virtues of his tenants, equally indifferent whether happiness or misery be their lot, so that his rents are regularly remitted—the fate of too many inhabiting districts, which do not, like this, hold forth an inducement for the residence of the wealthy."

IMPROVEMENT of ESTATES.—*Draining.*—P. 30. "Draining is much attended to by all good farmers, and is found to be of more benefit than any other mode of improvement that has lately been introduced on the clayey soil of the district. They were formerly made of *wood;* but that mode is now justly abolished. It looked well in *theory*, but was found to fail in *practice.* Drains are now wholly made of *stone;* and if carefully executed on the present plan, will not only produce the intended effect, but will also last for ages *."

DIVISION

* It cannot be foreign to my views to remark, here, tho it may be somewhat discreditable to the landed gentlemen of Herefordshire, that most of the *improvements*, or attempts at improvement, that have recently taken place, have been prosecuted under the auspices of "the Governors of Guy's Hospital."

DIVISION THE SECOND.

WOODLANDS.

WOODS.—P. 31. "This county is in general well wooded, and the coppice wood is kept under a most regular and rational system. The softer woods, such as ash, sallies, alder, are regularly cut from twelve to fourteen years growth; the oak from eighteen to twenty years. One standard is left to each forty-nine square yards, here called a lugg; or two standards, on three luggs, as they can be best found. These standards, when they can be had, are *maiden-trees*, and not old *stumps*, which are left clear of all incumbrance, in order to enable them to produce the greater quantity of young shoots."

P. 32. "The cultivation of HOPS has lately contributed to raise the value of woodlands in this county, in a very remarkable degree, which produces not only a sufficiency for its own consumption, but a vast quantity is annually sent to the Severn for the Bristol and other markets, mostly used in making hoops and hop-poles."

P. 65. "*Hedge-row Timber*—is most plentifully dispersed over most of the district. The elm is the most general."

DIVISION THE THIRD.

AGRICULTURE.

FARMS.—*Sizes.*—P. 14. "*The size of the farms* is in general pretty extensive, from 400l. to 500l. the large, and from 50l. to 100l. the small."

The following sensible remarks place the relation, between farmers and labourers, in a new, if not the true, point of view; and may serve as a useful reproof to those who are desirous to unite the two vocations.

P. 74. "Let us now look to that obnoxious character, a large farmer: he gives daily employment to twenty or thirty people, besides his own family, through the whole year.

year. A certainty of being able to provide for the demands of the day, holds forth an inducement to marriage, which is still strengthened by the reflection, that a wife and children, so far from being a burthen, will be an assistance to a man, because every good farmer will always find employment for the wives and children of his labourers when they are able to work. Most of the cottagers in this county live much more comfortably than little farmers in general. The only advantage which *these* have over *those*, is, that they can be idle for a day when they please: but it remains yet to be proved, that idleness contributes to the happiness of man, although the contrary be pretty evident. But one man to have so large a tract of land, and so many people obliged to obey his orders? To this it is to be replied, that in farming, as in most other occupations, men of the greatest talents generally get to the head of their professions, while others are left by the way; and whoever will examine the extent of the intellects of the general run of mankind, employed in any branch of business, will find, that Nature, in allotting to each his respective portion of her gifts, had it in view that the province of ninety-nine out of an hundred was to receive, not to give orders. In respect to the humility of so many being obliged to obey one man, every officer in the navy or army might make the same objection; yet the first nobility of the nation, our sovereign's sons not excepted, cheerfully submit to the orders of any superior officer whom chance has placed over them. The man who feels obedience unpleasant, is not very likely to have it soon in his power to command.

"I have intruded upon the reader's patience the longer on this point, because I know there are many men of good sense, property, and worth in this county, who entertain very different sentiments on this subject from those which are here delivered."

Fences.—P. 30. "*Plaching*—(that is laying old hedges) from four-pence to six-pence a perch. This is done very neat. The plants are cut almost wholly through, in order to encourage the young shoots to spring round the old stump."—A judicious method which is not peculiar to Herefordshire.

Homesteads.—The Reporter gives an unfavourable account of the farm-buildings of Herefordshire. But, as what may be called the Herefordshire method, forms a *variety* in rural architecture, I think it right to let the Reporter of the Herefordshire practices give his own description of it.

P. 57.

P. 57. " *Farm Buildings.* These are, in general, constructed in a manner that does no great credit to the rural architecture of the county. It is, however, much the same in most of the woody districts in the kingdom." (No.) " The foundation is, for a foot or two above the surface, stone wall, with a clay or mud cement. The house formed of timber frame-work is then erected upon this wall. The vacancies in the frame-work are then filled up by laths, interwoven in a basket-like form. This again is plastered over; and, when newly white-washed, looks well at a distance; but upon a nearer inspection, the tottering fabrick, leaning in different directions, and kept together only by the strength of the beams that unite the frame-work, discovers the infirmity of the crazy foundation to which the whole trusts for support. The stone-wall having only mud or clay for a cement, the rain soon washes it off. The stones, then loose, fall down, and the frame-work erected on the top of this wall, or rather a collection of loose stones, nods its heads in different directions.

" The thick flags used here, in place of tiles, add much to the mischief, by increasing the evil of an infirm foundation."

The shell of a building erected, in the manner described, is certainly not so firm,—so stiff,—as one that is built with studwork and weather boarding (see p. 238, aforegoing) but may require less workmanship. Timber of every species, however, is now become too valuable for the *walls* of farm buildings. I therefore register the method under notice, merely, as a memento of the practice of former times; when timber, especially in the more central parts of the island, was of little value.

P. 58. " There are, however, a number of good brick, and stone and lime buildings within this county, lately erected; the most conspicuous, and the best executed that I have met with, are those upon the estate of Guy's Hospital, situate in this county *."

PLAN of MANAGEMENT, and GENERAL STATE of HUSBANDRY.—P. 14. " Grain and hop are the crops, and neat cattle the stock to which the farmer must look for support. Sheep and pigs are also articles of some importance. Cider, it is true, forms a very extensive branch of the wealth of this county. This, however, is an article upon which

" * The plantations upon this estate are also well attended; for every tree cut, I am informed that there are at least fifty young ones planted. This does much credit to the gentlemen intrusted with the management of it."

which the farmer must not lay any considerable stress; for, even when *a hit* does take place, there are a number of avenues, besides the farmer's *pockets*, with gaping mouths ready to swallow the production of his blooming orchards. This forms at best but a precarious property, upon which prudence forbids any *material* dependance to be laid.

"The principal part of the land is employed in tillage. The most intelligent farmers say, that there is too large a proportion under corn. It is calculated in general that two-thirds of the farms are thus employed: one-third is too small a proportion for meadow and pasture; since rearing more than they now do, of their own inestimable breed of neat cattle, would pay better than grain.

"This, like many other evils, might have originated in the nature of the common fields. There a man must keep his land in tillage, which might have contributed to render this a corn county *first*, and even after inclosures had taken place, the practice was still continued. Habits once established are not easily eradicated."

P. 21. "Some of the most intelligent men of this county admit, and lament the foulness of their corn lands; but give the quantity of work to be done, and the scarcity of hands, as a reason. Here are *four harvests*, the hay, the corn, the hop, and the cider.

"From an attentive examination of the natural fertility of the soil, compared with the small return of grain which the district now under review yields to the occupier, a train of unwelcome reflections obtrude themselves on the dejected mind."

These reflections, however, are too figuratively fine to assimilate, well, with the more sedate and scientific matter of this register. And yet I cannot resist the temptation to insert one paragraph: its justness and useful tendency are obvious.—P. 22. "But although man *be indolent*, *Nature is active;* every spot of ground that he neglects, *she* appropriates to some use. HER family is numerous; she finds a tenant for every soil. Hence upon the best lands we find the thistle, nettle, couch, dock, ragwort, maywide, wormwood, wild mustard poppies, with an hundred others of the same *active tribe*, which nature seems to have sent as *overseers* to watch the *sluggard*, and to punish his idleness, by converting to their own use that wealth which the farmer's indolence has suffered him to neglect."

OCCUPIERS.—The genius of indolence, however, does not possess the husbandman of Herefordshire, in the mass. There are, we are told, "many good farmers in this district,"

trict," (p. 60). Two of their names are mentioned; namely, Thomas King, esquire, and Mr. John Yeald; and some account is given of their "system, on a large tract of land, in the parish of Pembridge, seven miles below Kington." But the detail furnishes nothing new or excellent. It is merely that of uninteresting facts, thrown together, after the manner of tourists.

Succession.—P. 17. "The *rotation of crops* varies much in different quarters of the county. In the rye lands the old system was, 1. a fallow, 2. wheat, 3. barley, 4. pease, 5. barley, and 6. and 7. rye-grass and clover. But some of the superior managers are now beginning to introduce the Norfolk husbandry on the lighter sandy soil.

"On some of the clay lands, north of the city, the rotation is, 1. a fallow, 2. wheat, 3. pease, 4. a fallow, 5. wheat, 6. barley, and sow clover."

WORKPEOPLE.—The subjoined account of wages, liquor and hours of work, in Herefordshire, in 1794, may, with similar accounts, in other counties, at the same period, be at least interesting, in times to come.

Yearly Wages.—P. 29. "Men hired by the year, from six to nine guineas. Boys from two to three ditto. Women from three to four ditto, Time of hiring in May."

Day Laborers.—"Six shillings a week in *summer*, and a *gallon of drink* to each man.

"Five shillings a week in winter, with three quarts of drink.

"In harvest, *fourteen pence* a day, with meat and drink.

"*Women*, six-pence a day, with *two quarts* of drink all the year, except in harvest, when they have also meat."

Hours of *Working.*—"In harvest, as early and late as they can see; in winter from light to dark; and in summer from six to six."

Harvest Laborers.—"The grain is cut by persons who come from the mountainous parts of Wales annually for that purpose, mostly from Cardiganshire. A *foreman* generally agrees for a whole farm at a stated price per acre, who finds the requisite number of hands to fulfil his contract, at whatever price he can."

Thrashing.—"Wheat for three pence halfpenny per bushel, of ten gallons.

"Barley, pease, and beans three half-pence, per bushel of ten gallons.

"Also three quarts of drink per day to each man."

WORKING ANIMALS.—P. 79. "There is great room for improving the breed of horses in this county. The Derbyshire kind would suit this district extremely well. Many are

are annually brought from thence. An immense sum of money might be saved, by introducing that or some other good breed, and rearing their own horses. There is, however, little prospect of such an event taking place, since the whole of the farmer's ambition is confined to the selection of the best sort of the inestimable breed of oxen, in which this county abounds. The worthy inhabitants, however, have not committed any great blunder in making the oxen their favourite hobby-horse. Any attempt to change the present breed of neat cattle, would exhibit the most glaring instance of folly and profligacy."

IMPLEMENTS.—P. 24. "The plough in general use is the long heavy one of the district. It contributes to the ease of the ploughman and the burthen of the cattle, by its great length."—A just remark on the Herefordshire plow!—I have measured it more than thirteen feet in length.—" Some of the best farmers," we are told, "have introduced a lighter implement."

MANURES.—P. 23. "Abstracting from the vicinity of large towns, the principal manure is *lime*, and the production of the land, to which the bottom of ponds, and scrapings of lanes, are added by good farmers : the makings of *mixens*, however, is not properly attended to in general.

"The price of lime at the kilns varies according to the distance from coal, from seven to fourteen shillings a load, of *fifty-four* Winchester bushels, with three or four gallons of drink for the quarry men. The quantity laid on an acre is from one load to one and a half; but nearer the kilns, where the frequent application of that *stimulus* has exhausted the land, a greater quantity is used."

The practice described, in the subjoined passage, is too *extraordinary* to be lost to the public.—P. 24. "If the land be *foul*, the lime is watered immediately when it is brought from the kiln. Next day it is spread on the land, and harrowed into the ground *as fast* as possible. The following day the wheat is sowed and ploughed down under a thin furrow. This practice, however, is not general."

TILLAGE.—A practice equally as extraordinary as the above, is likewise found in this Report.—P. 18. " In *some* quarters of the kingdom, the Writer would expect his veracity to be called in question, when he mentions a circumstance so improbable as a *whole* summer's fallow *after* turnips. It is, indeed, with much reluctance that he relates a circumstance so disgracefcl to the agriculture of so very respectable a county."—The particulars of this practice it is not necessary to register, here.

In

In the Appendix to this Report we find the Herefordshire method of making summer fallows. It resembles that of Glocestershire; where they are considered as profitable sheep walks. Part of the Reporter's remarks however are very much to the purpose.—P. 79. "The intention of the husbandman ought to be, in making a fallow, to destroy the native weeds of the soil, that he may plant more profitable crops in their place. Yet here they are left so green as to feed sheep for a considerable part of the summer. Strange infatuation, that for the paltry consideration of a few shillings worth of grass, the weeds should be suffered to exist in the ground, to injure the succeeding crops, and, in some degree, to frustrate the very intention of a summer's fallow."

SEMINATION.—What we have on this subject is a sort of hearsay report, about "changing all kind of seeds" (p. 65.) What is related, however, only serves to convey, to my mind, that the writer is a *fresh* farmer. The changing of seed corn is a subject apparently new to him. Something, is said about seed time (p. 24.) But it only relates opposite opinions, that are of no weight, on either side.

REARING CROPS.—The following personific strictures on the destruction of weeds, may serve to rouse the sloven from his slumber, with better effect, than plain prosaic injunctions.

P. 22. "There does not appear to be any thing in the practice of the agriculture of this county so very reprehensible as the little attention that is paid to the destruction of weeds. There seems to be a degree of *liberality* interwoven along with the other desirable qualities of the good inhabitants of this county; for they consider that there is *enough* of food for the grain, and *enough* for the weeds: their benevolence would be, however, still more laudable, if in place of the weeds, they would direct their attention a little more to the practice of *hoeing* and *weeding*, by which women and children might subsist comfortably upon that part of the earth's production, which has long been appropriated to the nourishment of weeds.

"Weeds are the ancient natives of the soil; they are *nature's children*, and by no means *useless*; for she made nothing in vain. Yet, in respect to the farmer's purpose, they are not only *useless*, but highly *hurtful*, because they avail themselves of his industry in manuring and cultivating the soil, and appropriate to their own use that nourishment, which he had intended for more profitable crops. The farmer ought, therefore, to consider them as not only intruders, but enemies; and their destruction and

and extirpation should claim his most serious and unremitting attention."

GRAIN CROPS.—Under the head, "Produce, of the different Grains," is comprized all that is related of their cultivation; excepting the above remarks, on tillage, semination, and weeding.

P. 20. "*Wheat* on the skirts of the county; the quantity is 160, and on the richer lands 200 gallons per acre*. When the strength of the soil and the mildness of the climate are duly considered, this quantity will appear very small. The land of this county has been long noticed as being uncommonly congenial to the growth of *wheat*, the quality of which is admitted to be superior to that produced by the surrounding districts. Hence it would seem, that the smallness of the quantity ought to be attributed to some other cause than either the soil or the climate. If so, it must follow as a consequence that the defect is occasioned by a quick repetition of exhausting crops, without the requisite application of proper manures; or what is more likely, by a deficiency of tillage, and suffering the weeds to appropriate to themselves a part of that food which ought to be wholly reserved for the support of the wheat.

"*Barley*.—The major part of this county being composed of a clayey soil, the cultivation of barley is not very general. On the south side of the county, where the soil is inclined to be sandy, barley, however, is a principal article. The produce may be 300 gallons an acre, but in the Ross quarter much more.

"*Pulse*—whether pease or beans, are sown *broad-cast*. The strong clayey soil is well adapted for this species of crop; yet from the quantity produced, the fact would seem to be otherwise, since the average produce cannot be estimated at more than 200 gallons per statute acre. This is not to be wondered at, considering that they are sown broad-cast in the spring, and left to share the land with flourishing crops of luxuriant weeds, who, being the ancient natives of the soil, come in for more than their share.

"*Beans*—are sometimes set, but not in regular rows, with an intention to keep the land clean by hoeing. The principal advantage therefore seems to be, that the birds cannot pick up the seed, and that the saving in the quantity of the seed sown will pay the women's wages for *setting*, and something more." TURNIPS.

"* This alludes to the general run of the county; for 300 gallons is not uncommon on WYE SIDE."

TURNIPS.—P. 19. "The cultivation of turnips has been but recently introduced into this district. It was found that a good crop of turnips could be had *without hoeing.* The eye *thus* fixed on the *present* gain seems to have lost sight of the *future* prospect. When barley was sown after unhoed turnips, the crop, *choaked up by the weeds,* was found to be unproductive. Hence the practice was given up, and the fault was assigned to some defect in the *soil,* and not to the real cause, the *superabundance* of the *weeds.*

"There is a principle inherent in the human mind, which proves rather an obstacle to any rapid improvement in agriculture; I mean that species of *pride* that prompts a man to support *his own practice* like *his own argument,* be it right or wrong."—A truth well conveyed.

With the view to supple this stubborn pride, Mr. Clark suggests, in a note, p. 19, that—"A fund, raised by a subscription among the land-owners in the county, to be distributed annually among the tenants of the *subscribers* for the best crop of *hoed turnips,* would be attended with consequences beneficial to themselves and the public.

"The *farms* might be divided into *ten* classes, from 500l. and upwards, down to 50l. a year; and one or more premiums to be given to each class: this would give the *little* farmer a *chance,* by contending with rivals of *equal* strength to his own."

And, in a note p. 59, we are informed that the Governors of Guy's Hospital gave a premium of a piece of plate, with the same view. "The Governors of Guy's Hospital gave a premium of a piece of place, value twenty pounds, annually, for the best crop of hoed turnips that could be produced upon their own estate in this county. This produced every visible good effect on the estate of the Hospital. Persons accustomed to the hoeing of turnips were sent for, from a distance, to some quarters where the operation had never been performed before. So far the Governors deserved much praise; but it is unpleasant to add, that at the end of three years only, this enterprising spirit, just then opening its tender buds, received a sudden check, by the premium's being discontinued."

HOPS.—The culture of this valuable crop, as it is practised in the SOUTHERN COUNTIES;—in the neighbourhoods of *Canterbury, Maidstone,* and *Farnham;*—I have studied and registered with peculiar care; and in such a manner, I believe, as to enable any practical and sensible husbandman,

bandman, or gardener, to raise it in perfection, without other instructions.

But, in the WESTERN DEPARTMENT,—in *Worcestershire* and *Herefordshire*,—I have had less opportunity of examining the various processes of its culture, and the management, necessary to prepare the produce for market*. I therefore gladly embrace any probable mean of furnishing my readers; especially those of the midland and northern provinces (whose climature better accords with that of Herefordshire, than with that of Kent or Surrey);—with the required information.—What I find in the Herefordshire Report, however,—even admitting it to be sufficiently authentic,—will go but a little way toward conveying to them a competent knowledge of the subject. On the interesting business of *harvesting* the crop, the difficult process of *curing* it, or the proper method of *preserving* it, and rendering it *saleable*, at market,—not a word! I insert all I find—*on the authority of the Reporter*.

P. 46. "*Hops*—form a very considerable article in the rural economy of the county of Hereford, and seems to be of all others the farmer's peculiar favourite. Time was, however, when the case was otherwise. Upon the first introduction of hop into this latitude, it met with a most unwelcome reception; for a petition was presented against it to parliament, in the year 1528, in which it is stigmatised as a most pernicious and wicked weed; and the national vengeance was requested to be hurled at the heads of those who should propagate it on their lands. The wicked weed, however, did not remain long in disgrace; for in 1552 it is mentioned with some respect, and in 1603 was finally taken under the protection of the legislature. A penalty is inflicted on those who shall be found to adulterate hops, with a view to add to the weight; so rapidly had the wicked weed ingratiated itself into the good graces of our ancestors.

"It is generally, I believe, admitted, that the best aspect for a hop-yard is a south-east one. Men of long experience wish to have a border of some plantation or other to the west; and when that cannot be had, they suffer the hedges in that point to grow as thick and high as they can get them. The time of picking hops is, in general, about

* My own knowledge of the practice of WORCESTERSHIRE, which may be considered as the prototype of that of Herefordshire. will be shown in reviewing the Report, from the former county.

about the autumnal equinox; and the wind being then, mostly, from that quarter, shelter is found to be of advantage. Others of equal experience and knowledge, however, have hop plantations on flat land; and towards other points of the compass, on side lands. It is admitted, in general, that in a good year the aspect is of no importance; but that in a bad year, some situations are found to bear a crop, while others have failed.

"If it be a wet summer, it is found that hops do not grow so well upon a clay, as upon a sandy soil. The reverse is also said to hold true, of the sandy soil.

"*Rearing Hops.* The land preferred by the planter, in this district, to be converted into hop ground, is meadow or old pasture, when it can be had; but any land that has lain for years in grass he prefers to tillage. The land is ploughed from the middle of November to Christmas, by skimming over the ground with a thin furrow, in order to bury the sward. The plough goes immediately along the former furrow, and raises a second deep furrow, which is thrown on the top of the first, raising thereby *a pale* of the depth of six or eight inches.

"The sward thus buried, and out of the reach of the air, begins to rot, and causes a degree of fermentation in the sub-soil; and the top mould, by being exposed to the influence of the atmosphere for the space of two months, becomes, in some degree, pulverized, and after cross harrowing, is then prepared for the reception of the young *sets.*

"The sets consist of cuttings, taken from the old stocks, of the length of four inches. To each set it is requisite to have two or three joints. From one of these joints there is a moral certainty of having shoots. Three or four sets are planted on each hill.

"There are two modes of planting. The one by digging a square hole six inches wide, and as deep as the plough went. This hole is afterwards filled up with some of the finest mould by a spade; and then pressed together, by two or three strokes with a round rammer, nearly of the size of the hole, as close as possible.

"In the mould thus pressed, holes are made with a wooden pin, of the same depth, and a little wider than the sets, in which they are planted. The tops of the sets are then covered with a little fine mould, rubbed between the hands, in order to prevent any hard clods from hindering the vegetation of the young shoots.

"The other method of planting is less expensive, and is

is said to be attended with equal success. This consists in making an impression with the rammer, after the land is harrowed in the spot where the hills are to be made, and then planting the sets within the circumference of this impression, without digging any holes. Some of the most intelligent planters use this last method, although many prefer the former. If theory might presume to intrude her suggestions, it would seem that lands of different degrees of stiffness require different management.

"The distance of the holes should be varied according to the richness of the land, since the richer land will produce a greater quantity of bine than the poorer; a greater distance must be left for the free circulation of the air, the want of which would be apt to render the crops 'foul.' The distance between the centre of the holes on good land should be six feet each way; that on the poorer land from five feet to five feet six inches.

"When the hops are thus planted, the land must be kept perfectly clean from weeds by the hand-hoe.

"The manner of planting, when the plough is to be used, is different, and the holes are made at a greater distance from each other. On good land, the distance between the rows is from eight to nine feet, and three feet in the rows; that on inferior is from six to seven feet between the rows, and three feet in the rows.

"They use a line, or chain, with marks at the distance at which the sets are to be planted from each other. A man takes a parcel of sticks of the length of two feet and an half, he sticks one firmly in the ground opposite to each mark, not perpendicular, but forming an angle with the ground, of about sixty degrees. This stick is to receive the young shoots, care being taken to direct them to it on their first appearance above the surface. Time of planting about the beginning of April.

"The first hoeing should take place about the beginning of June, if the ground, by purging or throwing up weeds, should not require it to be done sooner, taking care to weed round the young stacks with the hand, in order to guard against the hoes injuring the young shoots. In a month or six weeks, another hoeing should take place. About Michaelmas the mould should be gathered into hills round each set of stacks; taking care to leave open the eye of the shoots, by leaving a cavity of the form of a tundish on the top of each hill. In another month this cavity should be filled up with fresh mould by the spade. The space between the base of the hill should not be wider

wider than the breadth of the spade, leaving the alleys as even and level as possible. This finishes the operation of the first year.

"In order to have some benefit during this time, potatoes or turnips are, in some instances, planted in the alleys; but this is a puny piece of parsimony, reprobated by all good judges.

"The business of the second, and every succeeding year, commences by throwing down the hills, about the middle of April, with the hoe, and making the land even. The shoots are then cut off level with the surface, with a crooked knife. The top of each bed of sets is then covered with a small quantity of fine mould, raised in a pyramidical form, in order to point out where the stacks are, in case they should not all spring up at the time of pulling, which is sometimes the case.

"When the shoots make their appearance above the ground, the poles are put up in holes made to receive them, with an iron bar. When the bines are twelve inches high, they are tied to the poles with rushes, but not too tight, the consequence of which would be a stoppage in the circulation of the sap. This business is generally performed by women. The same operation is repeated until the wires are above the reach of a person standing on the ground. But sometimes the wind blows the top of the bine out of its perpendicular direction, and turns the point downwards; in that case a ladder with a stand is used for another tying.

"In six weeks after, the ground is to be hoed again; and about the beginning of July the hills are made. A hollow is made on the top of each hill, which is to be filled up occasionally with fresh mould; this will strengthen and invigorate the plant until the commencement of the picking season*.

"Poles of ten or twelve feet long, are used the second year; afterwards longer ones are requisite.

"*The Furnham-white, the Kentish-grape, and Red-vine*, require poles of twenty-one or twenty-two feet; but for most others, from fifteen to eighteen feet is the common length.

"The

"* The soil of a hop-yard should be clayey, for they are not found to succeed on a sandy soil. Too much moisture subjects the plants to the *mould*. The muck should be fully rotted, and mixed with earth and lime a year before it is used. They should have a little of this manure every year, not much at a time."

"The price of hop-poles, from ten to fifteen shillings a hundred, in the wood. If stript of the bark, they will last seven or eight years; if that operation is neglected, the softer wood will be useless in three years: yet, wonderful as it must appear, this trifling trouble is sometimes dispensed with. The subsequent operation, probable produce, and *profit*, I pass over, as forming no part of the plan of the Honourable Board, which is to discover the most likely means of enabling the soil to bring forth the greatest possible increase, and not to pry into the amount of the well earned wages of honest industry."

The close of the last period is good! very good!!—but it will not cover the sin of omission, as above stated.

GRASS LANDS.—P. 25. "*The hay* of this district is uncommonly well adapted to the feeding of cattle: the farm horses seldom eat a handful of oats, yet they are in good condition all the year. Whether this be owing to the natural goodness of the soil, or superior management in the mode of making and time of cutting, is probably not quite ascertained."—Not a syllable, however, as to either of the latter.

Irrigation.—P. 12. "Although the Wye is too haughty to yield to the husbandman's wish, by submitting to be turned over his meadows, yet here are other streams more humble and more useful, that are quite tractable, from whose invigorating streams the farmer derives no small portion of wealth.

"The Lugg rises in Radnorshire, near Llangunllo, and entering this county near Presteign, and passing by Leominster, empties itself into the Wye below the city, after having for twenty-five miles, watered a district*, which, taking it all in all, is perhaps not to be equalled by any other in this island, of equal extent.

"The Arrow, a beautiful little stream, rises near Gladstree in Radnorshire; it passes through Kington, and flooding many thousand acres of rich meadows, joins the Lugg below Leominster. The water of the Arrow is found to be uncommonly beneficial to the land over which it is turned. This is not to be wondered at, when it is remarked, that the water springs from hills that are mostly composed of a calcareous or a siliceous stone."

ORCHARDS.—The Orchards of Herefordshire have long been celebrated, in works on rural subjects. It was, therefore, to be expected that, in a Report of the Rural Practices

* We are not told in which or what manner.

practices of the County, those respecting ORCHARDS and CIDER would have been conspicuously brought forward; and we are not entirely disappointed, in our expectations. We look in vain, however, for any thing resembling analytical detail, or synthetic combination.—Nothing is discovered but floating opinions of practitioners; and speculative remarks of the collector of those opinions.

Having formerly studied those subjects, with singular attention,—traced their various branches, and minor ramifications, and registered the best practice, concerning each, together with the evident improvements which they appear to me to be capable of, (in the RURAL ECONOMY of GLOCESTERSHIRE, &c. &c.),—I am the better enabled to estimate the materials collected by the writer under notice. Whatever I can perceive in the collection that can in any way add useful information to my own Register, I will extract; leaving the remainder to the fate of the Board's Reports at large.

On the *situation* of Orchards, we find the most ample materials. But very few of them are adapted to the desired purpose;—excepting the following passage; which is in Mr. C's own manner. After dwelling some time on the striking variations, in the opinions of men of experience and observation,—Mr. C. adds,—P. 37. "It is agreed upon all hands, however, that the spring frosts and May blights do mischief to the fruit, and are perhaps the only cause why there is not a crop of apples and pears every year as regularly as there is a crop of corn. The blight spreads terrors much more tremendous, than those exacted by the *frost*, which if it does not come on suddenly while the blow on the trees is moist, does no harm. It seems pretty generally agreed also, that the critical period of time at which the fruit is accessible to the devastation of the blight is but of short duration. If one might venture to hazard any thing in the shape of an opinion upon so intricate a subject, it would be, a recommendation to watch with much attention the operation of Nature in this business. for a single fact from her volume, properly authenticated, is preferable to all that we can learn from the united wisdom of philosophical speculation. It is well known, that Nature has endued some apple trees, such as the redstreak, foxwhelp, early marlet, junettin, &c. with the power of maturing their fruits earlier in the season than others, as the hagly crab, golden-pippin, golden rozet, brefling, &c. It would seem, at least, probable, that there could not be any danger in our taking a hint from the operations of Nature in this instance, so far as to lend her all the assistance we can, in her apparent endeavours to obtain those ends which she seems to have in view. We know that a southeasterly aspect and a light sandy soil (moderately so) will assist the early fruits to get faster forward (perhaps out of danger's way) than they could do in any other soil or aspect. We know equally well, that planting trees on a flat or a northerly aspect, and on a strong clayey soil, will keep the fruit back, perhaps till the enemy has passed, and longer than if they had been planted in any other soil or aspect.

"If this conjecture has any foundation in Nature, then all early fruit trees should be planted in a southern, and all late trees in a northern aspect."

If the comings of frosts and blights were certain and fixed, like the festivals in the Almanac, the above suggestions would be truly valuable. But they come like thieves in the night; without warning or previous notice. The season of frosts is uncertain, and that of blights is too irregular to be guarded against, with any thing bordering on certainty. Mr. C's remarks have, nevertheless, the merit of being ingenious; and his rule may have the chances in its favour.

Indeed, in p. 34, there is a passage on aspect, which is valuable: but it may be said to be my own. (See GLOCESTERSHIRE, &c. II. 225.) It is as follows,—"Those who prefer the south-east side of the hill, observe that the morning sun directs his animating rays to that quarter before any other; that the trees being sooner relieved from the cold chill of night, enjoy a longer day than those placed in any other situation. The hills forming an angle of twenty or thirty degrees of elevation, throw the sun's ray back upon the fruit, in the nature of a garden wall: this brings the fruit quicker forward, and thereby affords it a better chance, by being sooner out of the power of the blight to injure it, than fruit in another aspect, which, by its slower growth, requires more time to pass the period of its nonage; and is, of course, longer within the reach of danger."

Mr. Clark agrees with me, (p. 38.) in that it is prudent to plant Orchards with different aspects, (where of course a choice can be had) in order to increase the chance of having some fruit every year.

Soils.—P. 38. "The apples, like different kinds of grain, affect, some a light sandy, and others a strong stiff clay.

"It is a fact well ascertained, that cuttings from the same tree, grafted upon similar stocks, and planted in different soils, will produce different cider. It is also found, that the early fruits obtain their greatest perfection in a sandy soil; and that the late fruits succeed best when planted in a

strong

strong clay. Some of the most valuable apples, such as the stive," (Stire) " hagly crab, and golden pippin, are said to be fond of a light sandy soil. The best orchards, however, are on a strong clayey soil. It seems to be admitted, that the cider from trees in clay, is stronger in the body, and will keep better than cider made from trees that are on a sandy soil." These popular notions I insert, merely as such.

On *raising stocks*, for apple trees, we find, at least, one idea worthy to be registered. After censuring the common practice of raising apple stocks, from the uncrushed kernels, lodged in the refuse or residue, of the cider press, (by reason of the fairest of the pippins being bruised in the operations of grinding,—a cause of alarm which, in the ordinary practice of the County, is seldom to be apprehended),—as well as that of propagating them from apple kernels in general,—Mr. Clark offers a hint to proprietors, which, received in a limited sense, may be useful to themselves and their successors.

P. 43. " The reason assigned for grafting on the apple-stock is, that the tree will bear fruit three or four years sooner than that on the crab-stock. But when it is considered, that the crab-stock will support the tree for twenty or thirty years longer than the apple-stock, that it, in some degree, protects it from the havock of the moss, and the still more fatal operation of the canker, and that the expence of protecting the tree on the apple-stock, during its infancy, is greater than that on the crab, because it is much longer before it arrives at maturity, (?) it seems to be worthy the attention of the land owners to inquire how far it would be proper to restrict their tenantry from planting their orchard trees on apple-stocks."

But this (like many other of this Reporter's suggestions) is too general to be just.—See the RURAL ECONOMY of GLOCESTERSHIRE, II. 213.

On the *planting* of orchards, we find nothing to preserve; excepting an idea relating to the distance of the trees.

P. 38. " The degree of elevation should determine, in a great measure, the distance at which trees ought to be planted from each other. If the situation be high, they ought to be planted thick, about eleven or twelve yards distant; because they shelter and protect each other by being thus close. If the situation be a low flat, double that distance will in the general run be found to answer best."

Unfortunately, however, for the observance of this, as a general rule, the upper fruit grounds (of Herefordshire) are for the most part kept in tillage; while the mere orchards, about farmsteads, are mostly in lower situations

To

To perennial pasture lands, the rule may be best applied.

What Mr. C. recommends, in regard to the depth at which apple trees ought to be planted, is like most of the speculations of unpractised writers, on practical subjects, *too general.* The depth should be regulated according to the given plants to be put in, and the given land to receive them. See, as above, (Ed. 1796) Vol II. p. 239.

On the *enemies* of orchard trees, there is, in Mr. Clark's Report, a particular or two to be noticed. In a note, p. 35, we have a *circumstantial* account of the origin and progress of the *blight.*—" If a mat, or piece of white paper be thrown over a tree at night, and examined in the morning, if there has been a blight, there will be little black spots, like the point of a pin, visible when viewed. They seem lifeless; but if the sun shine, by twelve o'clock they will be in motion. By next morning, they will be gone from the mat, and then, but not till then, they go into the leaves of the trees, where they form nests, and do the mischief. It happens very unfortunately, that these insects are more fond of apple-trees than any other food. In two or three days after the blight has infected an orchard, the leaves of the trees will be curled. If with a powerful miscrocope the inside be examined, there will be a thousand small insects seen: these will seize upon the half-formed *embryo*, and destroy it in the midst of its feeding leaves.

" When wounded by the insects, the leaf curls from an impulse similar to that by which a man is prompted to put his hand to his face when a fly stings him there. When the host of little vermin begin to wound and devour its inside, the point of the leaf bends with sympathy to the wounded part; but cannot relieve it. In a few days the little insects acquire so much strength as to be able to fly off, and then the leaf rears itself. If the blow be not on the tree, nor the fruit formed, when these vermin arrive, they do no mischief; or they lurk into holes, and the blow leaf escapes them, at least it is not more infected with them than any other leaf; but if the young apple be just formed, and not of sufficient strength to repel their attack, it is so much the food they want, that it falls an immediate sacrifice to their depredations."

By whom those curious particulars have been ascertained is not mentioned. All we find, concerning them, are the broad assertions above quoted.

On the disease of *Hidebound* is this notice.—P. 44. " When the trees are unkindly 'hide-bound,' they are 'scored,'

'scored,' by cutting the bark wish the point of a knife, from the bottom to the top of the stem."—This is not an uncommon operation of orchardmen, which, in some cases, is pretty evidently found useful.

The following well conveyed censure, on the "orchardists" of Herefordshire, regarding the *misletoe*, I have great satisfaction in transcribing. A more glaring instance than that under notice, of inattention and slovenliness, I know not, in the whole circle of rural affairs; excepting that of suffering the ivy to destroy the oak.

P. 45. "The destruction which the misletoe does to the trees, is so universally admitted, and the removal of it, by cutting off the branch on which it grows, is so easy, that I did imagine that some fragments of the Druidical superstition still remain in this district, and that the people were thereby deterred from destroying this pest to the orchards. For, since a labourer could clean fifty or sixty of the trees in one day, I could scarcely believe, that, to save a shilling, any man of common sense could see his trees lingering under disease, and suffer an annual loss of some hogsheads of cider. Upon repeated inquiries, however, I found that no other cause than laziness was assigned for the destruction of the orchard. 'Cannot do every thing at once,' was all the answer I could get to my repeated remonstrances on this subject. At the side of the river Wye, I found one small orchard quite clean from misletoe. Imagining that there was something in the soil or aspect that might be the cause of this, I waited on the occupier, and asked how his orchard came to be so clean, whilst all his neighbours' were covered with misletoe? He said, 'We have a small orchard and a large family, so must make the most of it. I pulled off all the misletoe some years back, and we never had any more of it; and you cannot believe how well our trees have been since.'

"'Cannot you prevail upon your neighbours to do the same?'

"'It is in vain talking, sir; they have large plantations, so have plenty of apples, and plenty of misletoe also.'"

Fruit Liquor.—If we find little that is estimable, in this Report respecting orchards, we discover still less relating to the manufacturing of Cider;—for which the County under Report has so long been proverbial. The Reporter, however, evades the subject, with a degree of adroitness (equal to that employed, relative to the harvesting and management of hops. See p. 288, aforegoing.) Having given outline descriptions of the mill and the press, he adds

adds—P. 40. "The extreme simplicity of the mill and press renders them peculiarly well adapted to be put into the rough careless hands destined to use them. But when the period arrives when the manufacturing of cider, like the distillery or brewing, shall form a profession by itself, it will then occupy the attention of scientific men, and machines very different in power at least, if not in principle, from those now in use, will be adopted. Men of large concerns are obliged to leave the making of cider to their common servants; and it may reasonably be conjectured, that their orders are not always punctually obeyed.

"Many farmers consider cider-making as an intrusion upon operations of greater importance, and often wish there had not be an apple-tree in the county. While the most part of the cider is manufactured by men in this humour * "

Now, the fact is—the principal part of the prime cider, sold in London and elsewhere, is manufactured by professional men;—by men who make a business of manufacturing and *rectifying* cider; even as distillers, rectifiers of spirit, and brewers, follow their businesses or professions; and like them, too, conduct their operations, more or less, on scientific principles. I do not mean to say that the art of cidermaking has yet reached its highest degree of perfection; even at Glocester, or Upton; for, like every other art, it is doubtlessly capable of improvement.—And, as I find, in a fresh bundle of the Board's publications, that Herefordshire has been re-reported; and by a man of learning, at least, if not of science; we may reasonably hope to find, in that Report upon Report, principles that may lead to further improvement.

CATTLE.—Herefordshire has not been less celebrated, during a length of years, for its breed of cattle, than for its fruit liquors. Yet, almost incredible to relate, we find not, in the Herefordshire Report, a word respecting the *breed, breeding, milking, working, grazing,* or any other part

" * The following conversation, which passed the other day, will shew what reception any person would meet with, who would propose an amendment in the cider mill:

" 'Master, what horse shall I take to drive cider mill?'

" 'D——n the cider and the mill too; you waste one-half of your time in making cider, and the other half in drinking it. I wish there was not one apple in the county. You all think of cider, no matter what comes of plough.' "

part of the management of this most valuable variety of English cattle!—excepting a few unprofitable remarks, on *stall-fatting* *; and excepting the subjoined, on their *winter management*.—P. 25. "*The winter* feeding of cattle is here well conducted. Round the sides of the yards (folds) a row of *cribs* is made, by sticking stakes firmly into the ground; wallings or withies are then wrought along these in a basket-like manner. In these cribs the cattle are fed; the young horses and brood mares in 'beoks' under a shade."—and, further, excepting a valuable Paper, in the Appendix, concerning the disease of GUT-TIE, by JOSEPH HARRIS of Wicton near Leominster;—who designates himself—"neither an ox-leech, nor a professional man, but a Herefordshire farmer." p. 76. His Paper, however, shows that he (or some friend who has assisted him) has made what is aukwardly termed "comparative anatomy," in some part, his study.

The symptoms and method of cure of this disease might doubtlessly have been given in fewer words, and less technical phrases. But, as the account wears marks of authenticity and accuracy, it will be right to transcribe it, at length; for the perusal of professional men.

P. 77. "The symptoms of the *guttie* are the same as an incurable *colic volvulus*, or mortification of the bowels. The beast affected with this complaint will kick at its belly, lie down, and groan: it has also a total stoppage in its bowels, (except blood and mucus, which will it void in large quantities) and a violent fever, &c. To distinguish with certainty the guttie from the colic, &c. the hand and arm of the operator must be oiled, and introduced into the anus, through the rectum, beyond the os pubis, turning the hand down to the transverse and oblique muscles, where the vessels of the testicles enter the abdomen. There the string will be found united to the muscles, and easily to be traced to the stricture, by the hand, without pain to the beast.

"This stricture, or guttie, as it is called, is occasioned by an erroneous method of castrating the calves, which the breeders practise throughout Herefordshire, and is as follows; they open the scrotum, take hold of the testicles with their teeth, and with violence tear them out, by which means all the vessels thereto belonging are ruptured. The vasa

* For a full account of stall-fatting, in this quarter of the kingdom, see my GLOCESTERSHIRE, &c. I. 233.

vasa deferentia, entering by the holes of the transverse and oblique muscles into the abdomen, pass over the ureters in acute angles; at which, turning by their great length and elastic force, the peretonæum is ruptured, the vasa deferentia are severed frem the testicles, and springing back, form a kind of bow from the urethra, where they are united, over the ureters, to the transverse and oblique muscles; and there again unite where they first entered the abdomen. The part of the gut that is tied is the jejunum at its turning from the left side to the right, and again from the right to the left, forming right angles under the kidney, and attached to the duplicator of the peretonæum, to which it was united, where the rupture happened. There the bow of the gut hangs over the bow of the vasa deferentia, which, by a sudden motion, or turn of the beast, form a hitch or tie of the string round the bow of the gut (filled with air) similar to what a carter makes on his cart-line. This causes a stoppage in the bowels, and brings on a mortification, which, in two, or four days at most, proves fatal.

"To this accident is the beast, castrated as above, liable from the day that he was castrated till the time of his being slaughtered. I have cut them of the guttie, from the age of three months to nine years. The only method of cure that can be safely ventured upon, is to make a perpendicular incision four inches under the third vertebra of the loins, on the left side of the ox, over the paunch, or stomach, and introduce the arm to find the part affected; if possible keep the beast standing, by the strength of proper assistants. The knife I make use of to sever the string, is in the form of a large fish-hook, with an edge on the concave side, fixed to a ring which fits the middle finger, which crooks round the back of the knife, the end of the thumb being placed on its edge. The instrument thus secured in the hand is a certain security against wounding the surrounding intestines. With this instrument, I divide the string, or strings, and being out, one or both as circumstances require. Here it is to be observed, that great care must be taken by the operator not to wound or divide the ureters, which would be certain death. I then sow up the divided lips of the peretonæum very close, with a surgeon's needle, threaded with strong thread, eight or ten double, sufficiently waxed; and also the hide, leaving a vacancy at the top and bottom of the wound sufficiently wide to introduce a tent of surgeon's tow, spread with common digestive and traumatic balsam, covering the incision

cision with a plaster made of the white of eggs and wheat flour. The wound thus treated and dressed every day, will be well in a fortnight. The medicine I give to remove the stoppage in the three stomachs, occasioned by the tie, and carry off the fever, is four ounces of glauber salts, two ounces of cream of tartar, one ounce of sena, infused in two pounds of boiling water; adding half a pound of oil olive, working it off with plenty of gruel, mixed with a large quantity of infusion of mallows and elder bark. Administer the gruel and infusion, for at least two or three days, by which time the beast will be well; will eat his provender and chew the cud; and will for ever be relieved, and remain safe from this fatal disorder."

Mr. Harris's method, or rather methods, of prevention differ, entirely, from that which I registered, in YORKSHIRE (II. 189). But they appear to me, on paper, to be less facile, and less likely to be efficient, than the method I there saw practised. It would, nevertheless, be wrong to refuse Mr. Harris's practice a place, here.

P. 78. "The following simple and easy method of castration will effectually prevent the guttie. Open the scrotum, loosen out the testicles, and tie the several vessels with a waxed thread, or silk, or sear with a hot iron to prevent their bleeding, as is the common way of cutting colts. This method can never displace either the vessels of the testicles, bladder, kidneys, or intestines; all of which remain covered or attached to the peretonæum, or lining of the abdomen of the beast, which renders it impossible that there should ever be a stricture or tie on the gut."

SHEEP.—Herefordshire has also long prided herself on her breed of 'Ryland sheep.' Yet, in the body of this Report, not a word is said, respecting that or any other breed!—In the Appendix, are the following loose remarks. —P. 79. "The Herefordshire breed of sheep may be said to be perfect of its kind; the animal is compact, well built and healthy; and the wool surpasses in fineness, any other in this quarter of the kingdom. The larger weighs from seventeen to eighteen pounds a quarter, the fleece from four to five pounds; but those kept on the old hilly pasture considerably less. Yet the superior quality of the wool, not making a full recompense for the inferiority of the quantity, and the smallness of the carcass, the time seems fast approaching when this breed will be wholly extinct, in order to make way for a more profitable one."

Respecting the SWINE, and the minor species of domestic animals, of Herefordshire, we are left, by this Reporter, entirely in the dark.

"GENERAL VIEW

OF THE

AGRICULTURE

OF THE

COUNTY OF HEREFORD:

DRAWN UP FOR THE CONSIDERATION OF

THE BOARD OF AGRICULTURE AND INTERNAL IMPROVEMENT.

BY JOHN DUNCUMB, A. M.

SECRETARY TO THE AGRICULTURAL SOCIETY OF THAT PROVINCE.

1805."

RESPECTING the identity of this REPORTER, nothing is to be gathered from the volume under Review; excepting what appears in the title page.

In regard to his QUALIFICATIONS, for the task he has undertaken, not one distinct ray of light is discernible. From the glimmerings which the work in general affords, it is evident that Mr. DUNCUMB has very little (if any) practical knowledge, in either of the three subjects (namely Natural, Political, and Rural Economy) on which he has here written. Some acquaintance with the ancient writers, on those subjects, is evinced in different parts of his book. But we find little in it, which any other A. M. tho fresh from College, might not have *done* as well.

Yet this is a recent publication, and is of course one of the "reprinted Reports,"—about which we are now hearing so much. (See the foregoing Advertisement.) But what renders the puffings of the Board's publisher the more

more ridiculous, this "reprinted" Report takes no notice, whatever, of the ORIGINAL REPORT, by Mr. CLARK; whose name, or production is not once mentioned! It is just another sketch—a *second Original*. Does the Editor of the Board mean to *sink* Mr. Clark's labors? which have at least as much *useful* knowledge to recommend them, as Mr. Duncumb's. Yet the publisher, or his employer, is scoffing at one, for bestowing a serious thought on the original Reports!

There are of course no *annotators*, to this, as to the really reprinted Reports. May it be asked what are become of the *notes* made on the margins of Mr. Clark's sketch;—if any such there were?

Mr. Duncumb, however, has modestly, and wisely, called in an ASSISTANT,—a Mr. *Knight*;—that is to say, one of the Mr. Knight's of literary celebrity;—and as it would seem,—from what appears in the section "Orchards,"—Mr. Knight the orchardist:—with what advantage will best be shown in reviewing the various chapters, in which Mr. K. comes forward.

The number of pages, in the body of the work, one hundred and sixty two;—in the Appendix, six.

A map of soils, and four other unuseful engravings, *embellish* the volume.

SUBJECT THE FIRST.

NATURAL ECONOMY.

EXTENT.—P. 10. "The gross number of acres in the county are estimated at 600,000: deducting 30,000, or one acre in twenty for the sites of towns, roads, water, houses, yards, and buildings, and 50,000 more for waste lands and woods, there remain 520,000 acres of cultivated ground."

On *elevation* and *surface*, nothing appears.

CLIMATURE.—P. 8. "In this county, no air, generally speaking, is more harsh and unkind than that, which proceeds from the west.

"This is probably to be attributed to the extensive tracts of mountainous country, which in that direction is seldom without snow during the winter, and is often bleached with it even late in the spring."

WATERS.

WATERS.—P. 11. "The principal rivers and streams of Herefordshire are, the Wye, the Lug, the Munnow, the Arrow, the Frome, the Teme, and the Leddon."

The courses and branches of those several rivers, are described, and a small sketch map of them given (similar to that which every map of the county affords, on a larger scale);—by whom does not appear.

Nothing of sufficient importance to the "Agriculture," or to the "internal improvement" of the county, or the kingdom at large, is found in this section; excepting what relates to *Inland Navigation* (of which in its place); and excepting some interesting remarks on

Salmon.—P. 14. "The principal fish taken in the Wye, is the salmon, which is well known to leave the sea at various periods, and penetrate, as far as is practicable, towards the sources of the greater rivers, where they deposit their spawn secure from the ebbing and flowing of the tides. Other motives appear also to attract them, as the season of coming is not confined to that of spawning, nor does it seem to depend, in any particular degree, on a greater supply of food than usual; an occasional change of water is probably grateful, if not essential to them.—They are found in the Wye at all times, (?) but they are only in perfection from December to August. The assertion of Dr. Fuller, that 'the salmon of the Wye are in season all the year long*,' is very erroneous.—They formerly, however, abounded so much, that it was a common clause in the indentures of children apprentice in Hereford, that they should not be compelled to eat salmon more frequently than twice in every week.

"But the various obstructions to their passage made by the erection of ironworks, which prevent their advancing further, unless the river be swelled far above its usual height, together with some illegal means of taking them by *cribs*, have of late years rendered precautions of this kind altogether unnecessary. It seems also probable, that the rivers Severn and Wye, independent of these grounds of complaint, have not been frequented of late years by salmon in that abundance, which formerly prevailed.

"The price of salmon in Hereford market was formerly one penny per pound; it now varies from eightpence to half-a-crown, according to the time and other circum-

" * Dr. Fuller's Worthies, p. 34."

circumstances. The degrees of perfection, in which they are taken, vary not only with the season, but also in proportion to the time elapsed since they have quitted the sea. After a short continuance in fresh water, they tend rapidly to impoverishment; and as they are stationary at no other time, but when there is not a sufficient stream to admit of their proceeding, a moderate swell puts the *new fish* in motion, and enables the fishermen to calculate their approach with considerable accuracy. They are very rarely found to advance against a current of very cold or very hard water; when therefore the Wye is swelled by snow dissolving in large quantities from the sides of the mountains towards its source, which occasionally happens as late as April or even May, all attempts to take them are suspended for the time. Nor are they frequently intercepted by the fishermen, when returning to the sea, as it is known that the *voyage* which they have performed has deprived them of their principal value (!); and in this state they are denominated *old fish.* The spawn, deposited in the river, produces fish of a very minute size, which about April becomes as heavy as a gudgeon, but more taper and delicate in their form; these are in some parts termed salmon-fry or salmon-pinks, but are here known by the name of *last-springs*, from the date of their annual appearance, and are readily taken by the artificial fly. And if this mode of catching them was alone resorted to, the supply of salmon would probably be far more abundant than it now is. Two kinds of last-springs are found in the Wye; the one, which is the larger and more common sort, leaves the river during the spring floods; the other is termed the gravel last-spring, and is met with particularly on shoals, during the whole of the summer. The general opinion is, that the last-springs, having made a voyage to the sea, return *botchers* in the beginning of the following summer. Botchers are taken from three to twelve pounds weight; they are distinguished from the salmon by a smaller head, more silvery scales, and by retaining much of the delicate appearance of the last-spring.—In the third year they become salmons, and often weigh from forty to fifty pounds each. These are the generally received opinions respecting the progress of the last-spring to the botcher and salmon; but it must not be omitted, that some able naturalists of the present time contend, that the last-spring and botcher are each distinct in their species from the salmon, and that the botcher resembles the *suin* taken in the Welsh rivers, or even that it it is the same fish. A question has also been suggested, whether the gravel last-spring may not proceed from the botcher."

These observations, it may be said, tho interesting, are not of high importance. It may, therefore, be proper to mention, that an additional motive, in extracting them, is to embrace a fair opportunity of suggesting (what has long been familiar to my mind) that if naturalists,—instead of gratifying a childish desire for what is *curious*, and a still weaker for what is *rare!*—would employ their ingenuity, and the ability which some of them possess, in developing the *useful*, in what is termed Natural History—whether in the animal, or the vegetable, world,—their benefit, to society at large, might be rendered highly valuable. But, unfortunately, at present, the productions of nature which are of the most essential use to the human species, and without which the species could not exist, in its present state of population,—are, as subjects of natural history, less studied,—and less *known*,—than is the most worthless fungus, or the meanest animalcule, of the farthest Ind.

SOILS and SUBSTRATA.—P. 9. "The soil of Herefordshire in its general character is a mixture of marl and clay, of great fertility, and containing a certain proportion of calcareous earth. No beds of chalk or flint are found within its limits, but, as in all clays, small particles of flint in the form of sand enter into its composition. Below the surface are strata of limestone, often beautifully intersected with veins of red and white, somewhat resembling calcareous spar. Near Snodhill Castle, in the hundred of Webtree, it becomes a species of that genus of fossils which is called marble, and was in considerable use and estimation as such during part of the seventeenth century.

"Towards the west borders of the county, the soil is often cold and ungenial, but still argillaceous or clayey, resting on nodules of impure limestone, or on a base of soft crumbling stone, which perishes by exposure to air and frost. That part of the county, in the aggregate, can boast of no high degree of fertility; its climate also is comparatively cold from greater elevation, as well as from the other causes noticed in the preceding section.

"In many places towards the east, the soil is loose and shallow, covering stone of small value, provincially termed the *dun-stone*: the more favored spots in this direction are found well adapted to the culture of hops. Deep beds

beds of fine gravel are particularly met with on the site and in the vicinity of the city of Hereford, which occupies a situation nearly central in the county.

"A large proportion of the hundred of Wormelow, on the south, consists of a light sand, which has been much improved in value, by the introduction of lime as a manure. The heaviest crops of wheat are produced in a clayey tract extending from Hereford towards Ledbury*."

FOSSILS, and MINERALS.—Herefordshire (as has been said) is not a *mining* county:—differing much, in this particular, from the adjoining county of Salop.

Beside what appears, in the above extract, we find, in the section "Minerals," the following fossil and mineral productions noticed.—P. 11. "Of the more rare kinds of earths and clays, there have been found, red and yellow ochres, fuller's earth, and tobacco-pipe clay; but probably from the want of an adequate supply, or from some imperfection in their qualities, they are now generally procured from other places. Fuller's earth is, however, still dug occasionally for sale, in small quantities, on the estates of the late Honourable Edward Foley, of Stoke Edith."

P. 10. "Iron-ore was discovered in the sandy district of Wormelow hundred as early as the time of the Romans in Britain, and many of the hand-blomaries used by them have been met with on Peterstow Common, and also considerable quantities of ore imperfectly smelted."—Again. —"Of late years, however, no iron has been manufactured in Herefordshire; but very extensive works are situated in the Forest of Dean, at the distance of a few miles only from the tract alluded to; a richer ore is probably met with there, and the situation and other circumstances being more favourable to the improved modes of extracting it, the practice has gradually been discontinued here. Small particles of lead ore have occasionally been found in the lime rocks situated on the north-west parts of the county; but it does not appear that any other mineral has been discovered. Many attempts to find coal have recently been made; but although first appearances have been flattering, no success has hitherto attended them."

SUBJECT

* Prefixed to this volume is a colored "Map of the Soil of Herefordshire:"—by whom is not said. Its authenticity may therefore be questionable.

SUBJECT THE SECOND.

POLITICAL ECONOMY.

POLITICAL DIVISIONS.—Mr. Duncumb, as Mr. Plymley, gives a list of hundreds and parishes:—to what end we are left to conjecture. See p. 206, aforegoing.

STATE of APPROPRIATION.—Speaking of "wastes and unimproved lands," Mr. D. says—p. 97.—"Lands of this description form a very inconsiderable proportion of Herefordshire. The greatest extent is on the east side of the Hatterell or Black Mountains: and there, unfortunately, in the steepness of the hills, and the poverty of the soil, oppose serious obstacles to all improvement."

P. 49. "Enclosures, under the authority of an act of Parliament, have been resorted to, within late years, much moie frequently than at distant periods. The additional value, which land invariably acquires by enclosing, has been generally found to repay the expenses of the process; but new inducements now offer themselves in the increased demand for corn, and the consequently advanced prices which it affords. Still, however, many commons remain without this improvement, but their aggregate bears a small proportion to the enclosed part of the county.

"The practice of allotting land in lieu of tithes prevails generally, and is one of the most popular, and perhaps beneficial, conditions."

And, under the head "Means of Improvement,"—Mr. D. recommends, p. 162, that—"Lastly, the waste and unimproved lands in the county should be put into such states of cultivation as they will admit of, from the growth of wheat, to a plantation of Scotch firs; and a general bill of enclosure should be submitted to the legislature, ascertaining the rights of all the parties concerned."

PROVISIONS. The following table, if it really may "be relied on," is valuable; as affording interesting data, in Political Economy.—P. 140. "Some idea of the increase in the prices of the necessaries of life in this county, within

within the last hundred years, may be formed from the following table, the accuracy of which may be relied on.

	1691		1740		1760		1804		
	s.	d.	s.	d.	s.	d.	£.	s.	d.
Wheat, per bushel of ten gallons,	3	0	3	0	3	0	0	10	6
Rye, (very little sown of late years)	2	0	....		....		....		
Oats,	0	10	0	11	1	0	0	4	0
White peas,	....		....		2	6	0	8	0
Barley,	....		....		3	6	0	6	0
Malt,	....		....		4	0	0	12	0
Butcher's meat per *lb.*	....		0	1	0	1½	0	0	7
Pigs for bacon per *lb.*	....		....		0	4	0	0	6½
A goose,	....		0	10	1	0	0	4	0
A roasting pig,	....		....		0	10	0	3	6
A couple of fowls,	....		0	6	0	7	0	2	4
Pigeons per doz.	....		....		1	6	0	4	0
Fresh butter per *lb.*	....		....		0	4½	0	1	3
Best cheese,	....		....		0	3	0	0	9
Fresh salmon,	0	1	0	2	0	4½	0	1	3
Coals per ton,	....		11	0	14	0	1	4	0"

FUEL.—P. 141. " Coal is in general use as fuel by as many of the inhabitants as can afford the purchase of it, except for the demands of the farmer's kitchen. The Forest of Dean in Gloucestershire supplies the south side of the county and the provincial metropolis; the Clee-hills of Shropshire furnish it for the northern and eastern parts; and the western procure it occasionally from Abergavenny. The town of Leominster has experienced some benefit in this respect from that part of the canal from Stourport which has been executed.

" The price of coal varies according to the distance from the pit, and the means of conveyance. When brought to Hereford in barges on the Wye from the Forest of Dean, it now sells at twenty-four shillings per ton; when conveyed by waggons, it brings three or four shillings more; and the latter mode is in favour of the consumer from the size and superior quality of the article, the refuse of the pit being generally mixed with the heap designed for the barges. A still inferior sort is sold for the use

use of blacksmiths' forges, from twelve to fourteen shillings the ton."

MANUFACTURES.—In the section, "Commerce and Manufactures," we learn—p. 146, that—"unprovided with any manufacture of general consumption (except that of gloves, which is carried on in the city on a very limited scale), the articles of commerce in Herefordshire must principally be confined to those immediately concerned with agriculture."

In the section, "Poor and Population," p. 148, we are informed that attempts have been made to introduce manufactures of different kinds, in order to afford employment for the lower classes (first, by Lord Scudamore of Home Lacy, and, since, by Mr. George Bradford of Hereford); but without the desired success. We are told, however, in p. 150, that—"a small manufactory for flannel is now established in Hereford, and it seems at present to promise that success which the proprietors so well deserve, and that employment, of which the industrious poor are in so much want."

POOR RATE.—P. 40. "Unprovided with manufactories, or other modes of employing women and children, so as to enable them to acquire their own maintenance, the county of Hereford must necessarily contribute largely to the plan adopted by the legislature for the support of the poor.

"That plan was doubtless founded on the most benevolent principle, and its provisions reflect honor on the country.

"But the public manner in which relief is afforded under it, is attended with consequences injurious to the community, by destroying that spirit of independence, and those ideas of honest pride, which stimulate a man to use his utmost exertions in support of himself and his family. The rates or loans applied to this purpose are gradually increasing, and they are severely felt by the numerous class of small house-keepers, particularly in towns. During the unprecedented price of grain in the year 1801, more than one instance in the city of Hereford occurred, within the observation of the writer of this Report, when a house-keeper, with a shop and decent connexions, was compelled to dine frequently on potatoes and water, in order, that eighteen-pence might be saved to meet the demands of the overseer!

"The returns made under the act of 26 George III. report the net expenses for maintaining the poor throughout the

the county of Hereford, in the year 1776, to have been 10,393*l.* 7*s.* 2*d.* The average of the years 1783, 4, and 5, as returned under similar authority, was stated at 16,727*l.* 18*s.* 2*d.*; at present they nearly amount to 20,000*l.* being in round numbers, double the sum raised thirty years ago."

In the chapter, "Rural Economy"! Mr. D. submits a plan for the melioration of the condition of "the Peasantry." *

I insert the plan, at length; not, however as I think it altogether free from objections,—or, indeed, altogether practicable; but because I am desirous to collect every thing on the subject, which is likely to furnish a probably useful idea, on a practical matter, so difficult as that which relates to the equitable maintainance of those who are *unable* to maintain themselves and their families. Mr D. appears to have thought more upon this, than on most other subjects of his performance.

P. 138. "To improve the condition, and to increase the comforts of this valuable class of the community, must be deemed a most desirable object by every liberal and patriotic mind. According to the ideas of the writer of this Survey, the principle, on which friendly societies are established, affords the means of promoting this object. The interference of Parliament in these establishments has hitherto been viewed with a jealousy hostile to their success; but it is conceived, that the occupiers, or at least the principal occupiers of land, in every parish or larger district, in concert with the clergy, might patronize a society, to consist of all the labourers and male servants within its limits.

"The general obligation should consist in the contribution of one penny per day from the wages of each member, to be left in the hands of their employer. A fund would thus be created, which should be considered as the sole property of the contributors, but liable to be applied to no purposes but those of the society. After a certain period, and in all cases of illness, age, large family, or accident, the payments should suddenly or gradually cease, and

* PEASANTRY.—This is a hateful, because injuriously humiliating, appellation,—when applied to the country people of this island. Let it be confined to the live stock in human shape,—in Russia, and in other nations of demi-slaves. Is so degrading a distinction calculated to promote "the honest independence of Englishmen," so much *talked about*, in the Board's Reports!

and a certain allowance per week should become due to each subscriber. When members removed from one district to another, they might be entitled to a certificate of the amount of their property in the funds of the district quitted, and their allowance be made payable from those of the district in which they should reside. An annual adjustment of accounts, amongst the different societies in a county, would render this practicable without difficulty; and in cases of removal beyond the limits of the county, some similar arrangements might be adopted.

"The comfortable prospect of a provision in old age or distress, would probably afford sufficient inducement to the young peasantry to engage in a plan of this nature, if properly explained and encouraged by their employers. It would also stimulate, whilst it rewarded industry; and a decided preference, if not an increase of wages, would naturally be given to members of such societies, by those who are in the habits of employing labourers and servants.

"If made a national establishment, a parliamentary grant of a few thousand pounds would materially aid the funds in the infancy of the plan, and convince the lower class, of the attention of the legislature to their comforts.

"The reduction of the poor-rates would prove one of the beneficial effects to be secured by an institution of this kind; and the honest independence of an Englishman would be flattered and confirmed."

TITHES.—On this topic, likewise, Mr. Duncumb has bestowed some attention, and on this, too, has offered his plan.

The following passage acquaints us with the *existing state* of tithes, in Herefordshire.—P. 36. "Most of the lands in Herefordshire are subject to the payment of tithes, and they are collected in kind in very few instances. The average composition in lieu of them varies from three shillings and sixpence, to four shillings for every pound of money paid in rent.

"This is certainly less heavy than the compositions for tithes in many other places, although they have been much increased since the enormous price of grain in the years 1800 and 1801. They are still however paid with reluctance, and invariably considered by the occupiers and proprietors of land, to be serious obstacles to agricultural improvements.

"Coppices are usually retained by the owner, and previous to the sale of their fallage by auction (which is generally practised), an agreement is made on the subject of tithe,

tithe, viz. one tenth of the sum they produce; and subsequent disputes are thus prevented "

The writer, next, produces a *plan* for a *general commutation* of tithes.—P. 37. " Of the various modes proposed to effect the desirable object of a general commutation of tithes, that of a corn-rent seems to have met with less objections than most others which have yet been proposed; still however nothing has been seriously attempted, and the subject remains open to further discussion.

" It has not perhaps occurred to every one, that tithes in their present form, have a direct and powerful tendency towards increasing the prices of wheat and every other grain, by creating obstacles to its culture, and thus diminishing the quantity which would otherwise be grown. But the single fact, that, an acre of land under the culture of wheat, is liable to a deduction on account of tithe, in nearly a ten-fold proportion to an acre of land, grazed by cattle or sheep, is surely sufficient evidence that tithes must operate unfavorably to the culture of grain, and consequently to its abundance and cheapness. How desirable then is such a commutation as would render this payment equally heavy on every acre of land according to its value, whether it be applied to the culture of grain, or to the production of animal food!

" Under this impression, it is now proposed, that in lieu of tithe, a tax be imposed (on the principle of an equal land-tax) on every estate, according to its value, for the support of the clergy. The wisdom of parliament would easily determine, how many shillings in every pound of rent would be equal to the revenues to which the clergy have a claim, and the measure would be much facilitated by the investigations occasioned by the income or property act now in force. The tenant might be made liable in the first instance to the payment of the duty proposed as a substitute for tithe, but in case of his defalcation, the landlord might be made ultimately responsible."

Mr. Duncumb then proceeds, with his assisting friend, " Mr. Andrew Knight," to point out the advantages of such a plan of commutation, and the evils of the present practice, of levying tithes; thus closing his strictures:— P. 39. " The plan now proposed for a commutation would, it is presumed, counteract or prevent these serious evils; encouragement would be given to an extended culture of grain; and a new motive to industry and exertion would be found in the consideration, that the most indolent farmer

must

must contribute an equal sum with the most active and successful cultivator.

"The effects of tithes in a religious view are obvious and important. The terms which too generally prevail between the clergyman and his parishioners, prevent habits of intercourse, expose him to attacks. and destroy the purpose of his labours. And to this source, may perhaps be ascribed in some degree the rapid increase of sectaries, and the comparatively greater influence possessed by their preachers, than by the ministers of the church of England."

The above plan is beautifully *simple*, and so *obvious* that it must have struck many a one. But its defects being almost equally evident, any man, of ordinary penetration, must perceive them.

One of the principal objections to tithes, taken in kind, or by the valuation of crops, is their operating as a tax on, and of course a check to, IMPROVEMENTS. But how will the plan proposed prevent this evil tendency?—and, at the same time, give the required security to the rector?

At the outset, it is true,—"the most indolent farmer must contribute an equal sum with the most active and successful cultivator."—But supposing the value of money to continue to lessen, with the same rapidity that it has lately done, the rector would soon find himself left in the rear. If, on the contrary, its value should as rapidly be increased, the cultivator would experience a similar hardship; owing to a nominal fall in the prices of his produce.—Hence, the plan in its nature pre-supposes, (tho nothing of the kind is expressed!) that the value of the lands should of course be ascertained, from time to time; and, of course, *together with the improvements* that may have been made in them, since the original estimate.—And, hence, we may safely advance that to *tithe* the *rent*, would be to proceed on a wrong principle.

Tithe is issuable out of *produce*, and out of that, only, can it be properly drawn. Corn can best be taken as a medium, for the existing prices of predial productions; and has long appeared to me to be the best, if not the only safe and equitable basis on which a commutation of tithes can be founded. I am, nevertheless, ready to listen to the opinions and plans of others.

Now, when the prices of corn are sufficiently ascertained, and regularly registered, under the authority of Government, there can be little doubt, that whenever tithe owners may

may prefer the peace and social order of parishes, and the prosperity of the present religion of the realm, as by law established,—to the unchristianlike gratification of possessing the power of oppression,—an equitable and happy SUBSTITUTION, for TITHES may be effected, through the medium of the CORN RETURNS,—*duly qualified.*

INLAND NAVIGATION.—*Navigable Rivers.*—P. 11.—"The Wye is the most beneficial on the immediate purposes of agriculture; in the conveyance of wheat and flour to Bristol, of coal for burning lime-tone, and also in the conveyance of lime from the kiln to distant parts of the county."

P. 13. "Various articles connected with husbandry are conveyed to, and from Hereford on the Wye, in barges containing from eighteen to thirty tons; but either a large or small supply of water is equally fatal to the navigation.

"The latter is experienced during the greater part of a dry summer, when shoals barely covered with the stream occur very frequently; in winter, heavy rains, or snow dissolving on its banks within this county, have the effect of gradually adding a few inches to the depth; but, when these rush in torrents into its channel from the mountains of Brecknock and Radnorshires, they occasion an almost instantaneous overflow, and give it a force, which defies all the ordinary means of resistance or controul.* By this impetuosity, large quantities of land are frequently removed from their situations, on the one side or the other, and new channels have thus been formed in various places."

P. 14. "Some attempts have been made to effect a safe and regular navigation on the Wye; with this view, an Act of Parliament passed 14th Charles II.; but no further steps were then taken. A similar Act passed 7th and 8th William III. and heavy assessments were levied on the county, with little or no effect. At the present time the subject is again under agitation, and an engineer is engaged to make a report on the practicability of scooping out channels through the principal shoals which obstruct the navigation at low water; of confining the current in those places within narrow limits; and for making a towing path for horses instead of men."

P. 18. "A similar inconvenience, with respect to navigation,

*The greatest flood experienced of late was occasioned by a fall of rain and the melting of snow on the 5th of February, 1795, when the river rose fifteen feet in twenty-four hours, and did enormous damage through the county, destroying bridges, drowning cattle and sheep, and sweeping off valuable plank and timber from the wharfs.

gation, is experienced when the Lug is swelled by partial rains, which have not equally affected the Wye; a rapidity and force are then given to the Lug in its discharge into the Wye, which it will probably be ever difficult to restrain or correct. An Act of Parliament passed in 1663, and a second about thirty years after, for the purpose of rendering the Lug navigable, but unforeseen difficulties arose, and nothing was effected. A private subscription was applied in the year 1714, with more success for a time, and a few barges navigated as far as Leominster; but either from want of skill in the architect, or from the obstacles before stated, a high flood, which followed soon afterwards, so materially injured the locks and all that had been done, that no attempts to repair or renew the works have been subsequently made."

Canals.—P. 143. "Inland navigation is beneficial to a county; first, in proportion to the heavy goods which it has to export, and next, in proportion to the quantity it has to receive. Where the soil is deep, the roads difficult to be formed, and expensive in repairs, (as experienced here,) this mode of carriage must be doubly advantageous. Herefordshire depends wholly on coal from other counties, and produces within itself large supplies of timber for navy and other purposes; an almost peculiar article of export in its provincial liquor, and a considerable excess of grain beyond its own consumption."—Again—"The precariousness of conveyance by the Wye has already been noticed, and no other river in its present state is even of partial utility in this way, excepting the occasional carriage of pigs of iron in small boats to a forge on the Lug, called Tidnor, which is about two miles distant from the junction of the Lug and Wye, and of coals to Lugwardine, about one mile further. An act of parliament was therefore obtained in the year 1791, for making a navigable canal from the city of Hereford, and by the town of Ledbury, to the Severn at Gloucester, with a lateral cut to the collieries at Newent."

P. 144. "An act for another canal to extend to Kington, from Leominster and Stourport, was obtained soon after the former. Lime and coal from Shropshire were stated to be the principal objects of importation, and the usual produce of the county, those for export.

"The expense from Kington to Leominster was estimated by an engineer at 37,000*l.* between Leominster and Stourport at 83,000*l.* A part of the latter extent was completed in the year 1796, and has effected some reduction in the

the price of coal, without reaching so far as Stourport. A miscalculation of expenses, similar to that of the other canal, has stopped, for the present at least, all further progress; and the two instances afford a useful lesson of caution to those who may in future engage in speculation of this nature."

Bridges.—Speaking of the impetuosity of the Wye, Mr. Duncumb favors us with the following interesting particulars respecting its Bridges.—P. 13. "To this impetuosity is also to be ascribed, the want of a number of bridges, adequate to a safe and easy communication between different parts of the county, and so highly essential in agricultural concerns. The original cost of building, and the heavy expense of repairs, have so much discouraged undertakings of this kind, that in the whole extent of the Wye through Herefordshire, there was only one bridge, that of Hereford, until the year 1597.

"An Act of Parliament, which stated in the preamble, the inconveniences of the ferry, and the number of lives lost in the passage, was then obtained for erecting a second, at Wilton near Ross. Since that date two more have been added, in order to facilitate the intercourse with Wales. One of these was built at Bredwardine, under an Act passed in 1762, and the other at Whitney, under an Act passed in 1780. That of Bredwardine, which is composed of brick, after sustaining great damage by the flood of 1795, has continued to resist the violence of the current; but that at Whitney has already been twice destroyed, and was again renewed on stone piers, A. D. 1802."

ROADS.—On this subject, we find not a word to our purpose. Mr. D. says—"the roads of Herefordshire were *once* proverbially bad." And if Mr. Clark is to be believed, they were not at the time he wrote, much better. See p. 270.

MARKETS.—P. 63. "A very considerable surplus of wheat is produced in the county, beyond the internal consumption, and admits of a large exportation every year to Bristol and other places, notwithstanding the quantity has been much diminished by the conversion of some of the best arable lands to other purposes."

P. 159. "The following are the peculiar weights and measures now in use in this county.

A pound of fresh butter,	Eighteen ounces.
A stone - - - - - -	Twelve pounds.
A customary acre, -	Two thirds of a statute acre.
A hop acre, - - -	That space of ground, which contains 1000 plants; viz. about half a statute acre.

A lugg, - - - - - -	Forty-nine square yards of coppice wood.
A wood acre, - - -	Three eighths larger than a statute, i. e. as 8 are to 5.
A day's math, - - -	About a statute acre of meadow or grass land, being the quantity usually mown by one man in one day.
A perch of fencing, -	Seven yards.
A perch of walling, -	Sixteen feet and an half.
A perch of land, - -	Five yards and an half (as statute).
A bushel of grain -	Ten gallons.
A bushel of malt, -	Eight gallons and an half."

In an "Appendix," the Reporter expatiates on the stale topic—"*The sale of corn by sample.*" The point has been, some time settled It would be folly in the extreme to prohibit the practice.

He likewise appropriates a section to "Observations on *Dealers* in *Corn* and *Cattle.*" But still we have—"much ado about nothing." While there is no law against *producers* taking their products to distant markets, no serious complaint can lie against *dealers.* If they can convey surplus produce to a distant market, cheaper than the producers,—surely, *consumers* are benefited by them; and ought to be thankful.—In regard to dealers in *livestock*, it is ridiculous to speak gravely on the subject And, in respect to *grain*, unless in times of extreme scarcity, there is little room for argument.

Another section of the Appendix relates to the extortion and tricks of *millers.* But the ancient custom of "the peasantry" carrying their bread corn to the mill, would seem to be on the decline, in Herefordshire.

SOCIETIES.—Mr. Clark's suggestion appears to have been attended to. See p. 273.

P. 157. "An Agricultural Society was established in Herefordshire in the year 1797, and it comprises most of the principal proprietors and many of the principal occupiers of land, throughout the county: the number of members at present exceeds one hundred and twenty."

The *Secretary* proceeds, unassumingly, to speak of the views of the Society. But I find not a line to instruct the Public; nor even the Managers of other Societies of a similar nature.

SUBJECT THE THIRD.

RURAL ECONOMY.

DIVISION THE FIRST.

TENANTED ESTATES,

Their IMPROVEMENT and MANAGEMENT.

ESTATES.—*Proprietors.*—P. 22. "The greatest estates in Herefordshire belong to, the Governors of Guy's Hospital in London, the Duke of Norfolk, the Earl of Oxford, the Earl of Essex, Sir George Cornwall, Bart., R. P. Knight, Esq., S. Davies, Esq., &c. &c."—"The extensive property now held by the Governors of Guy's Hospital formerly belonged to the Brydges family. The late Duke of Chandos had his residence at Aconbury, four miles south from Hereford; he was an active promoter of every measure, which had for its object the prosperity of the county, or the city of Hereford. His hospitality was liberal and diffusive; and a considerable part of his wealth was expended on the spot which furnished it; but disappointed in his expectations of support in a political contest, he became disgusted with his situation, and disposed of his residence and all his estates in the county, to the present possessors.

"Thus they remain under the mortifying change, that the rents are annually remitted to the metropolis, and the mansions destroyed, or converted to purposes far humbler and less generally useful, than those for which they were designed.

"The large estates of the Duke of Norfolk were acquired by marriage with the heiress of the Scudamores of Hom Lacy; and much of the land of Somerset Davies, Esq. was purchased from the Crofts of Croft Castle."

Tenures.—On this topic, we find some interesting particulars, in the Report under review. I insert them, here, on the authority of the Reporter,—as a man of *reading.*

P. 23.

P. 23. "A considerable part of the hundred of Wormelow is called *Irchenfield*, and is situated near Ross. Much of ancient history attaches to this district, which seems to have been one of the petty states into which Wales was formerly divided."

P. 24. "Amongst other peculiarities, the tenure of gavel-kind has prevailed in this district, from the remotest periods to the present time. The leading feature or principle of this tenure is well known, viz.

"That in cases of persons dying intestate, the law of primogeniture has no effect, and lands descend not to the eldest, youngest, or any one son only, but in equal divisions to all the sons together. But the privilege and the security of disposing of property by will are now so fully understood and experienced, that the provisions of this ancient and peculiar tenure are rarely resorted to.

"In the manor of Hampton Bishop, which belongs to the see of Hereford, another tenure prevails, which occurs nearly as seldom as that above mentioned; it is that of *Borough English*, by which the youngest son succeeds to the burgage, tenement, &c. on the death of his father, to the exclusion of his eldest and other brothers. Littleton supposes this tenure to have been founded on the principle, that the age of the youngest more particularly required the assistance of the parent. Other authors have given a less grave reason for this custom; they suppose that the lord of the fee had anciently a right to violate the seventh commandment with his tenant's bride on the wedding night, and that, therefore, the tenement descended to the youngest son as the more certain offspring of the tenant. The custom certainly prevailed in Scotland, and was abolished by Malcolm III. Amongst the Tartars it was general, and perhaps amongst many other nations at that early period, when they existed in a pastoral state; for in that situation of life, the elder sons successively left their parents, (probably with some assistance from them,) as soon as they were able to manage for themselves, and consequently the youngest son, who remained at home, had the best claim, and also the greatest occasion for a provision for himself.

"It will be imagined that this tenure, like gavel-kind, is not often acted on, but one instance at least has occurred here within a very short period from the present time.

"Copyhold property is not so common in this as in many other districts, and in consequence, courts are less regularly held, and the privileges of the lords, being in various instances inconsiderable in value, are less tenaciously preserved.

served. The continual expenses attending property of this description, the vexatious litigations to which it gives rise, and the distress to which families are frequently reduced by its operations, render it an object much to be wished, that some general criterion might be established by law, so that the landlord might purchase the interest of the tenant, or the tenant obtain that of the lord, by a fair and known compensation.

"Leasehold estates" (Q. Lifeleasehold?) "are more common, and are liable to many of the objections against copyhold property.—They seem to be relics of the feudal system, which is no inconsiderable argument in favour of their abolition.

"The principal lessors are, the Bishop, the Dean, the Chapter, the Prebendaries and other members of the Cathedral Church, the Corporation of Hereford and other towns, the College of Vicar's Choral, &c. Perhaps in round numbers, it may not be far from accurate to state, that two-thirds of the whole county is freehold, and the remaining third under the other tenures, which have been particularized above."

IMPROVEMENT of Estates.—On this subject we cannot reasonably expect much useful information, from an unpractised Reporter.

On the Improvement of *Homesteads*—something will be found, under that head, ensuing.

Draining.—The Reporter appears to be entirely unacquainted with this valuable art. And his assistant, is still, pretty evidently, in his noviciate, with regard to it

Sodburning.—The following instance of successful practice is worth preserving. P. 101. "Many parts of Herefordshire are doubtless susceptible of great improvements from this measure: but it has hitherto been confined to a few persons only. A general knowledge of the following fact will perhaps induce others to afford it a fair trial.

"About twelve years ago, an extensive tract of hilly ground, over-run with gorse and fern, was purchased by James Phillipps, Esq. with other lands in the parish of Dewchurch.

"The value of such grounds is not always known, but fortunately in this instance it is ascertained with the greatest precision; it being valued to him in the purchase as worth three shillings per acre of annual rent. Soon afterwards Mr. Phillipps engaged proper workmen from Gloucestershire, who cut the gorse in bundles at two shillings per hundred: they then pared and burnt the surface, and spread the

the surface, and spread the ashes at twenty-five shillings per acre. It was then ploughed for wheat, and the produce was no less than twenty-six bushels per acre.

"In the spring it was properly prepared for turnips, and brought a very good crop. It was next sown with barley and seeds, and has from that time remained an excellent pasture, and any of the neighbours would gladly rent it at sixteen or even eighteen shillings per acre."

Mr. K. however,—who would seem to possess an inordinate share of the spirit of opposition; and who is of course prompt to speak on every controvertible subject,—enters upon that of "Paring and Burning." But, on this, as on other occasions, nothing either new or excellent is to be found, in his remarks; which are only—"about it—and about it."—Finding himself superior, in some things, to the generality of occupiers, in the district in which he resides, he ventures (like many other men under similar circumstances) to talk on every topic, whether prepared or not; and does not appear to have been aware, that, by suffering his immature strictures to be sent to the press, he was in effect trusting himself out of Herefordshire;—and speaking among men who are more fully informed on rural subjects.

It must, by this time, be well understood (seeing how much has recently been published concerning it) that *burning* the sward acts as a *stimulant*, and is principally applicable to particular cases. In which cases, if the land be presently returned again to a state of herbage, the improvement is often very great. On the contrary, when foolishly relying on that stimulus, the improvident, or dishonest, occupier continues to take, and carry off, exhausting crop after crop, the effect will ever be *similar* to that mentioned by Mr. K. (in p. 102). The facts there adduced, however, are too few, and too loosely stated, and the "opinion" drawn from them, too vague, for insertion, here. I hope Mr. K. will follow up his conception, in order to make out, in a circumstantial and intelligible manner, that the success of paring and burning depends, in some sort at least, on the degree of *elevation* of the lands on which the operation is performed;—and this notwithstanding the extraordinary instance of improvement by it (above noticed) on "an extensive tract of hilly ground."—But a truce to trifling.

EXECUTIVE MANAGEMENT of Landed Estates.—*Leases.*—P. 41. "Leases of old dates were generally binding for twenty-one years; but from the extraordinary advance in the

the prices of grain, which has been so often alluded to, landed proprietors now grant leases more frequently in three terms of seven years each, determinable at either of those periods by landlord or tenant.

"The advantages of this mode, preponderate in favor of the landlord, whilst the uncertainty of the time checks the improvements of the tenant, and induces him to limit the capital which he employs. In proportion as these effects are produced, the public are sufferers."

Covenants.—P. 41. "The provisions in the clauses of Herefordshire leases have few peculiarities. Those granted by R. C Hopton, Esq. of Canon-Frome, after binding the tenant to keep the premises in repair, further stipulate, that the landlord, with proper persons, shall have power once in every year, to survey the state of the buildings, and make a report to the tenant of what appears necessary to be done on the premises, under that particular clause. This regulation has been attended with the best effects, and it is presumed, is worthy of general adoption."

He must be an improvident proprietor, indeed, who does not covenant for such a power.

P. 30. "The houses and buildings of all kinds are usually put into good repair by the proprietor, at the commencement of a lease, and the tenant engages to preserve them in good condition afterwards; having sometimes the advantage of unconverted timber from the estate when necessary."

P. 36. "In particular situations, the tenant further devotes the use of his waggon for a few days in the year to the service of his landlord; and this is usually applied to the conveyance of coal for the consumption of the latter."

Rents.—P. 36. "The best arable lands are rented on an average at twenty shillings per acre; the best meadow at forty shillings. In the vicinity of towns, and in other situations particularly eligible, meadows are let at four pounds an acre, or even more; and the produce of that meadow frequently exceed two tons of hay in good seasons. The poorer arable may be rented at ten shillings or less; and meadows of inferior quality and in distant situations, at eighteen or twenty shillings."

P. 63. "The heaviest crops of wheat, generally speaking, are produced in the vicinity of Hereford, and thence through the clays towards Ledbury. Lands thus situated are now rented from eighteen to twenty shillings the statute

tute acre; but abstracted from the pasture and meadow, the average price of all the arable land in the county, is probably not more than ten shillings."

Receiving Rents.—P. 36. "When a person becomes tenant of an estate at Candlemas, he is required to discharge half a year's rent at the Candlemas following, and to make a similar payment at the expiration of every six months afterwards."

DIVISION THE SECOND.

WOODLANDS.

WOODS.—P. 94. "Almost every part of Herefordshire abounds in woods, and old plantations of timber, or rather perhaps with fine trees of oak and elm, for which the proprietors are more indebted to nature, than to art. At a distant period a large proportion of the province must have been altogether woodland and coppice: the clearing naturally began in the most fertile spots, particularly near streams and rivers. Reference is made to the 'assart' or cleared lands near Aconbury, in grants to a religious house there, in the fourteenth century. But even at present, an eminence one mile east from the church and village of Mordiford, affords at once striking specimens of Herefordshire in its original state, and in that to which it has been brought by cultivation and refinement. Looking from this point towards the east, an immense expanse of woodland is seen, as far as the eye can reach, with a white cottage and a cultivated acre occasionally intervening. Deep and winding roads intersect the whole with a narrow track, and a bleak and barren common which appears 'far from the busy haunts of man,' completes the cheerless scene."

GROVE and HEDGE TIMBER.—To the westward, however, trees only serve to ornament the face of the country. On the demesne lands of men of fortune, and in various parts of the county, we are told, much valuable timber is found.

COPPICES.—P. 96. "Some of the most extensive coppices are situated in the parishes of Fownhope, Woolhope, and Little Birch; and in the vicinity of Ledbury. They consist principally of ash, oak, and willow, are generally cut

cut down once in thirteen years, and bring at a public sale from 18*l.* to 35*l.* per wood-acre, the size of which bears a proportion to the statute acre as eight to five. In falling a coppice, a certain number of store trees are left as standards on every acre: and these would furnish an adequate supply of timber from the spot, but they are too often cut down at the second fallage, and replaced perpetually after, with younger stores. The ash is converted into hoops, for which the county itself has of course a large demand; the oak and willow furnish poles for hops, and materials for laths; whilst what are termed *black poles*, which are those of larger size, and confined to oak, are applied in rafters and other purposes in building."

PLANTATIONS.—In a county so well stocked with fortuitous timber and coppice woods, it is no wonder that the *propagation* of woodlands should be neglected, or avoided.

For a novel suggestion on *Planting Hedges*, see *Farm Fences*, below.

DIVISION THE THIRD.

AGRICULTURE.

FARMS.—In the chapter, "Estates," we meet with some account of the *sizes* of Farms.—P. 22. "These estates" (the larger ones enumerated aforegoing) "are divided into farms comprising on an average, from two hundred to four hundred acres each."

In the legitimate section, "Size of Farms," the Reporter, disdaining the ground on which he stood,—the district about which he was professing to write,—launched, adventurously, into the sea of speculation, concerning the sizes of farms *politically* considered! And, after flounsing some time, reached a firm landing place (erected by mine own hand*) and spake as follows:—P. 35. "On the whole, it is submitted to the consideration of land-owners, whether they will not most essentially contribute to that public good and prosperity, (of which their own constitutes an individual part,) when they arrange their property

* See TREATISE on LANDED PROPERTY, p. 144.

perty in divisions of various extent, from five to five hundred acres, and thus afford to every class, the means of improving their condition by habits of industry, and of promoting the general welfare by individual exertion."

Fences.—After being informed that—"New enclosures are ditched, with posts and rails on the bank; but quickset or hawthorn plants should invariably be used on these occasions; and the agricultural society of the province has endeavoured to excite more attention to this excellent mode of fencing, by offering premiums for 'the greatest quantity of hawthorn quick properly planted for fencing an estate, or fairly sold by a nurseryman for that purpose'" (p. 49); and learning how fences may be raised, with such plants kept clean for two or three years, (how backward must Herefordshire be in this art, to require a premium to raise a hedge in the most ordinary manner!) —we are led to the following valuable suggestion.

P. 50. "But perhaps it would be a material improvement in this very useful practice, if the plants were permitted to remain in the nursery in rows distant one yard from each other, until they become of a size which would make an immediate fence, and require no protection.—The enormous expense of posts and rails would thus be saved."

This suggestion, however, rises inaptly out of the subject of "New Inclosures." For how, under the proposed management, could the parcels of newly appropriated lands be said to be *inclosed*, during the years which the plants would require, to raise them to sufficient maturity, for the intended purpose? The lands must of course continue to lie *open*, during that period.

Nevertheless, the plan of raising hedge plants, in a nursery, to a stature fit, or nearly fit, to form a fence, without guarding, is not altogether vague. On large estates, a nursery of that description would frequently be found highly useful: not only in parting large fields, but in filling up gaps, and unnecessary gateways.

Three feet intervals, however, would not be wide enough, for the purpose. A quarter of a statute rod would be found to be a more eligible width:—the middles of the intervals being dug deep, and a spade-width wide, from time to time, to cut off the straying roots (thus preventing those of adjacent rows from interweaving with each other) and keep the feeding fibers near the stems. By this treatment the plants would differ widely from those raised in hedges; which seldom thrive well when transplanted; by reason of the smaller roots and feeding fibrils

fibrils being cut off, and left in the ground, while the stems and larger naked roots, only, are removed.

Homesteads.—P. 29. "The old farm-houses of Herefordshire, as well as of other counties, are inconvenient, and the offices ill adapted to the purposes for which they were designed. Water and shelter appear to have been principally consulted in selecting a spot for building; these are confessedly objects of no trifling importance, but there are other objects also, which equally require and deserve attention. In the new ones (of which there are many), the defects of the old are generally supplied, to the great advantage and comfort of the farmer. The Governors of Guy's Hospital are in this, and I believe in every respect, particularly attentive to the interest and convenience of the tenants. Under the management of their present steward, James Woodhouse, Esq. several of the old houses have been taken down, and others substituted on better sites, and on the most approved plans. When practicable, a gentle declivity towards the south, which implies some eminence, is generally preferred: the building is adapted to the size of the farm to be occupied with it; the walls are constructed with stone, and the covering is of slate."

Prefixed to this Report is a "ground plot of Arrendall farm house, yard, and buildings, at Lide in the county of Hereford;"—belonging to the Governors of Guy's Hospital; but I perceive nothing in it of superior excellence. The long-square form is much inferior to that of an elongated octagon.—See TREATISE ON LANDED PROPERTY.

Cottages.—P. 30. "The cottages in Herefordshire are generally of very humble and inferior construction: many are built on waste ground by their proprietor, whose means are far from adequate to the attainment of comfort and convenience."

The following information may serve as a hint, in situations that will admit of the practice.—P. 31. "Of late years a valuable addition has been made to the minor objects of agriculture, by the introduction of *strawberries* in cottagers' gardens. On light soils, when proper care is taken to keep the roots free from weeds, and the plants well watered at the season of blossoming, very considerable profits are derived from this practice. Parts of the waste lands on Aconbury and Shucknell Hills, have been particularly applied to those purposes, with great success and little trouble. The red Carolina, or Bath scarlet, are generally preferred; and their fruit sold readily in in July at ten-pence per full quart in the Hereford market."

OCCUPIERS.—P. 35. "The old-fashioned farmer of Herefordshire receives any new experiment in agriculture with great hesitation, if not reluctance. When its utility is confirmed by repeated trials, he slowly and gradually falls into the practice; but he wisely leaves the experiment and the risque to those who recommend or suggest it; and happily the county at this moment is well provided with agriculturists, who possess the means and the spirit, to undertake the patriotic task."

PLAN of MANAGEMENT of Farms.—The succeeding account of the rural management of Herefordshire exhibits a forbidding view of the state of its agriculture; and shows how much the "means and the spirit" of improvement are there wanted.

P. 51. "Wheat is the grand dependence of the farmer, who is situated on the stiff clays, with which this county abounds; but it is conceived, that the following course, which formed the old routine of crops on that description of land, is liable, with this management, to serious objection. A good fallow on a clover-ley, well worked, limed, and manured, produces on an average about twenty bushels of wheat per statute acre. In the following spring it is sown with peas, sometimes beans, after one ploughing, and without measure; the produce is from twelve to fourteen bushels per acre. After two ploughings and a partial dressing, or much more frequently with no dressing whatever, it is again sown with wheat in October; and if this *brush* crop, as it is termed, produces somewhat more than half the quantity yielded by the fallow, the grower is satisfied. In the following spring it is sown with barley and clover seeds after two ploughings, but still without manure, and as may be expected from the exhausted state of the land, it generally affords a very inconsiderable crop.

"Sheep are turned on the young clover as soon as the barley is removed. Sometimes oats or turnips precede the barley on a small part of the land, and a few winter vetches are occasionally introduced, but still without manure, or any preparation, than one or two ploughings.

"After mowing one crop of clover, it is fed with cattle in the following spring, and afterwards a part remains for seed. The fallowing then recommences, and nearly the same system is repeated. In this manner almost one-third

third of the arable land is constantly under the culture of wheat, and that third, during its preparation for the seed, is termed the *odd mark*."

P. 52. "It will not be supposed, that the routine above described is still invariably adhered to; it is given merely as the old-fashioned course, from which many farmers are deviating daily with success. The county at present may boast of many, who turn their attention to agricultural pursuits in such a way, that no danger can be apprehended of the want of progress in agricultural improvements, or of a want of trial in every reasonable experiment."

In the section, "Fallowing," much is said in praise of aration; and a statement presumptuously made (in the debtor and creditor manner) between land in *tillage*, and that under *pasturage* (p. 60):—a statement which sufficiently shows the maker of it to be a bold man, and a man of figures. But figures in the hands of inexperience are too often the instruments of misrepresentation.

WORKPEOPLE.—P. 136. "The price of labour throughout the county, except during the period of harvest, averages six shillings per week in winter, and seven shillings in summer, with liquor and two dinners. These prices are somewhat higher than those paid forty years ago; but in the opinion of the writer of this survey, the increase is not proportioned to the increase in provisions and every article of life since that date.

"Wheat was then sold in Hereford market at three shillings per bushel on an average. The labourer, therefore, who between Monday morning and Saturday night could earn four shillings and six-pence, that is nine pence per day, earned the value of one bushel and an half of wheat in our provincial measure of ten gallons: but at the present period, the labourer, who carries home even seven shillings and six-pence per week, carries the average value of three pecks of wheat only: for no one who considers the advanced rents, taxes, and other circumstances of a farm in 1805, will, I think, contend, that wheat can be produced by a tenant, with a fair and reasonable profit, at a less rate than ten shillings the Herefordshire bushel, or one shilling the gallon."

On these premises Mr. D. speculates; and brings forward his plan of reform; which is to fix, by law, "a certain proportion between the price of labor, and the average price of wheat" (p. 137); and to let the prices of labor increase and decrease, with the rise and fall of grain.

This

This plan (even were it practicable) is founded on false principles; as it would tend to enable laborers to consume as much corn, in a time of scarcity, as in that of plenty:—a political error which has been detected;—in the NORTHERN DEPARTMENT, p. 377. But seeing the great disparity in the prices of labor, in different districts and situations, and the great difference in the value of the work of individual laborers, in each,—I do not perceive how the law could well interfere, in regulating their wages, by a common standard*.

Mr. D. however, returns to the charge (in p. 155). But I find not a word to convince me that a *general* law, of the nature proposed, would be proper. His concluding suggestion, nevertheless, is entitled to attention. It is fraught with justice and humanity, and is not only practicable, but political:—I mean, if an increase of population be so, without an increase of appropriated territory.

P. 156. "These would be removed by a general law, which, under the present rates of labour, might provide, that when wheat exceeded one shilling per gallon, the labourer should receive from the overseer a certain stipulated aid for every child † beyond the number of three; and it would be more congenial to the feelings of the writer of this, if the labourer might become entitled to this relief as his right, rather than be obliged to sue for it as a boon."

If the laboring class, at all times, had a similar *right*, a rapid increase of legitimate population, could scarcely fail to be the consequence.

P. 65. "The price of labour is seven shillings weekly, in summer, with liquor and two dinners; in winter, six shillings, with similar privileges."

P. 139. "The following are the average prices of wages now given to servants in the house by a Herefordshire farmer:

Waggoner

* It has long been a popular idea that "the day wage" of a workman in husbandry ought to be "a peck of corn:"—that is to say—a peck of wheat. A few years ago, a peck of wheat sold for five shillings, and is at present worth from three to four shillings. But wheat is, nowadays, only one article of a laborer's food; and a *temporary rise*, in that, does not advance the prices of other articles, in proportion. Hence, the plan above suggested may be deemed, altogether, inequitable and unjust.

† *Unable to earn its bread* ought, here, to have been inserted.

Waggoner - - -	10 to 12 guineas per annum.
Bailiff or cattleman	8 to 10 ditto.
Dairy maid - - -	6 to 7 ditto.
Under maid - -	2 to 3 ditto."

P. 138. "The hours of labour in winter are from light to dark; in summer, from six in the morning to the same hour in the afternoon.

"In harvest, when the wages are nearly doubled to those engaged for that period only, the time is regulated by the emergency of business. In this season they often work during fifteen hours."

For alien *harvest* people, see the head *Wheat*, ensuing.

WORKING ANIMALS.—P. 116. "The rearing of oxen for the purposes of agriculture prevails universally: nearly half the ploughing is performed by them, and they take an equal share in the labours of the harvest.

"They are shoed with iron in situations which frequently require their exertions on hard roads; but it has already been noticed, that grazing is not generally pursued except for provincial consumption."

P. 128. "The following return was made by an intelligent and extensive farmer, on the subject of comparing the different values of the horse and the ox in the common purposes of agriculture. 'Whether oxen or horses ought to be preferred by the husbandman to till his glebe, and perform the neces ary labours on his estate, is of greater importance in my opinion than people in general are disposed to admit.

"I believe most persons will allow, that population has increased, and that the necessaries of life have been advanced to very exorbitant rates: the public benefit, therefore, requires, that every method should be taken to encourage the use of those animals in agriculture, which consume the least valuable food, and which afterwards supply the markets, in preference to those which have not such qualities. But as the public good unfortunately is not always so strong a stimulus as private interest, it appears advisable to form an estimate of the comparative profits of the horse and the ox, in order that they, who are not too much prejudiced in favour of the former, may be induced from a prospect of gain to adopt the use of the latter, as much as their situations will admit. I am fully aware, that horses are a most valuable and useful race of animals, and that their services in agriculture are indispensable; but I am of opinion, that on dry and sound land their number may

may, and ought to be, reduced, in the proportion of one half, or even more.

"I used oxen several years, but thinking that they could not be managed without a man and a boy, I adopted horses to save the expense of a second attendant, placing three to a plough, and engaging one person only to turn it, and drive. Experience soon convinced me, that four oxen in harness, with one man, or able boy, could execute as much work as three horses with the same attendance; but I prefer four oxen in the yoke, thinking that they lie more immediately under the arm and eye of the driver, and that they make a more steady purchase.'"

This "intelligent and extensive farmer" closes his strictures with a debtor-and-creditor statement of the comparative advantages of oxen and horses;—concluding with the subjoined inference;—which I insert, here, rather as a matter of *opinion*, than of *fact*.

P. 131. "Thus the loss of 32*l.* 1*s.* 6*d.* on horses, and the gain of 12*l.* on four oxen, make a balance of 44*l.* in favour of the latter."

Oxen, we are told, p. 132, "are generally worked under the yoke." But "several farmers, influenced by the recommendation of the Acricultural Society, have adopted harness." And the *Secretary* informs us that "the harness cannot be too light and simple, and in many instances, *cords* have been found no mean substitutes as *traces*, instead of the more expensive material of *leather*." (!)

IMPLEMENTS.—P. 45. "The implements of husbandry used in this county have few peculiarities. Waggons, intended for frequent use on the turnpike roads, have usually wheels of six inches in breadth, carry about three tons and an half in weight, and are drawn by six horses abreast.

"One waggon of this description is usually attached to every considerable farm; the others are on narrow wheels, as better adapted to husbandry, roads, and common purposes; these are drawn by four horses, and convey a load weighing two tons and an half."

MANURE.—P. 103. "Of the several kinds of manure laid on lands in this county, that procured from the fold or *farm-yard* is used in the most considerable quantity.

"*Lime* is next in request, the beneficial effects of which are fully felt and acknowledged, but it is conceived, that its chemical properties and modes of action are not yet thoroughly understood.

"A skilful and experienced farmer of Herefordshire made

made the following observations in reply to queries submitted to him on this occasion."

Those observations are too interesting to be lost. Some of them agree with what I gathered, in Norfolk, on this subject:—Others are quite new.—P. 103. "In whatever way lime is applied, the succeeding crop or crops receive more benefit from a hot, than a cold summer.—Wheats, on fallows limed during the spring or summer previous to their sowing, seldom appear better than on unlimed lands under similar husbandry, until the weather becomes hot in May or June.

"Grain of all sorts on limed lands is later in getting ripe, than on those where no lime has been used.—When large quantities are applied, this effect is particularly discernible. Hence I infer, that lime has a tendency to make the land cool, perhaps by exciting or attracting more moisture; and I never recollect to have seen a crop suffer from a dry hot summer, when the land had been previously well limed. On stiff soils I prefer putting the lime on the fallows when it is hot, and the land somewhat wet, ploughing or harrowing it in as soon as possible.

"On light soils, I think it is used with the greatest advantage on young grass in the spring, where it soon reaches the roots of the plants; but, when placed on fallow land of this description, it appears to sink too deeply, to be beneficial to the crop on the surface. Lime should be exposed as little as possible to the sun,(?) particularly when spread thinly over the ground for manure; it seems to force the different particles of the earth into action, and I have no doubt, but that constant liming must be ever injurious to land under the plough, particularly if applied in large quantities.

"Lime ought to be put on the land some days at least before the sowing takes place, otherwise in wheat crops, it will cause the ground to ferment and lie too closely round the seed during the winter; or in barley crops, it will prevent the growing of many of the grains, if hot weather immediately succeed the sowing."

To those extraordinary strictures succeed a string of suggestions, by Mr. Knight;—well calculated to soften off the farmer's strong conceptions. And, to these, some learned remarks of the *ostensible* Reporter;—who, in the section "Fallowing," informs us that

P. 57. "The district now under consideration is termed the Rye-lands, and was reported by Dr. Beale, in the year 1636, to 'refuse wheat, peas, and vetches,' and to be adapted

adapted only to the culture of 'rye, hemp, flax, turnips, and parsnips*.'

"By the subsequent introduction of lime as a manure, it has been so fertilized, as to be successfully applied to the growth of every grain. The pastures also, which in Dr. Beale's time were stated to consist of 'short and poor grass, or of a coarse and sea-green blade,' have been improved in an equal degree."

And, in the section "Manuring" (in continuation of the remarks above mentioned) he says;—p. 107. "A practical proof of the use of lime on light soils is supplied by the district of Irchenfield in this county. This district, which, as before noticed, was reported by Dr. Beale 'to refuse wheat, peas, and vetches,' and to be adapted only to the culture of 'rye, hemp, flax, turnips, and parsnips,' has been so essentially improved by the use of lime as a manure, that it not only produces plentiful crops of barley, peas, &c. but is also successfully applied to the growth of wheat and other grain."

"Of *other manures* used in Herefordshire, the sweepings of towns is very valuable in those situations, which by their proximity will admit of its use. Common ashes and those from the soap-boiler's furnace, are applied to pastures with great effect. Night-soil is also mixed with earth and other ingredients, and forms a very forcing compost. The shovelings of roads, scouring of ditches, mud from ponds, and other resources of the active farmer, are occasionally resorted to, but not so often as they might be with profit."

TILLAGE.—In the section "Fallowing," we find crouded, in a sort of literary mob,—not only what properly belongs to that subject, or to that of tillage in general;—but to *manure*, *wheat*, *tax* on *horses*, *tax* on *malt*, *markets*, *rent*, *harvest work-people*, *oats*, *grass lands*, *barley*, *peas*, *hops*,—all hustled together,—in one of the *crack* reports of counties!—One of the sacred books of the "Philosophers Bible;"—one of the immortal chapters of the "famous doomsday book" of modern times;—one part of a "book of authority—unequalled in any nation of the world."—What an honor to "ENGLISH LITERATURE!!!!!" †

The fragmentary parts that relate to tillage, and require to be preserved, are the two which follow.

P. 53.

"* Herefordshire Orchard, 1656."

† Mr. Duncumb's name is enrolled in the document of which mention is made, in the prefix to this volume.

P. 53. "Fallowing, or repeated ploughing, is found in all cases the best preparation for sowing."

From this first line of the section, it will readily be perceived that Mr. D. is a fallowist; and he, accordingly, dissertates, at some length, on the pulverisation of soils; but without appearing to be aware,—that pulverizing, like most other valuable operations, may be carried too far; or that a clover ley,—that is to say—soil interwoven and held together in a state of firmness, with the roots and fibers of vegetables, is frequently preferable to a fallow, as a matrix for the seed,—especially of wheat:—the almost only grain crop that is mentioned in this Report of an arable county!

Mr. D's recapitulation of the advantages gained by tillage is brief:—P. 55. "Ploughing tends to dissolve the too great adhesion of stiff soils, it facilitates the introduction of manure, it destroys weeds, it opens the pores of the earth to receive readily the dews and vapours of the atmosphere, it enables the roots of plants to shoot more vigorously, and it brings the land into that state, which most easily admits of the depositing of seed."

A due proportion of tillage may certainly contribute toward these several benefits. But an excess of it, especially when applied to tenacious soils, is capable of rendering them entirely barren;—by causing them to flux, with water, as metals do, by fire;—thereby, not only rendering them, when indurated by draught, impervious to the tender fibrils of plants, but suffocating those which may have been formed, when the fluxion took place.

Wheat.—Even this. which, as has been said, is the only grain crop whose culture is in any way described, is very imperfectly treated of. Howevcr. by gleaning from different chapters and sections, and arranging the scraps picked up, in the natural order in which they succeed each other, in practice, I have been enabled to make out some account of the Herefordshire practice,—so far as it has been incidentally noticed by the Board's Reporter.

Of the *varieties* of wheat that are cultivated in Herefordshire, I find no notice.

Some idea of the *soils* on which wheat is cultivated, there, may be caught in the following account of the

Tillage in use, for the wheat crop.—P. 56. "The particular modes in which this practice" (ploughing) "is now generally pursued in Herefordshire, on different soils under the preparation for the culture of wheat, are as follow: on the clays, the first ploughing for a fallow commences

mences on a clover-ley, as soon as the Lent grain is sown, that is at the end of April or beginning of May. Previous to this, about one hundred and twenty bushels of lime are spread on each statute acre, and are ploughed in, by shallow furrows, so as to mix most effectually with the turf of the surface. Six weeks afterwards, the fields are cross-ploughed, and in the beginning of August, sometimes with a little dung, but more frequently without any, they are ridged up for the sowing, which commences in the vicinity of Dore, where the management of this branch at least, is generally good, by the last week in September or the first in October. The produce, as before mentioned, averages from twenty to twenty-five bushels per acre; but the system, it is thought, would be improved by beginning to fallow immediately after wheat sowing, instead of deferring it until May, and this would more than compensate for the small share of feed which sheep derive from the clover-leys during the winter. The second ploughing then takes place immediately after the Lent grain is sown, the third in six weeks after, at the fourth, it is ridged up before the harvest begins, and at the fifth it is sown in the beginning of October. This practice gives an additional ploughing, and it has been adopted by several farmers with great success; Mr. Knight, however, is unfriendly to this mode, and contends, that crops on clays may be injured by too much pulverization. On the light lands near Ross, the first ploughing for a fallow is postponed to the end of July, or even to the beginning of August, in order that the sheep may avail themselves of whatever pasture the clover-leys may afford, until they are sold at Ross fair on the 20th of July. In the month of May, the dung is hauled from the fold and placed in convenient heaps for spreading on the clover, as soon as the sheep are removed. As their heaps are to be exposed to the sun and air during two of the hottest months, a turf is generally laid on the top of each of them, that their virtues may not be exhaled and lost, before they are mixed with the soil. The second or crop-ploughing takes place six weeks after the first, and the third after an equal interval, when lime is introduced in proportion to the deficiency of dung, and the whole is ridged up for sowing in November."

The Reporter, however, recommends a "better practice;" and proceeds, in the didactic way, and the true pharmacopean manner, to impress it on the mind of his reader. But "the D——l a bit, the better Herring."

Manure

Manure for wheat. See the general article, *Manure*, aforegoing.

Semination.—On this stage of the wheat culture, we find a few particulars, beside those mentioned under the head Tillage: they are as follow:—

Time of sowing; as aforegoing.

Choice and preparation of the seed.—P. 58. "Considerable care is taken, and very deservedly, in the selection of wheat for sowing. The produce of the chalk-hills of Oxfordshire is often procured for this purpose, and with good effect; but the farmer is more frequently satisfied with the finest seed he can obtain from soil of an opposite description to his own. The seeds being procured, his next attention is directed towards the steeping, which is generally considered to be of the utmost importance.

"In this process the wheat is immersed in a large tub of urine or strong brine. By repeated stirrings the light and imperfect grains are brought to the top, and carefully skimmed off: the remainder is taken from the brine, after one night's soaking, and being thinly spread on a floor, it is powdered over with sifted lime, and put into sacks for use."

Method of sowing.—P. 52. "Wheat is sown, with very few exceptions, and those for experiment on a small scale, in the broadcast manner. Drilling or setting by the hand has been very rarely resorted to here."

Quantity of seed.—P. 59. The quantity sown on an acre varies from twenty to twenty-five gallons."

On covering the seed, or on the adjustment of the Soil, so as to preserve the seed and the seedling plants against their enemies, during the autumnal and winter seasons,—nothing appears.

Weeding.—P. 108. "Weeding is very rarely practised in Herefordshire, except the hoeing of thistles on wheat crops in the month of May be considered as an operation of this kind."—The hoeing of wheat does not seem to be a practice, in Herefordshire, as it is in Glocestershire.

Harvesting of wheat.—P. 64 "Wheat is generally reaped by parties of Welshmen from Cardiganshire, and other parts of South Wales; but it is now gradually becoming a branch of labour amongst our natives."—Again—"The companies of Ancient Britons vary in number according to the extent of the work which they have previously contracted for. To four or five men there generally belongs one horse, unincumbered with bridle or saddle, on this they ride in succession, taking little rest, and performing

forming their journey with great expedition. One of the party understands enough of the English language and roads, to act as interpreter and guide.

"They avoid as much as they can, the society of our natives; are temperate, laborious, and grateful; easily irritated and easily pleased."

On the *Barn* or *Farm-Yard* management, relating to this prime crop, (or indeed to any other crop, notwithstanding the full-faced farm-yard affixed to the volume) I have *found* not a syllable.

The *produce* of wheat is shown in its tillage; and in p. 65.—"The average produce of wheat per statute acre on a good fallow and tolerable soil, has already been estimated at twenty bushels."

Markets for wheat. This may be seen under the general head, aforegoing.

MESLIN.—P. 66. "Rye, which with an equal proportion of wheat, constituted the bread-corn used in religious houses before their suppression, is now sown but sparingly, but grain thus mixed in flour during a time of scarcity or dearness, still retains the name of *monk-corn*, from the circumstances above-mentioned."*

POTATOES.—Still we find the potatoe a *fresh* crop, in the Western Department.—P. 66. "Potatoes are gaining ground every year: near towns in particular, they are found a very profitable crop, by sale in the market: and in all situations when plentiful, they are applied to fatten pigs with great success: they are generally boiled for this purpose.

"Their culture is conducted with the plough or the spade, according to the extent of the plantation: the former implement is always used where there is room in setting, cleaning, and getting up."

BULBOUS RAPE.—P. 67. The Swedish turnip has been introduced but a few seasons, and has made very considerable progress; its superior ability to resist the attacks of wet and cold weather, are well known, and form very strong recommendations to its culture.

"The county is indebted to James Woodhouse, Esq. steward under the Governors of Guy's Hospital, for the introduction of this valuable species.

"Mr. Knight and Mr. Davis of Croft Castle, sowed them also

* The term in use, for this mixed, mongrel crop, throughout the northern districts, at least, of the Western Department, is, very properly, *mong* corn; doubtless, from the obsolete verb MONG, to mix; from which root, with equal aptitude, has sprung the epithet *mongrel*, and the preposition *among*.

also about the same time. Mr. Knight is trying to improve their size and growth by introducing the farina of the English turnip into the blossoms of the Swedish; but the experiment is not yet complete."

This is a bold attempt, seeing that they are, pretty evidently, two distinct *species* of plants. I shall wait with a degree of solicitude for the result of Mr. K's experiment.

On *Turnips*, I have *discovered* not a word; excepting in the chapter, "Implements,"—(p. 47.) wherein it is said—"Turnips have been drilled by Mr. Knight with the best effects; and where hoeing them is not generally practised, nor well understood, drilling has many recommendations, from the facility afforded of keeping the ground clear between the rows. and setting out the plants at proper distances."—These remarks plainly enough show that the turnip crop was, in 1805, an alien in Herefordshire.

On LUCERN pretty much is said; but nothing to my purpose.

On CICHORY—(CICKORY—CICHORIUM *intybus)* are these particulars.—P. 72. "Chicory has been used by way of experiment in two instances. Mr. Towne, of Trevase, sowed a proper quantity with barley in the broad cast manner, on half a field, of light sand, and sowed the other half with the usual proportions of clovers and grass-seeds: the latter proved far superior in every respect; like lucerne, it seems not adapted to broad-cast culture. The second experiment was by drilling in rows; but in this mode, it was not found equal to lucerne, nor did horses and cattle appear to eat it with equal avidity."

SAFFRON.—P. 169. "Considerable quantities of saffron were formerly produced in this county, and in the gardens situated in the suburbs of Hereford."—Again—"Its culture, however, has long been discontinued here."

HOPS.—The subjoined paragraph, *(found* in the section fallowing) is all I can discover respecting the culture of hops, in Herefordshire.—P. 65 "Hop plantations prevail in different degrees throughout the county, but abound most towards Worcestershire. They were probably made here soon after the introduction of hops into England, which was about the year 1524: the mode of culture is similar to that adopted in other counties," (!!) "Five hundred weight are esteemed as the fair produce of a provincial *hop-acre*, which contains two thousand poles, each root having on an average

average two poles. The plantations are more generally worked with the plough than with the spade, and this branch of agriculture has very much increased within these few years." What a fund of instructive intelligence!

But judging from the following passage, in the section, "Orchards,"—it may be said that Mr. D. is not a *Hopist*. P. 93. "The number of acres now employed in raising hops, and poles to support them, might be greatly reduced; and this alone would prove an immense advantage to agriculture. Hops at present occupy the best ground the farmer has to give them. They take his best manure; they are too often the principal objects of his attention; and whilst their culture injures the crops of corn in every district where they abound, it may be questioned whether the produce of a thousand acres, annually afford nutriment sufficient to support a single human being." And may not nearly as much be said of cider?

ORCHARDS.—In reviewing the preceding Report, by Mr. Clark, I have mentioned my own Register of the ORCHARDS and FRUIT LIQUORS of Herefordshire and the adjacent counties.—In Mr. Clark's performance I found little, on those subjects, either to praise or censure.—When I took my leave of it, I expressed a hope, that, in a corrected edition, with additions, I might find something bordering on perfection; especially, on the latter subject. But I have been lamentably disappointed,—even tho learning and science would seem to have been joined in the attempt.

The ostensible Reporter, conscious, perhaps, of his own inability, prudently accepted the assistance of his friend Mr. Knight, the Orchardist; whose treatise, we are told, in a note, p. 93,—"has been repeatedly alluded to, and by the obliging permission of the author, as freely adopted in this part of the Survey."—And, it may be added, has been repeatedly quoted, instead of its original.—There are few ideas,—very few indeed,—to be found in this lengthened chapter,—whether held out as being the Reporter's or his assistants', that may not have emanated from my Register.

Suffice it to notice an instance of one that has been bandied about as an important discovery of Mr. Knight, relating to the transitory nature of the varieties of orchard fruits:—

In the Rural Economy of Glocestershire, &c. section Orchards, first published in 1789, I have said,—"The DURATION of VARIETIES may, however, depend much upon management; for altho Nature wills that the same wood, or the same set of sap vessels (for the wood which is produced by grafting is, in reality, no more than a protrusion

sion of the graft—*an extension of the original stock)* shall in time lose its fecundity: yet it is probable that the same art which establishes a variety may shorten or prolong its duration."

Herefordshire Report.—P. 80. "Mr. Knight observes that the branch, from which a graft is taken, evidently partakes of the life of the tree to which it belongs; and that it is equally evident, that, when part of a tree is detached, no new life is communicated, whether it be used as a graft, or placed to emit roots as a cutting."—Again,—"Hence Mr. Knight infers, as before mentioned, that the cutting must partake of the life, and consequently of all the habits of the original tree."—P. 81. "In short, a tree, like an animal, has *its infancy, its flowery spring, its summer's ardent strength, its sober autumn, fading into age, and its pale concluding winter**."

How *appropriately* flowery and fine! Mr. K's being the *embellishment* of my theory! Alas! poor Forsythe!—to fall into, and fall by!

Mr. Knight, however, having gained, I understand, no small share of credit, as an Orchardist, and being as we are told, in the Herefordshire Report, (through the medium of which, only, I will view Mr. K. at present)—A man,—"whose abilities as a Naturalist are well known,"—I will the more carefully examine the joint effort of Messrs. Knight and Duncumb, on "Orcharding;"—and try if I can discover any thing that may usefully add to my former Register.

This, however, I find will be no easy task. The chapter under consideration, tho of some length, is in a manner void of arrangement. No regular subdivision of the subject:—"Orcharding," and Cider-making (that is to say the branches of these subjects that are here touched upon) are hurled together in strange confusion. The distinct operations, frequently, have not even a *break* to separate them. In the same paragraph, perhaps, two or three different topics are included:—the particular items of information being as difficult to find, as are those of a law deed of equal length.

The first particular which arrests my attention is a notice respecting the present spirit for raising NEW VARIETIES, or Sorts, of orchard fruits. I am "free to confess," however, that I mention it, rather to gratify my own feelings, than to convey profitable information to my readers.

Some twenty years ago, seeing the impracticability of prolonging the old varieties of superior worth, I urged the Orchardmen

" * Mr. Knight's Treatise."

Orchardmen of Herefordshire, and Glocestershire, to apply themselves, with ardor, to the discovery and propagation of new varieties of similar excellence, and offered them practical directions for that purpose. And, in the Herefordshire Report, now under review, I find the exhortation has not been altogether unavailing.—P. 79. "The introduction of others equally good, cannot be too strongly urged, and the public spirit of the present age has not been indifferent on the occasion; more endeavours have perhaps been directed towards this object within the last twenty years, than during a century preceding."

On *planting* Orchards, we find the following dictate.—P. 83. "The rows should extend from north to south, as in that direction, each part of every tree will receive the most equal portions of light and heat."

Lest this direction should fall into the hands of young planters, and give them much unnecessary trouble, in particular situations, it may be right to say—that in forming drills of beans, in laying out convex arable ridges, and in setting up corn shucks, such a direction would be perfectly right; but it is not requisite in planting orchards. Apple trees take semiglobular forms, and stand, or ought to stand, distant from each other;—not in *rows*, but *aquincunx*. They never can, if planted at proper distances, shade each other, like corn plants; nor can one plant receive more sun than another (by reason of their juxtaposition) like corn on opposite sides of raised ridges. The Reporter, probably, having seen similar directions given, in the cases above noticed, has unwittingly *generalized* them to Orchards. This, among a thousand instances, shows how mischievous it may be, for unpractised men to write on practical subjects.

The passage, which immediately follows the above, corresponds with Mr. Clark's ideas on the same subject. (see p. 291). "The distance between each row, as well as the space between each tree, should depend on the situation and soil. When the former is high and exposed, the trees should be closely planted to afford each other protection; and when the latter is poor and shallow, their growth will in course be less luxuriant, and they will consequently require less room. But in low and sheltered situations, and in deep and rich soils, wider intervals should be allowed." p. 83.

Among some popular notions, concerning the *colors* of *apples*, and mysterious quackery, about *mixing* the *liquor* of *fruits* for *cider*, we meet with the following remarks.

marks, on the *sizes* of apples; and an interesting experiment on separating the rinds and cores, from the pulps of the same fruits.—P 84. "Apples of a small size are always, if equal in quality, to be preferred to those of a larger, in order that the rind and kernel, which contain the flavour of the liquor, may bear the greatest proportion to the pulp, which affords the weakest and the most watery juice.—This is no new idea, for Batty Langley, who published his Pomona in folio in the year 1727, observed in that work, 'the smaller the apple, in reason the better the fruit, is a constant rule amongst us.' This was on the subject of Devonshire fruits; but had no such opinion been given, the fact has been fully ascertained by William Symonds, Esq. M. D. of Hereford, a gentleman well versed in every thing relating to planting, orcharding, and the manufacturing of cider. A few years ago, he made one hogshead entirely from the rinds and cores of apples, and another from the pulps of the same fruit. The former was of most unusual strength and highly flavoured: the latter was watery, and possessed not one recommendation."

This experiment must necessarily be ill reported. Mere rinds and cores are nearly destitute of juice. It would require several Orchards of fruit to make a hogshead of cider from those, alone. But see Worcestershire.

Mr. Knight's experiments on the comparative specific gravities of the juices of different cider fruits, is also interesting.—P. 87. "Mr. Knight has endeavoured to ascertain the specific gravity of the juice of different apples and pears by the hydrometer; and he is of opinion, that the strength of the cider, to be produced by any of the new fruits, may be thus calculated with considerable accuracy. The failure of a crop of apples, during the last two years, has been unfavourable to the experiment, but Mr. K. has already discovered, that the juice of the Stire far outweighs that of our ordinary apples; and that the specific gravity of the juice of a ripe and perfect Longland pear is 1053, and that of the Holmer pear 1060, in the same soil."

These experiments are founded on good theory.—*Sweets* being heavier than water, and the strength of cider depending on the quantity of *Sugar* which the juice contains,—the value of this (the juice) necessarily is as its specific gravity, or weight;—and, in ascertaining the quality of the fruit of a young tree, of a new variety, (before it it has borne a sufficient quantity to make cider from) a practice founded on that theory might perhaps become valuable*. But the given season must ever be duly weighed, as well as the juice of the fruit. In a cool moist season, all fruits are comparatively watery. In a warm one, comparatively sweet.

Further, admitting that sugar gives a *yellowness* to the pulp of the fruit: (p. 83) *Color* may be a useful criterion, in judging of the qualities of the first fruits of new varieties. But this by the way.

I have dwelt the longer on these topics, as on them, almost solely, rests the whole of the *profit* which *my* readers are likely to reap, from the Herefordshire Reports, concerning its orchards and fruit liquors.

In p. 90 of this Report, we find Mr. K. so sanguine an Orchardist as not to dispare of making an apple tree *ornamental.*

Mr. K. it appears, in different parts of it, is *crossing* English apples with the Siberian Crab; with what success, time only can show.

The subjoined passage, on the *herbage* of orchards, I insert as a hint to my friends in Devonshire;—where it is almost entirely wasted.—P. 91. "The grass produced in an orchard comes very early in the spring, when it is peculiarly valuable to the farmer. Under judicious management it is never suffered to grow long or coarse, and an orchard in this condition will be found to support a very considerable quantity of stock."

This may with truth be deemed the most appropriate morsel of Report in the volume under review. If the herbage of orchards be kept closely grazed, it becomes of considerable value;—but, by no means, equal to what it would be, without the trees;—unless during a week or two, in the spring. Pasturable herbs of almost every species grow weak, vapid, and spiritless, in the shade.

The following passage I must not pass over, unnoticed.—P. 92. "The apple and pear are found quite as highly flavoured and as perfect in many other counties as in this; and Mr. Knight is of opinion, that if the planter were at

* Admitting the transitory nature of varieties, it behoves the planter of Orchards to lose no time, in *extending* a valuable variety, over his grounds. Of course, a mode of discerning the quality of the fruit of a seedling plant, *while young*,—before it has reached a degree of maturity sufficient to bear fruit enough to make cider from,—and thereby, of course, gain several years of duration,—would doubtlessly be valuable. After it has arrived at that state of maturity, no other criterion can be wanted.

at liberty to choose his soil, a loam of moderate depth, with a sub-soil of chalk, would be found equal to any, which the counties now celebrated for orchards, could supply."

Now, it may be fairly asked where the description of land, here recommended, for apple and pear trees, is to be found? "Chalk" is confined to a few districts of this island, and in those districts, very little land is adapted to orchard ground; by reason of the elevation and bleakness of the situation. It is true that in the vallies of the chalk hills of the southern counties, there are some eligible sites for orchards; and many or most of those are already appropriated to that purpose.

In GLOCESTERSHIRE, I have said,—'the stire apple, on the *limestone* lands of the forest of Dean, yields a cider which is marked by richness (sweetness) and fulness of flavor; while the same apple, in the vale of Glocester, a strong deep rich soil, affords a liquor whose predominant qualities, without great diligence, in the manufacture of it, are roughness and strength. The hagloe crab, too, seems to require a *calcareous rock* to give full richness and flavor to its liquor.'—And in the SOUTHERN COUNTIES, I have noticed, that, in the district of Maidstone, (celebrated for its orchard fruits)—'The lands in the best repute, for orchard grounds, are Coomb, on *calcareous* rubble, and deep loam on *rock* of a *similar nature.*—For apples these lands are singularly eligible; affording fair and saccharine fruit.'

How Mr. K. could recommend a substratum that is rarely to be had, and leave unnoticed one that is more or less common, in every department of the kingdom (namely limestone) is not easily to be conceived. Surely, not under the color of disguise! Perhaps, Mr. K. as has been the fate of many a great genius, has fallen into the hands of an unskilful commentator.

The finale of this invaluable chapter may be entitled to some consideration.—P. 93. "By an extended culture of the apple and pear, many millions of bushels of barley, now converted into malt, might annually be saved, and applied to better purposes.

"The ground now employed in its culture might be made to produce wheat, or other articles immediately necessary to society; and that the juice of the apple and pear will afford a liquor as wholesome as any which can be obtained from malt, is sufficiently evinced by the general

neral appearance to the natives of this and other cider counties." (!) See Pitt's Staffordshire.

In some general observations, on fruit liquor as an object in Rural Economy, made at the close of my account of orchards and fruit liquors in Glocestershire and Herefordshire, I have shown, and I trust satisfactorily, that, under the present imperfect management of them, it is a matter of doubt whether they are a blessing or a curse, on the country; but that, under more judicious treatment of fruits of superior kinds, they may become valuable advantages.

The most mischievous tendency of the practice is that of promoting an inordinate desire of *drinking*, among laborers in husbandry *:—a mischief that has doubtlessly spread over a considerable portion of the kingdom, from the cider counties—Shropshire (see p. 181,) would seem to have been the *conductor*, between Herefordshire and the Midland Counties;—where an excess of malt liquor, equal almost to that of cider, in Glocestershire, &c. prevails. And the same waste of malt takes place in the cider counties, whenever fruit liquor fails. There will, I believe, be no risk in asserting that there is more malt consumed, by laborers, on a par of years, in Herefordshire, &c. (over and above the ocean of cider there drank) than in almost any part of the northern provinces, of equal extent.

More might be advanced, on this head; but it would be leading me away from the main purpose of my present undertaking.

Grass Lands.—*Mowing Grounds.*—P. 65. "The richest meadows are those on the banks of the Wye, Lug, and Frome."

P. 72. "Crops of clover and ray-grass are generally cut in July, and the meadow grasses soon after. The clover is turned once only, unless an unusually heavy crop, or wet weather, render it necessary to repeat the turning. Meadow grass when mown, is immediately spread thinly over the whole surface, and this operation is in this, as in some other counties, called *tedding*. It is then turned, and placed successively in rows, small cocks, beds, and large cocks. When sufficiently dried, the last process before hauling is that of collecting it into what are called wind-

* And let it be added, the consequent debilitated habits (effects of the cholic, and calculous complaints) to which cider-drinking laborers appear to be peculiarly liable.

wind-cocks; each of these contain about half a ton: in this state, they are considered as secure from any material injury under any weather whatever, and are frequently permitted to remain unmoved during a week or ten days, as best suits the convenience of the farmer."

P. 73. "Hay thus prepared, is usually brought into a bay formed in the manner of a Dutch barn, that is, open on the sides and covered at the top, where it continues until leisure is found to rick and to thatch it."

From this imperfect account, it seems, that hay, in Herefordshire, as in Glocestershire, is double-fermented.

After Grass.—The following instance of practice (or experiment) with the remarks thereon, I insert—further to agitate an interesting subject. See NORTHERN DEPARTMENT, p. 151.

P. 69. "A mode of managing sound meadows and pastures has lately been tried, and attended with a great increase of produce. The grass is mown as soon as it is in blossom, and consequently previous to the formation of seed. The after-grass is not grazed until it begins to contract a yellow appearance in the latter end of October or beginning of November. In this case, the ground remains covered during the winter with a portion of dead herbage, through which the young grass springs with the greatest vigour at an early period of the succeeding spring. Mr. Knight contends, that the sap in all plants ascends through the alburnous vessels of the root, and is dispersed over the leaf, whence it is returned to form new roots and buds, and to prepare them for vegetation. According to this theory, if the leaves be eaten off on mowing grounds, as soon as they are re-produced, the roots are deprived of their nutriment, and the plants, in consequence, vegetate weakly in the succeeding spring."

Dead herbage, left to rot on the surface, doubtlessly, like buckweet or turnips plowed into the soil, acts as a manure, to the crop which follows. But, in the instance under notice, we are not informed whether "the portion of dead herbage" be left on the land, as *manure*, or is eaten off (together with the young grasses that shoot through it early in the spring as in the case of preserved pasture grass) for *spring feedage!*

On the *Pasture Grounds*, of the first breed of cattle in the kingdom, not a word!

On *Irrigation*, we have the following learned notice.—P. 108. "The fertilization of Egypt by the annual overflowing of the Nile possibly first suggested the experiment of of irrigation in other places. Virgil seems to have understood the beneficial effects of the practice, when he observes, that

'Humida majores herbas alit;'

and again, he expresses himself more fully in these words

———'Huc summis liquuntur rupibus amnes,
'Felicemque trahunt limum.'"

—Yet, almost in the same breath, we are told that the father of Irrigation, in Herefordshire (ROWLAND VAUGHAN, who wrote on it, in 1610, and a great part of whose treatise the Board's *Reporter* has copied!)—was led to it in the following very probable manner.—P. 109. "In the month of March I happened to find a mole or wont's nest raised on the brim of a brook in my meade, like a great hillock; and from it there issued a little stream of water, (drawn by the working of the mole) down a shelving ground, one pace broad, and some twenty in length. The running of this little streame did at that time wonderfully content me, seeing it pleasing greene, and that other land on both sides was full of moss, and hide-bound for want of water.—This was the first cause I undertook the drowning of grounds."

HORSES.—P. 127. "The horses used in Herefordshire have no peculiarity; and perhaps no animal has been more altered, or in an agricultural point of view less improved, than the horse has been within the last twenty or thirty years. Its height, its bulk, and its powers for short and sudden exertion, have been considerably increased, but by this of size, it has been rendered much more subject to disease and accident, and much less capable of bearing long and continued labour."

CATTLE.—P. 116. "The cattle of Herefordshire have long been esteemed superior to most, if not to all, the breeds in the island. Those of Devonshire and Sussex approach nearest to them in general appearance. Large size, an athletic form, and unusual neatness, characterise the true sort: the prevailing colour is a reddish brown with white faces."—Again—"The show of oxen in thriving condition at the Michaelmas fair in Hereford, cannot be exceeded by any similar annual collection in England: on this occasion they are generally sold to the principal graziers in the counties near the metropolis, and there perfected for the London markets. An original account book, kept by William Town, in the vicinity of Hereford, has

has the following entry: '25 Aug. 1694, sold the nine oxen at 52*l.*; the money to be paid into the Exchequer within a month.'

"The price was therefore five guineas and a half each; and they were probably sold fat in London. Since that date, the size of oxen has doubtless increased very considerably, and the price has also advanced in at least a six-fold proportion."

The Reporter and his friend then venture out into the general subject of English cattle, and speak familiarly, if not prophanely, of the Leicestershire, or Bakewellian breed.

After laying down the law of good breeding, in a *master-like* manner, we are favored with the following *instructive* information.—P. 118. "The Leicestershire cow, such as it is at present, will never breed a rival to the Herefordshire ox. The whole attention of the Leicestershire breeder has been directed to the improvement of his cow; and for the use of the grazier, he has made her an excellent animal. The Herefordshire breeder on the contrary, has sacrificed the qualities of the cow to those of the ox: he does not value his cow according to the price which the grazier would give for it, but in proportion as it possesses that form and character, which experience has taught him to be conducive to the excellence of the future ox. Hence the cow of Herefordshire is comparatively small, extremely delicate, and very feminine in its character."

Admirable doctrine! What an opportunity, this, for Mr. Knight (whose communication, we are told, in a note, this is) to exercise his talent at controversy. The present *fashionable dictation* among *scientific* breeders, is (or a few months ago was) that the *female* (throughout all nature) ought to be *larger* than the *male*; forasmuch as nothing of symmetry, strength, or power of great exertion, can be produced by any other means. Yet, according to the *newer* doctrine, (it would seem) here laid down, the Herefordshire ox—the most powerful of the *Bovian* race—is to be bred from a female—"comparatively small,—extremely delicate, and very feminine in its character."—In what light, airy, pleasant times we live!—when the spirit of *opposition* is the life, not only of politics, but of science!!—Let but a "modern philosopher" *assert*,—no matter how absurd his assertion,—and he will have thousands to follow him:—until another literary Charlatan asserts the opposite; when the credulous flock of followers are seen to move in the

the contrary direction;—truth, which lies in the midway, being thus trodden underfoot.

How could Mr. K. *imagine* that "the whole attention of the Leicestershire breeder has been directed to the improvement of his cow." ?—When it is well known, to those who really know any thing of the principles of the Leicestershire breeders,—that their main object was, is, and must be, that of producing *males*—bulls—of extraordinary excellence; as, on these, their profits principally depend. In doing this, it is true, they, as a natural consequence, have bred females of extraordinary beauty. As to *oxen!* the leading breeders never reared any,—unless for shows.

Had I not understood that Mr. Knight has acquired a *name* among men of science, I should not have impeded my direct pursuit, by these animadversions.

Fatting Cattle.—P. 73. "Grazing and feeding cattle are seldom pursued in Herefordshire, except for the purpose of provincial consumption, and that almost invariably confined to heifers and cows. Smithfield, however, has often been supplied immediately from hence, with the fattest and most valuable oxen in the market: but from the impracticability of driving them so many miles in that condition without injury, it is much more usual to dispose of them at the Michaelmas fair in Hereford, when five or six years old in a thriving condition, to the graziers of Buckinghamshire and other adjacent counties, where they are prepared for the London markets.

"In fattening cows and heifers for provincial use, they are generally brought forwards by grass, and sometimes fattened with it altogether: in other cases, hay and turnips are added in stalls, and occasionally oil-cake."

Dairy.—In the chapter, "Grass," we find the following remarks (apparently by the *ostensible* Reporter) on—"the Dairy of Herefordshire."—P. 68. "Herefordshire has no pretensions to rank amongst the dairy counties. It is supplied from Wales with excellent butter in tubs, for winter use; and from Shropshire and Gloucestershire with cheese; for although very good cheese is made in various parts of this county, it has generally been confined to private consumption, including all the demands of the farm-house. Of late, the improved modes of other counties have been adopted with some success; and the vicinity of Bromyard produces cheese, which in the market of Hereford rivals the best of Shropshire in quality and price."

Yet,

Yet, here, I am again retarded in my progress, by the broad assertion of Mr. Knight,—or his admiring friend,—in the passage which succeeds the above.—"The general soil, however, of Herefordshire appears to be unfavourable to the making of cheese. Mr. Knight, with that accuracy and skill which he is known to possess on all subjects connected with agriculture" (!) "and natural history in general, has proved by experiments, that equal quantities of milk in Herefordshire and Cheshire, will produce unequal quantities of curd, highly to the advantage of Cheshire: and further, that better cheese has been produced in that county, from milk, half of which had been previously skimmed, than is produced in this, from milk altogether unskimmed. The want therefore of complete success in this valuable branch of rural economy, is not solely to be attributed to a want of skill in our dairy-maids; and the cause of failure is rendered more difficult of discovery, and consequently more difficult to be remedied, from an observation that the plants were nearly the same in the Herefordshire and Cheshire pastures, on which the above experiments were made: white clover abounded in each, with the crested dog-tail grass, and rye-grass mixed with others in small quantities."

"Proved by experiments"! What description of experiments? How conducted? or how often repeated? and by *whom!* does not appear. It would require some years of *attentive experience* by well educated dairywomen, to *prove* the fact above asserted *.

SHEEP.—P. 120. "The provincial breed of sheep is termed the Ryeland; the district so named is in the vicinity of Ross, and often alluded to in the course of this survey; being particularly favourable to them from the dryness of the soil, and the sweetness of the herbage.

"They are small, white-faced, and hornless, the ewes weighing from nine to twelve and fourteen pounds the quarter; the wethers, or *wedders*, from twelve to sixteen and eighteen pounds. In symmetry of shape, and in the flavour of their meat, they are superior to most flocks in England; in the quality of their wool, they are wholly unrivalled. They lamb in February and March; but during winter, and particularly in time of lambing, the store flocks are generally confined by night in a covered building

* Let the reader wait to hear what Mr. DAVIS (a man of *mature experience,* in "all subjects connected with agriculture") has to say on this point,—in the district NORTH WILTSHIRE, ensuing.

building provincially termed a *cot*, in which they are sometimes fed with hay and barley straw, but much more frequently with peas-halm. Some breeders accustom them to the cot only in very severe weather, and in lambing time.——

"The manure made from the peas-halm is excellent, and in large quantity; whilst the cotting materially contributes to the health of the animal, and the fineness of its fleece. The quantity shorn from each of the small original breed does not average more than two pounds, but the quality is such as almost to rival that imported from Spain. The price has often been as high as thirty-three shillings the stone of twelve pounds and a half untrinded, when coarse wool has brought but ten or twelve shillings. A cross has been made between the Rye-lands and the new Leicester sorts, to the advantage perhaps of the *breeder*, who is situated on good land, but certainly to the detriment of the wool.

"The preservation of the original fineness of this great staple commodity, or its improvement, are perhaps objects worthy of national attention

"A cross between the Rye-land and real Spanish seems the most probable mode of adding to the fineness and value of the wool, and amongst many spirited breeders who are now making the experiment, Colonel Scudamore of Kentchurch, sold the fleeces of a flock so crossed at forty shillings per stone, in the fair at Ross, in the course of last year. The first stage of the cross materially detracts from the beauty of the Rye-land's form: but by continued attention, this objection will probably be removed; and the flavour of the mutton is uninjured."

On this occasion, too, Mr. Knight steps forward to combat the Leicestershire breeders, and to appreciate their stock. I insert the following passage, without comment. It is merely Knight *versus* Bakewell,—"and his followers." —P. 123. "The quality of Mr. Bakewell's wool is inferior to most sorts in the island, nor does it appear that the quantity shorn from each is remarkably great; whilst, according to the modern system, the sheep being brought to market before it is two years old, the wool is of small value, if compared with that of the ground which the animal has occupied.

"The quantity of animal food, however, which is thus produced for the market is very considerable, but according to Mr. Knight's experience, it is far short of what the same weight or value of herbage would supply, if given as formerly

formerly to the labouring ox or cow. 'A well-bred heifer of three years and a half old, after supplying the market with a calf, if moderately kept and fattened, will not weigh less than six hundred pounds when slaughtered. This weight is equal to that of six sheep of twenty-five pounds the quarter; and I am of opinion that four sheep of that weight cannot be brought to market at the same expense to the community as a single heifer. A very coarse and indifferent pasture will suffice for the heifer in the summer, and it will be fed with straw and a few turnips in the winter. The food of the large sheep is of a much more expensive kind; and the calf and hide of the one will be found an ample equivalent for the wool and skins of the others. My pasture only will not fatten the new Leicester, and I have always been able, in rearing cattle for stock, to give my crop of turnips to the Herefordshire cow and ox, with much greater advantages than to sheep of any kind; and I have not yet found a sheep of one or two years, which would fatten in the same number of weeks, with a heifer of that breed. It is said by the admirers of Mr. Bakewell's sheep, that they consume less food than any other breeds: but I observe, that they are always kept in pasture where they have the power of eating much; and I can safely attest, that those which I have fattened had remarkably good appetites*.'"

The Southdown breed is next compared with that of Herefordshire. Little however, is to be learnt from the discussion. The following period (by Mr. Knight) I copy, for my own satisfaction.—P. 125. "The experience and opinions of some of my acquaintance who have made similar experiments, induce me to think the South-down much inferior to the Rye-lands, or fine-wooled breed of Herefordshire, which, till lately, has but little attracted the public attention."

It would have been but civil in the writer to have told his readers to whom his favorite breed, the Rylanders, are indebted for their present celebrity; if not for their existence. It is acknowledged by their greatest admirer, and patron, that the breed would probably have been lost,---nothing but its name would, now perhaps, have remained, had it not been for my representations.—See the Rural Economy

"* These observations were obligingly communicated by Mr. Knight, in answer to queries submitted to him, on the occasion of making this Survey."

ECONOMY of GLOCESTERSHIRE, &c.—Article *Sheep* of *Herefordshire.*

For several years past, experiments on a large scale have been made, to mix the Ryland with the Spanish breed, and with good success; so that it may now be said to have become a practice.—The Ryland breed, I believe, are found the most eligible of the English breeds wherewith to mix the Spanish; for the purpose of growing fine wool, in England:—not merely, I understand, as their being *naturally* a fine-wooled breed, but, likewise as they assimilate the best with the native, or established breeds of Spain.

The following general remarks, by Mr. Knight, at the close of his communication on sheep, abound in good sense; and tho I may not, in every particular, agree exactly with Mr. K. yet I can with great truth say that I have much satisfaction in transcribing them. They appear to have been written with a considerable degree of forethought.

P. 126. "If the sheep be to remain, what I apprehend Nature has made it, a mountain animal; if it is to collect its food in situations where the ox and the cow cannot subsist; and if wool be still considered as an object of national importance to Great Britain, I have no hesitation in asserting, that either of the preceding breeds, the Ryeland, or the South-down, deserve a preference to that of Mr. Bakewell.

"If, on the contrary, we are, in imitation of the Leicester, the Northampton, or the Warwickshire farmers, to convert our richest and most productive tillage into pasture; if the sheep be intended to banish the labouring ox and the cow, and be brought to market at a year and a half old, when it can supply the manufacturer with only a small portion of very indifferent wool, we cannot hesitate to pronounce Mr. Bakewell's sheep to be the best in the island. Its merits in fattening easily and abundantly, and being ready for the market at an early age, and in considerable weight, cannot be denied. In short it is an excellent animal in its way, but it is not such a one as is best adapted to a country which has recently imported corn in a single year to the amount of ten millions of money. The cow and the labouring ox are wanted; and were these made to resume the rich pastures now occupied by the sheep; were our tillage extended as formerly to supply these with straw during winter; and were our sheep suffered to acquire their full growth in their third year, our manufactories would be better

better supplied with wool both in quantity and bulk; and our markets be better supplied with animal food."

Management of Sheep.—P. 127. "The *sheering* in Herefordshire is performed by women."

SWINE.—P. 132. "No one breed of hogs, or of pigs as they are provincially termed, are peculiar to Herefordshire."

Different sorts are noticed; particularly "a small sort said to be Mr. Bakewell's,"—of which the Reporter speaks favorably. But Mr. Knight discovers in it much fault. He prefers his own kind of far greater size. And—"Mr. Knight naturally concludes, that the present predilection for small animals of this kind is not well founded." p. 133.

In this case, however, as in every other, the purpose for which a production is intended should first be consulted. For farm house servants, and hard working people in general, a large breed of hogs may be the most eligible. But not so when the palates of the indolent are to be pampered.

POULTRY.—P. 134. "Poultry have doubled their price within the last fifteen or twenty years; and the accumulation of several small farms into one, has contributed essentially to this alteration; the increased rates of other articles must also have had its share in producing an effect, much and severely felt by small housekeepers. In the year 1740, a fat goose, ready for the spit, brought ten-pence on an average in the market at Hereford; in the year 1760, it had only advanced to one shilling; in the present year 1804, it is worth four shillings at least. Fowls and pigeons have increased in the same rapid proportion. A couple of fowls in 1740 brought sixpence; in 1760, seven-pence; in 1804, they bring two shillings and four-pence. Pigeons in 1760 were worth eighteen-pence the dozen; in 1804, four shillings and six-pence. A roasting pig has increased in price, within the same period, from ten-pence to four shillings."

BEES.—P. 135. "Bees are confined to the cottager's garden, and are not there found in any abundance."

WORCESTERSHIRE.

THE outlines of Worcestershire (a few irregular outer-skirts excepted) may be said to be, at once, natural and political:—a circumstance which, I believe, is peculiar to Worcestershire. It is, nearly, but not entirely, *one* NATURAL DISTRICT; (the northern extreme of which penetrates, as has been said, aforegoing, into Shropshire);—one and the same widely spread rivered Vale;—reaching from TEWKSBURY to near BRIDGENORTH. That part of "the Vale of Evesham," which is situated in Worcestershire, north of the Bredon hills, is strictly a portion of

The VALE of WORCESTER.—This I have traversed, incidentally, in various directions;—as in the lines between Tewksbury and Worcester,—Evesham and Worcester,—Newent and Worcester,—Worcester and Tenbury,—Worcester and Bridgenorth,—Worcester and Broomsgrove. Nevertheless, I have *examined* it less than many other counties;—excepting its more southern parts; to which I paid particular attention, during my residence in Glocestershire; and excepting the Tenbury, or *hop-growing* district, which, as has been mentioned, I afterwards inspected. In the fertility of its soils, and the amenity of its situation, surface, and natural embellishments, very few passages of this fair isle, of similar extent, are equal to it;—scarcely one excels it.—Productive red lands are prevalent, in different parts of it. And its Agricultural products are not only more abundant, but more various, than those of other districts:—Not corn, cattle and dairy produce, only; but fruit liquors and hops rank among its productions.

"GENERAL

"GENERAL VIEW

OF THE

AGRICULTURE

OF THE

COUNTY OF WORCESTER,

WITH

OBSERVATIONS ON THE MEANS OF ITS IMPROVEMENT.

By WILLIAM THOMAS POMEROY,

OF FAIRWAY, NEAR HONITON, IN DEVONSHIRE.

DRAWN UP FOR THE CONSIDERATION OF

THE BOARD OF AGRICULTURE AND INTERNAL IMPROVEMENT.

1794."

OF Mr. POMEROY'S QUALIFICATIONS for the task he entered upon, we must judge from his performance, alone. Even his *profession* does not, in any way, appear. The reason why he was "sent," from afar, to report the rural practices of a county to which he was, pretty evidently, a total stranger, is seen in the "conclusion" of his Report. It requires but little discernment to discover, by whom it was written.

P. 76. "In concluding this account of the Rural Economy of this beautiful county, the person to whose lot its survey has fallen, wishes to observe, that throughout the whole, it has been his endeavour to state the several circumstances of it, in as accurate and distinct a light as possible: but little claim of originality is made, and he trusts no no charge of inaccuracy, from a neglect of earnest exertion, can be brought. Where any improvement is proposed, it is the result of frequent consultation with some of its first managers; it is their practice particularized, in hopes that, if these sheets ever reach the hands of the less informed tenantry, they may have that merit, at least, of directing their attention where they cannot imitate without improvement.

"To the nobility and gentry, and several of the principal tenantry, many thanks are due, for a most favourable reception, and kind assistance; to the Board, and their respectable President, some apology perhaps, for the lateness of the return: this, however, was, in a great measure, influenced by circumstances not to be remedied either by zeal or industry."

To this text, is appended the following note.—"The only particulars, about which the Author found any difficulty in procuring information, was in regard to hops and fruit. The planters of these, were in general inclined to be tenacious of their knowledge, at least few, actually engaged in the business of raising either, seemed disposed to be very communicative upon the subject. This, it is believed, might be principally owing to the apprehension of taxation, the cyder tax not being yet forgot. This jealousy, however, it is to be hoped, will soon be removed, as it is only by a free communication of ideas, and comparing the result of experiments made in different parts of the kingdom, that either hop plantations, or orchards, or the making of cyder and perry, or indeed any other art, can be much improved. It was principally with a view of comparing the practices of Devonshire and Worcestershire, in regard to fruit, and the liquors thence extracted, that the Author was sent by the Board of Agriculture from the one county to the other; and from the information accumulated upon the subject, by the survey of this and of other districts where hops and fruit are attended to, the art of raising, and the proper management of both, will probably be brought to perfection."

There can be little risk in saying that the close, at least, of this note betrays the pen of the first President. Who else, could have the assurance, even in 1794, to intimate, that the loose, flimsey, incoherent crudities of those *original Reports* that are, now, held in such contempt (see the Advertisement prefixed to this volume) could be capable of bringing any art to *perfection!*

In regard to Mr. P's MODE of SURVEY, we have no clew to

to serve us. His method of collecting information seems to have been (in some considerable part at least) that of sending round lists of queries to those whom he had been led to understand were best enabled to furnish the required answers

This is a mode of proceeding which I have at different times practised. But never, I think it right to embrace this opportunity of saying, until I had maturely surveyed the country, at large,—and its various practices, individually,—and had digested the materials, so collected. My *enquiries* have merely been made to fill up such blanks as I found remaining open, in my register; after I had digested the matter collected *from my own observations*;—or, in a very few instances, to gain some particulars of a district, situated at a distance from the STATION in which I had fixed my residence. It has ever been a standing rule with me—in studying and registering the nature and practices of a country,—*not to ask a question*, until I had *mastered my subject*: lest I should, thereby, receive false impressions that might improperly influence my judgement, and damp my endeavors to ascertain, *from my own knowledge*, the facts belonging to the nature and practices of the country under Survey;—on which, alone, I have ever formed the groundworks of my registers.

The performance, under notice, being an ORIGINAL REPORT, there are no annotators. The CONTRIBUTORS are those to whom the lists of queries had been sent:—

Mr. Darke of Bredon, and

Mr. Oldaker of Fladbury;—are the only ones that I shall quote.

The number of pages, in the body of the work, seventy seven;—in the Appendix, seventeen.

No map, or other engraving.

SUBJECT THE FIRST.

NATURAL ECONOMY.

ELEVATION and SURFACE.—P. 7. "The face of this county, when viewed from any of the surrounding eminences, approaches rather that of a plain; the gentle slopes and risings to the east and west of Worcester, remaining scarcely any longer discernible."

CLIMATURE.—P. 9. "The air is temperate; even on its highest situations, it is not so bleak as to considerably impede vegetation; nor are there any extensive tracts in the low lands, of boggy soil, to injure it by their exhalations."

P. 15. "The harvest season, is from the last week in July to the end of August; but the fickleness of the weather frequently drags it on to a greater length."

SOILS and SUBSOILS.—In a matter so extremely difficult to ascertain, as the soils and substrata of an entire county, (requiring a length of time and minute examination, to come nearly at the truth,) Mr. Pomeroy, I hope, will pardon me when I recommend to my readers, to receive the following detail (and others of a similar nature) with caution. If Mr. P. really paid that minute attention to this and other subjects of his Report that they required, he should, through one mean or other, have taken some method of making his readers sensible of it.

P. 8. "The soil is various: to the north of Worcester, which is situated nearly in the centre of the county, it chiefly consists of rich loamy sand, with a small proportion of gravel; there is some very light sand; a few spots of clay; of black peat earth the same; but chiefly inclining towards the east. In this quarter (the east) the prevailing soil is, for the most part, a strong clay. The waste land, which is very considerable, in general a deep black peat earth. To the south, between Worcester and the Vale of Evesham, the soil is partly of red marl, and part strong loamy clay; other parts sandy loam; and there is a small vein of land which partakes of each of these qualities; the sub-soil, more especially under the second division, limestone. In the Vale, the soil is particularly deep, of a darkish colour earth, with a sub-stratum of strong clay and some gravel. Beyond this, on the confines of the county

county, and in the small detached parts, including the Cotswold-Hills, a lime-stone prevails on the upper land, and a rich loam on the lower. To the south, between Worcester and Malvern, the general character of the soil is a clay, mixed with gravel in different proportions; the former prevailing in the lower, and the latter in the higher situations. To the left of this line, including Malvern Chase, a deep surface of clay is found in some places; in others, a rich loam, inclining to sand; sub-stratum *supposed* to be marl. To the right, till we approach a central point between the west and north, the proportion of clay increases gradually, till at last, a strong clay occurs; this again becomes gradually more gravelly, till it joins the light sands on the north. Below, partly marl, partly soft sandy stone, with some lime-stone, is found. In each of these districts, some very rocky land, and in most, some loose stony soil, or what is here called stone brush, or brash, is met with; but no where are there any traces of flint or chalk."

MINERALS.—*Salt.*—For incidental notices of the salt springs and salt works of DROITWICH, see the heads, *Manufactures, Covenants*, and *Manures*, ensuing.

SUBJECT THE SECOND.

POLITICAL ECONOMY.

STATE of APPROPRIATION.—On this subject, Mr. Pomeroy has collected sundry items of information. In the section, "Waste Lands," p. 17, the subjoined extract appears.—"The waste lands in this county, contain, at a very low computation, from 10 to 20,000 acres: the medium 15,000. They are in general depastured by a miserable breed of sheep, belonging to the adjoining cottagers, and occupiers, placed there for the sake of their fleeces, the meat of which seldom reaches the market, a third fleece being mostly the last return they live to make.

"Most of the common, or waste land, is capable of being converted into tillage of the first quality; of this description, Malvern Chase, extending some thousands of acres, and enriched by the soil and manure washed down from the extensive sheep walks on the adjoining hills, and above all, well supplied with the waters of their numerous springs, stands foremost; nor is there in this county

county (rocks excepted) a part not accessible to the plough, but would produce most excellent timber. As to the present mode of commonage, it is so radically bad, as not to admit of improvement, without a total alteration."

In the section "Inclosures,"—P. 15. "The lands are in general inclosed: here are, however, some considerable tracts in open fields. The most extensive are in the neighbourhood of Bredon, Ripple, and to the east of Worcester.

"The advantages from inclosing common fields, have been evidently very considerable; some few objections have been started, but they do not appear, on the whole, to have considerable weight: the rent has always risen, and mostly in a very great proportion; the increase of produce is very great, the value of stock has advanced almost beyond conception; in one parish alone, where the quantity inclosed has been pretty considerable, it is stated on unquestionable authority, to have amounted, in sheep and wool only, to full 1000l. a year. The improvements that may be made in stock in general, if properly attended to, are too obvious to be insisted on: it may be said in general terms, that there is but one opinion throughout the county on this subject; indeed it is in inclosures alone, that any improvement in the line of breeding in general can be made." Again, p. 16.—"Considerable inclosures have been made of late, some by authority of Parliament, others by mutual consent of the parties interested in them; more would certainly take place, were it not for the expence which attends the procuring Acts of Parliament for that purpose. A division of some of the common fields and meadows is under consideration."

In the section "Woods, &c."—P. 21. "The smaller tracts of woodland are chiefly inclosed, and under the management of the proprietors; some of the larger are thrown open, after a certain number of years from the last cutting; and the freeholders claim the privilege of turning in horses, horned cattle, &c. The injury this practice must do the young timber trees, is very great; nor can the advantage to those who claim the privilege, in any degree be thought to compensate it."

And, in the Appendix, Mr. Darke (one of the gentlemen to whom lists of queries had been submitted) furnishes some striking and valuable facts, concerning the unappropriated, and partially appropriated, lands of his neighbourhood;—the border of Glocestershire. I insert them in the order in which they stand.

App.

App. p. 2. "The lands being in common fields, and property much intermixed, there can be of course but little experimental husbandry; being, by custom, tied down to three crops and a fallow: first, barley, second year, beans (which always produce abundantly), or clover or vetches, which are ate off as green crops by the horses, tied with stakes and ropes, made with the rhind of wych hazle (a nasty habit peculiar to the Vale of Evesham); yet there are well-informed gentlemen, who highly commend this mode of husbandry. The third, wheat, which is sown on the bean stubble, or clover sward; and this mode invariably succeeds better than sowing it on fallow ground—a doctrine in general disbelieved by those who are strangers to the Vale of Evesham, so remarkable for its high ridges and deep furrows.

"The mixture of property in our fields, prevents our land being drained, and one negligent farmer, from not opening his drains, will frequently flood the lands of ten that lie above, to the very great loss of his neighbours, and community at large. Add to this, that although our lands are naturally well adapted to the breed of sheep, yet the draining, &c. is so little attended to in general, that out of at least one thousand sheep annually pastured in our open fields, not more than forty, on an average, are annually drawn out for slaughter, or other uses: infectious disorders, rot, scab, &c. sweep them off, which would not be the case if property was separated. Draining the lands, is the principal, and first good effect from inclosures. In our uninclosed hamlets, the meadow and pasture are fairly proportioned to the arable, which is, on a computation, about one thousand six hundred acres: the pasture one thousand three hundred, and the Avon meadows eight hundred. There are, besides, five hundred acres of commonable lands, which are of little or no value; being over-stocked, produce a beggarly breed of sheep, of no use to the owner, for being constantly brought off the high lands in autumn, to pasture and feed on the lands subject to floods, they are there baned, which consequently prevents the public from that produce which might assist population and commerce."

App. p. 3. "In other hamlets, there are commons for young cattle; these are usually overstocked, consequently the breeds of no note; nor will they be improved, unless the commons and fields are inclosed; we should then vie with our neighbours, in the best breeds; our meadows, rich from the washing of the manure and sheep-folds of Warwickshire, and the Vale of Evesham, would naturally enlarge

enlarge the growth of our stock, and excite in us emulation in our breeds."

Same p. "Now I am noticing meadows, if ever an inclosure takes place, the meadows should be lotted, to lay property together, but not divided by fences."

Mr. Darke is here speaking of *common* meadows,—a species of property that is unknown, in many parts of the kingdom. In situations where they lie dry, and do not require ditches to drain them, Mr. D's idea (which is to me—new) may be right:—I mean, where it may be eligible, to continue them in a state of perennial mowing ground. Much land, and expence of fencing, would be saved,—and good drying ground be preserved. The aftergrass would, of course, become a stinted pasture.

App. p. 4. "I have every reason to speak in praise of inclosures: about twenty years back, I obtained an act to inclose a parish in Gloucestershire, of strong clay lands; my allotment was about four hundred and fifty three acres, which, in its uninclosed state, averaged about eight shillings per acre, and will now bring upwards of thirty shillings. We must allow some part of the increase to the times, but the improvement is greatly owing to its turning from indifferent arable to most excellent pasture. Before the inclosure, the cattle and sheep were infamous; they are now of the first quality. My zeal for inclosures has carried me from Worcestershire to Gloucestershire. I hope the digression will be excused. From my commencement of farming, I have converted five hundred acres and upwards, of arable land, into pasture, and greatly increased its value." *

App.

* It will only be fair, however, to hear what Mr. Oldaker (tho he may write like a prejudiced man) has to say on this subject.

App. p. 10. "In regard to new inclosures, I have known farms not worth the old rent after an inclosure; and I have known others, nearly double the rent; but this must arise from the high or the low price they were let at before the inclosure took place. It can hardly be said to have paid common interest for the expence attending it in this neighbourhood. Where a proprietor had several small farms, to save the expense of dividing into small pieces, and repairing a number of small old buildings, by turning the whole into one, he may perhaps find an advantage. How far such practices, which must tend to depopulate, and in a measure monopolize, are a national concern, I will not pretend to determine In poor lands, when inclosed, the quality and quantity of corn will increase; but in good lands, the quality, when the fences are grown up, will not be so good, and the quantity no more. There is certainly a great opportunity to improve stock,

in

App. p 5. "Very few inclosures have been made in this district of the county; but as we lie at the extreme southern part, we are intersected on all sides by Gloucestershire, where there have been various inclosures, some very near; and in general, where they have been completed fifteen or twenty years, property is trebled, the lands drained; and if the land has not been converted into pasture, the produce of grain very much increased; where converted to pasture, the stock of cattle and sheep wonderfully improved. Where there are large commons, advantages are innumerable, to population as well as cultivation, and instead of a horde of pilferers, you obtain a skilful race, as well of mechanics as other labourers."

I think it proper to remark, here, that when ever Government may have leisure and inclination, to institute an enquiry, with a view toward a more civilized and rational plan of appropriation of the kingdom's territory, than at present exists, Mr. Darke's observations may be admitted as good evidence.—As a proprietor, an active magistrate, I believe, and an occupier, on a large scale, and for a length of years, he is of course well acquainted with the entire range of country concerns.

MANUFACTURES.—P. 27. "The principal manufacture of this county, is that of gloves; carried on chiefly at Worcester. It employs a considerable number of men, and a much larger proportion of the working women and girls of the city, and county round to the extent of seven or eight miles, from the age of eight or nine, and upwards. Any calculation of their number, must be extremely vague; it is, however, at a certainty so great, as to be severely felt through the neighbourhood.

"The hands employed at Worcester, in the china, and carpet

in an inclosed farm, which cannot be the case in uninclosed fields and commons." Again.—"It is reckoned to take about five years rent to inclose a farm.

"In the Vale of Evesham, and neighbourhood, the inclosures have very much decreased population, and every year will have still less occasion for labourers. This will be more the case, where the farms are converted from small into large ones; but where large commons and waste lands only have been inclosed, it must tend to increase population."

It is to be remarked here, that the instance above mentioned, by Mr. Darke, is among the comparatively few, in which rich deep-soiled, *grazing-ground land,* has been converted, after inclosure, into perennial pasture ground; thereby, of course, reducing the produce of corn, and the population, *of that particular part of the country.* See p. 268, aforegoing, on this subject.

carpet manufactories, are not very numerous; those employed at Kidderminster, in the latter business, are considerably more so. The carpet manufactory may be properly considered as a part of the œconomy of that town and neighbourhood. On the confines of Warwickshire and Staffordshire, many of the lower class are employed in the manufacture of nails; others, in that of needles and fish-hooks.

"The manufacture of salt at Droitwich, is chiefly deserving notice, from the immense revenue, compared with the size of the place. It pays annually to government, the lowest average, about per ann. That of glass, at Stourbridge, is very considerable, and employs many hands. There are also some iron works and collieries. Upon the whole, though this county is far inferior in its manufactories, to some of the adjoining ones, the numbers engaged in this line, bears no small proportion in that of its inhabitants; and their effect on its markets, and the value of the landed property, must be very great; nor does there appear to be room to doubt, but that they have uniformly operated to the advantage of agriculture*."

TITHES.—I insert the following passage, tho I confess I do not clearly see its practicability. But I am willing to draw together every idea that may, in any way, seem to lead to a rational and equitable substitute for tithes.

P. 43. "If the payment of tythes in kind, and mortmain tenures, are found obstacles to improvement, might not such obstacles be removed, by a law, enforcing a composition for tythes, to be assessed, not by the value of any particular estate, but by the average value of a considerable district, and re-assessed at different periods; confining the assessment to the value of the land in a common course of husbandry; that is, excluding all extraordinary improvements, such as buildings, plantations, &c. and by regulating renewals of the tenures under the church, in the same manner as the proportion of rent claimed as a fine, being ascertained by the value fixed for the tythes of the district."

This is still but tithing the rent. See p. 310, aforegoing.

ROADS.

"* One great effect which manufactures have upon agriculture, is that of raising the price of meadow land; and hence much arable land is necessarily converted into pasture."

ROADS. An admirable institution has been set on foot, by gentlemen in the "Vale of Evesham" and its environs; for the better management of the roads of that district; so far as they are personally concerned in them; and to enforce, by legal means, the improvement of those roads over which their own influence cannot prevail; by which means, we are told, p. 23,—"they have the pleasure of seeing their district assume a new face under their auspices; and instead of its being studiously avoided, as formerly, from the inconvenience, and even danger of travelling, they have now to congratulate themselves and the public, on a very safe and pleasant communication."

In the Appendix, p. 15, are inserted—"Rules and Regulations for the establishment of a Society to be called the Vale of Evesham Road Club."—And as nothing seems more likely to improve the roads of the kingdom at large, to the required degree of perfection, than similar establishments, I will here extract what may be useful in setting on foot such institutions.

Art. I. "That the Society shall commence, on the first Thursday in September 1792, and the members thereof consist of persons resident in the neighbourhood of Bredon Hill.

Art. II. "That the members shall dine together, on the first Thursday of every succeeding month.

Art. III. "That any three or more of them shall have the power of transacting business relating to the Society.

Art. IV. "That all who become members, shall accede to an agreement of the inhabitants of Beckford, Overbury, Kemerton and Bredon, entered into the 18th of September, 1788, in the following terms:

"We the undersigned inhabitants of Beckford, Over-
"bury, Kemerton and Bredon, feeling very sensibly the
"inconvenience arising from the bad state of the roads in
"our neighbourhood, and wishing to act cordially and
"unitedly, in the best manner, for the improvement of
"the said roads, do declare, that it is our intention from
"this time, to exert our utmost influence, by advice and
"example, to put the laws relating thereto in strict exe-
"cution; and for this purpose, we will be ready and will-
"ing to serve (at least in our turns), as Surveyors of the
"Roads in our respective parishes; and we strongly re-
"commend to the parishioners to appoint such persons,
"as shall be most likely to execute the duties of that
"office, with regularity, impartiality, and diligence.

Signed, "William Wakeman, John Darke, James
"Martin,

" Martin, R. Speediman, John Parsons, Henry White, " J. Biddle, Roger Parry, William Heekes, William Free- " man, Thomas Gibbs, Charles Tidmarsh, John Bricknell, " John Alcock, Isaac Nind.

" The above Subscribers give notice to all parishes ad- " jacent, that if the repairs of their respective roads are " not more seriously attended to than they have been " (the Statute Labour for which, duly performed, will in " a great measure be sufficient), they are determined to " unite in indicting such defaulters.

" That in order to excite the steady attention of the several members of this Society, to the improvement of the roads in their respective parishes, and diffuse a general knowledge of the plan and intent of this institution; these rules and regulations, together with the following advice to Surveyors, shall be printed on a large paper, in the most legible manner, and framed and fixed up in the hall or most frequented room, in the dwelling-house of each of the said members, as well as on the church doors, in the markets, and other places of public resort, in their neighbourhood."

In their *advice* to *Surveyors* (also inserted in the Appendix) I perceive not much (though of considerable length) that can be useful to the public at large. Nevertheless, a few of them are entitled to a place, here.

In a deep-soiled district, like that of the Vale of Evesham, (where in general, I believe, no hard foundation can be reached, by merely removing the soil) the following method of forming a road may be eligible.

App. p. 16.—" The intended road being laid out, the surface of the natural soil should not be reduced to a dead level, but left rounded from the trenches that are made to carry off the water; it should then be laid with small brushwood (such as is cut from the hedges), the twigs lying crosswise the road, or with furz, or both mixed, and upon that the stones, placing the largest at the bottom, and decreasing in size to the gravel, or whatever small materials you have for the last finish to the covering."

In a district, where the materials of roads are stones of a soft friable nature, when raised out of the quarry, but which acquire hardness by being exposed to the air:—the following regulation is admirable.—" No stone should be used for making or repairing the roads, but such as has been exposed to the air for twelve months at least; as when first taken out of the quarry, it is soft and mouldering."

They should of course be broken, as soon as they are raised,

raised, that the labor may be the less, and that the atmosphere may have a greater surface to act upon.—With stones that are liable to perish by the weather, a contrary line of conduct ought to be pursued.

For the purpose of filling up ruts, and otherwise keeping the surface of the road in due order, the Society recommend—"that each parish should leave a sufficient number of labourers for that particular work; and that each of those labourers should be appointed to take care of a certain portion or extent of road, and to keep the part allotted to him in perfect order."

On *passing* the *accounts* of road surveyors, the Society have pointed out some wise regulations.—App. p. 16. "If the method prescribed by the general Road Act, of the 13 Geo. 3. for the stating and settling of Surveyors' accounts, was more strictly observed, instead of the manner too generally adopted, of passing those accounts, without any previous examination, at the special sessions held annually for the highways, when (by reason of the short time allotted for the business of that meeting) it is impossible for the magistrates to enter into a thorough investigation of such accounts; it might have a very serviceable effect upon the conduct of Surveyors, by compelling them to a more punctual and regular performance of so necessary a part of their duty: it is therefore to be wished, that the magistrates who attend at such special sessions, would resolve in future, that all Surveyors shall render a full and particular account, as well of all work and duty performed by teams and labourers; as also of all assessments, compositions, and sums of money by them received and expended, for the amendment and preservation of the highways within their respective parishes; and that no such accounts be passed at such special sessions, unless it shall appear to have been previously produced at a public meeting of the inhabitants (testified by the signature of at least two of them), and afterwards examined and allowed by a proper magistrate, according to the directions of the beforementioned Act of Parliament: and, in order that all the Surveyors may have due notice of such resolutions, it is proposed, that the same be inserted in the instructions subjoined to their warrants of appointment. It may be reasonably presumed, that the Legislature intended the Surveyor's accounts should be examined by the nearest magistrate, who, from his own observation, or from local evidence, might be able to judge in what manner the duty had been performed."

MARKETS.—In the Appendix, Mr. Oldaker of Fladbury, (who would seem to have had a list of queries delivered to him), says. p. 11.—" I will here beg leave to give my opinion, that a general regulation by weight, would be much preferable to equalizing the measure, for several reasons; but a most principal one is, it would be a much fairer way to set an assize of bread from, than measure; for I know very well, that a bushel of wheat in Worcestershire, of the growth of 1791 or 1793, will make on the average, seven pound of dough, or six pound of bread, more than the produce of 1792."

Surplus Produce.—Mr. Pomeroy has been particularly full and intelligent, on this subject. How far his statements are accurate (they being of course, in great part, the fruits of enquiry) I cannot say. Some thought appears to have been bestowed upon them.

P. 28. " The produce *exported*, is chiefly fruit, cyder, perry, and hops; a considerable number of fat cattle, sheep, and hogs, are also sent to London, and the large manufacturing towns of the counties of Warwick and Stafford. The quantity of wool is estimated at two thousand packs, 240lb. each, value from 10l. to 16l. per pack. But the principal source of wealth, in its commerce with the different parts of this, and other countries, arises from its fruit, perry, cyder, and hops. The former is now growing into an article of considerable consequence, and deserves particular attention, more especially as the demand for it in the large manufacturing towns of the north, and all the intermediate country, increasing yearly, promises a certain and ample recompense for the greatest exertions that can be made in this branch of its rural economy. Some idea may be formed, from the following circumstances, of the quantity exported, and the price it bears. The average tonnage of fruit sent by water into the north, for the last three years, amounts to fifteen hundred tons; (in the year 1791 it exceeded two thousand and ninety-four tons), each ton weighing equal to fifteen horse pots, the measure by which it is commonly sold, making twenty-two thousand five hundred pots. The pot holds about five pecks.

" The fruits sold in Worcester market, is allowed to amount to (and the circumstance is fully confirmed by the rent given for the toll paid on it) one thousand pots per week, on an average of the last five months of the year.

" In ascertaining the value of the produce, as an article of commerce, the two preceding months may be safely included;

cluded; for though the number in these certainly falls short of this estimate, the superior value of the early fruits will amply compensate for the deficiency. Seven months, or thirty weeks, at one thousand pots per week, give thirty thousand—supposing one half of this quantity to be sent by water, and making part of the home consumption, there will remain fifteen thousand pots not accounted for in the estimate of the water carriage. Under these two heads, some part, the produce of Herefordshire, is included, perhaps an eighth of the whole; which, when deducted, leaves the number twenty-eight thousand one hundred and twenty-five pots. Not more than half the produce in this line exported, is supposed to pass through Worcester; allotting, therefore, to the markets of Bewdley, Kidderminster, Bromsgrove, &c. &c. and the rest of the county, north of this city, thirty thousand pots, the whole amount may be fairly estimated at fifty-eight thousand one hundred and twenty-five pots. The price varies considerably, from three shillings to six shillings the pot, and some of the inferior sorts, under. Four shillings is deemed a low average.

"The quantity of cyder exported, as far as can be collected from the opinions of several principal planters and merchants, may amount to about ten thousand hogsheads, of one hundred and ten gallons; the average price for about ten years past, 3l. per hogshead, as it is delivered from the planter to the merchant. The delivery is often a circumstance of considerable consequence, as they frequently live ten, twelve, or fifteen miles apart. That is the price of the greater part of the cyder sent out of the county; there are some few particular sorts, such as styre and golden pippin, which bring from 7l. to 10l. per hogshead; the quantity of these is not very considerable. The quantity of perry falls short of that of cyder, perhaps it does not reach one-tenth; but little is exported excepted the prime sorts, such as the real taynton squash, huffcap, &c. these bring from 4l. to to 7l. per hogshead.

"The number of acres in the county, planted with hops this year, is 5988. The lowest average, places the produce, at six cwt. per acre; the lowest average price above 3l. 3s. Calculating upon these low estimates, the whole may with much probability be stated with the exports."

P. 21. "There are employed every week, on an average, from twenty to thirty horses, in conveying the productions of the butter and poultry-market from Worcester alone, for the consumption of Birmingham and its neighbourhood, besides what is procured from the markets of Droitwich and

and Bromsgrove. Those employed in carrying vegetables and other produce, raised by the Evesham gardeners, are still more numerous."

SOCIETIES of AGRICULTURE.—Under this head will properly come the following reflections.—P. 45. "In regard to exciting a spirit of improvement, *premiums on produce*, although approved of by many, are not, perhaps, the best judged rewards. Land being of such different value, some worth ten shillings, and others worth thirty shillings, and even upwards, all hopes of a prize, would be given up by ninety-nine people out of an hundred, unless they were to rob one part of the farm to enrich a particular spot."

SUBJECT THE THIRD.

RURAL ECONOMY.

DIVISION THE FIRST.

TENANTED ESTATES,

Their IMPROVEMENT and MANAGEMENT.

IMPROVEMENT of ESTATES.—*Consolidating intermixed Lands.*—I insert the following suggestion of Mr. Oldaker of Fladbury, without comment.—App. p. 12. "There is one inconvenience much against improvements in farms, where the old inclosures run very small, as from one to three or four acres each, intermixed, and the owners not inclined to accommodate each other, which I am very often sorry to see; but when they are disposed so to do, circumstances often occur to prevent it, such as part belonging to leasehold property, and part freehold. An Act of Parliament, appointing Commissioners for such purposes, in general might remedy it."

Draining.—Mr. Darke, in his paper inserted in the Appendix to this Report, mentions a successful instance of improvement, by open drains. App. p. 6. "The most skilful drainer I know in Worcestershire is the present Earl of of Coventry: his part of the County was a morass, not half a century back, and is at this present time (though formerly a moorish, fœtid soil), perfectly dry, sound for sheep, and other cattle. He has but few under-drains. His principal drains are open formed, thus:

turfed to the bottom, so that cattle can graze without any loss of herbage; no water ever stands: and Croome is now noted for its dryness."

Where a moory soil of moderate depth rests on a firm basis, *in* which the channels of the drains can be formed, deep enough to prevent the water from communicating with the spungy mold, this method of laying the land dry is very ingenious; and may evidently be eligible, in several situations.

IRRIGATION.—Altho the watering of lands is not an established practice of Worcestershire, it has the credit of exhibiting one instance, whose general economy, and judicicious regulations, might well be held out as a pattern, to any county or district, of the kingdom.

Mr. TURNER in a letter to Mr. Pomeroy, the substance of which is printed in the Appendix, gives the following concise, yet clear, description of this masterly work.— App. p. 1. "The plan of watering the lands in this neighbourhood, belonging to the FOLEY family, is shortly as follows:—It is in the first place necessary to observe, that all the mills on the brook, or stream of water, as soon as it enters on their property, until it unites with the river Stour, for near three miles, belongs to them, of course they have the controul of the water. At the upper end of the stream, are three or four water-courses, made for several miles upon a level to the different farms that are watered, and the old stream divided in a manner proportioned to the quantity of land each course is intended to water. The farms that receive this valuable acquisition, are eight or nine, and the quantity of land watered upon the whole of them, is between three and four hundred acres. The quality of the soil, in general, is a very light sand, and many parts of it mixed with gravel: by the division of the stream as above, each farm has its portion of water repeated from two days to a

week

week, every three weeks throughout the year; and in order to prevent the least dispute between the tenants, respecting the distribution of the water, a person is appointed to turn it from one person's land to the next in turn, at certain stated times fixed for this purpose.

The farmer then takes to the management of it, and floods such part of his lands as is generally prepared to receive it."

EXECUTIVE MANAGEMENT of Estates.—*Tenancy.*—P. 9. "The estates are, in general, tenanted, and mostly by tenants at will, with no other restrictions but those which custom has introduced. The landlords appear, in general, to have great objections to granting leases: when granted, they chiefly are what are called running leases, for twenty-one years, determinable every seven."

P. 25. "It has been observed that there is an objection among the proprietors in general of this county, to the granting of leases. An ill-grounded jealousy on the part of the landlord, and the frequent disputes, and law-suits, occasioned by the present vague mode of drawing up these covenants, and the difficulty or trouble of drawing them up in such manner, as to adapt them properly to the peculiar circumstances of each farm, are the principal source of this opposition. Those granted, are generally for twenty one years, determinable every seven, at the option of either party; some for shorter terms, and determinable at shorter periods."

The following remarks I insert, here, with some hesitation.—P. 26. "That state of independence in which a long lease is supposed to place the tenant, is no longer a grievance, when he does his duty by the farm; it is from the negligent or dishonest occupier alone, that any thing is to be apprehended; and, *could the present tedious and expensive course necessary to eject the tenant, not complying with the conditions of this agreement, be altered, and the proceedings be conducted in a more summary way*—perhaps by a verdict of twelve neighbours, before an adjoining justice—this difficulty might be wholly removed. Those misunderstandings also, which arise where nothing dishonest is intended by either party, would be greatly diminished, were the simple language of common conversation introduced, instead of the present circuitous and intricate language of the law. The difficulty and trouble of framing leases adapted to the peculiar circumstances of each farm, would not, perhaps, be found so great, as at first sight they may appear to be: one form, drawn up by a person well acquainted with the business of a neighbourhood, might, with

with little variation, serve a considerable district. The principal source of this objection seems to be this, that leases are, in general, drawn up by professional gentlemen, who, having but few opportunities of more minute information, are under the necessity of copying from those who have gone before them."

Covenants.—P. 25. "The land-tax and repairs are paid by the landlord. He reserves the timber trees. The restrictions by which the tenant is bound, are, not to break up the meadow or old pasture grounds; not to sow more than a certain quantity of the tillage, and that proportioned to what he may be supposed to be able to manure properly with the produce of the estate; to spend all the hay, straw, green fodder, and dung, on the premises; or if hay or straw are sold, to procure a proportionate quantity in return, and to leave the farm in a proper course of husbandry. These are the general clauses by which the tenant is bound. Others, in some instances, are introduced, adapted to the peculiar circumstances of the estate, but they are not such as can convey general information."

DIVISION THE SECOND.

WOODLANDS.

WOODS and HEDGEROW TIMBER.—P. 20. "The extensive woods and forests of this county, so very considerable in early times, have almost disappeared. Feckenham Forest has sunk entirely under the continued demands of the salt works at Droitwich; these, however, having been worked for years with coal, that demand ceases. The woods of Hagley and Uffmore, are still of considerable extent, and some idea of the former abundance may be formed as yet, on those parts which border on Herefordshire. Through a considerable part of the county, small tracts of woodlands are frequent, and they furnish timber, chiefly oak and ash, with some beech, of excellent quality. The hedge-rows are every where crowded with elm, and though the present custom of lopping and pollarding must certainly injure their growth, they often produce timber of considerable dimensions.

sions. Elm is considered as the principal growth; there is, however, in many parts, as fine oak and ash as the kingdom produces.—The principal uses peculiar to this county, to which the underwood is applied, are hop-poles, and the making of charcoal for the iron works."

DIVISION THE THIRD.

AGRICULTURE.

FARMS.—P. 9. "The farms are small, from 40*l.* to 300*l.* a year: there are certainly more under the former, than above the latter value."

Fences.—P. 16. "The new fences are chiefly made with hawthorn, secured by post and rails; on the Bredon and Cotswold Hills they are of stone."

Homesteads.—Nothing appears on this subject, except that their situations are generally too low; and excepting that the middling and lower sized farms are much in want of sheds for cattle, in winter, p. 24.

OCCUPIERS.—P. 9. "The number of gentlemen who occupy land, has increased considerably of late; and some there are, who hold forth very laudable examples of experimental improvement."

PLAN of MANAGEMENT,—and GENERAL STATE of HUSBANDRY.—On these topics, I register the following scattered remarks.

Section, "Mode of Occupation."—P. 9. "The land, if the waste be considered as a part of the pasturage, is, probably, very nearly divided between that and husbandry."

Section "Crops,"—P. 12. "Of the land appropriated to husbandry, nearly an equal quantity is employed in the production of wheat, and barley; rye is likewise sown on the light soils, chiefly to be grazed by sheep; the different kinds of pulse are also cultivated; vetches, both summer and winter, are common; sainfoin has been raised hitherto but in small quantities; oats are sown sparingly, under an idea that they impoverish the land; hemp and flax are likewise grown; but chiefly on small tracts, occupied by little proprietors."

The

The "Appendix," P. 3 (by Mr. Darke)—"Some of the finest pastures at Mitton and Bredon, are employed in feeding oxen of the best Herefordshire and Devonshire sorts, for the London markets. We likewise breed some of the best Gloucestershire hill sheep; we touched on the Leicestershire, but found them, (though handsome,) rather too small for our rich pasture. We feed what sheep we breed, for the London markets. Our other pastures are used, in general, in dairies; some of these are employed in making butter for the Birmingham markets, and a skim cheese they call two meals, or seconds; these sell for eight shillings per cwt. less than the one meal, or best making. The dairies that make best cheese, make no butter, but depend entirely on the cheese. Where they make the skim cheese, the land is deemed too rich for one meal, as it causes it to heave, and that produces a strong rank flavour."

Section, "Crops,"—P. 13. "Except in the common fields, no particular rotation of crops prevail: the peculiar circumstances of the seasons, &c. seem to determine, and ought to decide this point."

The "Appendix,"—P. 12 (by Mr. Oldaker)—"I have seen two farmers upon the same sort of soil, manage their land very differently, according to the custom of each county; yet both live well, and both get money."

In the section, "Spirit of Improvement," we have a list of—"Queries drawn up by an intelligent farmer, in Worcestershire;" which conveys to us, in a striking manner, the *existing state* of *Agriculture*, in that county.—P. 44.

"*Queries respecting the Improvement of Worcestershire.*

"Whether turnips, and cultivated grasses, might not be more cultivated, and with greater advantage?

"Whether turnips ought not always to be hoed, and kept clean?

"Whether marl might not be more advantageously managed, and more generally used?

"As the hop-grounds are of great consequence to the farmer, whether more labourers ought not to be employed in cultivating the hops, as well as other parts of the farm; for, without a sufficiency of hands, either the one or the other must be neglected?

"Whether the pasture grounds should not be cleared of the alders, and ash plantations made, and properly inclosed, on every farm, according to its size?

"Whether

"Whether the fallows do not follow each other too frequently?

"Whether potatoes ought not to be more cultivated?

"Whether beans ought not to be sown in drills, instead of broad-cast?

"Whether improvements in stock, ought not to be more generally attempted?

"Whether more cottages, for labourers, ought not to be built?"

See also the head, *Grain Crops*, ensuing.

WORKPEOPLE.—P. 17. "The hours of labour are, from six in the morning to six in the evening, during the summer; in some parts, they are from five till seven, with a proportionate increase of pay:—in winter, from day-break till the close of the evening. During the harvest months, there are no fixed hours of beginning, or leaving work. The average price of labour, with drink (beer, cyder, or perry), is a shilling a day, or fourteen-pence without, at the choice of the person employed.

"A true idea of the expence of furnishing drink, will not be formed from the proportion the two prices bear to each other, or from what is usual in most other parts: two gallons a day is now pretty generally considered as the fixed allowance to each man. In the harvest months there is no restriction. In extenuation of this abuse, it is said that a part is taken home to the families; but this, when it happens, may be set down as an exception to general custom. Hired servants have the same.

"The price of labour, mentioned above, is to be understood as that of common day labourers: those who are qualified to undertake, and are entrusted with the care of any particular part of the business, such as the management of feeding cattle, or the care of sheep, receive from ten to twelve shillings a week. Women have six-pence with, or eight pence without drink. The price of piece-work varies in different parts of the county; the customary daily wages being the rule by which it appears to be regulated. The yearly wages of an able man servant, are from 5*l.* to 7*l.* a year, exclusive of diet, washing and lodging; some few and those chiefly such as are entrusted with the care of the team horses employed on the farm, receive from eight to twelve guineas. Women servants from 50*s.* to 4*l.*"

WORKING ANIMALS.—P. 11. "The breed of horses is chiefly confined to those sorts that may be useful in the cultivation of the land; they are, however, much heavier, and

and of course slower, than appear necessary for that purpose. Perhaps the general construction of the ploughs, and the unwieldy weight of the waggons, together with the badness of many of the parochial roads, may be thought to render them necessary. From the number of horses kept in Worcestershire, and the quantity of food they devour, it is said that they consume two-thirds of the produce of the land."

See also the head, *Cattle*, ensuing.

MANURES.—On this subject, we find little or nothing to be noticed; excepting what relates to "foul salt," from the "brine pits" of Droitwich, in this county.—P. 34. "The brine pits of Droitwich afford a manure, and in such quantities, as would deserve attention, were it not for the tax laid some years back on foul salt. This now acts almost as a prohibition; its usefulness has been fully ascertained, when used judiciously. There are those in the neighbourhood, who, after considerable expence, prefer it to most others, and employ it, though subject to a tax of 4d. per pound on the spot. No argument against it can be drawn, from the effect which the constant draining from the banks of the Droitwich canal (often very highly impregnated with it) has on the herbage immediately adjoining, no more than from any other injudicious excesses, which must always be detrimental."

For opinions, respecting this matter, in Cheshire, see pages 25, and 143, aforegoing.

GRAIN CROPS.—On this main object of *agriculture*, little, very little, information has been collected, by the Board's Reporter. The subjoined short extracts, comprize the whole of it.

P. 15. "The seed-time for wheat, varies, from the beginning of October to the end of December—for barley, from the middle of March to the beginning of May—pulse, the latter end of February and beginning of March—winter vetches, the latter end of September; those for summer, March, April, and beginning of May; the former are generally found to answer best."

P. 33. "The average produce of the tillage, bespeaks ample room for improvement, on land equal to any the kingdom can boast, the highest seldom exceeding twenty bushels of wheat per acre, and falling frequently under fifteen: the average of the county at large, cannot be placed so high as fifteen—barley twenty five bushels on the poorer lands, up to forty five, as they improve;—oats and beans about the same;—pease very uncertain. The deficiency

ciency of the crops, considering the advantages of the county, is notorious; to account for it, would be rather an invidious task; something, however, may be suggested, and it is hoped, without offence."

FLAX.—I insert the following account, as it is almost the only one (except on orchards) which the Reporter seems to speak of, from his own personal knowledge.—P. 36. "If the growth of flax was more generally introduced on the middle soils of this county, much advantage might be derived from it. The prejudice under which it labours, has been noticed, and may render the following instance of the benefit to be gained from it, not unworthy of attention.

"On part of an estate held by the life of a very infirm man, after it had been almost wholly exhausted by successive crops of corn, flax was sown as a last resort—it thrived well, the invalid lived, wheat was tried again without manuring: the crop on it proved equal to any of those formerly gained after a moderate dressing. The unexpected success of this first attempt, induced the holder of the property to make farther trial of it; and such has been the uniform advantage arising from it, that in a very considerable district of the county of Devon, flax is now very frequently adopted as a very useful and lucrative shift crop."

This district of Devonshire has, hitherto, eluded my observation.

On the CULTIVATION of HERBAGE; or on the MANAGEMENT of GRASS LANDS;—I perceive nothing, in the Worcestershire Report, that is entitled to extraction. It is on the subject of *hops*, *orchards*, and *fruit liquors*, we are to *expect* from it much useful information.

HOPS.—When I formed my register of the practice of KENT, in 1790 (see p. 283, aforegoing) I was unacquainted with that of Worcestershire, respecting this crop. But, in 1797, previously to my publishing it, I took a cursory view of the latter practice, in order to catch any variations in the outlines of management, that might there exist; and thereby enlarge my ideas concerning the general subject.

In that transient view, I perceived a wide difference between the two districts, in what I have usually termed the SOIL PROCESS; namely, in the culture and management of the soil. In Kent, the plow is rarely used; unless to break up the ground for planting. Whereas, in Worcestershire, much of the work is done with that implement. Yet, in most other respects, the two practices are not unsimilar.

To speak of Mr. Pomeroy's Report of the Worcestershire

shire practice, relating to the hop culture, I have to say—that it does not *contradict* my own minutes, made on the spot. But that—viewing it as a register or record of a practice, for the purpose of conveying useful knowledge, concerning it, to the public at large,—it is extremely deficient. It is little more than a desultory account; such as we frequently meet with in the works of other travellers,—speaking of what has fallen, incidentally, under their notice. Little method, and no distinctness of arrangement is observed. Separate branches of the subject, and different operations belonging to it, being not unfrequently united in the same paragraph.

But Mr. Pomeroy had no *precedent* to go by, in regard to *hops*, as he and others of the Board's Reporters have had, with respect to *orchards*, *fruit liquors*, *dairy produce*, and other complex and difficult subjects in Rural Economy. For altho I *formed* my register of the Maidstone practice, in 1790, I did not revise and *publish* it, until some time after Mr. Pomeroy wrote his Report. Mr. P. is therefore the less to be censured, for the irregularity and insufficiency of his report of this practice. His instructor had no former work, to plagiarize, and pillage of HEADS, for *this* chapter. The CULTURE of HOPS had not, *then*, been publicly treated of, analytically, or in a scientific manner.

My register of the MAIDSTONE practice (see the Rural Economy of the SOUTHERN COUNTIES) comprizes, I believe, every essential topic relating to the culture and management of hops; and it is of course a *complete groundwork*, for studying and registering those of any other district.

In the district of CANTERBURY, I registered the *variations* of practice, peculiar to that department of the Kentish culture.

And, in the district of FARNHAM, in Surrey, I pursued the same line of conduct; noticing the several *varieties* of practice pursued, in that celebrated district, for the culture of what are termed *fine hops.*

It is now my intention to point out, in the best manner which Mr. Pomeroy's remarks, and my own observations, will enable me, the *peculiarities* of practice that are carried on, in WORCESTERSHIRE: and thus endeavor to raise the cultivation and general management of hops, in England, to that state of "perfection," which the Board's editor has been *talking* about*.

The

* The NOTTINGHAMSHIRE, or "North-clay," practice, only, now remains to be registered. The quantity, there raised, is inconsiderable,

The *district* which produces what, in the London market, is termed "Worcester hops," is not wholly comprized within *Worcestershire;* but extends into *Herefordshire* and *Shropshire;* being, in the first, confined to that quarter of it which borders on the two last mentioned counties.

On the *extent* of the "Worcester-hop" plantations I have no accurate information. Mr. P. in his section "Commerce," p. 30, says—"the number of acres in the county" (of *Worcester*) "planted with hops this year, is 5,988." As every grower of hops is legally obliged to enter, on or before a certain day, in every year, the number of acres he has in cultivation, the number, in each hop-growing district of the kingdom, and the proportional extent of the growth of each, may no doubt be readily ascertained, by a reference to the proper offices, or documents, of Government.

The *varieties*, or sorts, of hops, cultivated in Worcestershire, Mr. P. reports as follows.—P. 46. "The different sorts of this valuable plant, cultivated here, are ranged under three general heads: the red, the green, and the white. A various cultivation, the real source probably of these first distinctions, has introduced a variety of different species, though differing little more than in name and degree, of the same colour, shape, and size. There are two, however, in more particular esteem, both with the planter and merchant; the Golding Vine, brought from the neighbourhood of Canterbury," (Maidstone) "and the Mathon White, the name of which denotes it to be a native of this plantation, and of the parish of that name."

Respecting the *sites* of hop grounds, there, I perceived no uniformity of choice. Mr. P. remarks, p. 46,—"The plantations of this county are principally to the west of the Severn, increasing as they approach the banks of the Teame, and the confines of Herefordshire. The situations preferred, are a gentle descent, with a south, south-west, or western exposure, screened at a distance to the north and east by high ground, or plantations of timber; but not so as to prevent a free ventilation."—They are, however, seen in almost all *aspects;* but mostly in *low situations.*

The *soil*, on which Worcester hops are chiefly grown, is deep

able, when compared with that of the kingdom at large. In reviewing the Board's Reports, from the MIDLAND DEPARTMENT, some information concerning the North-clay hop-culture may perhaps be found.

deep red loam. Nevertheless, in the bottoms of vallies, they are observable on brown, waterformed lands; and some on black moory soil, as in Nottinghamshire.

Regarding the *subsoils* of those lands I have had no opportunity of examination; nor have I been able to detect any thing concerning them, in Mr. Pomeroy's Report; tho much of the prosperity and duration of a hop ground depends upon it.

The methods of *forming* hop grounds, in Worcestershire, varies considerably from that of Kent; so much, indeed, as to make it seem that thay had not originated from the same stock; or had not been copied from, or after, each other. But, on more mature consideration, it appears probable, that the present difference, observable in the two practices, have arisen from the dissimilarity of the soils, or rather of the substrata over which they were respectively matured; and from which the *established customs* of the two districts severally arose.

The present practice of the district of Maidstone was, doubtlessly, matured and established, on the *absorbent* lands of that neighbourhood;—that of Worcestershire, on the clayey loams of the hop district of that county;—a species of soil which I have, in various parts of the kingdom, and uniformly, found resting on a *retentive* base. Hence, on the lands of Kent, where no superficial drains were required, the soil was deposited *flat*:—whereas, in Worcestershire, where the substrata are not equal to the absorption of heavy and long continued rains, it was found expedient to relieve the soil from superfluous moisture, by artificial means;—by moulding the surface into *inequalities*, and placing the roots of the hops somewhat above the natural level of the ground:--moreover, forming channels, at proper distances from the roots, to carry off a redundancy of rain, superficially *.

The method which the Worcestershire planters have fallen upon, to adapt their practice to the given nature of their lands, is twofold.

The one is to gather some considerable part of the soil into hillocks of nearly a semi-globular form, *by hand*; and to plant the hops in the centers of these hillocks. This was probably the first successful expedient hit upon, in the *garden* culture

* The folly of the Kentish planters, in not pursuing the same method, on lands that require it (namely those with retentive bases) has been shown in its proper place. See SOUTHERN COUNTIES, vol. I. p. 188.

culture of hops, to answer fully the required purpose, on the *retentive* lands of *Worcestershire.*

But that laborious method requiring more hands than a merely agricultural and recluse situation could furnish, a more expeditious and practical method was struck out, to carry the Worcestershire plantations to a greater extent, than the hand-labor method allowed; namely, that of gathering the soil into narrow ridges, or beds, *with the plow;* leaving interfurrows, to carry off the superfluous rain waters, and give the hop plants the required geniality of situation, on the ridges, or middles, of the beds.

To this day, we see the larger grounds cultivated with the plow, the smaller, only, by hand.

In the *preparation* of the soil, the *plants*, or the method of *planting*, no striking difference, in the practice of the two districts, is observable.

The custom of breaking up the ground (for a fresh plantation) by trench-plowing, is, perhaps, more prevalent, on the retentive lands of Worcestershire, than on the absorbent grounds of Kent;—and this is perfectly consonant with the natures of those lands. The deeper the soil is broken, and rendered porous, the more genial will be the situation of the young plants, near the surface.

The *distance* of the plants, and the direction of the lines they are placed in, differ with the mode of cultivation. HILLOCKS—provincially "Tumps,"—are generally placed, aquincunx; the distance between plant and plant being, in this case, six feet, more or less;—on BEDS, the plants stand in rows, about half a statute rod, asunder; and about half that distance, in the rows. Hence, in either case, a statute acre receives upward of twelve hundred plants.

The plants, as in the Kentish practice, are either recent cuttings, or nursery plants; *one* of the latter, according to Mr. P. (p. 47.) being "sufficient for a stock;" that is, to be planted in each hillock: a practice (if really such) that is not, I believe, to be recommended.

In the *rearing* of young hops, I have perceived nothing of excellence, in the Worcestershire practice.

And but little in the *management* of *grown hops.* In *manuring*, the Worcestershire agrees with the Kentish method. The species of manure is chiefly compost of dung earth, and lime; which last appears to be freely used in Worcestershire; and probably with good effect.

In the operation of *Dressing;*—the HILLOCKS are thrown down, and the roots laid bare, with a large hoe,—provincially a "kerf;" which is used as a hack, or mattock.—

The

The BEDS are turned back from the plants with the plow.

In the business of *Poling*, I saw nothing to notice; excepting the prevailing practice of setting up only two poles to each plant, or hillock; and these very short, compared with those in use, in the southern counties.

In *training* the *Vines*, three, I found, was the usual number led to each pole. They are tied with dried rushes, as in the district of Farnham.

In *cleaning* the *intervals*,—of the HILLOCKS,—the kerf, or hacking hoe, is used. Those of the BEDS are cleaned with the plow.

Respecting the *diseases* of hops, I met with nothing in Worcestershire (or in the Worcestershire Report); excepting the practice, or the expedient, of laying the crowns of the roots bare, in winter, to "chill" them, and thereby to prevent, or check, the mould. I notice this; as I had it from an experienced planter; and as it agrees, perfectly, with my own conceptions, respecting this disease.

Picking.—This operation, it would seem, from Mr. P's very imperfect description of it (I did not see it) is performed, in the district under notice, somewhat in the same manner, as in the *Maidstone* quarter of Kent. The pickers are drawn from the surrounding country, mostly from Wales. Mr. Pomeroy speaks of their picking "six or eight bushels per diem:" (p. 49.) whereas in Kent, each grown person picks from fifteen to twenty bushels and upward, a day.

Drying.—Neither in the *kiln*, nor in the *operation* of drying, nor in that of *packing*, do I perceive, in Mr. P's account, any thing peculiarly excellent, in Worcestershire.

On the *produce* of hops, by the acre, I have found no notice, in the Report of that county. From the inferior number and size of the poles, we may conceive that the crops of Worcestershire are not, on a par of years, equal to those of the southern counties. The truth might be come at, by ascertaining the number of acres entered, and the quantity of hops paid duty for, in the several districts.

Of the *expence* of the Worcestershire hop culture, Mr. Pomeroy has bestowed the most ample share of attention; and, in doing this, has gone over the ground, a second time:—but still without bringing out any thing like accurate, *practical* information;—such, I mean, as will enable a man, who is a stranger to the culture of hops, to set about

about trying it on the lands which are in his occupation:—much less to improve and *perfect!* the management of those who are in the habit of cultivating them, imperfectly.—The total expence is summed up, thus:—P. 53. "The average of the expences in general, is thus estimated: that of workmanship, from twenty-five shillings to thirty shillings per acre: those of picking, drying, charcoal, sack and duty, thirty shillings per hundred weight."

On the *duration* of the Worcestershire hop grounds, Mr. Pomeroy, speaks, as follows:—P. 53. "When the hop grounds are come to perfection, it is the general practice to exclude every other growth, and trust to them alone for a return of the great expence at which they are cultivated. Under this management, those which have been uniformly attended to in their prime, and not weakened by over poling, will continue to produce plentifully from twenty to thirty years; and in some instances, much longer, care being taken to replace the stocks that accidentally decay. On the other hand, fresh grounds are generally allowed to produce the finest hops, and in greatest abundance. A question of some difficulty arises at what time it will answer best to give up the old, and plant new grounds, and must at last be determined by the peculiar circumstances of each plantation."

I examined a flourishing ground which I was assured was twenty years old.—Quere, is there any thing of a calcarious nature beneath the soils of the Worcestershire hop grounds; or does the lime, which is there used, in manuring them, serve to prolong their duration?

Mr. P. strongly recommends the planting of Orchard trees with young hops. But Mr. Pomeroy (as Mr. Duncumb) is an Orchardist; and not a hopist. There certainly is no better way of raising fruit trees, than in a hop ground. In Kent, this practice is not uncommon.

The almost only point of practice, which struck me as being new or excellent, in Worcestershire, was that of RENEWING A HOP-GROUND, by *planting* the *intervals* of a worn-out Plantation. Thus, not only obtaining young vigorous plants, but changing the situation of the roots; and thereby, giving them fresh ground to feed in.

On HOPS, as a CROP in HUSBANDRY, we have the following popular remarks, in the Report under notice.—P. 34. "In the hop districts, these most certainly engross too much time and attention; the plantations run away with the greatest part of the manure, whether home made or bought; and the hop planter, looks down on the other branches

branches of husbandry, as a sort of secondary business, deserving but little notice, when put in competition with his darling hops; and what is rather extraordinary, though no one wishes for a general full crop, every one exerts himself, and strains every mean to procure one for himself."

For GENERAL REMARKS on this subject, see my SOUTHERN COUNTIES, Vol. I. p. 288.

ORCHARDS, and FRUIT-LIQUOR.—From the reason alleged (see p. 354) for sending a stranger to make a Report of the practices of a distant county, we had some right to expect a full and well digested detail of those relating to orchards and fruit liquors, in that county:—such a one as would, at least, have surpassed, if not have rendered null and void, all that had previously been written on those subjects. The disappointment on perusing the Worcestershire Report, therefore, must necessarily be great. As an *account*, it falls short, even of that given of the hop culture of that county. See the last head.

The Reporter speaks of his experience; and, as the planter (it would seem) of an orchard, on retentive land, he has some merit; as will presently be shown. He likewise speaks, intelligently, on rearing stocks for apple orchards. It is moreover pretty evident that the Reporter has seen something of cider making, in the *eastern* part of Devonshire; where a sort of mongrel practice prevails;—a kind of *cross*, between the Somersetshire practice, and the best practice of Devonshire; namely, that established in the *western* parts of the county,—in the South-hams, and the district of Plymouth. See the RURAL ECONOMY of the WEST of ENGLAND;—districts, *West Dorset*, &c. and *West Devon*.

Nevertheless, from the evidence before us, it may seem that the Board (or the first President thereof) "sent" Mr. Pomeroy to teach the good men of Worcestershire the arts of orcharding and cidermaking!

Mr. Pomeroy's Report, however, concerning these topics, is not altogether devoid of good sense and discrimination. I will therefore extract and digest; that is to say, arrange in their natural order; the particulars that I find scattered in his account; and which, I conceive, may serve as useful additions to my own detail of the practices of superior managers in the MAY-HILL DISTRICT,—including parts of *Herefordshire*, *Glocestershire*, and *Worcestershire*;—the whole forming one united practice; without any precise distinction, in regard to the adventitious outlines of those counties. See the RURAL ECONOMY of GLOCESTERSHIRE.

Sites

Sites of Orchards, in Worcestershire.—P. 59. "The situations are generally chosen, so as to avoid the extremes, which either expose too much, from their elevation, or are liable to suffer from moisture, by being low. A gentle declivity, and south or south-west aspect, with a view to secure them from the chills of the north and east, is sought for: some distant screen also to the west, to protect them from the violence of the winds proceeding from that quarter, is required."

These remarks, I conceive, are neither practically, nor theoretically, just:—a *south-easterly* being, I believe, a favorite and proper aspect.

Soils.—P. 59. "Different soils are well known to influence both the quality and flavour of the produce; some attention has been paid, in this particular, but by no means all that it is capable of; the size to which the several trees naturally grow, and the predominant characters of the fruit, being but little attended to, in fixing on them for the culture of the different sorts. Those preferred are, the deep loamy lands, and strong clays, when perfectly dry. The former, on the soft sandy stone, which prevails in some of the western parts of the county, though without any considerable depth, is esteemed particularly well adapted for cyder plantations. The gravelly clays, frequent in many parts, are also deemed favourable. Marl, when duly meliorated, is in much esteem; perhaps, strictly speaking, many of the plantations, said to be on a clay soil, are growing on a meliorated marl." What is meant by "meliorated marl," as a *soil*, I do not understand.

Stocks.—(on which to graft orchard trees).—What follows, we find among the Reporter's didactic remarks, as a Devonshire planter.—P. 69. "The stock should be raised under the eye of the planter, or under his who has a still greater interest in the success of the plantation, the proprietor's of the estate. In the nursery, a proper distinction should be made, of those raised ftom the seed of the crab; those from an austere, and those from more mellow fruits; that they may be each applied to the growing of fruit of that character they suit best, or may be most likely to improve. There certainly is no sufficient reason why those from the crab should be uniformly preferred; the others may, without doubt, in many instances, have a preference: they decay sooner, but they also come to perfection sooner; and when the seed is selected with care, from young vigorous trees, as that of every kind ought to be, are found to possess every requisite to form handsome and

and lasting plants. Owing to inattention in adapting the stock to the size of the tree it is intended to support, it is very common to see the upper part of the trunk, that growing from the graft, several inches larger in girth than the lower; that which remains of the stock, forming a considerable projection where the graft was inserted.* Great care should be taken in the choice of stocks, independent of that to ascertain the seed from which they are raised. At a very early date, a pretty accurate judgment may be formed of the future success of the plant; at two or three years growth, many will be found to put out thorns; others will be disposed to throw up shoots from their roots; both should be invariably removed immediately."

Grafting.—P. 70. "An improved practice in grafting, has been lately introduced, and deserves to be more generally adopted. Instead of taking off the entire head of the stock, it is left on till the boughs are large enough to receive the grafts. An injury to which the trees in general are liable (splitting in the crown) is by this means in a great measure avoided."

I am happy to find that my injunctions, respecting this operation, have not been thrown away. See as above: Art. *Grafting.*

Planting.—Distances.—Mr. P. in prefacing his chapter on "Fruit Plantations,"—says (p. 58)—"The plantations may be considered as consisting of those in the old orchards, and those of later date; of those under the present improved management in the hop-grounds, and the single trees, either in hedge-rows or elsewhere."—And speaks rather slightingly of the first class; as being too much crouded with trees,—"their greatest distance being, whether in pasture or tillage, twenty feet between the rows; and on an average, much less betwixt the trees (frequently, no order in the planting is discoverable); the heads of course, have not sufficient room to spread, but are much entangled with each other, and form a shade so thick, as to injure materially, not only the fruit, but the crops also that grow beneath. In many instances, there is scarce an evil to which they are liable, though easily remedied with moderate attention, by which they have not suffered in a great degree."

Now, in Devonshire proper (as a fruit-liquor district) the

* This is most observable when a free-growing variety has been grafted on a crab stock. Apple trees, thus raised, I have seen bearing well, at a great age.

the prevailing distance is only fifteen to eighteen feet:—in some instances, not more than twelve feet.—See as above, Art. *Planting Orchards.**

In giving *directions* on planting, p. 71, Mr. P. says (generally, or without exception)—" six inches is the depth at which trees ought to be set."—There is no precise general rule (as has been said aforegoing) about the depth at which fruit trees ought to be planted. The soil, and more particularly the substrata, are ever to be consulted; as well as the nature and habit of the trees to be planted.

The following is the passage on planting, before alluded to. I have given Mr. Pomeroy the credit of the spirited instance of practice he relates. He speaks of it as if it were his own; and does not say any thing to the contrary.

P. 72. " The following instance of successful management in this particular, deserves to be recorded, more especially, as there are many situations in this county that now lie neglected, on which it might be adopted with every prospect of success. The ground planted was in pasture, with a gentle declivity; the soil, a shallow strong clay, on a solid calcareous marl. (?) About the middle of March, circular holes were opened, about four feet in diameter; the sod, with the surface soil, to the depth of about six inches, was thrown up on one side, on the other, that beneath, so as to leave an opening two feet deep: during the summer, the whole was repeatedly turned, and as winter came on, the earth being then dry, was thrown up separately into round tumps, by the sides of the opening; on the approach of the following spring, small gutters were made level with the bottom of the holes, opening on the surface below, so as to carry off all the water that could collect in these basons formed in the marl.† In planting the trees, the method already recommended, was observed, and the following winter, a circular trench, two feet wide and two deep, was dug out round the outsides of the first openings; the soil left exposed, and turned as before; and the ensuing summer, it was nearly filled with furze, before the soil was returned into it, with the view to keep it loose, and by that means invite the

* The Reporter has prudently left unnoticed the prevailing distance of Orchard Trees, in *his* Devonshire. I have not, at least, been fortunate enough to hit upon any mention of it in his Report.

† A very ingenious, but expensive, way of rendering land, naturally not well adapted to an *Apple* Orchard, sufficiently absorbent for that purpose.

the shooting of the roots. The gutter was also extended, and carefully preserved. On the adjoining ground, the situation and soil exactly similar, a plantation was made in the usual manner, the trees being set when the openings in the first were made. The latter was repeatedly manured, and managed throughout with attention: on the former, no manure has been used. The trees of each plantation were young and thriving, about the same age when planted, and every other circumstance, exclusive of the method of planting the same. The result of the experiment, for such it may be called, though accidental, is this—the trees of the former plantation are at this time (about fourteen years from the first opening of the ground) full twice the size, some even three times, that of those in the latter, which are nevertheless allowed to be well grown The difference of the produce is equally great. One circumstance, however, ought not to be omitted, and may probably be thought to have contributed in some measure to the superior growth of the former; they are trained so as to form low spreading heads, branching off at about two feet from the ground. The latter, on the contrary, to form what has been termed the upright besom-head, with a stem about five feet long, which is the usual height in the more western parts of the kingdom."

Some remarks on this extraordinary instance, in Orchard Planting, will appear at the close of this section.

For the *market* of sale fruit, see p. 366, aforegoing.

FRUIT LIQUOR.—Mr. P's account of the *Devonshire* practice; as it relates to the GATHERING (if not the MATURING) of fruit is contradictory of the legitimate practice of that county;—where, only, I have seen apples gathered *in rain;* and, generally speaking, *wet or dry.* It cannot well be otherwise; seeing the moistness of the climature, the lowness of the trees, and the tallness of the grass and weeds growing under them.

Grinding.—The following ingenious suggestion Mr. Pomeroy, I believe, may claim as his own. It is highly creditable to him, even tho it shall not be found eligible, in practice on a large scale.—Dr. Symonds, probably, took Mr. P's hint. See p. 339, aforegoing.

Having spoken of the *mill* of Worcestershire (similar to that of Glocestershire) Mr. P. says, p. 66.—" The only defect complained of in the mills, is this—they do not always break the kernel sufficiently (it must certainly be very difficult to fix so small, hard, and slippery a part, when

when dispersed through large quantities of soft matter in machines of such dimensions), nor is it probable any improvement of the present simple, but excellent construction, can wholly obviate it. Nor do the different contrivances hitherto proposed, seem likely to be very generally adopted. Such, however, is the price the more perfect liquors bear, as to make any moderate additional expence not of material consequence. In preparing these, picking the fruit, so as to separate that which has been damaged, is particularly recommended by the first managers. When this is done, might not the person thus employed, with a circular scoop, take out the core of the apple with but little additional trouble? The form of the instrument conceived under this idea, is as follows: the cutting part of it cylindrical, open at both ends, half an inch, or rather, more in diameter, and about two inches long; from each side proceeds an upright piece, three inches, or something longer than the largest fruit, to give room for the core to fall out between the top of the cylindrical part and the handle: this is formed by these two pieces meeting in the middle, and entering a cross piece of wood. It is conceived, that with little practice, this might be used with considerable expedition by children, at very low wages: bone would be the most eligible material to make it of. Should metal be used, the inside of the cylinder might be armed with two or more cutting edges, crossing the diameter, or rising along the inside; these would serve to divide the core still more. The kernel, thus separated from almost the whole of the pulpy part of the fruit, would, if ground by itself, be with more certainty brought under the action of the mill; or would be reduced with much less trouble, by any of the other machines that are used, or have been proposed, for grinding fruit. The method of using it would be this—a piece of deal, or any soft wood, must be fixed before the person employed, on which to rest the fruit, while the scoop is forced through it, and a pail, or bucket, underneath, to receive the core as it drops from the scoop, each forcing out that which preceded it. Should the idea, as thus stated, be approved, it may be carried still farther. The fluted iron rollers, used in some parts of Herefordshire for a cyder mill, might be adapted to this grinding of the kernel; and contrived, without much additional machinery, to work with the present mill, or the construction of the malt mill could be easily applied; the nut being fixed on the inner arm of the axle-tree, the box secured by a support, projecting

jecting above and below from the upright shaft. All this, however, is only conjecture, no attempts having been made as yet, to put it in practice. Should it be found to answer, or lead to any other improvement, by directing the attention of the ingenious to this defect of the present mill, every end proposed will be fully attained."

Pressing and *Casking*.—P. 63. "What follows, with respect to the making of cyder, must be understood as relating to the general practice of the county. When deemed in a proper state, the fruit is conveyed into the mill, and ground with great care, so as to reduce the whole pulp, rind and kernel, as much as may be, into an uniform pap. When removed from the mill, it is thrown into a vat, where it remains for a day or two,* till some degree of fermentation is observable.† It is then put into separate hair-cloths, each being, when the sides are raised over the contents, about six inches thick; and from six to ten of these are placed, one on the other, beneath the press, where they are continued, under a most powerful pressure, so long as any juice can be forced from them. The liquor is then put into other vats, and when the grosser fæces have separated, it is drawn off into casks of sixty-three gallons" (110 gallons) "each, leaving both the scum that had risen to the top, and what had settled to the bottom, behind. This being strained through a three-corner bag of linen, or woollen cloth, is added to the other liquor, and is supposed to be the best of the whole. This last part of the process is omitted till after the principal part of the liquor has been racked once, or oftener, as it is found necessary to check the fermentation; and the fæces separated at each time, are collected, and the whole strained as above. The liquor thus gained by straining, is found to possess considerable power to retard fermentation; it is accordingly added to each vessel, in proportion as it seems more or less disposed to ferment." ‡

FER-

* If this be really the "general practice" of Worcestershire, the ciderists, there, are much more accurate than those of Glocestershire and Herefordshire.

† This is new; and may be excellent. It leads to a wide field of experiment.

‡ This, too, if a "general practice," places the ordinary cidermakers, of Worcestershire, in an advanced state of forwardness, in their

Fermenting.—Of this, the *nicest*, most difficult, and "refined," part of cider making, the Reporter takes an elevated, if not a sublime, view.—P. 64. "The management of the fermentation and fining, is an art so refined, so enveloped in mystery, that mortal language is not equal to the describing of it; though communicated some way or other to numberless votaries, they have all acquired it they know not how; of course they cannot, perhaps will not, give any information on the subject."

The LAND of ORCHARDS.—In a comparison between what the Reporter names "the Devonshire practice," and that of Worcestershire, we find a *waste* of land, indirectly recommended to the attention of the Worcestershire orchardmen.—P. 68. "There are other circumstances in which the fruit management of the two counties varies considerably. The following instances may possibly be found deserving the attention of the planters of this.—The orchards of Devonshire are wholly appropriated to this produce; no other crop, except now and then a little garden stuff, is ever expected from them. It is, as before observed, a general clause in their leases, that they shall not be stocked; and though horses, and perhaps calves and pigs, are turned in, in the spring and beginning of summer, it is mostly a trespass upon the covenant. Sheep are universally excluded, and this, from a well-grounded apprehension, that the grease, or whatever it may be they leave on the trees after rubbing against them, is peculiarly prejudicial." *

In pursuance of the same recommendation, it would seem, the Reporter the more readily brought forward the extraordinary instance of success, in planting, inserted above; in which the trees are not of the "upright besom-headed" sort, but—"are trained so as to form low, spreading

their art. But this superior trait of practice, it is possible may have been caught, in *reading*, rather than in *observation*. For it cannot even be *hoped* that the Worcestershire Orchardmen, "in general," have been studying the superior excellencies of their art, in the RURAL ECONOMY of GLOCESTERSHIRE.

* SHEEP in ORCHARDS.—While the trees are young, and their barks smooth, thin, tender, and easily injured, such an apprehension may, doubtlessly, be well founded. But after the bark has acquired a hard firm texture, and a rough scabrous surface, little or no danger, I believe, is to be apprehended. In Somersetshire, I have observed flocks of sheep depasturing in orchards of a middle age; and, I have been informed, with advantage to their productiveness.

ing heads; branching off, at about two feet from the ground."—(p. 73). Thus ingeniously precluding the necessity of the clause in leases (aforementioned), to preserve them from injury.

Under free growing apple trees, with two feet stems, and loaded with fruit, scarcely a hare could pasture.

These *excellencies* of the Devonshire practice appear to have been brought forward, the more solicitously, as—"some liberty has been taken in reprobating what appears to be the general management of the county, with respect to the fruit plantations."—p. 69.

Having already spoken *my* sentiments, freely (that is to say with "liberty") yet faithfully and fairly, I trust, on this topic,—I now leave the point, respecting the application of the lands of orchards, to be settled by Mr. Pomeroy and Mr. Knight!—See p. 340, aforegoing.

For the MARKETS of fruit liquor, see p. 367, aforegoing.

HORSES. I find no information, regarding this species of livestock; excepting what I have copied, aforegoing, under the head, *Working Animals.* See p. 374.

CATTLE.—P. 38. "The cattle of the country, are chiefly bought in from those of Hereford, Stafford, and Gloucester. Those that have been bred, in general, are a mixed breed, without any particular improvement in view. Some few have now turned their attention this way, and the experiments are in judicious hands, such as will spare neither expence nor care, in perfecting them. Were more oxen introduced into the working stock, it would undoubtedly, be a very advantageous improvement. One objection of some weight is this, that they cannot be worked in yokes, upon the declivities of the present high ridges."

For a few particulars relating to the *dairy* of Worcestesshire, see the head, *Plan of Management*, aforegoing; p. 372.

SHEEP.—P. 10. "By far the greatest part are a small sort of sheep, without horns, and with mottled faces, originally from Wales. (?) They are interspersed throughout the county, and occupy almost universally the waste lands. In point of number, those called the Ross sheep, stand the next; most of which are brought out of Herefordshire, though they are now bred in the western parts of this county: they are short legged, short, but particularly broad, on the back, without horns; their fleeces, for fineness, are supposed to stand unrivalled throughout the kingdom.

"There

"There are a breed peculiar to the Cotswold Hills, part of which are in Worcestershire; these are very general in the southern parts; they are without horns, long woolled, and of large size; having broad loins and full thigh, but rather light in their fore quarters."

Of the other species of domestic animals, propagated in Worcestershire, we have no account, in this Report; and no other, I understand, has yet been published, relative to that county.

GLOCES-

GLOCESTERSHIRE.

THIS county, as Worcestershire and Shropshire, is divided by the Severn. It differs from Worcestershire, in having more Uplands within its limits, and in its Vale lands being more confined, in width; but of more extended length.

The NATURAL DISTRICTS of Glocestershire I have formerly separated and described*. They are as follow:—

The VALE of GLOCESTER;—extending from the Bredon hills, in the neighbourhood of Tewksbury, to the Matson hillocks, which contract the Vale lands, a few miles below Glocester; but including the Vale lands, only, that are situated on the east side of the river.

The "OVER SEVERN" DISTRICT.—This, tho divided from the last mentioned by the river, only, differs essentially from it in surface, in soils, and in management; partaking of the upper grounds of Herefordshire, rather than of the Vale lands of Glocestershire.

The VALE of BERKELEY.—This, likewise, is confined to the east, or rather the southeast side of the Severn; extending, downward, from the Vale of Glocester, to the broken, many-soiled Uplands, below Thornbury; which may be named the BRISTOL QUARTER of Glocestershire.

The FOREST of DEAN occupies the upper grounds, on the northwest side of the river, opposite to the Vale of Berkeley; being bounded, on the west, by the banks of the Wye;—namely a narrow line of the country, termed "WYE SIDE;" as a similar slip of lower ground, on the northwest bank of the Severn, (between the river and the forest, below Newnham) I have heard termed "SEVERN SIDE."

The COTSWOLD HILLS form the eastern boundary of the Vale of Glocester; rising from it with a steep front. The STROUDWATER HILLS, in like manner, bound the Vale of Berkeley: and the SOUTH WOLDS, the Bristol quarter:—the

* In the RURAL ECONOMY of GLOCESTERSHIRE.

the three forming a line of calcareous heights, which reach from near Evesham, in Worcestershire, to near Bath, in Somersetshire.

A skirt of low land, which lies at the southeast foot of the Cotswold Hills, is naturally a part of the Vale lands of Northwiltshire.

Having, in the years 1783 and 1788, resided many months, in Glocestershire, for the sole purpose of examining its respective districts—registering its several practices—preparing my register for the press—and superintending its printing,—it would be tedious and unprofitable to particularize my various routes across the country. The only parts, which were, then, left unexamined, are the last mentioned Vale lands, and the southwestern extremity of the county, near Bristol:—both of which I have since been over.

"GENERAL VIEW

OF THE

AGRICULTURE

OF THE

COUNTY OF GLOUCESTER,

WITH

OBSERVATIONS ON THE MEANS OF ITS IMPROVEMENT.

BY GEORGE TURNER, OF DOWDESWELL.

DRAWN UP FOR THE CONSIDERATION OF

THE BOARD OF AGRICULTURE AND INTERNAL IMPROVEMENT.

1794."

OF Mr. TURNER's QUALIFICATIONS, as a Reporter of what relates to *Agriculture*, proper,—and especially to that of the *Cotswold Hills*,—(on the margin of which Mr. T is, or was, a respectable practitioner) I can speak from some personal knowledge.

As a Reporter of GLOCESTERSHIRE, a man of less ability than Mr. Turner might have sufficed. The *harvest* had been

been already reaped. As a *gleaner*, Mr. T. is entitled to much commendation. His Report, tho concise, is not void of useful information.

Mr. Turner has properly divided the county into its NATURAL DISTRICTS, similar to those which I had previously marked out; and has reported them in the following order.

"Cotswold Hills,"—which may be considered as the district of *his* STATION.

"The Stroudwater Hills,"—an adjacent, and somewhat similar district.

"Vale of Berkeley,"—a low-lying dairy district.

"The Vale for a few miles round Glocester,"—namely, a small portion of the Vale of Glocester; and little more, it would seem, than the environs of the town.

"The Vale of Tewksbury, or what is more generally called the Vale of Evesham,"—meaning, of course, such part of the Vale of Evesham as lies within the county of Glocester.

"The Over-Severn district."—This indefinite appellation is applied to that part of the Vale of Glocester which lies on the west side of the Severn. The Reporter says (p. 46)—"It chiefly consists of the red lands of Herefordshire."—It is true that, in regard to soil, if not to management, it resembles Herefordshire rather than the Vale lands of Glocestershire that are situated on the east side of the river.

Away from the waterformed lands,—the present banks of the river,—the surface of the Over Severn District is broken; and the soil of a mixed quality; resembling, in these particulars, a mountain-skirt district,—which, in reality, it is;—being situated at the immediate foot of the May Hills,—a range of mountain heights that divide in this part, the counties of Glocester and Hereford.

SEEING the very few particulars that require to be extracted, in either of those districts, I will bring the whole into one arrangement, noting the respective district to which each article of information belongs.

The number of pages fifty seven.

No map, or other engraving.

SUBJECT THE FIRST.

NATURAL ECONOMY.

CLIMATURE.—P. 7. (Cotswold Hills)—"The Cotswold hills, are milder than could be supposed, from their heighth and deficiency of shelter. The harvest, this last season, was begun in many places, the first week in August, and pretty generally by the second. There is however a difference of from one to three weeks, in the ripening of corn, in the different parts of the district under survey, which cannot be accounted for by management, or any outward circumstances." See the RURAL ECONOMY of GLOCESTERSHIRE, &c. on this interesting fact.

P. 41. (Vale of Tewksbury)—" In climate, this district in general is earlier than round Gloucester."

SOILS.—P. 7. (Cotswolds) —" *The soil*—is various; the greater part, what is here termed 'stone brash,' a loam intermixed with stones, on a subsoil of calcareous rubble or rock: the average depth of ploughing not much exceeding four inches: there is however some quantity of stiff sour land interspersed on these hills, many farms and one or two whole parishes are chiefly of that nature. Near Fairford and Cirencester the soil is richer and deeper; particularly about the former a deep sandy loam prevails, producing great crops in a favourable time, but apt to burn and parch up in dry seasons; at which times they likewise labour under great inconveniences for want of water, with which the greater part of these hills is abundantly supplied."

P. 41. (Vale of Tewksbury)—" *Soil*, varies from sandy loams to clay, but mostly deep and rich."

MINERALS.—*Coals*.—P. 55. (Over the Severn)—In a letter to the Reporter, we find the following notice, respecting the coals of the Newent quarter of Glocestershire *.—" In answer to your enquiries, respecting the vein of coal lately discovered at Borlsdon, near Newent, it was seven feet thick when they left off working. The great obstacle

* In the Forest of Dean (which Mr. Turner has not reported) coals are found, and worked, in great quantities.

obstacle to continuing the works, was, the want of an engine to draw off the water. The property in that neighbourhood, is divided into small parcels, coal probably is under the grounds of all the different proprietors thereabouts, and should any one person erect a fire engine, he would drain the adjacent grounds, as well as his own, and would of consequence, subject himself to be undersold. To work the pits therefore, to advantage, either a company should be formed, or stipulations entered into by the neighbours, to make one common purse for the engine."

SUBJECT THE SECOND.

POLITICAL ECONOMY.

STATE of APPROPRIATION.—To this important subject of political concern, Mr. Turner's industry has been commendably directed. The common-field and common-meadow state of agriculture,—*now* so disgraceful to the political economy of a country which has more inhabitants than it can support,—we find scarcely any where more prevalent than in Glocestershire; where of course its pernicious tendency is most evident and best understood.

P. 10. (Cotswolds)—"Probably no part of the kingdom has been more improved within the last forty years, than the Cotswold Hills. The first inclosures are about that standing; but the greater part are of a later date. Three parishes are now inclosing; and out of about thirteen, which still remain in the common field state, two I understand are taking the requisite measures for an inclosure; the advantages are great, rent more than doubled, the produce of every kind proportionably increased."

P. 23. (Cotswolds)—speaking of "the burdens that the farming world in general labor under," Mr. T. says,—"Among these, the payment of tythes in kind deserve to be mentioned. In the new inclosures, this load has been got rid of by giving up a part of the property in lieu of it. One-fifth of the arable, and one-ninth of the pasture, and in some instances, two-ninths of one, and one-eighth of the other, has been asked, and agreed to. As the impropriator is exonerated from all expences, except inside fences, the part that he takes is more than equal to a fourth of the arable land, even when one-fifth is allowed; but even

even then the improvements being entirely the proprietors, they have been obliged to acquiesce."

P. 39. (Vale of Glocester). "I know one acre which is divided into eight lands, and spread over a large common field, so that a man must travel two or three miles to visit it all. But though this is a remarkable instance of minute division, yet, it takes place to such a degree, as very much to impede all the processes of husbandry. But this is not the worst; the lands shooting different ways, some serve as headlands to turn on in ploughing others; and frequently when the good manager has sown his corn, and it is come up, his slovenly neighbour turns upon, and cuts up more for him, than his own is worth. It likewise makes one occupier subservient to another in cropping his land; and in water furrowing, one sloven may keep the water on, and poison the lands of two or three industrious neighbours. If the several interests in these fields could be reconciled, the different properties laid together, and an inclosure take place, there is no doubt, but, from the improved state of the land, from its being laid dry and healthy, with the introduction of a correct course of crops, more than double the quantity of corn would be raised."

P. 41. (Vale of Tewkesbury)—"A large proportion of this district is arable, and mostly common field, but subject to a regular course of crops.

"Here, as in the neighbourhood of Gloucester, there is a considerable quantity of lot meadow, which is common after hay-making. There are likewise in several parts of the district, summer common pastures for cattle and sheep."

P. 44. (Vale of Tewksbury)—"*The parish of Kemerton* was inclosed, and exempted from tithe, about the year 1772, since which time the rent is very much advanced, and the produce more than doubled. Population likewise very much increased."

P. 49. (Over Severn)—"Part of the district is inclosed with live hedges; some part is still common field. I am informed from good authority, that between 300 and 400 acres of common field in the tithing of Aure, now let at about 10s. per acre, would, if inclosed, be worth more than 25s. being much better adapted for pasture than tillage. This tithing has likewise a very rich common pasture of about 100 acres, which joining other commons, and, as is generally the case, being much trespassed and encroached on, is of very little use to the proprietors, but might by inclosure be made very valuable.

"The

"The quantity of common and waste land in the district is considerable. The forest of Dean, now pretty much thinned of its timber, subject to common rights, and considerably encroached on, consists chiefly of stiff soil, and might, if appropriated, be converted to the purposes of agriculture with very great advantage to the nation.

"*Corse Lawn* contains about 2000 acres, 1400 of which are situated in the parish of Corse. The proprietors are now making application for an inclosure. A paper printed and distributed by the promoters of this application, containing some very good reasons in favour of the inclosure, will accompany this Report for the inspection of the Board.*

"*Huntley Common*, a considerable tract of land, now of very little use, might, by inclosure, be rendered very valuable to the proprietors and the nation.

"*Gorsly Common* contains from 300 to 400 acres of land, chiefly on a lime-stone rock, very applicable for orcharding and corn, but in its present state nearly useless.

"These are the principal waste lands in the district; there are other smaller tracts: these wastes, in their present state, are not only of very little real utility, but are productive of one very great nuisance, that of the erection of cottages, by idle and dissolute people, sometimes from the neighbourhood, and sometimes strangers. The chief building materials are store poles, stolen from the neighbouring woods. These cottages are seldom or never the abode of honest industry, but serve for harbour to poachers and thieves of all descriptions."

For some particulars relating to the *present state* of the *common fields*, in the vale of Tewksbury,---see the head, *Sheep*, ensuing.

PROVISIONS.—Mr. Turner is not an enemy to *alehouses*, only; but to *chandlers' shops*. It may be remarked, however, that VILLAGE SHOPS (now become common in most parts of the kingdom) may in some situations, save much time of workpeople, which might otherwise be spent in attending distant markets; thereby alienating their attention, from home, and constant employment; and spending more money in idle company, than they might save by the cheapness of their bargains. I will, nevertheless insert Mr. T's remarks; as they are evidently the result of some thought on the subject.

P. 26. "*Chandlers shops* are nearly as great a nuisance in

* This paper does not appear.

in country places as ale-houses. They retail, in small quantities and at extravagant rates, the worst of commodities; and draw that money out of the pockets of the poor for tea, sugar, butter, and other unnecessary articles, which, if taken to a proper market, and well laid out, would support themselves and families in health and comfort. If a plan could be devised to furnish the poor in their respective parishes with necessary articles, good in quality, and at the lowest market price, I know of nothing that would so effectually relieve them. Here are some neighbouring instances of a saving of 18d. or 2s. a week, for a family of five or six people, in the article of bread only, by their being supplied with flour at the best hand."

Mr. Turner's plan, in regard to FLOUR, (in districts, at least, where grist millers are not employed to grind corn, for workpeople) is practicable:—But not, I apprehend, properly so, in any other respect. A large occupier might easily lay in a stock of flour, and retail it out to his workpeople. But certainly not, with conveniency, other chandler-shop wares.

Where there is more than one retailer of the necessaries and comforts which laborers are entitled to, and of course a *contention*, in a village or hamlet, no *advantage* is likely to be taken. And it may be wise, in those who employ many workpeople, to promote the required *competition*.

MANUFACTURES.— P. 23. (Cotswold) — "The woollen manufactories supply spinning work to the poor women, in many parts of the district, but the earnings are very low."

P. 31. (Stroudwater Hills)—" *The woollen manufactory* is carried on to great extent in this district; the fine trade is at present at a stand, but the coarse for army clothing and the East-India Company remarkably brisk. The introduction of machinery, for every process the wool goes through to the loom, has thrown many hands out of employ; and several gentlemen, I have consulted, attribute the enormous rise of poors rates entirely to that cause; these, I have been credibly informed, amount, in some instances, in the immediate vicinity of the manufactories, to six shillings in the pound and upwards yearly."

P. 41. (Vale of Glocester). " *Manufactories.*—The only one carried on in this district is the pin manufactory, which chiefly employs the poor in Gloucester, and a great deal round the country. Spinning is likewise brought into the neighbourhood from the clothing country."

POOR TAX.—On this topic, Mr. Turner makes some sensible remarks. There are those, however, who may think

think his sentiments concerning it, rather too rigid, if not severe.

P. 25. (Cotswold) "The administration of the poor laws, not only takes a large sum yearly, from the agriculturist, but, in its effects, greatly injures him, by encouraging idleness and profligacy, among the labouring poor. The liberal orders for relief, which an artful tale, and an appearance of poverty and wretchedness, most generally occasioned by sloth and debauchery, has too often obtained, has held out a means of support independent of manual labour and exertion, and quite destroyed that laudable pride, which, a few years ago, was often to be observed among the labouring poor, of keeping themselves independent of their parishes; on the contrary, the most trifling accidents now bring them to the overseers, and from thence to the magistrates, for relief. Real policy, justice, and humanity, require that parish relief should be administered in such a sparing manner, as to convince those liable to be beholden to it, that they must look to their own exertions and industry alone for a comfortable subsistence."

For an instance of the high rate of the poor tax, see the head, *Manufactures*.

P. 41. (Vale of Glocester)—"*Poor's Rates* in the villages round Gloucester run from 2s. to 2s. 6d. in the pound; rather decreasing than otherwise. In Gloucester they are very much reduced, owing to a gentleman very much interested in them, having taken upon himself the direction of the workhouse, and obliged all who wanted relief to come into it."

TITHE.—(Vale of Glocester)—P. 39. "*Tithes* are chiefly compounded for; arable land at 6s. and grass land at 2s. 6d. or 3s. per acre; but only yearly, and therefore, in the event of an improved husbandry, the full value of the tithe would doubtlessly be exacted."

PUBLIC WORKS.—*Drainage*—P. 45. (Vale of Tewksbury)---"The observations made on this head, in the neighbourhood of Gloucester, are equally applicable here. The wet state of the land is entirely owing to the brooks and ditches not being properly scoured and opened, to carry off the surface water. An enforced attention to this, and to the cutting new drains, if wanting, all through the vale, for this necessary purpose, would be the first and grand step towards one of the greatest improvements that can be suggested*." I am

"* In one of the open arable fields, I observed a considerable quantity of land, which, being too wet for the plough, lay neglected and covered

I am concerned to find that my suggestions, on this subject, had not, in 1794, been carried into effect. By a COMMISSION of DRAINAGE, duly planned and regulated, and faithfully executed, the marketable products of the vale lands of Glocestershire might be encreased many thousands, or tens of thousands, annually. I know no vale district of equal extent, which requires an act of public drainage more than that of Glocester.

MARKETS.—For remarks on village shops, see the head, *Provisions*, aforegoing.

SUBJECT THE THIRD.

RURAL ECONOMY.

DIVISION THE FIRST.

TENANTED ESTATES,

Their IMPROVEMENT and MANAGEMENT.

ESTATES.—P. 8. (Cotswolds)---" *The properties* are mostly large, and the occupations likewise; there are however some exceptions in both."

P. 32. (Vale of Glocester)—" A vast deal of land in this district is the property of the church. The whole parish of Barnwood, a great part of Wooton and Cranham, and nearly all Tuffley, with many estates in every parish in and near the city, belong to the dean and chapter of Gloucester; the parish of Maisemore to the bishop of Gloucester; and several estates to colleges at Oxford. The church has likewise the tithes of several parishes."

IMPROVING Estates.—*Sodburning*.—P. 21. (Cotswolds) ---" *Paring and burning* is very much practised and approved;

covered with rushes and trumpery, affording only a little ordinary keep to a few cattle, but which, if properly drained, would be equal in value to any part of the field."

proved; old sainfoin lays and all turf of a sufficient texture are usually broke up in that way. Turnips are often the first crop; and from the freshness of the land, and the good effects of the ashes, a large crop is generally obtained. But as the time is too short to get the land in proper tilth for the succeeding crops of barley, seeds, &c. it is thought a better method to sow wheat first, on one ploughing; after which, the ashes being still fresh in the ground, a crop of turnips may be as safely relied on, and there is plenty of time to get the land in complete tilth. Grassy wheat stubbles, that will produce a tolerable quantity of ashes, are frequently pared and burnt for turnips with great success. In short, whenever followed with the turnip and clover husbandry, its good effects are indisputable; but like every other practice, it is liable to abuse in the hands of designing men, who have sometimes made use of it to force repeated crops of corn, 'till the soil has been completely worn out and rendered incapable of any useful production *."

P. 45. (Vale of Tewksbury)---"I do not find that this is practised in any part of the district, except on Oxenton Hill, in the neighbourhood of Kemerton. This is a cold thin clay soil, more adapted for pasture than corn, but occasionally broken up. Mr. John Bricknell, who is represented to me as the introducer of this practice, thinks it exceedingly beneficial. He ploughs and burns for wheat; after harvest the stubble is breast-ploughed, and left through the winter to rot; in spring the land is ploughed and sowed with oats, and laid down with ray grass and clovers."

Irrigation.—P. 18. (Cotswolds) "Watering meadows, has long been practised in this district,† there is, probably, no considerable quantity of land capable of that improvement, without interfering with the mills, where it is not done."

Some account of the meadows of South Cerney, and its neighbourhood, might have been a valuable addition to this Report; in order, more particularly, to have corroborated, or contradicted, the account that has been blazoned about, concerning them. EXECU-

"* Down Ampney and its neighbourhood, the part of this county that borders on Wiltshire, is the only place in which I have met with any objection to this management; the soil here consists of stiff clays and gravels; on the clays they do not think it answers, but approve of it on the gravels."

† Rather say, on a corner of its southeastern margin.

EXECUTIVE MANAGEMENT of Estates.—*Tenancy.*—P. 23. (Cotswolds)—" I know of nothing commendable in the leases of the district; a good plain form, equally protecting the interest of landlord and tenant, is much wanting, if possible to be drawn. At present they are chiefly in professional hands, who either content themselves with antiquated copies, or, in order to guard against trifling inconveniences, cramp the industrious tenant, so as often to prevent improvements to the advantage of himself, his landlord, and the community; whilst, at the same time, they do not prevent the knave and sloven from running into the contrary extreme."

P. 33. (Vale of Glocester)—" The property belonging to the colleges is now mostly sold out on lease for twenty-one years, renewable every seven. The bishop's land is in general sold out for three lives; when one drops, putting a fresh one in as the parties can agree."

DIVISION THE SECOND.

WOODLANDS.

ON the Cotswold Hills, Mr. Turner follows up my recommendation, to propagate small coppice woods; at once, for shelter, fuel, and various uses of farms. At present, the country is almost naked; and straw an article of fuel.

P. 54. (Over Severn) A contributor says—" All this district abounds with wood: there is near a thousand acres, in the parish of Newent: Oxeuhall, Dymock, Hempley, Pauntley, and Bromsberrow, are, I imagine, in full proportion. The principal part is coppice, though interspersed thickly with timber trees, oak and elm: the oak thrives most on the clay soil, the elm grows almost spontaneously on the sand: the coppice consists chiefly of oak, and ash, though plentifully mixed with hazle, beech, sally, alder, &c. It is suffered to grow according to circumstances, from fourteen to twenty years; the prime part is devoted to the lath, some to hurdles, hoops, &c. and the remainder to cord wood, for the iron furnaces, at Powick, Lidney and Flaxley."

DIVISION

DIVISION THE THIRD.

AGRICULTURE.

FARMS.—*Sizes.*—P. 8. (Cotswolds)—" It is the opinion of experienced men, that farms of from 200 to 500 acres, can be managed with much greater advantage to the farmer and the public, than smaller ones."

Homesteads.—Dung Yards.—P. 18. (Cotswolds)—" The formation of the fold yards, so as to prevent the rain water from washing the dung heaps, as well as preserving the liquid part of manure, is not at all attended to, though so much deserving of attention; on the contrary, from the sloping situations of many of the fold-yards, it might be imagined, that the prime object in laying them out, was to diminish the value of the dung heaps as much as possible."

This is applicable to three-fourths of the farm yards of the kingdom. I thank Mr. T. for assisting me to censure them.

Mr. Turner complains, in different parts of his Report, of a want of close yards, and sheds, for cattle, implements, &c.; and this with much propriety. The following remarks are sensible and just.

P. 29. (Stroudwater Hills)---" There appears to be a great deficiency of shed room in this district. Implements of husbandry of all sorts, are either left in the grounds, where last used, or at best, have only the shelter of a tree to preserve them; nor are the yards much better accommodated for wintering cattle. This is a very material object; the injury sustained by having the implements thus exposed, is, perhaps, more than equal to the fair wear of them, and would well pay for the construction of sheds for their preservation. In regard to live stock, it is still worse; cattle fed on straw, in exposed and unsheltered situations, are sure to sink considerably; and are liable, when spring comes on, to the yellows, and other complaints, which greatly injure, and sometimes prove fatal to them. Dairy cows, in the open fields, down in the vale, are known to sink very much, in bad winters, though foddered with good hay. On the contrary, where good yards are constructed, with plenty of shed room, and attention is paid to littering them

them down occasionally, and keeping the cattle dry and comfortable, they sometimes even improve on the straw, and are sure to come out healthy and thriving in spring."

PLAN of MANAGEMENT of Farms.—P. 8. (Cotswolds)—"In the vallies, and where the land is of a sufficient staple for permanent meadow and pasture, it is mostly in that state. Sheep and cow downs are likewise frequently met with: but the quantity of land thus employed, bears but a small proportion, to that which is occasionally under the plough; some few parishes on the sides of the hills however, are an exception to this rule, in which perhaps half the land is meadow and pasture, worth from 20 to 30s. per acre. In these situations, dairying is mostly followed, in preference to grazing; the sort of cows chiefly Gloucestershire, frequently crossed and improved from other breeds. Most farmers dairy a little for home consumption; and though the nature of the soil renders sheep the live stock chiefly to be attended to, yet a sufficient quantity of cattle, generally are, and always ought to be, intermixed with them to improve the pastures, and make the most of the keep."

P. 10. (the same.)—"In the open field state, a crop and fallow was the usual course. What is here called the 'seven-field husbandry' now generally obtains; that is, about a seventh part sainfoin, and the remainder under the following routine; turnips, barley, seeds two years, wheat, oats."

P. 15. (the same.)—"On the heavier soils, attention is paid to the state in which they work best. The stiff sour land is frequently fallowed and dunged for wheat, over which broad clover is often harrowed in; in spring, after lying one or two years, it is broke up for wheat, followed by oats; or sometimes oats are sown on the lay, according to the state of the land. Turnips are sometimes sown on this sort of land, but, perhaps, had better be omitted; the poaching, in eating off, possibly doing more injury, than the teeth of the sheep recompences, rendering it unfit for any crop but oats, and probably injuring them. Wheat, clover, and oats, seem to be the crops best adapted to these soils." See the head *Manures*, ensuing.

State of *Husbandry*.—P. 38. (near Glocester)—"I do not think Mr. Marshall's account of the bad management and foulness of the land at all exaggerated, in many instances some years back; but, am happy to learn, that the slovenly managers are fast disappearing, and better practice tices daily getting ground." I am happy and *proud* to hear this.

For some particulars, relating to the state of husbandry, in the vale of Tewksbury, see the ensuing section, *Sheep*.

WORKPEOPLE.—P. 20 (Cotswolds)—" *Prices of Labour* are considerably increased; from 12d. to 14d. a day in winter; 18d. to 20d. haymaking; harvest 2s.; beer or an allowance in malt in some places, is gaining ground, and as much as possible, is done by the great. Women from 6d. to 8d. and 9d. in haymaking; in harvest 12d. Hours of work from six to six, when day-light permits; late hours in haymaking, and harvest generally recompenced with beer, &c."

P. 39. (Vale of Glocester.)—" *Wages* in winter 12d. in summer 18d. and beer. The harvest month about 30s. and board. Much work of all kinds done by the piece."

Mr. Turner forgets, in this place, to mention the swinish guzzling of laborers, in the vale of Glocester.

P. 44. (Vale of Tewksbury)—" In winter 12d. to 13d. summer 18d and beer; women 7d. or 8d. for the harvest 30s. and diet, or 3l. and $1\frac{1}{2}$ bushel of malt without."

The following I hope and trust is true Report.—P. 55. (Over Severn)—" *Wages*, in part of this district, have been low in money, but in some part recompenced by an extravagant allowance in cyder, which has introduced very bad habits amongst the labourers, and occasioned great expence, and inconvenience to the farmer in scarce years of fruit. I find from respectable authority, that this abuse is now likely to be rectified, and that the farmers in general, are curtailing the allowance of drink, and advancing the money price of labour."

See the ensuing head, *Orchards*, on this subject.

WORKING ANIMALS.—P. 19. (Cotswolds)—" *Horses and Oxen* are both used, the latter in harness, and getting ground, but not so much as they ought. One team of horses is necessary for carrying out corn, on our rough and hilly roads, but where more than one team is kept, oxen certainly are in every respect the most eligible."

P. 27. (Stroudwater Hills)—" I saw here an application of turnips, quite new to me. Mr. Hayward gives them in quantity to his farm horses, which he finds keeps them very healthy, and induces them to eat the barn chaff, and other dry meat, with a better appetite;—they were, when I saw them, in very good condition, though, I was informed, they had had no corn for half a year past, and were constantly worked."

P. 49.

P. 49. (Over Severn)—"*Oxen* are much used in tillage, particularly on the sandy soils. It is thought the canal now cutting through this country, will, when completed, be the means of reducing the number of horses, and bringing oxen into general use, by saving the road work."

IMPLEMENTS.—*Rollers.*—P. 29. (Stroudwater Hills)—"I saw two rollers in this neighbourhood, on a construction new to me; one of them was procured from the neighbourhood of Marlborough—a common roller, of about fourteen inches diameter, is surrounded with wheels nine inches distant from each other, and three feet in diameter; the spokes being let into the roll. The other is an improvement from this: a smaller roll is the axis, on which are put solid wheels, about three feet in diameter, and one-half inch thick; made alternately of wood and cast iron: the wooden ones are made to fix at any distance; between two of these an iron one is put one-half inch less in diameter, and with room sufficient to play up and down, so as to give way to any obstacle, and to press down into the hollows; it likewise, by these means, is rendered less liable to choak up in rough land. For breaking clods, or in light land, where great pressure is wanting, these appear to be very effective implements." These are *novel* and, judging from the above description, they are at least *ingenious* contrivances.

MANURES.—*Dung.*—P. 17. (Cotswolds)—"*Manures* are chiefly those of the fold-yard. The wheat stubbles are frequently mown or raked for litter, and cattle kept in sufficient quantity to eat the straw, but this is not always the case; large heaps of straw are seen in some parts of the district, rotting at the barn doors, for want of cattle to eat and tread it into dung, and this generally for want of a sufficiency of pasture to support the stock in summer; but surely, the keeping more land down to grass, or raising some sort of vegetable food for such stock, would be ultimately attended with increase of produce and profit to the farmer, and advantage to the public."

Lime.—P. 18. (the same)—"Lime is too expensive for manure: nor from two or three experiments that have come under my observation, does it seem worth attention, if that was not the case."

P. 48. (Over Severn)—"*Lime* is here in very high estimation as a manure, both for arable and pasture land. In the common practice it is laid in small heaps on the arable land to the quantity of two waggon loads per acre, if the land is very poor; if not, three loads to two acres, and spread, and ploughed in as soon as slaked. But in the neighbourhood

neighbourhood of Newent, it is found that their best and strongest lime, which is burnt from stone on Gorsley Common, requires a different management, the small heaps crusting, and not slaking properly; whereas, if put in heaps of a waggon load, or more together, it soon falls to a fine flour, digging out quite hot; this method is therefore followed in the best practice, though attended with additional trouble. It is thought equally beneficial on light and stiff soils, binding the one, and opening and ameliorating the other. This may be called a modern manure, in the district under notice."

Marl.—P. 49. (the same)—" Marl was formerly in great request, as appears by the number of old pits, but has not been in use in the memory of any person now living."

The species of marl is not here noticed. It is probably the red earthy substratum which appears to have formerly been used for manure, in every red-land district of the kingdom, perhaps; and which has, of later years, been superseded by lime. The red-lands of Nottinghamshire, however, I have not, yet, sufficiently examined.

Sheep-fold.—P. 18. (Cotswolds)—" Folding sheep is very little practised or approved of."

TILLAGE.—P. 16 (Cotswolds)—" It may be right to notice, in this place, an error of Marshall's in his Rural Economy of Gloucestershire, vol. 2, page 43. He represents the Cotswold farmers as ' wishing to plough for every crop, when the soil is wet, and working even their fallows, when they are moist.' This mistake originated, no doubt, from the account given him of the wheat process, as just related.* The fact is, the farmers here are as desirous of working their fallows in dry weather, and find the same good consequences resulting from it, as in other districts. Attention is likewise paid to sowing the barley in dry weather. The old adage respecting pease, ' if you sow in a flood, they will come up in a wood,' seems verified on this soil; as for oats, their hardiness requires no particular nicety. Such an error is very excusable in an account which is only given as an excursion. Mr. Marshall's account of this county contains much valuable information, and has greatly shortened mine."

Mr. Turner's surmises are, here, groundless. I never heard of the particulars of practice, which are above alluded to (and will presently appear) until I read his Report; which I did previously to my printing a new edition of my Register. On that occasion, I referred to my *original minutes*, respecting this matter; and there found, not only the practice

* See the ensuing section, *Wheat*.

practice recorded; but the reason for pursuing it explained.

Beside the general reason, respecting *Fallows*, published in my first edition (which Mr. T. ought to have noticed) I found the following, relating to the *wheat fallow.*—"Mr. ——— is clearly of opinion that the last stirring of a fallow for wheat should be *wet*, to give a degree of *sourness*"—(tenacity)—"to the soil; otherwise, the wheat dies, for want of foot-hold:"—An argument that is full of good sense, and was, doubtlessly, dictated by experience,—*on a crumbly soil.*

Mr. Turner has not quoted, *accurately* (a great crime in a critic):—I do not say for *every* crop, but for *a* crop. It was to the *wheat* crop, and to that grain crop alone, to which I paid particular attention, on the Cotswold hills. I do not even mention the *barley* crop; nor say a word about *pease.*

These circumstances having been duly considered, I did not, in reprinting my Register, find myself warranted, to make any alteration of the first edition; excepting that of inserting, in a parenthesis, after the words—for a crop—"that of barley, perhaps, excepted."

Doctors differ in Agriculture, as in Physic. Mr. T. may not have had the *best advice*: or he, or his friends, perhaps, may have been *talked*—perchance *laughed*—out of the *best practice*,—by men who cultivate lands, differing in their nature, from those of the Cotswold hills.

Beside, it would only have been justice, in Mr. Turner, to have apprized his readers, that the facts alluded to were not registered with the view, either of censure or praise, of the Cotswold practice; but solely, and declaratorily, as interesting facts, relating to the "PRINCIPLES of TILLAGE.* And if Mr. T. read my writings (which from his sentiments, if not his expressions, I am happy in thinking he does) he must I trust be convinced that I do not build castles in the air;—that I am not liable to catch up, hastily, and fly off with an idea, because it is new to me;—or suffer myself to be carried away by any newfangled notion that may happen to come across my mind:—much less to raise theories, or attempt to establish principles, without examining, carefully, the foundation I have to build on.

I am far from being offended by Mr. T's noticing what he might think was an error,—tho, by the way, he does not appear

* See the Rural Economy of Gloucestershire, (Edition 1796) Vol. II. p. 44.

appear to have been quite convinced that my statement was erroneous; or he would not have *stretched* it, the better to answer his purpose.

On the whole, I am much indebted to Mr. Turner, for giving me this opportunity of explaining myself; and still more for furnishing me with another firm foundation stone, on which to erect an enlarged theory concerning tillage;—namely, that of there being circumstances, and perhaps many, certainly more than has heretofore been admitted,—in which *tillage* (no matter whether by the plow, the harrow, the roller, or other implement) ought to be performed, while the soil is *moist*, or even *wet*. The method, reported by Mr. T. of putting in the wheat crop of the Cotswold hills, unsays, in effect, all that he has fairly said about my misrepresentation of the Cotswold practice. It is as follows:

WHEAT.—P. 15. (Cotswolds)—"The method of sowing this grain in the district under notice, is rather singular. The land is ploughed from two to six weeks before sowing, as circumstances permit; if it gets quite grassy, it is thought better. The first rain that falls in August in sufficient quantity to thoroughly soak the land, begins the seed time; from thence to the middle of September is thought the best time. The seed is dragged in with heavy drags, working the land till the furrows are well broke, but rather wishing to leave it rough than otherwise; if frequent showers fall during the dragging in, so as just to allow the drags to work, it is thought better by most people. Experienced men say, that our land being naturally too light for wheat, is by these means, rendered more suitable to it, at the same time that weeds are very much checked, which is a very material object, where the corn is so long on the ground. I have seen adjoining lands, the previous management of which had been exactly similar, the one part sown wet, produced a very good crop for the country, and quite clean; the other, sown dry, was not half so good, and devoured with filth This method is practised on the dry sound loams, of which the district chiefly consists."

P. 43. (Vale of Tewksbury)—"*Wheat* sowing begins towards the latter end of October, the bean stubbles are brushed soon after harvest, and again ploughed at seed time; if the stubbles are grassy, they are breast ploughed and burnt, in the best practice, if the weather permits. The clover and vetch lands, are generally ploughed some time before sowing; after the seed is harrowed

rowed in, the land is *trod* evenly and firmly *by men*, two treading a team's work.

"A superior manager, Mr. Stephens, of Pamington, *rakes* his wheat, as soon as the land is dry enough in spring, with *common wooden rakes*, raking the land two or three times in a place, so as thoroughly to stir the surface, at the expence of two shillings per acre; it is afterwards twice hoed in the common practice of the district; he finds this method very beneficial, and has generally superior crops to his neighbours, who, I do not find any of them follow his example." Those are novel practices.

BEANS.—P. 43. (the same) "*Beans* are all set by hand, as early as the weather permits in February, in rows twelve inches distant, used formerly to be planted lengthways of the lands, but it is now thought better to set them cross ways, being more convenient to clean, and lying better to the sun. They are twice hoed and hand weeded. Pease are not approved here, not so well admitting the hoeing and weeding as clean beans."

TARES.—The method of consuming vetches on the ground, with sheep, by the means of open hurdles, when the crop has been suffered to get too high, is ingenious. P. 17. (Cotswolds)—"*Winter Vetches* are, in the practice of a *few individuals*, sown in quantity to eat off with store sheep; they are usually sown after wheat, as soon after harvest as opportunity allows. The sheep are put on them the latter end of May, or beginning of June. They are commonly hurdled off in the same manner as turnips; but if a bulky crop, the better way is to give them through rack hurdles, which are made the same as the common five railed ones, only leaving the middle rail out, and nailing spars across at proper distances, to admit the sheep to put their heads through. A swarth of vetches, being mown across the lands, a sufficient number of these hurdles, allowing one to five sheep, are set close to it; at noon the shepherd mows another swarth, and throws it to the hurdles, and the same at night; next morning, a swarth being first mowed, the hurdles are again set; thus moving them once in twenty-four hours; by this trifling additional trouble the vetches are clean eaten off, and the land equally benefitted. As fast as the lands are cleared, they are ploughed, and sown with turnips, in which way good crops are often obtained in kind seasons, on land cleared in tolerable time, but it cannot be depended on for the main crop. When a succession is wanted, spring vetches are

are sometimes sowed; but at the time they are sown, labour is more valuable, and besides, they are not so much to be depended on."

CULTIVATED HERBAGE.—*Sainfoin.*—The following account of the cultivation of sainfoin, on the Cotswold hills, may serve to corroborate what I had written on the subject, and bring to conviction some who might have doubted the accuracy of my statement.

P. 11.—"*Sainfoin.*—This district stands one of the first in the cultivation of this excellent grass; the usual management has been to sow it with barley, after turnips, three bushels per acre, to which is generally added about five pounds of trefoil, which generally improves the first year's produce, and by occupying the soil, prevents the weeds from getting a-head till the sainfoin has established its roots. There are some very superior managers, however, who having been induced from an accidental occurrence to think a different procedure would be more advantageous, tried it with so much success, that they have constantly adhered to it since. The method alluded to, is to sow it on land exhausted by repeated cropping and full of couch grass, the sainfoin rooting so deep, does not draw its nourishment like corn, from the surface soil, and therefore is not injured by its impoverished state, whilst its greatest enemy, the black bent, is effectually kept under by the couch grass. In this practice it is likewise sown with barley, and very thin, not more than a bushel per acre, it having been noticed by the same attentive observers, that, when sown thin, the roots are larger and more vigorous, and in two or three years get full possession of the land, producing greater crops, and lasting longer than the thicker planted. There are other practitioners who object to thin sowing, observing that the hay being chiefly wanted for sheep, although it may produce as much or more in quantity, the stems are much larger and not so palatable to that animal, occasioning great waste in the consumption. It must likewise be observed, that the method of sowing it on foul exhausted land, having been tried in the neighbourhood of Guiting, on a less genial soil, has in two instances, that have come to my knowledge, failed; it might therefore be advisable, when the culture is new, to make small experiments first * In the neighbourhood of Stowe,

* The KENTISH practice of sowing *clover* with sainfoin is obviously preferable to that of sowing it among *couch grass*, to keep down weeds, the first and second years. See the RURAL ECON: of the SOUTH. COUNT. Art. *Sainfoin.* This practice has recently been introduced, in Yorkshire, with the best effect.

Stowe, I am informed, a fourth part of the land is appropriated to this grass; but as it requires a great many years to intervene before land that has once borne it, can be cropped with success, that probably may be found too large a proportion. The duration of sainfoin depends a great deal on the management; mowing it before its full blossom is detrimental, the roots bleeding very much and mildewing; for the same reason seeding of it is accounted beneficial; if wished to last, it should never be fed but in the months of October and November, and then only with cattle, sheep biting too close; the lattermath is, however, excellent food for weaned lambs, and therefore often applied to that purpose."

What follows is new to me.—P. 12. "Indeed the farmers in general do not wish it to last longer than seven years; the land being in that time thoroughly rested and fit for corn, whilst other land under the plough wants rest; but if desired, it might, with proper management, last ten or twelve years. The hay, if well made, is, in the fore part of the season, equal to any meadow hay in the district for most purposes. When worn out, so as not to be worth mowing, it is generally pastured a year or two, which thickens the turf, and of course produces more and better ashes, when pared and burnt, in which method it is always broken up."

On other cultivated herbs, I see nothing to notice;—except that (p. 13.)—"White Dutch" (no doubt *Trifolium repens)* "is getting out of repute for sheep feed:"*—and excepting that Mr. PACEY has—"cultivated the *Orchis* grass,—a broad-leaved grass that springs directly after the sithe"—(doubtlessly the *Orchard* grass—*Dactylis glomorata)* "with success."—I can speak of it, from my own experience, as a valuable species of cultivated herbage.

ORCHARDS.—A correspondent of Mr. Turner writes to him in the following desultory way, respecting the orchards of the Over-Severn district†.—P. 52. "It is, I believe,

* A maturely experienced husbandman, whose opinions, in agriculture, are seldom ill founded, asserts, that white clover is not well affected by sheep; and, generally, that it is much less nutritious than red clover, or ray grass.

This and the above notice I insert here, without comment, as the opinions of professional men, in distant parts of the kingdom.

† And this is all we find, in the Report under Review, respecting the Orchards of Glocestershire.

belive, impossible to make any accurate calculation, with respect to our quantity of orcharding in this district, without an actual survey. The produce of the inferior fruits, being used as small beer, and the allowance to the labourer large, not less than one gallon per day the year round, and two gallons a day in harvest; the farmer is naturally anxious, to have as much orcharding as will supply him with a sufficiency, without his having recourse to the maltster; he will also, supposing he has cellaring sufficient, always keep a reserve; for it has been observed of late years, that there is not a hit, as it is provincially called, that is, the trees do not universally bear a good crop, above once in four years. Our prime fruit trees by no means flourish, as they formerly did; the old fruits are apt to canker speedily; and the different experiments of having grafts and stocks from Normandy, having totally failed, the idea has been taken up, that the land is tired of them, or in other words, that the particular pabulum necessary for the support of apple and pear trees, is entirely exhausted. It may be worth while to give Forsyth's recipe a fair trial; and were this done scientifically, I should have little doubt of its being as successful with fruit, as with timber trees. Very possibly, we do not take so much pains with our plantations as formerly. In my own remembrance, wine was seldom produced, but at superior tables, and then only occasionally. The principal gentlemen of the county rivalled each other in their cyders: but now, the case is altered; and cyder, and perry, are seldom introduced but at dinner, and then only for a draught, as small beer: after the cloth is taken away you must treat with foreign wines, or incur the imputation of not making your friends welcome."

CATTLE.—P. 8. (Cotswolds)—" Of these not so many are bred as formerly, Gloucester market weekly affording great choice from Herefordshire, Wales and Somersetshire; of these, the Glamorgan and Somerset appear most eligible as working cattle for the hills, being active in harness, and when turned off, feeding in less time than the larger breed of Herefordshire. In stall-feeding, hay, chaff, barleymeal, oats and bran are the articles of food chiefly used."

DAIRY.—P. 32. (Vale of Berkeley)—" For the account of this part of the county, I must beg leave to refer to Mr. Marshall, his very respectable sources of information, and the pains he has taken in describing every thing worthy of notice in the district, has put it out of my power

power to make any useful additions. For the same reason I leave in his hands the dairy management of the county; his account of the process in manufacturing cheese and butter, is, to the best of my knowledge, perfectly accurate and just."

SHEEP.—P. 9. (Cotswolds)—"The native *sheep* of these hills in their unimproved state, was a small light carcassed, polled animal, bearing in the memory of an experienced agriculturist now living, a fleece of fine wool of about 3 lb. weight, but lighter and finer before that period. They were cotted in former times, but that practice has not been in use since the remembrance of the person alluded to, from which circumstances it is very probable that the assertions of ancient authors, that the Spaniards procured their breed of fine woolled sheep from the Cotswold Hills, are founded in fact, though contradicted by some modern writers."

I have only to say, in opposition to those remarks, that while I was on the Cotswold Hills, I made particular enquiry concerning that subject; and especially of one of the oldest, most sensible, and best experienced agriculturists thereon; but without coming nearer to the probability of the Cotswolds' having formerly been inhabited by a breed of fine-wooled sheep, (differing much from the present established breed) than that of common field-sheep having been changed from a smaller to a larger size, and from a shorter to a longer-wooled variety,—by inclosure, cultivated herbage, and the turnip husbandry. Mr. T's pardonable prejudice towards the honor of *his* country may have warped his opinion, respecting this unimportant circumstance. It is not certain, nor is it, I conceive, very probable, that the Spanish breed of fine-wooled sheep originated on the banks of the Severn or the Wye; or indeed received any material improvement from thence. If the Cotswolds really had a fine-wooled breed, it was in all probability, similar to the existing breed of Herefordshire. I only gave the *reputed* honor to the Ryelands, inasmuch as I thought that they were *more probably* entitled to it.

My words were these (RUR. ECON. of GLO. II. 199.)—"*If* the Spaniards improved their wool, by any breed of English sheep, it was, *most probably*, by that of the Ryelands of Herefordshire, not by that of the Cotswolds of Glocestershire." For a circumstantial evidence in favor of that idea, see p. 350, aforegoing.

Mr. Turner continues, p. 9.—"Since that time the inclosure

closures and better management taking place, and good rams being procured from Warwickshire and other counties, the Costwold sheep have considerably improved in weight of carcass and quantity of wool, which, though coarser than formerly, is in very great esteem as combing wool, being of a good length and very mellow quality. The fashionable Leicestershire sheep have been occasionally introduced into this district, and, for a cross or two when chosen with judgment, have been found to improve the breed in shape and disposition to fatten, but where persisted in, they have greatly reduced the carcass in size, and considerably lessened the wool in quality and quantity: nor is this reduction in size recompenced by their requiring less food, or fattening quicker than the other breeds, qualities which have been so strongly insisted on, and on which the merit of the breed has been chiefly founded; on the contrary, experienced graziers in this district who have paid particular attention to them, are convinced, that they require full as much time and room as the larger native breed."

I have registered those opinions of the "experienced graziers" of the Cotswold Hills:—not through any prejudice against the Leicestershire breed of sheep. But, as the men of Leicestershire have long been in the habit, of giving their opinions pretty freely, and *showing* off their breed in the most public manner, I think it is but fair that other districts should be entitled to similar privileges.

On the same principle, I indulge Mr. T. by inserting the following notice; tho not very intelligently given.—P. 27. (Stroudwater Hills) "*Sheep*, on the hills, are the chief stock; these are mostly of the horned Wiltshire breed, the fleeces average nine to the tod of 28 lbs. worth this year 26s. 6d. per tod. Average weight, when fat, wether 24 lbs. ewe 22 lbs. per quarter. This breed is liable to a disorder called the Goggles, which sometimes occasions very heavy losses. The only method of prevention is, entirely changing the flock once in eight or ten years. One practitioner, Mr. Hayward, of Baverstone, has been induced, from this circumstance, to try the Cotswold breed, and having, for three or four years past, used rams of that breed, he will very soon entirely get rid of the Wiltshire blood; and, I am inclined to think, will find a great advantage in so doing."

Common-field Sheep-husbandry.—P. 42. (Vale of Tewkesbury) "Though the greater part of the district under

under notice is very subject to the rot, insomuch that it is reckoned they lose their flocks once in three years on on average, there is a considerable quantity kept, the farmers being persuaded they could not raise corn without them. The arable fields after harvest, are stocked without stint. When spring seed time commences, they are confined to the fallow quarter of the field, and stinted, in proportion to the properties; they are folded every night, and kept so hard, that scarce a blade of grass, or even a thistle escapes them; and this management is thought essentially necessary, especially on the stiff soils, to keep them in good order, such soils being too hard to plough in very dry weather, and of course, not eligible in wet. The grass and weeds, without this expedient, would often get so much a-head as not to be afterwards conquered. The fold likewise is reckoned very valuable. Wether sheep are bought in for this purpose, an ordinary hardy mixed breed."

"GENERAL VIEW

OF THE

AGRICULTURE

OF THE

COUNTY OF GLOUCESTER.

DRAWN UP FOR THE CONSIDERATION OF

THE BOARD OF AGRICULTURE AND INTERNAL IMPROVEMENT,

BY THOMAS RUDGE, B. D.

1807."

ON Mr. RUDGE'S QUALIFICATIONS, for the task he has undertaken, it is difficult to judge; even from his book; excepting so far as the body of the work, as well as the title page, bespeaks him to be a man of education. Mr. R. moreover appears to be tolerably well *read*, on rural subjects;

subjects; and to have bestowed some time in *observing* the rural management of Glocestershire; tho the time, or the mode, of observation does not appear. But, having pretty evidently had no *practice*, whatever, in either of the branches of Rural Economy, his qualifications to *write* upon them must, of course, be *very incomplete*.

But, as has been observed in regard to Mr. TURNER, the harvest had been, previously gathered; and Mr. T. having performed the gleaner's part, the *after harvest*, alone, remained for Mr. Rudge. All that could be wanted was a handsome well sized volume, written in a readable style, and embellished with a few engravings; and this Mr. R. has furnished.

In Glocestershire, however, where crops are reaped, in rather a singular manner, some scanty portion of grain will not unfrequently be collected, even in the *second harvest*, which, there, usually takes place. I will therefore assiduously search Mr. R's collection, and faithfully lay up what Mr. Turner and I may have missed. For, as in collecting stubble, a few ears of corn will be gathered, so, in examining Mr. R's Report, a few useful ideas will be found.

Perceiving little, in Mr. R's account, that militates against my own, and seeing the errors that he may have fallen into cannot be the cause of serious apprehension to the *agricultural* public (weighty as Mr. Rudge's sentiments may be *in his own profession)* all I have to do, in this case, is to register what appears to be worthy of preservation; especially, regarding the *Natural* and *Political* Economy relative to Glocestershire; as, on these topics, Mr. R's remarks may be preferable to those of a mere practitioner in RURAL ECONOMY.

It will previously be proper to remark that Mr. Rudge divides the county into three "natural divisions;" namely, the "Cotswolds—Vale—and Forest" (p. 12).—This however is an error that I must take cognizance of. Such a division is by no means the "best adapted to an agricultural Survey."

The "Vale" is upwards of fifty miles in length, and its agricultural management, variable. The Vale of Glocester is an *arable common-field* district, with only a portion of grass land. That of Berkeley, on the contrary, is, almost purely, a *grass-land, dairy district*.—And the country toward Bristol is *entirely different*, in soil and management, to either of them; tho included in the general

sweeping

sweeping district—"the Vale."—Nevertheless, in the subsection "Potatoes" (!)—we find that last mentioned, spoken of as a distinct district.—Further, the "Forest of Dean"—(chiefly an open and partially woodland passage) is as different from the Over Severn (an inclosed district under mixed cultivation) as almost any two passages of territory in the kingdom.—However, for the secondary purpose which Mr. R. must consciously have had in view, the simple division he has made may serve.

This being another *second original* (see p. 299) there are of course NO ANNOTATORS. Nor have I found the first original itself once noticed! And this notwithstanding the subjoined "Advertisement," is prefixed to the volume,—doubtlessly, by the first President."

"The desire that has been generally expressed, to have the AGRICULTURAL SURVEYS of the KINGDOM reprinted, with the additional Communications which have been received since the ORIGINAL REPORTS were circulated, has induced the BOARD OF AGRICULTURE to come to a resolution to reprint such as appear on the whole fit for publication.

"It is proper at the same time to add, that the Board does not consider itself responsible for every statemen contained in the Reports thus reprinted, and that it will thankfully acknowledge any additional information which may still be communicated.

"N. B. *Letters to the Board, may be addressed to Sir* JOHN SINCLAIR, *Bart. the President, No.* 32, *Sackville-Street, Piccadilly, London.*"

How are these things to be reconciled to reason, common sense and propriety? They must either have arisen from some strange mistake, or must be considered as an insult offered to the discernment of the public.

Are we to conclude, from this mystical mode of procedure, that Mr. TURNER's Report, with the NOTES it may have accumulated, were intended to have been thrown aside, and rendered useless to the public? And this notwithstanding what has been said of Mr. CLARK's Report of Herefordshire (see p. 299) may be repeated of Mr. Turner's Glocestershire? *I* am by no means offended with this unaccountable misconduct; as it will serve to render my abstract (or shall I say CONCENTRATED EDITION) of the Board's Reports, whether *original* or *secondary*, still more comparatively valuable, than the Reports at large.

This

This Report, however, has to boast of two CONTRIBUTORS of high consideration.

Mr. SHEPPARD, on Spanish wool; and

Mr. WEBB, on draining.

Messrs. LUMBERT and ROGERS, on Working the Mole Plow, are also entitled to praise.

The number of pages, in the body of the work, Appendix and Index, four hundred and eight.

Five maps, or other engravings.

SUBJECT THE FIRST.

NATURAL ECONOMY.

WATERS.---In this Report of Glocestershire, the rivers and minor streams are not only enumerated, but the *names* of their several sources, as well as of the places situated near the courses of the larger ones, before they enter the county, are detailed.

This is a sort of information which any one, who is possessed of a Map of England, may readily give (and extend to any length he pleases); and, of course, no man possessing such a map requires a *verbal* description.

A description of the *substructure*, or *internal strata, out of which the branches of a river issue*, or of the *soils off which the rain waters are collected* in times of floods,---may be of real utility to the agriculture of a county.

Moreover, to describe, or even to enumerate, the various species of *fishes*, natural to a river, might be right in a Report concerning NATURAL HISTORY; but the SALMON, and its kind, alone, require notice, in one relating to "Agriculture and internal Improvement."

The following particulars relating to the *Salmon fishery* of the Severn, corroborate the accounts given of that of other large rivers in the kingdom.

P. 27. "The salmon, which has ever been reckoned the pride of the Severn, and in former times caught in great abundance, is become comparatively a scarce fish. A considerable decrease of the species, difficult to be accounted for, satisfactorily, is allowed by all who are employed in this branch of fishery. Great mischief is thought to be done

done by the use of small mashed nets, which take the young fry, generally known here by the name of samlet. The alliance of these to the salmon is disputed; it is, however, known that they also are much diminished in quantity *."

P. 343. (speaking of commerce) "Salmon also find their great market in the metropolis; and, it is said, that, for salmon alone, 4000*l.* is annually remitted into the country." —Quere,—*has been* remitted into this county?

SOILS.—Relating to this topic, the Report under notice comprizes much information. Its authenticity, however, requires to be examined into. Not only has Mr. Rudge given us a verbal description; but somebody has prefixed to his work a colored "map of the soils of Glocestershire." The letterpress and the engraving, however, contradict each other, in so flagrant a manner, as to render it more than probable that they are not the productions of the same mind. As, for instances,—

Mr. R. after having described the "general character of the hill soil,"—as a blowing sand! (p. 15.)—as will appear under the head, Wheat,—says (p. 16)—"there is a part of the Cotswolds, lying chiefly to the south of the turnpike-road from Oxford to Bath, which has a soil very different in nature from that first described. It extends, more or less, from Burford, through Cirencester and Tetbury, to Bath. The surface-soil consists of a mixed loam, to the depth of from nine to twenty-four inches, under which lies a stratum of rock in thin lamina, rubbly or broken, and mixed with light loam, to the depth of from four to twenty-four inches, and then a stratum of clay of various depths. This land is naturally wet, and rots sheep pastured on it, owing to the water in heavy rains sinking through the upper surface, and lodging in the second stratum, where it is retained; and when additional rains fall, this stagnant putrid water, not finding a vent below, is forced back upon the surface, and materially injures the vegetation of all the most valuable plants growing upon it. This soil is, however, interrupted by large breadths of land of very stiff clay, and others of a good loamy sand."—Whereas in the map, the

"* In 1803 some samlets were taken, about four miles below Gloucester, and thrown back into the river, with their fins cut; in the following season they were again taken, having in one year increased to three pounds weight. This fact I had from a respectable gentleman, who is largely concerned in fisheries, and have, therefore, no reason to question it."

I have heard of fine wire being fastened in the fin, with a similar result.

the entire range of hill, from Campden to near Bath, comprehending the Cotswolds, proper,—together with the Stroudwater, and the South Wold hills,—is of the same uniform *buff color:* and this notwithstanding the varieties of soil, above specified, and notwithstanding the obvious distinctions which Mr. Turner (another of the Board's Reporters) had previously pointed out, in a very satisfactory manner, (see p. 396, aforegoing). It is true, the outskirts of the Cotswold hills are distinguished by a different color, *blue.* But these are a natural part,—the northern margin,—of the wide spreading vale lands of Northwiltshire.

Again.—Mr. R. speaking of the soils of the vale,—says—P. 18. "In the parishes of Deerhurst, above Gloucester, and Berkeley, Rockhampton, &c. below it, as also at Iron Acton, Winterbourn, and Frampton Cotterel, the soil is of a strong ferruginous colour; in the former it is argillaceous; in the latter a sandy loam."

True it is that, in the neighbourhood of Deerhurst, there is a passage of red land of the peculiar kind found in various parts of the kingdom, and of the very first quality as such:—a sort of land which must forcibly strike any man who is accustomed to, or capable of making, observations on the soils of a country. Yet, in the map, no such passage appears. Even the water-formed lands, on either side of the Severn, in some places of considerable width, and well described by Mr. Rudge,—are not seen on the map; which is uniformly covered, in those parts, with the same *yellow* color, which, according to the "explanation of the coloring," denotes "brown clay, generally on a subsoil of blue clay."

Lastly, the red lands, west of the Severn, similar to those which prevail in parts of Herefordshire and Worcestershire, are noticed by Mr. R. but are not visible on the face of the map.

Mr. Rudge very properly says—P. 20. "In the foregoing distribution of soils, the general character only of the county is attempted; it would be tedious and useless to remark every transition, on so large a surface of land; especially where the transitions are sudden and frequent."

Why will the *editor* of the Board persevere in leading the public astray; merely, for the vain purpose of exciting—or endeavouring to excite—a momentary gape of the ignorant and credulous,—who are ready to swallow any thing, no matter how unworthy or absurd; provided it be set off in a plausible manner,—like the map of the soils of Glocester-

Glocestershire! It is splendidly specious. Nothing but the peacock's tail, which it much resembles, could be more fascinatingly imposing.

FOSSILS.—*Limestone.*—P. 22. "The forest of Dean, Longhope, and adjoining places, furnish a good lime-stone of the compact kind, for building and agriculture; but inferior to that which is found in vast beds at the southern extremity of the county, beginning at Cromhall, and expanding on each side elliptically, till the rocks meet again in Somersetshire. Within this circle, it is said, that coal is every where to be found.

"The lime made from this stone is of a peculiar whiteness and great strength: that which is burnt at St. Vincent's rocks, near Bristol, is the best. The lime, when slaked, is compressed closely in casks, and becomes a considerable article of foreign and internal commerce. For the purposes of agriculture it is highly valued, and superior to any which is made from the calcareous grit of the Cotswolds, or the blue clay-stone of the vale."

Gypsum.—P. 24. "Aust Cliff, in the parish of Henbury, has a fine bed of alabaster (gypsum), which furnishes a plentiful supply for stuccoing, &c. to the masons of Bristol, Bath, and other places; and might doubtless (?) be employed to advantage in agricultural improvements, though it has not yet found its way into practice in this neighbourhood.

"Derbyshire alabaster is esteemed of superior value by the marble masons, and is sold at Gloucestershire Quay, for fifty shillings per ton, while that from Aust, is so low as twenty-two."

Ironstone.—P. 20. "In the Forest of Dean, iron ore is in great abundance, but a small quantity only is raised. The greater part used in the furnaces is brought from Lancashire, which, under all the expences of carriage, on account of its richness, is more profitable for working."

MINERALS.—P. 20. "The Cotswolds contain no metallic ores, as far as discoveries have hitherto been made."

Coals.—P. 21. "The pits in the Forest" (of Dean) "are numerous, not fewer perhaps than one hundred and fifty. Many of these are worked at a shallow depth, for want of mechanical powers to exhaust the water. The steam-engine, on account of the great expence of erecting it, is beyond the reach of those who generally own and work the pits: for all free miners and colliers claim a right to dig for coal and ore; and as they are a species of adventurers without capital, few of the modern improvements

can

can be expected to take place. There are, however, at this time, three engines; and, from the pits connected with them, coal of good quality has already been raised; though in all, much sulphur is contained, which in burning emits unpleasant, if not unwholesome, vapours, and from its known property of dissolving iron, makes a rapid waste in the bars of the grates, wherein the coal is burnt.

"Three sorts are delivered from the Forest pits: house coal for the use of the kitchen, at about seven shillings per ton; smiths' coal, at five; and lime coal, at four. The lower part of the vale, including the parishes of Cromhall, Yate, Iron Acton, Westerleigh, Puckle-church, Stapleton, Mangotsfield, Bitton, Siston, and St. George's, within the Forest of Kingswood, equally abound in coal, but of a less sulphureous quality. The pits within this district are very numerous, and supply, besides that of the neighbourhood, the vast consumption of the Bristol manufactories, and in some degree of Bath. Here every advantage is derived from the steam-engine, and the pits are sunk to the depth of sixty fathoms or more. The price, at the pit's mouth, is about eight shillings per ton, or nearly three shillings per quarter, of eight bushels."

SUBJECT THE SECOND.

POLITICAL ECONOMY.

POLITICAL DIVISIONS.---Mr. Rudge, as Archdeacon Plymley, and Mr. Duncumb, inserts a list of the hundreds and their respective parishes; which, to the *agricultural* public, can have no other effect than that of enlarging the volume to be purchased.

APPROPRIATION of Commonable Lands.---P. 89. "The advantage of inclosing waste, and laying into severalty common field lands, have been so clearly proved by experience, that, in spite of the heavy expences attending the present mode, a great deal had been done within the last forty years, in comparison of what has been done in more early periods. The first Act of inclosure in this county was of Farmington (12 Anne), in 1714, and the only one during

during that reign. In the following reign, three parishes were inclosed; in the reign of George II. eleven; and, in the present reign, more than seventy Acts have passed the Parliament for inclosing, or laying into severalty.

"By these proceedings, the landlord and occupier are benefited; the former in an advance of rent, the latter in the increase of crops. On the Cotswolds, many thousand acres are brought into cultivation, which before were productive of little more than furze and a few scanty blades of grass. In the Vale, by the inclosure of common fields, lands have been laid together, and rescued from the immemorial custom or routine of crops---wheat, beans, and fallow; and the farmers have found, to their great advantage, that clover, vetches, and turnips, may be raised in the fallow year, which was before attended only with labour and expence."

Mr. R. then proceeds to particularize five advantages: namely, 1. An increase of crops and rent. 2. The commutation of tithes. 3. The drainage of the lands. 4. The removal of the injury and disputes arising from "turning on the head and fore lands" of others. 5. The encoragement of population.

Having remarked, at some length, on each of these advantages, Mr. R. adds—P. 91. "On these accounts, it is greatly to be desired, that one general and uniform plan, less clogged with expences, were sanctioned by an act of the legislature. I am well aware, that the subject has had the consideration of some intelligent and public spirited gentlemen, and doubt not but that their unremitted attentions will eventually conquer the difficulties which at present prevent the full effect of their intentions. Posterity, however, will scarcely believe, that the expences of inclosing 1000 acres, without taking in the subsequent costs of fences and buildings, amounted to 4,500*l.* in the year 1795; which was the fact in the parish of Turley. Great as may be the future advantages of an inclosure, this operates as an obstacle to the general adoption of the plan. It is probable, in the instance now referred to, the fee-simple of the land, in its waste state, would not have much exceeded in price the actual expences incurred. With this heavy burden, however, attached to it, the change has been in favour of the landlord, tenant, and public. Land which before was only valued for a few miserable sheep depastured upon it, and often subject to rot, is now in a state of profitable cultivation, eagerly rented at 30*s.* an acre, and adding 20,000 bushels of corn

at

at least to the stock of the market annually, or some produce equal to it."

Further, on the *effects* of appropriation.—P. 250. "The common or waste lands in the Vale, are seldom stinted to a definite quantity of stock, in proportion to the number of acres occupied; but the cottager claims by custom to stock equally with the largest land-holder. It is justly questioned, whether any profit accrues to either from the depasturing of sheep, since the waste commons, being under no agricultural management, are usually poisoned by stagnated water, which corrupts or renders unwholesome the herbage, producing rot, and other diseases, in the miserable animals that are turned adrift to seek their food there.

"The supposed advantages derived by cottagers, in having food for a few sheep and geese on a neighbouring common, have usually been brought forward as objections to the inclosing system. This question was much agitated with regard to the inclosure of Corse Chase, in this county; but if the present state and appearance of it, since the inclosure in 1796, be contrasted to what it was before, or its present produce of corn to the sheep that used to run over it, little doubt can remain of the advantageous result in favour of the community: 1350 acres of wet and rushy waste were inclosed, and, in the first year of cultivation, the produce was calculated at 20,250 bushels of wheat, or some other crop in equal proportion. If it could even be proved, that some cottagers were deprived of a few trifling advantages, yet the small losses of individuals ought not to stand in the way of certain improvements on a large scale. Besides, the augmentation in demand for the cottager's labour, will much overpay his loss by this trifling privation."

In the Appendix, Mr. Rudge brings forward still further evidence of the good effects of appropriation,—in two parishes on the Cotswold Hills; namely the parish of Aldsworth, and the township of Eastington, in the parish of North Leach.—In the former, the produce of grain, by the inclosure, rose from 720, to 2.360 quarters; giving an annual increase of 1.640 quarters. In the latter, the average produce of grain increased from 690 to 2.100;—the increase being 1.410 quarters;—the rental of the lands rising, in this case, from 500 to 1.460*l.* a year. Mr. R. adds—P. 381. "It is an argument not a little in favour of the inclosing system, that it has operated to the encouragement of labour. It is remarked, that labourers, who formerly were under the necessity

necessity of seeking employment in London and other places, now find it in sufficient quantity at home in their respective parishes."

Regarding the *principles* of appropriation, we find a valuable suggestion, which reflects much credit on the discernment of Mr. Rudge;—and which I, here, insert.—P. 92. "In all acts of inclosure, it might perhaps be proper, as it would certainly be equitable, to relieve the pressure, which weighs on small proprietors, in a degree not proportioned to the advantages they derive from them: for it should be remembered, that the expence of fencing a small allotment, is considerably greater than that of a larger one, according to the quantity; that is, a square piece of land containing ten acres, will cost half as much as forty, though only of one-fourth value. This disproportion occasions much reluctance in the class of proprietors before mentioned; and though it is frequently overcome by the superior influence of the great landholders, yet the injustice of it cannot but strike the considerate mind with conviction."

POPULATION.—Mr. Rudge has inserted a table of great length, in his Report; showing the population of each parish, in the county, at three distinct periods; namely, at the commencement, and the middle, of the last century, and at the beginning of the present:—the first, on the authority of Sir Robert Atkyns; the second taken from Rudder's History of the County; the last, from the Abstract of Returns made by order of Parliament, in 1800.

It makes no part of my present design, to register the population of counties; as the few scattered fragments, found in the Reports to the Board of Agriculture, could not be of much use to the public. A statement of that of the kingdom at large, as well as of its individual parts, is before the public. I will, nevertheless, insert the result of the comparative statement of the population of Glocestershire, at the three periods, above mentioned,—as set down by Mr. R.

P. 362. "The population of the county and city, was at the beginning of the last century, 128,341; had increased to 161,693 near the middle of it, and is now 210,267. After deducting 2,219 for a few instances of decrease, the actual increase during that period is 84,145."

FUEL.—P. 330. "In the immediate neighbourhood of the Forests of Dean and Kingswood, coal is of course a cheap and reasonable article; but in other places dearer, as more or less distant from the pits. In the former district, coal is sold at 7*s.* per ton, and at the latter 3*s.* per quarter

quarter of eight bushesls; or, if a bushel be reckoned at half a hundred weight, about 7*s.* 6*d.* per ton."

The following apt remark, tho it may be applied to private families, is equally applicable to an es ate; whose aggregate value (as well as the rental value of its individual farms) is more or less influenced, by the price of fuel, in its neighbourhood.

P. 331. "Situation in regard to fuel, is a matter of much importance in selecting a place of residence; so that the expenditure of a family at Stow will nearly be in the proportion of six to one of a family near the pits; or, stating the year's consumption at twenty tons, the cost to the first will be at least 35*l.* and to the last from 6*l.* to 7*l.*"

MANUFACTURES.——Glocestershire is a manufacturing county; and, as such, is here entitled to attention. Mr. Rudge's Report is intelligent on this subject.

P. 341. "The principal manufactures of the county, are those of woollen broad-cloths, of various sorts, but chiefly superfine, made of Spanish wool; and of fine narrow goods in the stripe and fancy way, to a very great extent. These are carried on in that district, which, by way of distinction, is called the Bottoms, including parts of the several parishes of Avening, Painswick, Pitchcomb, Randwick, Minchinhampton, Stroud, Bisley, Rodborough, Stonehouse, King's Stanley, Leonard Stanley, Woodchester, Horseley and Eastington. Extensive works are also carried on at Dursley, Cam, Uley, Alderley, Wickwar, and Wotton-under-Edge.

"The scarlet, blue, and black dyes are applied to cloths, in very high perfection, in these districts.

"At Cirencester, thin stuffs, composed of worsted-yarn, which are called Chinas, are manufactured. Carpet-weaving is also carried on in a small way, and a few woollen cloths are made for the army and India Company, which are sent undyed to London. Many labouring people are employed in sorting wool from the fleece: this, however, though forming a considerable part of the trade of the town, is much decreased within the last forty years, as also spinning woollen-yarn and worsted, since the introduction of machinery.

"At Tewkesbury, the stocking-frame-knitting is the principal manufacture, and finds employment for the greatest part of the lower class.

"At Dursley, Stroud, and Wotton-under-Edge, wire cards are made for the use of the clothiers.

"Rugs

"Rugs and blankets are manufactured at Nailsworth, Dursley, and North-Nibley.

"At Froombridge, in the parish of Frampton-upon-Severn, is an extensive set of works for making iron and brass-wire; and at Framilode, in the parish of Eastington, is a manufactory of tin-plate.

"Brass and wire are made at Baptist's-Mills, near Bristol; at Warmley, in the parish of Bitton, and other places in that neighbourhood.

"The pin-manufacture flourishes to an important extent at Gloucester; and on a smaller scale at Warmley, and other places."

Other manufactories, of minor note, are enumerated.

The *effects* of manufactures.—P. 345. "In many parts of the manufacturing districts, the manner in which the poor live, is miserable in the extreme. The interior of their habitations exhibits every appearance of wretchedness and poverty. The mischief is with more facility traced to its cause, than prevented. Independent of the usual effects produced among large associations of workmen, of various tempers, ages, and degrees of depravity, much evil arises from the toe common custom of paying the workmen's wages at the public-house, of all places the most improper and dangerous; since it is almost impossible for a man, however temperate in his inclinations, to resist temptation, thus powerfully offered to his appetites, and encouraged by example.

"The poor are maintained at a heavy expence through the county; and it is proved (chap. 4. sect. 4,) that nearly a seventh of the rental is expended on this and other incidental circumstances, which are provided for by the poor's-rate. The late period of scarcity brought with it more ill consequences, than what merely resulted from the dearness of provisions: it obliged many to apply for parochial relief, who before felt the conscious pride of independence; and that pride having once been broken, has not yet been, nor probably ever will be recovered. No more disgrace is now attached to such applications, than as if they were for the regular earnings of industry.

"In the clothing district, the weight of parochial assessments falls uncommonly heavy on landed property. During the late scarcity, the average charge might be 4*s.* 6*d.* through the county; while, at the same time, it amounted to at least three times that proportion in some of the parishes, where the clothing manufacture is carried on. It surely wears the appearance of unreasonableness and injustice,

injustice, that personal property or stock should not, as the letter of the law directs, assist in relieving this heavy and oppressive charge on the landed interests."

POOR RATES.—P. 66. "It appears, that, in this county, 33,113 persons are relieved in and out of workhouses, at the expence of 3*l.* 1*s.* 7¼*d.* per head, or 102,013*l.* 12*s.* 8*d.* total; which, taking the rental at 1,128,312*l.* gives about 1*s.* 9½*d.* in the pound *per annum.*"

For the unfortunate effect of a scarcity and dearness of provisions, on the moral sentiments of the laboring classes, see the preceding head, *Manufactures.*

Mr. Rudge condemns, not only alehouses and village shops (see p. 399, aforegoing) but *pawnbrokers.* (p. 344) These, however, can only be incident to manufacturing districts;—scarcely, to merely agricultural ones.

TITHES.—On this subject, it would be unjust not to give Mr. Rudge a full hearing. He may, *here,* be considered as speaking, *professionally.*—P. 59. "Within the last century, more than ninety Acts of Parliament have been passed for the inclosure of waste and commonable lands, in this county; by which a considerable part has been exonerated from tythes, besides demesne lands, glebe, and others, which have been discharged by private agreement between the impropriator, and land-owner, or under the Act for the Redemption of the Land-tax.

"In the inclosing of waste, where it has been a part of the plan to exonerate from tythes, a portion of land has been allotted to the tythe-owner, and the same in common fields and old pasture, where practicable: where it has not, owing to the smallness of the properties, or other reasons, corn-rents have been fixed, liable to an alteration of increase or decrease, on an average price of corn for the preceding seven or fourteen years. The general rule laid down and pursued by the commissioners, has been, to give a fifth of arable, and a ninth of pasture, by way of compensation; without any expence to the late owner of the tythes, either towards the charges of the act, inclosing, planting with quicksets, walling, or other modes of ring fencing, and keeping the fences in repair for the seven following years.

"The loss of a tenth part of the improved produce of land, has long been considered as a grievance, and, it must be allowed, not altogether without reason; but that it has operated as a check to agricultural improvements, to such an extent as some writers have endeavoured to carry

carry it, cannot be conceded. In this county, a solitary instance may possibly be produced, where a small quantity of land has been suffered to lie in a neglected state, to defeat the demands of the tythe-owner: but this is a trifling loss in the superficies of a county, and cannot have a sensible influence on the total produce."

Because there are few men so lost to reason and common sense, as to suffer their lands "to lie in a neglected state, to defeat the demands of the tithe owners,"—can this be well brought forward, directly or indirectly, in evidence that—"the loss of a tenth part of the improved produce of land" is not to be considered as a grievance nor as operating, to any great extent, as a check; to agricultural improvements? *One tenth* of the increase of *produce* may be *the whole* of the increase of *profit*; and if the tithe owner take this, what return has the spirited and patriotic cultivator, for his skill, industry and toil; and for the principal and interest of the money laid out on the improvement?

P. 61. "In this county, the instances of tythe being taken in kind, are not numerous; at least among the clergy; and compositions are moderate. In few cases, does the demand exceed 6 *s.* or 7 *s.* per acre, for the produce of arable land; or half-a-crown in the pound, on the rack-rent, of pasture and meadow. Such a demand cannot be deemed inequitable; and it is a justice due to the occupiers to observe, that it is generally submitted to without reluctance

"Where, however, the tythes are taken in kind, a different conduct often prevails: though the lands are continued in the usual course of cultivation, yet unkind feelings are excited on both sides, and all advantages, honourable or otherwise, are taken. A scrupulous exactness, in demanding the utmost which the law allows, and all the jealousy of suspicion, are found on one side; and, on the other, every obstacle, arising from subterfuge, equivocation, and chagrin. Hence, mutual animosities, kept up by repeated irritation, law-suits and enormous expences, which sometimes terminate in ruin. To this may be added, a defeat of the very end of the original establishment, by a dereliction of religious duties on the part of the occupier, and at best a languid and unsatisfactory performance of them on the part of the clergyman. These are evils of sufficient magnitude, even without throwing in the weight of agricultural interests, to induce every well-wisher to the promotion of religion and social comfort,

fort, to look forward with hope of the entire adoption of a plan favourable to peace, and satisfactory to the claims of both parties." These I have long been of opinion must necessarily be the sentiments of all rational and really pious members of the church.

Mr. Rudge's strictures relating to an equitable commutation, or recompense, for tithes, are fraught with ingenuity and good sense; and although he does not explicitly make out a practical plan to proceed upon, he evidently founds his proposals on the true ground, on which, and on which alone, I believe, a just and lasting provision, for the clergy of the established church can be safely raised. I transcribe his remarks, with singular satisfaction.

P. 62. "That a plan, indeed, embracing so many interests and views, can be proposed, free from objection, is hardly to be expected. To make the commutation in land, entirely, is impracticable in many old inclosed parishes; nor is it to be desired. There are some serious objections to the accumulation of this species of property in the Church, which have been sufficiently explained by writers on the subject: nor ought it to consist entirely of money payments: might not both be blended in such a manner as to secure the interests and couveniences of all? To every benefice, let a sufficient portion of land be allotted, where practicable, near the house, to enable the owner to provide some necessary articles for the consumption of the family, without being obliged to have recourse to a distant market: this, however, should not be large enough to constitute a farm, in the strict sense of the word, so as to be the occasion of engaging the occupier too deeply in the business of the world. To ascertain the exact extent of such a glebe, is difficult, as depending on relative circumstances; but it should in some measure depend on the value of the living; and a maximum, or minimum, might be determined at first setting out, above or below which it should not extend. Some benefices are already so well supplied with glebe, as to require no addition; and these might afford certain points, on which calculations might be made for others.

"Money payments can be settled no other way than as corn-rents, secured on the produce of the lands: an investiture in the public funds is liable to serious objections. The rents should vary with the price of corn; and this might be ascertained by a reference to the sessions records, as is usual under private acts. The only alteration I would

I would wish to suggest, is, to leave the choice of that reference to three years, instead of seven or fourteen, with either party. Fourteen, or even seven years include a considerable portion of an incumbent's life; and by looking back on what has passed within the last five years, the disproportion of any corn-rent which might have been fixed ten years before, is obvious. The income of a clergyman should receive an increase proportioned, as nearly as possible, to the advance of prices, since he must feel the inconvenience arising from it; and the same will hold good, in an inverse ratio, on a decrease. The equity of this plan is felt by the occupier also. Supposing, that during the preceding term, corn should have arisen to an extraordinary price, and the corn-rent be fixed accordingly for the next period; from that average, the occupier will pay an unreasonable composition for his tythes, greater perhaps, and more oppressive, than he would have experienced under the ancient system."

The only remark I have to make, on this subject,—to which I have long been attentive,—is, that the money payment for tithes ought to be ANNUALLY adjusted, by the corn returns of the PRECEDING YEAR:—that is to say, at whatever stated time the returns shall be made, and transmitted, by order of Government, to the Incumbent and Church-wardens of each parish, at such time and agreeably to such return, the annual payment shall become due, and its amount be regulated.

Thus, suppose the tithe of a parish to be estimated at two hundred pounds, when wheat (for instance,—or corn in the aggregate) is worth ten shillings a bushel, it may be readily found what the money payment ought to be, when the average price is nine shillings, or eleven shillings, or any other price which the returns may specify. See p. 310 aforegoing.*

PUBLIC DRAINAGE.—P. 258. "On the lands adjoining the Severn, the influx of tide-water is prevented by flood-gates, placed in the large reens or ditches, so contrived that the gate is closed by the weight of water as it rushes from the Severn, and the progress checked; but on the subsiding of

* The above suggestions, as well as those referred to, which have spontaneously presented themselves, in the pursuance of my present undertaking, I wish to have considered as parts of a whole that I hope I shall, hereafter, be able to bring before the public, in a *practical form*;—difficult as the subject may seem to be, and doubtlessly is.

of the tide, the gate is again set at liberty, to let out the water which has been collecting on the upper side from the streams. With all these precautions, however, great inundations are often experienced, and attended with considerable damage. Of late years, much has been prevented by the Commissioners of the Sewers, who have the regulation of the banks, or sea-walls, flood-gates, &c. The parishes, within the jurisdiction of this commission, are rated to the general repairs, in proportion to the number of acres in each, exposed to inundation. Between Arlingham and the lower extremity of the county, at the efflux of the Avon into the Severn, 12,130½ acres are under this management, and may truly be said to be kept in a state of utility by the attention of the Commissioners."

I wish Mr. Rudge had favored us with the outlines, at least, of the history of this Commission of Drainage;—when it was instituted, and to what part of the lands of the county it relates. It would seem to be incident, merely, to the marsh lands of the lower margin of the Severn: whereas public drainage, in the vales of Glocestershire should pervade every portion of them; to free the arable lands, in the flatter parts, effectually, from surface waters, in wet seasons. In the upper vale, this excellent improvement is most required:—not only private property; but the public roads; and the health of the country;—would be thereby ameliorated. See p. 402, aforegoing.

The following most ingenious method of draining a low, flat, swampy country is peculiarly entitled to notice, here. It does the inventor of it very great credit. There are many cases in which it might be successfully applied.—P. 263. "The most curious and scientific mode of open drainage which has been effected in this county, is at Kempsford: it is new, and interesting, and reflects credit on the ingenuity of Mr. Edward Webb, of Stow, under whose direction the plan was carried into execution.

"Where there is a large body of water to carry off by the general drainage, Mr. Webb has taken the upper drains, which collect the principal part of the water, two or three feet above the lower level of the lands, for the purpose of driving a wheel, by which the water is raised from the lower parts. On this principal drain, two wheels are fixed on one shaft: the broad wheel six feet wide, and eight high, driven by the fall out of the upper drain: the narrow wheel one foot wide and fourteen feet high, by which the water is raised three feet out of the lower drain to run off."

This

This is, in effect, the marsh draining mill, turned by water, instead of the wind.

This principal is particularly applicable to the swampy base of a valley, with a natural stream falling through it. By diverting the stream to one side of the valley, above the ground to be drained, and running a catch drain (if required) on the opposite side, to cut off all waters that may be liable to enter the swamps, on that side, and conduct them into the main channel,—the only waters to be got rid of, by the draining wheel, would be those that fall upon, or rise within, the ground to be drained; which, in many cases, might be drawn off by this beautifully simple apparatus.

Also, in a wide flat of country, where low-lying watery grounds are situated by the side of a river, having a sufficient current, the same principle is, in some cases, applicable. Some years ago, in contemplating a tract of country of the last mentioned description, it struck me that, by merely placing a common lave wheel, in the river (not in this case liable to high floods) and fixing on the same axle a wheel to work within a case, in the manner of the marsh mills of Norfolk, &c. the waters of the swampy grounds, conveyed by drains to the side of the river, might thus be raised into it;—and the lands, by such inexpensive contrivance, be relieved.—Mr. WEBB would seem, from the above description, to have had the superior merit of striking out, and executing with success, what I had merely conceived, in theory.

Where the stream to be employed is weak, reservoirs might be formed (especially in a valley) above the site to be drained, to collect water in ordinary seasons, to be used with greater effect when the season is moist, and draining most required.

A map of the site accompanies the verbal notice; but without affording much, if any, *general information,* that is *practicably* applicable to *other sites;* no two, generally speaking, being the same. But the principle is so simple and evident, that any one, practically conversant with the subject of drainage, may easily apply it.

The following is the letterpress "explanation of the plate annexed;"—and all that is further said, concerning this (tho not well reported) by far the most interesting and useful part of the body of the work under review.

P. 264.—"The grand drain is twelve feet wide at the bottom of the lower extremity, and diminishes in its progress upwards: at some places, it is nine feet deep below the surface.

"The

"The embankment of the embanked drain, is four feet high on the lowest land, and diminishes to a point at the upper part.

"The lower meadows are embanked, to keep off smaller floods. The draining-wheel, B. drains the water off three meadows, three feet below their surface, by trunks through the embankments, and takes off all the upper waters; this wheel is driven by water from the upper drain.

"One thousand acres are drained by the grand drain, and three hundred by the embanked drain. The land which requires this mechanical contrivance to get rid of its water, has of course no natural fall for common drainage, lying on the banks of the Thames, whose surface is generally above that of the adjoining meadows."

CANALS.—Three canals have of late years been planned, and wholely, or in part, executed, in Glocestershire:—namely, the "Stroudwater Canal," which joins the waters of the Thames and the Severn;—the "Hereford and Glocester Canal,"—to join, in effect, those of the Severn and the Wye; and "the Berkeley Canal;" which, we are told (p. 30) "was intended to form a shorter and more easy, as well as more safe communication for vessels of large burden, between Gloucester and the Severn, in its wider parts. The expectations of the first projectors were sanguine, and probably well grounded; but the calculations which were made of the supplies necessary to the completion of it, proved so erroneous, that after 120,000l. had been expended, scarcely 5 of 17 miles and a half were finished. The bason, at Gloucester, was begun in 1794; the canal is 70 feet wide at top, 20 at bottom, and 18 deep."

Mr. Rudge (who is *not* a violent canalist) states the loss of lands, by the canals above named, thus:—P. 337. "The Berkeley, according to its original plan, 215 acres at least; the Stroudwater, with the Thames and Severn in their passage through this county, upwards of 200; and the Hereford, more than 100; making in the whole a sum total of 515 acres lost to the purposes of agriculture, besides a considerable quantity rendered almost useless by the oozing of the water through the banks." But Mr. R. adds,—P. 338. "The time is probably fast approaching, when the iron rail-road will supersede the further use of canals, for the conveyance of materials and commodities of all kinds, through the interior parts of the island."

This, however, may be saying too much. Canals and railways are both good, in their proper situations. And, in in regard to the loss of land, by canals, it may be right to remark, that the saving of hay and corn (for horse provender) by water carriage (on the two canals first above-mentioned) will probably throw into the public market the produce of manifold the number of acres destroyed by their courses. Many of the existing canals are highly beneficial to agriculture, and superiorly so, to the community at large. And it is more than probable,—I will venture to say certain,—that there are several lines, in this island, along which canals may yet be cut, with similar advantages. I am happy to find, however, (as I have elsewhere mentioned) that the mania of canal making has abated;—never, I hope, to rage again. Railways may, in numerous situations, be formed in preference to canals. But let not a rage for railways succeed that for canals. Let each take the lines for which they are, respectively, best adapted.

SUBJECT THE THIRD.

RURAL ECONOMY

DIVISION THE FIRST.

TENANTED ESTATES,

Their IMPROVEMENT and MANAGEMENT.

ESTATES.—P. 34. "The largest property does not, probably, exceed 8000l. a year among the nobility, and from 3000l. downward, among the gentry. The number of yeomen who possess freeholds, of various value, is great, as appears frum the Sheriff's return of the poll, at the election for a county member in 1776, when 5790 freeholders voted, and the number since that period is much increased."

Proprietors.—Mr. Rudge has inserted, in his Report, a long list of landed Proprietors in Glocestershire. It certainly is creditable to his industry. But it is rather adapted to the use of a candidate for the county membership, than to that of the Board of Agriculture.

Tenure

Tenures.—P. 35. "The greater part of the property of this county, is freehold, some is copyhold, and about a fortieth portion of the whole is held under corporations, ecclesiastical or temporal. A considerable part of the latter has been enfranchised under the late Act of Parliament for the redemption of land-tax.

"Estates under the See of Gloucester, are leased out upon lives; and the usual mode is, to renew on the falling of a life at a year and a half improved annual value of the estate. Three lives in possession, and three in reversion, are upon copyholds. Under the Dean and Chapter, estates are held by leases of twenty-one years, renewable every seven, on a fine of one year and a half improved value.

"The tenure under the Corporation of Gloucester is nearly the same.

"Under proprietors, not corporate, the renewal of a single life is usually made at two years annual value."

Improvement of Estates.—*Draining.*—Mole plow.—

Mr. R. Lumbert of Risington Wick, in this County, has invented a "Mechanical Apparatus" for working the mole plow, *by hand*, instead of with horses; namely, by eight men, instead of twelve horses.

And Mr. Rogers of Withington, also in Glocestershire, has improved upon Mr. Lumbert's plan, by working this, in many cases, valuable implement, with *one horse*, instead of eight men.

The principle of the apparatus is that of the capstan, fixed in the centre of a broad-based frame of wood; and worked by levers:—A *Cable*, that is a strong rope or chain, being firmly fastened, with what may be termed an *Anchor*, at some distance from the machine, the implement is thereby impelled forward.

Under Mr. Rogers's improvement, a single lever is used, and of such length that thereby "one horse gains a power equal to thirty." (p. 261.) The horse, being harnessed, or *hamed* (we are not told which) to the end of the lever, works (*it would seem*;—for the descriptive part of this, as of that concerning draining, is unfortunately defective) round the apparatus; which, of course, keeps moving forward, as the rope or chain is wound round the pillar of the capstan;—the cable being prevented from rising too high (as it winds up the pillar) and thereby hindering the horse (it would seem!) from stepping over it,—by a friction wheel or wheels, fixed in the fore part of the frame; and a drag, fixed to the hind part of it, to prevent it (no doubt!) from lifting

lifting, when the cable rises high up the pillar of the capstan.

This is another beautifully simple, yet practical, contrivance that does Glocestershire considerable honor. Instead of the ground being partially torn to pieces, by eight or ten horses, drawing in a double line, (which I have ever considered as the chief objection to the mole plow,)—the whole surface is not only lightly, but evenly, trodden. For, owing to the progressive motion of the machine, and the rotatory movement of the horse, the animal must, necessarily, be constantly treading fresh ground,—can never step twice on the same surface.

On this occasion, as on that relating to draining, an engraving is given.—But, in this instance, the pencil and the pen are equally inexplicit; and, jointly, cannot answer any other good purpose, than that of an *Advertisement.*

Irrigation.—Mr. Rudge has not, like Mr. Turner, passed by, unnoticed, the famed water meadows of South Cerney; which are politically situated within the verge of Glocestershire; but, which as has been mentioned, are naturally a part of the vale lands of North Wiltshire;—having no natural relation to the Cotswold hills of Glocestershire; proximity only excepted. However, being included within the limits of Mr. R's precinct, it was his duty to bring them forward; which he has done in the following manner.

P. 275. "The practice of watering, or irrigation, is chiefly pursued in those vallies of the Cotswolds which are intersected by rivulets, and particularly in the meadows adjoining the Coln, and the Churn. In the parish of South Cerney, which is watered by the latter, it is carried to greater perfection, than elsewhere. The practice first began here, and has received all its improvements under the care and direction of the Rev. Mr. Wright, who has communicated the results of his experiments to the public in a treatise on the subject. To the judicious observations which he has made, little can be added; and those who wish to see the whole management fully explained, will refer to the pamphlet itself."

These meadows have no *natural* connexion with Glocestershire, and are in themselves too inconsiderable, had I even heard of them, while I was stationary in the county, to have engaged my particular attention.—Wiltshire, not Glocestershire is the county proper to be studied for practical knowledge on the watering of grass lands. But Mr. Wright's first edition having fallen into my my hands (the most empty publication on Agriculture, I have, even to this day, read) I made this corner of Glocestershire in my way from London to South Wales, in July 1804;—went over a considerable part of the extended flat of meadow lands, on the Isis and the Churn, whether situated in Wiltshire, or in Glocestershire; and particularly those of South Cerney;—even its Mill Meadow,—*classic* ground!—with one of the principal occupiers in the parish; of which Mr. Wright, I understood, was for some time Curate.

In South Cerney, there is a considerable extent of meadow lands. In the lower parts of the parish, they mostly lie in a flat, swampy state; being irrigated, merely, by the waters flowing out of the ditches, in times of floods. Nearer the village, something of organization appears:—but still such as a "drowner" of Salisbury or Amesbury would smile at. In the immediate neighbourhood of the village, it is true, a tolerable *imitation* of the Amesbury and Salisbury meadows is observable:—I mean in regard to the general distribution of the water. But, with respect to the forming of ridges, or beds, to receive it,—even Mill Meadow bears no resemblance to the well formed water-meads of the CHALKHILL DISTRICT of Wiltshire. I saw no appearance of the soil having been artificially moulded into convex beds,—to give due acceleration to the motion of the water. The only *forming* which I observed, even near the village, was that of dividing the meadow with shallow, and, where the turn of surface would admit of it, parallel drains; with intermediate channels, raised a few inches above the natural surface, to receive the water;—the beds themselves (between the floats and the drains) lying in their natural state;—leaving it to "time to round the beds." I saw the water on one of the meadows, where it appeared to lie dead upon the ground; there being scarcely any perceptible current. What a practice, this, to boast of, and write about!

The only particular that struck me in going over those meadows, and which appeared to be, in any way, peculiar to them, and eligible to be imitated,—is the practice of stirring up the mud of the ditches, to enrich the water passing through them to the land.—This, where the mud is of an enriching quality, as that which is deposited by calcareous waters, or by the washings of a town, as in the case of South Cerney,—whose waters issue from the Cotswold Hills, and wash the large town of Cirencester,—is obviously eligible.

Enquiring

Enquiring as to the age of the practice of watering meadows, in this parish, I was shown some meadows which, it was believed, had been watered upward of one hundred years. But, in general, they are, I understood, of more modern date.

Mr. Rudge refers, as above, to Mr. Wright's book;—and as I saw, some time ago, an *advertisement!* purporting that Mr. W. had published another edition of his performance, it may hereafter come, in its place, under my examination.

Mr. Rudge's own remarks, on Irrigation, (notwithstanding his reference to Mr. Wright's pamphlet) might have been spared,—after what had previously been written and published, on the subject, by those who well understood it.

EXECUTIVE MANAGEMENT of Estates.—On *Leases* and *Covenants* something is said. But I find nothing that requires particular notice, here.—"Covenants (we are told p. 66) are generally the same as in other counties."!

DIVISION THE SECOND.

WOODLANDS.

WOODS.—The beautiful chain of woods and timber groves, mentioned in the following extract, have not, I find, been noticed, in my own *agricultural* register. I therefore thankfully bring them forward, here.

P. 239. "The declivities of the hills which border the Cotswolds towards the Vale, almost along the whole extent, and particularly from Birdlip to Wotton-under-edge, are covered with the most luxuriant beeches, which present to the Vale a continued verdant skreen. The most extensive are those of Sir William Hicks, at Witcomb; Mr. Sheppard, at Hampton and Avening; Mr. Kingscote, at Kingscote; but above all, in extent as in beauty, the magnificent woods at Spring Park, and on the Frocester and Stanley hills, belonging to Lord Ducie.

"As these beech-woods re-produce themselves from seeds self-sown, they generally come up so thick as to require

quire to be constantly drawn for the first twenty or thirty years. The remaining trees then stand for timber, and are supposed to come to their perfection in seventy or eighty years. Woods of the best timber will then be worth from 80*l.* to 100*l.* per acre. They are sold to dealers, who convert the timber on the spot, into proper scantling for gun-stocks, saddle-trees, bedsteads, chairs, and other cabinet work; and of late years a considerable portion has been converted into what is called, in the West Indies, lumber, or staves for sugar-hogsheads. These several articles, deprived of waste bulk, are carried on at a cheap rate to Birmingham and Bristol, for exportation; but the cost of carriage prevents the supply of them to a London market."

The subjoined particulars (which I take for granted are sufficiently authentic) relating to the FOREST of DEAN, are valuable.

P. 242. "In the Forest of Dean, notwithstanding the continual depredations committed, there still remains a large quantity of valuable timber.* Under the direction of Government, the number of trees has at different times been well ascertained. In the reign of Charles I. there were growing within the limits of the Forest 105,557 trees, containing 61,928 tons of timber, 153,209 cords of wood. This number has been considerably diminished during that reign, by an imprudent grant made to Sir John Wintour, as appears by the survey of the following reign, when there were found 25,929 oaks, and 4204 beeches, containing, besides cordwood, 11,335 tons of ship-timber. The grant was renewed; and so much diligence was employed in the destruction of the trees, that, in 1667, of 30,133 oaks and beech mentioned in the preceding survey, only 200 remained; and, of the 11,335 tons of ship-timber reserved, not more than 1100 had been delivered. In the 20th Charles II. 11,000 acres were enclosed, planted, and carefully protected; and on these, the principal timber for the supply of the King's dock-yards immediately from this Forest, has of late been felled. In 1714, there were computed to be 27,302 loads fit for the navy, and 168,051 trees, of about sixty years growth. In 1783, on a new survey it was computed, that there were 90,382 oak trees, containing 95,043 loads; and in 1788, the timber growing in

* In the section "Wastes," p. 252, Mr. R says—"The Forest furnishes about 1000 loads of navy timber annually."

in the Forest, and immediately belonging to the Crown, was as follows: 24,000 oak trees, measuring about 30,000 loads; and 22,000, about 11,000; besides unsound trees, which were numerous, and a considerable quantity of fine large beech, and young growing trees, sufficient to furnish an annual supply of 1500 loads for seventy years from that time, which, by proper management, and well protected inclosures, might be made perpetual.

"Besides the oak timber growing on the royal demesne lands, there is a considerable quantity on the estates of individuals, which are held under the Crown, within the district, in purlieus of the Forest, as well as of other land-owners in the parishes of Dimock and Longhope, adjacent to the Forest, and within what is agriculturally considered as the Forest district."

PLANTING.—P. 244. "In the Forest of Dean, within the last thirty-five years, nearly 3000 acres have been planted, chiefly with oak.

"The usual time of planting acorns in the Forest, is as soon after Christmas as the weather will permit. This practice is founded on the idea, that they are likely to be eaten by mice and other vermin, if planted before; but an intelligent planter belonging to the Forest is of opinion, that autumn planting is best, because at that time there is sufficient food for these animals, and more easily obtained; and that in spring, after the acorns have lain in the ground for the winter, they become sour and unpalatable.

"The method of planting is, first, to mark out the ground; then taking off about a foot square of turf, to set two or three acorns with a setting-pin; afterwards to invert the turf upon them, and, by way of raising a fence against hares and rabbits, to plant two or three strong whitethorn sets round. They are seldom thinned till they have attained the size of hop-poles, and then are left at twelve feet distance from each other, with the view of again thinning them, by taking out every other one, when they are thirty years old, and have attained the size of five or six inches diameter. By growing thick, no side-shoots are thrown out, which supersedes the necessity of pruning.*

"The young trees which are drawn at the first thinning,

* In raising timber for the use of the house carpenter, this is an eligible practice; but not for growing valuable ship timber.

ning, are transplanted, and, as it is thought, grow equally well with those that have not been removed, and produce timber as full at the heart, compact, strong, and durable, as that which is raised immediately from the acorn.

"An elevated common called Woolridge, in the parish of Maisemore, was planted about the year 1735, by Bishop Benson, with 1200 small oaks, collected from the neighbouring coppices. On the inclosure of the common, in 1793, the greater part were cut down: they had taken their growth with different degrees of vigour, but in general measured from five to six feet round, near the ground. Of those which were left, one was cut down this year (1805), which measured nearly eight feet round, and in length about fourteen feet: the timber is perfectly solid, without a blemish or decayed part in it."

The following notice of the *walnut tree* is worthy of being registered.—P. 245. "Among trees which bespeak the attention of the agricultural planter, both for its timber and fruit, is the walnut *(juglans regia)*. It will grow almost in any soil, wants no pruning or care, and, in less time than the oak, will make a large tree. The wood is too valuable to apply to the usual purposes of timber trees, but is always used either in cabinet work or for gunstocks: for the latter, indeed, so great has been the demand for a few years past, from the Birmingham gunmakers, that the county has been ransacked for this wood, and high prices have been held out to tempt the sale of it. In consequence of this, the stock has been much diminished, and, with very few exceptions, only here and there is a solitary walnut-tree seen growing. In the parish of Arlingham there are more, perhaps, than in many other parishes combined; so abundant, indeed, is the fruit this year, (1805,) that it is become an article of commerce, and two vessels are now (October 11) being laden with walnuts for Scotland, at Arlingham, as low as 4s. or 5s. a thousand. Even at this price, the produce of a tree is highly valuable, as 20,000 are not considered an extravagant calculation for a large tree."

In Wales, and it would seem on the Welch side of Glocestershire, the bark of trees is substituted for hemp, in making ropes of every description; halters and plow traces not excepted. Mr. R. in mentioning the *lime tree*, gives the subjoined imperfect account of preparing the bark, for such purposes.—P. 247. "Of the inner bark are made ropes for cyder-presses, draw-wells, and fishing-boats.

boats. To the latter purposes, they are excellently adapted, as not contracting or expanding from moisture or draught. The bark is stripped off about Midsummer, dried like hay in the sun, and is called "bast:" it is either manufactured on the spot, or removed to other places for the same purpose. Bast-ropes are sold at a hundred yards length, in pairs, for 14s. per pair."

DIVISION THE THIRD.

AGRICULTURE.

FARMS.—The *sizes* of farms, politically considered, is a topic which most men feel themselves equal to discuss; and is a subject on which almost any man may say or write a great deal. Mr. R. has stained nearly half a sheet of *precious* paper with it:—Yet without furnishing one idea, I believe, which was not, previously, before the public.

Homesteads.—As on the subject of agriculture, proper, little practical knowledge can be reasonably expected, from an unpractised writer, I shall seize with the greater avidity any hint that may be occasionally dropt, in this Report, and which can be in the least useful, to the practical husbandman.—P. 44. "Where the stack happens to lean so much on either side as to require aid to prevent its falling, it is a good practice to arm the props with a sheet of tin, nailed round them, half way up, in the form of a funnel inverted; this stops vermin in their progress to the stack, and tin, on account of its polished surface, is best adapted to the purpose."—It is not unusual to nail plates of tin, *flat*, upon a shore, or support, set up against an ill built stack. Raising it from the pole, on the lower side, is an obvious improvement.

Cottages.—This is another topic on which any man, who has the use of the pen, can write to any extent; and, like that relating to the sizes of farms, has employed the pens of numbers. Clergymen are, or ought to be, in the nature of their profession, the best judges of the wants and comforts of cottagers. I shall therefore collect several passages,

sages, from different parts of Mr. Rudge's Report;—not so much, however, from their containing what is new; as to corroborate what has been repeatedly urged.—Mr. Rudge "must be a sensible man; because he thinks as I do."

From the section "Cottages,"—P. 48. "A cottage, which merely protects the inhabitant from the inclemency of the weather, is an incompleat provision: sound policy requires some concomitant advantages to attach him to his dwelling. I do not think that a cow is one of the necessary appendages to a cottage, or generally productive of good. In particular cases, the experiment has succeeded well, as reported by Lord Winchelsea, on his estates: and it will, perhaps, succeed in others, where the influence of a great land proprietor extends over the whole parish, or district; but property, in few instances, is thus consolidated. Besides, the management of a cow is attended with considerable trouble, requires more utensils than the earnings of a day labourer can well supply, and more conveniencies of building than are usually attached to a cottage. Capital is the sinew of husbandry, and, unless it be proportioned to the undertaking, the efforts will be weak, and the success uncertain.

"There is also reason to doubt, whether the labourer or his wife will be able to spare the time from their respective employments, and should it so happen, the evil will overbalance the good. It is pleasing to see a good garden, and a pig attached to the cottage: but neither of these interfere with the daily services of the labourer, or withdraw him from the necessary attention to the business of the farmer.

"The greatest of evils to agriculture would be to place the labourer in a state of independence, and thus destroy the indispensable gradations of society. The great body of mankind, being obliged to live with, and by each other, must necessarily consist of proprietors and workmen; and if it be allowed that the dependance of a regular supply of crops rests, among other things, on the regular services of the latter, it is surely an experiment not altogether without danger, to place them in such a situation as will cause them to remit a portion of their labour, at a time, perhaps, when it is most wanted."

In the section "Poor Rates," however, Thomas Estcourt, esquire, it appears, has an opinion (rather new, in England) that something more, of an arable nature, than a mere garden, is requisite, or adviseable, to meliorate the condition

dition of laborers; and relieve the public burden. He says,—P. 65. "If a cottager occupies an acre of land, so situated as that the plough may be admitted to the cultivation of it, and he can prevail on his master to lend the use of his team to plough the land, and cart out the manure, the whole of the rest of the work may be done by the family, without the labourer's losing an hour's time on it." Mr. R. adds, "This opinion is founded on the experience of several instances, in which it has been performed; and particularly in three, where widows, with each a large family, have maintained them by their labour."

In the Highlands of Scotland, a practice of this kind prevails. An "Acreman" is one step above a mere cottager. But, there, he is generally appendant to a small farmer; who is obliged, by the terms of his holding, to plow and harrow the acreman's plot of land; which thus becomes a constant cause of strife between them; and the produce of it, of course, is frequently of inferior value. And were the project, above recommended, to become general, farmers in England would find themselves frequently embarrassed; or the laborer's acres be ruinously neglected. Beside, the cottager's acre could seldom be attached to his dwelling; and his attention, in this case, would be led not only from his employer's business, but from his own home: or, if attached to his garden in a village, his crops would be liable to the depredations of wild and domestic animals.

In the chapter, "Gardens and Orchards," we find the following sensible remarks.—P. 196. "The gardens of the village labourers exhibit various instances of industry; and the character of the inhabitant may usually be determined by the appearance of cultivation without. Most of the cottages in the county possess, in a greater or less degree, this useful appendage; few, however, in a quantity sufficiently large to effect any great advantage. To what size, indeed, cottage gardens may be extended, with safety to the interests of agriculture, can only be ascertained by long continued experiments on a large scale. It has been already observed (chap. 3. sect. 3), that they ought not to be so far extended as to occupy too great a portion of the labourer's time; his attentions being wanted elsewhere. Wheat should not be among the productions of small inclosures; because it is a lure to the depredations of small birds; and the trouble of the different processes, before it is ready for the mill, probably overbalances the profit, besides the difficulty of finding manure sufficient to keep

the

the land in a good state of cultivation. Plantations of beans, peas, cabbages, and potatoes, will assist the cottager, in the keep of a pig, more than any other vegetable. In summer, the refuse of the cabbage, with wash, &c. will be sufficient for food; the straw of the beans and peas, with the haulm of the potatoes, will supply litter; while the less valuable of the potatoes, boiled or steamed, the gleanings of the harvest, and a little additional corn, will fatten him. If field peas or beans be cultivated, a part may be gathered green for eating, and the remainder left to ripen for the use of the stye. By this management, manure will be made for the land, as almost the whole of the produce will be again returned to it in the state of dung."

Again. P. 197. "Culinary productions being so advantageous to the cottager, the exertions of those, who, anxious for the increased comforts of the poor, have proposed rewards as an encouragement, for the best managed gardens, are highly wise and humane. The premium, however, should be given to him, who, without diminishing the attentions due to the farmer, with the least loss of time and regular earnings, as well as the least encroachment on Sabbath duties, has cultivated his garden with superior neatness and success. Loss of time is a material consideration, because every day, which does not bring in its proper return of money, is really lost to the family, and must occasion a reduction of some articles necessary to their comfortable subsistence. The industrious cottager, who has an eye to all these circumstances, will employ in his garden the extra hours, before he begins, and after he leaves off, the regular work of the day: this becomes a real saving, being so much time gained from idleness, and so much added to the stock of comforts, which others, under the influence of a lounging and indolent disposition, throw away."

After considering, at some length, and with much ability, the best size of a cottager's garden (calculating the number of leisure hours a day laborer in husbandry has in the course of a year, before and after the usual hours of work, and the quantity of labor they would allow him to perform) Mr. Rudge proceeds to draw the plan, and point out the general economy of a COTTAGE GARDEN. I insert his proposals here, as they appear to have been the result of much attention bestowed on the subject.

P. 200. "Concluding, that at present half an acre will in few instances be exceeded, and that it will be in most cases

cases sufficient for the labour of one man, without interfering with his usual engagements, I shall draw the plan of a cottager's garden, with the probable method of managing it to advantage.

"The ground is supposed to be of good quality, well fenced, and adjoining the house. A small portion may first be allotted to herbs and small seeds; then the remainder parted into three divisions; one for carrots, parsneps, onions, cabbages, borecole, &c.; the second for beans or peas, according to the nature of the soil; and the third for potatoes. The crops should succeed in regular rotation, and the manure always used with the potatoes. The occupier should be supplied with seeds and plants for the first year, after which he may contrive, from his own crops, to keep on a succession, or sell enough for necessary change.

"One-third of the ground may appear large, for what are usually called culinary productions; but it is of great consequence, that a poor man's family should be well supplied with vegetables; and if there be an overstock, nothing will be lost, as it will afford a present supply for the stye, and save the potatoes for winter use."

I have to remark, on this subject, that, as a *standard*, half an acre of ground is, in my opinion, too great a quantity for a cottage garden. As the *maximum* of extent, I can allow it. There is an objection to a *large* garden attached to a cottage. It is capable of alienating, not only the attention, but the labor, of its occupier, from the daily task of his constant employer. Most laborers (not all) who have much hard work to go through, in the evening, will not fail to favor themselves, during the day; and, perhaps, endeavor to desert their master's work, for their own, ere their honest day's work be done. Nor does a man who has been working hard, during some hours, in the early part of the morning, fall to his daily labor with the required alacrity. This is notorious, when day laborers are permitted (or otherwise engage) in the summer season, to perform "taken work," before and after "working hours." From a quarter to half an acre, I have long considered as the proper size of a cottage ground. See TREATISE on LANDED PROPERTY. Art. *Cottage Grounds.*

I will here suggest,—as a probable mean of exciting the industry of cottagers, and thereby abating the rise of the poor rates,—that cottage gardens ought to be liable to the inspection of the overseers of the poor, whenever their occupiers apply for relief;—and that (under ordinary

nary circumstances) relief should be withheld, or lessened, to those who *idly* neglect their gardens.

OCCUPIERS. For remarks on the *Agricultural profession*, and the *profits* attached to it, see the close of the Review of this Report.

PLAN OF MANAGEMENT.—Mr. Rudge has noticed two remarkable instances of practice, or expediency, in two extreme parts of Glocestershire.—The first is at the foot of the Cotswold Hills, bordering on Wiltshire, where barley was grown *pereniallу!*—P. 106. "A field in Shipton Moigne is asserted, by the inhabitants and the tenant, to have been for thirty years, preceding 1800, sown with barley, except once only with wheat, and once with turnips. The wheat is said to have run chiefly to straw, and little corn: the average crop of barley was from twenty to twenty-four customary bushels of nine gallons and a half, per statute acre."

The other, in the Bristol quarter.—P. 146. "The land is kept 'two years up and two years down.' When broken up from the clover ley, wheat is sown, then barley, with seeds. This course is seldom interrupted, except occasionally by a crop of potatoes before the wheat, and, where the soil is more loamy, oats instead of barley before clover." This is the less probable of the two.

WORKPEOPLE.—P. 328. "The general price of agricultural labour per day, through the year, except during harvest, is 1*s.* 6*d.* and about a gallon of drink."—In 1788, the ordinary day wage was one shilling:—a rise of fifty percent, having taken place, in twenty years.

WORKING ANIMALS.—Mr. R. enters pretty largely into the controversial topic of "horses and oxen compared as to their use in husbandry." But, for reasons repeatedly given, I will only extract the facts which he has adduced, relative to instances of practice, in Glocestershire.—P. 318. "The operations of husbandry are more generally performed with horses than oxen, in the Vale, where the soil is heavy, and will not bear much treading. On the Cotswolds, on the sandy lands of the Forest district, and in the southern parts of the Vale, oxen are generally used; one team at least, on most large farms. The Herefordshire breed have the preference, for two reasons; first, because they are smaller in the bone, and more active than the Gloucestershire, northern, or long-horned; secondly, because they are more profitable, going on with less food during their work, and, when put to the stall, from their aptitude

aptitude to feed, producing more beef, with less food, and in less time.

"Wherever oxen have come into use, the advantages of them have been great; and it seems to be more the effect of ancient prejudice than experiment, that they are not used with profit even on stiff soils. At Shipton-Moigne, a principal farmer employs an ox-team on strong clay land; they go single, and do as much, if not more work per day, than any horse team in the parish.*"

TILLAGE.—The section, Tillage, is sufficient to convince any practical man, that the Reporter, is unpractised, in matters of Agriculture. I am happy, however, to find, in his Report, that the practitioners of the Vale are lowering their ridges, in the manner I recommended.

N. P. 103. "A great improvement is now adopted by some sensible farmers, to get rid of these deep furrows; which is, by ploughing up a small ridge between the two high ones; this renders the land much drier, and more healthy, by raising the furrows, and thereby causing a better draught for the surface water."

GROWING CROPS.—Mr. R. gives a sort of catalogue raisonne of some of the corn weeds of Glocestershire; and speaks, in a didactic manner, of their destruction. I am not disappointed, however, at finding nothing new or excellent in his strictures. I have only to mention his notice of the *cuscuta*, or dodder, as a weed among pulse; which I insert, here, on Mr. R's authority; having not observed it myself, in that character.—P. 162. "Dodder *(cuscuta europæa)*

"* It has been asserted by some writers on agricultural subjects, *(see Baird's Survey of Middlesex, p. 41, note,)* that oxen will not stand constant work on hard roads. This doctrine, however, is opposed by the following fact.

"T. Estcourt, Esq. of Estcourt, near Tetbury, M. P. a few years since employed a team of horses and another of oxen, for two years, during the time his house was building, for the purpose of drawing timber and other materials, great part of which was brought from the distance of fourteen miles. The team of four horses, and the other of five oxen, used to go twice every week; they set out together in the night, and returned the next day; but it was observable, that the oxen so far out-walked the horses as to be at home about two hours before them. The horses were black, stout, and able; the oxen of the Herefordshire breed, and they brought the same weight. They were worked in harness, as horses, and shod; and their shoes lasted generally as long as those of horses. Their food was grass in summer, and hay in winter, but no corn. Hence it appears, that oxen will, if properly tutored to it, walk with a load as fast, and work on the road as well, as horses. *Extract from a Communication of T. Estcourt, Esq. to the Board of Agriculture.*"

europæa) is a great enemy to beans, vetches, and some other plants, but is never seen among wheat, barley, or oats. As soon as it has fixed on the plant, it separates from the root, and, like other parasitical weeds, draws all its nourishment from the plant it has embraced. Large quantities of beans are often ruined completely by it, so as not to carry a single pod; and no method has yet been discovered to destroy it; for though the root cannot be found, yet it surely returns in some part of the field, where it has once begun to grow, whenever the plants on which it feeds, form the crop of the season."

WHEAT.—*Tillage*.—Cotswold Hills.—P. 110. "In the neighbourhood of Stow, and other places, where the land is 'tough,' it is the practice, in dry seasons, to plough one furrow and leave one; which is called 'risbalking,' or 'strike balking.' The land is immediately 'scuffled,' or torn to pieces with the scuffler, and left in that state till sowing time.

"The land at the time of sowing is oftentimes quite green with weeds; and indeed some farmers say, the greener the better."—This I insert as another *variety* of the innovatory practice of those hills. See p. 411, aforegoing.

Semination of wheat —Season of sowing.—P. 114. "On the Cotswolds, seed-time commences immediately after the first sufficient fall of rain in August: on these soils, plentiful showers are necessary at the time of sowing; and when the chance of such a season is lost, the seed lies a considerable time in the ground without shooting, for moisture soon sinks away through the crevices of the sub-rock; and if a long drought follows a dry seed-time, the blade does not acquire sufficient strength to withstand the cold winds of winter; besides the loss sustained from birds, vermin, and insects, during its unvegetating state."

Preparing the seed.—The following experiments, relating to the *smut* of wheat, being the only proof that Mr. Rudge has given us of his own experience in agricultural affairs, I readily copy his recital. But whether these experiments were made in the field, or the *garden*, is not mentioned.—P. 112. "The wheat of the Cotswolds is little liable to smut, and experienced farmers assign two reasons; one, the use of old seed; the other, sowing on stale furrow. Perhaps it may be difficult to explain the rationale of this; yet smut certainly does not prevail so much on the Hills as in the Vale, though it is found more frequently there than formerly, and, as it is supposed, from

from want of care in the choice of seed, or sowing too soon after ploughing.

"That smut will sometimes produce smut, is evident from the following fact. Some cottagers, who occupy small portions of land in the neighbourhood of Tetbury, (which run long and narrow, in the nature of common field land, and adjoining to each other in the same field and same soil,) sowed with wheat in 1801. A few of these cottagers bought some smutty wheat of a farmer in the parish, for seed, because it was sold cheap,* the others sowed good seed. The first had smutty crops, not exceeding four bushels to the quarter of an acre; the latter had a crop perfectly free from smut, and from eight to ten bushels on the same proportion of land, though adjoining to, and intermixed with, the other lands which bore a smutty crop.

"That this, however, is not always the case, appears from the following experiments made by myself in the two last years. In November 1804, I sowed three parcels of wheat: the first was the half of some fine seed from the Cotswolds; the second, the other half, well mixed and compleatly tagged with smut-powder, taken from a smutty ear which grew in the Vale; the third, was picked from smutty ears, and well tagged with smut-powder from the same ears. The seeds were sown in drills, at a considerable distance from each other, in ground that had been some time *dug*. They all produced good ears, well filled, and without smut. In November 1805, I sowed some grains, taken from a quantity in the market, as black as if they had been shaken in soot: the ground had been dug a month before; the wheat grew luxuriantly, and the result was the same as in the former experiments. Still, whatever is the cause of smut, it is not prudent to risque a crop, on the chance of getting good corn from smutty seed."

More fresh *varieties* of practice.—P 111. (Cotswolds) —"The methods most in use are, (according to the broadcast system,) either below or above furrow. In the first, the land is ploughed about three inches deep; it being the opinion, that on these light lands, if the plough went deeper, the best prepared mould would be buried in the subrock. The seed being sown, and thus ploughed in, the harrow is lightly dragged over. In the second, the seed

* This is an evidence against *acre* farming. See p. 447, aforegoing.

seed is dragged in without ploughing; and in both cases, if the land be light and moist, it is, immediately after, well trodden with sheep and other cattle, with the view of giving firmness to the soil, and enabling it to retain its nutritious juices. This treading is sometimes repeated, when the wheat first makes its appearance, with this difference, that *dry* weather is *now* chosen for the purpose."

Drilling.—P. 111. "The drilling system is only followed, where the soil is pretty clear from stones; for, in some parts, they lie so abundant and large on the surface, that it is very difficult to preserve a straight course with the plough, and, of course, to deposit the seed regularly.

"On the declivities of the Hills, in the Vale and Forest district; similar methods of putting in are observed; but in the two latter, drilling is every season more and more practised." The latter part of this extract I insert on the authority of the Reporter.

A new variety in *field* semination.—P. 146. (Bristol quarter)—"The seed is often drilled by hand: women make channels with the hoe, across the beds, which have been formed by the plough to the width of half a lug, and drop the seed into them, leaving a distance of about seven inches between each channel: this is esteemed a good method, particularly for late work. The expence is about 7*s.* per acre, and the quantity of seed used about six pecks."

In the section, "Soil, &c." we have the following notice, concerning the semination and vegetating process of wheat.—P. 15. "It is often known (and was particularly the case in 1803,) that strong easterly winds blow the mould away from the wheat in the month of April, and lay the roots almost bare. To remedy this, or provide against it, the land is trodden with sheep and other cattle, not only by folding immediately after the wheat is sown, but by driving them repeatedly over it, in the spring. This process not only gives firmness to the soil, but is thought also to check the growth of poppies and other weeds, to which the land is subject."

Many good farmers may exclaim—"can it be right to sow wheat on such land?" Yet we see it grown on similar lands,—namely, thin-soiled, calcareous hills,—in different parts of the kingdom. And *if* it be right to grow it on such soils, and in such situations, the Cotswold practices are worthy of study.

Flax.—The only particular entitled to notice, on this head, in the Report under review, is the method of freeing

ing the young crop from vermin.—P. 153. "To stop the progress of the *grub*, it is found to be a good practice, to turn into the field, at night, a large quantity of *young* ducks, which will search for these *insects* with great regularity, without doing mischief to the tender plants."

Slugs, no doubt, are here meant. They are very mischievous to the flax crop; they feed by night, and hungry ducks will do the same; in the early part of it, at least. For turnips, infested with slugs, (as Mr. R. observes, p. 137) the same expedient might be adopted:—in preference (it may be added) to night-rolling.

TEASLES.—This species of Agricultural produce is incidental to the woolen-*cloth*-making districts; which are three in number; namely, Yorkshire, Glocestershire, and Somersetshire. Some account of cultivating teasles, in Yorkshire, is registered in the NORTHERN DEPARTMENT. The practice, in Glocestershire, as reported by Mr. Rudge, differs, in some particulars, from that of Yorkshire. I therefore, copy it, at length. Having, as I have before said, had no experience in its cultivation, I register the following account of it, on the authority of the Reporter.

P. 155. "Teasles were formerly much cultivated in the middle Vale, as appears by the mention made of them in the ancient tythe terriers; but now not a hundred acres are planted in the county.

"Preparation. Old leys are preferred; they will, however, grow on the same land for many successive years, so long as couch and other weeds can be kept under; and during all this time manure is said not to be required.

"Old pasture lands are once ploughed, and on the inverted sod the seeds are sown broad-cast: they are brushed in with thorns fastened to a hurdle, because the tines of the harrow would let in the seed too deep.

"The same preparation is used on old tillage lands, except where more ploughings are required to make them clean.

"Seed. From two to three pecks upon an acre. A sufficient quantity is easily collected from the plants when ripe and dry, as they shed upon the slightest motion. When a farmer first begins to plant any part of his estate, he purchases them of a neighbouring grower, and the price su sually the same which wheat bears at the time.

"Time. About the middle of March, or within a week after ploughing, according to the season; but sowing is not esteemed favourable, after the beginning of April.

"Cultivation. When the plants are come into larger leaf,

leaf, they are thinned to about twelve inches distance; and those which are drawn, may be transplanted to fill up intervals in the same ground, or on any other plantation. About the beginning of June, in the first year, they are 'spittled;' that is, the workman, with a 'shoe,' or small spade, turns over the surface-mould carefully between every plant. About two months after, they are 'grited;' that is, the mould is turned up four or five inches under, and thrown to the plants: if the land is filthy, the same operation is repeated about October, and the mould brought close round the roots with the common hoe. In the March following, they are again grited, and sometimes 'tumped,' or moulded, close round, to make them 'haddle' out, or throw forth side-shoots.

"Spittling generally costs a guinea and a half an acre; and griting, 25*s.* with drink.

"Harvesting. About the latter end of July, or early in August, they begin to ripen, and then are cut in the following manner. First, the central shoot of each plant, called the King, is cut with a small hooked instrument, like a pruning knife, which has a string run through the handle, for the purpose of hanging it on the wrist, when, as it often happens, it is necessary to strip off the leaves. They are cut with about nine inches of stem, and, being tied round a stick, are carried directly from the field to the drying shed, which is a building well covered, but open on the sides to the free circulation of air. About nine days after, the cutter goes over them again, taking off such as are ripe, and repeats the operation at the same interval, as long as any remain worth cutting. After they have been properly dried, which will probably be in a fortnight, they are taken off the stick, and sorted.

"The produce of the second and subsequent cuttings are sorted, according to their size, into Queens, which are the best teasles; Middlings, next in value; and Scrubs, which are but little esteemed, except in years of scarcity, or when the clothing trade is unusually brisk. The Kings, which are large and coarse, are generally sent into Yorkshire, to be used on cloths of coarse texture.

"Being thus sorted, they are tied up in bunches, or 'glens,' each glen containing twenty teasles. Twenty-five glens are fastened on a staff, and forty staffs make a pack, which thus contains twenty thousand teasles. Of Kings, a glen contains only ten; a staff thirty glens; and a pack thirty staffs, making nine thousand.

"In this state they are stacked, in a close building, in the

the form of a small rick; and, if they sweat a little, the quality and smell are improved; but if they are too moist, they are spoiled. In the following March, they are fit for sale, and the average price of Queens per pack may be fixed at five pounds; they have been sold as high as twelve guineas.

"Produce. Ten packs upon an acre are esteemed a fair crop, though they have been known to rise to twenty.

"The teasle *(dipsacus fullonum)* is a biennial plant; those which 'run,' or bear heads t e second year, immediately die; but there are always some which do not run, till the third year; these are called 'vores.' To supply the place of those that have run, it is usual to transplant young ones from other beds; or, if it be intended to keep the land several years in te sles, fresh seeds are sown in the vacant spaces; and thus the ground is constantly replenished, and produces successive crops, without exhibiting any signs of diminution in point of strength, or wanting manure: manure, indeed, is esteemed injurious, as running the plants too much to stalk, and less to head. There is now a field in the parish of Eastington, seven miles below Gloucester, which has borne this crop for more than twenty years without change; it would, however, now be good husbandry to plough it up, and give it a year's fallow, for the purpose of destroying the couch, &c. with which it is overrun.

"Teasles, when sown on an old ley, and continued only for two or three years, are an excellent preparation for wheat: the rotting sod, on which it is always improper to put wheat, on account of the grubs and insects which harbour in the roots, gradually reduces the soil to a state of great richness; and the necessity of keeping it clean during the three years, leaves it in a fine state of cultivation.

"The fly, and too much moisture, are the principal enemies of this plant: the former sometimes attacks the young leaves, but seldom with such mischievous effects as to turnips.

"Much rain during the time of blossoming, often rots the head; this, indeed, is what the planter has most to fear, as likely to be material y injurious to his crops.

"The operations of cutting, &c. are usually performed by day labourers; sometimes, which is more desirable, by men, who undertake to cut, dry, and make fit for sale, at 10s. per pack, with drink, carriage excepted."

POTATOES.—Mr. R. as most amateurs in farming, speaks with particular interest on the potatoe crop. He bestows several

several pages upon it. A fact or two, in the established practice, of an extreme part of the county I did not particularly examine, requires to be noticed, here:—namely, the Bristol quarter; where a practice somewhat peculiar prevails. It resembles that of the midland counties.

P. 140. "Old pasture ground is preferred; and this is dug neatly into beds of half a 'lug,' or perch, wide, about the beginning of March: the turf is cut up with the spade, to the depth of seven or eight inches, turned over with the sod downward, and the new surface is lightly loosened, or skimmed, with the spade, to produce a small depth of mould, provincially 'cutting a cotton.' Early in April, the setting begins, and continues through May."—The sets are "planted across the beds, with a pin or dibble, in rows of fourteen or sixteen inches apart:"—In this particular, varying from the midland practice*.

TURNIPS.—The Cotswolds team with new ideas in agriculture. What must be the astonishment of a Norfolk man, on reading the following grave remarks.—P. 137. "The Cotswold farmers are not agreed as to the quality of nourishment afforded by turnips, nor have experiments been made to ascertain it†. It is the opinion of many, that they have no feeding qualities in themselves, and that if sheep and other cattle are put upon them in low condition, they will merely not sink or lose ground. The general practice of giving hay with them, in the proportion before stated, shews that they are considered, either as a food, too watery of themselves to be safe, or not nutritious enough to fatten. A ton of hay should nearly of itself finish six or eight sheep, if already forward; and this being the allowance to an acre, little dependence seems to rest on the turnips; but the great advantages which the farmer looks forward to, are the improvement of a light and poor soil, by the manure and treading of the sheep; and, without these, his land is of little value.

"A cultivator of Turkdean, who has been all his life employed on Cotswold farms, thinks, that the nutritious qualities

* GRINDING POTATOES for SWINE.—In the section "Feeding," we meet with the subjoined trait of practice, in preparing potatoes for the fatting of hogs, which I do not recollect to have fallen under my own observation.—P. 193. "Potatoes ground in a cyder-mill, and mixed with flour, are found to answer the purpose well, and saves the expence of fire-fuel, which in many situatious is of material importance. With this mixture the hogs are allowed no water but what the potatoes supply."

"† A score of middling sized sheep may be kept on an acre for three months."

qualities of turnips are such as to increase wool and carcase, but not to produce fat; and that, while sheep are on this food, they should be allowed as much hay as they can eat without wasting it."

A passage, which precedes the above, ought not to be lost!—P. 136. "Turnips, however, on which so much depends on a Cotswold farm, being, in spite of the best management, a precarious crop, the following plan has been recommended to prevent a total disappointment, in case of their failure. Let one-third part of the land intended for turnips, be sown with peas or oats, and let the whole be eaten on the land, as if it had been sown with turnips; that is, thrash out the corn, cut up the straw, and give the whole to be eaten on the land where it grew, by folded sheep, which perhaps would improve the soil more than if the whole had been in turnips. In this case, the land certainly raises its own manure, and leaves a saving of that from the yard for the turnip land; these crops will also suit the stiffer soils, which are not so proper or certain for turnips."

For a hint, on destroying slugs, see the head, *Flax*, aforegoing.

CULTIVATED HERBAGE.—The following spirited method of renewing the sward of thin-soiled sheep walks, without taking a corn crop, adds to Mr. PEACEY's well earned fame, as a hill farmer.—P. 253. "Mr. William Peacey, on a farm he occupied under Lord Sherborne, in the hamlet of Eastington, in the parish of Northleach, was by his lease restricted from breaking up and converting a certain portion thereof, called Eastington-downs, adjoining his Lordship's park. The herbage was a coarse sedge-grass, of very bad quality, intermixed with a dwarf prickly thistle, which, in the summer season, covered more than half the ground, and annoyed the sheep very much in grazing. It was obvious that this land was capable of great improvement; and on application being made to Lord Sherborne, and the intended mode of management being explained, consent was obtained for the conversion of it.

"The experiments were made on eight acres only, in the following order:

"First year. The land was pared and burnt, and sowed with turnips; then fed off with folded sheep as usual.

"Second year. Sowed with turnips again, and fed off. As soon as the crop was cleared, the land was worked with the scuffler and hoe, and, by repeated operations, laid level, so that no vestige remained of the plough. Having previously collected, with great care, the seeds of the best natural

natural grasses from his own meadows, he mixed them with one bushel of his own (Peacey's) ray-grass, and one pound of white or Dutch clover; so that the quantity for an acre, including the ray-grass, clover, and natural seeds, was four bushels, which were sown on the 3d of September.

"Third year. The whole was summer-grazed with sheep and beasts, and continued to be so, with the intermission of a fortnight only in the fourth season, for the purpose of skimming the bents.

"Second experiment on seven acres more.

"First year. Pared, burnt, sown with turnips, and fed off, as before.

"Second year. Sown with turnips, early in the season, and eaten off in October; then immediately ploughed, and sown with winter-tares.

"Third year. The tares were eaten off in the summer with sheep, and again sown with turnips, which were eaten off, and the land ploughed immediately; then scuffled as before, and sown with seeds early in September.

"Fourth year. Mowed in May, and the aftermath fed off with sheep and cattle.

"Fifth year (1800.) Mowed in May as before.

"Third experiment.

"First year. Pared, burnt, sown with turnips, and fed off as before.

"Second year. Sown with turnips, and fed off with sheep. The ground immediately ploughed, and worked very fine with scuffler and harrows; then rolled down, and sown with seeds about the latter end of May. In the beginning of September following, it was stocked with 300 sheep for feeding. They continued on the land two months; and then it lay untouched till the 19th of May 1800, when it was mowed, and, though so early in the season, was supposed to produce a ton and half per acre.

"Mowing the first crop is preferred, because the high condition of the land from two years turnips, gives a very luxuriant growth to the stronger grasses, which require so great a weight of cattle to keep them down, that the more delicate ones are always injured, and sometimes destroyed; whereas, by early mowing, the more luxuriant sorts are cut down, and laid open to the influence of the sun and air: the finer ones, which have been protected by the shade of the other, then acquire strength to keep pace in their growth with the after-grass.

"The allowance of seeds in the first experiment having turned

turned out too much, half a bushel in the ray-grass, and as much in the collected seeds, were afterwards omitted, making the whole quantity three bushels."

The only remark I have to make, on this very interesting instance of practice, regards the mowing for hay, and carrying off a ton and a half an acre, from naturally weak land. But unless the texture of the soil of the site under experiment had been duly reported,—namely, as to whether it is the "sour" tenaceous kind, or the loose friable "stonebrash" sort, which prevails on the Cotswold hills (see p. 396, aforegoing) no accurate judgment can be formed of the strict propriety of management, nor any safe conclusion be drawn, for the guidance of others.—Land of the latter description requires to be trodden, can scarcely be overweighted,—surely not with sheep,—even the first spring, unless the season prove extraordinarily wet.

Dill.—In the section "Artificial Grasses," we find this extraordinary species of cultivated herbage reported.—P. 181. "Dill *(anethum segetum)* has been sown on the Cotswolds fifty or sixty years, and is now become frequent. It makes an excellent hay for all kinds of cattle, but best for ewes with sucking lambs, producing milk highly nutritious and abundant. It possesses also, the property of growing freely on poor, thin, and impoverished lands, where other seeds would make a scanty return. The seeds are, in colour, inclining to red; in form, resembling a vetch, but smaller; they are generally sown broad-cast in March or April, at the rate of a bushel and half on an acre; soon cover the ground, and require no hoeing or other attention, till ready for cutting, which, in the most favourable seasons, is seldom the case before the middle or latter end of September, if left for seed. Some cultivators, indeed, cut it for hay, before the blossom withers, and then it produces about a ton on an acre: this, however, is considered as the least beneficial mode, because the straw, after the seed has been thrashed out, is but little, or not at all, inferior to the early mowed. The kid or pod resembles that of a pea, and must be fully ripe before it is harvested; but, if it be too ripe, easily sheds. The produce of seed is often twenty-four Winchester bushels on an acre, and the price varies from 5s. to 8s. per bushel. Ground with barley, it is excellent food for fattening cattle and hogs."

To this ample account, the following learned note is appended.—"Not having seen any account of this plant in the modern agricultural books which have fallen under my notice, I merely conjecture that it is the *anethum segetum*

of

of Linnæus, and a native of Portugal. In the new edition of Linnæus, by Turton, is the folowing description: Anethum egetum. Portugal, Jacq. hort. 2. tab. 132. *Leaves* twice or thrice pinnate, with filiform leafets. Mortimer mentions, 'dill as raised of seed, which is ripe in August.'

"I am not informed whether dill is grown in other counties; it is certainly deserving of trial, on weak and hungry soils, any where."

These observations abundantly evince that Mr. R. (notwithstanding the *lists* he has given us) is either a book botanist, merely, or no botanist, at all.—Scarcely any two plants in nature are less alike (except in *name!)* than the dill of the gardens, and the dill of the Cotswold hills. The different species of *anethum* are *umbelliferous* plants—of the carrot, parsley, carraway and *fennel* tribe.—The Glocestershire dill is an *ervum*,—a *podded* plant; as Mr. R. describes it! It appeared to me, from what I saw of it, to be a cultivated variety of *ervum hirsutum* of Linneus; and as such I noticed it, in the PROVINCIALISMS of GLOCESTERSHIRE - not deeming it of sufficient importance, at this day, to be brought forward in the body of the work.

PERENNIAL GRASS LANDS.—In speaking of these, too, as of corn lands, a list of some weeds is given, with remarks thereon. But I perceive nothing new, excellent, or in any sort noticeable; excepting what is said of the *yarrow*, or millfoil.—P. 173. "Common yarrow *(achillea)* is plentifully intermixed with the herbage of the Vale, particularly where it has been much fed with horses. Some agriculturists have supposed that cattle are not averse to it; but I have observed that this weed has remained uneaten, till every blade of grass has been cropped close to the ground; and therefore, at the expence of manual labour, with the spade or three-pronged fork, it ought to be eradicated."—I insert this; as the yarrow has become a *fashionable* species of cultivated herbage.

ORCHARDS and FRUIT LIQUORS.—With accounts of these, Mr. Rudge has filled thirty six pages. But without furnishing a line that can usefully add to what I had previously published. It may doubtlessly amuse those who have read nothing else on these subjects; but cannot practically instruct men who are unacquainted with the arts that belong to them;—much less tend to improve those who practice them, imperfectly. It is rather to be regretted that Mr. R's time and talents should have been so unprofitably employed;—as his performance is pretty evidently not the mere

mere product of reading, but has been assisted by observation. There is only one short passage that require to be noticed, here.

P. 210. "The supposition of an able agriculturist, that the pear, being naturally saccharine, delights in a soil totally deprived of calcariosity; while the apple, abounding with acidity, thrives best among calcareous earth, the natural destroyer of acidity, seems too refined, and not supported by fact; otherwise, the best situations for apple-orchards, would be found on the Cotswolds; but in truth, apples and pears are indiscriminately planted on the same ground, and flourish so equally, as to make it difficult to say, which has the superiority."

If the above honourable appellation is meant to be applied to the writer of the Rural Economy of Glocestershire, the author of the Glocestershire Report would seem to have read with inattention, or to have censured unfairly:—as may be seen by referring to my register,—article *Soils* of *Orchards;*—where it plainly appears that the "supposition" *is* "supported by fact." consequently, the inference drawn, which is altogether futile (as not being *practicable)* and the finale of the remark, which is entirely sophistical (as not being strictly to the point) can require no reply.

How different are the sentiments of Mr. Rudge and Mr. Knight, concerning this diffidently suggested theory. See p. 340, aforegoing.

CATTLE.—On this head, I find nothing that could instruct, or in any way benefit my readers; excepting the following instances of casualties, which are related to have been incident to cows; and which, tho extraordinary, may usefully serve to put cattle farmers on their guard.

P. 287. "In January 1805, in consequence of some fences being broken down by a violent wind during the night, a pack of cows belonging to a farmer in Sandhurst entered an inclosed shrubbery, where were many yew-trees growing, and continued in it till the morning. Soon after they were driven out, all of them were seized, more or less, with a kind of madness, or such acute pains as made them run about in a very furious manner, sometimes leaping to a considerable height, then beating their heads against whatever opposed them, and at last falling instantly dead. Oils of different sorts were poured down their throats, as there was an opportunity of securing them, which seemed to produce a good effect on some; but notwithstanding every effort, nine out of thirty died in a few hours after they

they were discovered. On their being opened, it appeared that the whole quantity they had eaten, put together, would not have filled a peck."

N. P. 297. "Some cows are perhaps by constitutional weakness, or bodily imperfection, more liable to warp than others; accidental circumstances, however, which produce sudden fright, often prove the cause. In an inclosure in Arlingham, near to which was a dog-kennel, eight heifers and cows of twenty warped, in consequence, as was supposed by the farmer, of the frequent exposure of flesh, and skinning of dead horses before them: the remainder were removed to a distant pasture, and did well."

P. 302. "On the morning of the 26th of July 1805, two cows of about twenty, at Hempstead, were found dead in a pasture, where they had been kept for some weeks; no cause could be assigned but over eating of white clover *(trifolium repens)*, with which the herbage abounded, in consequence of rain after a series of dry weather."

Dairy.—On this most important department of the rural practices of Glocestershire, the Reporter has bestowed a sheet of letterpress. But his account of it, like that relating to orchards and cidermaking, might well have been spared. Nothing new or excellent is to be found in it. The two short passages that follow are all that is entitled to insertion, here.

Butter Milk.—The opinions of the husbandmen of Glocestershire, as related by this Reporter, are as singular, in regard to butter milk, as they are in respect to turnips. See p. 459, aforegoing.

P. 298. "Butter-milk, or that which is left from churning, whether from the cream of milk or whey, is reckoned of little value: where it is made in small quantities, it is sometimes saved in the whey-tub, though, according to the opinion of judicious farmers, it were better thrown away. Hence the provincial proverb: 'Whey feeds a hog, and starves a dog: butter-milk feeds a dog, and starves a hog.'"

Cheese.—The following eligible, tho minutial, particular of practice has, I find, escaped notice, in my own register. P. 290. "The cheese-tub is first 'laid,' that is, placed on a small 'tram' or bench, and then wetted with cold water. This prevents the milk from adhering to the wood; the same is done with pails, cloths, bowls, and other utensils."

Sheep.—Mr. Rudge enters upon the ungrateful task of comparison, between the Cotswold, the new Leicestershire, and the Southdown breeds, and their crosses. But I have

no

not been able to find anything, in his strictures, that can usefully interest the agricultural public, at large. I will, however, transcribe his concluding paragraph; as it relates particularly to the Cotswold breed.—P. 308. "Speaking generally of the Cotswolds, the opinion is in favour of a cross with the new Leicester, though pure Cotswold sheep are still found on several farms. At Daglingworth and Hampnett are to be found the largest and purest flocks of the old breed."

The subjoined account of a disease incident to sheep, in Glocestershire, I insert, here; as I am desirous to collect every thing that may throw any glimmering of light on this dark and neglected part of Rural Economicks, in England.

P. 316. "Giddiness, or the 'blood,' is a fatal disease, considered as the consequence of great fullness of blood, and usually attacking sheep which are removed from poor to rich keep, and particularly young luxuriant grass in May. The effect is sometimes momentary; at other times the animal runs round as in giddiness, and after some exertions falls dead. As a preventative, it is useful to bleed moderately, before the sheep go to new pasture; and when attacked by the disease, if there is time, the same remedy offers itself; and the practice of the farmers is to cut off part of their ears or tails immediately, to promote a plentiful discharge, and freer circulation of blood, which is often attended with the desired consequence."

In the Appendix of this volume we find "A Letter from Edward Sheppard, Esq" (of Uley near Dursley) "to Sir John Sinclair, Bart." (as President of the Board of Agriculture, in consequence of a request to that purpose) "on the subject of his experiments regarding the improvement of the fine-wooled breed of sheep, in this kingdom."

On perusing this valuable Paper, we find united, in Mr. Sheppard, a manufacturer, a sheep farmer, and a writer, of great merit and consideration. It may be deemed a masterly performance. It is of considerable length (occupying fourteen large octavo pages):—and altho much of it relates not particularly to Glocestershire, and ought rather to have been inserted in the "*Communications*" to the Board, than in any County Report,—it contains too much good sense and useful intelligence, to be passed over in silence, here.

Mr. Sheppard's experience is thus stated.—P. 391 "Anxious to ascertain to what degree of perfection wool might be brought in this country, by means of the Spanish cross on fine-woolled English sheep. and wishing to be satisfied

tisfied whether, under the common circumstances of the husbandry of the country, such wool would retain its fineness, I commenced the following experiments, considering myself, from being largely engaged in the manufacture of superfine cloth, and in the practice of buying and working up very considerable quantities of Spanish wool yearly, entitled to form, with some accuracy, an estimate of the relative quality and value of such wools as might be produced in this country, in competition with the wools of Spain. Accordingly, in the year 1800, I sent twenty Ryeland ewes to a Spanish ram of Lord Bathurst's, by his Lordship's obliging permission; this ram was from his Majesty's Merino flock.

"In the produce of this first cross, I found a surprizing improvement in the wool, partaking very strongly of the nature of the Spanish; to which I think it might be fairly considered as having approached half-way. I carefully preserved a large specimen of it, with a view to ascertain the important fact of subsequent depreciation. The weight of the fleece was increased one half, by the cross with the Spaniard.

"In the year 1801 I was favoured, through the medium of Sir Joseph Bankes, with a Spanish ram and three ewes, from his Majesty's flock; and I purchased from four to five hundred Ryeland ewes, in that and the two following years. I selected, with great caution, the finest woolled sheep from the best flocks in Herefordshire, where I found an assemblage of all sorts under the name of Ryelands, and not above one in twenty that I could chuse for my use.

"In the course of the years 1803 and 1804, I purchased a considerable number of ewes from a reputed Spanish flock in Herefordshire, Mr. Ridgeway's; who had for many years been in possession of part of his Majesty's Merino sheep, obtained, as well soon after their arrival, as at subsequent periods, through the means of his landlord, General Price. This Spanish race Mr. Ridgeway ingrafted on his own Ryeland flock; and I found the produce, as might be supposed, a very mixed and unequal breed. I could only purchase ten ewes of him in 1803, as he had just sold a quantity to the Marquis of Exeter, which were afterwards disposed of by auction at Burleigh, on the Marquis's death. In 1804, I purchased one hundred more ewes of Mr. Ridgeway, which he permitted me to select from his flock; of course, I drew such as were the least degenerated from the Spaniard; and amongst them I found many that were very little, if at all, inferior in wool to his Majesty's pure breed. I pur-

I purchased forty ewes of the same description from a mixed flock of Lady Caroline Price's; and classed the whole, according to their respective qualities, as second, third, and fourth crosses from the Spaniard.

"In the year 1805, I was enabled, from the increase of my flock, to dispose of all my Ryeland ewes. At this year's shearing, the average weight of my fleeces was 2¾lb. washed on the sheep's back.

"In the present year, 1806, my Spanish and mixed flocks amount to 986, exclusive of lambs; and the average weight of each fleece, washed as above, exceeds 3lb. The value of my wool, from the different crosses thrown together, I estimate at near 4s. 6d. per lb. and that of the fleeces exclusively Spanish, R's at 6s. 4d. when in the same state as the wool brought from Spain; the price of the best Spanish wools of this year's import being 6s. 9d. per lb."

Mr. S. next adverts to the method of WASHING the WOOL. The *Spanish* method is as follows.—P. 399. "In Spain, the wool when shorn is taken to the washing places, where, first with warm, and afterwards with cold water, the grease is in a great degree discharged: it is then exposed to a burning sun, and, when scorched thoroughly dry, is squeezed into packages, and compressed so closely, that, on being opened in this country, it has acquired such hardness as frequently to make it difficult to divide the flakes. The feel of the wool in this state is so unlike that of wool kept in a portion of its natural grease, that I very much doubt its capability of again recovering its original temper, even in the softening processes of the manufacture. It would be difficult to procure the Spanish wool in the unwashed state; and the duties being paid by the weight, would prove an insurmountable impediment. The Spanish lambs' wool, which comes in more of its native grease, has all the softness of feel that can be wished."

Mr. Sheppard, however, has found it more expedient to wash it on the sheep's backs; agreeably to the ordinary method in *England*;—P. 394. "For, although the wool of the real Spaniard is so close and compact as to admit of but little impression on the grease, at the root of the fibre, from common washing, yet the dirtier part of the fleece, near the surface, is considerably cleansed; and the more yolky and pure grease yields easily to the usual process of the manufacturer. In proportion as the cross from the English approaches the Spanish breed, it acquires the same property of *yolk*; but in every instance that I have seen, it parts much more easily with its grease in the washing

The

The process of shearing is also much facilitated by the wool having been washed on the sheep's back, which is otherwise very tedious and difficult."

P. 395. "I have not found it expedient to shear or wash my *lambs*, as I find them winter better with their coats on, and the wool is but of comparatively little value, and not marketable. It makes an addition to the more valuable fleece of the next year, in which state it is worked up better by the manufacturer, and the cost and trouble of twice shearing is saved."

On the ELIGIBILITY of growing fine wool, in England, and propagating the Spanish breed of sheep, for that purpose, Mr. Sheppard's observations are highly judicious.— P. 395. "The first reflection that occurs on the adoption of this breed of sheep, is, whether it is likely to be advantageous to the community; and on this head I cannot but give a decided opinion, that the judicious culture of fine wool must be productive of the greatest benefit to the agricultural, as well as to the commercial interests of the country. In the great variety of soil and situation which England produces, there are numberless districts where this breed of sheep may be cultivated with the greatest success, to the expulsion of the wretched and unprofitable flocks that now infest them. I am of opinion, that there is not a breed of clothing-woolled sheep in England, which would not produce a fleece, from four or five repeated crosses with the Spaniard, worth at least 4s. per lb. washed on the sheep's back. It seems therefore apparent, that it must be to the interest of the farmer and the community, that poor and mountainous tracts of land should be applied to the growth of this sort of sheep. As to the more rich and highly cultivated parts of the kingdom, I acknowledge a different opinion: I would wish such to be left in possession of the large and long-woolled flocks, which thrive so well upon them; for I am satisfied they would not be so well adapted to that sort of culture, the main object of which is the fineness of the fleece."

On the EFFECTS of CLIMATE and FOOD, on the wool of sheep, Mr. S's remarks are equally satisfactory.

The mixed breeds.—P. 396. "The comparison of four years successive produce from the same sheep, has satisfied me, that, without extraordinary care, to guard against the effects of climate, and a strict abstinence from the more nutritious and succulent kinds of food, the wool of the mixed breeds will materially degenerate. I have now before

fore me, large samples of the wool of my first crosses, from Lord Bathurst's ram on my Ryeland ewes, shorn in 1802, (having been shorn as lambs the year preceding,) and of the wool from the same sheep, shorn in the present year, 1806. The quality of the wool in the course of that time, has so much degenerated, that I should conceive the lapse of a similar period would reduce it to the coarseness of the maternal stock. It may be proper to observe, that these sheep have been kept on rich pasture land, and fed this spring on turnips and vetches: it must be observed also, that they were only the first cross from the Spaniard, which, as I shall afterwards explain, I do not consider as possessing equal preventatives with those of higher blood, against the causes of degeneracy."

The pure Spanish.—P. 396. "I have found also the wool of his Majesty's ram much degenerated, from the comparison of specimens in 1803 and the present year. He has been kept in the highest state possible, on the best pastures in the summer, and with corn in the winter, and has been very hard worked. I do not find such depreciation in the wool of the female produce from his Majesty's ewes; they have not been kept in such high condition, and their fleeces are as fine as those of the original ewes, which died after bringing two lambs each.

"In the *pure Spanish breed*, there is a wonderful capacity for resisting the effects of climate on the quality of the wool. The extreme exudation from the body of the animal, yielding a yolky consistence at the interior of the fleece, and, by its mixture with the soil, forming a kind of coat of mail on the outside, makes the wool almost impervious to wet, and protects the sheep exceedingly from the injuries of climate. The same quality attends the mixed breed, in proportion to its approximation to the pure Spanish; and I have no doubt that the more it inherits of this quality, the more capable it will be of resistance to the causes of degeneracy."

The method of PREVENTING this DETERIORATION OR DEGENERACY of the wool of the mongrel breeds, is of course obvious and easy.—P. 397. "I do not consider the fact of deterioration under the common circumstances of the husbandry of the country, as affecting, in any serious degree, the value arising from the growth of fine-woolled sheep. The preventative is always at hand—a frequent recurrence to the Spanish ram will be necessary, and will at all times be adequate to remedy the evil. A sort of wool will be produced that will be highly valuable to the manufacturer; and

and if we grow, in considerable quantities, wool worth 5s. 6d. per lb. which will be very practicable, (the comparative price of the best Spanish wool being taken at 6s. 9d.) we shall rival two-thirds of the import from Spain. It is to be observed, that the Spanish wool, coming in so much cleaner condition, adds 6d. per lb. to its value, compared with that of our own growth, washed on the sheep's back, of equal fineness.

"But in order to keep up the means of perpetuating the fine-woolled mixed breed, and of supplying the growers with the pure blood, there should be a *depot* of the real Spanish race carefully preserved, and protected from any mixture or degeneracy. The flock now in his Majesty's possession is eminently fitted for the purpose; and, under such beneficent and patriotic auspices, I have no doubt, will have every attention paid to the preservation of its purity. I am satisfied that a breed of sheep so pure as those are, with strict caution both to the nature of their food, and to their complete protection from the effects of climate, would remain for a century in the same state of fineness and perfection: indeed, we have no experience that will assign any period to their decline. In Saxony, under those precautions, the mixed breed retains the greatest possible degree of fineness: the best wools from that country equal, in smallness of fibre, and exceed in softness of feel, the finest wools of Spain, and are eagerly purchased, at even higher prices, by the manufacturers in this country, who have no difficulty in ascertaining the value and the waste, in the greasy and half-washed state they appear in; though the timid growers of fine wool here, are alarmed at the apparent difficulties which the sale of their wool meets with in similar condition. They may be assured, that, when a quantity can be produced sufficient to attract the manufacturer's attention, there will not be much difficulty in his ascertaining the value, let the condition or the grease be what it may.

"The mixed breed of English and Spanish, partakes very much of the soft and silky feel of the Saxon wool, and, was the same attention given to its culture, I have no doubt might be brought to equal fineness. That the cross with a coarser wool should have produced a softer and a finer wool than that of the fine parent fleece, is an extraordinary fact; but we now know it to be true from the indisputable proof of the Saxon wools. I am, however, disposed, to attribute much of the softness perceptible in Saxon, and Anglo-Spanish wools, to the management in washing.

washing. In Saxony, as with us, the wool is washed on the sheep's back, and remains for a long time afterwards in its native grease, till sent into this country, not hardened by any process."

Mr. Sheppard then notices the races of Spanish sheep, in SAXONY, in SWEDEN, and in FRANCE; and M. de Lasteyrie's Treatise on Spanish wool;—concluding his admirable paper in the following instructive manner.—P. 402. "To conclude—I do not assert, that it is impracticable to produce, and to preserve in England, wool equal to the finest quality in Spain, with the same management as is practised in countries under climates somewhat similar; but that, where land is so valuable, and where a regular course of husbandry is adopted on a comprehensive scale, as with us, I do not think such management can be looked for. The culture, however, of such wool, as I have before pointed out, may be pursued with the greatest ease, as well as advantage, in the many districts of less fertile land throughout the kingdom; where, I am convinced, the farmers, in the course of three or four successive crosses with the Spaniard, would obtain fleeces worth from 10s. to 15s. each, from almost any sort of short-woolled sheep.

"To those who can afford to chuse a sort of sheep to breed from, I should recommend a judicious selection of fine-woolled Ryelands, in preference to South Downs, or any other. The South Down flocks are equally mixed with the Ryelands, of coarse and fine woolled sheep; but the finest hair of the South Down sheep bears no proportion, in point of softness, to that of the Ryeland.

"Nor are the sheep from such cross with the Spaniard, less healthy, nor more subject to the foot-rot, or any other diseases. As lambs, they are tender; and it is necessary the ewes should yean as late as the month of March: the lambs fall very naked, and must be sheltered from bleak and exposed situations. After shedding their lambs' teeth, they are as healthy and strong as any sort of sheep whatever: they keep themselves in good order upon bare pastures; they go well to fold, which they stand equal with the South Downs; and I have found them fatten very handsomely. I have, in the past week, sold half a score six-toothed wethers of the first cross, fatted on grass and hay; for which I received from the butcher 22l. 15s. exclusive of the wool. I cut 5½lb. of wool, in the grease, from one sheep, which, when clean scowered, produced 3¼lb. well worth, in that state, 5s. per lb. The other fleeces average

average rather less. This great growth of wool since last shear-time, I attribute to the great fatness and enlarged size of the sheep, which weighed 21lb. per quarter; the average weight was 19lb. per quarter; the whole value of carcase and wool exceeding 3 *l.* in addition to the fleece at last shear-time, worth 15s. I readily obtained a penny per pound more than the market price, on account of the beauty of the meat, and its great fatness; and I must not omit the testimony, both of amateurs and adversaries, to the mildness and excellency of the mutton."

In the section, "Expence and Profit," (an *Article* which the Board's Reporters have *given out* to them) Mr. Rudge makes the following judicious remarks, concerning the Rural Profession; and the pecuniary profits attached to it.

P. 67. "The expenditures and profits of a farm, depend so much on the industry, attention, and activity of the occupier, that it is difficult, from the calculations of one, to form an estimate of all. The difference which a few years have made, both in the appearance and mode of living among the yeomanry, has generated an opinion, that the profits of farming are very high. In whatever degree this opinion may be just with regard to the great renters, it certainly does not hold good among the small ones: they still, in a great measure, keep up the old appearance, live frugally, spend little, and seldom die in the possession of much property. Hence, it would seem, that the actual profits of agriculture are not considerably increased: where, however, a strong capital is employed on a large farm, the several small profits which would arise from divided parts of it, in the aggregate, make a considerable sum; and, surely, if a man brought up in the agricultural line, is possessed of more money than his neighbours, he is equally entitled to an increased return from it, with others, who by employing a less capital in trade, make a more splendid appearance, and perhaps a greater interest. If the departure from the ancient character of a farmer, in dress and living, has, in some instances, produced in the landlord a determination of raising his rents, the effect is felt by the occupier, and does not, I conceive, extend to the community. The little farmer, though he preserves the exterior of ancient manners, feels no relief from high rents on that account; but if there be a difference, he holds his estate at a higher proportionable rent than the other; and this, for the obvious reason, that his farm, being within the reach of many, excites a greater degree

degree of competition, and is therefore often rented at a higher price, than is compatible with the reasonable profits of the cultivator."

Had the Reporter stopped, here, he would have left favourable impressions on the minds of practical readers; and have deserved well of the agricultural public, by his general sentiments on the subject. But an unpractised man to enter into the labyrinth of calculation, and blot twelve pages of paper with figures, arranged in the debtor and creditor manner, and this without experience, and of course without sufficient judgment, to guide him,—could only *prove* his own temerity. If men not only of the very first ability, but of the most mature experience, in rural concerns, be liable to fall into error, in attempting this most difficult proposition in the whole circle of the agricultural science, it were in vain to look for any thing like accuracy of statement from one, who,—learned and capable as he may be, and, from what appears in the Glocestershire Report, doubtlessly is, in *his own profession*,—can have no fair claim to such a qualification.

NORTH

NORTH WILTSHIRE.

WILTSHIRE, at large, was ably reported,—" by THOMAS DAVIS of Longleat, Wilts; steward to the most noble, the MARQUIS of BATH,—in January 1794.

What appears most strange, Mr. DAVIS's Report has not, even yet I believe, been *reprinted;* but remains in its *original* state; and, of course, virtually *unpublished*, to this day!—And this, while it contains, within itself, more valuable information, than is to be found in some half dozen of the Board's Reports, that have been published, and puffed off, in the octavo form.—So irrationally would seem to be conducted, the *literary* labors of the Board.

The principal part of Wiltshire; namely, the CHALK HILLS and their vallies; are not only in situation, but in soil and substrata, naturally a portion of the SOUTHERN DEPARTMENT of England; they being, in nature, as well as in agricultural management, separable, or distinct from the VALE LANDS, of North Wiltshire:—which, forming a link of the extended chain of vale lands that reach from the banks of the Mersey to those of the Somersetshire AVON, are naturally a district of the WESTERN DEPARTMENT.

Mr. DAVIS has properly drawn the same, or a similar, line of distinction.—P. 6. " In speaking of this county, it is usual to separate it into two districts, viz. 'South Wiltshire,' and 'North Wiltshire;' and the division is generally made, by supposing an east and west line passing through the county at or near Devizes, thereby leaving *Marlborough Downs* in *North Wiltshire;* but in treating of the county *agriculturally*, it will make a more natural division to draw an irregular line *round the foot of* the *chalk hills*, from their entrance into the north-east part of the county from Berkshire, to their south-west termination at Maiden Bradley, thereby comprehending *the whole of Wiltshire Downs*, with their intersecting vallies and surrounding verges, under the name of '*South Wiltshire*,' or, perhaps, more properly speaking, '*South-east Wiltshire*,' and

and calling the residue of the county 'North Wiltshire,' or more properly 'North-west Wiltshire.'

"The natural appearance, as well as the agricultural application of the two parts of the county, well warrant this division into south-east and north-west Wiltshire, the first comprehending the chalk hills, usually called Wiltshire Downs, whose general application is to corn-husbandry and sheep-walks; and the latter being remarkable for its rich pasture land on the banks of the Lower Avon and the Thames, so famous for the feeding of cattle, and still more so, for the production of one of the most excellent kinds of cheese this island can boast."

Mr. D. in consequence of this natural difference, judiciously treats, separately, of the two divisions:—*necessarily*, however, (in a *County* Report!) including, in the northwestern district, that part of the Cotswold, or Southwold, hills which are politically comprized, within the fortuitous boundary of Wiltshire.

By uniting, in one description, those two naturally dissimilar parts, his account is of course rendered less distinct and clear, than it would otherwise have been. It is to the VALE LANDS, however, his observations are chiefly confined. And what I may here extract, concerning the LIMESTONE UPLANDS, will serve as an addition to that which has been collected from the *Glocestershire* Reports, relating to the COTSWOLD HILLS.

NATURAL ECONOMY.

SOILS and SUBSTRATA.—P. 115. "The north-west verge of the county, viz. from near Cirencester, by Malmsbury, and on the west side of the road from London to Bath, may be truly called the Cotswold part of Wiltshire.

"Its external appearance, and internal component parts, are nearly the same with the Cotswold hills of Gloucestershire; except where the vein of clay lies so near the surface, as to make it colder.

"This part is, on account of the thinness and looseness of its soil, *usually*, and, in many instances, *necessarily*, kept in an arable state; while the adjoining land, viz. about Chippenham, and from thence southward, through Melksham and Trowbridge, which happens to have a greater depth of soil, and has a pure warm rock, without the intervening

vening vein of cold clay, is capable of grazing the largest oxen, and is, perhaps, one of the most fertile parts of the county, unless, possibly, the vein of gravel next described may be excepted.

" There is a vein of gravel, of a most excellent small pebbly, shelly kind, and, in general, covered with a good depth of rich loam, which runs in a broken line from Melksham, through Chippenham to Cricklade; but its greatest body extends from Tytherton, through Christian Malford and Dantzey to Somerford, and perhaps the richest part of it is at or near Dantzey.

" It is a most excellent undersoil, warming and drying the top mould, and it is only to be lamented, that its quantity in this district is so small. It is used for roads and walks, and when washed or skreened, for drains in the cold, clay lands which border upon it.

" There are two principal veins of sand in this district. They are in general red, and of a sharp, loose, gravelly texture, and, of course, not so fertile as the tough, close sands of South Wiltshire. One of these runs from Redburn, by Seagry, Draycott, and Sutton Benger, to Langley Burrell, near Chippenham. And another begins at the opposite corresponding hill at Charlcot, and runs through Bremhill to Bromham.

" From this last vein there are two detached masses at Rowd and Seend to the south, and probably the detached masses appearing at different places to the north of it, viz. between Charlcott and Swindon, are parts of the same vein.

" All these detached masses have a mixture of some other soils, and are generally more fertile than the principal veins. Under the sand land at Swindon, lies a singular rock of stone of a most excellent quality, serving equally, in its different beds, for the purpose of building houses, paving, and covering them.

" The greatest part of the residue of the soil of this district, and particularly from Highworth, by Wotton Basset to Clack, lies on a hard, close rock, of a rough, irregular, rustic kind of bastard limestone, of very little use but for the roads. The soil over this kind of stone is various, but generally cold, owing to its own retentive nature, and to the frequent intervention of a vein of clay.

" Badon Forest, (between Cricklade and Malmsbury) is an exception to the whole. It is a cold iron clay to the very surface; so bad, as to be called, by way of distinction, ' Badon

'Badon Land,' and was never so well applied, as when in its original state of woodland."

CLIMATURE.—P. 116. "The climate of this district is various, and though, in general, milder than that of the high lands in the south-east district, is nevertheless cold, and, in general, unfavourable to the purposes of early spring vegetation, owing probably to the cold retentive nature *of the undersoil of a great part of this district.*"

P. 135. "The north-west, or driest part of the stone-brash land, is sown and harvested nearly as early as the downs of the south-east district, while the low, cold lands, are frequently a month behind in both."

POLITICAL ECONOMY.

APPROPRIATION.—P. 117. "This district is for the most part inclosed, though not entirely so, there being still a few common fields remaining, and some commons, but no very extensive tracts of either."

P. 136. "Although the greatest part of this district appears to be inclosed, and it contains no very extensive entire tracts of waste land, yet there are numerous small commons in almost every part of it, in a very neglected, unimproved state: and there are many parishes, in which there are still common-fields; and those in a very bad state of husbandry.

"The greater part of the common-fields lie on the stone-brash land, on the north-west side of the county; and others, in the deep strong land, from Calne by Broadtown, towards Highworth; but the commons lie chiefly in a north-east line, from Westbury to Cricklade, through the centre of the richest land in the district.

"There are numerous instances, in which the common-field arable land, lets for less than half the price of the inclosed arable adjoining; and the commons are very seldom reckoned worth any thing, in valuing any estate that has a right on them.

"Although great part of this district appears to have been, at no very remote period, in a commonable state; and although the improvement on the lands, heretofore inclosed, has been so very great, the progress of inclosure therein

therein has been very slow during the last fifty years. The reason seems to have been, the very great difficulty and expence of making new roads in a county naturally wet and deep, and where the old public roads were, till within the last few years, almost impassable. But this reason having now nearly ceased, by the introduction of several new turnpike roads through the district, and by the spirit which now so generally prevails, of making good the approaches to them from the interior villages; it is to be hoped, that so great an improvement as that of inclosing and cultivating the commonable lands, will no longer be neglected.

"The tract of commons which are mentioned to lie in a line from Westbury towards Cricklade, are detached and dispersed in numerous pieces, and belong to a variety of parishes, but the whole content of them is supposed to exceed three thousand acres. And though the greater part of them at present turns to very little account, not only from the wet, rotten state, in which they lie every winter, but from the unprofitable kind of stock that are usually kept on them; they want only inclosing and draining, to make them as good pasture land as many of the surrounding inclosures.

"The improvement by inclosing them might, in many instances, be taken at from fifteen to twenty shillings per acre; and, indeed, inclosures of commons of this description frequently improve, not only the commons themselves, but also the *adjoining inclosures, by preventing the occupiers from continually mowing the latter, and carrying off the hay.*

"There are a few heaths in this district, (and but a few) which might be improved by plowing. There being but few instances where there are alterative manures, such as lime, chalk, marle, &c. which are properly adapted to them, to be got very near them, the greater part of them, particularly those about Badon Forest, would, in general, pay better for planting.

"Very great improvements might be made, by inclosing the common-fields in this district; and particularly those which are in need of draining, such as those in the deep, cold vein of land about Broadtown, Elcombe, &c. many of which would be much more valuable, if turned into pasture land, than in their present arable state. Even the common-fields in that part of this district, which is apparently the driest, viz. the north-west part, are so much in need of draining, that few of them are safe for sheep in in a wet autumn. This can only be remedied by inclosure; and no greater proof can be adduced of the necessity of it."

In speaking of "obstacles to improvement," Mr. Davis, after noticing mills, as an obstacle to Irrigation, says—P. 161. "The other obstacle to improvements in agriculture, is the impediment thrown in the way of inclosures of commonable lands, particularly where the quantity of land is small, or the number of proprietors large, by the difficulty and expence of procuring acts of parliament for that purpose.

"It has been already remarked, that there are a great number of common-fields still remaining in Wiltshire, particularly in the south-east part of the county; and that in the north-west part, there are still many open common pastures. These are undoubtedly obstacles to all improvements in agriculture, and ought to be divided without delay.

"There have been many common-fields lately inclosed in the south-east part of the county; but in the north-west part, inclosures have gone on very slowly for some years past. One reason has already been given for this, viz. the badness of the roads, and the difficulty and expence of making such new ones, as would be necessary in case of an inclosure. This impediment will soon be removed in North Wiltshire; and good roads will enable the owners of the adjoining commonable land, to make the most of it. And there is not a doubt, but that the greatest part of the commonable lands in the county would soon be divided, provided the *legal difficulties* which stand in the way of inclosures could be removed.

"It is well known, that no commonable land, *be it ever so small,* can be inclosed or divided without an act of parliament, unless by the consent of *all* the parties. That consent is always difficult to be got, and sometimes (particularly where some of the proprietors are *minors,* or under any other *legal disability)* impossible. An act of parliament is then the only resort. But it frequently happens, that the quantity of open land belonging to one manor, is insufficient to afford an expence of, perhaps, near 300l. for an act, besides the subsequent expence of working a commission. And although the land-owners of *two or more* manors might join in one act, yet it is a difficult matter to get them to agree on the terms of it; especially when, as is often the case, their interests, or, at least, their claims, on on the commonable lands, clash and interfere with each other.

"The expences of an act of parliament for an inclosure, are not entirely occasioned by the *fees* of the two Houses, but by the delay and uncertainty of attendances in London, owing to the multifarious and increasing business of parliament; and which an annihilation, or even a reduction of those fees, would tend much more to increase than prevent.

"*Remedy proposed.*—But there seems to be a mode by which this difficulty might be, in a great measure, obviated, and *small* common fields or commons divided at a trifling expence, viz. by empowering the justices of the peace to receive applications for that purpose at the quarter sessions; and particularly in those cases, where a very *great majority* of the proprietors were consenting, or where the objections were chiefly founded on *legal disability*.

"Notice of the proposed application to the justices might be given (in the way now prescribed by parliament) in August or September. The bill of the proposed regulations of the inclosure, might be delivered at the Michaelmas sessions, and made public immediately after. Objections might be heard at the Epiphany sessions, and the bench might then determine for or against an inclosure.

"Those who doubt the competency of a court of quarter sessions, to do this business properly, will consider, that the local information, so essential to the proper framing an inclosure bill, may be obtained, and the objections of parties aggrieved may be investigated, not only much *cheaper*, but much *better*, on the spot, than can possibly be done before parliament. And those who think it would be giving *too much power* to justices of the peace, will consider, that they have already a greater power than this, viz. the hearing and determining appeals that may come from parties aggrieved, under inclosure acts passed by parliament.

"And, indeed, if it were thought necessary, all possibility of partiality might be prevented by prescribed rules and regulations, as to the *proportional majority* of consenting proprietors, absolutely necessary to the passing an order for an inclosure."

The only remark I have to make, regarding these valuable strictures, is that Mr. Davis (the *late* Mr. Davis I am concerned to be compelled to put) from his extensive transactions in business, for a length of years,—and from

from his having, I believe, been in the habit of acting as a Commissioner of Inclosure,—is entitled to an attentive hearing, on the subject of the appropriation of English territory.

RURAL ECONOMY.

TENANTED ESTATES.

ESTATES and *Tenures*.—P. 117. "This district was formerly, and at no very remote period, possessed chiefly by great proprietors, who leased out the greatest part of it in small estates for *lives renewable*, at which time the country in general was in an open common field state, and most of the lessees lived on their own holdings. But since that period, many divisions of property have taken place, and freeholders been created by the dismemberment of manors, and gradual extinction of lifehold tenures, particularly in those parts which have been inclosed and laid down to pasture. Many manors, nevertheless, remain in their original common field state, and are still granted out on the same lifehold tenures, particularly those in mortmain, belonging to churches, colleges, schools, and other pious and public foundations; but upon the whole, property is much more divided than in the south-east district of the county."

P. 144. "In the dairy and grazing parts of the county, (which being the best land, were probably inclosed first) there are fewer traces of lifehold tenures remaining."

For the advantage accruing, in some cases, from an EXCHANGE of LANDS, see the head, *Dairy*, ensuing.

IRRIGATION.—It is in *South* Wiltshire, Mr. D. very properly speaks, at large, (and with superior ability) on the watering of meadow lands. Yet the following remarks, on the advantages of irrigation, on a *dairy* farm,—in order "to shorten the winter," and give a certain supply of valuable summer grass,—are aptly enough brought forward in the district now under notice.

P. 125. "On the banks of the Avon, and on some of the principal branches that lead to the Thames;* water meadows,

* As the banks of the Churn, for instance. See p. 440, aforegoing

meadows, though very practicable, are not much in request; the land being supposed to be 'good enough already.'

"But although it may, perhaps, be not easy to prove, that watering those rich meadows would improve *their quality*, it certainly would be of some advantage to a dairy farmer, to make the winter a month shorter, and to be able to turn his cows into *a flush of grass early in April*, instead of waiting till May, especially in a country where, on account of the great demand for, and high price of winter veal, a great part of the calves are sold off fat by the beginning of April; and if at that period the cows have no other food but hay, (unless the hay is very good) they frequently shrink their milk, and never fully recover it during the whole summer. A few of the dairy farmers have seen this advantage in this light, and have made water meadows, particularly near Somerford, where, though the expence must have been, at least, twelve pounds an acre, the improvement pays exceeding good interest for it. The very advantage of such land, not only requiring no manure itself, but affording manure for other land, is an object of more consequence than is generally imagined.

"*Objections against water meadows refuted.*—In a country like North Wiltshire, where grass land is plenty, and hay (of course) not so great an object as it is in South Wiltshire, it has been frequently remarked, that one of the great objects of a water meadow, 'that of producing a large and almost certain crop of hay' *is lost*; because, in such a country, hay of a much better quality than what usually grows in water meadows, is always to be got at a reasonable price. I answer to this, that the coarseness usually attributed to water mead hay, is in general not so much the fault of the herbage, as the covetousness of the owner, in letting it stand to increase the quantity till it is too ripe.

"Water mead hay, if cut young, is not only as good as that of dry meadow, but cows are *more* fond of it, on account of it's peculiar softness, than of the hard benty hay, that is produced on upland meadows, and it will produce more milk; though I will allow that, on that very account, it is not so saleable, nor, perhaps, so proper *for horses*.

"But, perhaps, it would not be difficult to prove, that water meadows, in many counties, and particularly those on dairy farms, will answer a better end to be summer-fed than to be mown at all.

"The advantage of the first flush of grass, a month before

before the upland meadows will produce it, is already pointed out, and is obvious to every one. When this is eat up, the land intended for summer-feeding will be ready to take the stock.

"The water may then be thrown over the water meadows for a fortnight, and a new supply of grass produced, that will again take the cows, by the time they have eat off the first shoot of the summer-pastures, and then they may be fed during the summer; and the quantity of grass they will produce, and the particular milky nature of that grass, is inconceivable to those who have not tried it, especially during a dry summer.

"In case of a wet summer, the meadow will not want watering after the second time, and indeed the drier they can be kept the better; but if the summer is dry, the water should be thrown over them whenever they appear to want it, and the cattle taken out, until the ground is dry and firm again. Two days watering, *and, in very hot weather, even a few hours,* will be sufficient; always remembering to stop it, before the water begins to leave a scum on the land.

"This plan of *summer-feeding* water-meadows, has been adopted by a few farmers in this district with success. In South Wiltshire it has been reduced to a system, in the neighbourhood of Hungerford, and applied to breeding lambs, and fatting them for the London market, in a way that is well worthy of imitation, in those counties where the *sheepfold* is not indispensably necessary."

For further remarks, on this head, see that of *Grass Land*, ensuing.

EXECUTIVE MANAGEMENT of Estates.—P. 144. "*Leases* are granted for various terms of years, in this district; sometimes for 21 years, but 14 seems the most general term.

Covenants.—"The landlord is usually bound to repair the buildings, and the tenant the fences.

"The landlord puts the gates in repair, and the tenant usually keeps them so, being allowed rough timber, or sometimes (and perhaps a better mode) being allowed as many new gates per annum, as the farm is supposed to require; the tenant putting them up, and keeping them in repair. The tenant is usually bound not to sell hay, or straw, and to spend the whole on the premisses.

Removals.—"The entries are various; some at Michaelmas, and some at Lady-day; but, in general, at Lady-day. On the corn farms, and even on those dairy farms that have arable

arable land annexed to them, the quitting tenant frequently takes an off-going crop of corn."

AGRICULTURE.

FARMS.—P. 144. "The land is, in general, divided into large farms, with the house in the most convenient part of them: and, perhaps, nothing contributes so much to the excellence of the dairy system of this district, as the convenient situation of houses in general, for reasons already given.

"North-Wiltshire dairy farms are, in general, exceedingly well accommodated with conveniences, and particularly with milk-houses, and cheese-lofts.

"The latter are frequently on a very large scale, as most of the North-Wiltshire cheese, being sold to factors, who contract for it by the year, requires to be longer kept than in countries where it is sold to chance customers.

"The cow-sheds, calf-houses, and milking-yards, are also, in general, on a much superior plan to those in many other countries; and nothing encourages the landlord to make these conveniences so much, as the remarkable neat style in which they are, almost uniformly, kept throughout this district."

PLAN of MANAGEMENT.—P. 117. "The stone-brash land, on the north-west verge, is chiefly arable.

"A great part of the residue is in grass land, and a great proportion of that part is applied to the dairy, particularly to the making of cheese. But although so great a portion of this district, is now in a state of inclosed pasture land, it does not appear to have been so from any remote period of antiquity.

"The straitness of the hedges, the uniformity of the inclosures, and the evident traces of the plough, are convincing proofs, that a great portion of it was originally in an open common field arable state, not excepting some of the very best meadow land on the fertile banks of the Avon.

"The difficulty of tilling and cropping land naturally wet and heavy, and its aptitude to run quickly to grass, has occasioned, from time to time, great quantities of it to be laid down to pasture, and the increase of the rents of the land when so applied, occasioned in a great degree by the excellence

excellence and increasing fame of the cheese made in this district, has contributed to keep it in that state, and daily to increase its quantity."

The subjoined remarks show the compass of mind and good sense of their writer.—P. 127. "It has been often said, that men are more apt to be led by custom and imitation, than by reason and observation. This is particularly the case in this part of North-Wiltshire. When this distric was in open common fields, (and which it appears to have been at no very distant period) the same system of sheep-folding was pursued, and perhaps very properly, as is still used on South-Wiltshire downs. And the same system is still pursued at this time, when the greatest part of the county is inclosed, and where they have neither down land, nor water meadow, nor very little pasture land, and frequently upon land neither proper, nor at all times safe for sheep, and the same kind of sheep, which, in South-Wilts, are kept to walk five or six miles a day, are here kept (comparatively speaking) to stand still."

Grass Lands.—P. 131. "The management of grass land has been entirely changed within a few years. It was formerly thought a sufficient manure for the grass land, to fodder the cattle upon it with the hay growing on the estate. But in deep, wet lands, this management did more harm than good: the treading of the cattle poaching the ground, and making it wetter, when its great fault was, the being too wet already.

"This has occasioned many land-owners to build stalls and sheds for wintering cattle, not only fat cattle, but dairy cows; whereby the occupiers are enabled to take their cattle off the land in November or December, or sooner, if the season requires it, and keep them off it until the grass is fit to take them in the spring; and as straw is necessary for this management, a little arable land is a necessary appendage to such a farm."

Manuring Grass Land.—P 132. "The dung made by such stall-foddering, is spread on the land in different modes and at different seasons; but the most approved mode is, to carry it out as soon as the cattle are gone from the stalls, and lay it in heaps near the spot where it is to be used, and to spread it in July or August; and it is reckoned the best husbandry, to put it on the land that has been mowed, soon after the hay is cleared off.

"A few farmers have dung enough, to cover all their grass land oftener than every eight or ten years; the loss of so small a part of the after-grass is immaterial, and is fully recom-

recompensed by the certain gain of a plentiful bite in September or October.

"This husbandry, with the addition of draining where necessary, (particularly with covered drains) winter haining, and early mowing, and the practice, now become general where it is practicable, of mowing and feeding every piece of land alternately, has been the chief cause of the late great improvements of the grass land of this district. The natural tendency of these improvements is, to get an early bite of grass in the spring, and thereby, in fact, *to shorten the winter;* an object of very great consequence to a dairy farmer. And those who are lucky enough to be able to shorten it still more by early water meadows, find an advantage in it that is not easy to estimate." See *Irrigation*, aforegoing.

Haymaking.—P. 135. "The dairy farmers, and, in particular, the graziers, are much more attentive to the quality than the quantity of their hay. It has been already remarked, that they make a point of haining up their meadows as early as possible in autumn, and, of course, are able to mow early in the summer.

"It is not uncommon to see grass mown, not only before it is in blossom, but even before it is *all in ear;* and to this it is owing, that it is more common to fat cattle with *hay alone*, in North Wilts, than, perhaps, in any county in the kingdom.

"And by this, the dairymen are able to keep up the milk of those cows that calve early, and from which calves are fatted, which would otherwise shrink before the springing of their grass, and never recover during the summer. And the advantage they get by early after-grass, and by the duration of that after-grass till a late period in autumn, fully compensates for the loss of quantity in their hay crop."

Cows.—P. 120. "It does not appear, at this time, what was the original kind of cow kept in this district; probably, the old Gloucestershire cow—a sort now almost extinct, or, perhaps, as is now the case in Somersetshire, a mixture of all kinds. But the universal rage, for upwards of twenty years past, has been for the long-horned, or, as they are called, the 'North-country' cows; and at this time, perhaps, nine-tenths of the dairies in this district, are entirely of that kind. The reasons given for the general introduction of this sort, are the nearness of their situation to the north-country breeders, where they can get any quantity they want at any time, cheaper than they can

can rear them in a country where land is in general too good, and rented too dear for that purpose; and, especially, as in consequence of the great demand for the Bath and London markets, calves will pay better to be sold for veal, than to be kept for stock; but, perhaps, the real reason is, that 'pride of stock,' which, operating like the pride of sheep and horses in South Wiltshire, has gradually led the farmers to an emulation in *beauty* and *size*, more than in *usefulness* and *profit;* and which pride, the breeders have not been wanting in using every artifice to create and promote."

P. 147. "Whether the dairymen are wrong, or right, in their choice of the kind of cows, will, probably, be hereafter determined. If they could buy another kind of cows, *immediately fit for the pail*, as easily as they can the long-horned ones, it is probable, that kind might not be so universal; but it is clear, that they think they get *nothing* by *breeding* their own stock, and, perhaps, they may *think right.*

"The cows they buy, are bred in a country whose cheese does not stand so high in repute as that of North-Wilts, and, of course, may be bred cheaper than they could breed them at home; but if this argument is well founded, are the North Wiltshire dairy-men right in fatting calves?"

For some account of the *management* of cows, see the preceding head, *Grass Lands.*

THE DAIRY.— P. 147. "The management of the dairy part of this district has been a source of so much profit, as well as credit, to the county, that it certainly must, in its principle, be right; and while there is so much to admire, it would be invidious to cavil at trifles."

P. 118. "The cheese of this district, was for years sold in the London markets by the name of Gloucester cheese, but is now perfectly well known by the name of 'North Wiltshire cheese.'

"It was at first doubtless an imitation, and perhaps an humble one, of that made in the vale of Gloucester, but is now, in the opinion of many, at least equal, if not superior, to that of the favorite district of Gloucestershire, the hundred of Berkley.

Mr. Marshall, who has so fully examined, and so ably described, the present state of the dairy in both districts, leans strongly to that opinion.

"Although this district varies as much, apparently, in soil and situation as almost any two counties can do, it is amazing

amazing how strong the predilection is to the dairy, and particularly to the making of cheese in every part of it; and still more so, that the cheese produced on soils and situations totally dissimilar, should frequently be found, when under skilful management, to be equally good. A strong proof, that although soil and situation may, in some measure, contribute to the production of that necessary article, yet art contributes more, or, perhaps, in other words, the dairy-women of this district, who happen to be situated in soils and situations, naturally unfavourable to the making of cheese, have, by attention and observation, found out the causes and the remedies for the faults peculiar to cheese made from their own dairies; and nothing has contributed more to excite that attention and observation, than the rivalship necessarily produced in a district, anxious, at first, to rival their neighbours in the vale of Gloucester, and then to keep up the superiority in goodness, and of course in price, which North Wiltshire cheese had, by degrees, acquired."

The following general observations, on the dairy of North Wiltshire, we find under the head, "Beneficial Practices."—P. 145. "The system of making cheese, as managed in North-Wiltshire, would certainly be of the greatest service, in many parts of the kingdom, if it could be introduced into them; and the production of good cheese, in this district, from land totally dissimilar, as stated in the preceding observations, shews that the goodness of this article does not depend so much on soils, or situations, as is generally imagined. Indeed, it is well known, that the fame of this district, for good cheese, is not very ancient. The circumstance, of its being sold for Gloucester cheese till within these few years, shews, that Gloucestershire had the *name* first; though the quantity now made in that county, is far less than what is made in this district, according to the report of Mr. Marshall, who spent much time in both districts, for the purpose of examining into this particular branch of rural œconomy.

"Indeed, many of the best dairy farms in the district appear, as has been already stated, to have been in an uninclosed state of arable, at no very remote period of antiquity; and many of the farm-houses and buildings appear to be of modern erection.

"The convenient situation of the houses and buildings of a great part of the dairy farms of this district, shews, that many exchanges in property must have taken place, before

before this desirable circumstance could have been obtained.—An object well worth imitation, in all countries where it can possibly be adopted; and, perhaps, there is no *single*, local circumstance, that contributes so much to the excellence of the dairy system of this district, as the general convenient situation of the lands round the houses, as a common center; so that the dairymen are able to drive all their cows home to milking, and, thereby, to put all their milk together of an equal temperature; and, by beginning their work much earlier in the morning, they can make cheese twice a-day during the whole season.

"This is impossible to be done, where servants must be sent to milk cows in detached and distant inclosures; as is too frequently the case in many dairy countries, and particularly in the county of Somerset.

"Good butter is made in every part of the kingdom, because the process is simple, and known every where; and if the same methods were practised in making cheese, in other countries, as are used in this, there seems no good reason why cheese, of equal goodness, might not be made in many other countries.

"As Mr. Marshall has so fully detailed the methods used by the North-Wiltshire dairy-women, it is unnecessary to repeat them here."

GRAZING CATTLE.—P. 119. "But although the dairy has from time to time, made great inroads on the arable lands of this district, *that* has likewise, in its turn, lost ground and particularly on the most fertile lands, by the rage for grazing.

"The rich and the lazy find this a pleasant resource; and the dairy, though much more profitable, is obliged to give way to it.

"Even those who are professedly dairy farmers, can seldom resist a propensity of applying a little of their best land to the purpose of grazing their own dry cows, and of fatting a few sheep in winter, or taking in stock sheep to winter for the down farmers.

"It may, therefore, be fairly asserted, that notwithstanding the strong natural predilection of this country to the dairy, and the peculiar excellence of the dairy-women in the making of cheese, at least one-fourth of the grass land in this district is applied to grazing."

P. 123. "The cattle consists chiefly of long-horned cows, turned off from the dairies, and of oxen bought

bought from different countries, particularly from Devonshire. They are usually bought-in very early in the spring, so as, if possible, to be finished with grass; but the largest and latest are taken into the stalls, and finished with dry meat, chiefly hay.

"Corn is but little in use for fatting cattle in this district; of late, potatoes have been introduced for winter fatting, dressed with steam, and mixed with cut hay or straw, as is mentioned in the description of the south-east district, and found to answer. Bath takes off many of the fat cattle of this district; many are sold at Salisbury market or the consumption of Hants, and the adjoining counties, but the greatest part go to Smithfield."

SWINE.—P. 122. "Pigs are looked upon to be a necessary appendage to every dairy farm; a great number are bred with the whey and offal of the dairy, and many fatted; barley-meal, mixed with the whey, is the general fatting food; pease are not so much used as formerly."

How delightful the task of reviewing the work of a sensible experienced man, writing in his own profession; and where, of course, the unpleasant service of censure is little, if at all, required.

NORTH

NORTH SOMERSET.

THIS portion of Somersetshire partakes of Glocestershire and Wiltshire, both in soils and agricultural management. It includes calcareous heights and vale lands. The dairy produce is similar to that of the rest of the Western Department. Even its cattle are of a kindred nature:—very different,—a distinct variety,—from those of South Somerset, and the other parts of the Southwestern Department

The natural line of separation is given by the marshes and sedgemores of the Brue and its branches; which, now, doubtlessly occupy what was, heretofore, an estuary or arm of the sea, that more determinately separated those two natural districts from each other, and the damnonian peninsula from the main land. Hence, not only the Mendip hills, but their southern skirts, form parts of the district under notice. The towns of Axbridge, Wells, and Shipton Mallet stand on its southern verge.

North of this line, grass land produce is principally applied to the CHEESE DAIRY; to the south of it, it is chiefly appropriated to GRAZING, or the BUTTER DAIRY.

For further particulars, relating to this natural and agricultural line of demarcation,—see the RURAL ECONOMY of the WEST of ENGLAND,—district the seventh, and minute sixty five.

SOMERSETSHIRE, at large, was reported, *originally*, in 1794, and published in a *reprinted* form, in 1798,—by Mr. BILLINGSLEY;—a man of considerable ability and information. His GENERAL QUALIFICATIONS, as a Reporter of rural concerns, will be most aptly considered in examining his Report of the principal part of the county,—as a portion of the SOUTHWESTERN DEPARTMENT.

By the extracts that will, *here*, be adduced, the reader will perceive that Mr. Billingsley's experience, in agriculture, has arisen (in one particular, at least) from an extensive

tensive practice. It will likewise be apparent to *professional* occupiers, that Mr. B's strictures are those of an *improver*, rather than of one who has long been in the habit of paying *personal* and close attention to the *minutiæ* of practice. It is to be observed, however, that, in many respects, a mind accustomed to consider the outlines and general economy of an art is more likely to afford a comprehensive view of it, than a mere pracitional professor;—who, on the other hand, is better qualified to describe existing practices, so as to convey them intelligibly to the minds of other practitioners. How seldom do we find the two qualifications united!

In some "preliminary observations," Mr. B. (it is proper to mention, here) has obligingly favored his readers (contrary to the usage of most other of the Board's Reporters) with some information concerning the work he was offering to the Board and the public. The close of the statement is the only objectionable part of it.—P. ix. "The following remarks on the present state of agriculture in the county of Somerset having been made without an actual survey, those readers who are conversant with the subject will be able, no doubt, to point out many *defects*, *errors*. and *omissions*.

"The writer, however, presumes, that though he may not have specifically and expressly touched on all the practices and improvements of the best farmers, yet that no kind or class of these matters has been absolutely overlooked.

"He does not profess to have given a complete detail of the various branches of rural management, but to have discussed the most *important* ar icles belonging thereto; and he has done his utmost to treat the subject in such a manner, and to express his meaning in such a language, as might be best adapted to the understanding and comprehension of common farmers."

NATURAL ECONOMY.

CLIMATURE, SURFACE, and SOILS.—P. 17. "The surface of this district being very irregular, and intermixed with lofty hills and rich fertile plains, the climate is consequently exceedingly varied. On the western side, including

cluding the hundreds of Winter-Stoke and Portbury, the soil is, for the most part, a deep and rich mixture of clay and sand; being originally a deposit by the sea, which, in antient times, flowed up a considerable way into that part of the country." *

FOSSILS.—For *Marls*, see the ensuing head, *Manures*.

MINERALS.—*Lead*.—P. 20. "The Mendip hills are famous for their mines, particularly of lead and lapis calaminaris. The former are nearly exhausted, or at least the deep working is so incumbered with water, that little can be done, and in all probability millions in value may remain concealed in the bowels of this mountain, 'till spirit enough be found in the country to perforate it by cutting a level, or audit, through its base, namely, from Compton-Martin to Wookey-Hole.

"The distance is about five miles, and the depth from the surface about one hundred and fifty yards; such a tunnel would not only convey off all water, but the driving it, or the sinking of the shaft or perpendicular pits, might lead to a discovery of veins of lead hitherto unexplored, and perhaps as valuable as that now at West-Chewton, which, tradition, says, yielded 100,000*l*. within the space of an acre."

Lapis calaminaris.—P. 21. "In the parishes of Rowberrow, Shipham, and Winscomb, there are valuable mines of lapis calaminaris. This mineral is sometimes found within a yard of the surface, and seldom worked deeper than thirty fathoms. Between four and five hundred miners are constantly employed in this business, and the average price is about five pounds per ton. In the parishes of Compton-Martin and East-Harptry are also many of a similar nature, and a considerable number of men are constantly employed therein."

There are other parts of the Mendip district in which this fossil is found.

I cannot withstand the temptation to insert, here, the following curious notice.—P. 22. "The general method of discovering the situation and direction of these seams of ore

* Mr. Billingsley speaks, at some length concerning the improvement of these marsh lands; and inserts in his work an engraving concerning them. But their nature, and the mode of their improvement, being similar to those belonging to the central parts of the county (already in a state of improvement) Mr. B's plan will, hereafter be considered, with better effects, when the county more at large shall come under consideration.

ore (which lie at various depths, from five to twenty fathoms, in a chasm between two benches of solid rock) is, by the help of the *divining-rod*, vulgarly called *josing*; and a variety of strong testimonies are adduced in support of this doctrine. Most rational people, however, give but little credit to it, and consider the whole as a *trick*. Should the fact be allowed, it is difficult to account for it; and the influence of the mines on the hasel-rod seems to partake so much of the marvellous, as almost entirely to exclude the operation of known and natural agents. So confident, however, are the common miners of its efficacy, that they scarce ever sink a shaft but by its direction; and those who are dexterous in the use of it, will mark on the surface the course and breadth of the vein; and after that, with the assistance of the rod, will follow the same course twenty times following *blindfolded*"

Coals.—P. 26. "This district abounds with coal, and with respect to this article is reducible to the separate divisions of northern and southern. The former, including the parishes of High-Littleton, Timsbury, Paulton, (with Clutton and Sutton adjoining to the west, and Camerton and Dunkerton to the east of the district) Radstock, and the northern part of Midsummer-Norton. The latter, the southern part of Midsummer-Norton, Stratton on the Foss, (Halcombe and Ashwick adjoining the district) Kilmersdon, Babington, and Mells.

"These, meaning the *latter*, are what were heretofore known by the name of Mendip collieries, and probably they were once within the verge of that extensive forest, though now in the midst of old inclosures. They being still frequently described in ordinary books of topography by the same name, (now obsolete in the neighbourhood) this remark was thought necessary for the purpose of identification.

"In the northern collieries the strata of coal form an inclination of the *plane* of about nine inches in the yard: these are in number nineteen. In thickness variable, from ten inches to upwards of three feet. If less than fifteen inches, they are seldom worked. Coal is now working generally from seventy to eighty fathoms in depth: in a few places deeper; and by a late introduction of machinery to raise it by the steam-engine, a much greater depth of working will be obtained *." The

"* As it may be a matter of consequence to all such coal-works whose situation in regard to water will admit of it, it ought to be noticed, that at Welton, a work in the northern part of Midsummer-Norton,

The following desultory remarks are full of information. —P. 28. "The southern district is on a more limited scale of working. The strata of coal form an inclination of the plane from eighteen to thirty inches in the yard; in some the plane is annihilated, and they descend in a perpendicular direction. They are in number twenty-five; in thickness from six inches to seven feet; seldom worked under eighteen inches; in depth from thirty to sixty fathoms at the present working. By the steam-engines, which are now erecting in this district, a much greater depth will be attained. Profits in the aggregate of working very trifling, if any, owing to the consumption of timber, and the expence of drawing water. The coal of various quality; some nearly equal to that of the northern district; but the greatest part less firm, of shorter grain, and less calculated for distant carriage; but free to burn, wholly divested of sulphureous stench, and durable. The small coal excellent for the forge, and when reduced to a cinder, called *coke*, by a process of very ancient usage, it furnishes a fuel for drying malt, which, from its purity and total exemption from smoke, cannot be excelled, if equalled. The south-western parts of Wiltshire, the northern of Dorset, and the eastern and southern parts of Somerset, are the markets for consumption.

"The quantity now raised is from eight hundred to a thousand tons weekly, which, in the course of a few years, might be extended to two thousand tons, if sale could be found. Boys and men employed at present amount to from five to six hundred. An improved method of working has been lately adopted in some parts of this district, by which the springs are prevented from inundating the deep working; whereby its extent and duration will be considerably promoted.

"A canal to the works in this district, which might be cut at an easy expence, has been for some time in contemplation *; and which not only would benefit the proprietors

Norton, the coal has lately been drawn up by a water-wheel on a new construction; the machinery appendant to which is so contrived as to answer the purpose in the most perfect and cheap manner; the use of horses, as in the old way, being entirely superseded; and the consumption of fuel, as in the new way by the steam-engine, altogether saved. R. P."

"* This is now (Jan. 1797) in execution, and the tonnage, &c. of coal to Frome (nine miles) will not exceed 2s. per ton."

prietors of the works, by extending the consumption, but also reduce the price to the more distant consumers more than half.

"The average price of coal in this district is three-pence three-farthings per bushel.

"Should the works in the northern district be stopped, the probable increase of the poor-rates would be 2000*l.* per annum. In the southern (much more burthened with poor) to seven or eight shillings in the pound.

"At Clapton also, a village lying to the north-west of Leigh-Down, there is a coal-work which possesses the advantage of a land-level of forty-four fathoms. At this pit are landed about 240 bushels daily. The best coal is sold at three-pence halfpenny per bushel, and the small is shipped at Portishead-point for Wales, where it is used for burning lime.

"South-east of Leigh-Down is a vale of rich grass land, extending from Bedminster at the north-east, to Brockley and Nailsea at the south-west.

"Under this level are supposed to be inexhaustible veins of coal. At present they land 2500 bushels a day. The best coal is sold at three-pence halfpenny, the middle sort at three-pence, and the small at two-pence, per bushel. One of the works is under contract to serve the glass-houses, some time since erected in the parish of Nailsea, at one penny farthing per bushel.

"These glass-houses consume about 2000 bushels weekly. The deepest work is forty-two fathoms. The principal vein is five feet thick; sometimes more. The coal takes a south *pitch*, or inclination, never exceeding two feet in a fathom. Little timber is used; but they are much incommoded with water; for the rock which lies above the coal so abounds with fissures, that it is difficult to prevent the *land water* from pervading the bottom of the works.

"When the top veins are exhausted, and the proprietors compelled to go deeper, it is a matter of doubt whether any power of a steam-engine may be competent to the task of keeping them dry.

"Many people are under alarming apprehensions lest the coal-mines may be exhausted by the extra demand produced by the extension of sale established by the canals; —but such disquieting ideas will vanish, when they are told that more than treble the present quantity could be raised from the pits already in use, did the demand require it; and

and the increased quantity might be supplied for several hundred years."—Such, at least, would seem to be the Reporter's opinion.

POLITICAL ECONOMY.

APPROPRIATION.—P. 130. (chapter "Waste Lands") —"In this district there are many commons uninclosed; the principal of which are, Broadfield-Down near Wrington, and Lansdown near Bath. The former contains two thousand five hundred acres, and is for the most part a good soil, deep in earth, and easily ploughed.

"Surely the inclosing and cultivating a tract like this, situate only eight miles distant from the city of Bristol, could not fail of being a great advantage to the proprietors; particularly as it abounds with excellent lime-stone, and the coal-pits are only a few miles distant.

"Lansdown comprehends nearly one thousand acres; but as the soil is thin, and the surface perfectly smooth, and remarkable for its excellence in feeding sheep, to which it imparts a delicate flavour, it might not be prudent to break it up, especially as it affords a luxurious and beautiful ride to the sojourners in Bath.

"Inclosing has been of long standing in most of these parts; many have exemplified an advance of rent more than two-thirds."

P. 19. (section "Climate, Soil, &c.") "Leigh Down. This is a tract of elevated land, extending from Cleveden to the Hot-Wells, near Bristol. It is principally fed with sheep, and consists of nearly three thousand acres. A large portion of this down will not admit of cultivation, the lime-stone rock being within two or three inches of the surface. It is probable that this land will pay more as pasture than any other way. But the chief inconvenience arises from the unlimited right of stocking, by which it is burthened with double the number it ought to have; the breed of neat cattle is greatly injured; and, in respect to sheep, the quantity of wool lessened. To illustrate this observation, respecting over-stocking, I shall state a case in point. A farmer of this district, some years since, put twenty-five head of steers and heifers into a piece of commonable land: the spring being unfavourable

to

to the purchase of cattle, and a considerable fatality having prevailed the preceding winter, the common was *moderately* stocked; in consequence of which a profit of two pounds per head was made between the months of April and November. Encouraged by this success, and flattering himself with the prospect of similar profit, he purchased the next year one hundred head; but others following his example, he, to his great mortification, found that, instead of profit, he suffered a loss of nearly one hundred pounds.

"From these premises, may it not fairly be inferred, that the *inclosing* and *dividing* of commons, even in cases where the plough cannot prudently be introduced, are beneficial both to the individual and the public; as the owner can then apportion the stock to the quantity and quality of his land, and can have them at all times under his eye?"

P. 48. (chapter "Inclosing, &c.") "Mendip Hills. This chain of mountainous land extended, according to the ancient boundary, from Cotle's-Oak, near the town of Frome, to a place called the Black-Rock, in the Bristol channel near Uphill, being a distance of more than thirty miles. A great portion of this land having been inclosed, divided, and cultivated, in the course of the last forty years, and nearly an equal portion still remaining in its open uncultivated state, I cannot forward the views of the respectable Board, under whose auspices this Report will be brought forward to the public, in a better way than by a minute description of the origin, progress, and success of those undertakings.

"And first, let us begin with taking a view of the objections which have been started to this species of improvement, and see if we cannot prove them to be for the most part either false or frivolous.

"1st. Invasion of the rights and interests of the cottagers.

"2dly. A supposed injury done to the breeding system.

"3dly. The expences attending the act of parliament with those of commissioners, and other subordinate agents employed in its execution.

"4thly. The expence of buildings, such as farm-houses, barns, stables, stalls, and pools, for the purpose of creating distinct farms, superadded to the expences of cultivation and fencing, altogether constituting an expenditure which the improved value will not reimburse.

"5thly. Injury done to the woollen-manufacture, by lessening the number of sheep, and deteriorating the quality of the wool.

6thly.

"6thly. A supposed diminution of the rent of the old farms, to which such commons were appurtenant."

These objections are answered at considerable length. But as the Reporter's strictures are not confined to the north of Somersetshire, but extend to the moorish commons, in the central parts of the county, they properly belong to the County more at large.—As a man of general information, as well as an experienced Commissioner of "Inclosures," Mr. Billingsley's statements are well entitled to consideration.

Provisions.—On this topic, Mr. B's remarks are ample, and many of them interesting and valuable;—evincing the energy and compass of mind that dictated them.—P. 152. "In the year 1793 wheat was six shillings per bushel, (Winchester) barley four shillings and sixpence, oats three shillings and three pence, beef four pence halfpenny per pound, mutton four-pence halfpenny, pork five-pence, butter ninepence,* and cheese, six months old, forty shillings per cwt. Now, viz. January 1797, wheat is at seven shillings, barley three shillings, oats two shillings and three-pence, per Winchester bushel; beef at six-pence, mutton five-pence halfpenny, pork seven-pence, butter one shilling per pound, and cheese fifty-six shillings per cwt. The prices of all grain are declining rapidly; and it is probable, that before the conclusion of the year 1797, they will be very low indeed.

"In the alarming scarcity of bread-corn, and the dearness of all other grain, which was felt in the years 1795-6, the attention of mankind was naturally directed to an investigation of those causes from which that distressing evil might have originated. Various were the opinions of mankind on this subject; and the chief causes stated, were, the *consolidation of farms, the combination of farmers, jobbers, and millers*; *the consumption made by the distillers, the oppression of tithes, the sale of corn by sample*, and lastly, the *increased luxury of the times*.

"Though all these causes have undoubtedly contributed in part to produce the effect, which we have had so much reason to deplore, yet I think the great operating causes have been, *scanty crops of corn, the prevailing disposition of converting arable to pasture*, and the *unavoidable waste which must inevitably accompany war*.

"From

"* In the years 1795-6 wheat was at fourteen shillings per bushel, barley five shillings, oats three shillings and nine-pence, beef five-pence, butter tenpence, and cheese fifty shillings per cwt."

"From the year 1791 to 1796 we had not a first-rate crop of corn. The summer and autumn of 1792 were a continued series of wet weather; both corn and hay were greatly injured in harvesting, and consequently the little corn that was well secured, advanced in price; but under all these unfavourable circumstances, the old stock in hand was so considerable, that the price in 1793 did not exceed (in the county of Somerset, at least) seven shillings and sixpence per bushel, Winchester. The produce of 1793 being a middling crop, wheat did not experience much advance, till a probable deficiency in the crop of 1794, accompanied with nearly a total failure in the crop of pulse, was discoverable. Its advance then was very rapid, and great part of the old stock being exhausted, apprehensions were entertained of an absolute famine. We may, therefore, from the foregoing statement, draw this fair inference, that three out of the five years before referred to were *deficient in produce*; and that the crops of 1791 and 1793, though tolerable, were not sufficient to make good the deficiency of the three unproductive years."

Again—P. 154. "From the statement made in the first Report of the Select Committee appointed to take into consideration the means of promoting the cultivation and improvement of waste land, it appears that the total increase, in the consumption of cattle and sheep, for the last sixty-two years, amounts to the enormous number of 32,854 head of cattle, and 203,290 sheep, or nearly one third *for the metropolis alone*; and as the size and weight, both of cattle and sheep, have probably increased at least one-fourth since 1732, such augmented proportion ought to be added to the calculation of consumption. This denotes such an increase, both of inhabitants and of luxury as must have been attended with a proportionate consumption of butter, cheese, hay, &c.; and if extended to the whole kingdom, clearly accounts for the increased price of the before-mentioned articles, and is a sufficient apology for that predilection for *pasture* land, which, for many years past, seems to have been universally manifested.

"In the course of the last thirty years, the price of labour, butter and cheese, beef and hay, have advanced in price nearly fifty pounds per cent. Barley and oats have also advanced thirty or forty per cent. Not so *bread corn*. If we except the last two years, that article has advanced but little; and perhaps the average price of the last thirty years, namely, from 1764 to 1794, is not much higher than that from 1734 to 1764."

Mr

Mr. Billingsley next adverts to the consolidation of farms, as a cause of dearness. But arguments, on that point, appear to be no longer requisite. The prices of grain have of late years been as low as, under existing circumstances, they can be grown;—and this while the sizes of farms have probably been increasing. Mr. B. concludes—P. 158 "If the foregoing observations are founded on fact, we may safely infer that the late dearness of wheat is easily accounted for, without having recourse to the combination of farmers, the monopoly of jobbers, or to any other of the causes before enumerated.

"It arose from *three years out of five of deficient produce. The almost total failure of pulse in the year* 1794, *and the destructive ravages of war*, which has not only lessened importation, but has inevitably produced in our fleets and armies a wasteful expenditure of this necessary article of human food."

MANUFACTURES.—P. 160. "The principal manufactures in this district are those of woollen cloth, and knit worsted stockings, which, in the town of Frome, as well as Shepton-Mallet, are considerable; and from the number of hands therein employed, must have some effect on the agriculture of the neighbourhood.

"The town and parish of Frome are found to contain nearly seventeen hundred families, or about ten thousand people; more than one-third of which are actually and immediately supported by the manufactures spoken of; besides a vast number of the lower order of people, in the adjacent villages. In this town, the annual quantity of cloth manufactured has lately been found to be more than one hundred and fifty thousand yards In Shepton, the inhabitants may be reckoned six thousand, and the cloth manufactured one hundred and twenty thousand yards."

Mr. Billingsley then enters, with appropriate feeling, upon the important topic,—the use of *Machinery* in modern manufactories. This, however, is no farther connected with my present views, than in as much as it tends to sever agriculture and the manufacture of its produce; and thereby to prevent them from mutually assisting each other.—See NORTH. DEPART. p. 344.

Viewed in this light, the use of modern machinery, in the woollen and linen manufactories, has ever appeared to me a serious evil.—Beside (as Mr. B. suggests in the close of the subjoined extract) the danger of thereby more easily transfering the lucrative manufactures of this to any other Country. To be expert in *manual* operations requires

requires some years of experience; and, to carry on extensive manufactures, by that means, requires numbers to execute them;—who, in that case, must emigrate in a body, with the art they practise;—as did the Flemmings, with the woollen manufacture, and the French with the manufacture of silk, to this country.—Whereas, a few individuals, or a single person, with the art in his head and drawings in his pocket, may readily erect a "spinning jenny," in any quarter of the world.

P. 162. "The assistance of machinery was had recourse to by the manufacturers of Frome and Shepton from absolute necessity; for had they continued in the old method, their trade must have been lost; and indeed *now* the North-country manufacturers are beforehand with them, particularly in the application of water, the best *primum mobile* of all machinery.

"It is much to be feared, that the improvements already made, and those now going on, will ultimately be the means of disseminating manufactures in other countries, to the prejudice of the export trade of Britain."

The *effect* of modern manufactures on *agriculture*, are mentioned in the subjoined notice.—P. 162. "There are also several mills on the Avon for preparing iron and copper, and sundry others for the spinning of worsted, and spinning and weaving of cotton. The effect on agriculture has been considerable; the pay of men, in the time of harvest, has been greatly advanced, and that of women and children doubled."

POOR RATE.—For the *effect* of *Mining*, on the poor rate, and of course on *Agriculture*, see the head *Minerals* aforegoing; p. 497.

CANALS.—For the advantages of a Coal-mine Canal, see Minerals, p. 496 aforegoing.

RURAL ECONOMY.

TENANTED ESTATES.

ESTATES.—P. 31. "There are in this district many large proprietors from 2000l. to 6000l. per annum; but still

still the greatest part is possessed by the middle class, holding from 50l. to 500l. per annum."

IMPROVEMENT of ESTATES.—*Drinking Pools.*—P. 89. (Mendip Hills)—"The next, and not the least important appendage of these farms, are *pools* or *reservoirs of water;* for on hills so elevated few springs can be expected. Nothing more strongly verifies the truth of the old adage, "Necessity is the mother of invention," than the skill exhibited by the masons of this district in buildings of this nature. Scarcely ever do these pools let through the water, and the cost, supposing it to be of the following dimensions, 40 feet long, 16 wide, and 6 feet deep in the middle, may be thus stated:

	£	s.	d.
Digging out for foundation - - - - -	2	2	0
N. B. In most instances this will furnish a sufficient quantity of stone for the building.			
Mason's labour - - - - - - -	10	10	0
Three hundred bushels of lime - - -	3	0	0
Ten loads of clay and carriage - - -	1	0	0
Eight loads of coal-ashes and carriage - -	1	8	0
	*18	0	0

"A pool of these dimensions, if properly situated, will supply eighty or one hundred acres with a sufficiency of water for the stock throughout the year; and if well made, may be kept in repair for six-pence a year."—Of the construction of, or the method of forming, those ponds, we are left to conjecture.

Introducing improvements.—In a note, to the section, "Woad,"—we find the following sensible remarks, by R. P.—Note, P. 115. "About forty years ago woad was cultivated in the neighbourhood of Mells; and there was in the parish a horse-mill for grinding, and sheds for drying it, the property of one HARVEY, who was more generally known by the appellation of the Woadman, than his own surname. Since his death it has been entirely discontinued.

"From whence this man originally came is unknown, but most

"* Some cautious people go to a considerable distance for lime made from the white-lyas stone, which is certainly a stronger cement under water than the lime burnt on these hills. In this case, an additional expence is incurred."

most probably from some part where this plant was in usual culture. Small plots of teazels, hops, &c. are sometimes seen in villages far distant from those parts where they are raised on a large scale. Hence one is led to observe the attachment which most men have to the local husbandry of the district in which they are born and brought up, and the consequent difficulty of introducing a new system of agriculture into any place. The person migrating carries his attachments and habits with him, whilst the neighbours, where he settles, are unconcerned, or perhaps contemptuous spectators of his proceedings; and though they see him flourish and do well, are scarce ever induced to relinquish their old ways and imitate his example."

For another notice, respecting this topic, see the ensuing head, *Tillage*.

EXECUTIVE MANAGEMENT of Estates.—*Receiving Rents.*—P. 35. " Rent is universally paid in money; and it is generally customary to receive the Michaelmas rent at Lady-day, and the Lady-day's rent at Michaelmas."

WOODLANDS.

WOODS.—P. 129. " The ancient forest of Selwood (on the verge of which the town of Frome stands) appears to have comprised a woody vale of about twenty thousand acres, about eighteen thousand of which are now cleansed and converted into pasture and arable land, with a small portion of meadow; the remainder continuing in a state of coppice-wood. The chief sorts of timber in these coppices are oak and ash, which, though not of large growth, are very good of their kinds, and find profitable markets in the neighbourhood; the oak selling from fifty shillings to three pounds sixteen shillings per ton, and ash from forty five shillings to three pounds. The underwood is chiefly hazel, ash, alder, withy, and birch; some of which, at eighteen or twenty years growth, sell as high as sixteen pounds per acre."

AGRICULTURE.

AGRICULTURE.

FARMS.—P. 34. "The farms in this district are not large, seldom exceeding 200 l. per year, and accompanied with a small proportion of arable. Some of the dairy farms are so small, as not to exceed 60 l. or 70 l. per year; and many instances can be produced of such little farmers breeding up a large family in a very respectable way. In such instances, it is generally found that the wife undertakes the whole management of the cows, and the husband goes to daily labour. There are few trades in which a small capital can be employed to greater advantage than this."

P. 99. "Though I am no advocate for farms of an *excessive* extent, yet I think, that on soils, and in situations such as Mendip hills, they should not be less than four or five hundred acres. I mean sufficient to keep a flock of sheep for the purposes of *folding*."

Homesteads.—P. 32. "On all the dairy farms, a shameful inattention prevails, in respect to out-houses and sheds for their stock to retire to in the winter months. Cattle are almost universally served with their provender in the field; and many a dairy farmer, with twenty cows, scarcely makes, in the whole winter, a quantity of dung sufficient to manure *one acre* of land. Corn being generally stacked, the barns are small, and principally *thatched* with wheat-straw unbroken by the flail, which gives to the roof a very neat appearance, and renders the building perfectly secure from rain."

OCCUPIERS.—Speaking of "Estates," Mr. B. says—p. 31. "Part is leased out on lives; part is in demesne, and let out for short terms; and no small quantity is the fee of the occupiers, constituting a most respectable yeomanry."

WORKPEOPLE. In noticing an instance of *ploughing by the acre*, (see *Tillage*, ensuing) Mr. Billingsley is led to the following ingenious and valuable considerations.—P. 101. "Let us pause here, and seriously consider the advantages

advantages of *contract* in comparison with *daily* labour*. The English labourer is naturally disposed to vigorous exertion, if encouraged thereto, either by an increase of wages, or by the exhilarating influence of good cheer.

"Do we not see in times of harvest a degree of activity exhibited, unknown at other times of the year? and this at a season when the heat of the weather naturally induces fatigue.

"Do not the manufacturer and artisan, almost of every description, have recourse to contract labour? And though their workmen earn from ten to thirty shillings per week, do they not find their account in so doing, from the emulation which it excites, and the perfection of workmanship which it produces?

"Must it not be acknowledged, that in those countries where *daily labour* is the prevailing mode, a slow and indolent habit is generated, which neither promises nor threats can entirely overcome, to the great injury of the commonwealth, as well as of the farmer. Suppose we allow the average rate of daily labour to be sixteen-pence, and admit that by contract, men will be excited to earn twenty-pence, what an addition of useful labour would be created, taking it in an aggregate point of view!"

WORKING ANIMALS.—*Oxen* and *Horses.*—P. 103. "It is the general opinion of farmers in this district, that oxen are preferable to horses, for the purpose of ploughing, but for harrowing and all other purposes, the contrary."

Some account of the extraordinary exertions which *oxen* are capable of, as beasts of draft, will appear under the next head, *Tillage.*

I insert Mr. B's calculation on the expences of keeping a "team" of oxen and a "team" of horses:—not, however, so much with the view of registering uncontrovertable facts, as to introduce the concluding remark.—P. 103. "The expences of keeping a team of each for the purposes

"* Many sensible and well-meaning men have objected to *contract labour*, under the idea of its being injurious to the health and longevity of the labourer;—but though I have been in the habit of letting my work by the job or task for twenty years past, I never perceived any ill effect on the health or strength of my workmen. Where great exertion and excess of wages are forerunners to drunkenness and debauchery, such consequences may follow;—but no practical man will deny, that where daily labour prevails, a considerable portion of the day is wasted in sauntering, holding tales, and in a sluggish use of those limbs which are capable of more lively motion."

poses of farming may be thus stated, and it will appear, that the superiority of oxen is not so great as some sanguine men have stated.

"HORSE TEAM, (4)

"The first cost, including harness, cannot be estimated at less than one hundred pounds.

	£.	s.	d.
To 30 weeks keeping at hay, 12 tons at 40s. -	24	0	0
Corn throughout the year - - - -	30	0	0
To twenty-two weeks keeping at grass, at 3s. 6d. each horse - - - - - -	15	8	0
Repairs of harness - - - - -	2	12	0
Farrier and shoeing - - - - -	4	0	0
	£. 76	0	0

"OX TEAM, (6)

"The first cost of these, supposing them to be the best North-Devon breed, and four or five years old, yokes, bows, and chains included*, 70l.

	£.	s.	d.
To twenty-six weeks at hay, twenty-four tons, at 40s. - - - - - - - -	48	0	0
Twenty-six ditto at grass, 2s. 6d. per week each ox - - - - - - - -	19	10	0
Repairs of yokes and bows, and chains - -	0	10	0
	£. 68	0	0

"Some farmers think that three horses are equal in exertion to six oxen; if that be admitted, the expences of the horse team will be less than those of the oxen.

"If an accident should happen whereby a horse is lamed, the value is much more lessened than in the case of an ox; but in all other respects they stand on equal ground; for horses, if purchased at the age of four or five years, are improving in value for two or three years, as much or more than oxen. And every intelligent farmer must be sensible of the folly of keeping a horse after he is six or seven years old; they should then be transferred to common carriers, &c. and agriculture should only be the medium

"* Oxen are now (January 1797) fifty per cent. dearer. J. B."

dium whereby a young horse becomes, by gentle labour, inured to more severe discipline."

If the horses, employed by "common carriers, &c." were three or fourfold in number to those required for the purposes of husbandry (instead of the *reverse* I apprehend) the above general suggestion might have conveyed practical and valuable advice. In the county of Wilts, and its environs, where such a practice, as that alluded to, has long prevailed, the hint may have its use;—and the writer, probably, did not recollect, at the moment, that he was conveying his sentiments to the united kingdom, at large.

Horses.—P. 148. "Few people are aware of the expences which attend the keeping of a team for *road* work.

"The following being taken (as an average of seven years past) from an account kept by a person whose accuracy may be depended on, needs no apology.

"TWO TEAMS, NINE HORSES.

	£.	s.	d.
Two waggoners 60l. turnpike 50l. expences 27l. 6s.	137	6	0
Corn of all sorts	110	10	0
Brewers' grains four-pence per bushel	38	19	0
Hay, at three pounds per ton	74	0	0
Harness-maker	9	12	0
Tilts, lines, &c.	11	0	0
Blacksmith	27	10	0
Farrier	3	1	0
Wear and tear of waggons	20	0	0
Ditto of horses	30	0	0
Straw	16	0	0
	£. 477	18	0*

Or nearly 240l. per team."

TILLAGE.—P. 100. (Mendip Hills)—"Formerly the ploughs used here were the most aukward, and ill-contrived, that could be conceived, but they have in a great measure given place to the *double-furrowed* plough, which was introduced to this neighbourhood by a speculative man who turned farmer on these lands, disregarded and despised by all practical husbandmen.

"Though

"* This calculation affords a very substantial reason why *traunters*, as they are called, (that is, men who keep horses and waggons for hire) seldom get rich."

"Though common farmers are for the most part backward in adopting new plans, yet I never knew any *valuable* discovery that they did not sooner or later fall into. So it happened with the double ploughs. For ten years, did the person above alluded to use this instrument, and was constant in season, and out of season, in recommending it to others; (for they who have a true taste for agriculture, enjoy themselves in the communication of every useful discovery) but all in vain, the more warm he was in enforcing its utility, the more reluctant were the common renters in adopting the use of it; and in all probability it would have remained to the present day, undistinguished for its superiority, had not the same been manifested at the different trials of ploughs exhibited under the direction of the Bath Agricultural Society.

"At present, scarce any other plough is used after the first breaking; and, I believe, I may truly assert, that in comparison with the old ploughs of the district, no less than fifty pounds per year is saved on a farm of five hundred acres.*

"Another mode of management has been for many years past introduced by the person before alluded to, namely, ploughing by the *acre* instead of the *day*.

"The contract is thus conducted; the master finds oxen and food, and the ploughman labour and driver. The latter is also bound to attend the cattle at all times, even when debarred from work by rain, snow, frost, or any other cause. The price is two shillings and two-pence per acre for the ploughing of the rough Mendip lands when first inclosed, (this is done with a single plough) and one shilling and two-pence for all other ploughings of every description, with the double plough.

"By this system of management he has annually had more ground ploughed by *one* team, than his neighbours by *two*; and it has been no unusual thing for his man and boy to earn regularly per week seventeen shillings and six-pence, that is, for two acres and half per day on an average. Nay, his man has repeatedly ploughed with six oxen (in yokes) twenty acres of land, statute measure, in forty-eight hours; I mean in six successive days, reckoning eight hours per day: the breadth of the plit according to

* On absorbent soils that admit of being laid flat, and where plowing with two horses without a driver is not in use, this implement is the most eligible.

to agreement not exceeding nine inches, nor the depth less than four inches, (when the soil was deep enough to admit thereof.")

Mr. Billingsley, very properly, mentions two objections to this *new* practice.—P. 103. " First, the possibility of cattle being injured by too great exertion; and secondly, imperfection in the execution."—Nevertheless, in a busy seed time, it might, in many situations, be found eligible. The plowmen have, in this case, an interest in taking due care of their teams.

MANURE.—*Lime.*—P. 90. " As *lime* is the grand manure of this district, by which the improvements of cultivation are in a great measure brought about, kilns for burning it are numerous, and generally thought well constructed; their form is that of a French bottle, the height seventeen feet, the length of the neck, in which the calcination is wholly effected, seven feet; its diameter four feet, and the diameter of the belly in the largest part twelve feet. They are built on the side of a hill, by which means the top is on a level with the adjacent *rock*."

How inadequate is this description. What " common farmer" (out of the West of England, at least) knows the shape of a " French bottle?" And how can the calcinations be " wholly effected" in its " neck?" How is the " belly," in the first instance, filled, and its contents calcined? These, and various other particulars, ought, surely, to have been explained.—Yet, with these slender helps, the reader is left (p. 91)—" to determine, whether kilns of this construction are or are not to be preferred to those in shape of an inverted cone."

This form differing widely from that of every other lime furnace, in the kingdom, and being the established form of the country under Report,—and its use, I believe confined within narrow bounds,—its history, and a minute description of it, might have been a valuable acquisition, in sites, in which it can be conveniently adopted.

P. 105. " Before we leave the subject of liming, it may be right to inform my readers, that some have dressed their old pastures with hot lime, by which the moss has been destroyed, and a fine herbage produced, highly grateful to the palate of all sorts of stock. The lime, after the rate of one hundred and sixty bushels per acre, is put on the land soon after it is mown, and its effects are very durable; being perceptible for fifteen or twenty years, and it quite alters the nature of the coarse sour grass, to which old layers are very subject."

The

The following striking results, related of the effects of lime on the Mendip lands, are of more consideration than the theory on which they are accounted for.

P. 105. "Having already stated that lime is the great article of modern improvement of these hills, I shall only add, that instances might be produced of lands letting at this time for thirty shillings per acre, which forty years ago were not worth four shillings; and the beginning of all these improvements has been by lime, whereby the acidity of the soil, impregnated with mineral exhalation, has been corrected, and crops raised on them as good as those on improved fields; and it is no less wonderful than true, that thirty cart-loads of rotten dung per acre, *previous to liming*, have had no sensible effect; but after the land has been once limed, the operation of dung is as perceptible here as on other lands."

Marl.—P. 132. "The parishes of Midsummer-Norton, Stratton-on-the-Foss, Kilmersden, Radstock, Timsbury, High-Littleton, Farmborough, Paulton, Ston-Easton, Binegar, and Chilcompton, comprehend a district of land, part of which is rendered remarkably fertile by the application of marl *.

"The soil consists of an earth more or less loamy, of a mixed colour, between brown and red, with a prevalence of one or the other; very stony, resembling that kind of soil usually denominated corn-grit, and naturally so barren, that when in common field, at the beginning of the present century, the lands were not set at more than three shillings and six-pence per statute acre.

"By a moderate computation, this soil may be said to occupy, in the parishes before enumerated, an average proportion of at least one-third. At a variable depth from the surface an inexhaustible store of black marl is constantly found, which, from properties equally singular as to fertility and duration, has advanced the lands from three shillings and six-pence to one pound eleven shillings and six-pence, and some to two pounds per statute acre; and this too with a very liberal allowance of profit to the occupier.

"This valuable manure is raised in the summer at the average depth of about seven or eight fathom, by sinking a pit or shaft of four feet diameter, the sides whereof are secured by timber props, interspersed with wreathings of brush-

" * Marl also may be found at Queen-Charlton, Chewton-Keynsham, and Burnett."

brushwood, and it is drawn to the surface by means of a windlass and buckets.

"The first bed of marl perforated is blue, two feet thick, of a stiff consistence, and on repeated trials found in a comparative degree useless. Below this lies a stratum of stone, nine inches thick, and of a blue colour; next to which is found a bed of marl, from three to four feet in thickness, nearly horizontal, of a colour approaching to black, and, towards the lower part, of a shelly substance; the greater predominance whereof is found proportionably to improve its fertilizing property.

"The expence of raising it, including that of sinking the shaft, is from eight-pence to one shilling per cart-load of twenty-four bushels. That, and carting out, spreading and brushing in, eighteen shillings per statute acre.

	£.	s.	d.
"Forty load is an ample dressing for a statute acre, which, at one shilling per load, amounts to	£.2	0	0
Carting, spreading, &c. - - - - - - - - -	0	18	0
The whole	2	18	0

"For which a manure is obtained that secures a luxuriant undiminished vegetation, not requiring any further assistance for fifteen or twenty years."

This would seem to be a rare variety of marl;—possessing very extraordinary powers. Of its specific quality, or component parts, we have no account. It appears, however, from what is here said of it, that it is singularly entitled to analysis. Judging from the subjoined passage, compared with the preceding, we may conceive it to possess some remarkable properties.

P. 137. "Marl has been repeatedly tried on the looser red earth lands, and on freestone grit soil, in different parts of the district, without producing any good effect. It has also been carried some miles out of the district, and applied to the light red earth of the lime-stone lands, with no better success."

P. 134. "The generation of moss manifests the declining effects of this manure. It is considered as an indication for breaking up the old sward, which is generally done. This developes a very curious and singular phœnomenon; namely, the marl spread on the surface forty or fifty years before, has only obtained the depth of between five and six inches, where it forms a regular, uniform, consolidated bed. Even at this depth its effects, although not exhausted, are never-

nevertheless so much impaired as to demand its renewal. Will not this fact tend, in some degree, to elucidate its modus operandi?

"While it remains within two or three inches of the surface, which is the case in some instances perhaps for twenty years or more, it may be supposed to form a kind of pan or reservoir for the nutritious and fructifying influences deposited by the atmosphere; which being there retained, and in contact with the roots of the grasses, form such combinations in the laboratory of nature as are best adapted to give vigour and permanence to the elementary principles of vegetation. These are evidently weakened when the marl, by its descent, gets below the roots of the grasses, and thereby deprives them of the matrix, which seems to preserve the means of their nutrition and support. This may account for the production and increase of moss on the surface, and the necessity of marling afresh, not only to impede its propagation but to destroy it."

I give these reveries a place, here, as they are those of a man whose speculations, even, are not to be wholely disregarded.

HARVESTING.—P. 97. "All the corn, wheat, barley, and oats, are bound into sheaves and mowed in the field. The price for barley and oats from three to five shillings; besides these prices, the men are allowed for wheat two gallons of beer, and for barley and oats one gallon and half, per acre.

"In situations subject to sudden and violent rain, this custom of mowing in the field cannot be condemned, as, in respect to wheat, the day's cutting is secured every evening, and the lent corn can be put together and secured much sooner than in the common method.

"The principal objections are, the bringing mice with the sheaves into the barn, or large mow; and the want of sufficient dryness in the corn for winter threshing.

"The men of this country are very dextrous in making these mows, so as to prevent rain from injuring the corn; and they frequently remain five or six weeks in the field without suffering any damage."—The Somersetshire "mows" are probably similar to the *arish mows* of Devonshire, and Wales. They are probably of Celtic origin. For a description, and the method of forming them, see the Rural Economy of the West of England.

HOMESTALL MANAGEMENT.—"Threshing," or "making,"—"*Somersetshire Reed.*"—The following extract, with its appendant notes, contain all the particulars that we find

find in this Report, concerning the singular practice of Somersetshire, in separating the grain from the straw of wheat. In what manner the ears are severed from the straw, how this is freed from the weeds and ravelled straws with which it is usually encumbered, or how the grain is extracted from the ears,—I have not been able to find any account, in the Somersetshire Report:—notwithstanding the practice may be said to be peculiar to that county. It is essentially different from the Devonshire practice.

P. 97. "Wheat is seldom threshed with the straw, but the ears are cut off, and the straw bound in sheaves tied very tight; the circumference of the sheaf at the bond should be six feet; this costs five-pence per sheaf, including the threshing of the ears. A good acre of wheat will produce three dozen sheaves, value eight shillings and sixpence per dozen*, and each sheaf should weigh fifty-six pounds. By this method, the firmness of the stalk is preserved, and rendered more valuable for the purposes of thatching buildings †, &c."

ARABLE CROPS.—Of the ordinary grain crops I find nothing that is entitled to notice, here; the preceding extracts excepted.

TEASLES.—This crop, as has been remarked aforegoing, accompanies the woolen cloth manufacture;—which has long been established, I believe, on the borders of Somersetshire and Wiltshire. The following is Mr. Billingsley's account of the culture, of the teasle, in *Somersetshire* ‡.

P. 110.

"* Ear-pitching is the provincial term for this management, and the sheaves thus prepared are called reed-sheaves. They are in general use for the purpose of thatching, for which, indeed, they are solely intended. The practice is not confined to Mendip, but is in common use through great part of the district. The workmen are very dextrous in making, and the thatchers no less expert in using it; and at the same time that it makes a covering more durable than any other of straw, it is of such superior neatness, that the thatched buildings of this neighbourhood excite the admiration of many strangers coming from other parts where this practice is not known.

"A dozen sheaves will cover a square of one hundred feet. Price of laying them up (new work) three shillings per dozen. A second or any succeeding coat, two shillings per dozen. Mending, four-pence per sheaf. R. P."

"† Some people dispute this point, and say, that the hollow tube of the wheat-straw admits the air, and that its decay is thereby accelerated, and assert (from experience) that *threshed* straw is more durable than *unthreshed*. J. B."

‡ For the *Yorkshire* practice, see the NORTHERN DEPARTMENT, p. 479; and for that of *Glocestershire*, see p. 456, aforegoing.

P. 110. "In the parishes of Wrington, Blagdon, Ubly, Compton-Martin, and Harptry, teasles are much cultivated. The head of this plant, which is composed of well-turned vegetable hooks, is used in dressing of cloth; and the manufacturers of this county and Wilts are, for the most part, supplied from these parishes. Large quantities are also sent (by water conveyance from Bristol) into Yorkshire.

"As this is a plant not generally known, I will describe its culture.

"The most favourable soil is a strong rich clay, or what is generally denominated good wheat land.

"Sometimes an old ley is broke up, and sometimes a wheat-stubble; the seed is sown, after the rate of two pecks per acre, in the month of April. During the summer the land is worked over three or four times with *long narrow spades* to destroy the weeds.

"In the month of November, if the plants are too thick, they are drawn out to fill up vacancies, and the plants are set at a foot distance. If, after this thinning, too many plants remain, another field is prepared, into which they are transplanted; but those plants which are never removed produce the best heads.

"At the next spring and ensuing summer the land is worked over three or four times with the narrow spades, by which it is kept thorough clean, and the plants earthed up. This is called speddling.

"In the month of July the uppermost heads begin to blossom, and as soon as the blossom falls, they are ripe. The gathering is performed at three different times. A man, with a knife made for the purpose, cuts the heads which are ripe, and ties them up in handfuls. After a fortnight he goes over the ground again, and at a third cutting the business is completed. On the day of cutting they are carried into a house, and if the air be clear, they are taken out daily and exposed to the sun till they are compleatly dry; but great care must be taken that no rain falls on them.

"The crop is very hazardous. A wet season rots them, particularly when there is much rain at the time of blossoming.

"In the year 1792 there were few worth harvesting. The crop this year is but indifferent. When dry they are separated into three different parts, called kings, middlings, and scrubs; and are, after that, made into packs, containing of kings nine thousand heads, and of middling twenty thousand. The scrubs are of but little value. The average price

price is forty shillings per pack; and sometimes the produce is fifteen or sixteen packs an acre, at other times a total blank. There is an amazing inequality in the produce of different plants; some stocks will send forth one hundred heads, others not more than three or four.

"Should not great attention therefore be paid to the selection of seed, namely, by taking it from those plants which appear to be most prolifick? This, however, is not done, but the seed is taken indiscriminately from the whole crop.

"As the goodness of the crop chiefly depends on the care taken to keep the land free from weeds, leaving the plants at proper distances, and earthing them up well; and as most of the common workmen will pay more attention to their own than to another person's interest, it frequently happens that a partnership is formed between master and man. The former finds ground and ploughing, and the latter seed and labour.

"At harvest the crop is divided, and each party takes a moiety."

Again, p. 112. "The working with the spade can only be done to advantage by the men accustomed to it, who are become, by habit, so dexterous in the use of this implement, that they will even thin out a crop of carrots.

"The common hoe has been tried, and though in the hand of a compleat turnip-hoer, it was not found to answer."

The dimensions of these spades, with the method of using them, might well have been noticed. They may, it is more than probable, be profitably used, on other occasions.

WOAD.—This, too, is an article of *field* produce, the *minutiæ* of whose culture have not fallen under my *examination*. It is on the eastern side of the kingdom, I believe, where we are to look for accurate ideas concerning it. Nevertheless the Somersetshire practice, as here reported, may be useful to collate with others that may be found, in going through the Board's Reports. It is of course registered, here, on Mr. Billingsley's authority.

P. 113. "This is an article of cultivation, which being important, as it relates to the woollen manufactory, must not be omitted. It is raised principally in the neighbourhood of Keynsham, and its quality is much esteemed.

"The farmers who raise it have an opinion that the parish of Keynsham is particularly favourable to the growth and perfection of it; but this is most likely a vulgar error, for experiments are attested of as good crops elsewhere. The

The soil must be strong and good where it flourishes; it delights most in a deep fat loam, of a dark colour, which must have so much sand as to admit of easy pulverization.

"As the excellence of woad consists in its size, and the succulency of its leaf, it requires careful management as well as a rich soil It is most commonly sown on land fresh broken up, and on narrow ridges.

"The first ploughing should be against winter; the second in the spring, when the ridges should be formed; a third in April; and the last in May or June, just before the sowing of the seed.* In the intervals of the ploughing, harrowing should take place, to destroy all weeds.

"The seed is sometimes sown by the best farmers in drills, for which purpose the surface should be harrowed very fine and level. The plants, in a moist season, appear in a fortnight, and in two or three weeks after are fit to hoe; they should be hoed out clean, to the distance of about six inches at least; some prefer a greater distance. In this neighbourhood, hand-weeding and thinning are generally used; and at the employ, women and children earn very high wages, especially since a cotton manufactory has been introduced in the parish. The success of the crops depends much on the hoeing and weeding, so as to keep the ground fresh and clean. Thus managed, three or four crops or gatherings will be produced in succession; but the first two are the best. The time of gathering is determined by the full growth of the leaves, and the first appearance of change of colour at the extremities; and this rule of course governs the succeeding crops.

"The leaves are cut by hand, and gathered into baskets by women and children, who carry them to a very deep large cart at the edge of the field. After two cuttings, the crop is suffered to go to seed for the next year, if seed be wanted; but if only one crop be taken, the seed will be the finer. When the pods turn of a dark colour, the seed is deemed ripe. The stalks should then be reaped like wheat, and spread abroad; and if the weather be favourable, the seed will be fit for threshing in four or five days.

"When the green crops are carted home, the plant is thrown into a mill, constructed with a heavy iron ribbed roller, something like that which is used for bruising bark and other substances; by this process it is cut and bruised to

"* Frequently woad is sown on *ley* ground, and on one ploughing, the surface being well harrowed."

to a pulp. It is then laid in small heaps, pressed close and smooth; and as the crust formed on the outside cracks, it is closed again to preserve the strength of the substance. After lying about a fortnight in this state, the heaps are broken up, the outside worked into the mass, and the whole formed by the hand, and sometimes by wooden moulds, into oval balls, which are then dried on hurdles, under a shed exposed to the sun.

"They turn black, or of a dark-brown, on the outside, when well manufactured, and are valued in proportion to their specific weight and a purplish cast in the inside. Thus they are sold to the dyer; and it is scarcely necessary to add further, that the use of this article in dying consists in forming the ground of the indigo blue. The crop is generally a profitable one. The quantity per acre near a ton and half. The nett profit of course must be governed by the goodness and price of the article. But it seems, on an average, to be so lucrative a culture, that few farmers who can raise it ever discontinue the practice. It however exhausts the land exceedingly, and more than two years crops must not in general be taken. To this crop succeed wheat and beans."

POTATOES.—P. 115. "The rapid extension of the cultivation of this root can only be equalled by its general utility as a food both for man and beast. Thirty or forty years ago it was an extraordinary thing to see an acre of potatoes in one spot, and in one man's possession; now there are many parishes in this district which can produce fifty acres. Nay, the writer of this Report has grown thirty or forty acres per year, for a succession of years; and once he had upwards of one hundred acres in one year."

From this extraordinary extent of practice,—if personally, and minutially, attended to,—an accuracy of ideas, and an excellency of management, could scarcely fail to result. The following are Mr. B's strictures, (at large,) on their *culture*.

P. 116. The soil most favourable is a rich sandy loam, newly broke up, and of a loose texture. The sorts cultivated are, the *kidney*, *white Scotch*, *magpie*, *rough red*, *purple*, and *silver-skin*. Rotten horse-dung is considered as the best manure; next to that, hog's dung; and after that, all sorts of farm-yard dung.

"Lime, marl, soaper's ashes, or rags, make the potatoes scabby. The season of planting is April or May, and the quantity planted per acre from five to eight sacks, (240 lb.) The seed should be changed every two years, and *large* cuttings

cuttings used from your *largest* and *finest* potatoes. Whole potatoes have been tried, and found not to answer. There are various methods of planting, but they may be reduced to two, viz. the drill and the promiscuous.

"If labourers are plenty, the promiscuous method is supposed to be the best. In this way the land is thrown into beds, five feet wide; intervals or alleys three feet, which are dug and thrown on to the beds.

"The sets are placed one foot apart. Let the season be ever so wet, the potatoes in this way lie dry. In hoeing* also, access is had to the plants without treading on them. They are not so liable to be injured by rooks; and such a putrid fermentation is excited by the close thick shade of the haulm, that the land is more meliorated, and the weeds more compleatly suffocated and destroyed than in any other method. In regard to expence there is no great difference, for in this way it may be done for a guinea an acre, and in the drill method it will cost at least twelve shillings. The same reasoning weighs still stronger in respect to taking up: dexterous labourers, by thrusting their spades under the potatoes, avoid cutting the roots. They also, in digging, separate the *small* from the *large*. They pulverize the soil more: they can dig clean, though the land be wet: and, on the whole, the expence of digging will not exceed that of ploughing out, more than *ten shillings* an acre. If the crop be a good one, the separating the small potatoes from the large will cost more than this difference. The produce varies from fifty to one hundred and twenty sacks (240lb. each) an acre; and the general price, as human food, is from four shillings to seven shillings per sack; and on particular occasions they have been sold at ten shillings.

"When dug, they are secured in pits, and if common care and attention be bestowed, they are preserved in this way through the most severe winter, without injury; but they will shrink in respect to measure about one sack in twenty."

To the *application* and *expenditure* of potatoes, and their *value* for *farm* consumption, Mr. Billingsley would seem to have paid closer attention.—P. 117. "From a series of experiments made by the writer of this Report, and communicated through the channel of the Bath Society's Papers,

"* In hoeing, be particularly careful to cut out all plants which appear curled in the leaf."

Papers, it appears that their value, when applied to the fatting of hogs, could not be made to exceed two shillings and sixpence, or three shillings, per sack, of 240l.: and from other experiments since made, it is probable, that no greater value can be affixed to them if applied to the sustenance of any other stock. However, this should be no discouragement, for on good land, and with good management, they may be grown for one shilling and sixpence per sack, and will furnish the farmer with a certain supply of food in those months wherein he is most distressed."*

On the *effects* of the potatoe crop on *land*, his remarks are less satisfactory.—P. 117. "Many object to the cultivation of this root *on a large scale*, considering it in the light of a great exhauster. If the produce of any crop, so productive as this is, be sold from the farm, and consumed at so great a distance that no return can be made, I will acknowledge that such must be the effect; but if potatoes are consumed on the premises, the return of manure, from the consumption of *one* acre, will be sufficient for *two* or *three;* and as the potatoe crop ought always to be highly manured, no deficiency need be feared in the subsequent crops of corn, grasses, &c. particularly if wheat be banished as a succeeding crop, and barley or oats substituted in its place †."

CULTIVATED HERBAGE.—Mr. Billingsley's "hints," on *laying down arable land* to *grass*, may well be taken, and his directions (in the outline at least) safely followed, in any

* For their value, compared with that of hay, see the close of the next note.

"† The reason why wheat frequently fails after potatoes, is because the frequent hoeings and digging render the land so light and porous, that it is more subject to the ravages of the grub, earth-worm, &c.; beside, in cold and exposed situations, the sowing is generally protracted till the month of November, which alone is sufficient to check the practice." (Not satisfactory.)

"*N. B.* The writer has known thirty-two successive crops of potatoes from the same field, and the produce as good at the latter part of the term as at the beginning. This will puzzle the theorist, with his *peculiar substances of nutrition.*

"A large cow, tied up a month after calving, ate 2cwt. and 18lb. of hay in one week, and on the ensuing week, being given four bushels (Winchester) of potatoes, the consumption of hay was reduced to 3qrs. and 26lb. It appears, therefore, that a sack of potatoes is equal to 1cwt. of hay. The quantity of milk was increased by the potatoes, but it was thinner in quality."

any district:—care being had to gather the "hay seeds" from a *kindred* soil and situation,—and to see the mowing ground diligently *weeded*, before the herbage be ready for the sithe.

P. 120. "Perhaps there are few things in husbandry more difficult to be accomplished than that of restoring worn-out arable to a good pasture. A few hints on this subject may not be unacceptable.

"The first step is to extirpate from the land all noxious weeds. This may be done by a compleat winter and summer-fallow; or, in place of the summer-fallow, by a crop of potatoes, well manured, and kept perfectly clean, and followed by winter vetches, fed off in the spring.

"At the latter end of May, or beginning of June, sow one bushel of buck-wheat per acre, and when that is up, and in rough leaf, harrow in (choosing, if possible, moist weather) two bushels of hay seed, collected from the best meadow hay, half a bushel of rye-grass, four pounds of marl grass, and four pounds of white Dutch clover. The buck is intended principally as a screen to the grass seeds.

"If, therefore, the harrowing should pull up some of the plants, so much the better. A thick crop is not desirable. After the buck-wheat is harvested, which will be some time in September, let the field be hayned, or shut up for the winter; and let it be fed the next summer with sheep, or any kind of cattle, except horses; the latter animal will tear up the young plants with his teeth."

Buckweet is well known to smother, or check, the growth of seed weeds; and serves of course to prevent the matting of chickweed,—the great enemy of young grasses that are raised without corn. But too thick a crop of it may endanger the seedling herbage. RAPE, if kept sufficiently stocked, in dry weather, to keep it down, is in my opinion preferable to buckweet:—either of them is to be chosen, when *perennial grass land* is in view, in preference to a crop of *corn*;—which, on the contrary, when a *temporary ley* of one, two, or three years, only, is required, will bring in a greater present profit, and be, on the whole, the most adviseable;—provided it do not lodge, and smother the young herbage.

Marl Grass.—P. 136. "Marl grass is the spontaneous production of the marl land. It was first noticed and collected fifty or sixty years ago by a Mr. JAMES, who lived on a farm belonging to the Marquis of BATH, in the parish of Chilcompton. By his assiduity in preserving and propagating

pagating the seed, in the course of a few years it became common, and has been considered ever since as a valuable substitute for red or broad clover, to which it bears rather a striking analogy; with, however, this difference, that it will continue much longer in the land."

This is, doubtlessly, the "cow grass" of other districts; —TRIFOLIUM *pratense* (not *alpestre*);—the common red trefoil of meadows and pastures;—the NATIVE CLOVER of this island.

GRASS LANDS.—There is much truth in the following remarks.—P. 119. "It has been already observed, that the grass land of this district greatly preponderates; and if it be not chilled by too much moisture, it may boast of almost a perpetual verdure.

"On the rich marsh land near the Bristol Channel, the grazing system prevails. In the vicinity of Bristol and Bath, the scythe is in constant use; and at a greater distance nothing is scarcely seen but the milking-pail. To which ever of these purposes the land is devoted, its bounties are not niggardly dispensed. If we view them comparatively, the hay system is perhaps the most injurious to the land, and the least productive of profit. This article seldom exceeds three pounds per ton; and if we consider the risk in making, the expence of carriage, the loss of time, and above all, the declining value of the estate so occupied, few arguments can be wanted to prove the impolicy of the system. In short, I never knew a hay-selling farmer get rich."

ORCHARDS.—P. 124. "The whole district is full of orchards, which let from three pounds to six pounds per acre; and the fruit produced at the northern base of Mendip hills, viz. at Langford, Burrington, Rickford, Blagdon, Ubly, Compton-Martin, and Harptry, affords a cyder strong, palatable, and highly esteemed as a wholesome *table* liquor. Many of these orchards have a northern aspect, and are sheltered from the violence of the westerly winds; and it is noticed, that orchards, so situated, are the most regular and uniform bearers." Near the western coasts of this island, requires to be here added.

P. 125. "Mr. Good, who occupies a large farm in Hutton, has a method of making cyder, which it may not be amiss to describe. The apples are ground by a horse-mill. The pummice is then wrung in hair bags; after which it is put into a tub and chopped. It is then ground over again, and made into a cheese, which stands in the press all night.

"In

"In the morning the press is strained as tight as it will bear by a lever or cap-staff."—This is eligible; but not new or peculiar.

P. 126. "Notwithstanding the apparent utility of extensive and productive orchards, many considerate and sensible men have hesitated in giving their unqualified a sent to this sentiment; alledging, that plenty of cyder is the forerunner of idleness, drunkenness, and debauchery, not only among the lower class, but also among the yeomanry themselves, who at these times spend successive days and nights in toping and guzzling at each others' houses. We ought not, however, to confound the abuse of a thing with its intrinsic value."

HORSES.—P. 148. "There are but few horses bred in this district—the farmers are principally supplied by dealers who attend the North-country fairs. Farriery is in the hands of men equally conceited and illiterate; and these useful animals frequently die of a disease called the *doctor*."

COWS.—What may be properly termed the *cheese dairy* of Somersetshire is, as has been shown above, p. 492, chiefly confined to the northern limb of the county.—But Mr. Billingsley divides his account of it. His general remarks, on *cows*,—their breeds and management,—are found, principally, in what he terms the northeast district." Whereas, we find his *note* on the *dairy*, in "the middle district;" where, also, is found some further observations on *cows*. I will, here, bring the several particulars (concerning cows) together; and place them in their natural order.

P. 142 (Northeast District)—"As the cows are all devoted to the dairy, preference is given to that sort which gives the most milk and of the best quality; or, in the farmer's language, to that stock which makes the most goods, whether it be butter, or cheese, or both; hence it follows, that in point of carcase they are very deficient. They are mostly of the short-horned breed,* and though the fine long-horned cows of North-Wiltshire have been tried, and strongly recommended by some, yet the general run of dairymen are strongly attached to their own breed.

"As this is a subject of some magnitude, let us bestow on it a few moments attention.

"In the choice of stock, the buyer should principally attend to the purposes for which that stock is designed, and to the nature and quality of his land.

"If

* Very different, however, from the *Dutch* or *Holderness* breed. See WEST of ENGLAND; *Cattle* of *East Somerset*.

" If his principal object be rearing, either with a view to fat himself or to sell to others, the form or shape of the parent stock should first be regarded.

" That frame of body, which is accompanied with the greatest portion of valuable flesh, and the least offal, is to be preferred.

" An aptitude to fat in youth is also an object of great importance. By an attention to these points, the farmers of Leicestershire and other counties have so attracted the notice of emulous breeders, as to sell their stock at a price scarcely credible to a plain old-fashioned farmer. But however we may admire their care and ingenuity, does it follow that we are to be led astray by the extravagant ideas which some people entertain of their superiority? A heifer of three or four years old, which discovers a disposition to fat, seldom proves a good milker, and is by our farmers turned out of the dairy. Beside, I have been informed that the great breeders are frequently obliged to have the assistance of Welsh nurses for their calves, through a deficiency of milk in the parent animal. Is this a recommendation of them to the dairyman?

" As a confirmation of the idea that handsome stock are seldom good milkers, I shall advert to the North-Devon breed, and I believe in all other respects there is not a more valuable in the kingdom.

" In that part of the kingdom, little attention is paid to cheese or butter; but if a cow produce handsome stock, it is all that is required of her; and it frequently happens that a farmer, with ten or twelve cows, has but little more of those articles than is sufficient to supply his family.

" The Somersetshire dairymen generally keep their good cows till they are ten or twelve years old, at which time their value is reduced to four or five pounds each. A long-horned cow, at that age, might be worth eight or ten pounds; (I mean of the middling breed;) here is then an apparent deficiency of four or five pounds; but when we reflect that the keeping of one is worth ten shillings a year more than the other, the loss is not so apparent; and if we admit, that the short-horned will make half a hundred of cheese more per year than the long-horned, the balance of profit is then in favour of the former.*

" I do not mean by what I have said to detract from the merit of Mr. BAKEWELL, or other great breeders of the North.

* This a North Wiltshire Dairyman might deem supposititious.

North. I only wish to recommend a discriminating principle, and to deter the credulous farmer from *too hasty* a dereliction of principles and practices founded in experience, and to which he has been long accustomed.

"I may be here told, that the foregoing premises, from which conclusions are drawn unfavourable to the long-horned cow, are delusive; that a North-country breeder would laugh at the idea of keeping a cow, till she is ten years old; that at six years, or at the farthest at seven, she ought to be in the possession of the butcher.

"But coolly and calmly, ask a practical cow-keeper at what period of life a cow makes the most goods, and he will tell you between the age of six and twelve years old. I have known cows continue good milkers till they have passed their twentieth year.*

"When cheese only is made, the annual produce per cow is from three to four cwt.

"Many dairy farmers, in the vicinity of Bath and Bristol, make butter and half-skimmed cheese; in either way, the annual produce per cow is from eight to twelve pounds, including the calf, and profit of pigs.

"From three to four acres of land will keep a cow throughout the year.†

"If kept on hay alone, a middle-sized cow will eat one hundred and three quarters per week during the winter month, and on an average thirty hundred in the whole winter; this calculation is formed on a supposition that she calves between Christmas and Candlemas. If turnips or cabbages be given, she will eat, of the former two hundred, and of the latter one hundred and half in twenty-four hours, and the quantity of hay will be lessened about one half.—Heifers are put to the bull when one year and half old; and very few calves are reared for bulls or oxen, and

"* The discriminating principle recommended, is a very necessary one, and deserves particular attention. It may here be observed in general, that in many parts there is a sort of cattle, as it were provincial, hardy, thriving, and well adapted to the soil on which it is bred. Let the cautious farmer furnish himself with the best of this sort which he can select, and if he must improve, as it is called, let him not lose sight of the discriminating principle, but do it with wariness and discernment. And as very little of the dairyman's profit is expected from sale of the carcase, if his cows are well kept, and yield him a good quantity of rich productive milk, it will be immaterial whether they have long horns, short horns, or any horns at all. R.P."

† P. 122. "Two acres, worth thirty shillings per acre, are necessary to summer a cow well, and one acre and half for her winter provender."

and no more of the female kind than just sufficient to keep up the stock.

"Next to the selection of a proper sort, good keeping when young is of the first importance: and it has been observed, that calves, after being turned out to grass, should have but little water given them. The first winter each calf will eat above sixteen hundred of hay."

These desultory remarks I have inserted entire; tho some of them may not appear to be strictly accurate.

P. 247. (Middle District.) "The cows of this district being intended chiefly for the purposes of cheese-making, the profit arising is in proportion to the quantity and quality of the milk; size, therefore, is not attended to, but principal regard is paid to the breed whence she sprung. The dairy-men think it more profitable to have a small breed *well fed*, than the best breed in the world *scantily kept;* and the cow that gives milk the longest is most esteemed. The time of calving is from the beginning of February to Lady-day, and they take great care to keep their cows well three weeks or a month before they calve; the milk will rise in proportion to the goodness of their keeping; very little attention is paid to the nature or sort of the bull."

P. 249. (same District) "The heifers are put to the bull in July, when they are about one year and a half old; and the prevailing opinion seems to be, that those which are kept from the bull a year longer do not turn out *good milkers.* The average produce of a dairy per day, may be calculated at about three gallons per cow, from Lady-day to Michaelmas, and from Michaelmas to Christmas one gallon per cow per day.

"Cows are kept till they are fourteen or fifteen years old."

P. 252. (the same) "The cows of this district are almost universally depastured in the fields both summer and winter; in consequence of which, the dung produced even by a large dairy is trifling indeed; hence arises a manifest declension in the fertility of the land, and you may distinguish a grazing from a dairy farm at a great distance. In this exhausted state the dairy land must remain, unless a different system of management be successfully inculcated. Were I to suggest a plan of improvement, it would be the following: Let all dairy farms be accompanied with a due proportion of arable, perhaps *a fourth part;* let proper stalls and bartons be erected as a residence for the cows during the winter months; let cabbages, turnips, and potatoes,

toes, be grown for their winter subsistence; but above all, let them be well littered, and kept perfectly clean. By these means, a large supply of dung may be procured at a little expence; and if the farmer wish to increase the quantity, he need only dig up the waste earth on the borders of the highways, and make a layer therewith in his farm yard. This will absorb the urine, and when mixed and incorporated with the dung, will constitute a manure highly fertilising."

P. 249. (the same) "Cows are subject to a disorder called *the yellows*, something similar to the jaundice in the human species. This disorder frequently affects the udder, and brings on a false quarter, that is a deprivation of milk in one teat, accompanied with a swelling and inflammation. For this, however, I can suggest a remedy which seldom fails, viz. flour of mustard mixed with any liquid, two ounces a dose, and repeating the same two or three times in the course of twenty-four hours."

The CHEESE DAIRY of Somersetshire.—*Note*, P. 247. —"The cheese of this district is much admired, particularly that made in the parishes of Mear and Cheddar.

"It is for the most part purchased by jobbers, and sent through the medium of Weyhill, Giles's-hill, Reading, and other fairs, to the London market, where it is sold under the name of *double Glocester*.

"The method of making has been so often described, that I shall not trouble my readers with a minute detail thereof. The annexed short account of the process I shall only premise, with observing, that cleanliness, sweet rennet, and attention to breaking the curd, are the principal requisites in cheese-making.

"*Process of Cheese-making.*

"When the milk is brought home, it is strained into a tub, and about three table-spoonfuls of good rennet put therein, (supposing the quantity of milk sufficient to make a cheese of twenty-eight pounds) which remains undisturbed about two hours, (!) then it becomes curd, and is properly broken; when done, three parts of the whey is taken therefrom and warmed, and then put into the tub again, where it remains about twenty minutes; the whey is again put over the fire, made nearly scald hot, and put into the tub to scald the curd about half an hour, and then part of the whey is taken away, and the remainder remains with the curd till it is nearly cold; the whey is then poured off, the curd broken very small, put into the vat and pressed,

pressed, where it remains nearly an hour; and then is taken out, turned, and ut in again and pressed till the evening, when it is taken out again, turned, and pressed till the next morning: it is then taken out of the vat, salted, put into it again with a clean dry cloth round it, and remains in the press till the next evening, when it is taken out again, salted, put into the vat without a cloth, and pressed till the next morning; and then it finally leaves the press, and is salted once a day for twelve days."

To whom it may be asked (without meaning to give offence) can the above account be profitable? Surely, something more—or nothing—should have been said.

SHEEP.—P. 145. "In the north-east part of this district, that is, in the vicinity of Bath, a very large and good race of sheep are bred; the wethers of which are commonly folded till they are between two or three years old, and then grazed. Some of these sheep, when well fatted, run to thirty or forty pounds per quarter. Mr. MOGER, of Woolverton; Mr. DAY, of Foxcote; Mr. YOUNG, of Camerton; Mr. HOLBROOK, of Corston; and Mr. SMITH of Twerton, are the principal breeders; and this sort of sheep, having a large quantity of tallow, is highly approved by the butchers. There is also the native Mendip breed, a sort that will thrive on the poorest soil, and fatten on such land as will scarcely keep other sorts alive. Pasturage ever so dry and exposed will feed this kind. They are very hardy and their wool fine. The mutton is also excellent for the table, being full of gravy and of a rich flavour.

"The large heavy loaded sheep of Leicestershire and Lincolnshire have been tried; but the great doubt lies whether this sort of sheep would bear folding; if not, they are inadmissible, as folding is the *sine qua non* of good husbandry, on the sheep and corn farms of this district."

SWINE.—*Breeds*.—P. 149. "The vast number of hogs fatted in this district are for the most part bought at Bristol market of Welchmen, or of the itinerant drovers, who travel through the county. They are fed chiefly with whey, sometimes a little corn is given to finish; and their flesh is of a fine colour and delicate flavour; their weight when fatted from ten to twenty score. Those few that are bred, are of various sorts:—1st. The native white, with large ears and long body. 2d. The Berkshire, black and white in colour, and of a compact round form. 3d. The Chinese. 4th. A mixed breed.

"In

"In *breeding* hogs, nothing should be more attended to than *warmth* and *cleanliness;* without these, the most liberal allowance of food will not avail; and as there is a great difference in the quantity of food necessary to support hogs of different sorts, though of the same age and size, experiments are wanting to ascertain their different degrees of perfection."—Again.—"The writer of this Report has been in the habit of *folding* hogs on his pasture land, feeding them with raw potatoes.

"The improvement of the land has been astonishing; and when hogs are kept on a large scale, the practice cannot be too warmly recommended."

RABBITS.—P. 150. "Some years since there were many warrens in this district, but the only ones now left are, Charter-House, Temple-Down, and Ubly, containing about sixteen hundred acres. Both the flesh and skin of the rabbits, bred on these warrens, are much esteemed; and they sell, when in season, (that is, from November to January) for two shillings and six-pence a couple, skins included."

POULTRY.—P. 150. "The great demand in Bristol and Bath naturally induces an attention to the rearing and fattening of all kinds of fowls. Of late it has been found that potatoes, boiled and mixed with the skimmings of the pot, or with any other fat or greasy substance, is the cheapest food that can be given to all kinds of poultry, and fattens them in a few days, making the flesh of a most delicate colour and flavour."

BEES.—P. 150. "It is to be regretted that these useful insects are so little attended to.

"Suppose in each parish of the county there were kept only ten hives, and the average produce of each hive was twenty pounds of honey, this would amount at the present price to near five thousand a year, besides the value of the wax."

THE END.

Mr. MARSHALL's other WORKS on RURAL ECONOMY.

1.

In two Volumes, Octavo, price 15s. in Boards,

MINUTES and EXPERIMENTS on AGRICULTURE; containing his own Practice in the Southern Counties; and moreover conveying, to practical Men in general, an accurate Method of acquiring Agricultural Knowledge, scientifically, from the Results of their Experience.

2.

In twelve Volumes, Octavo, price 4l. in Boards,

The established Practices of the higher Orders of Professional Men, in the six Agricultural Departments of England:

The Practice of the Northern Department being shown, in the RURAL ECONOMY of YORKSHIRE; price 12s.

That of the Western Department, in the RURAL ECONOMY of GLOCESTERSHIRE; price 12s.

That of the Central Department, in the RURAL ECONOMY of the MIDLAND COUNTIES; price 14s.

That of the Eastern Department, in the RURAL ECONOMY of NORFOLK; price 12s.

That of the Southern Department, in the RURAL ECONOMY of the SOUTHERN COUNTIES; price 15s.

That of the South-western Department, in the RURAL ECONOMY of the WEST of ENGLAND; price 15s.

3.

In two Volumes, Octavo, price 16s. in Boards,

A general Work on PLANTING and RURAL ORNAMENT; with the Management of WOODLANDS and HEDGEROW TIMBER.

4.

In one Volume, Quarto, price 2l. 2s. in Boards,

An elementary and practical TREATISE on the LANDED PROPERTY of ENGLAND: comprizing the Purchase, the Improvement, and the executive Management of Landed Estates; and moreover containing what relates to the general Concerns of PROPRIETORS, and to such Subjects of Political Economy, as are intimately connected with the LANDED INTEREST.

5.

In one Volume, Octavo, price 10s. 6d. in Boards,

A general Work on the MANAGEMENT of LANDED ESTATES; being an ABSTRACT of the above Treatise; for the Use of professional Men: including whatever relates to the BUSINESS of ESTATE AGENCY; whether it be employed in the Purchase, the Improvement, or the executive Management of Estates.

Also;

INDEX.

INDEX.

Duncumb's

Managers

T.

V.

W.

Y.

From the Office of
T. WILSON & SON,
High-Ousegate, York.